The Trombone

An Annotated Bibliography

G. B. Lane

The Scarecrow Press, Inc.
Lanham, Maryland, and London
1999

SCARECROW PRESS, INC.

Published in the United States of America
by Scarecrow Press, Inc.
4720 Boston Way
Lanham, Maryland 20706

4 Pleydell Gardens, Folkestone
Kent CT20 2DN, England

British Library Cataloguing in Publication Information Available

Library of Congress Cataloging-in-Publication Data
Lane, G. B. (George B.), 1943-
    The trombone : an annotated bibliography / G.B. Lane.
      p. cm.
    Includes index.
    ISBN 0-8108-3465-0 (cloth : alk. paper)
    1. Trombone—Bibliography. I. Title.
ML128.T76L36   1999
016.7889'3—dc21

          98-28420
          CIP
          MN

∞™ The paper used in this publication meets the minimum requirements of
American National Standard for Information Sciences—Permanence of
Paper for Printed Library Materials, ANSI Z39.48–1984.
Manufactured in the United States of America.

CONTENTS

FOREWORD by Thomas G. Everett   v

PREFACE   vii
    How to Use the Book   x
    Explanation of Terms in the A/S/K Line   xi
    Typical Search Strategies   xii

STANDARD ABBREVIATIONS   xiv

CHAPTER 1: General Reference
    Bibliographies   1
    Discographies   5
    Miscellaneous   9

CHAPTER 2: Biographies/General   18

CHAPTER 3: Biographies/Jazz, Popular, Studio   62

CHAPTER 4: Music   94

CHAPTER 5: Performance Practices   151

CHAPTER 6: Instruments and Equipment   205

CHAPTER 7: Pedagogy   261

APPENDIX I: Selected Periodical List   331

APPENDIX II: Obituaries
    Obituaries/General   345
    Obituaries/Jazz, Popular, Studio   346

APPENDIX III: International Trombone Association Award
    Recipients   349

APPENDIX IV: International Trombone Association
    Presidents   351

INDEX   352

ABOUT THE AUTHOR   425

FOREWORD

by Thomas G. Everett

The basic construction of the trombone and its method of sound production have not changed in five centuries. Although simple in design, in the hands of a creative and sensitive musician the trombone is capable of whispering a sensuous melody, producing innovative timbres, or representing the voice of God.

Today, the performer and teacher of trombone has available an incredibly wide range of research and historical information, musical literature, and equipment. Unfortunately, despite the significant work of such organizations as the International Trombone Association, such publications as the *Brass Bulletin*, and the camaraderie and willingness of trombonists to share information, there is simply too much diverse material for any one library or person to access.

G.B. Lane has undertaken a herculean "labor of love" that will require additions by the time *The Trombone: An Annotated Bibliography* goes to press. However, his text has provided us with a basic resource for locating materials related to all aspects of the trombone.

The text not only documents and educates but encourages each of us who knows and loves the trombone to pursue his or her own research and writing. G.B. Lane's work includes dissertations, reviews, biographies, specialized bibliographies, periodicals, and books.

It is important for the contemporary trombonist to be aware of performance practices of early music, chamber and orchestral music, and jazz. In addition, history, musicology, methodology, iconography, acoustics, literature, and instrumental design need to be considered.

Lane's cross-references in his book lead his readers into these diverse areas. They should prove intriguing not only to trombonists but to curious and knowledgeable musicians and historians of the arts.

Finally, though the book was intended as a research reference text, I have also found it fascinating and enjoyable simply to peruse and discover more about my chosen musical instrument.

Tom Everett, Founder and first president, International Trombone Association

Director of Bands, Harvard University, Cambridge, Massachusetts

PREFACE

Writing this book has been an almost Bunyanesque experience for me. I feel I have gone back over my life and filled in some gaps that I didn't realize were there. In the course of assembling this bibliography I have seen the trombone world change before my eyes, almost literally. I am able to better compare what the world of music thirty years ago was like for a young trombonist, naive and bursting with enthusiasm for his instrument, to what it is now. In addition, I have gained perspective for the more distant past.

Not as many positive changes have been accomplished as I had hoped. The number of outstanding solo performers on trombone who are able to make a living primarily as soloists is disappointingly small. Further, many opportunities for playing professionally in the jazz and popular markets have perished with the big bands. Colleges and universities are increasingly reluctant to employ full-time applied trombone teachers who have few traditional academic skills and credentials. For those who intend to pursue a career as a trombone teacher in higher education, my advice is to become not only proficient as a performer, but also as a composer, conductor, or researcher.

Many trombonists still seem to be reluctant to write and do research, even on their own instrument and its music. However, this attitude may be changing. As I progressed in a timeline in the preparation of this book, I noted more and better articles and books, and a proliferation of dissertations and other graduate documents. Though there is not enough yet to say that the trombone has come into its own, my research and experience have shown me that our instrument, and those who excel on it, equal any musical medium in the world. To paraphrase Charles Schulz's Linus, there is no heavier burden than a great potential, and the potential of the trombone is exciting. However, the musical world has yet to discover our Heifitz or to recognize our Chopin. The magnum opus of our Charles Rosen has yet to be published.

I hope that what I have gathered in this volume is enough to provide an incentive to begin or continue a number of projects which might address the last observation. At the least, I hope the book is considered user-friendly. It was written for trombonists primarily, but I believe that the broader research community will find it helpful in discovering information about some of the more arcane and esoteric topics about the instrument.

As my work progressed over the years I was able to use more on-line and other computer sources than were available to me at the beginning. My primary sources were *Music Index, DIALOG, Répertoire International de Littérature Musicale [RILM], Dissertation Abstracts, Journal of the International Trombone Association, Newsletter of the International Trombone Association, Online Computer Library Center [OCLC], International Index of Music Periodicals,* my personal library, several college and university libraries, indices in several music journals and magazines, and countless responses from colleagues and friends to my requests for information and confirmation. Many of the primary sources were available to me in several media (on-line, CD-ROMs, hard copies) at one time or another during my compilation period.

Mark Fasman's *Brass Bibliography* and Vincent Duckles and Ida Reed's *Music Reference and Research Materials: An Annotated Bibliography*, 6th ed., proved to be invaluable verification sources for me. David Lasocki's recurring bibliography in the *HBSJ* was particularly helpful in verifying sources about historical instruments and performance practices. All of these sources also occasionally led me to materials which I was not able to find in my primary sources. Bibliographies and lists in the publications of the International Trombone Association by Randy Kohlenberg, Randall Mark Jenkins, Jim Roberts, Stephen Glover, Richard Roznoy, Karl Hinterbichler, Edward Bahr, Larry Weed, Tom Everett, Vern Kagarice, and several others were also beneficial. David Fetter was generous with his time and swift to respond to my questions about specific materials in my entries.

At the heart of practically any substantive bibliography of materials on any brass instrument are the series of brass bibliographies compiled by Mary Rasmussen and others in her scholarly journal, *Brass Quarterly*. Her efforts, unfortunately suspended in 1964, spearheaded the gradual but steadily increasing interest of the music world in materials written for and about brass that culminated in the publication of such books as Fasman's *Brass Bibliography*. Rasmussen's work also contributed to the founding of such periodicals as the *HBSJ* and the various journals dedicated to individual brass instruments. Fortunately, her journals have been reprinted and are available (see appendix 1, listed under *Brass Quarterly*).

I am especially grateful to the music librarians at the University of South Carolina, Thomas Parkman, Jennifer Ottervik, and their staff, for their willingness to conduct searches, and to provide me with any materials they could. The librarians in the reference department at the Thomas Cooper Library at the University of South Carolina and the music library staff at the University of North Carolina at Chapel Hill went far beyond the call of duty in assisting me in finding information, particularly during the time before the new music library at South Carolina was put in place.

Tom Morton, Jason Trenary, and Elna Corwin, also on the staff at the University of South Carolina, furnished invaluable technical assistance. Tom came to my rescue many times just before I was about to pull the plug on my hard drive, Jason performed CPR on my computer, and Elna solved many formatting problems by inducting me into the mysteries of WordPerfect. One of our graduate students in music, Jeff Parker, was a thorough and helpful proofreader, especially in the early stages of assembling the information. Andy Johnson, a student in our Honors College, also served as a diligent proofreader for my index.

I wish to thank the University of South Carolina, and especially the former (and first) dean of the School of Music, Dorothy Payne, for granting me a sabbatical in order to complete most of the work on this book, in addition to encouraging and supporting me during its writing.

My wife, Connie, whose long-suffering has been monumental during the years I have been involved with this book and who assisted me during the crucial early proofing stages, has my eternal thanks and love. My daughter, Brandie, who also has my love, was generous in encouraging her Papa to get the book done and in offering me her wisdom when I ran into some of the frequent stumblingblocks that plague a project of this nature.

My long-time friend and colleague, Tom Everett, who founded the International Trombone Association and served as its first president, not only furnished a great deal of cited material for the book but also graciously consented to write a foreword for it. Tom's contributions to the trombone and music world in general include encouraging and doing research, writing, performance, and general evangelization of the instrument. I believe that much of what has been accomplished in research, promoting new compositions for trombone, and recognition of outstanding performers on the instrument would not have yet taken place without his efforts and encouragement.

Unattributed opinions expressed above and in the rest of this book are my own. It is my fond hope that many of the negative impressions I have garnered from my research will be altered or eliminated in the future, and that the positive things I have noted will be strengthened so that the trombone, those who perform well on it, and those who write well about it, may take their rightful places in our musical pantheon.

How to Use the Book

At first blush, this section might be considered patronizing to those who are experts in research techniques (if you don't need my advice, just skip over this section). But perhaps other people who are just beginning their adventures in research and reference, or who prefer to have things explained in detail, might save some time and frustration by establishing a clear understanding of how the book is constructed.

The book is classified alphabetically by author for each chapter (or section in the case of the first chapter). Each entry is numbered consecutively throughout the entire book, and the numbers are used to reference each entry in the index.

Many of the references cited are in books or media which may not be in many libraries or included in major on-line sources. Therefore, a selected list of addresses of journals and periodicals, which are still in print as of this writing has been included in appendix 1. Further information may be obtained by checking *LASOCKI*, *RILM*, Imogen Fellinger's articles, "Periodicals" in the *New Grove's Dictionary of Music and Musicians* or "Musikbibliographien" in the new *MGG*, and the January *Music Index* (see standard abbreviations below).

Basically, the material in the bibliography can be perused at three levels: (1) browsing through the broad classifications as divided by chapter; (2) using the cross-referenced material within the text for sub-classifications such as alto trombone, Moravian music, contrabass trombone, and so forth; (3) utilizing the index for author, subject, and keyword references, which include the author/subject/keyword line at the bottom of each entry, and materials, especially performance literature, which are contained in the cited entries, but do not necessarily appear in the annotations. Note that in the index the titles of the performance literature which do not appear in the annotations are indicated by asterisks (*). Obviously, by using the latter method one can discover the most material on any subject or keyword contained in this book.

Explanation of Terms in the Author/Subject/Keyword (A/S/K) Line

All doctoral papers are cited in the a/s/k line as *diss*, whether they are classified as documents, theses, monographs, dissertations, or any other terms utilized by the academic community. All master's papers are designated as *theses*. Other papers done for bachelor's degrees, or which were not completed as documents for academic degrees, are identified as *research*.

Some colleges and universities are identified in the a/s/k line by their current name (e.g., Washington State College is now known as Washington State University), although in the citation they are identified by the name in use at the time of the writing. Others are identified by their state affiliation (NorthCarolinaU), by their city if necessary (TexasU-Austin), or by their institutional names (NorthwesternU, Eastman).

References to brass instrumental organizations and well-known academic and cultural institutions are cited mostly as abbreviations (e.g., ITA, ITG, TUBA, NACWPI), with an explanation of the abbreviation either in the title of the publication or in the annotation. Information on some of the abbreviations may be found below in the section Standard Abbreviations and others may be found in appendix 1, *Periodicals*.

The a/s/k line may be regarded as an abbreviated annotation, that is, names, subjects, and keywords listed are referred to in the actual article or book even though they may not appear in the bibliographic annotation. For some searches it could save time to peruse the a/s/k/ line first, particularly on entries which have lengthy annotations and extensive cross-referencing, to determine if an author or subject might be included in the annotation.

In most instances where a work could be primarily classified either by format or by content, I have opted for content. Examples may be found in various annotated bibliographies of music, which are basically classified according to the principal type of music contained, with secondary references in the a/s/k line, including the term "Bib" [bibliography].

Much of the performance literature cited in the index does not appear in either the annotations or the a/s/k lines, primarily because of space considerations (such citations are indicated by asterisks [*]). I did not intend this book to serve mainly as a bibliography of trombone music but felt it incumbent upon me to direct the searcher to books and articles where there are annotations and discussions of music significant to trombonists.

Typical Search Strategies

As one example of how the book's features may be utilized, we can search for an unpublished, and until recently, unperformed work by an American composer written for a famous American trombonist of the 1930s. Scholars not familiar with trombonists from that time might choose to look through the index for American composers from that era (for instance George Gershwin, Roy Harris, or William Grant Still), while trombonists might be more likely to search for the performer (Tommy Dorsey, Vic Dickenson, or Jack Teagarden).

Both types of searchers will discover from the index that Roy Harris was the composer and Tommy Dorsey the performer when they read the annotation or a/s/k line for 587, Jonathan Winkler, "Jim Pugh discovers new 'Tommy Dorsey' work," *JITA* (*Journal of the International Trombone Association*) 25, no. 3 (Summer 1997): 34-35. The name of the work, *American Symphony—1938*, is also listed in the index, and if the searcher happens to know that the work was performed at a trombone workshop, he/she could search under workshops, or specifically an Eastern Trombone Workshop and find the same entry. The entry is also crosslisted under the modern performer, Jim Pugh, the Army Blues (the organization that performed the work with Jim Pugh), and various other entries concerning Tommy Dorsey.

Another search could be conducted for the identity of the trombonist who immortalized the "rink" or "doink" sound on recordings of the Spike Jones band. The non-trombonist searcher could search for the Spike Jones band, while the more experienced trombonist might prefer to search for the description of the sound itself (admittedly a more subjective path, but phonetic representations of the sound have become almost standard in trombone circles).

A search under Jones will reveal that Jones's name was actually Lindley Armstrong, and in this book his band is cited under his nickname of "Spike." A search under Spike Jones shows that the bandleader is mentioned in the annotation of 751. At the end of the annotation by Gerry Sloan, recently deceased West Coast trombonist and composer/arranger Tommy Pederson's claim to have originated the sound is revealed. Further information on Pederson is listed in entry 405, and more information and crosslistings for the entire topic of "the talking trombone" are given, including significant practioners of various mute and plunger techniques.

Obviously, thinking like a trombonist will help a person to use this book. But even if that accomplishment is neither desired nor possible, I believe the book still has substantial value in locating material about the trombone.

All mistakes, of course, are my responsibility, and I will appreciate any information which will help make a subsequent edition, whether mine or someone else's, more accurate and complete.

Finally, to those intrepid souls who may yet decide to join the ranks of those of us who sit in the darkest and most remote sections of the orchestra pit, who lounge through several movements of a symphony waiting for a few moments of glory, and whose hair has been parted in several different places by an iron-chopped lead trumpeter whose bell is only eighteen inches from the left ear, I leave you with a thought from Professor Stephen Shore, "Never trust an instrument that changes shape while it is being played."

STANDARD ABBREVIATIONS

BassTrb—Bass Trombone

BBIBC—Brass Bulletin—International Brass Chronicle. Jean-Pierre Mathez, ed. Brass Bulletin, P.O. Box 576, CH-1630 Bulle, Switzerland [on the Internet see http://www.editions-bim.ch or http://www.brass-bulletin.ch].

BRASSANTH—Brass Anthology: A Compendium of Articles from "The Instrumentalist" on Playing the Brass Instruments. Evanston IL: The Instrumentalist Co., 1980.

BRASSBIB—Fasman, Mark J. *Brass Bibliography: Sources on the History, Literature, Pedagogy, Performance, and Acoustics of Brass Instruments.* Bloomington: Indiana University Press, 1990.

BrassPerf-19thC—Brass Performance-19th Century (dates vary)

ChamMus-Trb—Chamber Music—Trombone

DA—Doctor of Arts

DIALOG—DIALOG Information Services, Inc., 3460 Hillview Ave., Palo Alto CA 94304 [800-334-2564, Fax 415-858-7069].

Discog—Discography

Diss—Dissertation

DM—Doctor of Music, sometimes abbreviated as DMus

DMA—Doctor of Musical Arts

HBSJ—Historic Brass Society Journal. Jeffrey Nussbaum, managing ed. Historic Brass Society, 148 West 23rd St., No. 2A, New York NY 10011 [also same address for the *Newsletter*].

Horn—International Horn Society

ITA—International Trombone Association (see below *JITA)*

ITG—International Trumpet Guild

JENKINS—Jenkins, Randal Mark. "An annotated bibliography of periodical articles related to the bass trombone," *Journal of the International Trombone Association* 11, no. 4 (October 1983): 7-12.

JITA—Journal of the International Trombone Association [ITA Journal]. Vern Kagarice, ed. International Trombone Association, Subscriptions Manager, P.O. Box 5336, Denton TX 76203.

JITG—Journal of the International Trumpet Guild

KOHLENBERG I and *II*—Kohlenberg, Randy. "Update on trombone related research, part 1," *Journal of the International Trombone Association* 17, no. 4 (Fall 1989): 22-26; part 2 in 18, no 1 (Winter 1990): 17-20.

LASOCKI—Lasocki, David. "A bibliography of writings about historic brass instruments, 1988-89." *Historic Brass Society Journal* 2 (1990): 190-202 [ongoing column].

MGG—Die Musik in Geschichte und Gegenwart [Music in history and the present] Friedrich Blume, ed. (Kassel, Germany: Basel: Bärenreiter-Verlag, 1949-1986). The new *MGG*, edited by Ludwig Finscher (Kassel, Germany: Bärenreiter; Stuttgart, Metzler) was issued initially in 1994 with the intention of publishing subsequent volumes at the rate of two per year for ten years.

Music Index—Harmonie Park Press (Informational Coordinators, Inc.), 23630 Pinewood, Warren MI 48091.

NACWPI—National Association of College Wind and Percussion Instructors

NITA—Newsletter of the International Trombone Association

OrchExcerpts—Orchestral Excerpts

PerfPrac—Performance Practices

RILM—Répertoire International de Littérature Musicale, RILM Center, City University of New York Graduate School and University Center, 33 West 42nd St., New York NY 10036

ROBERTS—Roberts, James. "Current research relating to the trombone." *Journal of the International Trombone Association* 12, no. 1 (January 1984): 31-32.

TrbChoir—Trombone Choir

TrbMusic—18thC—Trombone Music—18th Century (various dates of music cited)

TrbMus-Gen—Trombone Music—General

TUBA—Tubists Universal Brotherhood Association

UMI—University Microfilms, 300 North Zeeb Rd., Ann Arbor MI 48106

GENERAL REFERENCE

Bibliographies

1. EVERETT, Thomas G. "A handlist of trombone-related theses and dissertations published between 1983 and 1986." *JITA* 16, no. 1 (Winter 1988): 16-17.
   Everett is the founder and the first president (1972-1976) of the International Trombone Association.
   Diss/ITA/Research/Theses

2. ————. "Recent articles about the trombone and trombonists." *JITA* 18, no. 3 (Summer 1990): 13.
   See also the *JITA* 19, no. 3 (Summer 1991): 8, for an update.
   Bio/Jazz-Blues/Orchestra/Pedagogy

3. FASMAN, Mark J. *Brass Bibliography*. Bloomington IN: Indiana University Press, 1990.
   Described by the author as "sources on the history, literature, pedagogy, performance, and acoustics of brass instruments," criteria include (1) prose writing in book, journal, or dissertation form (reviews and most regular feature articles are not included); (2) appearance in a standard bibliography of brass sources, such as those in *Brass Quarterly, Music Index, RILM Abstracts*, various brass instrument societies'journals, etc.; (3) written in English, German, French or Italian.
   The book's sizable list of trombone materials is classified by subject and indexed by author and subject. It was used in the preparation of the present volume as a verification source for references for materials prior to 1988, the last year included

in Fasman's book. There are only a few annotations. It is cited as *BRASSBIB*.
Brass

4.   GLOVER, Stephen L. "A list of brass dissertations, 1976-1977." *NITA* 5, no. 2 (December 1977): 5.
        Glover's list was first published in the *JITG* 2 (1977): 48.
        Diss/ITG/Research

5.   HILLS, Ernie M., III. "Medicine and dentistry for brass players: A selected survey of recent research in the journal literature." *JITA* 15, no. 4 (Fall 1987): 32-37.
        See Edward R. Wolff, III, M.D., "Medical corner," *JITA* 22, no. 4 (Fall 1994): 16-17. Wolff now writes an ongoing column on medical problems for trombonists and other wind players, which began with the Fall 1994 issue. For an update on this article see Marc David Horowitz, "Trombone citations in recent medical and scientific literature," *JITA* 26, no. 1 (Winter 1998): 60-61.
        Dental/Horowitz,M./Medical/Wolff,E.

6.   HÜBLER, Klaus-K. "Die polyphone Posaune: Ein Vorschlag zur Notation [The polyphonic trombone: An introduction to its notation]." *BBIBC* 45 (1984): 31-33.
        Hübler's article is in English, French, and German and was one of the sources of Charles Isaacson's article on twentieth-century music for trombone and organ (see 472).
        Isaacson,C./Notation/Organ/TrbMus-Gen

7.   JENKINS, Randal Mark. "An annotated bibliography of periodical articles related to the bass trombone." *JITA* 11, no. 4 (October 1983): 7-12.
        Jenkins has assembled a helpful compilation of articles, dated through 1982, mostly annotated. References to materials in it are identified as *JENKINS*.
        BassTrb

8.   [KAGARICE, Vernon, et al.]. "International Trombone Association *Journal* and *Newsletter* index." *JITA* 11, no. 2 (April 1983): 40-43.

Volumes 1-10 of the *JITA* and all eight volumes of the *NITA* have been classified and indexed. See also vol. 14, no 3 (Summer 1986) for a classified index to volumes 1-13 of the *JITA* and all eight volumes of the *NITA*.
Bio/Indices/Instruments/Interviews/ITA/Jazz-Blues/Orchestra/Pedagogy/PerfPrac/TrbMus-Gen

9.   KEHRBERG, Robert. "Trombone degree-related research and performance: A listing from *Dissertation Abstracts*." *JITA* 17, no. 2 (Spring 1989): 32-33.
Entry data were compiled from a *DIALOG* computer search of *Dissertation Abstracts*.
Diss/Research

10. KOHLENBERG, Randy. "The Glenn D. Bridges Collection." *JITA* 16, no. 4 (Fall 1988): 18-20.
A brief biography of Glenn Bridges and an overview of his collection of brass recordings and other memorabilia now housed at the Glenn D. Bridges Archive-Library, University of North Carolina-Greensboro, are included.
Bio/Bridges,G./NorthCarolinaU-Greensboro

11. ———. "Preliminary results of a survey of trombone related research." *JITA* 15, no. 2 (Spring 1987): 18-19.
Diss/Research

12. ———, comp. "Update on trombone related research." *JITA* 17, no. 4 (Fall 1989): 22-26 and 18, no. 1 (Winter 1990): 17-20.
Kohlenberg has included research studies related to the trombone listed alphabetically by author from Adams through Kehrberg in part 1 and from Kidd through Yoder in part 2. He also has compiled a short bibliography of useful research sources. Projects are dated from 1941-1988 and include doctoral studies, master's studies, independent studies, and undergraduate studies. Materials cited from these references are identified as *KOHLENBERG I* and *II*.
Diss/Research/Theses

13.   [LANE, G.B.]. "Articles concerning trombone." *NITA* 2, no. 2
      (April 1975): 6.
      Periodicals

14.   LASOCKI, David. "A bibliography of writings about historic
      brass instruments, 1988-1989." *HBSJ* 2 (1990): 190-202.
          Lasocki's ongoing bibliography appears annually in the
      succeeding volumes of the *HBSJ*. The author is head of public
      services at the Indiana University Music Library.
          There are a few annotations, and at the end of each article are
      instructions on how and where to obtain the sources listed.
      Several sources on trombone, mostly from a historical viewpoint,
      appear in the citations. Listings taken from this bibliography and
      used in this book are credited to *LASOCKI*.
      Brass

15.   ROBERTS, James. "Current research relating to the trombone."
      JITA 12, no. 1 (January 1984): 31-32.
          Citations from this article are identified as *ROBERTS*.
      Research

16.   ROZNOY, Richard T. "A selected bibliography of English
      language material relevant to the trombone." *JITA* 3 (1975): 8-9,
      and 4 (1976): 23-29.
      EnglishLanguage/Research

17.   [SMITH, Henry Charles]. "Orchestral audition list." *NITA* 6, no.
      2 (December 1978): 8-9.
          Smith's list appeared in Karl Hinterbichler's ongoing column,
      "Literature reviews."
      Hinterbichler,K./OrchExcerpts

18.   STUART, David, comp. "Brass research projects." *JITA* 10, no.
      4 (October 1982): 5-9.
      Brass/Research/MusicEd

19.   SWANSON, Thomas L. "A comprehensive performance project
      in trombone literature with an essay consisting of an annotated
      bibliography of the articles in the *JITA* and *NITA*." [cited in

ROBERTS as graduate research for the DMA at the University of Iowa: projected date of completion, 1982]. The author is on the music faculty at Bemidji State University in Minnesota. Periodicals/Research

20. [WEED, Larry]. "Brass dissertations." *JITA* 8 (March 1980): 12. Brass/Diss/Research

Discographies

21. BAHR, Edward R. *A Trombone/Euphonium Discography*. Stevens Point WI: 1988.

    See also *Dissertation Abstracts* (August 1980): 41/02-A, 451, AAD 80-16922. Bahr's book is available from Index House, Box 716, Stevens Point WI 54481.
    Diss/Euphonium/OklahomaU/TrbMus-Gen

22. ———, ed. "Record reviews." *NITA* 3, no. 1 (September 1975): 21-23.

    Bahr's ongoing column appeared first in the *NITA* with Stephen L. Glover as the column's first editor (retiring from his position by the April 1975 edition), then continuing in the *JITA*, beginning with volume 10, no. 1 (January 1982): 37-40.

    Glover's first column in the *NITA* 2, no. 1 (April 1974): 10-11, contains a fairly complete list of recordings which were available in the early 1970s. Some are no longer available commercially. There is also a significant article in the *JITA* 17, no. 4 (Fall 1989): 39, which contains a bibliography focusing on periodicals available in the United States for those interested in purchasing trombone recordings (or recordings for other media as well).
    Bib/Glover,S./TrbMus-Gen

23. BRUYNINCKX, Walter. *Sixty Years of Recorded Jazz, 1917-1977*. [Privately printed.]

    Bruyninckx's multi-volume work is available from the compiler at Lange Nieuwstraat 121-2800, Mechelen, Germany. It includes short biographical sketches and detailed discographies of all major and many minor jazz artists through 1977.

The format is crude, typewritten, with many spelling and typographical errors, but it is the most complete compilation of its type in existence. It now has about eighteen volumes, with more to come. Many jazz trombonists are included, and it is a good source for birth and death dates.
Bio/Jazz-Blues

24. EVERETT, Thomas G. "J.J. Johnson on record: An overview."
     JITA 16, no. 2 (Spring 1988): 34-35.
     See Louis George Bourgois, 267 (cited in *ROBERTS* as Louis
     G. Bourgeois [*sic*] III). See also Jim Burns, 274, Thomas G.
     Everett, 299 and 300, Leonard Feather, 303, Gene Kalbacher 320,
     and Gerry Sloan, 749.
     Bio/Bourgois,L./Burns,J./Feather,L./Jazz-Blues/Johnson,J.J./
     Kalbacher,G./PerfPrac/Sloan,G.

25. [———]. "Recent jazz 'slides' on record." *NITA* 4, no. 3 (May
     1977): 19-21.
     Everett's listing later appeared as "Recent jazz slide sides" in
     the *NITA* 6, no. 2 (December 1978): 10-11, and vol. 7, no, 1
     (December 1979): 14-16+ (the article was printed twice). The
     series continued with this amended title in vol. 8, no. 2
     (December 1980): 12-14. It also appeared in the *JITA* 11, no. 1
     (January 1983): 15-17 and featured recordings made in Europe
     and Japan. A third version appeared in the *NITA* vol. 8, no. 4
     (September 1981): 35-36 as "Recent jazz trombone slides."
     Avant-Garde/Europe/Japan/Jazz-Blues

26. HANSEN, J.E., and J.D. MCENIRY, comps. "Discography of
     trombone solo literature." *JITA* 13, no. 2 (April 1985): 32-34.
     Hansen and McEniry's discography is organized by composer,
     composition, artist, and label. See Robert Kehle, 30.
     Kehle,R./McEniry,J./Solos/TrbMus-Gen

27. HEPOLA, Ralph. "The complete jazz and solo discography of
     Bill Watrous." *JITA* 14, no. 4 (Fall 1986): 42-45.
     These recordings are listed in chronological order through 1984.
     See a letter by Richard Renner in the *JITA* (Winter 1987)
     (mistakenly identified as volume 14, no. 4, but is actually volume

15, no. 1), page 4 for another album on which Watrous is heard but not listed in Hepola's discography. See also a letter from Gerry Sloan identifying yet another album in "The eighth position," *JITA* 15, no 2. A further update from Hepola may be found in vol. 16, no. 3 (Summer 1988): 2 (with a reference to a phantom addendum on page 30).

Jazz-Blues/Renner,R./Sloan,G./Watrous,B.

28. [HINTERBICHLER, Karl]. "Albert Mangelsdorff discography." *NITA* 6, no. 2 (December 1978): 9.

Mangelsdorff's discography is printed in Hinterbichler's ongoing column, "Literature reviews." It was reprinted with permission from *MPSsence* no. 6 (February 1978), a monthly newsletter of MPS (EMI) records. For references on Mangelsdorff, see George Broussard, 271.

Broussard,G./EMI/Jazz-Blues/Mangelsdorff,A./*MPSsence*

29. [JOYCE RECORDS]. *Tommy Dorsey and His Orchestra* and *Si Zentner and His Orchestra*.

These sources are listed by Edward Bahr in his ongoing column in the *JITA* 14, no. 3 (Summer 1986): 47. They are listed as being available from Mr. Nostalgia, P.O. Box 414201, Miami Beach FL 33141, and are perhaps by J. Wolfer [see his *Si Zentner and His Orchestra*, 2nd ed., Guttersloh, Germany, 1993]. For more information on Si Zentner, see "Video critique: *Swingtime Video Presents Meet the Band Leaders*" in *Cadence* 12 (May 1986): 65-66+. Information on Tommy Dorsey may be available from Paul Hunt (see his research presentation, "The legacy of Tommy Dorsey," given at the 1990 International Trombone Workshop).

See Fred Snyder, 66, and [Amy Lee], 323. See Jonathan Winkler, 587 for a discussion of a Roy Harris work discovered by Jim Pugh which was composed for Dorsey's band in 1938.

Bahr,E./Dorsey,T./Harris,R./Hunt,P./Jazz-Blues/Lee,A./ MrNostalgia/Pugh,J./Snyder,F./Videos/Winkler,J./Wolfer,J./Zentner,S.

30. KEHLE, Robert. "Addendum to 'Discography of trombone [solo] literature.'" *JITA* 13, no. 4 (October 1985): 34-35.

For notes on the original article see J.E. Hansen and J.D.
McEniry, 26.
Hansen,J./McEniry,J./Solos/TrbMus-Gen

31. MACHADO, Roberto L. *Basic Discography of Frank Rosolino.*
     2nd ed. Fortaleza, Brazil: Roberto L. Machado, 1996.
     Machado's book is available from the author at Caixa Postal
     1142, 60.000, Fortaleza, Brazil. It is also obtainable in the United
     States from W.G. Swanson, 7817 Tree Swallow Dr. SE, Grand
     Rapids MI 49508.
     Jazz-Blues/Rosolino,F./Swanson,W.

32. "Moravian trombone choir music recorded." *Moravian Music
     Foundation Bulletin* 21, no. 2 (1976): 9.
     See Jeff Reynolds, 541 and 734-735, Wesley Branstine, 606,
     Manfred Büttner, 610, Marion Grubb, 650, Harry D. Hall, 654,
     L.W. Hartzell, 659, Jerome Leaman, 694, Joseph Maurer, 706,
     Richmond Myers, 714, and William Reichel, 732.
     Branstine,W./Büttner,M./Grubb,M./Hall,H./Hartzell,L./Leaman,J./
     Maurer,J./Moravian/Myers,R./Reichel,W./Reynolds,J./TrbChoir/
     TrbMus-18thC/TrbMus-19thC

33. [SAN FRANCISCO TRADITIONAL JAZZ FOUNDATION].
     Turk Murphy: Just for the Record. San Leandro CA: San
     Francisco Traditional Jazz Foundation, 1984.
     This reference is cited in Edward Bahr's regular column
     "Record reviews," in the July 1984 issue of the *JITA.* The
     address given for obtaining the publication is P.O. Box 433, San
     Leandro CA 94577. See Douglas Yeo, 383.
     Jazz-Blues/Murphy,T./Yeo,D.

34. SLOAN, Gerry. "Suggested listening for jazz trombonists." *The
     Instrumentalist* 30 (March 1976): 82+.
     Jazz-Blues

35. SPILKA, Bill. "A recorded history of jazz trombone to 1958."
     NITA 3, no. 1 (September 1975): 18-19.

Spilka's listing is classified according to artist, label, and composition. He begins with Daddy Edwards in 1917 and ends with Kai Winding and his Septette in 1958.
Jazz-Blues

36. SWETT, James P. "A comprehensive list of solo recordings for trombone." *JITA* 2 (1973-74): 51-60.
Swett lists the works alphabetically by performer.
Solos

37. WINKING, Charles. "A discography of trombone, euphonium, and bass trombone solos and ensembles." *National Association of College Wind and Percussion Instructors [NACWPI] Journal* 28, no. 4 (1980): 6-15.
Considered by *JENKINS* to be of some value, many of the smaller record companies have their addresses listed.
BassTrb/Ensemble/Euphonium/Solos/TrbMusic-Gen

Miscellaneous

38. ASHWORTH, Thomas and James ten BENSEL. "How to organize a trombone symposium." *JITA* 19, no. 1 (Winter 1991): 30-32.
Ashworth and Bensel use the 1991 University of Minnesota Trombone Symposium as a model.
Minnesota/Symposia/Workshops

39. *AUSTRALIAN TROMBONE EDUCATION MAGAZINE [ATEM]*. 1 Oxley St., Naremburn 2064, Australia.
AustralianTromboneAssociation/Periodical

40. BAER, Douglas. "Baer's law." *JITA* 10, no. 2 (April 1982): 40.
Baer's article is a semiserious attempt to persuade the International Trombone Association to endorse a law (the enforcement of which is left to the imagination of the reader) that would set minimum distances between players, stands, equipment, and performers in works involving trombonists.
Equipment/Humor/ITA

41. [BAHR, Edward R.]. "Video." *JITA* 14, no. 3 (Summer 1986): 31.
    Listed in Bahr's ongoing column, "Record reviews," this article contains one of the earliest listings of videos featuring famous trombonists.
    Bib/Bio/Dorsey,T./Green,U./Jazz-Blues/Miller,G./Teagarden,J./Tizol,J./Videos/Young,T.

42. BAKER, Buddy. "Exit sliding: A report on the trombolympic games." *JITA* 17, no. 2 (Spring 1989): 22-23.
    After a rather lengthy hiatus, Baker, a past president of the International Trombone Association (1976-1978), and recipient of the ITA Award in 1974, returns to his first love, showing the humorous side of the trombone world. See the *NITA* 6, no. 2 (December 1978): 9-10, for an account of Baker's stint as an "extra" in the Universal Studios television movie production of *Centennial*. See also Buddy Baker, 82.
    Centennial/Humor/Television/Trombolympic

43. BAKER, Nicholson. "Playing trombone." *Atlantic Monthly* 249 (March 1982): 39-58.
    A whimsical but insightful short story, written by a bassoonist from Eastman, it concerns the trials of Zeno, the son of a miner, who played second trombone in the Mammoth Symphony Orchestra.
    Fiction/Humor/Orchestra

44. BUGLI, David. "Pity the people who play the trombone." *NITA* 6, no. 2 (December 1978): 6.
    A poem dedicated to Max C. Culpepper, it is a bittersweet reminder of what trombonists endure for the few moments of musical satisfaction the instrument bestows.
    Culpepper,M./Humor/Poetry

45. DOUAY, Jean. "Une expérience de la chirurgie sur les lèvres [Lip surgery—a report]." *BBIBC* 21 (1978): 53-57.
    At the time of this article André Féraud was the first trombonist in the Aimé Barelli Orchestra, which plays at the Sporting Club in Monte Carlo. He had been a jazz trumpeter but has had three surgical operations to modify his upper lip. The problem consisted of what is sometimes called a "cupid's bow," or fleshy

protuberance in the middle of the upper lip, which extends downward and sometimes becomes an obstruction to the air column of a brass player. The operations are explained in great detail, along with comments from Féraud, explaining his development from a trumpeter to a trombonist. This article is in French, German, and English.

Cupid'sBow/Dental/Embouchure/Féraud,A./Medical/MonteCarlo/ Surgery

46. *GLISSANDO.* [French trombone periodical]. 12bis, rue Louis Bouquet, Paris, France.
France/Periodical

47. GREEN, Katherine, "How about thirty-two trombones?" *Orbit Magazine* (June 16, 1974): 19.
PerfPrac/TrbMus-Gen

48. GREINER, Anthony. "Aldous Huxley's dedicatory address for the first performance of Igor Stravinsky's *In Memorium—Dylan Thomas.*" *JITA* 10, no. 3 (July 1982): 21-22.
ChamMus-Trb/Huxley,A./Stravinsky,I./Thomas,D./Vocal

49. *Holton's Harmony Hints (1914).* "Trombone makes first trans-Atlantic sound." N.p.
Contributed by Ted Kexel, then of Frank Holton & Co., to the *NITA* 2, no. 2 (April 1975): 7, this article gives a fascinating account of how a trombone was used to test the first trans-Atlantic wireless sound transmitter.
Holton/Kexel,T./Marconi,G./Trans-Atlantic/Wireless

50. *HOME PAGES: TROMBONE* [Selected]
International Trombone Association Web Page, http://www.niu.edu/acad/music/ita.html. This page is run by Paul Bauer, u40pdb1@wop.cso.niu.edu, and has many links to related home pages, which are springing up very rapidly.
Erik Nicklas Trombone Page (original trombone source on the web), http://www.missouri.edu.cceric/index.html. This page also contains information on how to join Trombone-L, and links to other pages.

Frank Rosolino Page, http://www.austexmusic.com/business/
atex/frank.htm. This page is maintained by Austex Music, 1706
East 38th St., Austin TX 78722.

Douglas Yeo, http://www.yeodoug.com (especially helpful for
bass trombone topics and links).

For further information see Randy Campora's ongoing column
"General news," in the *JITA*.

BassTrb/Bauer,P./Campora,R./Internet/ITA/Nicklas,E./Rosolino,F./
WorldWideWeb/Yeo,D.

51.   KAGARICE, Vern, ed. *NITA*. 1979-1981.
      Kagarice replaced G.B. Lane as editor of the *NITA* and
      continued until 1982, when the *JITA* and the *NITA* were merged.
      Kagarice remained as editor of the new *JITA*, replacing Larry
      Weed. Kagarice is now executive manager and publications
      coordinator of the International Trombone Association.
      ITA/Lane,G./Weed,L.

52.   LANE, G.B., ed. *NITA*. 1972-1978.
      Lane was the founder of the *NITA* and its editor for the first six
      years of its existence. Editorial duties for it were assumed by
      Vern Kagarice in 1979.
      ITA/Kagarice,V.

53.   LENTHE, Carl. "Competition experience." *JITA* 10, no. 4
      (October 1982): 14-15.
      Lenthe outlines the International Music Competition and the
      related trombone competitions in Europe, how they work, their
      basic formats, and their rewards.
      Competitions/Europe/International

54.   MARCELLUS, John. "The joy of trombone." *JITA* 12, no. 2
      (April 1984): 24-26.
      Marcellus gives a lighthearted (and perhaps lightheaded) look
      at the sometimes mundane world of *trombonisms*.
      Humor/Pedagogy

55.   MCCULLOH, Byron. *The Brass Larynx*. Pittsburgh: Sa-Voo Sa-
      Vah Press, 1989.

McCulloh's volume is a book of poems by the "self-proclaimed poet laureate of the trombone." See the *JITA* 17, no. 4 (Fall 1989): 2, for a nefarious "Foreword to *The Brass Larynx*," which is purported to have been found by John Marcellus, himself a poet of no mean repute. See also a review by Earl Schreiber in the *JITA* 18, no. 3 (Summer 1990): 38-39. See Bruce Tracy, 225 and Barry Catelinet, 1034. See also a letter from Ralph Sauer relating to McCulloh's comments on the trend in bass trombone sounds, printed in "The Eighth position," *JITA* 15, no. 2 (Spring 1987). A short biographical sketch of McCulloh appears in Ben Ivey's ongoing column, "General news," in the *NITA* 7, no. 2 (April 1980): 4-5. It contains a brief bibliography of McCulloh's compositions up to 1980.
Catelinet,B./Ivey,B./Marcellus,J./Poetry/Reviews/Sauer,R./ Schreiber,E./Tracy,B.

56. MERLINO, Diane. "Billy and his musical bones." *NITA* 6, no. 4 (September 1979): 9-10.
Reprinted from *The Pacifica Tribune* of Pacifica, California. Merlino's article deals with the formation and activities of a San Francisco area trombone choir, which premiered Henry Brant's *Orbits—A Spatial Ritual for Eighty Trombones*. See also Henry Brant, 407.
BayBones/Brant,H./Robinson,B./SanFrancisco

57. NOVA, Craig. *Trombone*. New York: Ivy Books, 1994.
Fiction/Novel

58. PEDICARIS, Steve. "TransAtlantic slide." *JITA* 19, no. 3 (Summer 1991): 32-33.
An American trombonist who performed in England with the City of Birmingham Symphony Orchestra on several concerts gives his observations on the typical lifestyles of British orchestral trombonists.
Birmingham(Eng)/CBSO/England/Orchestra

59. RILEY, Dan. "*Sonata vox Gabrieli* by Stjepan Šulek." *JITA* 23, no. 4 (Fall 1995): 37.

Riley has written lyrics for this originally instrumental work. For more information on the work see David Manson, 173, Michael Parnell, 530, and Robert Reifsnyder, 538.
Manson,D./Parnell,M./Poetry/Reifsnyder,R./Solos/Šulek,S./Trb Mus-20thC

60. *SCHALLSTÜCK, [DAS].* [German trombone periodical] Haydnweg 7, D-64342 Seeheim, Germany.
Germany/Periodical

61. SCHREIBER, Earl A. "Preserving trombonology." *JITA* 16, no. 4 (Fall 1988): 16-17.
Schreiber's article contains suggestions for trombonists who might be interested in chronicling the history of trombone music and performance.
PerfPrac/TrbMus-Gen

62. ———. "Trombone after-life." *JITA* 12, no. 4 (October 1984): 43
Schreiber gives a whimsical look at where trombones can go after they die.
Humor/Whimsy

63. ———. "Trombonology." *NITA* 7, no. 2 (April 1980): 30-31.
A poem is offered about the vagaries, foibles, and blessings of being a trombonist. The author is an English literature instructor. He has provided reference notes so that the reader can see from what works the allusions were taken.
Poetry/Trombonology

64. SMALL, Charles. "My partner." *JITA* 24, no. 2 (Spring 1996): 44-45.
The agonies of "getting in playing shape" are told from the perspective of Small's trombone, which had been neglected for several years.
Humor/Pedagogy

65. ———. "The studio musician." *NITA* 4, no. 3 (May 1977): 4-5.
Careers/PerfPrac/Studio

66. SNYDER, Fred ("Moe"). "True devotion (a true short story)."
    New York Brass Conference for Scholarships Journal (1984): 38.
    Synder gives a poignant account of a man who pretended to be
    Tommy Dorsey's son because of his admiration for Dorsey's
    music in the Big Band era. See [Joyce Records], 29 and [Amy
    Lee], 323.
    Bio/Dorsey,T./Jazz-Blues/Lee,A./Pugh,J.

67. SPELDA, Anton. "Die gegenseitige Maskierung (Verdeckung)
    der Orchesterinstrumente [Reciprocal masking or covering of
    orchestral instruments]." *De musica disputationes pragenes* 2
    (1974): 86-143.
    Spelda's article is in German and considers the perceived ability
    of musical instruments (including the trombone) and the human
    voice to mask and be masked or covered (as in being concealed
    or obscured) in various musical situations. See also Spelda's
    "Fluktuace ustalene hladiny dynamiky [Fluctuation at a stabilized
    level of dynamics]," *Hudební věda* 7, no. 2 (1970): 123-155,
    which gives a precise acoustical description of dynamic variations
    of held notes on several instruments, including trombone.
    Acoustics/Dynamics/Masking

68. SPILKA, Bill. "An alternate history of the trombone." *NITA* 4,
    no. 1 (September 1976): 5.
    An irreverent and humorous sketch about nearly 10,000 years
    of trombone history, Spilka's account is continued in vol. 4, no.
    2, (February 1977): 14-15.
    History/Humor

69. ———. "The ITW at Eton." *JITA* 17, no. 4 (Fall 1989): 30-37.
    In a report on the International Trombone Association's
    Workshop at Eton College in England, Spilka includes sketches
    and profiles of several well-known American and European
    trombonists. Photos accompanying the article were also taken by Spilka.
    England/Eton/ITA/Workshops

70. ———. "A tribute to Kai Winding." *JITA* 11, no. 4 (October
    1983): 5-7.

A New York musical tribute to Kai Winding, performed at The Village Gate, is reviewed. It featured trombonists Britt Woodman, Al Grey, Curtis Fuller, Dick Griffin, Eddie Bert, Wayne Andre, Slide Hampton, Bob Brookmeyer, and J.J. Johnson.
Bio/Jazz-Blues/NewYork/VillageGate/Winding,K.

71.   SVANBERG, Carsten. "Orchestras and musical life in Denmark."
      NITA 8, no. 2 (December 1980): 18-19.
          At the time of this article, Svanberg was solo trombonist with the Danish Radio Symphony Orchestra.
      Bands/Careers/Denmark/Military/Orchestra

72.   *THE TROMBONIST.* Anthony Parsons, ed.
          This periodical is the official publication of the British Trombone Society, whose editor, a former International Trombone Association vice-president for European affairs, may be contacted at 3 Christchurch Road, London N8 9QL, England. The URL is www.nthwood.demon.co.uk/bts/contra.htm.
      BritishTromboneSociety/England/Parsons,A./Periodical

73.   TUCKER, Albert. "Never look at the trombones." *JITA* 18, no. 3 (Summer 1990): 42-43.
          In compiling a psychological profile of a selected group of college and high school band trombonists, the author utilized the Myers-Briggs Type Indicator (MBTI). This test was first developed by the Educational Testing Service in 1962. See Alois Melka, 910.
      ETS/MBTI/Melka,A./Psychology

74.   UPCHURCH, John D. "Post-prehistoric origins of the trombone: A research milestone." *NITA* 7, no. 2 (April 1980): 24-25.
          A tongue-in-cheek view of the trombone is given as it might have originated in Egypt, if the Egyptians had not been so busy building the pyramids and trying to escape from the annual flooding of the Nile.
      Egypt/Humor

75.   VITALI, Carlo. "L'esame de assunzione di un musico palatino a Bologna nella prima meta del 1600 [The competition for

appointment of a town musician in Bologna in the first half of the 17th century]." *Carrobbio* 4 (1978): 417-434.

Vitali's article, in Italian, deals with an audition in 1628 for the appointment of a sackbut player for the "Concerto Palatino," which was a wind ensemble in the service of the city senate of Bologna during the seventeenth century.
Auditions/Baroque/Bologna/ConcertoPalatino/Italy/PerfPrac/
Renaissance/Sackbut

76. WATERS, David. "My first twenty years in Houston." *JITA* 15, no. 1 [mistakenly labeled 14, no. 4] (Winter 1987): 54-55.
BassTrb/Bio/Houston/Orchestra

77. WEED, Larry, ed. *JITA*. 1972-1981.
Weed was founder of the *JITA* and its editor for the first ten years of the International Trombone Association. Editorial duties for the *JITA* (merged with the *NITA* in 1982) were assumed by Vern Kagarice in 1982. See Vern Kagarice, 51, and G.B. Lane, 52.
ITA/Kagarice,V./Lane,G.

78. YEO, Douglas. "The view from the back row." *Christianity Today* 27 (January 1983): 40.
Orchestra/PerfPrac/Religious

79. ———. "You'll never get anything done by letting things slide unless you play the trombone." *JITA* 19, no. 4 (Fall 1991): 44-45.
Yeo's short essay was reprinted from the Boston Symphony Orchestra program guide for the week of March 9, 1989, and gives a touching glimpse of a professional trombonist's reasons for continuing to love and appreciate his instrument. At the time of the writing of this article, Yeo was bass trombonist of the Boston Symphony.
Boston/Orchestra/TrbMus-Gen

BIOGRAPHIES/GENERAL

80.   ADAMS, Stan. "Orchestra showcase: The Saint Louis Symphony
      Orchestra." *NITA* 8, no. 3 (April 1981): 20-24.
      Adams features an interview with Bernard Schneider, principal,
      Roger Davenport, second trombone, Melvyn Jernigan, bass
      trombone, and John Tafoya, utility trombone and librarian of the
      orchestra. Included is a roster of St. Louis Symphony low brass
      personnel from 1894-1981.
      Davenport,R./Jernigan,M./Orchestra/SaintLouis/Schneider,B./
      Tafoya,J.

81.   ALSCHAUSKY, Serafin. *Der kunsterlich perfekte Blaser* [The
      artistically perfect wind(player)]. Dresden: Rudolf Kraut, 1937.
      Alschausky's monograph is cited by Robert Reifsnyder, 540.
      See that entry for references on German trombone virtuosos of
      the nineteenth and early twentieth centuries. Alschausky was a
      noted European trombone virtuoso and teacher who flourished
      during that time.
      Germany/Pedagogy/PerfPrac/Reifsnyder,R./Solos

82.   BAKER, Buddy. "Exit sliding." *JITA* 2 (1973-74): 61-62.
      Baker is the author of several humorous sketches by this title,
      which occasionally recur in the *JITA* . This sketch deals mostly
      with Lewis Van Haney, who was the recipient of the ITA Award
      in 1973. For more biographical material on Van Haney see
      Randy Kohlenberg and Robert Thomas, 164, John Marcellus,
      176, and Bruce Tracy, 227. For other sliding exits by Baker, see
      JITA 3 (1975): 20, which includes stories about studio bass
      trombonist George Roberts, the 1982 recipient of the ITA Award,

and vol. 4 (1976): 22-23 for accounts of Phil Wilson. See also Buddy Baker, 42.
Haney,L.V./ITA/Kohlenberg,R./Marcellus,J./Roberts,G./ Thomas,R./Tracy,B./Trombolympic/Wilson,P.

83. ———. "Thomas Beversdorf retires from trombone teaching (an interview—a tribute)." *NITA* 6, no. 4 (September 1979): 4-5.
S. Thomas Beversdorf received the International Trombone Association Award in 1979. Baker, who was a colleague of Beversdorf, includes comments from several of Beversdorf's students. See also obituaries for Thomas Beversdorf (1924-1981) in *NITA* 8, no. 3 (April 1981): 15-16, which includes excerpts from Baker's article, and in the *BBIBC* 35 (1981): 3.
Beversdorf,T./IndianaU/ITA/Obituaries/Pedagogy

84. BALL, Donald. "Edward Erwin." *JITA* 23, no. 3 (Summer 1995): 36-38.
Erwin was assistant principal trombone with the New York Philharmonic for 35 years, retiring in 1993. See Randy Kohlenberg and Robert Thomas, 164.
Erwin,E./Kohlenberg,R./NewYork/Orchestra/Thomas,R.

85. BARBOUR, William. "Orchestral showcase: The Detroit Symphony Orchestra." *JITA* 11, no. 4 (October 1983): 13-17.
Barbour features interviews with Raymond Turner, principal, Joseph Skrzynski, associate principal, Nathaniel Gurin, second, and Thomas Klaber, bass trombone. He also includes a list of the music directors and members of the low brass section in Detroit from 1914-1983.
Detroit/Gurin,N./Klaber,T./Orchestra/Skrzynski,J./Turner,R.

86. BAUER, Paul. "Frank Crisafulli." *JITA* 17, no. 4 (Fall 1989): 13-17.
Crisafulli joined the Chicago Symphony Orchestra in 1938. He was the 1990 recipient of the ITA Award. See Stewart Ross, 200, Eileen Meyer, 1186, and Bob Rainer, 1211. See also the *NITA*, April 1980, for a listing of the CSO low brass personnel from the orchestra's earliest days.
Chicago/Crisafulli,F./Meyer,E./Orchestra/Rainer,B./Ross,S.

87.   BEYER, Werner. "Reminiszenz an Posaunisten der
       Vergangenheit [Reminiscences of trombonists of the past]."
       BBIBC 22 (1978): 37-44.
          Printed in German, French, and English, Beyer's report is
       concerned with the history of trombone performers in the
       Staatskapelle Dresden, whose unbroken history extends back to
       1667. There is a particularly interesting paragraph about Eugen
       Reiche, whose Concerto No. 2 in A Major is frequently
       performed by trombone soloists.
       Dresden/Germany/Orchestra/Reiche,E.

88.   BOWELL, Jeffrey. "Orchestra showcase: The Cleveland
       Orchestra." *NITA* 6, no. 3 (April 1979): 13-17.
          Bowell's article includes interviews with Robert Boyd,
       principal, James DeSano, assistant principal, Allen Kofsky,
       second, and Edwin Anderson, bass trombone. A list of Cleveland
       Orchestra trombone personnel from 1918-1978 is included. The
       list was taken from an alphabetical listing of personnel in the
       Cleveland Orchestra programs, so that in some cases it was not
       able to determine who held the actual chairs. See below Harold
       McKinney, 186, and Bruce Tracy, 225.
       Anderson,E./Boyd,R./Burkhart,W./Cleveland/DeSano,J./
       Kofsky,A./McKinney,H./Orchestra/Tracy,B.

89.   BRIDGES, Glenn D. "The Frank Holton story, 1858-1942."
       Music Journal 33, no. 3 (March 1975): 48-49.
          Holton was one of the premier trombone soloists around the
       turn of the twentieth century and the founder of the Holton
       instrument company.
       Holton,F./Instruments-20thC/Solos

90.   ———. "Trombone History." *JITA* 1 [1972-73]: 20-21.
          Bridges was probably the foremost authority on brass
       performance in the United States in the nineteenth and early
       twentieth centuries. He has written a fascinating sketch of
       trombonists and contemporary artists from that period. See also
       his "The trombone in America," *Brass World* 9, no. 1 (1974): 32-
       33. He was the author of *Pioneers in Brass*, rev. (Detroit: Glenn

D. Bridges, 1968). See *BRASSBIB* for a more complete bibliography of Bridges's work.
Cairns,W./Čimera,J./Clarke,E./Holton,F./Innes,F./Isele,R./
King,T./Martin,C./Müller,R./Pinard,A./Proctor,J./Pryor,A./
Randall,C./Simons,G./Smith,C./Spary,C./Weldon,A./Wiehe,L.

91. BRIGHT, Dudley. "Denis Wick." *JITA* 17, no 2 (Spring 1989): 24-28.
Wick was for many years the top symphonic trombonist in London and is now a respected teacher and businessman. He was the 1989 recipient of the ITA Award.
ITA/London/Orchestra/Pedagogy/Wick,D.

92. BROUSSARD, George. "A musician's odyssey: The life and times of Leo Arnaud." *JITA* 13, no. 1 (January 1985): 21-24.
This multitalented musician also known as Arnaud-Vauchant is best remembered as presumably the first trombonist to perform the trombone solo in Ravel's *Bolero* (see Joel Elias, 115). Broussard's article covers Arnaud's career to about 1934. A second article in the *JITA* 13, no. 2 (April 1985): 26-28, covers the succeeding period up to 1985. An obituary for Arnaud-Vauchant may be found in the *Jazz Times* 21, no. 8 (1991): 38. See Jean Douay, 623.
Arnaud-Vauchant,L./*Boléro*/Douay,J./Elias,J./France/Obituaries/
Orchestra/PerfPrac/Ravel,M.

93. BROWN, Keith. "Robert Marsteller remembered." *JITA* 13, no. 1 (January 1985): 8.
See Joel Elias, 116. See also Robert Marsteller, *Advanced Slide Technique*, San Antonio: Southern Music Co., 1966.
Elias,J./LosAngeles/Marsteller,R./Studio

94. BROWN, R.S. "An interview with Christian Lindberg." *Fanfare* 15, no. 4 (1992): 126-129.
See Thomas G. Everett, 118, and Richard Raum, 196.
See also Knud Ketting, "A musician also has to be an actor," *Nordic Sounds* (September 1987): 16-17; V. Vern, "Dansk hoest i Pumpehuset," *Nutida Musik* 33, nos. 3-4 (1990): 19; J. Kosinska, "Puzon . . . i nie tylko," *Ruch Muzyczny* 34, no. 10

(1990): 4; and S. Sagvik, "Christian Lindberg, trombonvirtuos," *Tonfallet* 6 (September 1987): 2-3. Lindberg was the 1991 recipient of the ITA Award.
Denmark/Everett,T./ITA/Ketting,K./Kosinska,J./Lindberg,C./Raum,R./Sagvik,S./Solos/Vern,V.

95.   BRUENGER, David. "Women at work: Trombonists in North American orchestras and universities." *JITA* 20, no. 2 (Spring 1992): 12-21.
Colleges-Universities/NorthAmerica/Orchestra/Women

96.   CALL, Glenn K. "Joseph Edouard Barat (1882-1963)." *Euphonia* 2, no. 4 (April 1977): 8.
Call's article was based on a biography sheet supplied by Alphonse Leduc, Editions Musicales, Paris. Essential information from the article may be found in Ben Ivey's ongoing column, "General News," in the *NITA* 5, no. 3 (1978): 5-6.
Barat,J.E./France/Ivey,B./Leduc,A./TrbMus-20thC

97.   CARLSON, Eric, and Blair BOLLINGER. "A tribute to Glenn Dodson." *JITA* 23, no. 2 (Spring 1995): 28-33.
Actually a series of biographical essays by Dodson's friends and admirers, Carlson and Bollinger compiled this article upon Dodson's retirement from twenty-seven years as principal trombonist with the Philadelphia Orchestra. For more references on the Philadelphia Orchestra, see Bruce Tracy, 229.
Bollinger,B./Dodson,G./Orchestra/Philadelphia/Tracy,B.

98.   CHAMBERLAIN, David. "Simon Karasick: An unsung hero." *New York Brass Conference for Scholarships Journal* 21 (1993): 4.
Karasick was one of the most active free-lance players and teachers in the New York City area from the 1930s through the present. See Simon Karasick, 875.
Karasick,S./NewYork

99.   CHASANOV, Elliot L. "Orchestral showcase: The National Symphony Orchestra." *JITA* 11, no. 1 (January 1983): 7-12.
Chasanov interviews Milton Stevens, principal, David Finlayson, associate principal, James Kraft, second, and Robert

Kraft, bass trombone. There are also special reminiscences with Robert Isele, who served as soloist with the Marine Band from 1937 to 1961 and as second trombonist with the National Symphony from 1964-1980. See Ken Shifrin, 207.
Finlayson,D./Isele,R./Kraft,J./Kraft,R./Orchestra/Shifrin,K./ Stevens,M./Washington,DC

100. ———. "Orchestral showcase: The Pittsburgh Symphony Orchestra." *NITA* 8, no. 2 (December 1980): 6-10.
Chasanov interviews Carl Wilhelm and Robert Hamrick, co-principals; Harold Steiman, second trombone; and Byron McCulloh, bass trombone. He also includes a list of Pittsburgh low brass personnel from 1926-1981.
Hamrick,R./McCulloh,B./Orchestra/Pittsburgh/Steiman,H./ Wilhelm,C.

101. COHEN, Albert. "The King's Musicians: A postscript." *Notes* 49, no. 4 (June 1993): 1390-1394.
Cohen lists players on sackbut and trumpet for the King's Musicians during medieval times. The list is a supplement to a previous article, *"L'Etat de la France*: One hundred years of music at the French court," *Notes* 48, no. 3 (March 1992): 767-805, cited in *LASOCKI*, 1994.
France/King'sMusicians/Medieval/Sackbut

102. [COLIN, Charles]. "Master brass teacher John Coffey: A symbol of greatness [John Coffey: Tape talk to Dr. Charles Colin]." *New York Brass Conference for Scholarships Journal* 5 (1977): 100-103.
Colin's interview includes a reprinted article by Lynne Richmond from the *Cape Cod Standard-Times*, December 1, 1970. The rest of Colin's article contains a partial list of Coffey's students (up to 1977) and an informal interview taped by Phil La Normandin. Donald P. Poole wrote a subsequent article on Coffey on page 68 of the 1982 *New York Brass Conference for Scholarships Journal*, "Nothing to it kid, just tongue and blow." See Donald Appert, 1001. See also an obituary for John Coffey (1907-1981) in the *NITA* 8, no. 3 (April 1981): 14-15. Coffey taught for many years at the New England Conservatory and was presented the ITA Award in 1977.

Appert,D./BassTrb/Coffey,J./ITA/LaNormandin,P./Obituaries/
Pedagogy/Poole,D./Richmond,L.

103. CONANT, Abbie. "An interview with Heather Buchman." *JITA*
19, no. 3 (Summer 1991): 10-13.

At the time of the writing of this article, Buchman was
principal trombonist with the San Diego Symphony. Conant also
wrote a review of a recital by Heather Buchman for *Oper und
Konzert* 27 (November 1989): 25. Abbie Conant was first vice-
president of the International Trombone Association from 1996-1998.
Buchman,H./Orchestra/SanDiego/Women

104. COOPER, Isaiah. "Orchestra showcase: The Buffalo
Philharmonic Orchestra." *NITA* 7, no. 1 (December 1979): 17-21.

Cooper interviews Richard Myers, principal trombone, Fred
Halt, second trombone, Donald Miller, bass trombone, and Don
Harry, tuba. He includes a chart of the low brass personnel of the
Buffalo Philharmonic from 1936-1979.
Buffalo/Halt,F./Harry,D./Miller,D./Myers,R./Orchestra

105. "Die Posaune und einer ihrer Pioniere [The trombone and one of
its pioneers]." *Die Musik-Woche* 9 (1941): 21-23.

This article is in German and deals with Prof. Friedrich Mater.
Mary Rasmussen cites an article by Mater in her "Brass
bibliography: 1941-1945," *Brass Quarterly* 1, no. 4 (June 1958):
232-239 (see Friedrich Mater, 705).
Germany/Mater,F./Pedagogy/PerfPrac/Rasmussen,M.

106. DIETRICH, Kurt. "Orchestra showcase: The Milwaukee
Symphony Orchestra." *JITA* 11, no. 3 (July 1983): 26-28.

Dietrich includes a chart of the low brass personnel from 1959-
1983 and interviews with Don Haack, principal, Gary Greenhoe,
second, and Dick Kimball, bass trombone.
Greenhoe,G./Haack,D./Kimball,D./Milwaukee/Orchestra

107. DILLON, Steve. "Arthur Pryor: Poet of the trombone."
Instrumentalist 40 (November 1985): 34+.

See John Dittmer, 109, Daniel E. Frizane, et al., 135, Loren
Luper, 171, Steve Wolfinbarger, 243, Glenn P. Smith, 556, and

Philip Jameson, 870. See also Suzanne Mudge, "Arthur Pryor: This is your life," *JITA* 15, no. 2 (Spring 1987):28-29.
Dittmer,J./Frizane,D./Jameson,P./Luper,L./Mudge,S./PerfPrac/ Pryor,A./Smith,G./Wolfinbarger,S.

108. "Directory of symphony trombonists [in the U.S. and Canada]." *Instrumentalist* 40 (November 1985): 40+.
See Vern Kagarice and John Marcellus, 163, and Douglas Yeo, 247.
Ballet/Canada/Kagarice,V./Marcellus,J./Opera/Orchestra/Yeo,D.

109. DITTMER, John S. "'Thoughts of Love': Reminiscences of Arthur Pryor." *JITA* 13, no. 2 (April 1985): 20-23.
This article features an interview, taped by Joel Elias, with Dittmer, who studied with Arthur Pryor in the 1930s. The interview took place at Humboldt State University, during the annual Brass Chamber Music Workshop. For some interesting responses see the *JITA* 14, no. 1 (Winter 1986) letters in "The eighth position," and Col. Dittmer's final response in the *JITA* 14, no. 2 (Spring 1986), also in "The eighth position." See Steve Dillon, 107, for more references to Arthur Pryor.
Dillon,S./Elias,J./Pedagogy/PerfPrac/Pryor,A.

110. DOUAY, Jean. "André LaFosse (1890-1975): Maitre es-trombone [André LaFosse (1890-1975): Trombone master]." *BBIBC* 70 (1990): 56-60.
LaFosse was for many years the trombone professor at the Paris Conservatory.
France/LaFosse,A./ParisConservatory/Pedagogy

111. ———. "Une femme au trombone [A woman trombonist]." *BBIBC* 29 (1980): 49-52.
Internationally acclaimed French trombonist Jean Douay introduces Yvelise Girard, the first woman in France to be appointed to an official musical post by means of a competition. His article is translated from French into German and English.
France/Girard,Y./Women

112. EISENBERG, Reinke. "Johann Doms: Performer, teacher, publisher." *JITA* 20, no. 3 (Summer 1992): 14-19.

Doms was the former solo trombonist with the Berlin Philharmonic. He also taught at the Hochschule der Kunst and the Karajan Academy.

Berlin/Doms,J./Orchestra/Pedagogy/TrbMus-Gen

113. ELIAS, Joel. "Interview with Eric Crees." *JITA* 24, no. 3 (Summer 1996): 22-24.

Crees is co-principal trombonist of the London Symphony Orchestra. He also teaches at the Guildhall School of Music and Drama in London and is musical director of the LSO brass. The article contains a selected discography of Crees's arrangements for brass ensemble. See Eric Crees, 819.

Crees,E./Discog/England/London/Orchestra

114. ———. "Ken Shifrin: Virgo man from Birmingham." *JITA* 17, no. 3 (Summer 1989): 28-30.

At the time of this interview Shifrin was the principal trombonist of the City of Birmingham (England) Symphony Orchestra. He is also the founder of Virgo Music. The article includes Shifrin's views about his controversial advertisement in the Fall 1987 *JITA*.

England/Orchestra/Publishing/Shifrin,K./Virgo

115. ———. "Miles to go: An interview with Miles Anderson." *JITA* 11, no. 4 (October 1983): 26-29.

Although this interview deals mostly with Miles Anderson's work with contemporary music and new techniques, there is a fascinating story concerning Leo(n?) Arnaud (see George Broussard, 92), who played the first performance of *Bolero* under the direction of Maurice Ravel. Anderson also gives his views on other outstanding trombonists. See Jean-Pierre Mathez, 183.

Anderson,M./Arnaud,L./*Bolero*/Broussard,G./ContempTech/ Discog/Electronic/Mathez,J./Solos/TrbMus-20thC

116. ———. "Robert Marsteller: In memoriam." *NITA* 3, no. 1 (September 1975): 15.

Marsteller was principal trombonist with the National Symphony and the Los Angeles Philharmonic, a teacher at the University of Southern California, and an active studio trombonist

in the Los Angeles area from the 1940s through the early 1970s. He was the author of *Advanced Slide Technique*, published by Southern Music. He was also the trombonist for whom Paul Creston wrote his *Fantasy for Trombone and Orchestra*. See Keith Brown, 93.
Brown,K./Creston,P./Marsteller,R./Orchestra/Studio

117. EVERETT, Thomas G. "The Boston Symphony Orchestra personnel history and interview." *NITA* 6, no. 4 (September 1979): 10-12+.
The trombone section of the Boston Symphony at the time of this article included Ronald Barron, principal, Norman Bolter, second, and Gordon Hallberg, bass trombone. Everett also includes a list of trombone personnel from 1881-1979.
Barron,R./Bolter,N./Boston/Hallberg,G./Orchestra

118. ———. "A conversation with Christian Lindberg." *JITA* 17, no. 1 (Winter 1989): 23-31.
Everett's interview was transcribed by John Kafalas. The article contains a discography and a transcription of Lindberg's cadenza from the Ferdinand David *Concertino*. See R.S. Brown, 94, for more references to Christian Lindberg.
Brown,R./Cadenzas/David,F./Denmark/Discog/Kafalas,J./Lindberg,C./Solos/Sweden

119. ———. "A conversation with John Swallow." *JITA* 14, no. 3 (Summer 1986): 13-18.
Swallow was for many years trombonist with the New York Brass Quintet, was an active free-lance performer in the New York area, and has been on the music faculty of several major schools including Yale University. See John Swallow, 1269-1271. See also Owen Wells Metcalf, "The New York Brass Quintet: Its history and influence on brass literature and performance," Indiana University, DM, 1978.
Metcalf,O./NYBrassQuintet/Orchestra/Pedagogy/PerfPrac/Swallow,J./TrbMus-20thC

120. ———. "Glenn D. Bridges (1899-1981): A biographical sketch." *JITA* 10, no. 2 (April 1982): 39.

Bridges was one of most prolific biographers of nineteenth- and early twentieth-century brass virtuosos, including trombonists such as Arthur Pryor, Leo Zimmerman, and Frederick Neil Inncs. An extensive bibliography of his work can be found in *BRASSBIB*. See Randy Kohlenberg, 10.
BrassPerf-19thC/Bridges,G./Kohlenberg,R./Obituaries

121.   ———. "History and update of ITA Scholarship winners." *JITA* 13, no. 1 (January 1985): 9-11.

Everett updates the last review (1979) of the ITA Scholarship recipients: Jan Moeller (1973), John Veselack (1974), Brad Bobcik (1975), David Foley (1976), Rock Ciccarone (1977), Stan Jeffs (1978), Stephen Witser (1979), Jeff Budin (1980), Randy Campora (1981), Doug Johnson (1982), Michael Finton (1983), and John J. DiLutis (1984).

For a related story see Eugene Grissom and Eileen Massinon, 307. For a further update on other ITA scholarship winners see Roy Pickering, Jack Robinson, and James Roberts, "The Don Yaxley Bass Trombone Scholarships winners: Where are they now?" *JITA* 26, no. 1 (Winter 1998): 44-48—Paul Eachus (1981), John Wasson (1982), Randy Campora (1983), Dan Satterwhite (1984), Bruce Blomquist (1985), Blair Bollinger (1986), Harold Van Schaik (1987), Matthew Guilford (1988), Robert Byrd (1990), Robert Fournier (1991), Sergei Fedianin (1992), Steven R. Brown (1993), Darren McHenry (1994), Norbet Laczko (1995), Matthias Dangelmaier (1996), Michael D. McLemore (1997).

Blomquist,B./Bobcik,B./Bollinger,B./Brown,S./Budin,J./
Byrd,R./Campora,R./Ciccarone,R./Dangelmaier,M./DiLutis,J./
Eachus,P./Fedianin,S./Finton,M./Foley,D./Fournier,R./Grissom,E./
Guilford,M./ITAScholarship/Jeffs,S./Johnson,D./Laczko,N./
Massinon,E./McHenry,D./McLemore,M./Moeller,J./Pickering,R./
Roberts,J./Robinson,J./Satterwhite,D./VanSchaik,H./Veselack,J./
Wasson,J./Witser,S./Workshops/Yaxley,D.

122.   ———. "An interview with Miloslav Hejda." *JITA* 2 (1973-74): 68-70.

Hejda is a noted Czech bass trombonist, teacher, and composer. At the time of the interview he was bass trombonist with the Czech Philharmonic. See also Larry Weed, 234.
BassTrb/Czechoslovakia/Hejda,M./Orchestra/TrbMus-20thC/Weed,L.

123. [———]. "New York City Opera trombonist dies." *JITA* 14, no. 2 (Spring 1986): 11.
Robert Wright, bass trombonist of the New York City Opera for twenty-one years, died on September 9, 1985. Wright was born in Canada but later enrolled at Hofstra University, where he became a member of the National Orchestral Association. He also was a member of the Air Force Band and the Si Zentner Orchestra before joining the Opera orchestra in the fall of 1963. Wright's obituary appeared in Everett's ongoing column, "General News."
BassTrb/NewYorkCityOpera/Obituaries/Opera/Wright,R.

124. ———. "A survey of orchestral bass trombonists." *JITA* 7 (1979): 23-26.
The names beginning with A-H are contained in this article. The survey is continued in vols. 8 (1980): 23-26 [K-M], and 9 (1981): 28-30 [P-W]. Everett's study is a sequel to a similar one he wrote dealing with studio and big band bass trombonists, which is cited as 301.
Aharoni,E./Alexei,E./Andresen,M./BassTrb/Biddlecombe,R./Boyd,F./Clark,J./Coffey,J./Destanque,G./Glover,B./Griffith,T./Hallberg,G./Harper,R./Harwood,D./Kleinhammer,E./Kublock,H./Lortie,S./McCulloh,B./Orchestra/Ostrander,A./Premru,R./Reynolds,J./Sakakibara,S./Vernon,C./Waters,D.

125. ———. "The second annual National Trombone Workshop," *Brass World* 7, no. 2 (1972): 146-151.
Biographical sketches of the faculty appear on pp. 146 and 147.
Baker,B./Bridges,G./Brown,L./Cramer,W./Haney,L.V./Humfeld,N./Pederson,T./Pressler,B./Roberts,G./Romersa,H./Watrous,B./Weed,L./Wiehe,L./Wilson,P.

126. ———. "The eleventh annual international trombone workshop
     preview." *NITA* 8, no. 3 (April 1981): 2-11.
     Biographical sketches of the workshop faculty are included in
     this preview.
     Baker,B./Christmann,G./Cryder,R./Dempster,S./DiStasio,E./
     Erdman,J./Haney,L.V./Hildebrandt,D.J./Knaub,D./Knepper,J./
     Middleton,A./Ostrander,A./Pearce,B./Pulis,G./Robinson,J./
     Shiner,M./Slokar,B./Upchurch,J./Wagner,I./Whigham,J./Wick,D.
     Wilson,P./Workshops

127. ———. "Twelfth annual ITW preview." *JITA* 10, no. 2 (April
     1982): 5-12.
     Everett's article contains biographical sketches of the workshop
     faculty.
     Andre,W./Brown,K./Chasanov,E./Cleveland,J./Cramer,W./
     Ervin,T./Gray,R./Janks,H./Kaplan,A./Lusher,D./Peck,B./Roos,I./
     Roznoy,R./Sanborn,P./Smith,D./Stewart,D./Streeter,T./
     Svanberg,C./Ward,C./Weed,L./Wheeler,M./Wigness,C./Workshops

128. ———. "Thirteenth annual ITW preview." *Journal of the
     International Association* 11, no. 2 (April 1983): 6-15.
     As in the previous articles, Everett's preview contains
     biographical sketches of the workshop faculty (also included is a
     discography for Armin Rosin).
     Anderson,L./Cravens,T./Discog/Fillio,L./Fink,R./Forsang,B./
     Fowler,B./Globokar,V./Grey,A./Hansson,A./Höna,G./Josel,R./
     Kagarice,V./Lindberg,R./Magliocco,H./Prussing,R./Rogers,D./
     Rosin,A./Schuller,G./Swallow,J./Trimmer,P./Ulyate,L./Vernon,C./
     Watrous,B./Weed,L./Whigham,J./Williams,J./Workshops

129. ———. "Fourteenth ITW preview." *JITA* 13, no. 2 (April 1985):
     6-19.
     Aharoni,E./Anderson,M./Arnaud,L./Barron,R./Bauer,P./Bell,R./
     Bucher,P./Chasanov,E./Covington,W./Douay,J./Drew,J./Erb,D./
     Erdman,J./Garvin,K./Green,U./Haney,L.V./Hartman,M./
     Humfeld,N./Lindberg,C./Marcellus,J./Matten,C./Olson,C./
     Peebles,B./Reichenbach,B./Rutherford,P./Sloan,G./Smith,L./
     Vogt,N./Weiss,R./Wiehe,L./Williams,J./Workshops

130. FADLE, Heinz. "A portrait of Willi Wather." *JITA* 22, no. 1 (Winter 1994): 33-34.

Reprinted from *Das Schallstück* (see 60 in this book under *General Reference/Miscellaneous*), Fadle's interview deals with one of the most prominent symphonic trombonists and teachers in Germany. Fadle was president of the International Trombone Association from 1996 to 1998.

Germany/Orchestra/Wather,W.

131. FAUNTLEY, Basil J. "Orchestral showcase: The CAPAB Orchestra." *JITA* 12, no. 4 (October 1984): 22-24.

The CAPAB [Cape Performing Arts Board] Orchestra is based in Cape Town, South Africa, along with another orchestra, the Cape Town Symphony. The orchestra, which was multiracial even in 1984, was part of an organization fully supported by production, technical, and administrative departments and boasting a full-time staff of 620, a full ballet company, an opera company with chorus, and a drama company.

Fauntley's article features interviews with Alan Griggs, principal, Joseph Stott, sub-principal, and Edgar Tyson, bass trombone.

CapeTown/Griggs,A./Orchestra/Scott,J./SouthAfrica/Tyson,E.

132. FETTER, David. "Daniel Speer." *JITA* 6 (1978): 5-6.

Based on Fetter's 1969 thesis, "Daniel Speer, Stadtpfeiffer (1636-1707)," UMI no. AA1 1301982, DAI vol. 0801 (Music), Ann Arbor: University Microfilms, his article contains a discussion of the diatonic system of slide positions found in Speer's *Grund-richtiger Unterricht . . .* (Ulm, 1697). Among other things, Fetter identifies Speer as the composer of the "Bänkelsängerlieder," which may be the most performed work in the history of modern brass quintets.

The thesis is not available at present but may be obtained from Fetter at 109 Hawthorne Rd., Baltimore MD 21210, or through interlibrary loan from the Friedheim Music Library, Peabody Institute, 1 East Mt. Vernon Place, Baltimore MD 21202. See Dale Voelker, 573, Arnold Fromme, 640, Heinrich Hüber, 676, Jeffrey Quick 728, and Henry E. Howey, 1122. For more information about the music of Daniel Speer, see Mitchell Neil

Sirman, "The wind sonatas in Daniel Speer's *Musicalisch-Türckischer Eulen-Spiegel* of 1688," The University of Wisconsin, PhD, 1972 [University Microfilms 72-29,512].
Bänkelsängerlieder/Fromme,A./Howey,H./Hüber,H./Instruments-17thC/PeabodyInstitute/Pedagogy/Quick,J./Sirman,M./Speer,D./Theses/TrbMus-17thC/Voelker,D.

133. ———. "Johannes Rochut (1881-1952)." *BBIBC*, no. 50 (1985): 41-49.
Fetter's article is in English, French, and German. Rochut was bass trombonist with the Boston Symphony and transcribed Italian tenor Marco Bordogni's (1788-1856) vocalises for trombone. A similar article by Fetter also appears in *JITA* 10, no. 3 (July 1982): 22-23. See Glenn P. Smith, 555, Neill Humfeld, 1124, Randall T. Mitchell, 1189, and Benny Sluchin, 1253.
Bib/Bordogni,M./Etudes/Humfeld,N./Mitchell,R./Pedagogy/Rochut,J./Sluchin,B./Smith,G./TrbMus-Gen

134. FOCACCIA, Laura. "Bartolomeo Sorte cantore e trombonista padovano [Bartolomeo Sorte, Paduan singer and trombone player]." *Il Santo: Rivista antoniana de storia dottrina arte* 32, nos. 2-3 (May-December 1992): 187-196.
Focaccia's article is in Italian.
Italy/Padua/Sorte,B./Vocal

135. FRIZANE, Daniel E., et al. *Arthur Pryor, Trombone.* Sedro Woolley WA: Crystal Records, N.d.
Frizane's insert to the cassette *Arthur Pryor Trombone with the Sousa Band and Pryor Orchestra* (Cassette C451) contains some of the most complete biographical sketches and discographies of famous brass virtuosos. Contributors include Glenn Bridges, Herbert L. Clarke, Clifford P. Lillya, Glenn P. Smith, and Leonard Smith. The insert also contains five photographs dating from Pryor's earliest career.
Frizane did his doctoral paper on "Arthur Pryor (1870-1942) American trombonist, bandmaster, composer," University of Kansas, DMA, 1984. See *Dissertation Abstracts* 46/05-A, 1122; MBB85-13825; AAD85-13825 [order numbers from various citations], and *RILM*83/3522dd29. See also a review of the

doctoral paper by H.T. Young in the *Council for Research in Music Education Bulletin* 97 (Summer 1988): 85-88. See Steve Dillon, 107, for more references on Arthur Pryor.

See also Henry Woelber, "Arthur Pryor: Band director and ace trombonist," *Jacobs' Band Monthly* 26 (March 1941): 8, as cited by Mary Rasmussen in "Brass Bibliography: 1936-1940," *Brass Quarterly* 2, no. 2 (December 1958): 63-77.

Bridges,G./Clarke,H./Dillon,S./Discog/Diss/KansasU/Lillya,C./Pedagogy/PerfPrac/Pryor,A./Rasmussen,M./Smith,G./Smith,L./Woelber,H./Young,H.

136. GADE, Per. "Anton Hansen (1877-1947)." *BBIBC* 27 (1979): 27-40.

Called by Gade the "Scandinavian king of the trombone," this Danish virtuoso's long career influenced composers and musicians to develop a greater appreciation of the musical capabilities of the trombone. Gade's article is in three parts. Part 1, cited above, tells of Hansen's childhood and youth in Copenhagen, and ends with Hansen's departure to Berlin, where he studied with Paul Weschke (see Carl Lenthe, 695).

Part 2, in vol. 28, ends with Hansen's experiences under the baton of Carl Nielsen in the Royal Orchestra in Copenhagen. Part 3, in vol. 29 (1980), deals with Hansen's association and friendships with French musicians such as Johannes Rochut and André Lafosse and recounts his experiences playing under the baton of Sibelius. See Per Gade, 137.

Denmark/Hansen,A./Jørgensen,A./LaFosse,A./Rochut,J./Weschke,P.

137. ———. "Axel Jørgensen (1881-1947): A biographical profile." *JITA* 11, no. 1 (January 1983): 6.

Gade's article, which first appeared in a Tokyo program of the International Brass Quintet, may interest trombonists because of Jørgensen's friendship with Danish trombonist Anton Hansen. Hansen influenced many of Jørgensen's works for brass, including his 1916 "Romance for Trombone and Piano," now available from Edition Wilhelm Hansen in Copenhagen. For more information on Hansen see Per Gade, 136. See also the *NITA* 7, no. 1 (December 1979) for a short biographical sketch on Danish-born trombonist Gade.

Hansen,A./Jørgensen,A./TrbMus-20thC

138. ———. "An Interview with Thorkild Graae Jörgensen." *JITA* 10, no. 2 (April 1982): 28-30.

Jörgensen was solo trombonist with the Danish National Radio Symphony and a leading teacher in Denmark. Gade also includes a discussion of Launy Gröndahl's *Concerto for Trombone and Orchestra* and a list of corrections for the reprinted 1974 version. Concertos/Gröndahl,L./Jörgensen,T./TrbMus-20thC

139. GAJDAMOVIC, Tat'jana, ed. *Mastera igry na duhovyh instrumentah Moskovskoj konservatorii: Ocerki* [Master wind performers of the Moscow conservatory: Sketches]. Moscow: Muzyka, 1979.

Gajdamovic's book, in Russian, contains two articles concerning the great Russian trombone teacher Vladimir Blazhevich: Boris Grigoriev, "V.M. Blazevic: Trombonist, pedagogue, conductor," and Viktor Batasev, "The pupil of V.M. Blazevic: V.A. Scerbinin." The book is located in *RILM*79/953bc29. See André Smith, 212, and Larry Weed, 240. Batasev,V./Blazhevich,V./Grigoriev,B./Moscow/Russia/ Scerbinin,V./Smith,A./Weed,L.

140. GARVIN, Keig E., and André SMITH. "Jaroslav Čimera (1885-1972): Virtuoso trombonist—master teacher." *JITA* 25, no. 1 (Winter 1997): 34-47.

Two of Čimera's students document the life and career of an outstanding teacher and virtuoso performer. Their essay will be expanded into a full biography of Čimera to be published by André M. Smith Music Co. See Traugott Rohner, 199, John Upchurch, 232, and Jaroslav Čimera, 1036. Čimera,J./Rohner,T./Smith,A./Upchurch,J.

141. GINSBERG, M. "Canadian scene." *International Musician* 87 (September 1988): 13.

Ginsberg's article contains information about Alain Trudel. For more information on Trudel, see vol. 91 (November 1992): 11. See also Robert Hough, 675. Canada/Hough,R./Jazz-Blues/Trudel,A.

142. GOODWIN, Peter. "Ray Premru: An appreciation." *JITA* 17, no. 1 (Winter 1989): 38-39.

Written by one of Premru's colleagues in the London Philharmonia, Goodwin's tribute deals with Premru as a performer, teacher, and composer. A representative discography of his performances with various ensembles and a list of the Philharmonia low brass sections since Premru joined them in 1958 are included. Ray Premru passed away in 1998. For information on his passing see Randy Campora, "General News," *JITA* 26, no. 3 (Summer 1998): 11.
BassTrb/Campora,R./Discog/London/Obituaries/Orchestra/ Philharmonia/Premru,R.

143. ———. "Venice preserved." *JITA* 15, no. 2 (Spring 1987): 24-26.

London Philharmonia trombonist Goodwin's ancestors in the Bassano family emigrated to England from Italy sometime in the sixteenth century. Some of them performed on sackbuts and, along with other musicians in the family, dominated the *King's Musick* under Henry VIII and his successors. Some of the English Bassano family apparently returned to Venice in the late sixteenth century, hence Goodwin's connection to the Italian city. See David Lasocki and Roger Prior, 167.
Bassano/*King'sMusick*/Lasocki,D./Prior,R./Sackbut/Venice

144. GUION, David M. "Felipe Cioffi: A trombonist in antebellum America." *American Music* 14 (1996): 1-41.

See also Guion, 145.
Cioffi,F./Solos/TrbMus-19thC

145. ———. "Four American trombone soloists before Arthur Pryor: Some preliminary findings." *JITA* 20, no. 4 (Fall 1992): 32-37.

Guion gives short biographical sketches of Felippe Cioffi, Frederick Letsch, Carlo Alberto Cappa, and Frederick Neil Innes. There are also several references cited in the notes at the end of Guion's article. For further information see Glenn Bridges, *Pioneers in Brass*, Detroit: Sherwood, 1965. See also Bridges, 90, Guion, 144, and Wolfinbarger, 243. For an update on Cioffi and some other nineteenth-century trombonists (Antonio Mariotti [c.1755-1838], Antoine Dieppo [1808-1878], and M? Schmidt [fl.

mid-nineteenth century in Germany]), see Guion's article, "Great, but forgotten trombonists: Some biographical sketches," *BBIBC* 97 (1997): 62-73.

For an article on Schmidt, see "Herr M. Schmidt, Tonkünstler auf der Posaune," 148. See also Mary Rasmussen, 194, where she relates a slight controversy about the relative performance merits of Schmidt (presumably the same person) and Queisser as recorded in *Allegemeine musikalische Zeitung* 32 (1830): 287.

See Hugh Callison [incorrectly cited in one of Guion's articles as *Cathson*], 613, for more information on Frederic Letsch (or Leetsch). For general information on brass instruments of this period in the United States see Robert Eliason, 832. Bands/Belcke,F./Bridges,G./Callison,H./Cappa,C./Cioffi,F./ Dieppo,A./Eliason,R./Innes,F./Letsch,F./Mariotti,A./Queisser,C./ Rasmussen,M./Schmidt,M./Wolfinbarger,S.

146. HARVISON, Emery. "The Meridian Arts Ensemble: An interview with Benjamin Herrington." *JITA* 24, no. 1 (Winter 1996): 38-43.

Benjamin Herrington is the trombonist for this versatile and exciting brass quintet whose repertoire, according to Harvison, "covers a wider range of styles than any other professional touring ensemble in existence." They have collaborated with and commissioned works by such composers as Frank Zappa, Milton Babbitt, Kirk Nurock, Ira Taxin, and Elliott Carter, and adapted music by Herbie Hancock, Jimi Hendrix, and Captain Beefhart. A short discography is included.
ChamMus-Trb/Discog/Herrington,B./MeridianArts/Rock-Popular

147. ———. "A tribute to Betty Glover." *JITA* 14, no. 2 (Spring 1986): 12-15.

Harvison has written a warm sketch about the career of one of the pioneer women trombonists who blazed a trail for other women who sought acceptance as professional trombonists.
BassTrb/Cincinnati/Glover,B./Orchestra/Women

148. "Herr M. Schmidt, Tonkünstler auf der Posaune [M. Schmidt, musical artist on the trombone]." *Monatsbericht der Gesellschaft der Musikfreunde* (1830): 8-9.

See the annotation to David M. Guion, 145. See also Mary Rasmussen, 194, where she quotes an account of a concert in Kassel in the 1830 *Allgemeine musikalische Zeitung*, which featured an M. Schmidt and relates a small controversy about the relative performance merits of Schmidt and Carl Traugott Queisser (see index for references to this outstanding nineteenth-century artist).
Belcke,F./Germany/Guion,D./PerfPrac/Queisser,C./Rasmussen,M./
Schmidt,M./Solos/TrbMus-19thC

149. HINTERBICHLER, Karl. "Orchestral showcase: The Dallas Symphony Orchestra." *JITA* 12, no. 1 (January 1984): 8-14.
Hinterbichler includes interviews with John Kitzman, principal, Philip Graham, second, and Daral Rauscher, bass trombone. There is also a list of music directors and trombone personnel in the Dallas Symphony from 1947-1983.
Dallas/Graham,P./Kitzman,J./Orchestra/Rauscher,D.

150. HOGG, Simon. "Harold Nash: A half century with the trombone on the British scene," *BBIBC* 98, no. 2 (1997): 70+.
See Harold Nash, 716, 916, and 1191.
England/Orchestra/Pedagogy

151. HUMFELD, Neill H. "Fifteenth ITW preview." *JITA* 14, no. 2 (Spring 1986): 16-25.
Anderson,S./Bahr,E./Brevig,P./Brown,K./Campbell,L./
Dempster,S./Ervin,T./Everett,T./Höna,G./ITA/Kleinhammer,E./
Leno,L./Mulcahy,M./Pugh,J./Rehak,F./Stuart,D./Whigham,J./
Workshops

152. ———. "Seventeenth ITW preview." *JITA* 15, no. 2 (Spring 1987): 30-31.
The biographical sketches of the faculty appear in an insert between pages 30 and 31.
Everett,T./Forbes,V./Friedman,J./Kagarice,V./Lawrence,M./
Lemke,F./Mandernach,C./Marsteller,L./Premru,R./Raph,A./
Sluchin,B/Smith,G./Stuart,David/VanLier,B./VanLier,E./
Watrous,B./Workshops/Xenakis,I.

153. ———. "[Eighteenth] ITW Preview." *JITA* 16, no. 2 (Spring 1988): 28-29.

     The workshop is misnumbered as seventeen. Biographical sketches of the faculty are located in an insert between pp. 26 and 27.

     Baker,B./Cramer,W./Elliott,D./Johnson,J.J./Lindberg,C./ Loucky,D./Mangelsdorff,A./McDougall,I./Plsek,T./Steinmeyer,D./ Stevens,M./Svanberg,C./Taylor,D./Wick,D./Workshops

154. [HUMFELD, Neill H., and John MARCELLUS]. "International trombone workshop XX: Faculty biographies." *JITA* 19, no. 2 (Spring 1991): insert [between pages 18 and 19].

     The twentieth International Trombone Workshop was held at the Eastman School of Music and celebrated the life and work of Emory Remington on the twentieth anniversary of his death.

     Crisafulli,F./Douay,J./Griffith,T./Haney,L.V./Marcellus,J./ McDougall,I./Norrell,S./Pugh,J./Remington,E./Sluchin,B./ Svanberg,C./Watrous,B./Wick,D./Workshops

155. HUNT, Paul B. "Orchestra showcase: The Denver Symphony Orchestra." *JITA* 10, no. 1 (January 1982): 16-19.

     Hunt's interview primarily involved John Dailey, principal, but Ron Arentz, second, and Dick Reed, bass trombone, also assisted in the preparation of the article. Paul Hunt is president of the International Trombone Association (1998-2000).

     Arentz,R./Dailey,J./Denver/Orchestra/Reed,R.

156. [IVEY, Ben]. "Leslie Bassett: A biographical profile." *NITA* 6, no. 3 (April 1979): 2.

     Bassett's profile appears in Ivey's ongoing column, "General News." A trombonist himself, Bassett, a Pulitzer Prize winner and Prix de Rome recipient, has composed many works for trombone in various settings.

     Bassett,L./PrixDeRome/PulitzerPrize/TrbMus-20thC

157. [———]. "Raymond Katarzynski: A biographic[al] profile." *NITA* 7, no. 2 (April 1980): 4.

     Katarzynski is one of the most well-known performers and teachers in Europe. At the time of Ivey's profile, which is

included in his ongoing column "General News," Katarzynski was principal trombonist with the Paris Opera.
France/Katarzynski,R./Orchestra

158. [————]. "Sonata for Trombone and Piano, cn[catalog number?] 292 (1977), Thom Ritter George." *NITA* 6, no. 2 (December 1978): 5-6.

The report on George's Sonata appears in Ivey's ongoing column, "General News." There is a short discussion of the Sonata, but most of the article comprises a concise biography of the composer.
George,T.R./Solos/Sonata/TrbMus-20thC

159. JAMESON, Philip. "Orchestra showcase: The Atlanta Symphony Orchestra." *JITA* 10, no. 4 (October 1982): 11-13.

The primary interview is with Harry Maddox, principal trombone. At the time of the article Richard Hansbery was second trombone and Donald Wells played bass trombone with the orchestra.
Atlanta/Hansbery,R./Maddox,H./Orchestra/Wells,D.

160. JAMESON, Philip, and David MATHIE. "The National Music Camp at age 60: A retrospective look at its trombone teachers and students from 1928-1988." *JITA* 16, no. 3 (Summer 1988): 32-33.
Intlerlochen/Maddy,J./Mathie,D./NationalMusicCamp

161. JOHANSEN, David P. "A conversation with Robert Lambert." *JITA* 25, no. 1 (Winter 1997): 26-33.

Robert Lambert was a former associate principal trombonist of the Philadelphia Orchestra under Eugene Ormandy, and the principal trombonist of the Chicago Symphony under Fritz Reiner. The author of the article is currently professor of low brass studies at Western State College in Gunnison CO, near where Lambert now resides. Included in the article is a tribute by Jay Friedman, currently principal trombonist with the Chicago Symphony.
Chicago/Friedman,J./Lambert,R./Orchestra/Philadelphia

162. KAGARICE, Vern. "A tribute to Neill Humfeld," *JITA* 18, no. 4 (Fall 1990): 28-30.

    See "Neill Humfeld (1928-1991)." *JITA* 19, no. 4 (Fall 1991): 3. See also Humfeld, 1124-1126. He was president of the International Trombone Association (1980-1982) and received the ITA Award in 1984.

    Humfeld,N./ITA/Obituaries/Pedagogy

163. KAGARICE, Vern, and John MARCELLUS. "Trombone personnel of American and Canadian orchestras and service bands." *JITA* 10, no. 1 (January 1982): 20-21.

    See an addendum in the *JITA* 12, no. 3 (July 1984): 44, which also includes Israeli orchestras. See also "Directory of symphony trombonists," 108, and Douglas Yeo, 247.

    Bands/Canada/Marcellus,J./Military/Orchestra/USA/Yeo,D.

164. KOHLENBERG, Randy, and Robert THOMAS. "Orchestral showcase: The New York Philharmonic Orchestra." *JITA* 11, no. 2 (April 1983): 16-24.

    A special interview is conducted with some of the legendary members of past trombone sections of the Philharmonic: Gordon Pulis (see Bill Spilka, 215), Lewis Van Haney (see Buddy Baker, 82, John Marcellus 176, and Bruce Tracy, 227), and Allen Ostrander (see Hal Reynolds, 197, Ronald G. Smith, 213, and Bruce Tracy, 223).

    The 1983 section of the Philharmonic included Ed Herman, Jr., principal, Edward Erwin, assistant principal (see Donald Ball, 84), Gilbert Cohen, second, and Don Harwood, bass trombone. Also included in this article, prepared with the assistance of Robert Resnikoff, a member of the publicity staff of the Philharmonic, is a list of low brass personnel of the orchestra, and conductors, dating from 1849 to 1983.

    Baker,B./Ball,D./Cohen,G./Erwin,E./Haney,L./Harwood,D./ Herman,E./Marcellus,J./NewYork/Orchestra/Ostrander,A./Pulis,G./ Resnikoff,R./Reynolds,H./Smith,R.G./Spilka,B./Thomas,R./Tracy,B.

165. LAKE, S. "Red brassman." *Melody Maker* 52 (April 1977): 40+.

    Paul Rutherford, the subject of this interview, is an English avant-garde trombonist. See also John Litweiler's interview with

Rutherford in the *Village Voice,* July 27, 1977, where he discusses Rutherford's album, *The Gentle Harm of the Bourgeoisie.* Rutherford makes use of mute and vocal effects to produce his unique sonorities. The album is also reviewed in *Coda—Canada's Jazz Magazine* 158 (November/December 1977): 14.

Avant-Garde/England/Litweiler,J./Mutes/Rutherford,P./Vocal

166. LAPIE, Raymond. "The Braun brothers: Two names, one method." *JITA* 23, no. 1 (Winter 1996): 30-31.

Jean Christophe (or Jean Frédérick) and André Braun were brothers who were active brass (including trombone) players in Paris during the latter part of the eighteenth and early part of the nineteenth century. André authored a popular tutor for trombone, *Gamme et méthode pour les trombonnes* [Trombone scale and tutor for alto, tenor, and bass trombones].

Lapie believes the significance of this tutor stems from the fact that it appears to be the first modern book on trombone pedagogy which gives "equal importance to the seven positions . . . and is also the first to consider the trombone as a B-flat instrument (non-transposing)." See also Howard Weiner, 1290.

Braun,A./Braun,J.C./Paris/Pedagogy/TrbMus-18thC/Weiner,H.

167. LASOCKI, David, and Roger PRIOR. *The Bassanos: Venetian Musicians and Instrument Makers in England, 1531-1665.* London: Scolar Press, 1995.

Members of the Bassano family numbered among the most influential trombonists of the Tudor and Stuart periods in England. The book is distributed in the United States by Ashgate Publishing Co., Old Post Rd., Brookfield VT 05036. See a review by Trevor Herbert in the *HBSJ* 7 (1995): 207-209. See also Peter Goodwin, 143.

Bassano/England/Goodwin,P./Herbert,T./Instruments-Renaissance/Instruments-17thC/PerfPrac

168. LIND, Michael. "Palmer Traulsen (1913-1975)." *BBIBC* 66 (1989): 28-31.

Lind deals with one of Denmark's outstanding trombonists and teachers of the twentieth century. See Carsten Svanberg, 220.

Denmark/Orchestra/Pedagogy/Svanberg,C./Traulsen,P.

169. LUCAS, Don. "Orchestra showcase: The Houston Symphony Orchestra." *JITA* 10, no. 3 (July 1982): 27-31.

Lucas's interview also includes a conversation with Albert Lube, who was the trombone teacher at the University of Houston and a former member of the trombone section of the Houston Symphony. At the time of the article the section included John McCroskey, principal, Allen Barnhill, co-principal, and David Waters, bass trombone.

Barnhill,A./Houston/Lube,A./McCroskey,J./Orchestra/Waters,D.

170. LUMPKIN, Royce. "Leon Brown—the man and teacher." *JITA* 11, no. 3 (July 1983): 5-8.

Leon Brown, considered one of the world's leading experts on trombone literature and a master teacher, was presented the 1983 ITA Award. He is profiled by one of his students who later became a colleague at the University of North Texas, president of the International Trombone Association (1990-1992), and currently serves as head of the music department at the University of North Carolina at Charlotte.

Brown,L./ITA/NorthTexasU/Pedagogy/TrbMus-Gen

171. LUPER, Loren. *Arthur Pryor: His Trombone, His Band, His Music.* [Santa Barbara CA: Loren Luper, 1987].

Luper's tantalizing book was the subject of an article by Suzanne Mudge, "Arthur Pryor: This is your life," in the *JITA* 15, no. 2 (Spring 1987): 28-29. Unfortunately, the author of the book, who knew Pryor and played in his band, died in 1987, shortly after making his book available. See Steve Dillon, 107, and Daniel E. Frizane, 135, for more references on Arthur Pryor.

Dillon,S./Discog/Frizane,D./Mudge,S./Pedagogy/PerfPrac/ Pryor,A.

172. MAGLIOCCO, Hugo. "A special endurance." *JITA* 20, no. 2 (Spring 1992): 22-28.

Magliocco gives an overview of the career and legal problems of Abbie Conant, who, at the time of the article, had been solo trombonist with the Munich Philharmonic since 1980. He deals specifically with her discrimination suit against the Philharmonic. See also an article on Abbie Conant in the *BBIBC* 55 (1986): 5,

and 68 (1989): 1. For a later account of Conant's legal issues see Randy Campora's "General News," in the *JITA* 21, no. 3 (Spring 1993): 11.
Campora,R./Conant,A./Legal/Munich/Orchestra/Women

173. MANSON, David. "Stjepan Šulek." *JITA* 16, no. 2 (Spring 1988): 8-9.
Manson's biographical sketch of Šulek may be used by those who are programming Šulek's *Sonata (Vox Gabrieli)*. The article is included in James Roberts's ongoing column, "Research." An earlier sketch of Šulek may be found in the *NITA* 1, no. 2 (April 1974): 9. See also Dan Riley, 59.
Bib/Riley,D./Roberts,J./Solos/Sonata/Šulek,S./TrbMus-20thC

174. MARCELLUS, John. "Blow freely: A salute to William F. Cramer." *JITA* 15, no. 3 (Summer 1987): 14-16.
See Marcellus and Christian Dickinson, 178. Cramer was the 1987 recipient of the ITA Award.
Cramer,W./Dickinson,C./ITA/Pedagogy

175. ———. "Larry Wiehe (October 17, 1929-August 7, 1992): A retrospective." *JITA* 20, no. 4 (Fall 1992): 26-28.
Marcellus includes reminiscences by Leon Brown, Col. Arnold Gabriel (who directed the U.S. Air Force Band during Wiehe's tenure as solo trombonist), Buddy Baker, and Royce Lumpkin.
Baker,B./Brown,L./Gabriel,A./Lumpkin,R./Wiehe,L.

176. ———. "Lewis Van Haney: June 14, 1920-May 2, 1991." *JITA* 19, no. 3 (Summer 1991): 24-25.
See Buddy Baker, 82, Randy Kohlenberg and Robert Thomas, 164, and Bruce Tracy, 227. Van Haney, who had a distinguished orchestral career with the New York Philharmonic, and was later professor of trombone at Indiana University, was given the first ITA Award in 1972 for outstanding contributions in the field of trombone performance and teaching.
Baker,B./Haney,L.V./IndianaU/ITA/Kohlenberg,R./NewYork/ Obituaries/Orchestra/Thomas,R./Tracy,B.

177. [————]. "Orchestra showcase: The Baltimore Symphony Orchestra." *JITA* 10, no. 2 (April 1982): 14-19.

     Marcellus interviews David Fetter, principal, James Olin, co-principal, Eric Carlson, second, and Douglas Yeo, bass trombone.
     Baltimore/Carlson,E./Fetter,D./Olin,J./Orchestra/Yeo,D.

178. MARCELLUS, John, and Christian DICKINSON. "William F. Cramer (1919-1989)." *JITA* 17, no. 4 (Fall 1989): 27-28.
     See also John Marcellus, 174.
     Cramer,W./Dickinson,C./Obituaries/Pedagogy

179. MATHEZ, Jean-Pierre. "Armin Rosin: Le pionnier de l'emancipation du trombone classique en Allemagne [Armin Rosin: The pioneer of the emancipation of the classical trombone in Germany]." *BBIBC* 81 (1993): 74-80.
     Mathez's article is in French, German, and English. Rosin is one of the outstanding European trombone concert artists.
     Germany/PerfPrac/Rosin,A./Solos

180. ————. "Branimir Slokar, un tromboniste heureux [a happy trombonist]." *BBIBC* 95, no. 3 (1996): 14+.
     See also an earlier sketch of Slokar by Mathez in *BBIBC* 59, no. 3 (1987): 10-16. Both articles are in French, German, and English. For another profile of Slokar, one of Europe's premier trombonists and a designer of instruments, see also Mathez, 903.
     Instruments-20thC/Slokar,B.

181. ————. "Dave Taylor." *BBIBC* 68 (1989): 18-19+.
     Mathez's article is in English, French, and German. See Douglas Yeo, 245, and Michael Bourne, 268. See also L. Kerner, "Outwardly mobile brass," *Village Voice* 32 (March 1987): 69, and H.J. Rippert, "Annie Whitehead, Ray Anderson, and Dave Taylor," *Jazz Podium* 38 (July 1989): 38.
     BassTrb/Bourne,M./Jazz-Blues/Kerner,L./Rippert,H./Taylor,D./Yeo,D.

182. ————. "In seventh heaven with the trombone." *BBIBC* 96 (1996): 77-81.
     In a capsule biography of the life and career of Jacques Marger, principal trombonist with the National Theater Orchestra of the

Paris Opera and trombone teacher at the French Conservatory, Mathez deals with his performance of new music. The article is in French, German, and English.

Avant-Garde/France/Marger,J./PerfPrac/TrbMus-20thC

183. [————]. "An interview with Miles Anderson." *BBIBC* 26 (1979): 55-58.

Mathez speaks to the then-youthful recording artist about his career plans. The interview is in English, French, and German. See also Joel Elias, 113.

Anderson,M./Avant-Garde/Elias,J./PerfPrac/TrbMus-20thC

184. [————]. "Une interview avec Jean Douay [An interview with Jean Douay]." *BBIBC* 10 (1975): 49-57.

Douay was the solo trombonist with the Orchestra National de France at the time of this interview. The article is in French, English, and German. See a subsequent conversation with Douay in vol. 73 (1991): 78-85.

Douay,J./France/Orchestra.

185. MCCARTY, Frank L. "An interview with Stuart Dempster." *Instrumentalist* 28 (May 1974): 36-38.

See Valerie Samson, 202, and Dempster, 621. One of the world's premier experts on contemporary trombone music, Dempster was the recipient of the 1978 ITA Award.

Avant-Garde/Dempster,S./ITA/Pedagogy/Samson,V./TrbMus-20thC

186. MCKINNEY, Harold. "Warren Burkhart: Looking back fifty-five years." *JITA* 13, no. 3 (July 1985): 10-12.

Burkhart was second trombonist of the Cleveland Symphony Orchestra from 1935 to 1964. See also Jeffrey Bowell, 88.

Bowell,J./Burkhart,W./Cleveland/Orchestra

187. "Mortal combat between trombone and cornet." *Musical Courier* 1 (1880): 391.

Cited in Guion, 145, as being abridged from the *New York Herald*, August 11, 1880, p. 11, this article is an account of the controversy between Jules Levy, cornet soloist with Patrick Gilmore's band during the late nineteenth century, and Frederick

Neil Innes, trombone soloist of the same band. Innes insisted on playing solos identified with Levy as encores to his own performances. See A.H. Rackett, 193.
Bands/Cornet/Gilmore,P./Guion,D./Innes,F./Levy,J./Rackett,A./ Solos/TrbMus-19thC

188. MUDGE, Suzanne. "Orchestra showcase: The Los Angeles Philharmonic Orchestra." *NITA* 8, no. 1 (September 1980): 17-22.
Mudge interviews Byron Peebles and Ralph Sauer, co-principals, Sonny Ausman, second, and Jeffrey Reynolds, bass trombone. She complains that much of the interview had to be edited and censored for publication purposes but hoped that "some of the utter zaniness that prevailed still shows through." The article contains a chart of Los Angeles Philharmonic Orchestra low brass personnel from 1919-1980.
Ausman,S./LosAngeles/Orchestra/Peebles,B./Reynolds,J./Sauer,R.

189. NIEMISTO, Paul. "Olavi Lampinen passes away." *JITA* 12, no. 1 (January 1984): 38.
Olavi Lampinen was a Finnish trombone teacher and performer who, until his death, had been "the teacher and mentor of practically every professional player" then active in Finland.
Finland/Helsinki/Lampinen,O./Obituaries/Pedagogy

190. OBREGON, Richard. "An interview with Tom Ervin." *JITA* 23, no. 1 (Winter 1995): 20-22.
Tom Ervin is professor of trombone and jazz studies at the University of Arizona. He is also a past president of the International Trombone Association (1978-1980).
Ervin,T./ITA/Jazz-Blues/Pedagogy

191. "Orchestra showcase: The Iceland Symphony Orchestra." *JITA* 24, no. 1 (Winter 1996): 20-22.
This article includes a chart listing the low brass personnel and music directors since the founding of the orchestra in 1950. The current low brass section includes Oddur Björnsson, principal, Sigurdur Thorbergsson, assistant principal, David Bobroff, bass trombone, and Bjarni Gudmundsson, tuba.
Björnsson,O./Bobroff,D./Iceland/Orchestra/Thorbergsson,S.

192. PRINCE, Howard. "A personal look at Roger Smith [1914-1975]." *NITA* 3, no. 1 (September 1975): 15-16.

Prince wrote his tribute from the perspective of a student of Roger Smith. See also the *NITA* 2, no. 2 (April 1975): 10; the May 1975 issue of the *Juilliard News Bulletin*; Bill Spilka's and Moe Snyder's articles in the *New York Brass Conference for Scholarships Journal* 4 (1976): 38-40+; and David Langlitz's "Tribute to Roger Smith," in the *NYBCS Journal* 5 (1977): 91-92.
Juilliard/Langlitz,D./MetropolitanOpera/Pedagogy/Snyder,M./Spilka,B.

193. RACKETT, A.H. "Frederick Neil Innes: The supreme master." *Musical Messenger* 19 (April 1923): 3.

Rackett's article is cited in Guion, 145. See also "Mortal combat between trombone and cornet," 187. Innes's dates are 1858-1927. A pamphlet titled *Innes and his Band: In combination with scenes from grand opera (not in costume) by grand opera singers*, New York: Wynkoop, Hallenbeck, Crawford & Co., 1902? may be found in the South Caroliniana Library on the Columbia campus of the University of South Carolina. The program contains dates and times of performances of Innes's band at the South Carolina Inter-State and West Indian Exposition held in the Charleston SC Exposition Auditorium in 1902.
Guion,D./Innes,F./SouthCaroliniana/TrbMus-19thC

194. RASMUSSEN, Mary. "Two early nineteenth-century trombone virtuosi: Carl Traugott Queisser and Friedrich August Belcke." *Brass Quarterly* 5, no. 1 (Fall 1961): 3-17.

Queisser and Belcke were two of the most famous European trombone soloists of the nineteenth century. Though both concertized on trombone all over continental Europe, Queisser was also active as a violinist and violist in Leipzig, while Belcke's career seemed to center in Berlin. Rasmussen's article is a definitive and well-documented study of their careers and the unusual circumstances which brought about their successes. See also Werner Beyer, 403, Michael Lewis, 495, Robert Reifsnyder, 540, Gary Shaw, 551, Larry Weed, 577, and Steve Wolfinbarger, 592.
BassTrb/Belcke,F./Berlin/Beyer,W./Concertos/Gewandhaus/
Instruments-19thC/Leipzig/Lewis,M./PerfPrac/Queisser,C./

Reifsnyder,R./Schmidt,M./Shaw,G./TrbMus-19thC./Weed,L./
Wolfinbarger,S.

195. RAUM, Richard. "Christian Lindberg." *BBIBC* 91, no. 3 (1995): 74+.
Included in Raum's interview are mentions of several works
which Lindberg, one of the few trombone soloists who has
succeeded strictly as a soloist on the concert stage, has recently
or will shortly perform: Elizabeth Raum's *The Olmütz Concerto
for Alto Trombone and Orchestra*, a new work by Xenakis for
trombone and percussion, a new concerto by Luciano Berio, and
several commissioned works (Stockholm Philharmonic and
Sydney, Australia, Festival) by Arno Pärt. See R.S. Brown, 94,
and Thomas G. Everett, 118. See also Knud Ketting, "A musician
also has to be an actor," *Nordic Sounds* (September 1987): 16-17;
V. Vern, "Dansk hoest i Pumpehuset," *Nutida Musik* 33, nos. 3-4
(1990): 19; J. Kosinska, "Puzon . . . i nie tylko," *Ruch Muzyczny*
34, no. 10 (1990): 4; and S. Sagvik, "Christian Lindberg,
trombonvirtuos," *Tonfallet* 6 (September 1987): 2-3.
Berio,L./Brown,R./Cadenzas/David,F./Denmark/Discog/Everett,T./
Ketting,K./Kosinska,J./Lindberg,C./Pärt,A./Raum,E./Sagvik,S./
Solos/Stockholm/Sweden/Sydney/Vern,V./Xenakis,I.

196. [————]. "Thomas Gschlatt: His career as eighteenth-century
court trombonist in Salzburg and city musician in Olmütz." *JITA*
22, no. 4 (Fall 1994): 25.
Listed and summarized in George Broussard's "ITW: Research
presentations," Raum's study was prepared and presented as a
paper at the 1994 International Trombone Workshop. Raum is a
professor at the University of Regina, Saskatchewan, Canada.
His presentation dealt with Thomas Gschlatt, who was
employed as a trombonist at the Salzburg court from 1756 to
1769. Raum's study was also published in three parts in a
fictional format similar to the one employed by him in his "From
the diary of a court trombonist, 1727" (see 731) in the *BBIBC*
beginning with "Thomas Gschladt: An historical perspective of
an eighteenth-century trombonist," 87 (1994): 10-29. Also see
Raum, 537, 729, and 730, C. Robert Wigness, 583, and Kenneth
M. Hanlon, 656.

AltoTrb/Broussard,G./ChamMus-Trb/Concertos/Eberlin,J./
Gschlatt[Gschladt],T./Hanlon,K./Haydn,M./Mozart,L./Olmütz/
PerfPrac/Salzburg/Solos/TrbMus-18thC/Vienna/Wigness,R.

197. REYNOLDS, Hal. "Allen E. Ostrander (1909-1994): A personal remembrance." *JITA* 23, no. 2 (Spring 1995): 16-18.
   Reynolds is currently associate professor of trombone at Ithaca College, where Ostrander attended school and later served on the faculty. Ostrander was the recipient of the 1981 ITA Award. See Randy Kohlenberg and Robert Thomas, 164, Ronald G. Smith, 213, and Bruce Tracy, 223.
   BassTrb/ITA/Kohlenberg,R./Obituaries/Orchestra/Ostrander,A./
   Pedagogy/Smith,R./Thomas,R./Tracy,B.

198. REYNOLDS, Mary E. "Emory Remington (1891-1971): Portrait of a legend." *JITA* 19, no. 2 (Spring 1991): 16-18.
   See Ralph Sauer's profile of Remington, 203, and Robert Swift, 221. See also the *NITA* 7, no. 2 (April 1980): 7-9, for a profile of Remington by Donald Hunsberger; the *New York Brass Conference for Scholarships Journal* 2? (1974): 67, for an account of the founding of the Emory B. Remington Alumni Association; and Roger P. Phelps, "Some impressions of Emory Remington, master teacher," also in the *NYBCS Journal* (1979): 44.
   Eastman/Hunsberger,D./Obituaries/Phelps,R./Remington,E./
   Sauer,R./Swift,R.

199. [ROHNER, Traugott]. "Musician extraordinary." *Instrumentalist* 8 (December 1953): 35.
   Rohner's excellent thumbnail sketch of the life and career of Jaroslav Čimera includes a mention of the Čimera-Sares mouthpiece, which Čimera designed in collaboration with one of his students. See Keig E. Garvin and André Smith, 140, and Čimera, 1036.
   Čimera,J./Garvin,K./Mouthpieces/Pedagogy/Sares/Smith,A.

200. ROSS, Stewart. "An interview with Frank Crisafulli." *Instrumentalist* 32, no. 3 (October 1977): 78-82.
   See Paul Bauer, 86, Eileen Meyer, 1186, and Bob Rainer, 1212.
   Bauer,P./Chicago/Crisafulli,F./Meyer,E./Orchestra/Pedagogy/Rainer,B.

201. RUBINSTEIN, L. "Profile: CMA [Chamber Music America]
      board member Robert Biddlecombe." *American Ensemble* 6, no.
      1 (1983): 7.
         Robert Biddlecombe performed as bass trombonist with the
      American Symphony and the American Brass Quintet, in addition
      to holding several college and conservatory teaching posts in the
      New York area. See also [Margaret Shakespeare], 205.
      AmericanBrassQuintet/BassTrb/Biddlecombe,R./BrassQuintet/
      ChamMus-Trb/Shakespeare,M.

202. SAMSON, Valerie. "An interview with Stuart Dempster." *NITA*
      6, no. 3 (April 1979): 19-24.
         Samson's article was originally published in *Composer
      Magazine*. See Frank L. McCarty, 185, and Dempster, 621.
      Avant-Garde/Dempster,S./McCarty,F./Theater/TrbMus-20thC

203. SAUER, Ralph. "Emory B. Remington: A profile." *BBIBC* 21
      (1978): 37-39.
         In French, German, and English, this article, written by the
      principal trombonist of the Los Angeles Philharmonic, a former
      Remington student, emphasizes Remington's skills in light of
      composer and former Eastman School Director Howard Hanson's
      famous quote about him, "Remington did not teach trombone, he
      taught people."
         See Mary E. Reynolds, 198, and Robert F. Swift, 221. See also
      Roger P. Phelps, "Some impressions of Emory Remington,
      master teacher," in the *New York Brass Conference for
      Scholarships Journal* (1979): 44, for a viewpoint of a non-
      trombonist who studied with Remington (whom he called "The
      Boss").
      Pedagogy/Phelps,R./Remington,E./Reynolds,M./Swift,R.

204. SCHNABEL, Wolfgang. "Adolf Müller: Sein Leben, seine
      Umwelt und sein Werk [Adolf Müller: His life, milieu, and
      work]." In *Musikgeographie: Weltliche und geistliche
      Bläsermusik in ihren Beziehungen zueinander und zu ihrer
      Umwelt.* 2 (Bochum: Brockmeyer, 1991): 177-225.
         See *RILM*1991-04122-as. Schnabel's study, in German,
      discusses Müller's work with trombone music and Posaunenchöre

(wind ensembles, particularly brass, used in churches in Germany) in Saxony around the turn of the twentieth century. See Müller, 518 and 519. See also A[dolph] Müller, *Unsere Posaunenchöre* (Dresden: Verbandsbuchhandlung, [1905]), cited by Mary Rasmussen in her "Brass bibliography: 1900-1905," *Brass Quarterly* 4, no. 3 (Spring 1961): 129-132. For more information on Posaunenchöre see the annotation on Wilhelm Ehmann, 629.
Ehmann,W./Germany/Kuhlo,J./Müller,A./Posaunenchor/Rasmussen,M./ Saxony/TrbMus-19thC

205. [SHAKESPEARE, Margaret]. "Robert Biddlecome [*sic*]: A conversation with the American Brass Quintet's departing bass trombonist." *New York Brass Conference for Scholarships Journal* (1991): 41-45.
See also L. Rubinstein, 201.
AmericanBrassQuintet/BassTrb/Biddlecombe,B./BrassQuintet/ ChamMus-Trb/Rubinstein,L.

206. SHARPE, Margaret. "Fred Cullum: G bass trombone champion." *JITA* 19, no. 3 (Summer 1991): 29-31.
Sharpe's article first appeared in the *Australian Trombone Education Magazine* in 1989. Cullum was one of the outstanding brass band bass trombonists in Australia for more than forty years.
Australia/BassTrb/BrassBands/Cullum,F./G-BassTrb

207. SHIFRIN, Ken. "Mr. Greased Lightning." *JITA* 22, no. 1 (Winter 1994): 22-29.
Robert Isele was a legendary soloist with the Marine Band from 1937-1961 and later a member of the National Symphony Orchestra from 1964-1981. Shifrin includes a letter, dated 1937, which Herbert Clarke wrote to Isele and in it states, "Your trombone playing is the nearest to Pryor's style and technic [*sic*] I have heard since Arthur's playing of over 35 years ago." See Elliott Chasanov, 99. Isele was the 1994 recipient of the ITA Award.
Bands/Chasanov,E./Clarke,H./Isele,R./Military/Orchestra/Solos

208. SHUKMAN, Henry. *Travels with My Trombone.* New York: Crown Publishers, 1993.

Shukman has written an autobiographical account of his performances with several Latin-American bands.
Jazz-Blues/Latin/PerfPrac/Salsa

209. SLUCHIN, Benny. "Michael Becquet." *BBIBC* 50 (1985): 11-16.
Becquet is internationally known as a trombone soloist and teacher. He has taught at the Hochschule für Musik in Cologne since 1989, and before that he taught at the Conservatoire National Superieur de Musique in Paris. He has participated as a member of the faculty of the International Trombone Workshop (Festival) a number of times.
Becquet,M./France/ITW

210. SMITH, André. "In memoriam, Robert S. Harper (1915-1991)." *JITA* 19, no. 4 (Fall 1991): 38-43.
The life and pedagogical style of the long-time bass trombonist of the Philadelphia Orchestra are recounted by one of his students. Smith gives Harper a tribute that any teacher could covet, "He gave form to drudgery and helped transmute self-indulgence into purpose." See Bruce Tracy, 229, where Tracy includes a conversation with Robert Harper.
BassTrb/Harper,R./Orchestra/Pedagogy/Philadelphia/Tracy,B.

211. ———. "Per Brevig: An enduring legacy in two cultures." *JITA* 24, no. 3 (Summer 1996): 32-38.
Smith has written a brief sketch of the life and career of Per Brevig, principal trombone with the Metropolitan Opera and long-time trombone teacher at Juilliard. It contains copious notes and a list of commissions and premieres for solo trombone by Brevig. This article, along with one published in the *New York Brass Conference for Scholarships Journal*, 1996, are part of a comprehensive biography of Brevig written by Smith, soon to be published by André M. Smith Music Company.
Brevig,P./Juilliard/MetropolitanOpera/Norway

212. ———. "Vladislav Mikhailovich Blazhevich (1886-1942): Some recollections on the semicentennial of his death." *JITA* 21, no. 1 (Winter 1993): 22-27.

Smith's thoroughly researched account of Blazhevich's life, teaching, and career, includes his record as a founding member and solo trombonist with the Persymfans (an acronym that is taken from the Russian for "First Symphony Ensemble of the Moscow City Soviet"). It was an orchestra owned and managed by the musicians comprising the orchestra, with no conductor (Blazhevich served without secure financial remuneration for ten years). The article's endnotes are as fascinating as the article itself, which Smith says is excerpted from a larger work in preparation, *The History of the Trombone in Russia, from Catherine II, The Great, to Prokofiev*, to be published by André Smith Music Co., New York. See Tat'Jana Gajdamovic, 139, and Larry Weed, 240.
Blazhevich,V./Gajdamovic,T./Persymfans/Russia/Weed,L.

213. SMITH, Ronald G. "The life and work of the orchestral bass trombonist, Allen Ostrander, and the development of his bass trombone methods and solos." Louisiana State University, DMA, 1992.
See *Dissertation Abstracts* 9301106 and *RILM*1992-09587-dd.
See Randy Kohlenberg and Robert Thomas, 164, Hal Reynolds, 197, Bruce Tracy, 223, and Ostrander, 1196-1198.
BassTrb/Diss/Kohlenberg,R./LSU/Orchestra/Ostrander,A./
Reynolds,H./Thomas,R./Tracy,B.

214. SPILKA, Bill. "Abraham Godlis (1911-1978)." *NITA* 6, no. 1 (September 1978): 22.
Godlis was a member of the New York Philharmonic trombone section when Leopold Stokowski was the conductor of the orchestra. He was also active for many years as a free-lance player and a studio and staff musician at several radio and television stations in the New York area.
Spilka's interview also appears in the 1979 *New York Brass Conference for Scholarships Journal*.
Godlis,A./NewYork/Orchestra

215. ———. "An interview with Gordon Pulis." *NITA* 5, no. 3 (April 1978): 21-26.

Pulis gained his greatest fame as principal trombonist of the New York Philharmonic. This part of Spilka's interview covers the early years up to about 1935, when Pulis graduated from Eastman after four years of study with Emory Remington. The interview was to have been continued in succeeding issues of the *NITA*, but only part 1 was published. Pulis was the recipient of the 1976 ITA Award. See Randy Kohlenberg and Robert Thomas, 164, and Pulis, 1209. See also Harvey Phillips, "Musical stories," *Instrumentalist* 46 (January 1992): 4. An obituary of Pulis appeared in the *JITA* 11, no. 1 (January 1983): 7.
ITA/Kohlenberg,R./Obituaries/Orchestra/Phillips,H./Pulis,G./Thomas,R.

216. ———. "The spit valve." *NITA* 3, no. 1 (September 1975): 19-20.
Spilka's recurring column primarily chronicles trombone events in New York City, including the Brass Conference and various jazz events, and gives brief biographical sketches of various New York performers. It appeared intermittently in the *NITA* until 1979, after which it has continued to appear in subsequent editions of the *JITA*, beginning with vol. 10, no. 1 (January 1982): 22-26.
Jazz-Blues/NewYork

217. ———. "The Tenth Annual New York Brass Conference." *JITA* 10, no. 3 (July 1982): 31-34.
See also Spilka's "Fourteenth Annual New York Brass Conference for Scholarships," *JITA* 14, no. 3 (Summer 1986): 40-44.
ConcertBand/Jazz-Blues/NewYorkBrassConference/Orchestra

218. STRICKLING, George F. "I knew Innes, Sousa, and Yoder!" *Instrumentalist* 21 (January 1976): 12.
See also David Guion, 145.
Guion,D./Innes,F./Sousa,J.P./Yoder,P.

219. SUPPAN, Wolfgang. "Rudolf Josel, Österreichs führender Posaunist [Rudolf Josel, Austria's master trombonist]." *BBIBC* 80 (1992): 56-59+.
Josel has served as principal trombonist in the Vienna Philharmonic since 1964.
Austria/Josel,R./Orchestra/Pedagogy/Vienna

220. SVANBERG, Carsten. "Danish trombone traditions." *JITA* 20, no. 2 (Spring 1992): 32-33.

Svanberg one of the outstanding trombonists in Europe, gives historical information about Anton Hansen (1877-1947) and Palmer Traulsen (1913-1975), two of the most famous Danish trombonists of this century. He recommends articles by Per Gade (see 136) on Hansen. See also Gade, 137, for an article dealing with Hansen's friendship with composer Axel Jørgensen. Svanberg further cites an article by Michael Lind on Palmer Traulsen (see 168).
Denmark/Gade,P./Hansen,A./Jørgenson,A./Lind,M./Orchestra/Traulsen,P.

221. SWIFT, Robert F. "Hail to the Chief: Emory Remington." *Brass and Percussion* 1, no. 5 (November 1973): 17-18.

See Mary E. Reynolds, 198, and Ralph Sauer, 203. See also Roger P. Phelps, "Some impressions of Emory Remington, master teacher," in the *New York Brass Conference for Scholarships Journal* (1979): 44, for a viewpoint of a non-trombonist who studied with Remington (whom he called "The Boss").
Eastman/Pedagogy/Phelps,R./Remington,E./Reynolds,M./Sauer,R.

222. SZEWCZUK, Janusz. "Juliusz Pietrachowicz." *JITA* 20, no. 4 (Fall 1992): 22-24.

Pietrachowicz was a former solo trombonist of the National Philharmonic of Poland, who, at the time of the article, was professor of trombone at the Warsaw and Lodz Academy of Music. He was also the 1992 ITA Award recipient. See also Pietrachowicz, 534.
ITA/Orchestra/Pietrachowicz,J./Poland

223. TRACY, Bruce. "A conversation with Allen Ostrander." *JITA* 12, no. 2 (April 1984): 9-14.

The famous bass trombonist of the New York Philharmonic and the NBC Symphony under Toscanini was born in 1909 (he passed away in 1994). See Paul Hunt, "Literature reviews," *JITA* 23, no. 1 (Winter 1995): 46, for a brief sketch of Ostrander's life.

See also Randy Kohlenberg and Robert Thomas, 164, Hal Reynolds, 197, and Ronald G. Smith, 213.
BassTrb/Hunt,P./Kohlenberg,R./NBC/NewYork/Orchestra/Ostrander,A./Pedagogy/Reynolds,H./Smith R./Thomas,R.

224.   ————. "A conversation with Byron McCulloh." *JITA* 15, no. 1 [mistakenly labeled as 14, no. 4] (Winter 1987): 18-25.

See also a letter from Ralph Sauer, relating to McCulloh's comments on the trend in bass trombone sounds, printed in "The eighth position," of the *JITA* 15, no. 2 (Spring 1987). A short biographical sketch of McCulloh appears in Ben Ivey's ongoing column, "General News," in the *NITA* 7, no. 2 (April 1980): 4-5, and contains a brief bibliography of McCulloh's compositions up to 1980. See also McCulloh, 55, and Barry Catelinet, 1034.
BassTrb/Catelinet,B./Ivey,B./McCulloh,B./Orchestra/Pedagogy/Pittsburgh/Sauer,R.

225.   ————. "A conversation with Edwin Anderson." *NITA* 8, no. 4 (September 1981): 23-29.

See also Jeffrey Bowell, 88.
Anderson,E./BassTrb/Bowell,J./Cleveland/Orchestra/Pedagogy

226.   ————. "A conversation with Raymond Premru." *JITA* 13, no. 3 (July 1985): 28-31.

See Peter Goodwin, 142. After his stint in England, Premru served on the music faculty at Oberlin College until his death in 1998.
BassTrb/Goodwin,P./London/Orchestra/Premru,R.

227.   ————. "Lewis Van Haney's career." *JITA* 13, no. 4 (October 1985): 8-12.

Tracy's article was reprinted in the *Instrumentalist* 40, no. 4 (November 1985): 4. See Buddy Baker, 82, Randy Kohlenberg and Robert Thomas, 164, and John Marcellus, 176.
Baker,B./BassTrb/Haney,L.V./IndianaU/Kohlenberg,R./Marcellus,J./NewYork/Orchestra/Thomas,R.

228.   ————. "Orchestra showcase: The Chicago Symphony Orchestra." *NITA* 7, no. 2 (April 1980): 10-15.

The main body of this article is an interview with Edward Kleinhammer, the bass trombonist of the orchestra at that time (see Douglas Yeo, 246). Tracy also includes a chart of the low brass personnel of the Chicago Symphony from its founding through 1980. The low brass section in 1980 was comprised of Jay Friedman, principal, James Gilbertson, associate principal, Frank Crisafulli, second (see Paul Bauer, 86), and Arnold Jacobs, tuba. Bauer,P./Chicago/Crisafulli,F./Friedman,J./Gilbertson,J./Jacobs,A./ Kleinhammer,E./Orchestra/Yeo,D.

229. ———. "Orchestra showcase: The Philadelphia Orchestra." *JITA* 12, no. 3 (July 1984): 9-19.
A list of trombonists in the orchestra from 1900-1984 is included. See Eric Carlson and Blair Bollinger, 97. A separate interview was conducted with Robert Harper, who had recently retired as bass trombonist. See André Smith, 210. Alessi,J./Bollinger,B./Breuninger,T./Carlson,E./Dodson,G./ Harper,R./Orchestra/Philadelphia/Smith,A./Vernon,C.

230. ———. "A profile of Robert Gray." *JITA* 20, no. 2 (Winter 1992): 26-31.
Gray, a past president of the International Trombone Association, is a distinguished trombone teacher and scholar who served for many years on the faculty at the University of Illinois. He is perhaps best-known for his research which culminated in a series of articles in collaboration with Mary Rasmussen that appeared during the 1950s and 1960s in Rasmussen's *Brass Quarterly* (see Gray, 648, and Gray and Rasmussen, 447 and 448). Gray,R./IllinoisU/ITA/Rasmussen,M./Research

231. "Unique master of the trombone, Davis Shuman." *1978 New York Brass Conference Journal* 6 (January 1978): 38.
This uncredited short biography is cited by Karl Hinterbichler in his ongoing column, "Literature Announcements," in the *NITA* 6, no. 1 (September 1978): 23. Included are an obituary which appeared in the *New York Times* in 1966 and a review of one of Shuman's recitals which appeared in the *International Musician* in 1949. Shuman is best remembered as a teacher at Juilliard, for his efforts to improve and expand the solo literature for the

trombone, and his trombone design, which angled the slide to the performer's right in order to facilitate technique in the outer positions.
AngledSlide/Concertos/Hinterbichler,K./Instruments-20thC/Juilliard/ Obituaries/Shuman,D./Solos

232. UPCHURCH, John. "An interview with Keig Garvin." *NITA* 7, no. 1 (December 1979): 13-14.
Garvin is a former soloist with the U.S. Army Band (1938-1961) and was a student of Jaroslav Čimera. See also Keig E. Garvin and André Smith, 140.
Bands/Čimera,J./Garvin,K./Military/Smith,A.

233. WEBER, K. "Die Posaunisten im Festspielorchester Bayreuth [The trombonists in the Bayreuth Festival Orchestra]." *Das Orchester* 28 (July-August 1980): 581-583.
Weber's article in is German. See also Kerschagl and Weidemann, 680.
Bayreuth/Germany/Kerschagl/Opera/Orchestra/Wagner,R./Weidemann

234. WEED, Larry. "Miloslav Hejda." *JITA* 7 (1979): 15.
See Thomas G. Everett, 122.
Czechoslovakia/Everett,T./Hejda,M./Orchestra/TrbMus-20thC

235. [———]. "The tenth annual international trombone workshop." *JITA* 8 (1980): 10-12.
Short sketches of the faculty of the tenth workshop are included.
Ausman,S./Baker,B./Brown,L./Coffey,J./Fontana,C./Hall,R./Hill,J./ ITA/Jazz-Blues/Lewis,G./Mangelsdorff,A./Marcellus,J./Masso,G./ McCulloh,B./Minick,L./Reynolds,J./Roberts,G./Sauer,R./ Stevens,M./Workshops

236. [———]. "International trombone workshop 1990." *JITA* 18, no. 2 (Spring 1990): insert [between pages 18 and 19].
Biographical sketches of the 1990 ITW faculty are included.
Anderson,R./Bassett,L./Buchman,H./Erdman,J./Eubanks,R./ Globokar,V./Handrow,R./Hawes/R./ITA/Kitzman,J./Trudel,A./ Turré,S./Workshops/Zadrozny,E.

237. [————]. "1993 international trombone workshop [Artist biographies]." *JITA* 21, no. 2 (Spring 1993): insert [between pp. 20 and 21].
Becquet,M./Brown,L.F./Dempster,S./Fadle,H./Fedchock,J./Glover, Betty/Gray,R./Hartman,S./Herwig,C./Kagarice,V./Shiner,M./ Smith,G./Trudel,A./VanDÿk,B./Whigham,J./Witser,S./Workshops

238. [————]. "Twenty-third international trombone workshop [1994]: ITW artist biographies." *JITA* 22, no. 2 (Spring 1994): insert [between pp. 24 and 25].
Anderson,R./Buchman,H./Kenny,J./Kitzman,J./Lindberg,C./ Nightingale,M./Olson,C./Ordman,A./Reynolds,J./Roos,I./ Smith,H.C./Wiest,S./Workshops

239. [————]. "Twenty-fourth international trombone workshop program [participants]." *JITA* 23, no. 2 (Spring 1995): insert [between pages 30 and 31].
Anderson,J./Anderson,M./Ashworth,T./Ausman,S./Bahr,E./ Bootz,W./Caravan/Conant,A./Ervin,T./Fontana,C./Guilford,M./ Herrington,B./Horgan,M./Klay,E./Lindberg,C./Liston,M./ Marcellus,J./McDougall,I./Pearson,N./PRISMA/Reynolds,J./ Roos,I./Sauer,R./Tall,D./Taylor,D./Trudel,A./Vining,D./Vivona,P./ Watrous,B./Whigham,J./Workshops

240. [WEED, Larry], trans. "Biography of V.M. Blazevich [*sic*]." *JITA* 7 (1979): 32.
This biography is part of a series of 132 of Russian trombone and tuba players translated by Weed and available from him (2221 Excalibur Dr., Orlando FL 32822). See the *JITA* 10, no. 1 (January 1982): 12-13. See also Tat'jana Gajdamovic, 139 and André Smith, 212.
Blazhevich,V./Gajdamovic,T./Russia/Smith,A./Tuba

241. WESSELY, Othmar. "Die Musiker im Hofstaat der Königin Anna, Gemahlin Ferdinands I [The musicians in the royal household of Queen Anna, consort of Ferdinand I]." *Fellerer Festschrift* (*RILM* 74/1645): 659-672.
Wessely's article is in German and discusses Queen Anna's circle of musicians in the eighteenth century, which included five

trombonists: Stephan Mahu, Rodolphe Nicolas, Thomas de
Berzizia, Herionymus Blasel, and Valentin von Strassburg.
Berzizia,T./Blasel,H./FerdinandI/Mahu,S./Nicolas,R./QueenAnna/
Strassburg,V./Vienna

242. WIEHE, Larry, Jr. (1929-1992). "My life as a trombone player."
     2 parts. *JITA* 21, no. 3 (Spring 1993): 18-23, and 21, no. 4
     (Summer 1993): 42-47.
     Wiehe's autobiographical sketch, edited by John Marcellus,
     chronicles Wiehe's trombone experiences from the age of four.
     Part 1 covers the years to 1951, while part 2 ends in 1985. Wiehe
     was awarded the 1993 ITA Award posthumously.
     Bands/ITA/Marcellus,J./Military/Solos

243. WOLFINBARGER, Steve. "The solo trombone music of Arthur
     Pryor." 3 parts. *JITA* 11, no. 1 (January 1983): 13-15, 11, no. 2
     (April 1983): 20-25; 11, no. 3 (July 1983): 20-25.
     The gist of all three sections of Wolfinbarger's article is mostly
     a biographical discussion of Pryor and some of his contemporaries.
     However, part 3 also contains brief structural analyses of Pryor's
     famous solos and illustrative diagrams of his compositional style,
     in addition to a bibliography and partial discography.
     For more references on Pryor see Steve Dillon, 107. See also
     Henry Woelber, "Arthur Pryor: Band director and ace trombonist,"
     Jacobs' Band Monthly 26 (March 1941): 8, as cited by Mary
     Rasmussen in "Brass bibliography: 1936-1940," *Brass Quarterly*
     2, no. 2 (December 1958): 63-77.
     Bib/Cappa,C.A./Čimera,J./Clarke,E./Dillon,S./Discog/Holton,F./
     Innes,F./Mantia,S./Martin,C./Proctor,J./Pryor,A./Rasmussen,M./
     Simons,G./Solos/Spary,C./Stacy,C.E./TrbMus-19thC/TrbMus-20thC/
     Woelber,H./Zimmerman,L.

244. YEO, Douglas. "A conversation with Kauko Kahila." *JITA* 15,
     no. 3 (Summer 1987): 18-22.
     Kahila was bass trombonist with the Boston Symphony (a
     positions Yeo now holds) from 1952 to 1972.
     BassTrb/Boston/Kahila,K./Orchestra

245. ———. "David Taylor, bass trombone: An appreciation and interview." 2 parts. *JITA* 19, no. 4 (Fall 1991): 30-36, and 20, no. 2 (Winter 1992): 14-23.
Part 2 also contains a bibliography of music commissioned or premiered by Taylor and a discography of his recordings. See Jean-Pierre Mathez, 184.
BassTrb/Bib/Bio/Discog/Mathez,J./Taylor,D.

246. ———. "Edward Kleinhammer: A tribute." *JITA* 13, no. 2 (April 1985): 4-6.
See Bruce Tracy, 228. Kleinhammer was the 1986 recipient of the ITA Award. See also Kleinhammer, 1147 and 1148, and Kleinhammer and Douglas Yeo, 1149.
BassTrb/Chicago/ITA/Kleinhammer,E./Orchestra/Tracy,B.

247. ———. "Personnel listing of symphony, opera and ballet orchestras (international)." *JITA* 12, no. 1 (January 1984): 15-19.
See the *JITA* 19, no. 1 (Winter 1991): 34-39, for an update. See also "Directory of symphony trombonists," 108, and Vern Kagarice and John Marcellus, 163.
Ballet/Kagarice,V./Marcellus,J./Opera/Orchestra

248. ———. "A pictorial history of low brass players in the Boston Symphony Orchestra, 1887-1986." *JITA* 14, no. 4 (Fall 1986): 13-21.
Adam,E./Aloo,M./Barron,R./Behr,C./Bolter,N./Boston/Coffey,J./ Gibson,W./Hallberg,G./Hampe,C./Hansotte,L./Kahila,K./Kenfield,L./ Lillebach,W./Mäusebach,A./Moyer,W./Orchestra/Orosz,J./Raichman,J./ Rochut,J./Smith,K./Stewart,G.

3

BIOGRAPHIES/JAZZ,POPULAR,STUDIO

249. [AEBERSOLD, Jamey D.]. *Fond Memories of . . . Frank Rosolino*. New Albany IN: Double-Time Records, 1996.

Aebersold's retrospective contains a book of Rosolino solos, transcribed by Conrad Herwig (the first winner of the Frank Rosolino Memorial Scholarship for Jazz Trombone from the International Trombone Association, 1979), along with other rare photos and information. The foreword of the book was prepared by Eugene Grissom (see his article with Eileen Massinon, 307).

In 1978 Rosolino (1926-1978) was given a special ITA Award in recognition of his contributions to the field of jazz and trombone performance, and as reported by Ben Ivey, "specifically the development of be-bop trombone stylings and, more importantly, fostering a friendship and spirit among trombonists and other musicians." See Gene Lees, 324, Marty Morgan, 333, Gerry Sloan, 345, Lee Underwood, 363, Conrad Herwig, 457, and Bruce Melville, 512.

Bebop/Grissom,E./Herwig,C./ITA/Ivey,B/Lees,G./Massinon,E./ Melville,B./Morgan,M./Obituaries/Rosolino,F./Sloan,G./Underwood,L.

250. ALLEN, Rex. "Jack Teagarden: An evaluation of his style and contribution to jazz." *JITA* 5 (1977): 35-41.

See Whitney Balliet, 252, Leonard Guttridge, 311, and Gerry Sloan, 348.

Balliet,W./Bib/Guttridge,L./PerfPrac/Sloan,G./Teagarden,J.

251. ATKINS, Jerry. "Carl Fontana interview." *Cadence Magazine* 5 (December 1979): 7-8+.

See Campbell Burnap, 273, Thomas G. Everett, 297, Nancy Grissom, 308, and Bob Rusch and B. Jenne, 341. Fontana was the 1998 recipient of the ITA Award. For an update on his career, and some edited excerpts of his solos, see Ken Hanlon, "Carl Fontana: The trombonist's trombonist," *JITA* 26, no. 3 (Summer 1998): 32-35.

Bebop/Burnap,C./Everett,T./Fontana,C./Grissom,N./Hanlon,K./ Jenne,B./Rusch,B.

252. BALLIET, Whitney. "Big T." *The New Yorker* 60 (April 1984): 47-53.

See Rex Allen, 250, Leonard Guttridge, 311, and Gerry Sloan, 348.

Allen,R./Guttridge,L./Sloan,G./Teagarden,J.

253. ———. "Profiles: Jimmy Knepper: A trombone mouth." *The New Yorker* 67, no. 13 (May 1991): 52-58.

See also Gerry Sloan, 346, and Les Tomkins, 359.

Cunningbird/Knepper,J./NewYork/Sloan,G./Tomkins,L.

254. ———. "Three tones." *The New Yorker* 57 (September 1981): 39-42.

See Grahame Columbe, 283, Stanley Dance, 287, and Lee Jeske, 319.

Columbe,G./Dance,S./Dickenson,V./Jeske,L.

255. BAUER, Paul. "A tribute to Grover Mitchell." *JITA* 22, no. 2 (Spring 1994): 24-29.

Mitchell was one of Count Basie's lead trombonists and later formed his own big band in the early 1980s. At the time of the article the band was still active.

Basie,C./Mitchell,G./PerfPrac

256. ———. "The trombones in the orchestras of Stan Kenton." *JITA* 10, no. 3 (July 1982): 23-26.

A capsule history of Stan Kenton's career is followed by a discussion of the trombone sections, how they were used, and some of the trombonists who filled the chairs. Chapter 1, "A chronological history of Stan Kenton and his orchestra," and chapter 2, "The development of the trombone section," appear in the issue of the *JITA* cited above. Chapter 3, "Trombone feature pieces performed by Stan Kenton and his orchestra," appears in vol. 10, no. 4 (October 1982): 16-24, along with a complete discography of the LPs recorded by Kenton's orchestra and commercially released, a complete listing of the trombone and tuba players on those recordings (giving the recordings on which each of them played), and an exhaustive bibliography which includes music manuscripts and unpublished materials.

"A complete chronological listing of the trombone and tuba personnel of Stan Kenton's orchestras" appears in vol. 11, no. 4 (October 1983): 24-25. In the *JITA* 25, no. 4 (Fall 1997): 48-54, Chris Moncelli has written a tribute to Bobby Burgess, who played lead trombone on many Kenton recordings. Burgess passed away June 9, 1997.

Bib/Burgess,B./Discog/Kenton,S./Moncelli,C./Obituaries

257. BERENDT, Joachim E. "Albert Mangelsdorff [interview]." *Jazz Forum* 7, no. 21 (1973): 41-45.

See a summary of this interview in the *BBIBC* 7 (1974): 97-103, under the title, "Albert Mangelsdorff (ein Posaunist, der sich vom Gesang der Vögel inspirieren lässt) [Albert Mangelsdorff: A trombone player inspired by bird song]," translated into French, German, and English. See *Down Beat* 44 (February 1977): 16-18. See also Berendt, 600, George Broussard, 271, Thomas G. Everett, 296, and Bill Smith, 349. For more information on the use of multiphonics in areas of music other than jazz, examine the index entries under the term, Multiphonics (e.g., Stuart Dempster, 621, and Richard W. Bowles, 1022).

Bowles,R./Broussard,G./Dempster,S./Everett,T./Mangelsdorff,A./ Multiphonics/PerfPrac/Smith,B.

258. BERNHARDT, Clyde. "Talking about King Oliver, an oral history excerpt." *Annual Review of Jazz Studies* 1 (1982): 32-38.

Bernhardt (1906-1986) recounts his experiences playing trombone with King Oliver's band from March to November of 1931. See also Bernhardt, 259.

Oliver,K./OralHistory/PerfPrac

259. BERNHARDT, Clyde, and S. HARRIS. *I Remember: Eighty Years of Black Entertainment, Big Bands, and the Blues: An Autobiography.* Philadelphia: University of Pennsylvania Press, 1986.

See *RILM*1988-06682-bm. Clyde Bernhardt was also known professionally as Ed Barron. See obituaries in *Down Beat* 53 (October 1986): 13; *Black Perspective in Music* 14, no. 3 (1986): 322; *Jazz Magazine* 353 (September 1986): 4, and 356 (December 1986): 9; *Variety* 323 (June 1986): 150; and *Jazz Podium* 36 (February 1987): 27. See also Bernhardt, 258.
Barron,E./Harris,S./Obituaries/PerfPrac

260. BERNOTAS, Bob. "Al Grey." *JITA* 22, no. 1 (Winter 1994): 36-39.
Bernotas's article originally appeared in *Windplayer* 8, no. 3 (1991) and was revised in 1993. It includes Rob Boone's transcription of Grey's plunger trombone solo on "It's Only a Paper Moon," from his album with J.J. Johnson, *Things Are Getting Better All the Time.*
Boone,R./Grey,A./Johnson,J.J./PerfPrac/Plunger

261. BERT, Eddie. "My friend Trummy Young." *New York Brass Conference for Scholarships Journal* (1975): 56-57.
See Mike A. Bloom, 263, Charles Colin, 280, Gudrun Endress, 292, Thomas G. Everett, 302, Robert Lindsay, 327, and Ira Nepus, 1193.
Bloom,M./Colin,C./Endress,G./Everett,T./Lindsay,R./Nepus,I./Young,T.

262. BLOOM, Mike A. "Brunis trombone presented to N[ew]O[rleans] J[azz]C[lub] collections of the Louisiana State Museums." *The Second Line (New Orleans Jazz Club)* 33 (Winter 1981): 26-27.
Bloom includes a short profile of George Brunis, known as "The King of Tailgate Trombone."
Brunis,G./Dixieland/Instruments-20thC/NewOrleans/Tailgate

263. ———. "Interview with Trummy Young." *Cadence* 7, no. 5 (May 1981): 5-8+.
Bloom's interview with Young was cited by Marta Hofacre in Karl Hinterbichler's ongoing column in the *NITA* 8, no. 4 (September 1981): 37, as a discussion with Young about his years with the bands of Booker Coleman, Earl Hines, and others. See Robert Lindsay, 327, for more references.
Hinterbichler,K./Hofacre,M./Lindsay,R./Young,T.

264. BOGLE, Michael. "'Slide' Hampton." *JITA* 18, no. 1 (Winter 1990): 12-16.

Bogle's profile includes observations about jazz performance in Europe and a transcription by David Baker of a Hampton solo, "Chop Suey," from the album, *The Fabulous Slide Hampton Quartet.* See also W.A. Brower, 272, Robin Verges, 369, and Stan Wooley, 380.

Baker,D./Brower,W.A./Europe/Hampton,S./PerfPrac/Verges,R./Wooley,S.

265. BOUCHARD, Fred. "Hal Crook." *Down Beat* 57 (February 1990): 14.

At the time of this article, Crook was performing with Phil Woods's quintet. Bouchard's interview gives a capsule biography of Crook's background and lists the jazz greats that Crook considers his mentors.

Crook,H./Woods,P.

266. —————. "Profile: Michael Gibbs." *Down Beat* 50 (September 1983): 50-51.

Gibbs had made an outstanding career as a trombonist and composer/arranger. At the time of the article he was preparing to reenter the jazz performance area after a teaching hiatus at the Berklee School in Boston.

Berklee/Gibbs,M.

267. BOURGOIS, Louis George. "Jazz trombonist J.J. Johnson: A comprehensive discography and study of the early evolution of his style." Ohio State University, DMA, 1986 [cited in *ROBERTS* as Louis G. Bourgeois [*sic*] III].

See *Dissertation Abstracts* 47/03A, 704; MBB86-12343; DA8612343; AAD86-12343 [order numbers from various citations]. See also Jim Burns, 274, Thomas G. Everett, 24, 299, and 300, Leonard Feather, 303, Gene Kalbacher, 320, and Gerry Sloan, 749. Johnson was the 1988 recipient of the ITA Award.

Burns,J./Discog/Diss/Everett,T./Feather,L./ITA/Johnson,J.J./Kalbacher,G./OhioStateU/PerfPrac/Sloan,G.

268. BOURNE, Michael. "Profile: Dave Taylor." *Down Beat* 55 (August 1988): 52-53.
See Jean-Pierre Mathez, 181, and Douglas Yeo, 245. See also H.J. Rippert, "Annie Whitehead, Ray Anderson, and Dave Taylor," *Jazz Podium* 38 (July 1989): 38, and L. Kerner, "Outwardly mobile brass," *Village Voice* 32 (March 1987): 69.
BassTrb/Kerner,L./Mathez,J./Rippert,H./Taylor,D./Yeo,D.

269. ———. "Ray Anderson: Bone from another planet." *Down Beat* 58 (August 1991): 16.
See Jeff Levenson, 325. See also H.J. Rippert, "Annie Whitehead, Ray Anderson, and Dave Taylor," *Jazz Podium* 38 (July 1989): 38.
Anderson,R./Discog/Levenson,J./Rippert,H.J./Taylor,D./Whitehead,A.

270. ———. "Steve Turré: Trombone straight from the hip." *Down Beat* 54 (December 1987): 28-30.
Turré has played for many years with the band featured on "Saturday Night Live," and has appeared at the International Trombone Workshop. See entries in this book under *Biographies/ General* for his various workshop appearances.
NewYork/SaturdayNightLive/Television/Turré,S.

271. BROUSSARD, George. "Multitalented multiphonic Albert Mangelsdorff." *JITA* 17, no. 3 (Summer 1989): 14-18.
Mangelsdorff is one of the pioneers in performing, analyzing, and teaching multiphonics for jazz trombonists. The article also contains a selected discography. See the *NITA* 7, no. 2 (April 1980): 28, for a transcription of Mangelsdorff's "Brief Impression of Brighton."
See also Joachim E. Berendt, 257 and 600, Thomas G. Everett, 296, Bill Smith, 349, and Richard W. Bowles, 1022. For information on multiphonics in areas other than jazz, examine the index for entries under the term, Multiphonics (e.g., Stuart Dempster, 621).
Berendt,J./Bowles,R./Dempster,S./Discog/Everett,T./Germany/ Mangelsdorff,A./Multiphonics/Pedagogy/PerfPrac/Smith,B./ TrbMus-20thC

272. BROWER, W.A. "Slide Hampton: A good guy who's working."
     Jazz Times (December 1980): 8-9.
     See Michael Bogle, 264, Robin Verges, 369, and Stan Wooley, 380.
     Bogle,M./Hampton,S./Verges,R./Wooley,S.

273. BURNAP, Campbell. "Carl Fontana—A virtuoso's virtuoso."
     Crescendo International 25 (November-December 1988): 24-25.
     See Jerry Atkins, 251, for more references on Fontana.
     Atkins,J./Bebop/Fontana,C.

274. BURNS, Jim. "J.J. Johnson: The formative years." *Jazz Journal
     International* 28, no. 8 (August 1975): 4-7.
     See Louis G. Bourgois, 267, for more information on Johnson.
     Bourgois,L./Johnson,J.J.

275. [CAMPORA, Randy]. "Pioneering trombonist Barry Rogers is
     dead at 56." *JITA* 19, no. 4 (Fall 1991): 11.
     Rogers was best known for his long-term collaboration with
     Eddie Palmieri and the jazz/fusion group Dreams. This obituary
     appeared in Randy Campora's ongoing "General news" column
     in the *JITA*.
     Dreams/Obituaries/Palmieri,E./Rogers,B.

276. [————]. "Trombonists celebrate Joe Howard's 75th birthday."
     JITA 23, no. 4 (Fall 1995): 16.
     This story appeared in Campora's ongoing column, "General
     news." See also Mike Millar's letter in "The eighth position,"
     JITA 24, no. 1 (Winter 1996): 2, which gives the date of the
     well-known Los Angeles jazz and studio trombonist's death as
     October 12, 1995.
     Howard,J./LosAngeles/Millar,M.

277. CATALANO, Nick. "Kai Winding: His long and winding road."
     Down Beat 45 (September 1978): 27+.
     See Piet van Engelen, 293, Sue Mudge, 336, Stan Wooley, 379,
     and Les Tomkins, 1278.
     Engelen,P./Mudge,S./Tomkins,L./Winding,K./Wooley,S.

278. CHADBOURNE, Eugene. "Wandering spirit song: Julian Priester talks with Eugene Chadbourne." *Coda—Canada's Jazz Magazine* 12, no. 2 [issue no. 134] (December 1974): 2-5.

Julian Priester was born in the United States in 1935 and has made several recordings with his own group in New York City. Chadbourne's article includes a discussion about an album, *Love, love, "Pepo Mtoto"* (ECM (G)1044), recorded in 1974, in which Priester performs on tenor trombone, bass trombone, alto trombone, baritone horn, post horn, percussion, and synthesizer. See also Mack Crooks, 285. For more information on Priester, see L. Means, "Profile: How the other half lives," in *Down Beat* 41 (June 1974): 34-35.

Crooks,M./Discog/Means,L./Priester,J.

279. COLIN, Charles. "A reflection of love: Interview with George Roberts." *New York Brass Conference for Scholarships Journal*, 10 (1982): 10-14.

Colin's article is cited by Elecia Hill, 313. See also Bill Spilka, 350. Roberts, who has been called "Mr. Bass Trombone," was the 1982 recipient of the ITA Award.

BassTrb/Hill,E./ITA/Roberts,G./Spilka,B.

280. ———. "Trummy Young: An interview with Charles Colin." *New York Brass Conference for Scholarships Journal* (1980): 114-122.

See Robert Lindsay, 261, for more references on Trummy Young.

Lindsay,R./Obituaries/Pedagogy/Young,T.

281. [———], ed. *New York Brass Conference for Scholarships Featuring: Urbie Green.* NY: New York Brass Conference for Scholarships, 1984.

This booklet contains biographical sketches, articles, a partial discography, accolades, and photos of the legendary jazz trombonist. See Herb Nolan, 337, and Bill Spilka, 351. See also Ira Gitler, "Urbie Green: The urban-rural scene," *Down Beat* 36 (February 1969): 15+.

Discog/Gitler,I./Green,U./Nolan,H./Spilka,B.

282. COLNOT, C., and B. DOBROSKI. "Bill Watrous." *Accent* 1, no. 1 (1976): 11-13.
    Some of Watrous's ideas on jazz performance and pedagogy are included in this article. For more of Watrous's ideas and opinions, examine the index for several other entries in this book which are about him or include him in their discussions (e.g., Harvey Phillips, 1203). See also Watrous and Alan Raph, 1289. Dobroski,B./Pedagogy/PerfPrac/Phillips,H./Raph,A./Watrous,B.

283. COLUMBE, Grahame. "How do they age so well? Lawrence, Dicky, and Vic." *Jazz Journal International* 29, no. 8 (August 1976): 4-6.
    The improvisational styles of Lawrence Brown, Dicky Wells, and Vic Dickenson are briefly surveyed. For other articles on Dickenson see Lee Jeske, 319. For an obituary on Lawrence Brown see Kurt Dietrich, 290. For obituaries of Dicky Wells see *Billboard* 97 (December 1985): 71; *Cadence* 12 (January 1986): 91; *International Musician* 84 (April 86): 14; *Jazz Educators Journal* 18, no. 3 (1986): 72; *Jazz Podium* 34 (December 1985): 43; *Jazz Times* (January 1986): 25; *Musical Times* 127 (January 1986): 45; *Orkester Journalen: Tidskrift for jazzmusiik* 54 (January 1986): 30; *Variety* 321 (November 1985): 123; and signed articles by D.A. Rodrigues, *Jazz Forum* 98 (1986): 33; and Grahame Columbe, *Jazz Journal International* 39 (January 1986): 20.
    Brown,L./Dickenson,V./Dietrich,K./Improvisation/Jeske,L./ Obituaries/PerfPrac/Rodrigues,D.A./Wells,D.

284. COOK, Eddie. "Roy Williams talking to Eddie Cook." *Jazz Journal International* 33, no. 10 (October 1980): 6-7.
    Roy Williams, an English traditional jazz trombonist, speaks of his background and his impressions of the Colorado Jazz Party. See "Trombonist Roy Williams offers a few tips to beginners," 1280. ColoradoJazzParty/England/Williams,R.

285. CROOKS, Mack. "Julian Priester." *Cadence Magazine* 4, no. 1 (April 1978): 12-15+.
    Cited by Karl Hinterbichler in his ongoing column, "Literature announcements," in the *NITA* 6, no. 1 (September 1978): 22,

Crooks's article discusses Priester's early jazz and trombone influences, "and his work with Sun Ra, Max Roach, Duke Ellington, and Herbie Hancock." See Eugene Chadbourne, 278. See also an article by L. Means, "How the other half lives," in *Down Beat* 41 (June 1974): 34-35.
Chadbourne,E./Hinterbichler,K./Means,L./PerfPrac/Priester,J.

286. CROSBIE, Ian. "Will Bradley." *Coda—Canada's Jazz Magazine* 150 (August/September 1976): 2-3+.
Trombonist Bradley and his dance band were popular during the 1930s swing era.
Bradley,W./Canada/Swing

287. DANCE, Stanley. "Vic Dickenson: A melody man at heart." *Down Beat* 31 (December 1964): 18-20.
Dance's article was reprinted in the *New York Brass Conference for Scholarships Journal* (1975): 45-47, with an addendum by Jack Bradley. See Whitney Balliet, 254, Grahame Columbe, 283. and Lee Jeske, 319.
Balliet,W./Bradley,J./Columbe,G./Dickenson,V./Jeske,L.

288. DAVIS, Francis. "Borscht-Belt trombone." *The Atlantic.* (September 1992): 103-108.
Jazz great Roswell Rudd was a prime force in free jazz who performed his music for jazz lovers in the Catskills. See also Bret Primack, 339, and B. Tepperman, 356.
Catskills/FreeJazz/Moncur,G./PerfPrac/Primack,B./Rudd,R./
Tepperman,B.

289. DEDRICK, Rusty. "My brother Art." *New York Brass Conference for Scholarships Journal* 3? (1975): 63-64.
Although Art Dedrick is better known as a publisher (Kendor), he began his professional musical career as a trombonist in several bands, including his own (as Art Wilson). Tragically, his playing career was cut short by a severe case of polio. See also an obituary in the *NITA* 7, no. 2 (April 1980): 3.
Dedrick,A./Kendor/Wilson,A.

290. DIETRICH, Kurt. *Duke's 'Bones: Ellington's Great Trombonists.*
      Rottenburg, Germany: Advance Music, 1995.
          Randy Campora, who cites this work in his column in the *JITA*
      23, no. 2 (Spring 1995): 12, says, "In addition to containing rich
      interviews and historical information, the book also features fifty
      solos and section transcriptions." The publisher's address is
      Advance Music, Maierackerstr. 18, 72108 Rottenburg, Germany,
      phone 7472-1832 or fax 7472-24621. The book is evidently based
      on Dietrich's dissertation, "Joe 'Tricky Sam' Nanton, Juan Tizol,
      and Lawrence Brown: Duke Ellington's great trombonists, 1926-
      1951," University of Wisconsin-Madison, DMA, 1989. See
      Dissertation Abstracts 50/11A, 3405, publication no.
      AAC9009559 and *RILM*1989-07356-dd. See a review by Chris
      Buckholz in the *JITA* 25, no. 3 (Summer 1997): 65-66.
          See also Dietrich, 622, and Grahame Columbe, 283. For
      obituaries of Lawrence Brown, see the *New York Times*,
      September 18, 1988, section 1, p. 67, col. 5; *Variety* 332
      (September 1988): 94; and *Jet* 75 (October 1988): 58.
      Brown,L./Buckholz,C./Campora,R./Columbe,G./Diss/Ellington,D./
      Nanton,J./Obituaries/PerfPrac/Reviews/Tizol,J./WisconsinU-Madison

291. DUDLEY, Paul. "Bomblight serenade." *New York Brass
      Conference for Scholarships Journal* (1975): 15-18.
          Dudley worked with the Miller band both before and after
      Miller's tragic death in 1944. This article is reprinted from a
      1946 issue of *Esquire*. See Leo Walker, 372. See also a story by
      Clinton W. Trowbridge, who recounts his experience at age 15 of
      seeing the Miller band play and of being allowed to play on
      Miller's trombone at the intermission of the concert. The story
      appears in the *Christian Science Monitor*, June 7, 1991, p. 16,
      col. 2. For more information on Glenn Miller, his tenure with the
      Army Air Force, and his band during the war years, see Edward
      F. Polic, *The Glenn Miller Army Air Force Band: Sustineo Alas
      = I Sustain the Wings* (Metuchen NJ: Scarecrow Press, 1989).
      Bands/Military/Miller,G./Polic,E./Walker,L./WWII

292. ENDRESS, Gudrun. "Trummy Young: Meine Jahre mit Earl
      Hines, Jimmy Lunceford, und Dizzy Gillespie." *Jazz Podium* 33
      (July 1984): 4-8.

Endress's article is in German. See Robert Lindsay, 327, for more references on Trummy Young.
Gillespie,D./Hines,E./Lindsay,R./Lunceford,J./Young,T.

293. ENGELEN, Piet Van. *Kai Winding: Discography, 1942-1982.* [N.p, n.d.].
Engelen's discography is listed by Edward Bahr in his ongoing column in the *JITA* 14, no. 3 (Summer 1986): 24. It was reviewed in *Cadence* (July 1986). Further information may be obtained from the magazine at the Cadence Building, Redwood NY 13679 (thanks to Edward Bahr for this information). See Nick Catalano, 277, and Sue Mudge, 336, for more references on Kai Winding.
Bahr,E./Catalano,N./Discog/Mudge,S./Winding,K.

294. ERVIN, Tom. "Jazz at Nashville '74." *JITA* 3 (1975): 5-7.
Among the jazz artists on whom Ervin reports are Urbie Green, Jaxon Stock, Eje Thelin, Bill Watrous, Phil Wilson, and several jazz trombone ensembles.
Green,U./ITA/Reviews/Stock,J./Thelin,E./Watrous,B./Wilson,P./ Workshops

295. EVANS, David. "Since ol' Gabriel's time: Hezekiah and the Houserockers." *Louisiana Folklore* 7, no. 2 (October 1982): 1-34.
The lives, musical influences, style, and repertory of a basically blues band located in Natchez, Mississippi, and across the river in Louisiana are examined. The band includes Leon "Peewee" Whittaker, who sings and plays trombone.
Bib/Louisiana/Mississippi/Whittaker,L.

296. EVERETT, Thomas G. "Albert Mangelsdorff interview." *NITA* 5, no. 1 (September 1977): 20-21.
Transcribed by Bob Rusch, Everett's interview originally appeared in *Cadence—The Jazz and Blues Magazine*. See George Broussard, 271, for more references to Mangelsdorff.
Broussard,G./Germany/Mangelsdorff,A./Multiphonics

297. ———. "Carl Fontana: Master of bebop." *JITA* 21, no. 2 (Spring 1993): 14-18.

Everett's article is in two parts. Part 1 focuses on Fontana's life and career, while part 2, "Carl Fontana on record and compact disc," *JITA* 21, no. 2 (Summer 1993): 26-35, deals with Fontana's recordings and includes a transcription of "A Beautiful Friendship," as recorded live in 1975 at the Concord Jazz Festival with the "Hanna-Fontana Band," on Carl Jefferson's Concord Jazz label. Part 2 also lists two video tapes on which Fontana appears, *Woody Herman and His Famous Alumni* and *The Great Rocky Mountain Jazz Party*. See Jerry Atkins, 251, for more references on Fontana.
Atkins,J./Bebop/Discog/Fontana,C./Videos

298.   ———. "An interview with Frank Rehak." *JITA* 15, no. 2 (Spring 1987): 36-45.
Part of Everett's interview (through 1984) was condensed from an article for *Cadence* magazine. An update by Sandy Rehak, Emily Quist, and Sue Hummel is included. Everett later included Rehak's obituary in his "General news" column in the *JITA* 15, no. 4 (Fall 1987): 10-11. See also Stuart Dempster, 621. In his "Appendix IV: John Cage and Frank Rehak," Dempster relates the story of Cage's *Solo for Sliding Trombone*, which was written for and premiered by Rehak.
Cage,J./Dempster,S./Discog/Hummel,S./Obituaries/Quist,E./ Rehak,F./Rehak,S./Synanon

299.   ———. "J.J. Johnson: On the road again." *JITA* 16, no. 3 (Summer 1988): 22-29.
See Louis Bourgois, 267, for references on Johnson.
Bourgois,L./Johnson,J.J.

300.   ———. "J.J. Johnson: The architect of the modern jazz trombone." *JITA* 16, no. 2 (Spring 1988): 31-33.
See Louis G. Bourgois, 267, for more references on Johnson.
Bourgois,L./Johnson,J.J.

301.   ———. "A survey of studio and big band bass trombonists." *NITA* 5, no. 3 (April 1978): 9-16.
Though somewhat incomplete, since many of the top studio bass trombonists were unable to respond to the author's

questionnaire, Everett's survey still gives a good overview of the backgrounds, equipment, playing experiences, and brief glimpses of the pedagogical ideas of a representative group of the "first call" bass trombonists in the late 1970s. See 124 for Everett's survey dealing with orchestral bass trombonists.
Baker,D./Bargeron,D./BassTrb/Conners,C./Faulise,P./Heather,C./ Jeffers,J./Keen,P./Knight,B./Lieb,D./McQuary,D./Mitchell,T./ Pedagogy/Premru,R./Raph,A./Roberts,G./Shroyer,K./Studio/ Tack,E./Waldrop,D.

302. [———]. "Trummy Young (1912-1984)." *JITA* 13, no. 1 (January 1985): 50.
  This obituary mentions Trummy Young's abilities as a vocalist, making reference to his recording of *Margie* with Jimmy Lunceford in 1938. See Eddie Bert, 261, for more references to Young.
Bert,E./Obituaries/Young,T.

303. FEATHER, Leonard. "Trombone renaissance?" *Los Angeles Times*, November 15, 1987, section C, p. 75, col. 1.
  A profile of J.J. Johnson, this is the first in a two-part series. See Louis Bourgois, 267, for more references to Johnson.
Bourgois,L./Johnson,J.J.

304. FRANK, Robert. "Third brother Delfeayo Marsalis is paying his own dues." *Boston Globe*, August 27, 1989, p. 76. col. 1.
  The trombonist brother of trumpeter Wynton and saxophonist Branford Marsalis is profiled as a performer and acoustic jazz producer.
Marsalis,D.

305. GIDDINS, Gary. "The '76 trombonist." *New York Magazine* (November 1975): 95.
  Giddins writes about Bill Watrous as a trombonist and band leader. See Steven Marks, 330, Zan Stewart, 354, E.T. Vögel, 371, Charles Winking, 377, and Scott Yanow, 381.
Marks,S./Stewart,Z./Vögel,E./Watrous,B./Winking,C./Yanow,S.

306. "Glory of jazz: Trombonists, old and new." *Music U.S.A.* 76
      (May 1959): 15-16.
      Bio

307. GRISSOM, Eugene, and Eileen MASSINON. "Workshop and
      festival scholarship winners: Where are they now? (featuring the
      Rosolino winners)". *JITA* 24, no. 4 (Fall 1996): 24-27.
      The young jazz artists who were awarded the Frank Rosolino
      Memorial Scholarship from 1979-1996 are featured: Conrad
      Herwig (1979), Chris Seiter (1980), Scott Bliege (1981), Paul
      McKee (1982), Tom Kordus (1983), Rob Boone (1984), Jim
      Martin (1985), Joel Adams (1986), John Moak (1987), Mike
      Christianson (1988), Eric Felten (1989), Matt Soule (1990),
      David Gibson (1991) [no winner awarded for 1992], Robert
      Stone (1993), Elliot Mason (1994), Jürgen Neudert (1995), and
      Nils Wogram (1996).
      For more references to Frank Rosolino see [Jamey Aebersold],
      249. For information about other ITA scholarship winners,
      including the Donald Yaxley Bass Trombone Scholarships
      through 1997, see Thomas G. Everett, 121.
      Adams,J./Aebersold,J./Bliege,S./Boone,R./Christianson,M./
      Everett,T./Felten,E./Gibson,D./Herwig,C./ITA/Kordus,T./
      Martin,J./Mason,E./Massinon,E./McKee,P./Moak,J./Neudert,J./
      Rosolino,F./Seiter,C./Soule,M./Stone,R./Wogram,N./Yaxley,D.

308. GRISSOM, Nancy. "Trombonist Carl Fontana." *Jazz Notes*
      5, no. 10 (April 1988).
      Jazz Notes is the newsletter of the Gainesville, Florida, Friends
      of Jazz. See Jerry Atkins, 251, and Thomas G. Everett, 297, for
      more references to Fontana.
      Atkins,J./Everett,T.Fontana,C.

309. GRUNO, Linda. "Eddie Bert." *Down Beat* 58 (July 1991): 14.
      Bert was one of the most prominent jazz trombonists before J.J.
      Johnson. Bert's wife recorded on a home disc-cutter some 1941
      airchecks featuring vibist Red Norvo's band, with whom Bert
      was playing. The recordings were released in 1994 by Music
      Masters as *Red Norvo and His Orchestra—Live at the Blue
      Gardens*. For more information on Bert's recordings and an

update on his career see Bob Laber, "The career of Eddie Bert: Sideman to jazz history," *Instrumentalist* 48, no. 10 (May 1994): 25-30+.
Bert,E./Laber,B./Norvo,R.

310. ———. "Fred Wesley." *Down Beat* 57 (April 1990): 15.
Wesley was known as "the funk trombonist of the seventies" because of his association as sideman and arranger for singer James Brown. His influence may be heard in the performances of several younger artists such as Steve Turré and Robin Eubanks.
Brown,J./Funk/Wesley,F.

311. GUTTRIDGE, Leonard. "Giants of jazz: Jack Teagarden," New York: *Time-Life* Records, 1979.
Teagarden's life and music are highlighted, while the recordings that accompany the pamphlet contain examples of his output from the 1920s through the 1950s. Guttridge's pamphlet is part of the *Time-Life* jazz recording series. See also Rex Allen, 250, Whitney Balliet, 252, and Gerry Sloan, 348.
Allen,R./Balliet,W./Discog/Sloan,G./Teagarden,J.

312. HELLAND, Dave. "Robin Eubanks: A true sense of perspective." *Down Beat* 56 (January 1989): 26-28.
Eubanks's style, based on traditional jazz but going beyond what some critics regard as its parameters, is discussed. At the time of the interview, Eubanks was playing with Art Blakey and working with new electronic and technological ideas with his group called M-BASE (macro basic array of structural extemporization). See also Eubanks, 634.
Computers/Discog/Electronic/Eubanks,R./M-BASE

313. HILL, Elecia. "George Roberts: Tribute to a legend." *JITA* 16, no. 1 (Winter 1988): 22-30.
One section is excerpted from Charles Colin, 279. See also Bill Spilka, 350.
BassTrb/Colin,C./LosAngeles/Roberts,G./Spilka,B.

314. HILLMAN, Chris. "Big Jim, 1892-1976." *Jazz Journal International* 29, no. 8 (August 1976): 16.

Jim Robinson was one of the members of the Preservation Hall
Jazz Band. See also Karl Koenig, 321.
Dixieland/Koenig,K./NewOrleans/PreservationHall/Robinson,J.

315. HÜGER, Florian H. "Ory's Creole Trombone: Transkription und
      Analyse der ersten Schallplattenaufnahme einer schwarzen New
      Orleans Jazzband [Ory's Creole trombone: Transcription and
      analysis of the first recording of a black New Orleans jazz
      band]." *Jazzforschung/Jazz Research* 23 (1991): 9-115.
      Dating from 1922, this recording of Edward (Kid) Ory is
      considered significant for its expression of the so-called New
      Orleans style of jazz. See also Franz Krieger, 688.
      Krieger,F./NewOrleans/Ory,K.

316. [IVEY, Ben]. "Quentin 'Butter' Jackson (1909-1976)." *NITA* 4,
      no. 2 (February 1977): 5.
      This brief obituary was included in Ivey's ongoing column,
      "General news." Jackson was one of the last jazz trombonists to
      play in the plunger "talking" style originated by "Tricky" Sam
      Nanton. See Bill Spilka's "Spit valve," on p. 9 of the same issue
      of the *NITA*. See also Bob Bernotas, 260, Jennifer Paradis-Hagar,
      720, and Gerry Sloan, 751.
      Bernotas,B./Jackson,Q./Nanton,S./Obituaries/Paradis-Hagar,J./
      Plunger/Sloan,G./Spilka,B.

317. JAMES, Betty A. "Bilingual bebop (Guy Levilain, jazz
      musician)." *Minneapolis-St. Paul Magazine* 11 (July 1983): 64.
      Bebop/Levilain,G./Minneapolis-StPaul

318. ———. "The return of Dicky Wells." *Jazz Journal International*
      31 (August 1978): 6-7.
      James's interview was held after Wells's hospital stay in 1978.
      See above Grahame Columbe, 283. See also Dicky Wells and
      Stanley Dance, *The Night People: The Jazz Life of Dicky Wells*,
      rev. ed. (Washington DC: Smithsonian Institution, 1991). A
      review by Steve Voce of the book may be found in *Jazz Journal
      International* 45 (October 1992): 16-17. Other reviews are in
      Billboard 104 (February 22,1992): 68; *Cadence* 18 (June 1992):
      19; *International Association of Jazz Record Collectors Journal*

25, no. 3 (1992): 71; and *Jazz Times* 22, no. 4 (1992): 63. Further information may be found in Jan Evensmo's monograph, *The Flute of Wayman Carter, the Trombone of Dicky Wells 1927-1942* . . ., (Hasle, Norway [1347 Postboks 50]: Compiler, 1983). Chris Sheridan's review of this book may be found in *Jazz Journal International* 37 (May 1984): 16.
Columbe,G./Dance,S./Evensmo,J./Reviews/Sheridan,C./ Smithsonian/Voce,S./Wells,D.

319. JESKE, Lee. "Vic Dickenson: Swing master escapes Condon gang." *Down Beat* 47 (March 1980): 24-25.
See Whitney Balliet, 254, Grahame Columbe, 283, and Stanley Dance, 287. For obituaries of Dickenson (1906-1985), see *Black Perspective in Music* 13, no. 2 (1985): 242; *Cadence* 11 (January 1985): 78; *JITA* 13, no. 2 (April 1985): 51; *Jazz Educators Journal* 17, no. 3 (1985): 80; *Jazz Podium* 34 (January 1985): 38; *Orkester Journalen: Tidskrift for jazzmusik* 53 (January 1985): 38; and signed articles by A. Morgan, *Jazz Journal International* 37 (February 1985): 84; A. Stevens, *Crescendo International* 22 (June-July 1985): 38; and J.H. Klee, *Mississippi Rag* 12 (January 1985): 4.
Balliet,W./Columbe,G./Dance,S./Dickenson,V./Klee,J./Morgan,A./ Obituaries/Stevens,A.

320. KALBACHER, Gene. "J.J. Johnson: Bringing it all back home." *Down Beat* 55 (March 1988): 16-19.
See above Louis G. Bourgois, 267, for more references on Johnson.
Bourgois,L./Discog/Johnson,J.J.

321. KOENIG, Karl. "Nathan 'Big Jim' Robinson: Jazz trombonist." *Second Line* 35 (Winter 1983): 24-35.
Jim Robinson (1890-1976) was a New Orleans trombonist whose style became an inspiration for many players. Koenig's article includes a history of the Sam Morgan band, with whom Robinson played from 1922 to 1929. See Chris Hillman, 314.
Hillman,C./Morgan,S./NewOrleans/Robinson,J.

322. ———. "Plantation bands, part 4: Harrison Barnes, Sunny Henry, and the Eclipse Marching Band of Magnolia Plantation." *Second Line* 34 (Summer 1982): 37-45.
       Harrison Barnes and Sunny Henry were two trombonists who were taught in and performed with the Eclipse Marching Band. Barnes,H./EclipseMarchingBand/Henry,S./Louisiana/ MagnoliaPlantation

323. [LEE, Amy]. "The Dorsey brothers played for pennies." *New York Brass Conference for Scholarships Journal* 4 (1976): 104-110.
       A reprint from the September 1940 issue of *Metronome Music USA* article dealing with both Tommy and Jimmy Dorsey, Lee's article includes many photos of the famous brothers in performance. See [Joyce Records], 29, and Fred ("Moe") Snyder, 66. See also Jonathan Winkler, 587, for a discussion of a Roy Harris work composed for Dorsey's band in 1938. Bahr,E./Dorsey,J./Dorsey,T./Harris,R./MrNostalgia/Pugh,J./ Snyder,F./Winkler,J.

324. LEES, Gene. "Why?" *JITA* 13, no. 1 (January 1985): 43-46.
       Lees relates a poignant and compelling narrative about the tragic death of the legendary jazz trombonist Frank Rosolino. See [Jamey Aebersold], 249, for more references to Rosolino. Aebersold,J./Rosolino,F.

325. LEVENSON, Jeff. "Ray Anderson: Slidin' into first." *Down Beat* 56 (August 1989): 27-29.
       See also Michael Bourne, 269. Anderson,R./Bourne,M.

326. LEWIS, Alwyn, and Laurie LEWIS. "Pictorial voyage of Phil Wilson." *Cadence* (1990).
       The Lewises' article was reprinted in the *New York Brass Conference for Scholarships Journal* 21 (1993): 7-24. Wilson,P.

327. LINDSAY, Robert. "A jazzman learns his trade." *JITA* 12, no. 2 (April 1984): 19-20.

An interview with Trummy Young, excerpts of which are included in this article, was conducted by Patricia Williard in July 1976 under the auspices of the Jazz Oral History Project of the Institute of Jazz Studies. See Eddie Bert, 261, Mike A. Bloom, 263, Charles Colin, 281, Gudrun Endress, 292, and Ira Nepus, 1193. For obituaries of Trummy [James Osborne] Young (1912-1984), see Robert Lindsay in the *JITA* 21, no. 1 (Winter 1993): 16; Floyd Levin, "Memories of Trummy," *Jazz Journal International* 37 (November 1984): 9 [Mr. Levin asserts emphatically that his article is not an obituary]; Thomas G. Everett, "Trummy Young (1912-1984)," *JITA* 13, no. 1 (January 1985): 50; and unsigned articles in the following publications: *Mississippi Rag* 11 (October 1984):3 and 12 (November 1984): 4; *Billboard* 96 (September 1984): 69; *Cadence* 10 (October 1984): 93; *Coda—Canada's Jazz Magazine* 199 (December 1984): 39; *Down Beat* 51 (December 1984): 14; *International Musician* 83 (November 1984): 13; *Jazz Magazine* 332 (September-October 1984): 4; *Jazz Times* (November 1984): 7; *Orkester Journalen: Tidskrift for jazz musik* 52 (October 1984): 34; and *Orkester* 32 (November 1984): 1000.
Bert,E./Bloom,M./Colin,C./Endress,G./Everett,T./Levin,F./ Nepus,I./Obituaries/Williard,P./Young,T.

328. LITWEILER, John B. "Profile: George Lewis." *Down Beat* 44 (August 1977): 36-38.
At the time of the interview, Lewis was performing with Anthony Braxton's group.
Braxton,A./Lewis,G.

329. MARCELLUS, John. "A survey of selected jazz trombonists 1920-1970." *JITA* 7 (1979): 7-10.
Marcellus's survey concentrates on performers who originated and developed new styles and techniques.
Bohanon,G./Brunis,G./Cleveland,J./Discog/Dorsey,T./Green,C./ Green,U./Harris,B./Harrison,J./Higginbotham,J.C./ITA/ Johnson,J.J./Mangelsdorff,A./Moncur,G./Morton,B./Ory,K./ PerfPrac/Rosolino,F./Teagarden,J./Winding,K./Young,T.

330. MARKS, Steven. "Bill Watrous: Swing refuge in the wilds of
      Manhattan." *Down Beat* 42 (June 1975): 14-15+.
      See also Burt Korall's column in the June 1975 issue of the
      International Musician. Marks's article was reprinted in the *New
      York Brass Conference for Scholarships Journal* 4 (1976): 48-50.
      See Gary Giddins, 305, for more references on Watrous.
      Giddins,G./Korall,B./Watrous,B.

331. MCNAMARA, Helen. "Murray McEachern." *International
      Musician* 73 (February 1975): 7+.
      McEachern was considered a consummate stylist by his peers
      in the studios of the West Coast. Dick Nash, Henry Mancini's
      favorite lead trombonist, has credited Murray McEachern for
      being at least indirectly responsible for the development of his
      sound and ballad style. See Nash, 715.
      McEachern,M./Nash,D.

332. MILKOWSKI, Bill. "Craig Harris: Renegade spirit." *Down Beat*
      58 (February 1991): 24-25.
      See also Francis Davis, "If it sounds good, it is good," *High
      Fidelity* 35 (October 1985): 75-77, and Lee Jeske, "Profile: Craig
      Harris," *Down Beat* 50 (April 1983): 44-45.
      Davis,F./Discog/Harris,C./Jeske,L.

333. MORGAN, Marty. "For Frank Rosolino." *National Association
      of Jazz Educators Journal* 11, no. 3 (March 1979): 76.
      See above Jamey Aebersold, 249, for more references on
      Rosolino.
      Aebersold,J./Rosolino,F.

334. MUDGE, Sue. "Conversations in Los Angeles with Charlie
      Loper, Dick Nash, Bill Booth, Roy Main, and Morris Repass."
      JITA 11, no. 1 (January 1983): 21-24.
      Some of the busiest and best studio trombonists in the Los
      Angeles area during the 1980s are introduced. The interviews are
      continued in vol. 11, no. 3 (July 1983): 32-35. For further
      information on Dick Nash see Les Tomkins, 357, and Bill Spilka,
      352. See also Leonard Feather's article in the *Los Angeles Times*,
      November 24, 1988, sec. 6, p. 4, col. 1. Roy Main retired in

April 1997 (see [Randy Campora], "General news," *JITA* 25, no. 3 (Summer 1997): 13).
Booth,B./Campora,R./Feather,L./Loper,C./Main,R./Nash,D./ Repass,M./Spilka,B./Studio/Tomkins,L.

335. ———. "Conversations in Los Angeles with Lloyd Ulyate." *JITA* 12, no. 1 (January 1984): 5-8.
Ulyate had been a Los Angeles studio musician since 1947.
LosAngeles/Studio/Ulyate,L.

336. ———. "'Jangles,' let's get on with it." *JITA* 11, no. 4 (October 1983): 4-5.
Mudge relates a poignant, sometimes humorous remembrance of Kai Winding (1923-1983) as narrated by Bill Watrous. See Nick Catalano, 277, Piet van Engelen, 293, Stan Wooley, 379, and Les Tomkins, 1278.
Obituaries of Winding are included in *Billboard* 95 (May 1983): 60; *Coda—Canada's Jazz Magazine* 190 (June 1983): 39, *Crescendo International* 22 (February-March 1984): 25 (there are also signed articles from the same magazine by Don Lusher in vol. 21 (June-July 1983): 38; and J. Goatham, "The warmth of Winding," (August 1983): 31). Additional obituaries may be found in the *International Musician* 81 (January 1983): 14; *Jazz Educators Journal* 16, no. 2 (1984): 109; *Jazz Journal International* 36 (January 1983): 15; *Jazz Times* (July 1983): 12, *Mens en Melodie* 38 (June 1983): 275; *Musical Times* 24 (July 1983): 44;, *Orkester Journalen: Tidskrift for jazzmusik* 51 (June 1983): 3;, and *Variety* 311 (May 1983): 117.
Catalano,N./Engelen,P./Goatham,J./Lusher,D./Obituaries/ Tomkins,L./Watrous,B./Winding,K./Wooley,S.

337. NOLAN, Herb. "Urbie Green: Studio slidemaster." *Down Beat* 43 (October 1976): 14-15.
See Charles Colin, 281, and Bill Spilka, 351. See also Ira Gitler, "Urbie Green: The urban-rural scene," *Down Beat* 36 (February 1969): 15+. Green was the recipient of the ITA Award in 1985.
Colin,C./Gitler,I./Green,U./ITA/Spilka,B./Studio

338. POTTER, Barrett. "Spiegle Wilcox, nearing eighty and still sliding." *International Association of Jazz Record Collectors Journal* 13, no. 4 (October 1980).
Karl Hinterbichler cited this article in his ongoing column, "Literature announcements," in the *NITA* 8, no. 3 (April 1981): 33. See also the *JITA* 24, no. 3 (Summer 1996): 2-3, for an interesting letter from Harry Price in Australia, updating information on Spiegle Wilcox, who is now in his nineties. See also Sinclair Traill, 360.
Goldkette,J./Hinterbichler,K./Price,H./Traill,S./Wilcox,S.

339. PRIMACK, Bret. "Roswell Rudd: Transmission from the soul." *Down Beat* 45 (October 1978): 24-25+.
See Francis Davis, 288, and B. Tepperman, 356. Davis,F./FreeJazz/Rudd,R./Tepperman,B.

340. REAVER, Doc. "Gigging with Bill Rank." *International Association of Jazz Record Collectors Journal* 9, no. 3 (Summer 1976).
See also the *NITA* 7, no. 1 (December 1979): 2, for a short obituary of William C. "Bill" Rank (1904-1979).
Obituaries/Rank,B.

341. RUSCH, Bob, and B. JENNE. "Carl Fontana interview." *Cadence Magazine* 16 (July 1990): 14-25+.
See above Jerry Atkins, 251, for more references on Fontana. Atkins,J./Bebop/Fontana,C./Jenne,B.

342. SCHNECKLOCK, Tim. "Guardians of the musical future: A gallery of contemporary music educators [David Baker]." *New York Brass Conference for Scholarships* (1979): 34.
Schnecklock's short sketch of the life, trials, and musical philosophies of jazz great David Baker was reprinted from an article dealing with Baker and several other musicians in *Down Beat* 44 (December 1977): 14-16. See also Gunther Schuller, 343. Baker,D./BassTrb/Pedagogy/Schuller,G.

343. SCHULLER, Gunther. "Indiana renaissance." *Jazz Review* 2 (September 1959): 48-50.

Reprinted in the *New York Brass Conference for Scholarships Journal* (1991), Schuller's article speaks of David Baker's early career as a jazz solo artist on bass trombone. See Tim Schnecklock, 342.
Baker,D./BassTrb/Indiana/Schnecklock,T.

344. SCHULZ, Klaus. "Erich Kleinschuster: Der Pragmatiker mit der Posaune [Erich Kleinschuster: Trombone pragmatist]." *Jazz Live: Österreichisches Jazz Magazin II* (November 1984): 4-10.

Erich Kleinschuster founded a jazz ensemble in Austria in 1966 and later became the leader of the Österreichischer Rundfunk Big Band. He taught jazz improvisation at the conservatory in Graz. Austria/Graz/Kleinschuster,E./ÖsterreichischerRundfunk

345. SLOAN, Gerry. "In memoriam: Frank Rosolino," *NITA* 6, no. 3 (April 1979): 5.

See Jamey D. Aebersold, 249, for more references on Rosolino.
Aebersold,J./Obituaries/Rosolino,F.

346. ———. "Jimmy Knepper: Cunningbird of the trombone." *Jazz Journal International* 33 (November 1980): 6-7.

In his article, Sloan has included a partial discography of recordings featuring Jimmy Knepper. See Whitney Balliet, 253, and Les Tomkins, 359.
Balliet,W./Cunningbird/Discog/Knepper,J./Tomkins,L.

347. ———. "Tommy Turk (1927-1981): A tribute." *JITA* 10, no. 1 (January 1982): 26-28.

Turk was one of the most respected but least known (to the general public) of the significant jazz trombonists who began their work in the 1940s. He influenced such jazz greats as Buddy Baker, Rich Matteson, and Carl Fontana. This article was reprinted from *Jazz Journal International*.
Obituaries/Turk,T.

348. ———. "You're in Teagarden country." *JITA* 14, no. 2 (Spring 1986): 27-32.

Included are an annotated, selected discography; a bibliography; addresses of people to contact to assist in learning more about

Teagarden's life and career; and a transcribed solo, "Lover," performed by Teagarden with La Vere's Chicago Loopers (1950). See also Rex Allen, 250, Whitney Balliet, 252, and Leonard Guttridge, 311.
Allen,R./Balliet,W./Bib/Discog/Guttridge,L./LaVere/Teagarden,J.

349. SMITH, Bill. "An interview with Albert Mangelsdorff." *Coda—Canada's Jazz Magazine* 168 (August 1979): 4-10.
See George Broussard, 271, for more references on Mangelsdorff.
Broussard,G./Germany/Mangelsdorff,A./Multiphonics

350. SPILKA, Bill. "An interview with George Roberts." *New York Brass Conference for Scholarships Journal* 12 (1984): 32-35.
See Charles Colin, 279, and Elecia Hill, 313.
BassTrb/Colin,C./Hill,E./ITA/Roberts,G.

351. ———. "An interview with Urbie Green, 10/10/75." *NITA* 5, no. 1 (September 1977): 22-27.
The original transcription was by Muriel Slater, and the interview was retranscribed on November 17, 1976. See Charles Colin, 281, and Herb Nolan, 337. See also Ira Gitler, "Urbie Green: The urban-rural scene," *Down Beat* 36 (February 1969): 15+.
Colin,C./Gitler,I./Green,U./Nolan,H./Slater,M.

352. ———. "Letter from Hollywood." *NITA* 6, no. 1 (September 1978): 16-22.
Spilka gives a narrative of his stay in Hollywood, where he wined, dined, and interviewed some of the best-known studio and jazz trombonists in the Los Angeles area. See also Sue Mudge, 334.
LosAngeles/Mudge,S./Studio

353. ———. "Small makes it big in the Big Apple." *JITA* 16, no. 3 (Summer 1988): 17-21.
In his review of the New York Brass Conference for Scholarships, Spilka outlines the career of Charlie Small.
BigApple/NewYork/NYBCS/Small,C.

354. STEWART, Zan. "Bill Watrous: Straight talking sideman."
Windplayer 2, no. 4 (May 1985): 12-15.
The issue also contains on p. 8 a transcription by Andy Weiner
of Watrous's solo on "Shadow Waltz," from his album, *La Zorra*.
See Gary Giddins, 305, for more references on Watrous.
Giddins,G./Watrous,B./Weiner,A.

355. STOKES, W. Royal. "The big band sound of Melba Liston."
JITA 13, no. 2 (April 1985): 35-37.
Stokes is a jazz performance reviewer for the *Washington Post*,
book editor of "Jazz Line," a frequent contributor to *Jazz Times*
and jazz broadcaster over WPFW-FM (Pacifica). His article was
originally printed in *Ms. Magazine*, January, 1983. See also Phil
W. Petrie, "Melba Liston: The woman, the horn, the dream,"
Essence Magazine 12 (October 1981): 13.
Liston,M./Petrie,P.

356. TEPPERMAN, B. "Rudd, Moncur and some other stuff." *Coda—
Canada's Jazz Magazine* 10, no. 2 (1971): 8-11.
See Francis Davis, 288, and Bret Primack, 339.
Davis,F./Moncur,G./Primack,B./Rudd,R.

357. TOMKINS, Les. "Benny Morton." *Crescendo International* 13
(January 1975): 14-16.
Tomkins has two other interviews in other issues of this
magazine with Don Lusher and Dick Nash. See vol. 12 (May and
June 1974) and vol. 13 (August 1974). See also Richard McRae, 710.
For obituaries on Benny (Henry S.) Morton (1908-1986), see
the *Los Angeles Times*, January 3, 1986, sec. 1, p. 33, col. 5,
Down Beat 53 (March 1986): 13; *Jazz Educators Journal* 18, no.
3 (1986): 40; *Mississippi Rag* 13 (February 1986): 5; *Orkester
Journalen: Tidskrift for jazzmusik* 54 (February 1986): 30; and
Variety 321 (January 1986): 146.
England/Green,C./Harrison,J./Lusher,D./McRae,R./Morton,B./
Nash,D./Obituaries

358. ———. "The musical inheritance of Chris Brubeck." *Crescendo*
19, no. 6 (January 1981): 16-17.
BassTrb/Brubeck,C.

359. ———. "Reflections of Jimmy Knepper." *Crescendo* 19, no. 7 (February 1981): 6-7.

See Whitney Balliet, 253, and Gerry Sloan, 346.

Balliet,W./Knepper,J./Mingus,C./Sloan,G.

360. TRAILL, Sinclair. "Goldkette memories." *Jazz Journal International* 33 (April 1980): 32-33.

Cited in Karl Hinterbichler's ongoing column, "Literature announcements," in the *NITA* 8, no. 1 (September 1980): 32, as "Goldhette [*sic*] memories," Traill interviews trombonist Spiegle Wilcox, who played with the Jean Goldkette band, along with cornetist Bix Beiderbecke, in the 1920s. Wilcox replaced Tommy Dorsey in the Goldkette Orchestra. See also Barrett Potter, 338.

Goldkette,J./Hinterbichler,K./Potter,B./Wilcox,S.

361. "Trombonists talk with Buddy Morrow." *Crescendo International* 10 (October 1971): 22.

Morrow's real name was Moe Zudecoff, and occasionally he added the name "Muni" in front of his stage name. See also C. Deffa, "Buddy of Tommy Dorsey," *Mississippi Rag* 17 (August 1990): 20-22; and "Talent in action [Buddy Morrow]," *Billboard* 94 (June 1982): 47.

Deffa,C./Dorsey,T./Morrow,B./PerfPrac/Zudecoff,M.

362. ULMAN, Edward J. "Jiggs." *JITA* 24, no. 1 (Winter 1996): 34-37.

Ulman's profile of jazz artist Jiggs Whigham includes a selected discography and a transcription of one of Wigham's choruses from "My romance," from one of his albums, *The Jiggs Up.* See also Joe Weisel, 374.

Discog/Germany/Weisel,J./Whigham,J.

363. UNDERWOOD, Lee. "Frank Rosolino: Conversation with the master." *Down Beat* 44 (November 1977): 18-19+.

Underwood's interview was conducted shortly before Rosolino's tragic death. See Jamey Aebersold, 249, for more references on Rosolino.

Aebersold,J./Rosolino,F.

364.   ———. "Profile: Alan Kaplan." *Down Beat* 47 (April 1980): 54-55.
        At the time of this profile, Kaplan was a prominent studio lead
        and jazz trombonist on the West Coast. See also Kaplan, 480.
        Kaplan,A./Studio

365.   ———. "Profile: Bruce Fowler," *Down Beat* 41, no. 20
        (December 1974): 26.
        Fowler was one of the young jazz stars who began to be
        noticed in the 1970s. The interview includes his musical and
        philosophical views. See Fowler, 639, and 1092.
        Fowler,B.

366.   ———. "Profile: Glenn Ferris." *Down Beat* 44 (December 1977): 42.
        Ferris, a versatile, iconoclastic trombonist was, at least at this
        time in his life, severely critical of the commercial music industry.
        The interview was reprinted in the *BBIBC* 23 (1978): 31-34.
        Ferris,G.

367.   ———. "Profile: Raul De Souza." *Down Beat* 45 (January 1978): 32.
        De Souza is one of the most significant jazz musicians to come
        out of South America. He has been very successful with his
        musical career in the United States.
        Brazil/DeSouza,R.

368.   VACHER, Peter. "Louis Nelson and the New Orleans Navy."
        Jazz Journal International 30, no. 10 (October 1977): 8-9.
        Nelson was an early New Orleans Dixieland trombonist. For an
        obituary, see [Douglas Yeo], 384.
        Nelson,L./NewOrleans/Yeo,D.

369.   VERGES, Robin. "Slide Hampton: Back at the right time." *Jazz
        Podium* 57 (1979): 34-37.
        See Michael Bogle, 264, W.A. Brower, 272, and Stan Wooley, 380.
        Bogle,M./Brower,W.A./Hampton,S./Wooley,S.

370.   VOCE, Steve. "Duke of bebop." *Jazz Journal International* 30,
        no. 7 (July 1977): 16-17+.
        In a tribute to jazz trombonist Bennie Green, who died in
        March 1977, Voce discusses Green's style, which combined

swing with bop technique. After a short but significant
performing career, Green became a noted writer and critic in the
jazz field. See obituaries in the *NITA* 5, no. 1 (September 1977):
35; *Jazz Journal International* 30, no. 6 (June 1977): 24; *Jazz
Podium* 26 (June 1977): 25; and *Orkester Journalen: Tidskrift för
jazzmusik* 45 (May 1977): 5. See also James Burns, "Dem bones,
dem bones, dem bopping bones," *Jazz and Blues* 2 (October
1972): 16-19, and a review of one of Green's albums, *Early
Bones*, in *Down Beat* 43 (December 1976): 36-39.
Bebop/Burns,J./Green,B./Obituaries/PerfPrac/Swing

371. VÖGEL, E.T. "Ein junger Posaunist sucht seinen Weg: Bill
Watrous [A young trombonist seeks his way . . .]." *Jazz Podium*
24 (September 1975): 15-17.
Vögel's article is in German. See above Gary Giddins, 305, for
more references on Watrous.
Giddins,G./Watrous,B.

372. WALKER, Leo. "Glenn Miller???" *The Big Bands* (January 1981).
Marta Hofacre cites this article in Karl Hinterbichler's ongoing
column, "Literature announcements," in the *NITA* 8, no. 4
(September 1981): 37, as containing a "short summary of the
mystery and a few recollections. The back cover includes a photo
of the Glenn Miller Air Force Band in the Yale Bowl." See Paul
Dudley, 291, for more references.
ArmyAirCorps/Bands/Dudley,P./Hinterbichler,K./Hofacre,M./
Military/Miller,G./WWII

373. WALTER, Cam. "An interview with Rob McConnell." *JITA* 22,
no. 4 (Fall 1994): 30-33.
Rob McConnell is well-known as a valve trombonist, band
leader, composer, and arranger who has lived in Toronto most of
his life. Included in the article is a transcription of his solo on
"Long Ago and Far Away," from his 1994 release, *Trio Sketches*.
Canada/Discog/McConnell,R./ValveTrb

374. WEISEL, Joe. "Meet Professor Jazz: An American in Cologne."
NITA 8, no. 2 (December 1980): 17-18.

Reprinted from the *International Herald Tribune* in Paris, Weisel's article deals with Jiggs Whigham's appointment to the first university-level chair for jazz studies in Germany, at the Kölner Hochschule für Musik. See Edward Ulman, 362. Germany/KölnerHochschuleMusik/Ulman,E./Whigham,J.

375. WESTIN, Lars. "Eje Thelin: Trials and tribulations of a Swedish trombonist." *Down Beat* 43 (October 1976): 18.
  Thelin, a jazz artist from Sweden, was on the 1974 International Trombone Workshop faculty. See Tom Ervin, 294. See also G.B. Lane's "Report on the 1974 International Trombone Workshop . . ." *Brass World* 9, no. 2 (1974): 101-107. James Robertson and Tom Senff contributed to the report and a biographical sketch of Thelin may be found on p. 101.
  Ervin,T./Lane,G./Robertson,J./Senff,T./Sweden/Thelin,E.

376. [WILLIAMS, Sandy]. "Confessions of a trombonist." *Jazz Journal International* 28, no. 2 (February 1975): 12-14.
  This article was distilled from Williams's words in an interview, conducted by Harry Whiston of Canadian Broadcasting and edited by Sinclair Traill. Williams toured with many of the best-known jazz groups from the 1920s through the 1960s.
  BlackMusic/Swing/Traill,S./Whiston,H.

377. WINKING, Charles. "Wild Bill Watrous on jazz trombone." *Instrumentalist* 36 (January 1982): 20-22.
  Winking's article is reprinted from one in *Accent* 6, no. 3 (January/February 1981). See Gary Giddins, 305, for more references on Bill Watrous.
  Giddins,G./Pedagogy/Watrous,B.

378. [WOLFINBARGER, Steve]. "In memoriam: James Kenneth Huntzinger, Jr. (1945-1994)." *JITA* 23, no. 2 (Spring 1995): [insert between pp. 30 and 31].
  Huntzinger was the trombone instructor at the University of Nevada-Las Vegas and a successful free-lance trombonist in the Las Vegas and Nevada area since 1968. Huntzinger was slated to have appeared as a solo recitalist at the 1995 International

Trombone Workshop but unfortunately succumbed to cancer in December of 1994.
Huntzinger,J./ITA/NevadaU-LasVegas/Obituaries

379. WOOLEY, Stan. "Meandering with Winding." _Jazz Journal International_ 32, no. 4 (April 1979): 14-15.
See above Nick Catalano, 277, and Sue Mudge, 336, for more references on Kai Winding.
Catalano,N./Mudge,S./Winding,K.

380. ———. "Slide Hampton: Interview." _Cadence_ 4, nos. 8-9 (September 1978): 3+.
See Michael Bogle, 264, W.A. Brower, 272, and Robin Verges, 369. See also Gary Giddins, 643.
Bogle,M/Brower,W.A./Giddins,G./Hampton,S./Verges,R.

381. YANOW, Scott. "Bill Watrous: Horn o'melody." _Down Beat_ 55 (May 1988): 19-21.
See Gary Giddins, 305, for more references on Watrous.
Discog/Giddins,G./Watrous,B.

382. [YEO, Douglas]. "Ashley H. Alexander (1935-1988)." [Obituary]. _JITA_ 16, no. 4 (Fall 1988): 11.
See other obituaries in the _Jazz Educators Journal_ 21, no. 1 (1988): 10; _Cadence_ 14 (December 1988): 93; _Jazz Times_ (December 1988): 8; and _Variety_ 332 (August 1988): 118. See also Alexander, 787.
Alexander,A./Instruments-20thC/Obituaries/Superbone

383. [———]. "In memory of Turk Murphy." _JITA_ 17, no 3 (Summer 1989): 9.
A poem in memory of Turk Murphy is included in this obituary. It was written by Ray Clark Dickinson of Stockton, California for trombonist April West. Murphy was one of the most influential Dixieland jazz artists from the 1940s through the 1970s. See also [San Francisco Traditional Jazz Foundation], 33.
Dickinson,R./Murphy,T./Obituaries/Poetry/SanFrancisco/West,A.

384. [————]. "Last Preservation Hall musician dies." *JITA* 18, no. 4 (Fall 1990): 8.

Louis Nelson, a jazz trombonist who was the last surviving musician of the original Preservation Hall bands, died at the age of 87. See also Peter Vacher, 368.

Nelson,L./Obituaries/PreservationHall/Vacher,P.

4

MUSIC

385. ADAMS, Stan R. "A comprehensive bibliography of works for trombone and percussion, together with an analysis of three selected compositions."

Adams's study is cited in *ROBERTS* as graduate research for the DMA at Arizona State University. For further information about other works for trombone in various chamber ensembles, see appropriate entries in the index, especially Chamber Music-Trombone. Also in the index, titles of several individual works are indicated by asterisks (*) according to the number of the publication in which they are discussed (even though the work may not be mentioned in the annotation). For instance, *One Man for Trombonist and Percussion* [B.Johnston] may be found in Stuart Dempster, 621, and Milton Stevens, 759.
Bib/ChamMus-Trb/Gifford,R./Percussion/TrbMus-20thC

386. ———. "Some thoughts on solo trombone literature." *The School Musician* 48 (November 1976): 8+.
Pedagogy/Solos/TrbMus-Gen

387. ———. "A survey of the use of trombones to depict infernal and horrendous scenes in three representative operas." *JITA* 9 (January 1981): 16-20.

The operas surveyed are *La favola d'Orfeo* (1607), music by Monteverdi; *Don Giovanni [Il dissoluto punito]* (1787), music by Mozart; and *Salome* (1905), music by Richard Strauss. See B. Gugler, 450, Egon Komorzynski, 683, and Don L. Smithers, 757.
Bib/Gugler,B./Komorzynski,E./Monteverdi,C./Mozart,W.A./Opera/Smithers,D./Strauss,R./TrbMus-17thC/TrbMus-18thC/TrbMus-20thC

388. ———. "Trombones in the orchestra." *The School Musician* 47 (March 1976): 8+.
Adams gives his ideas on learning the orchestral repertoire.
Orchestra/Pedagogy

389. ALLSEN, J. Michael. "Frescobaldi's 'Canzonas for Basso Solo' (1628-1634)." *JITA* 12, no. 3 (July 1984): 36-40.
See William M. Hughes, 467.
Baroque/Frescobaldi,G./Hughes,W./Solos/TrbMus-17thC

390. ANDERSON, Stephen C. "Giovanni Martino Cesare's music for trombone and cornett." University of Kansas, independent research project, 1987.
Information gleaned from this project (which is cited in *KOHLENBERG I*) and the one listed below on the music of Dario Castello were later used in some of Anderson's articles on trombone music in the seventeenth and eighteenth centuries. Cesare,G.M./Cornett/KansasU/TrbMus-18thC

391. ———. "Music for alto trombone." *JITA* 13, no. 2 (April 1985): 42-43.
AltoTrb/Bib/Discog/Pedagogy/TrbMus-17thC/TrbMus-18thC/ TrbMus-20thC

392. ———. "Selected Works from the seventeenth-century music collection of Prince-Bishop Karl Liechtenstein-Kastelkorn: A study of the soloistic use of the trombone." *JITA* 11, no. 1 (January 1983): 17-20; no. 2 (April 1983): 35-38; no. 3 (July 1983): 29-32; no. 4 (October 1983): 20-22; vol. 12, no. 1 (January 1984): 33-37; and no. 2 (April 1984): 32-38.
See also *Dissertation Abstracts* 38/04-A, p. 1722, AAD77-21358 and *RILM78*/1627dd45. The manuscripts cited in this study are located in the castle archives of Kromeriz Castle in Czechoslovakia, but microfilm copies were obtained by Don L. Smithers and constitute the Liechtenstein Collection in the George Arents Research Library for Special Collections at Syracuse University. Some of Smithers's citations of the collection appear in his article, "Music for the Prince-Bishop,"

Music and Musicians 18 (April 1970): 24-27. See also Craig A. Otto, 529.

AltoTrb/ArentsLibrary/Baroque/Bib/ChamMus-Trb/Collections/ Diss/KromerizCastle/Liechtenstein-C[K]astelkorn/OklahomaU/ Otto,C./PerfPrac/Smithers,D./SyracuseU/TrbMus-17thC/TrbMus-18thC

393.   ———. "The soloistic use of the alto and tenor trombones in the choral music of Franz Ignaz Tůma." *JITA* 14, no. 3 (Summer 1986): 48-53.

See also an independent research project on music by Tůma done by Anderson in 1983 at the University of Kansas (cited in *KOHLENBERG I*).
AltoTrb/Choral/PerfPrac/Research/TrbMus-18thC/Tůma,F.

394.   ———. "The soloistic use of the trombone in the music of Dario Castello." University of Kansas, independent research project, 1987.

This project is also cited in *KOHLENBERG I*. See Anderson, 390.
Castello,D./Cesare,G./KansasU/PerfPrac/Research

395.   ARLING, Harry J. *Trombone Chamber Music: An Annotated Bibliography*. Enlarged 2nd ed. Nashville TN: Brass Press, 1983.

According to the introduction, "This bibliography is a compilation of chamber music compositions involving trombone as the *only* brass instrument." It was also published as an article in *Music Educators Journal* 66 (September 1979): 88. The book was reviewed by Mike Allsen in the *JITA* 12, no. 4 (October 1984): 59, and by Peter Brown in *Notes* 36, no. 1 (September 1979): 103-104. See *Dissertation Abstracts* publication no. AAC0345751 [listed as not available] and *RILM*78/2288dd07. See also James W. Erdman, 431, Robert M. Gifford, Jr., 644, Robert E. Gray, 648, Michael Struck-Schlön, 762, and James D. Willis, 780.
Allsen,M./Bib/Brown,P./ChamMus-Trb/Diss/Erdman,J./Gifford,R./ Gray,R./Hindemith,P./IndianaU/Reviews/Struck-Schlön,M./ TrbMus-20thC/Willis,J.

396.   ARNOLD, Alan L. "Selected works for solo trombone with woodwind ensembles." University of Illinois, DMA, 1978.

Arnold's paper is cited in Randy Kohlenberg's survey in the *JITA* 15, no. 2 (Spring 1987): 18. See H.J. Arling, 395, James

W. Erdman, 431, Robert M. Gifford, Jr. 644, Robert E. Gray, 648, Michael Struck-Schlön, 762, and James D. Willis, 780.
Arling,H./ChamMus-Trb/Diss/Eastman/Erdman,J./Gifford,R./ Gray,R./Hindemith,P./IllinoisU/Kohlenberg,R./Solos/Struck-Schlön,M./TrbMus-20thC/Willis,J./Woodwinds

397. [ASHWORTH, Tom]. "Christian Lindberg to present world premiere at 1994 ITW." *JITA* 22, no. 2 (Spring 1994): 8-11.
Appearing in Randy Campora's ongoing column, "General news," Ashworth's article deals with the world premier of Toru Takemitsu's *Concerto for Trombone and Orchestra*, presented at the Ordway Theater in Saint Paul MN with Christian Lindberg as soloist and the Saint Paul Chamber Orchestra, June 3, 1994.
Campora,R./Concertos/ITA/Lindberg,C./StPaul/Takemitsu,T./ TrbMus-20thC/Workshops

398. [BABCOCK, Ron]. "The contributions of Johann Joseph Fux to the development of the alto trombone repertoire." *JITA* 23, no. 4 (Fall 1995): 29.
Babcock presented a paper at the 1995 International Trombone Workshop based on his doctoral lecture-recital at the University of North Texas, "A study of Sonata a Quattro, K. 347, and Alma Mater, K. 186, by Johann Joseph Fux: The historical significance," 1994. George Broussard reported on Babcock's research in his article on the 1995 International Trombone Workshop. In 1995 Babcock was on the music faculty at Portland State University. See also Klaus Winkler, 589.
AltoTrb/Baroque/Broussard,G./ChamMus-Trb/Diss/Fux,J.J./ Lecture-Recital/NorthTexasU/PerfPrac/TrbMus-18thC/ Winkler,K./Workshops

399. BAHR, Edward R. "A performer's interpretation toward performance." *JITA* 11, no. 4 (October 1983): 26.
Carl Vollrath, the primary subject of this article, was at the time of its writing on the music faculty of Troy State University in Alabama. His compositions for trombone are featured.
AltoTrb/BassTrb/PerfPrac/Solos/TrbMus-20thC/Vollrath,C.

400.   BAKER, Buddy. "Why? How about who, where, what,
       when?—The development of Berio's *Sequenza V.*" *JITA* 22, no.
       2 (Spring 1994): 30-33.
       The copy for this article, which consists of two taped interviews
       with Stuart Dempster and Vinko Globokar, was prepared by
       Debra Drake, an MM trombone performance student at the
       University of Northern Colorado. The purpose of the interviews
       was to establish some facts about how this particular piece came
       to be. It was commissioned by Dempster, but because of the
       recording by Globokar and his connections with Berio, the piece
       is thought by some people to have been commissioned by
       Globokar. See Douglas Weeks, 579, and Milton L. Stevens, Jr., 759.
       Avant-Garde/Berio,L./Dempster,S./Drake,D./Globokar,V./Grock/
       SequenzaV/Solos/Stevens,M./TrbMus-20thC/Weeks,D.

401.   BARTLETT, Clifford and Peter HOLMAN. "Giovanni Gabrieli:
       A guide to the performance of his instrumental music." *Early
       Music* 3, no. 1 (January 1975): 25-32.
       Music written for the typical large-scale instrumental ensemble,
       including trombones, which was used for performances in Venice
       around 1600 is discussed in this article. See Klaus Winkler, 590,
       and Arnold Fromme, 640.
       For further discussions of Gabrieli's music, including his vocal
       works which are scored with trombones, see two articles by
       Denis Arnold, "Brass instruments in Italian church music of the
       sixteenth and early seventeenth centuries," *Brass Quarterly* 1
       (December 1957): 81-92, and *"Con ogni sorti di stromenti* [With
       every sort of instrument]: Some practical suggestions," *Brass
       Quarterly* 2 (1958-59): 99-109; J. Bunker Clark's "The a capella
       myth," *Choral Journal* 9, no. 4 (January/February 1969): 28-31;
       and two sources by Egon F. Kenton, "The 'brass' parts in
       Giovanni Gabrieli's instrumental ensemble compositions," *Brass
       Quarterly* 1 (December 1957): 73-80, and his monumental *Life
       and Works of Giovanni Gabrieli*, Musicological Studies and
       Documents, [Rome]: American Institute of Musicology, 1967.
       See also Jack R. Bayes, "The proposed use of embellishment in
       the instrumental ensemble music of Giovanni Gabrieli: The
       canzone and sonate from the *Sacrae Symphoniae* of 1597,"
       University of Washington, DMA, 1977.

Arnold,D./Baroque/Bayes,J./ChamMus-Trb/Clark,J./Fromme,A./
Gabrieli,G./Kenton,E./Renaissance/Venice/Winkler,K.

402. BELET, Brian. "Toward a unification of algorithmic composition, real-time software synthesis, and live performance interaction." In *International Computer Music Association: Proceedings of the symposium in San Jose, California, October 14-18, 1992*, 158-161. San Francisco: International Computer Association, 1992.

The work featured, *.Discourse [GUTs 2a]* / (1992, for bass trombone and Kyma system), was composed by Belet. Symposium proceedings are cited in *RILM*1992-01388-bs.

Avant-Garde/Computers/ElectronicMusic/InternationalComputer
Association/Kyma/Symposia

403. BEYER, Werner. "Das klassische Solokonzert für Posaune und seine Interpreten im 19. Jahrhundert [The classical solo concerto for trombone and its interpreters in the nineteenth century]." *BBIBC* 25 (1979): 51-55.

Beyer discusses the origins of what is termed "the classical trombone literature." His information is taken primarily from the programs of the Gewandhaus Orchestra in Leipzig from the nineteenth century. Works by C.G. Müller, Ferdinand David, and Carl Maria von Weber, whose horn concerto, op. 45, had been transcribed for trombone by C.T. Queisser, are compared. One of the soloists, identified by Beyer as W. Rex, is named in an article by Michael Lewis (see 495) as Franz Rex. Beyer's article is in German, French, and English. See also Mary Rasmussen, 194, Robert Reifsnyder, 540, Gary Shaw, 551, Larry Weed, 577, and Steve Wolfinbarger, 592.

Belcke,F./Bruns[Bruhns?],A./Concertos/David,F./Gewandhaus/
Leipzig/Lewis,M./Müller,C./Müller,R./Queisser,C.T./Rasmussen,M./
Reifsnyder,R./Rex,W./Shaw,G./TrbMus-19thC/Weber,C.M.von/
Weed,L./Wolfinbarger,S.

404. BOCK, E. "Posaunen und Harfen [Trombones and harps]." *Christgemeinschaft* 16 (1939-40): 229-232.

Bock's article is in German.
ChamMus-Trb/Harp/Sacred

405. BOLTINGHOUSE, James. "Hoyt's Garage." *JITA* 24, no. 2 (Spring 1996): 32-35.

Boltinghouse, one of the younger members of the Los Angeles area group that meets in Hoyt Bohannon's garage, gives a fascinating account of the people and music that make up the legendary conclave of some of the best trombonists in that area. Though Hoyt Bohannon, himself an outstanding jazz and studio trombonist for more than forty years, died in 1990, his wife, Betty, has permitted the sessions to continue (actually they occur in a room adjoining the Bohannon garage).

Boltinghouse also gives a roster from the past fifty years, which lists most of the players who have participated in the group. It is estimated that among Hoyt Bohannon, Tommy Pederson, and several other contributors, there are over 500 works for trombone groups ranging in size from two to sixteen that have resulted from these sessions. Pederson, whose jazz trombone ensembles so captivated those who attended the 1972 International Trombone Workshop, died in 1998. See Michael Millar, "In memoriam: Tommy Pederson (1920-1998)," *JITA* 26, no. 3 (Summer 1998): 22-23.

Bohannon,H./Jazz-Blues/LosAngeles/Millar,M./Obituaries/
Pederson,T./Studio/TrbChoir/TrbMus-20thC

406. BOVERMANN, P. "Nochmal 'Posaunenmusik' [More trombone music]." *Zeitschrift für Kirchenmusiker* 11 (1929): 59.

Bovermann's article is in German.
Sacred/TrbMus-Gen

407. BRANT, Henry. "A new spatial symphony for eighty trombones." *NITA* 5, no. 2 (December 1977): 9-11.

Henry Brant was commissioned to compose this work by the International Trombone Association and it was to have been premiered at the 1978 International Trombone Workshop under the composer's direction. However, the premier was delayed because of an illness contracted by the composer.

The work, *Orbits—A Spatial Ritual for Eighty Trombones*, was finally performed by Billy Robinson's Bay Bones, plus players from all over the country, at Saint Mary's Cathedral in San Francisco in 1979 (see Diane Merlino, 56). Brandt discusses the

work from his own viewpoint. For a short biography of Brant and a bibliography of his work through 1978, see the *NITA*, vol. 6, no. 2 (December 1978): 7. Brant's discussion of his work was also published in *The Composer Magazine* 9 (1977-78).
BayBones/Bib/Bio/Merlino,D./Robinson,B./SanFrancisco/TrbChoir/
TrbMus-20thC

408. BREIG, Werner. "Neue Schütz-Funde [New discoveries of Schütz]." *Archiv für Musikwissenschaft* 27, no. 1 (April 1970): 59-72.

Breig identifies two previously unknown psalm settings by Heinrich Schütz, one of which, Psalm 137, is scored for eight voices and a five-part trombone choir ("An den Wassern zu Babel sassen wir und weineten [By the waters of Babylon we sat down and wept]"). The article is in German. See also Klaus Hoffman, 674, Frederick S. Miller, 712, and Richard R. Ross, 738.
Baroque/Choral/Hoffman,F./Miller,F./Ross,R./Sacred/Schütz,H./
TrbMus-17thC

409. BRICKENS, Nathaniel O. "Jazz elements in five selected trombone solos by twentieth-century French composers." University of Texas at Austin, DMA, 1989.

Works discussed include the *Concerto* (1958) by Henri Tomasi, [see below, Harold McKinney, 511], *Deux dances* (1954) by Jean Michel Defaÿ, *Ballade* (1944) by Eugène Bozza, *Sonatina* (1958) by Jacques Castérède, and *Concertino d'hiver* (1955) by Darius Milhaud. See also Michael Samball, 741.
Bozza,E./Castérède,J./Defaÿ,J.M./Diss/France/Jazz-Blues/
Milhaud,D./PerfPrac/Samball,M./Solos/TexasU-Austin/Tomasi,H./
TrbMus-20thC

410. BROWN, Leon, et al. "Annotated solo list for high school trombonists." *JITA* 8 (March 1980): 13-15.

Brown and a select committee from the International Trombone Association include materials from the Music Educators National Conference levels 3-6, for tenor and bass trombone. See Vern Forbes, 443, Martha Hylander, 471, Vern Kagarice, et al., 478, Joseph Nicholson, 527, Robert Reifsnyder, 539, William Richardson, 542, Glenn Smith, 558, and James Swett, 563.

Bib/Forbes,V./Hinterbichler,K./Hylander,M./Kagarice,V./Nicholson,J./
Reifsnyder,R./Richardson,W./Smith,G./Solos/Stevens,M./Swett,J./
Tennyson,R./TrbMus-Gen/Wagner,I.

411. ———. "Favorite studies and solos for trombone." *JITA* 12, no.
1 (January 1984): 28-31.
Concertos/Etudes/Solos/TrbMus-Gen

412. ———. *Handbook of Selected Literature for the Study of
Trombone at the University-College Level.* Denton TX: North
Texas State University [University of North Texas], 1972.
   Brown's handbook includes general texts and periodicals,
pedagogical literature, solo literature, ensemble literature, a short
discography, and a publisher's list with addresses. It is over
twenty-five years old and at one time was the only one-volume
source of trombone music available. Though out of print for
several years, it is still a valuable reference source for
trombonists seeking to build a good library of teaching and
performing materials.
Bib/Colleges-Universities/Concertos/Etudes/Pedagogy/Solos/
TrbMus-Gen

413. BROWN, Merrill. "Trombone solos performed in college student
recitals." *JITA* 5 (1977): 22-23.
   Solos are ranked by frequency of performance, and the list
includes works for both tenor and bass trombone. The article is
based on an earlier compilation by Brown dated 1971-1972, and
copyrighted in 1974. I was unable to determine whether or not
the earlier work was ever published.
BassTrb/Bib/Colleges-Universities/Solos

414. BRYAN, Paul. "A look at some eighteenth-century source
material for the trombone." *JITA* 4 (1976): 6-7.
TrbMus-18thC

415. BUNTAIN, William E. "The use of the trombone in the
Kammersonaten of Matthias Weckmann." University of North
Texas, MM, 1979.

Cited in *KOHLENBERG I*, Buntain's thesis discusses the work of one of Heinrich Schütz's students. Much of Weckmann's music illustrates the Schütz tradition of concerted music for chorus, solo voices, and orchestra without reference to chorale melodies. For more references on the music of Schütz see Werner Breig, 408.

Breig,W./NorthTexasU/PerfPrac/Schütz,H./Theses/TrbMus-17thC/ Weckmann,M.

416. BUSS, Howard J. "Trombone theater pieces." *JITA* 6 (1978): 6-10.
See James D. Kraft, 687, and Peter M. Vivona, 772 (see also *JITA* 10, no. 2 (April 1982): 3, for a "statement of correction" dealing with Vivona's article and that of Buss).
Avant-Garde/Bib/Kraft,J./Theater/TrbMus-20thC/Vivona,P.

417. CHAMBERS, Robert Lee. "Selected trombone virtuosi of the nineteenth century and their solo repertoire." University of Oklahoma, DMA, 1986.
See *Dissertation Abstracts* 47/03-A, p. 704; MBB86-09819; AAD86-09819 [order numbers from various citations]. Chambers's study deals with selected trombonists from Germany, France, England, and Russia, and their music. There are appendices listing nineteenth-century trombone music and nineteenth-century composers of trombone solo material.
Bib/Bio/Diss/England/France/Germany/OklahomaU/Russia/Solos/ TrbMus-19thC

418. CHRISTENSEN, Carl J. "Some uses of the trombone in the Mexican symphonic repertoire." *JITA* 4 (1976): 36-39.
See J.D. Shawger, 746.
Mexico/Orchestra/PerfPrac/Shawger,J./TrbMus-20thC

419. CHRISTIE, John M. "Music for bass trombone." *Instrumentalist* 15, no. 7 (1961): 44-45.
Once the most complete listing available of all types of music for bass trombone, it is cited and annotated in *JENKINS*. See *BRASSANTH* 288-289 and Christie, 1035. See also Thomas G. Everett, 432, and Todd Fallis, 439.
BassTrb/Everett,T./Fallis,T./Pedagogy/TrbMus-Gen

420. COE, John W. "A study of five selected contemporary compositions for brass." Indiana University, DM, 1971.
Located in *RILM*71/863dd28, Coe's dissertation contains a discussion of *Animus I for Trombone and Tape* by Jacob Druckman, among other works. See Stanley Pethel, 531, and Gary Shaw, 551, for further discussion of Druckman's compositions.
Avant-Garde/Diss/Druckman,J./ElectronicMusic/IndianaU/ Pethel,S./Shaw,G./Solos/Tape/TrbMus-20thC

421. COLLINS, William T. "Berlioz and the trombone." University of Texas at Austin, DMA, 1985.
See *Dissertation Abstracts* 46/11-A, p. 3185; MBB85-29811; AAD85-29811 [order numbers from various citations]. See Benny Sluchin and Raymond Lapie, 553, which deals with the valve alto trombone Berlioz favored for performing the first-trombone parts of some of his works. See Lewis Harlow, 856. See also Cecil B. Wilson, "Berlioz's use of brass instruments," Case Western Reserve University, PhD, 1971 (*RILM*71/821dd27).
Berlioz,H./Diss/Harlow,L./Orchestra/PerfPrac/TexasU-Austin/ Trombet/TrbMus-19thC/Wilson,C.

422. CONGER, Robert B. "J.S. Bach's 'Six Suites for Solo Violoncello,' BWV 1007-1012: Their history and problems of transcription and performance for the trombone: A lecture recital, together with three recitals of selected works by Paul Hindemith, Georg Christoph Wagenseil, Richard Monaco, Darius Milhaud, Nino Rota, Giovanni B. Pergolesi, and others." University of North Texas, DMA, 1983.
See *Dissertation Abstracts* 44/08-A, p. 2285, AAD83-27017. See also James F. Gould, 1104.
Bach,J.S./Baroque/Gould,J./Lecture-Recital/NorthTexasU/Solos/ Transcriptions/Violoncello

423. COX, Joseph L. "The solo trombone works of Kazimierz Serocki: A lecture recital, together with three recitals of selected works by W[alter] Hartley, P[ierre Max] Dubois, H[enri] Dutilleux, H[enri] Tomasi, G[ordon] Jacob, L[auny] Gröndahl, J[ean] Aubain and others." University of North Texas, DMA, 1981.

See *Dissertation Abstracts* 42/12-A, p. 4967, AAD82-11698. The lecture portion of Cox's presentation includes a discussion of neoclassicism in Poland.
Concertos/Lecture-Recital/Neoclassicism/NorthTexasU/Poland/
Serocki,K./Solos/TrbMus-20thC

424. CRAMER, William. "Munich Trombone Competition." *JITA* 3 (1975): 21-22.
Prizewinners of this 1974 competition include Ronald Barron (USA), Branimir Slokar (Yugoslavia), and Michel Becquet (France).
Barron,R./Becquet,M./Competitions/Munich/Slokar,B./TrbMus-18thC/
TrbMus-19thC/TrbMus-20thC

425. CRIDER, Joseph R. "American trombone solos written from 1960 to 1990 deserving greater recognition and exposure: An annotated bibliography." University of Northern Colorado, DA, 1991.
See *Dissertation Abstracts* 9216415 and *RILM*1991-00542-dd. Crider's body of solo trombone music written over the past thirty years is based on a review of recital programs from 1972-1990. See also Crider's master's thesis, "Two seventeenth-century chamber sonatas," Bowling Green State University, MM, 1988, which includes brass septets arranged for five trombones and two trumpets.
Bib/ChamMus-Trb/Diss/NorthernColoradoU/Solos/TrbMus-20thC

426. DEHN, [no first name given]. "Bei Gelegenheit eines Konzertino für die Tenorbassposaune [On the occasion of a concertino for the tenor-bass trombone]." *Berliner allgemeine musikalische Zeitung* 3 (1826): 391-392 (also pp. 351 and 383).
Dehn's article is cited in Mary Rasmussen's "Brass Bibliography: 1820-1829," *Brass Quarterly* 7, no. 4 (Summer 1964): 194-197, and in *BRASSBIB*, but with no indication of which concertino is referred to. The Ferdinand David *Concertino*, op. 4, was written after the publication of Dehn's article.
Though I have not perused the publication, I believe it is possible that Friedrich Belcke was the trombonist involved, since he had gone to Berlin as early as 1816 and remained there amid great acclamation until his retirement in 1858. Since he also published numerous works for trombone (see Mary Rasmussen,

194), including at least one concertino in or around 1829, it is also possible that one of his works is discussed. Belcke was known as a performer on both tenor and bass trombones.
Belcke,F./Berlin/Rasmussen,M./Solos/TrbMus-19thC

427. [DOUAY, Jean]. "Trombone-posaune." *BBIBC* 20 (1977): 11-14. Douay has classified a list of trombone music by studies, solos, concertos and ensembles, divided by composer, title, publisher, and current price. The article has been translated from French into German and English.
TrbMus-Gen

428. DREW, John Robert. "Classic elements in selected sonatas for trombone and piano by twentieth-century composers." University of Kentucky, DMA, 1978.
Works by Halsey Stevens, Richard Monaco, Klaus George Roy, John Davison, Paul Hindemith, George F. McKay, Robert W. Jones, Walter Watson, and Henry Cowell are included in this study. See *Dissertation Abstracts* 39/06-A, p. 3208, AAD78-24393 and *RILM*78/3829dd45. See Dean A. Farnham, 440, and Chang-Yi Lai, 489. Drew is currently first vice-president of the International Trombone Association.
Cowell,H./Davison,J./Diss/Farnham,D./Hindemith,P./Jones,R./ KentuckyU/Lai,C./McKay,G./Monaco,R./Roy,K./Sonata/Stevens,H./ TrbMus-20thC/Watson,W.

429. EISENBERG, Reinke, and Franz SCHULTE-HUERMANN. *Annotated Bibliography of Trombone Literature.* Detmold, Germany: Edition Piccolo, 1997(?)-.
Published in a loose-leaf format, the original intention was to publish about two hundred reviews of trombone compositions, studies, excerpts, tutors, and secondary literature every six months, beginning in the spring of 1995 (to my knowledge this project has yet to appear in print—GBL).
Bib/OrchExcerpts/Reviews/Schulte-Huermann,F./TrbMus-Gen

430. ENGLISH, Jon. "Some solo works for the trombonist." *NITA* 7, no. 1 (December 1979): 12-13.

Twentieth-century works, some by the author of the article, are catalogued with addresses (now probably mostly out of date) for those which had not been published at the time of the publication of the list.
Avant-Garde/Solos/TrbMus-20thC

431. ERDMAN, James W. "Trombone in chamber music with both woodwind and percussion instruments." Central Missouri State University, MM, 1980.
See H.J. Arling, 395, Alan L. Arnold, 396, Robert M. Gifford, Jr., 644, Robert E. Gray, 648, Michael Struck-Schlön, 762, and James D. Willis, 780.
Arling,H./Arnold,A./CentralMissouriU/ChamMus-Trb/Gifford,R./ Gray,R./Hindemith,P./Percussion/Struck-Schlön,M./Theses/ TrbMus-20thC/Willis,J./Woodwinds

432. EVERETT, Thomas G. *Annotated Guide to Bass Trombone Literature.* 3rd ed. Nashville TN: Brass Press, 1985.
Everett's book is generally considered the primary source for bass trombone literature. See the reviews by Michael K. Mathews in the *JITA* 13, no. 4 (October 1985): 52; Peter Brown in *Notes* 36, no. 1 (September 1979): 103-104; and Robert D. Weast in the *Brass World* 8, no. 2 (October 1973): 116. The first edition is cited in *RILM*73/2911rb07. For an update on significant bass trombone literature, see a compilation by Everett under Paul Hunt's "Literature reviews," *JITA* 21, no. 1 (Winter 1993): 48-49. See also John M. Christie, 419.
BassTrb/Bib/Brown,P./Christie,J./Hunt,P./Mathews,M./Reviews/ TrbMus-Gen/Weast,R.

433. ———. "Contemporary trombone quartet literature," *Brass World* 9 (1974): 18-20.
See Bruce N. Keeling, 481, Frank J. Musil, 521, Jay Hildebrandt, 668, Shelley Smithwick, 758, and Wallace E. Tucker, 769.
Hildebrandt,J./Keeling,B./Musil,F./Smithwick,S./TrbMus-20thC/ TrbQuartet/Tucker,W.

434. ———. "The literature of the Ars Antigua Trio: A ten-year
commissioning project." *JITA* 15, no. 3 (Summer 1987): 44-47.
Everett's article lists and annotates the works in the Ars
Antigua Commissioning Series from 1977-1987. The Ars Antigua
Trio is active in the Boston area. See corrections and updates in
the *JITA* 16, no. 1 (Winter 1988): 3. See Donald A. Hummel,
468, and Ronald Nethercutt, 524.
AltoTrb/ArsAntigua/Bib/Boston/Hummel,D./Nethercutt,R./
TrbMus-20thC/TrbTrio

435. ———. "Marsteller premiers Bellis *Concerto.*" *JITA* 10, no. 3
(July 1982): 34-35.
The premier of Bellis's work for trombone and concert band is
reviewed, with a capsule biography of Loren Marsteller included.
Richard Bellis is best known as a Hollywood film composer.
Bands/Bellis,R./Bio/Concertos/Marsteller,L./Reviews/TrbMus-20thC

436. ———. "Solo literature for the bass trombone." *Instrumentalist*
26, no. 5 (1971): 43-47.
Everett's information also appears in the first edition of his
Annotated Guide to Bass Trombone Literature (see 432). See also
John M. Christie, 419, and Todd Fallis, 439.
BassTrb/Christie,J./Fallis,T./Solos

437. ———. "The tenor/bass trombone and bass trombone literature
with pre-recorded tape." *JITA* 3 (1975): 10-11.
In part of a lecture-recital presented at the International
Trombone Workshop in June 1974, Everett summarizes his
findings.
Avant-Garde/BassTrb/ElectronicMusic/ITA/Tape/TrbMus-20thC/
Workshops

438. ———. "Unaccompanied bass trombone solos." *JITA* 1 (1972-
73): 23-27.
See Thomas E. Senff, 550, and Douglas G. Weeks, 579.
BassTrb/Bib/Senff,T./Solos/Unaccompanied/Weeks,D.

439. FALLIS, Todd. "Selected bass trombone literature."
Instrumentalist 50 (March 1996): 34+.

See John M. Christie, 419, and Thomas G. Everett, 432-438.
BassTrb/Bib/Christie,J./Everett,T./TrbMus-Gen

440. FARNHAM, Dean A. "The twentieth-century trombone sonata."
Boston University, PhD, 1969.
See *Dissertation Abstracts*, publication no. AAC0246189 [listed
as not available]. See John Robert Drew, 428, and Chang-Yi Lai, 489.
BostonU/Diss/Drew,J./Lai,C./Solos/Sonata/TrbMus-20thC

441. [FARWELL, Doug]. "Bibliography to works for solo trombone
and electro-acoustic music." *JITA* 23, no. 4 (Fall 1995): 29.
Farwell's paper, presented at the 1995 International Trombone
Workshop, is summarized in George Broussard's article, "Viva
Las Vegas," *JITA* 23, no. 4 (Fall 1995).
Avant-Garde/Broussard,G./ElectronicMusic/ITW/Research/Solos/
Tape/TrbMus-20thC/Workshops

442. FIEDLER, Andre. "The Equale." *JITA* 19, no. 1 (Winter 1991):
40-41.
In a discussion of Beethoven's and Bruckner's *Equali*, Fiedler
proposes that the so-called Mendelssohn "equali" were not
intended by the composer to be included in that genre. See
Othmar Wessely, 581 and 777.
Beethoven,L./Bruckner,A./*Equale*/Mendelssohn,F./TrbMus-19thC/
TrbQuartet/Wessely,O.

443. FORBES, Vernon. "Solos for grade school, junior high, and
senior high trombone players." University of Nebraska-Lincoln,
Independent Research, 1988.
Now retired, Vernon Forbes was for many years the trombone
professor at the University of Nebraska (and a maker of fine
trombone mouthpieces). See Leon Brown, et al., 410, Martha A.
Hylander, 471, Vern Kagarice, 476 and 479, James Kidwell, 485,
Joseph Nicholson, 527, Robert Reifsnyder, 539, William
Richardson, 542, Glenn Smith, 558, and James Swett, 563.
Brown,L./Hylander,M./Kagarice,V./Kidwell,J./NebraskaU-Lincoln/
Nicholson,J./Pedagogy/PublicSchool/Reifsnyder,R./Research/
Richardson,W./Smith,G./Solos/Swett,J.

444. FULKERSON, James. "Indeterminate instrumentation." *BBIBC* 12 (1975): 48-53.

Fulkerson's article, in English, German, and French, contains a suggested list of contemporary compositions which will help develop new ideas and technical skills on the trombone. See also Fulkerson, "Indeterminate instrumentation: A way of extending instrumental techniques," *JITA* 4 (1976): 3-4.

Avant-Garde/Bib/PerfPrac/TrbMus-20thC

445. GEORGE, Stanley P. "A descriptive list of baroque solo editions which may be practically integrated into the solo literature for trombone." American University, MA, 1969.

See *Masters Abstracts*, Ann Arbor: University Microfilms, 07/03, p. 137, AAD13-01836.

AmericanU/Baroque/Solos/Theses/Transcriptions

446. GRAY, Robert. "A starter list of works utilizing the trombone in advanced contemporary idioms." *JITA* 3 (1975): 16-20.

Avant-Garde/Bib/ChamMus-Trb/ElectronicMusic/TrbMus-20thC

447. GRAY, Robert, and Mary RASMUSSEN. "A bibliography of chamber music including parts for the trombone." *Brass Quarterly* 3, no. 3 (Spring 1960): 93-102.

Gray and Rasmussen use several standard sources which were available in the middle of this century, such as W.W. Cobbett, comp. and ed., *Cobbett's Cyclopedia Survey of Chamber Music*, Oxford: Oxford University Press, 1929, and Robert Eitner, *Biographisch—Bibliographisches Quellen—Lexikon*, Leipzig: Breitkopf & Härtel, 1900, to catalog the entries. See Robert E. Gray, 648, H.J. Arling, 395, Alan L. Arnold, 396, James W. Erdman, 431, Robert M. Gifford, Jr., 644, Michael Struck-Schlön, 762, and James D. Willis, 780.

Arling,H./Arnold,A./Bib/ChamMus-Trb/Cobbett,W./Eitner,R./ Erdman,J./Gifford,R./Hindemith,P./IowaU/Rasmussen,M./Struck-Schlön,M./TrbMus-20thC/Willis,J.

448. ———. "Three bibliographies of nineteenth- and twentieth-century concertante works." *Brass Quarterly* 6, no. 1 (Fall 1962): 10-16.

These bibliographies are classified by works for large and small ensembles with one or more solo parts for various brass instruments. Works with solo parts for trombone are listed on pp. 13 and 14.
Bib/ChamMus-Trb/Rasmussen,M./TrbMus-19thC/TrbMus-20thC/ Trumpet

449. GREENHOW, Ann. "The use of the trombone in the quintets of Victor Ewald." Western Michigan University, MM, 1989.
Greenhow's thesis is cited in *KOHLENBERG I*. See Marta Hofacre, 462, Michael Green, 649, Robert Lindahl, 696, and Robert Posten, 726.
BrassQuintet/ChamMus-Trb/Ewald,V./Green,M./Hofacre,M./ Lindahl,R./PerfPrac/Posten,R./Theses/WesternMichiganU

450. GUGLER, B. "Sind im zweiten Finale des *Don Juan* die Posaunen von Mozart [Did Mozart score the trombones in the second finale of *Don Juan*]?" *Allgemeine musikalische Zeitung* 2 (1867): 2-4, 13-15, 21-24, 35, 59.
See Stan Adams, 387, Egon Komorzynski, 683, and Don L. Smithers, 757.
Adams,S./*DonJuan*/Komorzynski,E./Mozart,W.A./Opera/ Smithers,D./TrbMus-18thC

451. GUION, David M. "French military music and the rebirth of the trombone." *Journal of Band Research* 21, no. 2 (1986): 31-36.
Bands/France/Military/TrbMus-18thC

452. ———. "The trombone and its music." University of Iowa, PhD, 1985.
See *Dissertation Abstracts* 46/06-A, p. 1435, AAD85-18834.
Guion begins with Daniel Speer's *Grundrichtiger . . . Unterricht der Musicalischen Kunst* (1697) and ends with Joseph Frölich's "Posaunenschule," in his *Vollstandige theoretischpracktische Musikschule* (1811). Twenty articles written between these two works are reproduced in the dissertation. See Guion, 853, David Fetter, 132, Dale Voelker, 573, and Henry Howey, 1122. For more information about the music of Daniel Speer, see Mitchell Neil Sirman, "The wind sonatas in Daniel Speer's *Musikalisch-*

Türckischer Eulen-Spiegel of 1688," The University of
Wisconsin, PhD, 1972 [University Microfilms 72-29, 512].
Diss/Fetter,D./Frölich,J./Howey,H./Instruments-18thC/Instruments-
19thC/IowaU/Sirman,M./Speer,D./TrbMus-18thC/TrbMus-19thC/
Voelker,D.

453. HAMMERBACHER, J. "Wert oder Unwert der Posaunenmusik
      [Worth or lack of worth of trombone music]." *Zeitschrift für
      evangelische Kirchenmusik* 6 (1928): 91-95, 120-124.
      Hammerbacher's article is in German.
      Germany/Sacred/TrbChoir

454. HARTLEY, Walter S. "The trombone in my music." *JITA* 2
      (1973-74): 18-23.
      Bib/Bio/TrbMus-20thC

455. HARVEY, Martin. "Weber's *Romance* with the trombone over?"
      JITA 19, no. 2 (Spring 1991): 12-13.
      Originally appearing in the Autumn 1990 issue of *The
      Trombonist*, the magazine of the British Trombone Society,
      Harvey's article was reprinted in Douglas Yeo's ongoing column,
      "General news."
      TrbMus-19thC/Valves/Weber,C.M.von/Yeo,D.

456. HELLER, Friedrich C. "Cesar Bresgens Konzert für Altposaune
      und Orchester [Cesar Bresgen's Concerto for Alto Trombone and
      Orchestra]." *Österreichische Musikzeitschrift* 36, nos. 7-8
      (July/August 1981): 402.
      Composed in 1980 as a commission from Branimir Slokar, this
      work was first performed in 1981 at the Salzburg Festspiele. The
      article is in German.
      AltoTrb/Austria/Bresgen,C./Concertos/Salzburg/Slokar,B./TrbMus-20thC

457. HERWIG, Conrad. "Frank Rosolino solo transcription." *JITA* 25,
      no. 2 (Spring 1997): 42-44.
      Herwig, the first winner (1979) of the Frank Rosolino Memorial
      Scholarship from the International Trombone Association has
      transcribed and commented on Rosolino's solo on "Free for All,"

as heard on the 1996 release, *Fond Memories of Frank Rosolino*, Double-Time Records DTRCD-113. See Jamey D. Aebersold, 249.
Aebersold,J./Bio/Jazz-Blues/Obituaries/Rosolino,F.

458. HINTERBICHLER, Karl G. "Evolution of the role of the solo trombone in the nineteenth-century and twentieth-century. University of North Texas, DMA, 1974.
See *Dissertation Abstracts* 35/07-A, p. 4587, AAD75-00884.
Diss/NorthTexasU/PerfPrac/Solos/TrbMus-19thC/TrbMus-20thC

459. [————]. "Large scale trombone choir transcriptions by Jay Friedman." *JITA* 17, no. 1 (Winter 1989): 49.
Classified by composer, title, approximate timing, and number of parts, the list is included in Hinterbichler's ongoing column in the *JITA*, "Literature." It is available from Chicago Trombone Productions, c/o P. Ignas, 6511 N. Sacramento, 3C, Chicago IL 60645. See Carl M. Lobitz, 496.
Friedman,J./Lobitz,C./Transcriptions/TrbChoir

460. ————. "The trombone in new music at Darmstadt." *NITA* 8, no. 2 (December 1980): 14-15.
Hinterbichler reports on the Darmstadt Internationale Ferienkurse für Neue Musik at its thirtieth anniversary session.
Avant-Garde/Darmstadt/TrbMus-20thC

461. ————, ed. "Literature [announcements]." *NITA* 4, no. 2 (February 1977): 5-6.
In an ongoing column which began in the *Newsletter* and switched to the *JITA*, beginning with vol. 10, no. 1 (January 1982), Hinterbichler originally included periodical articles and other writings of interest to trombonists. He now devotes the column primarily to music and performance programs.
TrbMus-Gen

462. HOFACRE, Marta. "The use of tenor trombone in twentieth-century brass quintet music: A brief historical overview with comprehensive listing of original, published twentieth-century quintets and a discussion of tenor trombone excerpts from selected compositions." University of Oklahoma, DMA, 1986.

See *Dissertation Abstracts* 47/07, pp. 2362A-2363A, AAD86-1175. The music discussed includes *Quintet*, op. 73 by Malcolm Arnold; *Laudes* by Jan Bach; *Commedia IV* by Richard Rodney Bennett; *Sonatine* by Eugène Bozza; *Music for Brass Instruments*, by Ingolf Dahl; *Quintet for Brass Instruments* by Alvin Etler; *Quintet* by Edward Gregson; *Brass Quintet*, op. 65 by Jan Koetsier; *Par Monts et Par Vaux* by Michel Leclerc; *Parable II for Brass Quintet* by Vincent Persichetti (see Mark Nelson, 523); *Suite for Brass Quintet* by Verne Reynolds; and *Music for Brass Quintet* by Gunther Schuller.

See Robert G. Lindahl, 696, for discussions of Jan Bach's *Laudes*, Alvin Etler's *Quintet*, and Gunther Schuller's *Music*. See also Ann Greenhow, 449, Michael Green, 649, and Robert Posten, 726.

Arnold,M./Bach,J./Bennett,R.R./Bib/Bozza,E./BrassQuintet/ ChamMus-Trb/Dahl,I./Etler,A./Gregson,E./Green,M./ Greenhow,A./ Koetsier,J./Leclerc,M./Lindahl,R./Nelson,M./ PerfPrac/ Persichetti,V./Posten,R./Reynolds,V./Schuller,G./ TrbMus-20thC

463. HOGG, Simon. "Duet for trombone and organ." *JITA* 23, no. 1 (Winter 1995): 34.

Warwick Music U.K. announces its publication of this recently discovered work by Gustav Holst. The work apparently was premiered in 1895 at Highbury Congregational Church in Cheltenham with Adolph Holst (Gustav's father) on organ and John Boyce on trombone. See also John C. Mitchell, 514.

Boyce,J./England/Holst,A./Holst,G./Mitchell,J./Organ/TrbMus-19thC/WarwickMusic

464. HOLBROOK, Jonathan. "The emergence of the trombone as a standard member of orchestral instrumentation." East Texas State University, unpublished undergraduate research, 1979.

Holbrook's research is cited in *KOHLENBERG I*. See Kenneth M. Hanlon, 656, Terry Pierce, 722, Jay Dee Schaefer, 743, and William A. Taylor, 767.

EastTexasStateU/Hanlon,K./Orchestra/Pierce,T./Research/ Schaefer,J./Taylor,W.

465. HOOPER, Jonathan. "A critical analysis of the use of the trombone in *L'histoire du Soldat*." East Texas State University, MM, 1987.

Hooper's thesis is cited in *KOHLENBERG I*. See Mark R. Williams, 585.

ChamMus-Trb/EastTexasStateU/*L'histoire*/Stravinsky,I./Theses/ Williams,M.

466. HORN, Erwin. "Anton Bruckner, Geistliche Motetten: Ecce sacerdos für 8-stimmigen gemischten Chor, 3 Posaunen und Orgel [Anton Bruckner, Sacred motets: Ecce sacerdos for eight-voice mixed chorus, three trombones and organ]." *Musica Sacra* 103, no. 1 (1983): 46-58.

Bruckner's motet was written around 1885 for the entrance of the bishop on the occasion of the 100th anniversary of the establishment of the Linz diocese. The motet is listed on page 110 of Mary Rasmussen, 536.

Bruckner,A./Choral/Linz/Rasmussen,M./Sacred/TrbMus-19thC/Vocal

467. HUGHES, William M. "The trombone in performance of the bass-solo canzonas of Girolamo Frescobaldi." University of Maryland-College Park, DMA, 1988.

See *Dissertation Abstracts* 49/10A, p. 2857, publication no. AAC8827147 and *RILM*1988-08009-dd. Hughes's study includes a comparison of the 1628 (*Il primo libro delle canzoni*) and 1635 (*Canzoni da sonare*) collections. See also J. Michael Allsen, 389.

Allsen,J.M./Baroque/BassTrb/Diss/Frescobaldi,G./MarylandU-CollegePark/Solos/TrbMus-17thC

468. HUMMEL, Donald A. "A selected and annotated bibliography of original works for trombone trio." University of Missouri-Kansas City, DMA, 1976.

Hummel's study was also published as "A selected list of original works for trombone trio" in the *JITA* 6 (1978): 16-17. It is cited as "Abstract: A selected and annotated bibliography of original works for trombone trio" in the *Missouri Journal of Research in Music Education* 3, no. 5 (1976): 119-120. See *Dissertation Abstracts* 37/05A, p. 2481, publication no.

AAC7712744. See Thomas G. Everett, 434, Vern Kagarice, 478, and Ronald Nethercutt, 524.
Bib/Diss/Everett,T./Kagarice,V./MissouriU-KansasCity/ Nethercutt,R./TrbTrio

469. HUNT, Paul. "A closer look at the world premier of Leslie Bassett's *Concerto Lirico for Trombone and Orchestra.*" *JITA* 12, no. 3 (July 1984): 30-32.
Bassett's work was premiered on April 6, 1984, with H. Dennis Smith as the soloist and the Toledo Symphony Orchestra under the direction of Yuval Zaliouk. Bassett wrote the concerto for Smith, and at the time of the premier both Bassett and Smith were on the faculty of the University of Michigan.
Bassett,L./Concertos/Smith,D./Solos/Toledo/TrbMus-20thC/Zaliouk,Y.

470. ———, ed. "Literature reviews." *JITA* 13, no. 4 (October 1985): 49-57.
Paul Hunt assumed the editorship of this column from Hugo Magliocco (see 501) with this issue and continued in that role until vol. 26, no. 1 (Winter 1997). He was succeeded by Michael Hall.
Hall,M./Reviews/TrbMus-Gen

471. HYLANDER, Martha A. "A selective list of graded trombone methods and solos." University of Rochester, Eastman School of Music, MM, 1948.
See above Leon Brown, et al., 410, and Vernon Forbes, 443 for more references on trombone methods and solos.
Bib/Brown,L./EastmanSchool/Forbes,V./Methods/Pedagogy/ Solos/Theses

472. ISAACSON, Charles F. "A study of selected music for trombone and voice." University of Illinois, DMA, 1981.
Isaacson's study was reviewed by Karl Hinterbichler in the *JITA* 11, no. 3 (July 1983): 61-62. See *Dissertation Abstracts* 42/09-A, p. 3802, AAD82-03495 and *RILM*81/3589dd45. The study includes a list of sixteenth-century works which combine trombones, voices, and other instruments. See also Mary Rasmussen, 536.
See Isaacson's "Twentieth-century music for trombone and organ" in the *JITA* 24, no. 4 (Fall 1994): 24. At time of the

article, he was associate professor of trombone at the University of Wisconsin-Oshkosh. His article on music for trombone and organ, which is international in scope, lists the works by composer and title, and he annotates each entry in a separate listing, with a key to sources and a bibliography. One of the primary sources for his article is Klaus Winkler, 588.

Bib/Diss/IllinoisU/Organ/Rasmussen,M./TrbMus-15thC/TrbMus-16thC/TrbMus-20thC/Vocal/Winkler,K.

473. JAMESON, Philip. "Guide to orchestral excerpts." *JITA* 13, no. 4 (October 1985): 30.

The material in this article is classified by composer, composition, and volume. See also Jameson's "Guide to the Alfred Stöneberg orchestral excerpt books," *JITA* 14, no. 1 (Winter 1986): 30. It classifies the excerpts in all ten volumes of the International Music edition of Keith Brown's excerpt collection by composer, composition, volume, and page number. See also Robert Kehrberg, 484, Loren Marsteller, 505, Thomas Matta, 509, James E. Roberts, 543, Milton Stevens, 561, and Robert Wagenknecht, 574.

Bib/Brown,K./Kehrberg,R./Marsteller,L./Matta,T./OrchExcerpts/Roberts,J./Stevens,M./Stöneberg,A./Wagenknecht,R.

474. JENKINS, Grant B. *Bibliography of music for the B-flat tenor trombone.* Glen Ellyn IL: Instrumentalist, 1949.

Listed in Richard Roznoy, *JITA* 3 (1975): 9, with annotation, this volume was also a Master of Music thesis (1948?) from Northwestern University. It is cited by Mary Rasmussen on page 174 of her "Brass bibliography: 1946-1950," *Brass Quarterly* 1, no. 3 (March 1958): 168-181.

Bib/NorthwesternU/Rasmussen,M./Roznoy,R./Theses/TrbMus-Gen

475. JENSEN, Niels Martin. "The instrumental music for small ensemble[s] of Antonio Bertali: The sources." *Dansk Årborg for Musikforskning* 20 (1992): 25-43.

Cited in *LASOCKI*, 1994, Jensen's article also includes music for trombone. For more references on the works of Bertali see Robert Reifsnyder, 538, C. Robert Wigness, 583, and Stewart Carter, 616.

Baroque/Bertali,A./Cartcr,S./ChamMus-Trb/Reifsnyder,R./
TrbMus-17thC/Wigness,R.

476. KAGARICE, Vern. *Annotated Guide to Trombone Solos with
      Band and Orchestra.* Lebanon IN: Studio/PR, 1974.
        Kagarice's 1973 Doctor of Music document at Indiana
      University has been revised and updated. It is located in
      *RILM*73/2920dd07. See a review by Hugo Magliocco in the *NITA*
      3, no. 2 (May 1976): 21. See also James K. Kidwell, 485.
      Bib/Concertos/Diss/IndianaU/Kidwell,J./Magliocco,H./Reviews/
      Solos

477. [————]. "Brass [and trombone] trios in the ITA collection."
      JITA 14, no. 1 (Winter 1986): 42.
        See also Kagarice, 478, "Trombone [and brass] trios."
      BrassTrio/ChamMus-Trb/ITA/TrbTrio

478. [————]. "Trombone [and brass] trios in the ITA collection."
      JITA 14, no. 1 (Winter 1986): 41-42.
        See Kagarice, 477, Thomas G. Everett, 434, Donald A.
      Hummel, 468, and Ronald Nethercutt, 524.
      BrassTrio/Everett,T./Hummel,D./Nethercutt,R./TrbTrio

479. KAGARICE, Vern, et al. *Solos for the Student Trombonist: An
      Annotated Bibliography.* Nashville TN: Brass Press, 1979.
        Number 8 in the International Trombone Association Series,
      this bibliography was prepared by a select panel of teachers and
      performers: Vern Kagarice, Leon Brown, Karl Hinterbichler,
      Milton Stevens, Robert Tennyson, and Irvin Wagner. Available
      recordings of the solos are also listed. See a review in the
      Newsletter of the International Trumpet Guild 7, no. 2 (1981): 12.
        See Leon F. Brown et al., 410, for more references on solo
      literature for trombone. See also Robert W. Stroetz, "A
      descriptive analysis of the solo literature for trombone with piano
      accompaniment," University of Southern California, MM, 1950,
      cited on page 174 of Mary Rasmussen's "Brass bibliography:
      1946-50," *Brass Quarterly* 1, no. 3 (March 1958): 168-181.
      Bib/Brown,L./Discog/Hinterbichler,K./ITA/Pedagogy/Rasmussen,M./
      Reviews/Solos/Stevens,M./Stroetz,R./Tennyson,R./Wagner,I.

480. KAPLAN, Allan R. "A performance analysis of five major recital works: Concerti for solo trombone and orchestra." New York University, PhD, 1978.
    See *Dissertation Abstracts* 39/08-A, p. 4582, AAD78-24091.
    See Lee Underwood, 364, and John Leisenring, 492.
    Concertos/Diss/Leisenring,J./NewYorkU/PerfPrac/Underwood,L.

481. KEELING, Bruce N. "The trombone quartet: A brief historical overview and a discussion of selected, original, published twentieth-century quartets." University of Oklahoma, DMA, 1991.
    See *Dissertation Abstracts* 9128667 and *RILM*1991-04804-dd.
    See above Thomas G. Everett, 433, for more references on the trombone quartet.
    Diss/Everett,T./OklahomaU/TrbMus-20thC/TrbQuartet

482. KEHRBERG, Robert. "Nine original trombone solos incorporating twentieth-century compositional techniques graded for the first ten years of playing." University of Northern Colorado, DA, 1983.
    See *Dissertation Abstracts* 44/05-A, p. 1236, AAD83-13977.
    Diss/NorthernColoradoU/Pedagogy/PerfPrac/Solos/TrbMus-20thC

483. ———. "'Tautophonic': A composition for trombone and four-channel tape delay." *JITA* 14, no. 1 (Winter 1986): 21-24.
    Kehrberg gives detailed instructions on the notation and performance problems of his complex work.
    Avant-Garde/ElectronicMusic/PerfPrac/Solos/Tape/TrbMusic-20thC

484. ———. "Trombone orchestral excerpts: A guide to published works." *JITA* 14, no. 3 (Summer 1986): 20-22.
    Fifteen different sets of books by composer, work, and all sets which contain the excerpt are classified. See Philip Jameson, 473, for references to orchestral excerpt materials.
    Bib/Jameson,P./OrchExcerpts

485. KIDWELL, James K. "An annotated performance-recording project of selected solo music for trombone with band accompaniment." University of Oklahoma, DMA, 1976.

See *Dissertation Abstracts* 37/12-A, p. 7394, AAD77-12744.
See Vern Kagarice, 476.
Bands/Bib/Concertos/Discog/Kagarice,V./OklahomaU/Recording/
Solos

486. KOHLENBERG, Randy. "The acquisition of facsimiles of manuscripts and printed music from the seventeenth and eighteenth centuries which contain soloistic passages for the trombone." University of North Carolina-Greensboro, unpublished independent research, 1987.

Kohlenberg is on the music faculty of the University of North Carolina at Greensboro, and serves as secretary/archivist of the International Trombone Association. See C. Robert Wigness, 583, and Kenneth M. Hanlon, 656.
Choral/Hanlon,K./NorthCarolinaU-Greensboro/Research/TrbMus-17thC/TrbMus-18thC/Vocal/Wigness,R.

487. ———. "The solo trombone music of Michael Haydn." University of North Carolina-Greensboro, unpublished independent research, 1987.

Cited in *KOHLENBERG I*, some of the information in this study may be found as notes to Haydn's *Concerto for Alto Trombone*, [extracted from *Divertimento in D* 1764], edited and arranged by Kohlenberg and published by Modern Editions, 1984.
See T. Donley Thomas, 566, and David Bruenger, 609.
AltoTrb/Bruenger,D./Concertos/Haydn,M./NorthCarolinaU-Greensboro/Research/Solos/TrbMus-18thC

488. KUZMICH, John. "A basic jazz solo repertory." *Instrumentalist* 29 (May 1975): 67-71.

Several transcribed jazz solos are included in Kuzmich's article. See also an update of his article in *Instrumentalist* 32 (January 1978): 75-77. See David Baker, 597, recommended by Kuzmich.
Baker,D./Jazz-Blues/Pedagogy

489. LAI, Chang-Yi. "An analytical study of nine selected sonatas for trombone and piano." Lamar University-Beaumont, MMED, 1993.

See *Masters Abstracts* AAC 1356182, MAI 32/04, p. 1097, August 1994. The works analyzed include transcriptions. The

sonatas selected are by J.S. Bach (Sonata No. 1), Leslie Bassett, Newell Kay Brown, Francesco Corelli (Sonata No. 7), Johann Friedrich Fasch (Sonata No. 11), Walter Hartley (Sonata Concertante), Paul Hindemith, Richard Monaco (Sonata No. 1), and Donald White. Short biographies of the composers and background material on the compositions are also included. See also John Robert Drew, 428, and Dean A. Farnham, 440. For more information on Donald White's sonata see Robert Mullen, 516.
Bach,J.S./Bassett,L./Bio/Brown,N./Corelli,F./Drew,J./Farnham,D./ Fasch,J./Hartley,W./Hindemith,P./LamarU-Beaumont/Monaco,R./ Mullen,R./Solos/Sonata/Theses/Transcriptions/White,D.

490. [LANE, G.B.]. "Orchestral repertoire for civic symphony trombonists." *National Association of College Wind and Percussion Instructors Journal* 25, no. 1 (Fall 1976): 38-40.
Lane's article appears in A. Keith Amstutz's ongoing column, "Brass forum." For more references on orchestral excerpts, see Philip Jameson, 473.
Amstutz,K./Orchestra/Pedagogy

491. LEBENS, James C. "An analysis of 'Keren' for solo trombone by Iannis Xenakis: Randomly generated music within a symmetrical framework and performance considerations." University of Washington, DMA, 1993.
See *Dissertation Abstracts* AAC 9417049, DAI-A 55/02, p. 177, August 1994.
Avant-Garde/Diss/Keren/Solos/TrbMus-20thC/Unaccompanied/ WashingtonU/Xenakis,I.

492. LEISENRING, John R. "Twentieth-century trombone concerti." University of Illinois, DMA, 1974.
See *Dissertation Abstracts* 35/07-A, p. 4591 BAK75-00352 and *RILM* 76/15006dd45. See also Allan R. Kaplan, 480.
Concertos/Diss/IllinoisU/Kaplan,A./TrbMus-20thC

493. LEMKE, Jeffrey J. "French tenor trombone solo literature and pedagogy since 1836." University of Arizona, DMA, 1983.
Lemke includes a history of the Paris Conservatory. See *Dissertation Abstracts* 44/03-A, p. 698; MBB83-15294, AAD84-

25538 [order numbers from various citations] and
*RILM*83/3789dd45. See a review by Chris Buckholz of J.
Mark Thompson and Jeffrey Jon Lemke, *French Music for Low Brass
Instruments: An Annotated Bibliography*, Bloomington IN:
Indiana University Press, 1994, in Paul Hunt's ongoing column,
"Reviews," *JITA* 25, no. 4 (Fall 1997): 80. See also Robert
Reifsnyder, 539, Glenn P. Smith, 558, and J. Mark Thompson, 567.
ArizonaU/Bib/Bio/Buckholz,C./Diss/France/Hunt,P./Paris
Conservatory/Pedagogy/Reifsnyder,R./Reviews/Smith,G./Solos/
Thompson,M./TrbMus-19thC/TrbMus-20thC

494. LESTER, Raymond David. "The emergence of the bass trombone
      in recent music literature." California State University, Long
      Beach, MA, 1981.
      See *Masters Abstracts* 20/02, p. 198, AAD-13-17459.
      BassTrb/CaliforniaStateU-LongBeach/Theses/TrbMus-20thC

495. LEWIS, Michael. "Solo trombone performances at the
      Gewandhaus in the eighteenth [*sic*, nineteenth] century." *JITA* 20,
      no. 3 (Summer 1992): 27-32.
      Solo trombone performances at the Gewandhaus during the
      nineteenth century apparently began on April 6, 1815. A table is
      included which cites the subsequent dates, compositions, and
      performers. Lewis's article is based on his doctoral lecture-recital,
      "Solo trombone performances at the Gewandhaus in the
      nineteenth century: A lecture recital," University of North Texas,
      DMA, 1990.
      In the course of his research Lewis found the trombone part to
      Ferdinand David's *Concerto Militaire* (a previously unknown
      second concerto by the composer), the second and third
      concertinos by C.H. Meyer, and twenty-eight previously unknown
      nineteenth-century works for trombone. See Werner Beyer, 403.
      Beyer and Lewis disagree on first name of the Gewandhaus
      trombone soloist Rex, identified by Beyer as W. Rex and by
      Lewis as Franz Rex.
      See also Robert Reifsnyder, 540, Larry Weed, 577, and Steve
      Wolfinbarger, 592. For more information on Queisser and Belcke,
      who dominated the trombone performances at the Gewandhaus
      and in Berlin during their careers, see Mary Rasmussen, 194.

BassTrb/Belcke,F./Beyer,W./Bruns[Bruhns?],A./Concertos/
David,F./Gewandhaus/Handrow,R./Kummer,F./Lecture-Recital/
Meyer,C.H./Müller,C.G./Müller,R./Nabich,M./Queisser,C./
Rasmussen,M./Reifsnyder,R./Rex,F[W?]./Shaw,G./TrbMus-19thC/
Weber,C.M.von/Weed,L./Wolfinbarger,S.

496. LOBITZ, Carl M. "Problems in transcribing and composing music for trombone choir." University of Oklahoma, DMA, 1969.
See *Dissertation Abstracts* 30/05-A, p. 2062, AAD69-18445.
An original work, *Symphony for Trombone Choir*, is used to illustrate important factors in composing for trombone choir.
See [Karl Hinterbichler], 459, Danny J. Hutson, 678, Paul Tanner, 766, and Irvin L. Wagner, 774.
Friedman,J./Hinterbichler,K./Hutson,D./PerfPrac/Tanner,P./
Transcriptions/TrbChoir/Wagner,I.

497. LOUCKY, David. "Contemporary notation and limited indeterminacy: Roger Reynolds's . . . *From Behind the Unreasoning Mask.*" *JITA* 24, no. 2 (Spring 1996): 36-42.
Loucky analyzes this work, written for trombone, percussion, assistant percussion, and four-channel tape. He also discusses some of the ideas and philosophies of Roger Reynolds, based on his writings and compositions. The article was originally published by *ex tempore: a journal of compositional and theoretical research in music*, 2 (Fall 1991). See also Per Brevig, 607, and Klaus-K. Hübler, 677.
Avant-Garde/Brevig,P./ChamMus-Trb/ElectronicMusic/*extempore*/
Hübler,K./Notation/Reynolds,R./Tape/TrbMus-20thC

498. LUND, Erik R. "The 'Discours' of Vinko Globokar: To speak <---> to play." University of Illinois at Urbana-Champaign, DMA, 1988.
Globokar's *Discours* are six works in series, one of which, *Discours II*, is for trombone quintet and one for brass quintet. See also Douglas Weeks, 579, John J. Bingham, 601, Cornelius Cardew, 614, Vinko Globokar, 647, Wolfgang König, 684, Rudolf Lück, 698, and Milton Stevens, 759, for further discussion of *Discours II*. A review by Dika Newlin is located in *Notes* 27, no. 2 (December 1970): 338-339.

Avant-Garde/Bingham,J./BrassQuintet/Cardew,C./ChamMus-Trb/
Diss/Globokar,V./IllinoisU/König,W./Lück,R./Newlin,D./
Reviews/Solos/Stevens,M./TrbMus-20thC/TrbQuintet/Weeks,D.

499. MACKENZIE, Kirk. "'Music for Wilderness Lake': Sonaré
1979." *NITA* 7, no. 2 (April 1980): 31-33.
Sonaré is an Ontario-based trombone choir of university
students and free-lance artists who gather to perform at the end
of each summer (see the *NITA* 6, no. 3 [April 1979]: 4, 7). One
of their primary goals is to promote the composition and
performance of new works by Canadian composers. "Music for
Wilderness Lake," was written by R. Murray Schafer and was the
result of over a year's work. The world premier was broadcast
over the CBC network on February 24, 1980.
Canada/Ontario/Schafer,R./Sonaré/TrbChoir/TrbMus-20thC

500. MAGLIOCCO, Hugo. "A trombone fest." *JITA* 2 (1973-74): 80-82.
Literature lists and discussions about trombone solo and
ensemble literature are included in this article.
Solos/TrbChoir/TrbMus-Gen

501. ———, ed. "Literature reviews." *NITA* 3, no. 2 (May 1 1976): 21-23.
Magliocco's ongoing column, first appeared in the *NITA*, and
later continued in the *JITA*, beginning with vol. 10, no. 1
(January 1982): 32-37. It was edited by Magliocco until vol. 13,
no. 4 (October 1985), when the editorial duties were assumed by
Paul Hunt (see 470).
Hunt,P./ITA/TrbMus-Gen

502. MANGSEN, Sandra J. "Instrumental duos and trios in printed
Italian sources, 1600-1675." Cornell University, PhD, 1989.
Instruments specified in this study include trombones.
Baroque/ChamMus-Trb/CornellU/Diss/Italy/TrbMus-17thC

503. MANSON, David. "The Ellen Taaffe Zwilich *Concerto for
Trombone and Orchestra*." *JITA* 17, no. 3 (Summer 1989): 20-22.
Excerpts from interviews with both the composer and Jay
Friedman, principal trombonist with the Chicago Symphony (who
premiered the concerto with the Chicago Symphony under the

baton of Sir Georg Solti, on February 2, 1989) are included in this article. The concerto has also been performed by Charles Vernon with the Chicago Symphony. See a review by John von Rhein of that performance in the *Chicago Tribune*, May 1, 1991, sec. 1, p. 22, col. 2. See also J. Mark Thompson, 568. Chicago/Concertos/Friedman,J./Reviews/Rhein,J.von/Solti,G./ Thompson,M./TrbMus-20thC/Vernon,C./Zwilich,E.

504. MARCELLUS, John R. "Lecture-recital: The alto trombone and the concerto literature." *JITA* 2 (1973-74): 31-42.

Marcellus's article is based on the lecture portion of his DMA lecture-recital at Catholic University. See *Dissertation Abstracts*, publication no. AAC279223 [listed as not available]. He presented his lecture-recital at the 1975 International Trombone Workshop, performing the "Larghetto" from *Alma Redemptoris Mater* by Marc Antonio Ziani, some solo movements for trombone by Leopold Mozart, the "Andante" from *Divertimento in D Major* (1764) by J. Michael Haydn, and J.G. Albrechtsberger's *Concerto for Alto Trombone and Strings* (1769). Marcellus is professor of trombone at the Eastman School of Music.

See Richard Raum, 196, 537, and 729-731 (see also his "From the diary of a court trombonist, 1727 [Leopold Christian, Sr.]," *BBIBC* 82 (1993): 56-69), Terry Pierce, 533, Benedict J. Smar, Jr., 554, C. Robert Wigness, 583, David Bruenger, 609, Stewart Carter, 616, Kenneth M. Hanlon, 656, Noreen E. Harris, 657, and Jay Dee Schaefer, 743.
Albrechtsberger,J./AltoTrb/Bruenger,D./Carter,S./CatholicU/ ChamMus-Trb/Concertos/Harris,N./Haydn,M./ITA/Lecture-Recital/Mozart,L./Raum,R./Schaefer,J./Smar,B./Solos/TrbMus-18thC/Wigness,R./Ziani,M.

505. MARSTELLER, Loren. *Complete Index of Orchestral Excerpts for Trombone*. La Cañada CA: Mco Publishing, [1987].

The publisher's address is P.O. Box 1426, La Cañada CA 91011. See above Philip Jameson, 473, for more references to orchestral excerpt materials.
Bib/Jameson,P./OrchExcerpts

506.   MASSINON, Eileen. "Joseph Alessi's premier of a Pulitzer Prize winner." *JITA* 24, no. 2 (Spring 1996): 26-31.
       Joseph Alessi, who premiered Christopher Rouse's *Trombone Concerto* on December 30, 1992, with the New York Philharmonic, Leonard Slatkin conducting, is interviewed. The interview was conducted on April 24, 1995, and is included in Massinon's document for the doctor of music degree from Indiana University. Massinon also interviewed Rouse for her document, and a summation of his comments is included in this article. Bernard Holland in the *New York Times*, April 17, 1990, sec. C, p. 15, col. 1, reviewed Alessi's earlier concerto performances with the New York Philharmonic.
       Alessi,J./Concertos/Diss/Holland,B./IndianaU/NewYork/Orchestra/ PulitzerPrize/Reviews/Rouse,C.

507.   MATHIE, David. "Heitor Villa-Lobos'[s] *Choros No. 4*: Background and errata." *JITA* 16, no. 4 (Fall 1988): 36.
       Mathie discusses Villa-Lobos's work for three horns and one trombone.
       Brazil/ChamMus-Trb/TrbMus-20thC/Villa-Lobos,H.

508.   ———. "A twentieth century alternative for the alto trombonist: Paul Hindemith's *Sonata for Alto Horn*." *JITA* 20, no. 1 (Winter 1992): 32.
       AltoHorn/AltoTrb/Hindemith,P./Solos/Sonata/Transcriptions

509.   MATTA, Thomas. "A ranking of seventy-three orchestral excerpts for bass trombone: A postal survey." *JITA* 20, no. 1 (Winter 1992): 45.
       See Philip Jameson, 473, for more references to orchestral excerpt materials.
       BassTrb/Jameson,P./OrchExcerpts

510.   MCGRANNAHAN, A. Graydon, III. "The trombone in German and Austrian ensemble sonatas of the late seventeenth century: A lecture-recital, together with three recitals of selected works of [William] Presser, [Eugène] Bozza, [Thom Ritter] George, [Ludwig van] Beethoven, [Halsey] Stevens, [Alec] Wilder,

[Donald] White, [Robert] Spillman, [Burnet] Tuthill and others."
University of North Texas, DMA, 1981.
See *Dissertation Abstracts* 42/07A, p. 2926, publication no.
AAC8128280. See Jeffrey P. Williams, 584, Ludomir Klucar, 682.
Austria/BassTrb/Beethoven,L./ChamMus-Trb/Klucar,L./Lecture-
Recital/NorthTexasU/TrbMus-17thC/Williams,J.

511. MCKINNEY, Harold. "'Tambourin,' from Tomasi's *Concerto for Trombone*: A harmonic and melodic analysis." *JITA* 10, no. 4 (October 1982): 9-10.
See Nathaniel O. Brickens, 409, and Michael Samball, 741. James Robertson, who is on the music faculty at Montana State University at Billings, related to me that he once performed the Tomasi with a pianist who had actually studied with the composer, and revealed a cadenza which was intended to be performed with the work but is not in the published edition.
Analysis/Brickens,N./Cadenzas/Concertos/Jazz-Blues/Robertson,J./ Samball,M./Tomasi,H./TrbMus-20thC

512. MELVILLE, Bruce E. "An analysis and comparison of selected improvised solos by Frank Rosolino (trombone)." University of Houston, MA, 1995.
See *Dissertation Abstracts* AAC 1361074, MAI 33/06, p. 1625, December 1995. Melville analyzes seven improvised solos which he has transcribed. They span a period from 1956 through 1978. See [Jamey D. Aebersold], 249, for more references to Rosolino and William R. Yeager, 783, for more references to improvisation.
Aebersold,J./Bio/HoustonU/Improvisation/Jazz-Blues/Obituaries/ Rosolino,F./Theses/Yeager,W.

513. MILLER, D[onald?], G. "Johann Störl and his Six Sonatas for Cornett and Trombones." University of Rochester, MM, 1962.
See Ludwig Plass, 724. For further information on Johann Störl (1675-1719) and his sonatas (actually tower sonatas), see Helmut Schultz, "Deutsche Bläsermusik von Barock bis zur Klassik [German wind music from the Baroque to the Classical period]," *Das Erbe Deutscher Musik*, Erste Reihe, XIV, 32-38, and Pattee Edward Evenson, "A history of brass instruments, their usage, music, and performance practices in ensembles during the

Baroque era," University of Southern California, DMA, 1960, pp. 408-415. For further information on tower music, see Robert Thomas, "The nature of the *Turmmusik* of Johann Pezel," Southern Illinois University, MM, 1959.
Baroque/ChamMus-Trb/Cornett/Evenson,P./Germany/PerfPrac/
Pezel,J./Plass,L./RochesterU/Schulz,H./Störl,J./Theses/
Thomas,R./TowerMusic

514. MITCHELL, John C. "Gustav Holst's duet for organ and trombone." *JITA* 18, no. 1 (Winter 1990): 22-25.
The referenced duet is an early work by Holst, dating from 1894, now in the British Library, Add MS 57864. At the time of the writing of the article, the author was working on a version of the work for trombone and piano. See Simon Hogg, 463. See also the summary of Jeremy Dibb's research presentation on this work at the 1995 International Trombone Workshop, cited in George Broussard's report on the 1995 ITW in the *JITA* 23, no. 4 (Fall 1995): 29.
Bio/BritishLibrary/Broussard,G./Dibb,J./Hogg,S./Holst,G./ITA/
Organ/Solos/TrbMus-19thC/WarwickMusic/Workshop

515. MORGAN, Robert P. "New music for solo trombone—and for virtuoso trombonist." *High Fidelity* 19 (April 1969): 64-65.
Morgan reviews Globokar's recording (Deutsche Grammophon #137005) of works by himself [*Discours II*, with Globokar playing all parts], Carlos Roqué Alsina [*Consecuenza*], Luciano Berio [*Sequenza V*], and Karlheinz Stockhausen [*Solo*]. See Buddy Baker, 400, for references on Berio and *Sequenza V*. See Erik R. Lund, 498, for references on Globokar and *Discours II*.
Alsina,C./Avant-Garde/Baker,B./Berio,L./Globokar,V./Lund,E./
Reviews/Solos/Stockhausen,K./TrbMus-20thC

516. MULLEN, Robert. "Donald H. White's *Sonata for Trombone and Piano*." *JITA* 13, no. 1 (January 1985): 40-43.
Mullen's larger paper, "The solo brass literature of Donald H. White," provided the material for this article. The article contains a short biography of White and a concise analysis of one of the most popular serial works for trombone. See

Mullen, 517, for information on White's *Tetra Ergon*. See also Chang-Yi Lai, 489.

Bio/Lai,C./Serial/Solos/Sonata/TrbMus-20thC/TwelveTone/White,D.H.

517. ———. "Donald White's *Tetra Ergon for Bass Trombone and Piano.*" *JITA* 13, no. 2 (April 1985): 24-26.
See also Mullen, 516.
BassTrb/Serial/Solos/TrbMus-20thC/TwelveTone/White,D.H.

518. Müller, Adolf. "Kirchenmusikalische Bedeutung der Posaunenchöre [Significance in church music of the trombone (brass) choir]," *Bausteine* 61 (1931), 189-193.
Müller's article is cited by Mary Rasmussen on page 123 of her "Brass bibliography: 1931-1935," *Brass Quarterly* 2, no. 3, 117-125. See Wolfgang Schnabel, 205, for information on Adolf Müller. See also Wilhelm Ehmann, 629, for a discussion of the Posaunenchor in Germany.
Ehmann,W./Germany/Posaunenchor/Rasmussen,M./Worship

519. ———. "Posaunenchöre in der Kirchenmusik [Trombone (brass) choirs in church music]," *Sächisches Kirchenblatt* 79 (1931), 670,685.
See Müller, 518, for references.
Germany/Posaunenchor/Worship

520. "Music for bass trombone." *Sounding Brass and the Conductor* 8, no. 4 (1979): 153.
Apparently a part of a series in *Sounding Brass*, this article is continued in vol. 9, no. 2 (1980): 31-32. A separate column, "Music for trombone," also appears in vol. 8, no. 4, on pp. 151-152.
BassTrb/Bib/England/TrbMus-Gen

521. MUSIL, Frank J. "A descriptive analysis of the trombone quartet *Bolos* by Jan Bark and Folke Rabe." East Texas State University, MM, 1983.
Musil's thesis is cited in *KOHLENBERG II*. See Thomas G. Everett, 433, for more references to the trombone quartet.
Bark,J./*Bolos*/EastTexasStateU/Everett,T./Rabe,F./Theses/TrbMus-20thC/TrbQuartet

522. MUSSELWHITE, Wayne. "The use of the trombone in three
      selected tone poems of Richard Strauss." University of North
      Texas, MM, 1975.
      Musselwhite's thesis is cited in *KOHLENBERG II*. See John R.
      Drew, 625.
      Drew,J./NorthTexasU/Orchestra/Strauss,R./Theses

523. NELSON, Mark A. "The brass parables of Vincent Persichetti."
      Arizona State University, DMA, 1985.
      Included in this study is the unaccompanied solo "Parable" for
      trombone, in addition to similar compositions for horn, trumpet,
      and tuba. See Marta Hofacre, 462.
      ArizonaStateU/Brass/Diss/Hofacre,M./*Parable*/Persichetti,V./
      Solos/TrbMus-20thC

524. NETHERCUTT, Ronald. "Trombone trios: Ronald Nethercutt."
      JITA 7 (1979): 19-21.
      See Thomas G. Everett, 434, Donald A. Hummel, 468, and
      Vern Kagarice, 478.
      Everett,T./Hummel,D./Kagarice,V./TrbTrio

525. NICHOLSON, Joseph M. "A historical background of the
      trombone and its music." DMA, University of Missouri at Kansas
      City, 1967.
      Listed in Roznoy, *JITA* 3 (1975): 8, with annotation, this study
      is located in *RILM*76/15024dd45. See also *Dissertation Abstracts*
      28/09A, p. 3706, publication no. AAC6803573.
      Diss/MissouriU-KansasCity/Roznoy,R./TrbMus-Gen

526. ———. "The history of the trombone as a solo instrument."
      JITA 16, no. 3 (Summer 1988): 34-36.
      See Leon Brown, et al., 410, for more references to solo
      literature for the trombone. See also Nicholson, 527.
      Bib/Brown,L./PerfPrac/Solos

527. ———. "The trombone and its solo literature." *Woodwind
      World—Brass and Percussion* 14, no. 3 (1975): 38+.
      See Leon Brown, et al., 410.
      Bib/Brown,L./Solos

528. O'LOUGHLIN, Niall. "Trombone." *Musical Times* 125 (April 1984): 217.

O'Loughlin reviews several twentieth-century works for trombone by Carlos Chávez [*Concerto*], Egil Hovland [*Concerto*], Robert Suderberg [*Chamber Music III:* "Night Set"], Yvonne Desportes [*Un Souffle Profound*], Frank Michael [*Epigramme*, op. 48], and Giovanni Schiaffini [*Canzon La Venexiana*].
ChamMus-Trb/Chávez,C./Concertos/Desportes,Y./Hovland,E./ Michael,F./Reviews/Schiaffini,G./Solos/Suderberg,R./TrbMus-20thC

529. OTTO, Craig A. "A checklist of compositions with significant trombone parts in the Liechtenstein music collection." *JITA* 9 (1981): 11-13.

The collection dates from the reign (1664-1695) of Karl Liechtenstein-Castelcorn and resides in the Collegiate Church of St. Maurice in the province of Moravia now in the Czech Republic. See Stephen C. Anderson, 392. See also Don Smithers, "Music for the Prince-Bishop," *Music and Musicians* 18 (April 1970): 24-27.
Anderson,S./Baroque/Bib/ChamMus-Trb/CzechRepublic/ Liechtenstein-C[K]astelcorn,K./Smithers,D./TrbMus-17thC

530. PARNELL, Michael. "The 1995 Eastern Trombone Workshop in review." *JITA* 23, no. 3 (Summer 1995): 22-28.

Normally coverage of regional trombone workshops is not cited in this book, but this particular article contains a list of addresses where new compositions and arrangements for trombone and wind ensemble can be obtained. The *Concerto* by George Walker is listed and has been reviewed by Eileen Southern in *Music Quarterly* 41, no. 4 (October 1975): 645-650. For a discussion of the Zwilich Concerto, see David Manson, 503.
Bands/Carvalho,U./Chestnutt,R./Cohen,A./Colegrove,J./Concertos/ Creston,P/Defaÿ,J.-M./Dubois,P.M./Hudson,F./Popp,H./PRISMA/ Simpson,C./Southern,E./Stojowski,S./Šulek,S./Taylor,M./TrbMus-20thC/TrbQuartet/Walker,G./Weber,C.M.von/Wells,S./ Wil[l]son,M./Zwilich,E.

531. PETHEL, Stanley R. "Contemporary composition for the trombone: A survey of selected works." University of Kentucky, DMA, 1981.

    See *Dissertation Abstracts* 42/07-A, p. 2928, AAD81-29757, and *RILM*81/2166dd07. Pethel's study deals with post-1950 literature for the trombone and includes works by Thomas Albert, Luciano Berio, Leonard Bernstein, Andrè Bon, Eugène Bozza, J.E. Brown, John Cage, David Cope, James Cuomo, Conrad de Jong, Jacob Druckman, Robert Erickson, Jere Hutcheson, Ernst Krenek, I. Mitsouka, Stan Pethel, Walter Ross, Elliot Schwartz, Phil Wilson, and Michael Zbar. See Milton Stevens, 759.

    See Buddy Baker, 400, for further discussion of Berio's *Sequenza V.* See John W. Coe, 420, and Gary Shaw, 551, for discussions of *Animus I for Trombone and Tape* by Jacob Druckman.
    Albert,T./Avant-Garde/Baker,B./Berio,L./Bernstein,L./Bon,A./ Bozza,E./Brown,J.E./Cage,J./ChamMus-Trb/Coe,J./Cope,D./Cuomo,J./ DeJong,C./Diss/Druckman,J./ElectronicMusic/Erickson,R./Grock/ Hutcheson,J./KentuckyU/Krenek,E./Mitsouka,I./Notation/Ross,W./ Schwartz,E./Shaw,G./Solos/Stevens,M./Tape/Theater/TrbMus-20thC/ Unaccompanied/Weeks,D./Wilson,P./Zbar,M.

532. PHILLIPS, Jeff. *Annotated Guide to Trombone Quintet Literature.* N.p., n.d.

    Cited by Paul Hunt in his ongoing column, "Literature reviews," in the *JITA* 13, no. 4 (October 1985): 49, the author was a graduate student at Western Kentucky University, Bowling Green KY, in 1985. His 1997 address was 227 Southburn Dr., Hendersonville TN 37075. For a further discussion of Vinko Globokar's *Discours II* for trombone quintet, included in Phillips's guide, see Erik R. Lund, 498.
    Bib/*Discours*/Globokar,V./Hunt,P./Lund,E./TrbQuintet/Western KentuckyU

533. PIERCE, Terry. "The trombone in the eighteenth century." unpublished independent research, 1980.

    Cited in *KOHLENBERG II*, see also Pierce, 722.
    AltoTrb/ChamMus-Trb/Concertos/Solos/TrbMus-18thC

534. PIETRACHOWICZ, Juliusz. "Polish chamber music for brass instruments since 1945." *JITA* 6 (1978): 3-5.

Pietrachowicz includes addresses of contemporary Polish composers (as of 1978). For more information on Pietrachowicz, the 1992 ITA Award recipient, see Janusz Szewczuk, 222.

ChamMus-Trb/ITA/Poland/Szewczuk,J./TrbMus-20thC

535. "Posaunenmusik." *Zeitschrift für Kirchenmusiker* 10 (1928): 184. This article is cited by Mary Rasmussen on page 164 of her "Brass bibliography: 1926-1930," *Brass Quarterly* 2, no. 4 (June 1959): 158-166. It apparently deals primarily with music for the *Posaunenchöre* (brass ensembles used frequently in German church services). See also C. Mahrenholz, 701.

Bib/Germany/Mahrenholz,C./Posauanenchor/Rasmussen,M./
Sacred/TrbMus-Gen

536. RASMUSSEN, Mary. "A bibliography of choral music with trombone ensemble accompaniment, as compiled from eleven selected sources." *Brass Quarterly* 5, no. 3 (Spring 1962): 109-113.

Rasmussen used a selected number of standard sources, including the *Composers Facsimile Edition—Basic Catalog, 1957* (New York: Composers Alliance, 1957) and F.F. Clough and G.J. Cuming, *World Encyclopedia of Recorded Music* (London: Sidgwick & Jackson, 1952) to compile this list. See also Charles Isaacson, 472.

Bib/Choral/Isaacson,C./Sacred/TrbMus-19thC/TrbMus-20thC/Vocal

537. RAUM, J. Richard. "Extending the solo and chamber repertoire for the alto trombone." *JITA* 16, no. 2 (Spring 1988): 11-23.

A valuable and extensive survey of a body of sacred music from the courts and churches of eighteenth-century Vienna and Salzburg, Raum's study contains solo or significant parts for alto trombone. It also contains several musical examples, tables, charts, and a bibliography. The article was the result of research conducted at the University of Regina in Canada.

For an interesting letter by Raum dealing with the performance of the Albrechtsberger *Concerto* on alto or tenor trombone, see the *BBIBC* 89 (1995): 103. See also Raum, 196, and 729-731, John Marcellus, 504, Terry Pierce, 533, C. Robert Wigness, 583,

Stewart Carter, 616, Kenneth M. Hanlon, 656, and Noreen E. Harris, 657.

For more information on sacred music in Vienna during the eighteenth century, Raum cites Bruce MacIntyre, *The Viennese Concerted Mass of the Early Classic Period*, Ann Arbor: UMI Research Press, 1986. Adlgasser,C./Albrechtsberger,J./AltoTrb/Boog,J./Caldara,A./ Carter,S./Casati,[P?]/ChamMus-Trb/Eberlin,J./Gschlatt [Gschladt],T./Hanlon,K./Harris,N./Hoffman/Krottendorfer/ MacIntyre,B./Marcellus,J./Neumann,[A?]/Öttl,M./Reutter,G./Roll/ Salzburg/Schmidt/Tischer/TrbMus-18thC/Tůma,F./Ulbrich,M./ Vienna/Wigness,R./Zechner,J./Zinsmayr,J.

538. REIFSNYDER, Robert. "A closer look at recent recital programs." *JITA* 11, no. 1 (January 1983): 25-27.

Reifsnyder shares his findings and conclusions from five years of record-keeping dealing with the literature which appears in the solo programs printed in the *JITA*.
Concertos/Solos/Sonata

539. ———. "The Paris Conservatory solos, 1897-1945." *JITA* 14, no. 2 (Spring 1986): 44-47.

Part of a series concerning "The pedagogical use of solo literature," Reifsnyder's article contains tables categorizing the solos in terms of endurance level, difficulty level of solo line, style, musicality, personal choices for teaching repertoire, and frequency of performance in contemporary times. See Jeffrey J. Lemke, 493, and Glenn P. Smith, 558.

Reifsnyder and Smith disagree on the dates of the inclusion of G.-J. Pfeiffer's *Solo de Trombone* as one of "Les Concours des Prix." Smith dates the solo as 1899 and 1906, while Reifsnyder dates it 1896 and 1906 (although because of the unavailability of Pfeiffer's composition he has not included the solo in his tables of comparisons). See also Benny Sluchin and Raymond Lapie, "Slide trombone teaching and method books in France (1794-1960)," *HBSJ* 9 (1997): 4-29, where in an appendix listing Paris Conservatory trombone solos from 1842-1960 they appear to agree with Smith's dates.

France/Lapie,R./Lemke,J./ParisConservatory/Pedagogy/
Sluchin,B./Smith,G./Solos/TrbMus-19thC/TrbMus-20thC

540. ———. "The romantic trombone and its place in the German solo tradition." 2 parts. *JITA* 15, no. 2 (Spring 1987): 20-23, and 15, no. 3 (Summer 1987): 32-37.

Brief biographies of the best-known trombonists in German orchestras of the nineteenth century, composers who wrote for trombone, and publishers who published music for the instrument are included in this study. Part 2 includes a listing of original works published for trombone in Germany between 1829 and 1913, classified by composer, title, publisher, and date of publication. See also "The eighth position," in the *JITA* 16, no. 2 (Spring 1988): 3, for a letter from Rolf Handrow, the bass trombonist in the Gewandhaus Orchestra of Leipzig, to Reifsnyder further shedding light on trombone performances in nineteenth-century Germany.

See Mary Rasmussen, 194, Werner Beyer, 403, Michael Lewis, 495, Gary Shaw, 551, Larry Weed, 577, and Steve Wolfinbarger, 592. For an update on trombone performance in Germany see Carl Lenthe, 695.

Alschausky,S./Belcke,F./Beyer,W./Bib/Bio/Bruns,A./Concertos/
Germany/Gewandhaus/Handrow,R./Leipzig/Lenthe,C./Lewis,M./
Müller,R./Nabich,M./Queisser,C.T./Raasch,H./Rasmussen,M./
Rex,F.[W?]/Shaw,G./TrbMus-19thC/Weed,L./Weschke,P./
Wolfinbarger,S.

541. REYNOLDS, Jeff. "Moravian trombone choir music." *NITA* 8, no. 2 (December 1980): 24-26.

Works for up to sixteen parts are classified in this bibliography. Some of the music may be heard on Crystal Records Stereo S222 (Crystal Records, Inc., 2235 Willida Lane, Sedro Woolley WA 98284). See also Reynolds, 734-735. For further references on Moravian trombone music see Wesley R. Branstine, 606.

Bib/Branstine,W./CrystalRecords/Moravian/TrbChoir

542. RICHARDSON, William. "Trombone and baritone solo and study materials." *Instrumentalist* 32 (February 1978): 60-61.

See *BRASSANTH* 793-794. Later reviews by Richardson also appeared in the *Instrumentalist* 35 (December 1980): 34-36; 36 (December 1981): 66-68; 37 (January 1983): 52-55; and 39 (February 1985): 77-79. See above Leon F. Brown, et al., 410, for more references on solo literature for the trombone.
Brown,L./Euphonium/Methods/Pedagogy/Solos/TrbMus-Gen

543. ROBERTS, James E. "A comprehensive performance project in trombone literature with an essay consisting of an annotated guide to orchestral excerpts for trombone." University of Iowa, DMA, 1977.
Dissertation Abstracts 37/07-A, p. 4010, AAD77-28531. See Philip Jameson, 473, for more references on orchestral excerpt materials.
Diss/IowaU/Jameson,P./OrchExcerpts

544. [———]. "A preliminary list of seventeenth-century chamber music employing the trombone." *JITA* 8 (1980): 19-22.
Many primary musicological and publishing sources such as the various *Denkmalern*, Eitner, *MGG*, Fétis, Breitkopf & Härtel, *Brass and Woodwind Quarterly*, and others were utilized in the compilation of this list. Roberts divided it into works by Italian and non-Italian composers. See Sandra Mangsen, 502, and Klaus Winkler, 590, for more information on Italian music from this period.
Baroque/Bib/ChamMus-Trb/Italy/Mangsen,S./Winkler,K.

545. ———. "Works with trombone in the Alfred Einstein Collection of sixteenth- and seventeenth-century instrumental music: A descriptive catalog." *JITA* 12, no. 4 (October 1984): 25-32.
Housed in the music archives of the Werner Josten Library at Smith College in Northampton MA, the collection was named after the famous musicologist Alfred Einstein, who served for many years on the faculty at Smith.
Catalogs/Einstein,A./SmithCollege/TrbMus-16thC/TrbMus-17thC/
WernerJostenLibrary

546. ROZNOY, Richard T. "A stylistic adaptation of the piano accompaniment of Paul Hindemith's *Sonata for Trombone and*

Piano, for wind ensemble." University of Wisconsin-Madison, PhD, 1976.
See *Dissertation Abstracts* 37/90-A, p. 5434, AAD76-28937.
Bands/Hindemith,P./Solos/Sonata/Transcriptions/TrbMus-20thC/ WindEnsemble

547. RYON, James P. "The use of the trombone as a solo and ensemble instrument in selected works of the seventeenth-century Moravian court composer, Pavel Josef Vejvanousky." Catholic University, DMA, 1978.
See *Dissertation Abstracts*, publication no. AAC0328615 [listed as not available].
CatholicU/Diss/Moravian/PerfPrac/TrbMus-17thC/Vejvanousky,P.

548. SCHULLER, Gunther. "Alec Wilder's *Sonata for Bass Trombone and Piano*." *JITA* 13, no. 3 (July 1985): 6-9.
Schuller responds to a review by Douglas Yeo of the Margun edition of Wilder's work. See Yeo, 593. Yeo updates his earlier comments in the *JITA* 18, no. 4 (Fall 1990): 16-17, and discusses the controversy surrounding who actually premiered the piece. See also a response by Donald Knaub in the *JITA* 13, no. 4 (October 1985): 39-40.
BassTrb/Knaub,D./Margun/Solos/Sonata/Wilder,A./Yeo,D.

549. SEIDEL, John A. "The trombone sonatas of Richard Monaco." University of North Texas, DMA, 1988.
See *Dissertation Abstracts* 50/02A, p. 297, publication AAC8908935. See John Robert Drew, 428, and Chang-Yi Lai, 489.
Bio/Drew,J./Lai,C./Lecture-Recital/Monaco,R./NorthTexasU/ Solos/TrbMus-20thC

550. SENFF, Thomas E. "An annotated bibliography of the unaccompanied solo repertory for trombone." University of Illinois, DMA, 1976.
Dissertation Abstracts 37/01-A, p. 28, AAD76-16191. Located in *RILM*76/82dm07. See Thomas G. Everett, 438, and Douglas G. Weeks, 579. See also Stanley E. Schumacher, "An analytical study of published unaccompanied solo literature for brass instruments," Ohio State University, PhD, 1976.

Bib/Diss/Everett,T./IllinoisU/Schumacher,S./Solos/
Unaccompanied/Weeks,D.

551. SHAW, Gary. "A comprehensive musicianship approach to applied music through selected trombone literature." University of Wisconsin-Madison, DMA, 1984.

See *Dissertation Abstracts* 46/01A, p. 16; MBB 84-28900. Shaw demonstrates some techniques for developing comprehensive musicianship through analysis and modeling using three works, including the allemande from the fourth unaccompanied cello suite by J.S. Bach, the *Concertino*, op. 4, by Ferdinand David, and *Animus I* by Jacob Druckman. See Larry Weed, 577, and Steve Wolfinbarger, 592, for further discussions of the David *Concertino*. See John Coe, 420, Stanley Pethel, 531, and Douglas Weeks, 579, for *Animus I*.
Bach,J.S./Baroque/Coe,J./David,F./Diss/Druckman,J./Pedagogy/
Pethel,S./Solos/TrbMus-19thC/TrbMus-20thC/Weed,L./Weeks,D./
WisconsinU-Madison/Wolfinbarger,S.

552. SLUCHIN, Benny. "The trombone in the sacred works of W.A. Mozart." *BBIBC* 46 (1984): 31-35.

Sluchin's article is in English, French, and German. See Sluchin, 753, and Felix Weingartner, 580. See also Derrick Parker, ed., "Mozart's *Requiem:* An Internet discussion on 16th April 1996 between Douglas Yeo and Howard Weiner," *The Trombonist* (Autumn 1996) (see online at www.nthwood.demon. co.uk/bts/contra.htm).
Eberlin,J./Mozart,W.A./Parker,D./PerfPrac/Sacred/TrbMus-18thC/
Weiner,H./Weingartner,F./Yeo,D.

553. SLUCHIN, Benny, and Raymond LAPIE. "Solo trombone passages in nineteenth-century French orchestra music." *JITA* 19, no. 1 (Winter 1991): 26-29.

The valve alto trombone, which Berlioz advocated using for "singing solos" in his *Traité d'Instrumentation et d'Orchestration*, is discussed in this article. See also William T. Collins, 421, and Lewis Harlow, 856.

AltoTrb/Berlioz,H./Collins,W./Couillaud,H./Dieppo,A./Harlow,L./
Lapie,R./Orchestra/Saint-Saëns,C./Thomas,A./TrbMus-19thC/
Trombets/Valves

554. SMAR, Benedict J., Jr. "Georg Christoph Wagenseil's concerto
for trombone and orchestra: An analysis—first movement." *JITA*
6 (1978): 2-3.
For more references on eighteenth-century trombone concertos,
see C. Robert Wigness, 583, David Bruenger, 609, Kenneth M.
Hanlon, 656, Noreen E. Harris, 657, and Richard Raum, 729-731.
AltoTrb/Bruenger,D./Concertos/Hanlon,K./Harris,N./Raum,R./
TrbMus-18thC/Wagenseil,G./Wigness,R.

555. SMITH, Glenn P. "Errata for Bordogni-Rochut's *Melodious
Etudes for Trombone, Book I*." *JITA* 5 (1977): 5-9.
Smith's errata are for sixty etudes. His article also includes the
locations of accompaniments in print, with aids to finding out-of-
print accompaniments, and etudes in original keys. See also Neill
Humfeld, 1124, Randall Thomas Mitchell, 1189, and Benny
Sluchin, 1253.
Bib/Bordogni,M./Humfeld,N./Mitchell,R./Pedagogy/Rochut,J./
Sluchin,B./TrbMus-19thC/Vocal

556. ———. "Match your skills with Pryor's." *JITA* 12, no. 4
(October 1984): 41-42.
Glenn Smith, for many years a distinguished trombone teacher
at the University of Michigan, discusses Arthur Pryor's
performances released on Crystal Records (cassette C451, Crystal
Records, Inc., 2235 Willida Lane, Sedro Woolley WA 98284)
with emphasis on Pryor's recorded cadenzas in "Thoughts of
Love" and "Blue Bells of Scotland." For more references on
Pryor see Steve Dillon, 107, and Steve Wolfinbarger, 243.
Cadenzas/CrystalRecords/Dillon,S./Pedagogy/PerfPrac/Pryor,A./
Solos/Wolfinbarger,S.

557. ———. "Original unaccompanied trombone ensemble music."
Instrumentalist 28 (February 1974): 52-54.
TrbEnsemble

558. ———. "Paris National Conservatory contest pieces for trombone."
        JITA 5 (1977): 23-24.
        Solos written from 1897-1975 and dates of some composers are
        included in the discussion. See Jeffrey J. Lemke, 493, and Robert
        Reifsnyder, 539. Smith and Reifsnyder disagree on dates of the
        inclusion of G.-J. Pfeiffer's *Solo de Trombone* as one of "Les
        Concours des Prix." Smith dates it as 1899 and 1906, while
        Reifsnyder dates it as 1896 and 1906. See also Benny Sluchin
        and Raymond Lapie, "Slide trombone teaching and method books
        in France (1794-1960)," *HBSJ* 9 (1997): 4-29, where in an
        appendix listing Paris Conservatory trombone solos from 1842-
        1960 they appear to agree with Smith's dates.
        Bib/France/Lapie,R./Lemke,J./ParisConservatory/Reifsnyder,R./
        Sluchin,B./Solos/TrbMus-19thC/TrbMus-20thC

559. ———. "A second look at Rimsky-Korsakov's trombone
        concerto with the original cadenzas." *JITA* 6 (1978): 20-22.
        Smith presents a comparison of Rimsky-Korsakov's original
        cadenzas with the versions of Davis Shuman, William Gibson,
        Thomas Beversdorf, a Kalmus edition (no editor or date given),
        Per Brevig, and Vicktor Batashov [Batasev].
        Batashov,V./Beversdorf,T./Brevig,P./Cadenzas/Concertos/
        Gibson,W./Rimsky-Korsakov,N./Shuman,D./TrbMus-19thC

560. STANLEY, William. "Annotated bibliography of compositions for
        trombone and string quartet." *JITA* 24, no. 3 (Summer 1996): 26-31.
        The works Stanley discusses are annotated with regard to
        bibliographic information, playing time, trombone range,
        difficulty indications, special effects or techniques, and recording
        availability. See also the *JITA* 23, no. 4 (Fall 1995): 28, for a
        summary by George Broussard of a paper given by Stanley at the
        1995 International Trombone Workshop. See Harry J. Arling,
        395, Thomas G. Everett, 432, and Robert Gray and Mary
        Rasmussen, 447 and 448.
        Arling,H./Bib/Broussard,G./ChamMus-Trb/Discog/Everett,T./
        Gray,R./Rasmussen,M./Research/StringQuartet

561. STEVENS, Milton. "One hundred fifty difficult excerpts for the
        orchestral trombonist." *NITA* 8, no. 1 (September 1980): 30-31.

See also Stevens's later article, "Essential orchestral excerpts for tenor trombone." *JITA* 23, no. 1 (Winter 1995): 28-29. At the time of the writing of this article, Stevens was principal trombonist with the National Symphony Orchestra. The excerpts are classified into six levels, according to order of difficulty. See a critique by Keith David Jones of the listing in "The eighth position," *JITA* 23, no. 2 (Spring 1995): 2. See also Philip Jameson, 473, for more references on orchestral excerpt materials.
Bib/Jameson,P./Jones,K./OrchExcerpts

562. [SVANBERG, Carsten]. "News from Carsten Svanberg." *NITA* 5, no. 3 (April 1978): 4-5.

Found in Ben Ivey's ongoing column, "General news," Svanberg, one of the most well-known trombonists in Europe, gives a short account of his activities and a brief bibliography of Danish music for trombone available in 1978.
Bib/Concertos/Denmark/Ivey,B./Solos/TrbMus-20thC

563. SWETT, James P. "A selected annotated list of published trombone literature." *Instrumentalist* 28 (February 1974): 76+.

See *BRASSANTH* 671-675. Swett's list of solo material is classified according to level of difficulty. His annotations are useful and comment not only about the solo trombone parts, but evaluate the piano accompaniments as well. He includes both tenor and bass trombone solos. See above Leon Brown, et al., 410, for more information about trombone literature.
BassTrb/Bib/Brown,L./Pedagogy/Solos

564. TENNYSON, Robert S. "Five anonymous seventeenth-century chamber works with trombone parts, from the castle archives of Kromeriz." University of Maryland, DMA, 1973.

See *Dissertation Abstracts* 34/06-A, p. 3459, AAD73-28906 and *RILM*76/9860dd25. See Stephen C. Anderson, 392, and Craig A. Otto, 529. See also Don Smithers, "Music for the Prince-Bishop," *Music and Musicians* 18 (April 1970): 24-27.
Anderson,S./Baroque/Bib/ChamMus-Trb/CzechRepublic/Diss/
Kromeriz/Liechtenstein-C[K]astelcorn,K./MarylandU/Otto,C./
Smithers,D./TrbMus-17thC

565. TESCH, John A. "An annotated bibliography of selected trombone duets." University of Arizona, DMA, 1987. ArizonaU/Bib/Diss/TrbDuet

566. THOMAS, T. Donley. "Michael Haydn's 'Trombone' Symphony." *Brass Quarterly* 6, no. 1 (Fall 1962): 3-8. Thomas based his article on the work of Lothar Herbert Perger, who edited several instrumental works by Michael Haydn for the Austrian Denkmäler in 1907. Perger found a "symphony" by Haydn which contained a trombone solo in its third movement (see the Austrian Denkmäler, Jg.XIV/2, section Ib/34). A "Larghetto," by Michael Haydn has been edited for trombone and piano by Charles Sherman, and is published by Ludwig Doblinger K.G. (Austria) [available from Robert King Music Sales, Inc., 140 Main St., North Easton MA 03256]. See Randy Kohlenberg, 487, David Bruenger, 609.
    See also Randy Kohlenberg's edition for alto trombone and keyboard of another work by Haydn which is titled, "Concerto for Alto Trombone (extracted from *Divertimento in D* [1764])," Modern Editions, 1984. Kohlenberg cites an orchestral version for this work by Kalmar Laslo, no. 7 in the Musica Rinata Series published by Editio Musica Budapest in 1973. Other information dealing with this and similar works may be found in writings by Charles Sherman and Reinhard Pauly.
    AltoTrb/Concertos/Haydn,M./Kohlenberg,R./Laslo,K./Pauly,R./Perger,L./Sherman,C./TrbMus-18thC

567. THOMPSON, J. Mark. "An annotated bibliography of French literature for bass trombone, tuba, and bass saxhorn including solos and pedagogical materials." University of Iowa, DMA, 1991.
    See *RILM*1991-00602-dd. See a review by Chris Buckholz of Thompson's and Jeffrey Jon Lemke's *French Music for Low Brass Instruments: An Annotated Bibliography*, Bloomington IN: Indiana University Press, 1994, in Paul Hunt's ongoing column, "Reviews," in the *JITA* 25, no. 4 (Fall 1997): 80. See also Jeffrey J. Lemke, 493.
    BassTrb/Bib/Buckholz,C./Concertos/Diss/France/Hunt,P./IowaU/Lemke,J./Pedagogy/Reviews/Saxhorn/Solos/Tuba

568. ———. "Ellen Taaffe-Zwilich: Concerto for bass trombone, strings, timpani, and cymbals." *JITA* 20, no. 2 (Spring 1992): 30-31.

Charles Vernon, for whom the work was written, premiered the work with the Chicago Symphony (where he was bass trombonist) on May 25, 1989, with Daniel Barenboim conducting. The article includes an excerpt of the first movement cadenza. See David Manson, 503.
Barenboim,D./BassTrb/Chicago/Concertos/Manson,D./Orchestra/ Vernon,C./Zwilich,E.(Taaffe)

569. TUCKER, Wallace E. "The solo tenor trombone works of Gordon Jacob, a lecture recital, together with three recitals of selected works by L[eslie] Bassett, W[alter] Hartley, B[oris] Blacher, E[rnest] Bloch, D[onald] White, F[erdinand] David, G[eorg Christoph] Wagenseil, J[acques] Castérède, L[ars-Erik] Larsson and others." University of North Texas, DMA, 1987.

See *Dissertation Abstracts* 48/03-A, p. 511, publication no. AAD87-13987. Tucker's lecture includes a brief biography of Gordon Jacob.
Bio/ChamMus-Trb/Concertos/Jacob,G./Lecture-Recital/ NorthTexasU/Solos

570. TYCHINSKI, Bruce. *"Encounters IV: Duel for Trombone and Percussion."* *JITA* 22, no. 2 (Spring 1994): 21.

Some of Kraft's insights and descriptions of this challenging work and descriptions of the techniques and equipment required to perform it are featured in this article. This work was commissioned by Karen and Tom Ervin, and they have recorded it on Crystal Records S641 (1973) [Crystal Records, Inc., 2235 Willida Lane, Sedro Woolley WA 98284].
Avant-Garde/CrystalRecords/Ervin,K./Ervin,T./Kraft,W./ Percussion/TrbMus-20thC

571. UBER, David. "New music catalog of unpublished compositions." *JITA* 2 (1973-74): 24-27.

The works by David Uber in this list utilize the trombone.
Bib/TrbMus-20thC

572. VAN DOVER, David L. "Three dissertation recitals featuring solo and chamber music performed on bass trombone." University of Michigan, DMA, 1987.
See *Dissertation Abstracts*, 48/06-A, p. 1354.
BassTrb/ChamMus-Trb/MichiganU/Solos

573. VOELKER, Dale. "The trombone music of Daniel Speer." *JITA* 16, no. 4 (Fall 1988): 38-43.
See David Fetter, 132, David Guion, 452, and Henry Howey, 1122. For more information about the music of Daniel Speer, see Mitchell Neil Sirman, "The wind sonatas in Daniel Speer's *Musicalisch-Türckischer Eulen-Spiegel* of 1688," University of Wisconsin, PhD, 1972 [University Microfilms 72-29,512].
ChamMus-Trb/Fetter,D./Guion,D./Howey,H./Sirman,M./Speer,D./ TrbMus-17thC

574. WAGENKNECHT, Robert E. "Index to orchestral excerpts for trombone." *JITA* 6 (1978): 22-31.
See above Philip Jameson, 473, for more references on orchestral excerpt materials.
Bib/Jameson,P./OrchExcerpts

575. WAGNER, Irvin L. "A new, original, seventeenth-century solo: A sonata for trombone and basso continuo." *JITA* 5 (1977): 41-43.
Wagner discusses a sonata which was written between 1660 and 1670 by an unknown composer, thought to be Czech or from Eastern Europe. The work was found in Brno, Czech Republic, and made available by Ludomir Klucar, principal trombone in the Brno Philharmonic.
AltoTrb/Baroque/Czechoslovakia/Klucar,L./Solos/TrbMus-16thC/ TrbMus-17thC

576. ———. "Trombone ensemble review." *JITA* 2 (1973-74): 88-89.
Allen Chase's *Rondo for Eight Trombones* is reviewed in this article. See also Wagner's article, "Trombone ensemble music," in the *Instrumentalist* 26 (August 1971): 80-81.
ChamMus-Trb/Chase,A./Reviews/TrbEnsemble/TrbMus-20thC

577. WEED, Larry. "Ferdinand David's *Concertino for Trombone and Orchestra*, op. 4." *JITA* 9 (1981): 26-27.
See above Werner Beyer, 403, for more references on David and trombone soloists from the nineteenth century.
Beyer,W./Concertino/David,F./TrbMus-19thC

578. ————. "Summary of performance materials: Three programs of trombone music." University of Michigan, DMA, 1979.
See *Dissertation Abstracts*, 40/05-A, p. 2349.
ChamMus-Trb/MichiganU/Solos

579. WEEKS, Douglas G. "A review and evaluation of selected contemporary literature for unaccompanied trombone." *JITA* 7 (1979): 21-23.
Weeks's reviews and evaluations of several works are included: Leonard Bernstein's *Elegy for Mippy II*, Leslie Bassett's *Suite for Unaccompanied Trombone* (see Stanley Pethel, 531, and a review by Halsey Stevens in *Notes* 27, no. 1 (September 1970): 154-55), John Cage's *Solo for Sliding Trombone*, Barney Childs's *Sonata for Solo Trombone*, Jacob Druckman's *Animus I* (see John Coe, 420, Stanley Pethel, 531, and Gary Shaw, 551), Luciano Berio's *Sequenza V* (see Buddy Baker, 400), and Vinko Globokar's *Discours II* (see Erik Ragnar Lund, 498).
For more information on Globokar's music see Globokar, 647, John Bingham, 601, Cornelius Cardew, 614, Wolfgang König, 684, Rudolf Lück, 698, and Milton Stevens, 759. See also a review by Dika Newlin in *Notes* 27, no. 2 (December 1970): 338-339]. For more references on unaccompanied works, see Thomas G. Everett, 438, and Thomas E. Senff, 550.
Baker,B./Bassett,L./Berio,L./Bernstein,L./Bingham,J./Cage,J./ Cardew,C./Childs,B./Coe,J./Druckman,J./Everett,T./Globokar,V./ König,W./Lück,R./Lund,E./Newlin,D./Reviews/Senff,T./Shaw,G./ Stevens,H./Stevens,M./TrbMus-20thC/Unaccompanied

580. WEINGARTNER, Felix. "Die Posaunen in Mozarts *Requiem* [The trombones in Mozart's *Requiem*]." *Die Musik* 5 (1905/06): 41-43.
Weingartner's article is in German. See Benny Sluchin, 552. See also Derrick Parker, ed., "Mozart's *Requiem:* An Internet

discussion on 16th April 1996 between Douglas Yeo and Howard Weiner," *The Trombonist* (Autumn 1996) (see online at www. nthwood.demon.co.uk/bts/contra.htm).
Choral/Mozart,W.A./Parker,D./Sacred/Sluchin,B./TrbMus-18thC/ Vocal/Weiner,H./Yeo,D.

581. WESSELY, Othmar. "Zur Geschichte des Equals [Concerning the history of the equale]." *Beethoven Festschrift*: 342-60.
The *Festschrift* is located in *RILM*71/133 and is in German. See Wessely, 777, for a discussion of Bruckner's *Equale*. See also Andre Fiedler, 442.
Beethoven,L./Bruckner,A./Equale/Fiedler,A./TrbMus-19thC/ TrbQuartet

582. WHEAT, James R. "The tuba/trompetta repertoire of the fifteenth century (France)." University of Wisconsin-Madison, DMA, 1994.
See *Dissertation Abstracts* AAC 9417222, DAI-A 55/03, p. 417, September 1994. Part of the study explores early examples of idiomatic instrumental compositions thought to be associated with the origins of the trombone.
Diss/France/Medieval/PerfPrac/Renaissance/Trompetta/Tuba/ Vocal/WisconsinU-Madison

583. WIGNESS, C. Robert. *The Soloistic Use of the Trombone in Eighteenth-Century Vienna*. Brass Research Series No. 2. Nashville TN: Brass Press, 1982.
Based on Wigness's doctoral paper at Iowa University, this study is one of the most helpful documents dealing with trombone music and performance practices in eighteenth-century Vienna and Austria. It contains selected instrumental and vocal works, brief biographies of eighteenth-century Viennese Imperial Court trombonists, and a table of performance requirements. See also *Dissertation Abstracts* 31/09-A, p. 4828, AAD71-05853 and *RILM*76/15058dd45.
Peter Brown reviewed Wigness's book in *Notes* 36, no. 1 (1979): 103. Stephen C. Anderson reviewed it in the *NITA* [identified as the *JITA* in *BRASSBIB*] 6, no. 2 (December 1978): 20-21, as did Anthony Baines in the *Galpin Society Journal* 34 (1981): 157-158.

See John Marcellus, 504, for more references on eighteenth-century trombone music and performance practices.
Albrechtsberger,J./AltoTrb/Anderson,S./Austria/Baines,A./
Bertali,A./Bib/Bio/Boog,A./Brown,P./ChamMus-Trb/Christian,C./
Christian,H.G./Christian,L.,Sr./Christian,L.,Jr./Christian,L.F./
Concertos/Diss/Eberlin,J.E./Fontana,J./Fontana,S./Fux,J.J./
Hammer,M./Haydn,M./IowaU/JosephI/Marcellus,J./Messerer,C./
Mozart,W.A./PerfPrac/Reutter,G./Reviews/Solos/Steinbruckner,A./
Steinbruckner,I./Tepser,S./Thomas,W./TrbMus-18thC/Tůma,F./
Ulbrich,A./Ulbrich,I./Ulbrich,J./Vienna/Vocal/Wagenseil,G./Ziani,M.A.

584. WILLIAMS, Jeffrey P. "The trombone in German and Austrian concerted church music of the baroque period: A lecture recital, together with three recitals of selected works of L[eslie] Bassett, L[auny] Gröndahl, W[alter] Hartley, V[incent] Persichetti, K[azimierz] Serocki, H[enri] Tomasi, D[onald] White and others." University of North Texas, DMA, 1974.
    See *Dissertation Abstracts* 35/09A, p. 6188, publication no. AAC7507076. See also A. Graydon McGrannahan, III, 510, and Ludomir Klucar, 682.
    Austria/Baroque/ChamMus-Trb/Germany/Klucar,L./Lecture-Recital/
    McGrannahan,G./NorthTexasU/PerfPrac/Sacred

585. WILLIAMS, Mark R. "The role of the trombone in selected chamber works by Igor Stravinsky." University of Texas at Austin, DMA, 1990.
    See *Dissertation Abstracts* 9116801 and *RILM*1990-08988-dd.
    See also Jonathan Hooper, 465.
    ChamMus-Trb/Diss/Hooper,J./Stravinsky,I./TexasU-Austin/
    TrbMus-20thC

586. WINKING, Charles. "Lower brass literature." *School Musician* 48 (April 1977): 48-49.
    Pedagogy/TrbMus-Gen

587. WINKLER, Jonathan. "Jim Pugh discovers new 'Tommy Dorsey' work," *JITA* 25, no. 3 (Summer 1997): 34-35.
    Winkler interviews Pugh about the discovery of a work by Roy Harris, written for Tommy Dorsey's orchestra in 1938. The work

was given the title, *American Symphony—1938*. Pugh and other musicians recorded the two existing movements in 1995, then Pugh premiered the two movements with the Army Blues at the 1997 Eastern Trombone Workshop.

Before that performance only one rehearsal is known to have taken place, in February of 1939 at the Rainbow Room in New York. For more references on Dorsey see [Joyce Records], 29, Fred ("Moe") Snyder, 66, and [Amy Lee], 323.

AmericanSymphony1938/ArmyBlues/Dorsey,J./Dorsey,T./ETW/ Harris,R./Lee,A./MrNostalgia/Pugh,J./Snyder,F./Workshops

588. WINKLER, Klaus. "Bibliographie der Kompositionen für Posaune und Orgel [Bibliography of compositions for trombone and organ]." *BBIBC* 51 (1985): 63-66.

Winkler's article is in English, French, and German. He has written two related articles, also in the *BBIBC*, "Posaune und Orgel: Dialog zweier Instrumente [Trombone and organ - dialog between the instruments]," part 1, in vol. 56 (1986): 75-89, and part 2 in vol. 57 (1987): 41-49. All the articles are in the three languages mentioned and are cited as sources for Charles Isaacson, 472.

Bib/Isaacson,C./Organ

589. ———. "Die Bedeutung der Posaune im Schaffen von Johann Joseph Fux [The importance of the trombone in the works of Johann Joseph Fux]." In *Johann Joseph Fux und die barocke Bläsertradition* (Tutzing, Germany: Schneider, 1987): 177-199.

See *RILM*1987-02247-as. See also [Ron Babcock], 398.

Babcock,R./Baroque/ChamMus-Trb/Fux,J.J./TrbMus-18thC

590. ———. *Selbständige Instrumentalwerke mit Posaune in Oberitalien von 1590 bis ca. 1650: Ein Beitrag zur Frühgeschichte der Instrumentalsonate* [Independent instrumental works with trombone in northern Italy from 1590 to ca. 1650: A contribution to the early history of the instrumental sonata]." (Tutzing: Schneider, 1985).

Winkler's dissertation is in German and includes a discussion of music for trombone in the compositions of Giovanni Gabrieli and other composers in and around St. Mark's in Venice during the early Baroque. See *RILM*1986-01680-bm. A review by Mary Rasmussen of the dissertation may be found in *Music and Letters* 75, no. 2 (1994): 261-63. See Winkler, 782, Clifford Bartlett and Peter Holman, 401, and George K. Halsell, 655.

See also Arnold Fromme's dissertation, "The compositions for three choirs in the 'canzoni et sonate' (Venice, 1615) of Giovanni Gabrieli," New York University, PhD, 1980, and C.G. Anthon, "Music and musicians in northern Italy during the sixteenth century," Harvard University, MA, 1943.
Anthon,C./Bartlett,C./ChamMus-Trb/Diss/Fromme,A./Gabrieli,G./
Holman,P./Italy/MainzU/Rasmussen,M./Reviews/StMark's/
TrbMus-16thC/TrbMus-17thC/TrbMus-18thC/TrbMus-19thC

591. WISNER, Gary. "Annotated excerpts of Schönberg, Stravinsky, and Shostakovich." [Cited in *ROBERTS* as graduate research for the DMA at the University of Miami].
Bib/MiamiU/Orchestra/Research/Schönberg,A./Shostakovich,D./
Stravinsky,I.

592. WOLFINBARGER, Steve M. "The nineteenth-century German tradition of solo trombone playing: A lecture-recital, together with three recitals of selected works of E[ugène] Bozza, W[alter] Hartley, A[rthur] Frackenpohl, A[rthur] Pryor, G[irolamo] Frescobaldi, L[auny] Gröndahl, Paul Bonneau and others." University of North Texas, DMA, 1989.
See *Dissertation Abstracts* 50/90A, p. 2073, publication AAC9005371. Wolfinbarger's study deals with solo trombone music in nineteenth-century Germany and the influence of Carl Traugott Queisser (1800-1846) and Friedrich August Belcke (1795-1874). Works discussed include Ferdinand David's *Concertino*, op. 4, Friedbald Gräfe's [*Grand*] *Concerto*, and Josef Serafin Alschausky's *Concerto no. 1* [*in B-flat Major*]. See Mary Rasmussen, 194, Werner Beyer, 403, Michael Lewis, 495, Robert Reifsnyder, 540, Gary Shaw, 551, and Larry Weed, 577.
Alschausky,S./Belcke,F./Beyer,W./Bio/David,F./Germany/
Gräfe,F./ITA/Lewis,M./Queisser,C.T./Rasmussen,M./
Reifsnyder,R./Shaw,G./Weed,L.

593.   YEO, Douglas. "A new edition of the Alec Wilder *Sonata* for
       bass trombone and piano." *JITA* 12, no. 4 (October 1984): 38-41.
          Yeo, bass trombonist of the Boston Symphony Orchestra, takes
       exception to many of the changes made by Gunther Schuller in
       the 1983 version of the Margun edition. See Schuller, 548. See
       also a response by Donald Knaub in the *JITA* 13, no. 4 (October
       1985): 39-40. Yeo updates his earlier response in the *JITA* 18,
       no. 4 (Fall 1990): 16-17, and discusses the controversy
       surrounding who actually premiered the piece (Alan Raph, Tom
       Everett, or Russ Schultz).
       BassTrb/Everett,T./Knaub,D./Margun/Raph,A./Remington,E./
       Roberts,G./Schuller,G./Schultz,R./Solos/Wilder,A.

594.   ZUBECK, Robin J. "Twenty-four transcriptions for trombone and
       mixed ensembles." University of Texas at Austin, DMA, 1994.
          See *Dissertation Abstracts* AAC 9428439, DAI-A 55/06, p.
       1418, December 1994. The transcriptions were prepared for
       students in the seventh through twelfth grades. The grading
       system is that of Kendor Music, Inc. Performance criteria and
       sources for the original works are included, along with a
       biography of each composer. See Robert B. Conger, 422, Stanley
       P. George, 445, Chang-Yi Lai, 489, and James F. Gould, 1104.
       Bach,J.S./Bio/ChamMus-Trb/Conger,R./Diss/George,S./Gould,J./
       Kendor/Lai,C./Pedagogy/PerfPrac/Roznoy,R./Solos/TexasU-
       Austin/Transcriptions

5

PERFORMANCE PRACTICES

595. ANDERSON, Stephen C. "The soloistic use of the alto and tenor trombones in the choral music of Franz Ignaz Tůma." *JITA* 14, no. 3 (Summer 1986): 48-53.

A brief selected bibliography and three appendices which identify the libraries where the Tůma manuscripts are located are included in this article. Anderson cites the works which contain trombone and works containing trombone parts which have not yet been examined.

See also Stephen C. Anderson, "The alto trombone in the music of Franz Tůma," University of Kansas, independent research project, 1983, cited in *KOHLENBERG I.*

AltoTrb/Choral/Czechoslovakia/TrbMus-18thC/Tůma,F.

596. BAKER, David. *Contemporary Techniques for the Trombone: A Revolutionary Approach to Dealing with the Problems of Music in the Twentieth Century.* New York: Charles Colin, 1974.

Basically a general pedagogy text, but with heavy emphasis on jazz techniques and style, it is located in *RILM75/2486bm45.*

ContempTech/Jazz-Blues/Pedagogy/TrbMus-20thC

597. ———. *Jazz Styles and Analysis: Trombone.* Chicago: Downbeat Music Workshop, 1973.

Baker's book contains 247 solos by 191 trombonists, including a solo by Phil Wilson on "My Favorite Things," Columbia 9157. The book is recommended by John Kuzmich in 488.

Jazz-Blues/Kuzmich,J./Pedagogy/Wilson,P.

598. BARRON, Ronald. "Being a concert trombone soloist." *BBIBC* 93 (1996): 63.

Ron Barron is currently principal trombonist with the Boston
Symphony but also has had a successful career as a solo recitalist
and recording artist. His article is in English, French, and German.
Pedagogy/Solos

599. BELLAY, F. "Le pupitre des trombones [The arrangement(?) of
the trombones]." *Musique et Radio* 50 (1960): 211-212.
Bellay's article is in French. It is cited by Mary Rasmussen on
p. 70 of her "Brass bibliography: 1960," *Brass Quarterly* 5, no.
2, pp. 69-72. She labels it as "uninformative."
France/Radio/Rasmussen,M./Studio

600. BERENDT, Joachim-Ernst. "Jazz in Germany." *Jazz Journal
International* 32 (January 1979): 9-14.
Berendt, a leading European jazz historian and critic, devotes
a large part of his article to the talents and achievements of
Albert Mangelsdorff. He credits Mangelsdorff with originating the
technique of multiphonics on the trombone (the skill of buzzing
one pitch with the lips through the mouthpiece and the instrument
while humming a second pitch, the acoustics of which produce
a third pitch, all of which sounding together gives a chordal
effect) and further credits Mangelsdorff with being the only
trombonist in the world who has mastered this technique.
Thomas G. Everett wrote a letter which appeared on p. 7 of the
August 1979 issue of *Jazz Journal International* in which he
points out that the technique of multiphonics on brass instruments
has been used for many years in a virtuoso manner by several
well-known brass artists. The technique was even known to have
been utilized as far back as the middle of the nineteenth century
(in Germany). See Berendt's interview with Mangelsdorff, 257.
See also George Broussard, 271, Thomas G. Everett, 296, and
Bill Smith, 349.
Broussard,G./Everett,T./Germany/Jazz-Blues/Mangelsdorff,A./
Multiphonics/Smith,B.

601. BINGHAM, John J. "The innovative uses of the trombone in
selected compositions of Vinko Globokar." University of Illinois
at Urbana-Champaign, EdD, 1984.

See *Dissertation Abstracts* 45/11-A, p. 3234, AAD85-02072. Four of Globokar's works, *Accord* (1966), *Discours II* (1967), *Echanges* (1973), and *Res/As/Ex/Ins-pirer*, are discussed as examples of his nonidiomatic use of the trombone. See Erik R. Lund, 498, Douglas Weeks, 579, For further discussion of *Discours II* see Cornelius Cardew, 614, Vinko Globokar, 647, Wolfgang König, 684, Rudolf Lück, 698, and Milton Stevens, 759. There is a review by Dika Newlin in *Notes* 27, no. 2 (December 1970): 338-339. See also Niall O'Loughlin, "Vinko Globokar, agent provocateur: Shock tactics in the concert hall," in *Provokacija v gladbe* [Provocation in music], Lubljana: Festival Lujubljana, 1993, pp. 177-186. See *RILM*1993-01602-bs. Avant-Garde/Cardew,C./Diss/Globokar,V./IllinoisU/König,W./ Lück,R./Lund,E./Newlin,D./O'Loughlin,N./Solos/Stevens,M./ TrbMus-20thC/Weeks,D.

602. BLANCHARD, Henri. "Le trombone." *Revue et gazette musicale de Paris* 20 (1853): 374.

Blanchard's article is in French and is cited in Mary Rasmussen's "Brass bibliography: 1850-1859," *Brass Quarterly* 6, no. 4 (Summer 1963): 187-189. It is also cited in *BRASSBIB*. See also Blanchard, 801.

France/Rasmussen,M./TrbMus-19thC

603. BLANDFORD, W.F.H. "Handel's horn and trombone parts." *Musical Times* 80 (1939): 697-699, 746-747, 794.

For further discussion see also *Musical Times* 81 (1940): 223. See also James Montgomery, 713.

Baroque/Handel,G.F./Montgomery,J./Oratorio/Orchestra

604. BOONE, Rob. "The Latin jazz soloist." *JITA* 25, no. 1 (Winter 1997): 24-25.

Boone, the 1984 recipient of the Frank Rosolino Memorial Scholarship from the International Trombone Association, gives a concise analysis of some Latin genres with suggested exercises for learning to play in a Latin or salsa band. For an update see Mike Bogle, "The Latin trombonist, part 2," *JITA* 26, no. 3 (Summer 1998): 24-26, which deals with several common Latin dance forms such as the Salsa, Merengue, Cumbia, Mambo, Bossa Nova, and Cha Cha. See also Henry Shukman, 208. Bogle/BossaNova/ChaCha/Cumbia/ITA/Jazz-Blues/Latin/Mambo/ Merengue/Pedagogy/Salsa/Shukman,H.

605. BOULTON, John. "The trombone." *Hallé* (May 1950): 12-14. England/TrbMus-Gen

606. BRANSTINE, Wesley R. "The Moravian church and its trombone choir in America: A lecture recital, together with three recitals of selected works by W[illiam] Presser, R[ichard] Monaco, L[eslie] Bassett, P[aul] Bonneau, E[ugène] Bozza, R[obert] Dillon, and others." University of North Texas, DMA, 1984. See *Dissertation Abstracts* 45/07-A, p. 1906, AAD84-23857. See also "Moravian trombone choir music recorded," 32, Jeff Reynolds, 547, and 734—735, Manfred Büttner, 610, Marion Grubb, 650, Harry H. Hall, 654, L.W. Hartzell, 659, Jerome Leaman, 694, Joseph A. Maurer, 706, and William C. Reichel, 732. Büttner,M./ChamMus-Trb/Grubb,M./Hall,H./Hartzell,L./ Leaman,J./Lecture-Recital/Maurer,J./Moravian/NorthTexasU/ Reichel,W./Reynolds,J./Sacred/Solos/TrbChoir/TrbMus-18thC/ TrbMus-19thC

607. BREVIG, Per A. "Avant-garde techniques in solo trombone music: Problems in notation and execution." Juilliard School, PhD, 1971. See *Dissertation Abstracts*, publication no. AAC0237626 [listed as not available]. An article, "Let's standardize trombone notation," was excerpted from this dissertation in the *Music Journal* 32 (July 1974): 18-20+. See also David Loucky, 497, and Klaus-K. Hübler, 677. Avant-Garde/Diss/Hübler,K./Juilliard/Loucky,D./Notation/ Pedagogy/Reynolds,R./Solos/TrbMus-20thC

608. BRUENGER, David. "Choral-orchestral balance: A view from the trombone section." *Choral Journal* 34, no. 4 (1993): 37-43. Choral/Orchestra

609. ———. "Designing classical cadenzas." 2 parts. *JITA* 23, no. 3 (Summer 1995): 30-35, and 23, no. 4 (Fall 1995): 42-45.

Part 1 of Bruenger's two-part article discusses stylistic matters such as length, harmonic content, character, opening and closing gestures, and structural function. Part 2 lists typical works where classical cadenzas may be used, such as the Georg Christoph Wagenseil *Konzert für Posaune in E-flat Major* and the Michael Haydn *Larghetto in F Major*. A helpful bibliography is included in Part 2. Bruenger based his article on his doctoral paper, "The cadenza: Performance practices in alto trombone concerti of the eighteenth century," University of North Texas, DMA, 1991, *Dissertation Abstracts* 9128691, and *RILM*1991-08904-dd. See John Marcellus, 504, for more references on eighteenth-century trombone music and performance practices.
AltoTrb/Bib/Cadenzas/Concertos/Diss/Haydn,M./Marcellus,J./
NorthTexasU/TrbMus-18thC/Wagenseil,G.

610. BÜTTNER, Manfred. "Bethlehem (USA) und der elteste noch heute existierende 'richtige' Posaunenchor: Gedanken anlalich mehrerer Besuche bei den Brüdergemeinen in der alten und neuen Welt [Bethlehem (USA) and the oldest extant 'authentic' trombone choir: Thoughts inspired by several visits to the Moravian communities in the old and new world]." In *Musikgeographie: Weltliche und geistliche Bläsermusik in ihren Bezienhungen zueinander und zu ihrer Umwelt. Vol. 2.* (Bochum: Brockmeyer, 1991): 253-259.

See *RILM*1991-08590-as. The article is in German. See Wesley Branstine, 606, and Richmond Myers, 714, for more references on Moravian trombone music and Bethlehem PA.
Bethlehem/Branstine,W./Moravian/Myers,R./TrbChoir

611. ———. "Zum Einflua der geographischen Lage auf die kultische Musik, insbesondere das 'Posaunenblasen' [The influence of geographical situations on ritual music, in particular trombone playing]. In *Musikgeographie: Weltliche und geistliche Bläsermusik in ihren Beziehungen zueinander und zu ihrer Umwelt. Vol. 1.* (Bochum: Brockmeyer, 1990): 177-206.

See *RILM*1991-12222-as. Büttner's study discusses the differences between the ritual musics of matriarchal and

patriarchal cultures, particularly with regard to whether priests or priestesses play ritual instruments, such as sacred trumpets or trombones. The text is in German.
Anthropology/Geography/Instruments/Ritual/Sacred

612. CAILLIET, Lucien. "The third trombone in the band." *Symphony* 6, no. 6 (1952): 13.

Cailliet's ideas are now considered somewhat dated, but this is still a useful discussion of the role of the bass trombone in the band, as opposed to its traditional orchestral role, with some references to the use of the instrument in marching bands. His article is cited and annotated in *JENKINS*. See also James C. Tanner, 765.
Bands/BassTrb/Orchestra/Tanner,J.

613. CALLISON, Hugh A. "Nineteenth-century orchestral trombone playing in the United States." Ball State University, DA, 1986.

Callison includes a review of the events leading up to the establishment of the New York Philharmonic, Boston Symphony, Chicago Symphony, Cincinnati Symphony, and the Philadelphia Orchestra. He includes a listing of all pieces performed by major orchestras during the 19th century. See *Dissertation Abstracts* 47/08-A, p. 2787, publication no. AAD86-25501, and *RILM* 1986-04883-dd. Callison's doctoral paper is cited incorrectly by David Guion, 145, as being by Hugh *Cathson*. See also William A. Taylor, 767.
Boston/Chicago/Cincinnati/Concertos/Letsch,F./NewYork/Orchestra/Philadelphia/Taylor,W./TrbMus-19thC

614. CARDEW, Cornelius. "Music in London." *Musical Times* 110 (January 1969): 50-51.

A performance of Karlheinz Stockhausen's *Aus den sieben Tagen*, featuring Vinko Globokar, is reviewed. For more information on Globokar see John J. Bingham, 601. See also Robert P. Morgan, 515.
Avant-Garde/Bingham,J./England/Globokar,V./König,W./Lück,R./Lund,E./Morgan,R./Stockhausen,K./TrbMus-20thC

615. CARTER, J. "Up the pole." *Crescendo International* 13 (June 1975): 19.
TrbMus-Gen

616. CARTER, Stewart. "Trombone obbligatos in Viennese oratorios of the Baroque." *HBSJ* 2 (1990): 52-77.
Composers discussed include Antonio Draghi, Marc'Antonio Ziani, Johann Joseph Fux, and Antonio Caldara. See J. Richard Raum, 537, C. Robert Wigness, 583, Kenneth M. Hanlon, 656, and John Hill, 669. See also Bruce MacIntyre, *Viennese Common Practice in the Early Masses of Joseph Haydn*, Munich: Henle, 1986.
AltoTrb/Bertali,A./Boog,A./Caldara,A./Christian,C./ Christian,H./Christian,L.,Sr./Christian,L.,Jr./Christian,L.F./ Draghi,A./Fontana,J./Fontana,S./Fux,J.J./Hammer,J./Hanlon,K./ Hill,J./JosephI/MacIntyre,B./Obbligatos/Raum,R./Sacred/ Steinbruckner,A./Steinbruckner,I./Tepser,S./TrbMus-17thC/ TrbMus-18thC/Vienna/Wigness,R./Ziani,A.

617. CASTELLENGO, Michelle. *Sons multiphoniques aux instruments á vent* [Multiphonic sounds of wind instruments]. Rapports IRCAM 34. Paris: Centre Georges Pompidou, 1982.
Castellengo discusses the acoustical properties and multiphonic sounds of various wind instruments, including trombone. His monograph is in French and is located in *RILM*82/1787bm86.
See Joachim-Ernst Berendt, 600, Stuart Dempster, 621, Bruce Fowler, 639, Benny Sluchin, 754, Milton Stevens, 759-760, Paul Warnex, 775, and R.W. Bowles, 1022. For more references on multiphonics in jazz see George Broussard, 271.
Acoustics/Avant-Garde/Berendt,J./Bowles,R./Broussard,G./ Dempster,S./Fowler,B./Mangelsdorff,A./Multiphonics/Sluchin,B./ Stevens,M./Warnex,P.

618. CHRISTMANN, Günther. "Free Improvisation." *JITA* 10, no. 2 (April 1982): 32-34.
See Thomas G. Everett, 126, for a biographical sketch and partial discography of Christmann.
Bio/Discog/Everett,T./Germany/Improvisation/Poland

619. DAVIS, Micha, and Douglas YEO. "The Bartók glissando." *JITA*
     20, no. 2 (Spring 1992): 34-35.
         Bass trombonists with two of the world's leading orchestras
     discuss the problem (and some solutions) of the B to F bass
     trombone glissandi in Bartók's *Concerto for Orchestra* and in the
     Miraculous Mandarin. They not only give their own solutions,
     but discuss those of various other bass trombonists, such as
     Eliezer Aharoni and Lewis Van Haney. The article gives
     particulars for two instruments specially designed for this
     performance problem: Davis's eight-position trombone, built by
     Hagai Beres, and the Osmun/Shires bass trombone, built by Steve
     Shires, also with eight positions.
         Aharoni,E./Bartók,B./BassTrb/Beres,H./Glissandi/Haney,L.V./
     Instruments-20thC/Orchestra/OsmunBrass/Shires,S./Yeo,D.

620. DEISENROTH, F. "Die Bläserkultur der Blechblasinstrumente in
     der Militärmusik unter besonderer Berücksichtigung der
     Weitmensurierten Bügelinstrumente mit Einschluss der Zug- und
     Ventilposaunen [The predicament of brass sections in military
     musical organizations because of the controversy over the
     inclusion of slide and valve trombones]." *Deutsche Militär-
     Musiker Zeitung* 60 (1938): 29-30, 41-42.
         Deisenroth's article is in German and is cited by Mary
     Rasmussen on p. 66 of her "Brass bibliography: 1936-1940,"
     Brass Quarterly 2, no. 2 (December 1958): 63-77.
         Bands/Germany/Instruments/Military/Rasmussen,M./Slide/Valves/
     ValveTrombone

621. DEMPSTER, Stuart. *The Modern Trombone: A Definition of its
     Idioms.* Berkeley CA: University of California Press, 1979.
         Dempster is one of the world's most well-known and highly
     skilled trombonists, whose particular specialty is contemporary
     music. He bases his conception of the modern trombone on his
     studies of the Australian aboriginal didjeridu (a hollowed-out tree
     trunk) in the sense that he regards the trombone as a "*resonator*
     [italics his] of whatever sound is introduced at the mouthpiece."
     His book includes recorded examples [on two phonograph discs
     in the original edition, but with a CD in the reprint now
     available] of the techniques he discusses.

Dempster's volume is arguably the most complete and scholarly work dedicated to avant-garde techniques on the trombone, particularly in the area of multiphonics. It is volume 3 in a series called *The New Instrumentation*, edited by Bertram Turetzky and Barney Childs, published by the University of California Press, and located in *RILM*79/3565bm45. For more information on Dempster, see Frank L. McCarty, 185, and Valerie Samson, 202.

For more references on some of the techniques explored in Dempster's book, including multiphonics and theater, see Howard Buss, 416, Michelle Castellengo, 617, Bruce Fowler 639, James Kraft, 687, Benny Sluchin, 755, Milton Stevens, 759-760, Peter Vivona, 772 Paul Warnex, 775, and R.W. Bowles, 1022. For more information on multiphonics in a jazz context see George Broussard, 271, Tom Everett, 296, and Bill Smith, 349.

Of particular interest to admirers of both avant-garde composer John Cage and jazz trombonist Frank Rehak is a discussion of Cage's *Solo for Sliding Trombone*, written for Rehak and premiered by him at New York Town Hall in 1977. For more information on Rehak see Thomas G. Everett, 298.

Avant-Garde/Berendt,J./Berio,L./Bib/Bowles,R./Broussard,G./ Buss,H./Cage,J./Castellengo,M./Childs,B./Didjeridu/Discog/ Druckman,J./Erb,D./Erickson,R./Everett,T./Fowler,B./Johnston,B./ Kraft,J./London,E./Mangelsdorff,A./McCarty,F./Moran,R./ Multiphonics/Pedagogy/Rehak,F./Samson,V./Sluchin,B./ Smith,W./Solos/Stevens,M./Theater/TrbMus-20thC/Turetzky,B./ Vivona,P./Warnex,P./Wilding-White,R.

622. DIETRICH, Kurt. "The role of trombones in *Black, Brown, and Beige (Duke Ellington)*." *Black Music Research Journal* 13, no. 2 (1993): 111-124.

See Grahame Columbe, 283, and Kurt Dietrich, 290. See also the *New York Times*, September 18, 1988, sec. 1, p. 67, col. 5, *Variety* 332 (September 1988): 94, and *Jet* 75 (October 1988): 58, for obituaries of Lawrence Brown, one of the trombonists in Duke Ellington's orchestra.

BlackMusic/Brown,L./Dickenson,V./Ellington,D./Orchestra/Wells,D.

623. DOUAY, Jean. "Le trombone dans le *Boléro* de Ravel [The trombone in Ravel's *Boléro*]." 2 parts. *BBIBC* 13 (1976): 59-62, and 19 (1977): 29-30.

Douay discusses his experiences of performing this work under several conductors and in various situations. See George Broussard, 92, for further information on the trombone solo in *Boléro*. See also Michel LaPlace, 692.

Arnaud-Vauchant/*Boléro*/Broussard,G./France/LaPlace,M./ Orchestra/Ravel,M.

624. DOWNEY, Peter. "In tubis ductilibus et voce tubae: Trumpets, slides, and performance practices in late Medieval and Renaissance Europe." In *Music and the Church*, eds. Gerard Gillen and Harry White. Irish Musical Studies. Dublin: Irish Academic Press, 1993, pp. 303-332.

Gillen,G./Ireland/Medieval/Renaissance/Sacred/White,H.

625. DREW, John. "The emancipation of the trombone in orchestra literature." *JITA* 9 (1981): 2-3.

Drew's article concentrates on the nineteenth- and early twentieth-century composers who gradually developed an orchestral style which gave the trombone increasing musical importance in their symphonic works. See Wayne Musselwhite, 522. See also Wesley L. Hanson, "The treatment of brass instruments in the symphonies of Gustav Mahler," Eastman School of Music, DMA, 1977.

Bib/Hanson,W./Musselwhite,W./Orchestra

626. DUERKSEN, George. "The voice of the trombone." *Instrumentalist* 19 (October 1964): 98-101.

See *BRASSANTH* 362-363. See also Duerksen, 826.

TrbMus-Gen

627. EASTER, Stanley E. "A study guide for the performance of twentieth-century music from selected ballet repertoires for trombone and tuba." Columbia University, EdD, 1969.

See *Dissertation Abstracts* 31/06A, p. 2953, publication no. AAC7018135.

Ballet/ColumbiaU/Diss/Orchestra/Tuba

628. ECCOTT, D.J. "The missing trombone." *Delius Society Journal* 48 (July 1975): 5-13.
TrbMus-Gen

629. EHMANN, Wilhelm. *Johannes Kuhlo, ein Spielmann Gottes* [a minstrel of the Lord]. 5th ed. Bielefeld: Luther Publications, 1974. See review (in French, German, and English) by the author in the *BBIBC* 18 (1977): 55-59. Ehmann's book, written "with great sense of humor," chronicles the activities of Johannes Kuhlo, a German pastor (he began his musical career playing alto trombone, but switched to flügelhorn) who was active in founding the first "Trombone Choir" [*Posaunenchor*] in Ravensburg, Germany, in 1843.

Actually the name "trombone choir" is slightly misleading to those not acquainted with the common use of the term in Germany, since all brass instruments could be used in this group. Ehmann speculates, "Probably the *Posaune* in the German Evangelical Bible translation ("trumpet" or "horn" in the English version) as a symbol of the Lord's voice influenced the choice of the name."

See Johannes Kuhlo, 1155. See also "Ein Brief von Johannes Zahn an Eduard Kuhlo [A letter from Johannes Zahn to Eduard Kuhlo]," *Jahrbuch für Liturgik und Hymnologie* 4 (1958/59): 135. In addition, see Friedrich Bachmann, "Pastor D. Johannes Kuhlo und das deutsche Posaunenwerk [Pastor D. Johannes Kuhlo and the German trombone choir]," *Musik und Kirche* 13 (1941): 87-90, and Wolfgang Schnabel and Manfred Büttner, "Johannes Kuhlo: Beziehungen zu seiner Umwelt und Auswirkungen auf die gegenwörtige Posaunenchorarbeit [Johannes Kuhlo: Connections with his milieu and influence on present-day trombone choirs]," in *Musikgeographie: Weltliche und geistliche Bläsermusik in ihren Beziehungen zueinander und zu ihrer Umwelt. Vol. 1.* 77-133 (Bochum: Brockmeyer, 1990).
Bachmann,F./Bio/Büttner,M./ChamMus-Trb/Germany/Kuhlo,E./
Kuhlo,J./Posaunenchor/Sacred/Schnabel,W./TrbMus-19thC/
TrbMus-20thC/Zahn,J.

630. ———. "Neue Trompeten und Posaunen [New trumpets and trombones]." In *Kirchenmusik, Vermächtnis und Aufgabe*, edited by Wilhelm Ehmann, 58-63. Darmstadt: K. Merseburger, 1958.

Ehmann is known for his historical research on brass instruments, including trombones. See his "New brass instruments based on old models," *Brass Quarterly* 1, no. 4 (June 1958): 214-225.
Germany/Sacred/Trumpet

631. ———. *Tibilustrium: Das geistliche Blasen, Formen und Reformen* [Tibilustrium. Church wind instruments, shaped and reshaped]. Kassel, Germany: Bärenreiter, 1950.
Germany/Instruments/Sacred

632. ———. "Was guett auff Posaunen ist [What is good(?) about the trombone]?" *Zeitschrift für Musikwissenschaft* 17 (1935): 171-175.
Germany/Instruments

633. EHRMANN, Alfred von. "Von Posaunisten und Tubabläsern [Of trombonists and tuba players]." *Die Musik* 28 (1935-36): 201-203.
Germany/Tuba

634. EUBANKS, Robin. "Wayne Shorter's solo on 'On Green Dolphin Street': A trombonist's analysis." *Down Beat* 56 (January 1989): 58-59.
See also Dave Helland, 312.
Helland,D./Jazz-Blues/OnGreenDolphinStreet/Shorter,W.

635. FADLE, Heinz. "St. Petersburg impressions." *JITA* 24, no. 1 (Winter 1996): 32-33.

Fadle, president of the International Trombone Association from 1996 to 1998, and professor of trombone in Detmold, Germany, gives an account of his visit to the St. Petersburg Conservatory in Russia accompanied by nine of his students. He discovered that "there certainly is a Russian school of brass playing, and even more certainly, there is a St. Petersburg way of trombone playing." See Thomas G. Everett, 1073, and Victor Venglovsky, 1287.
Everett,T./Russia/StPetersburg/Venglovsky,V.

636. FAULDS, John. "The trombone ensemble." In *Brass Today*, edited by Frank Wright, 111-112. London: Besson, 1957.
TrbChoir/TrbQuartet

637. FEATHER, Leonard. "La coulisse, le swing, et l'embouchure [Slide, swing, and embouchure]." *Jazz Magazine* 8 (October 1962): 20-25.
Leonard Feather is one of the most distinguished and prolific writers on the art of jazz performance. This article is in French.
Jazz-Blues/Pedagogy

638. FLOUER, Jack A. "A modern performing edition for trombone and piano of Francesco Geminiani's *Six Sonatas* for violoncello and continuo, Opera V (1739), with a study of eighteenth-century performance practice." Indiana University, DM, 1971.
Located in *RILM*71/430dd25.
Baroque/Diss/Geminiani,F./IndianaU/Transcriptions

639. FOWLER, Bruce. "Circular breathing [winds: vocal multiphonics]." *Down Beat* 47 (January 1980): 68-69. See also vol. 48 (January 1981): 59-62.
See Michelle Castellengo, 617, Stuart Dempster, 621, Benny Sluchin, 754, Milton Stevens, 759-760, Paul Warnex, 775, and R.W. Bowles, 1022. For more information on multiphonics in jazz see George Broussard, 271.
Avant-Garde/Berendt,J./Bowles,R./Broussard,G./Castellengo,M./CircularBreathing/Dempster,S./Everett,T./Jazz-Blues/Mangelsdorff,A./Multiphonics/Pedagogy/Sluchin,B./Stevens,M./Warnex,P.

640. FROMME, Arnold. "Evidences and conjectures on early trombone techniques." *JITA* 1 (1972-73): 3-7.
Fromme's study is one of the best summaries of research and insight into early trombone performance practices based on music and books from the Renaissance and early Baroque periods. See also Fromme's dissertation, "The compositions for three choirs in the *Canzoni et Sonate* (Venice, 1615) of Giovanni Gabrieli: A critical and performing edition," New York University, PhD,

1980, for a discussion of Gabrieli's scoring of trombones in his instrumental music.

See David Fetter, 132, which includes comparison tables for slide positions from Carse, Bate, Hüber, Sachs, and Speer, as well as a table of several Baroque trombone parts. See also Clifford Bartlett and Peter Holman, 401, Klaus Winkler, 590, John Hill, 669, Heinrich Hüber, 676, Hugo Magliocco, 700, Martha R. Nicholas, 717, Joseph Nicholson, 718 and 920, Jeffrey Quick, 728, David B. Smith, 756, Francis Galpin, 846, David Guion, 852, Keith McGowan, 908 and 909, Ephraim Segerman, 947, and Henry Howey, 1122.

For further information on the instrumental ensemble music of Giovanni Gabrieli see Jack R. Bayes, "The proposed use of improvised embellishment in the instrumental ensemble music of Giovanni . . . ," University of Washington, DMA, 1977. See also Anthony Baines, "Trombone," in *Grove's Dictionary of Music and Musicians*, 5th ed. (London: Macmillan, 1970), vol. 8, pp. 552-559, and Philip Bate, "Trombone," *New Grove Dictionary of Music and Musicians* (London: Macmillan, 1980), vol. 19, p. 166. Baines,A./Bartlett,C./Bate,P./Bayes,J./Diss/Fetter,D./Gabrieli,G./ Galpin,F./Guion,D./Hill,J./Holman,P./Howey,H./Hüber,H./ Iconography/Magliocco,H./McGowan,K./Mersenne,M./ NewYorkU/Nicholas,M./Nicholson,J./Pedagogy/Praetorius,M./ Segerman,E./Slide/Smith,D./Speer,D./Tinctoris,J./TrbMus-15thC/ TrbMus-16thC/TrbMus-17thC/Winkler,K.

641.   ———. "Performance technique on brass instruments during the seventeenth century." *Journal of Research in Music Education* 20, no. 3 (Fall 1972): 329-343.

Fromme includes a discussion of the techniques of trombonists during this period. See John Hill, 669.
Hill,J./Technique/TrbMus-17thC

642.   GARCÍA, Antonio J. "Choosing alternate positions for bebop lines." *JITA* 25, no. 2 (Spring 1997): 36-41.

García gives several examples from notable players to illustrate his ideas on articulation and slide positions in improvised performance. He is currently associate professor of jazz and integrated arts at Northwestern University.

See also his "Thematic dissonance—no wrong notes!" *Jazz Educators Journal* 23, no. 3 (Spring 1991): 28+. For more references to uses of alternate positions outside a jazz context, see Donald L. Banschbach, 1011.
AlternatePositions/Articulation/Banschbach,D./Bebop/Jazz-Blues/ Matteson,R./Pedagogy/Reichenbach,B./Rosolino,F./Slide/Watrous,B.

643. GIDDINS, Gary. "Weatherbird: Lawrence Welk's gift to jazz." *Village Voice* 25 (September 17-23, 1980): 64.

Gary Giddins is a noted New York jazz writer and critic. His column, "Weatherbird," recurs on a regular basis in the *Village Voice*. This issue features a report on the annual Colorado Jazz Party. Included is a discussion of the traditional jazz style of Bob Havens, who was featured frequently on "The Lawrence Welk Show," and a description of a jam session with Bill Watrous, Slide Hampton, Al Grey, and Carl Fontana.

Another column, ". . . The trombone's connected to the . . .," in vol. 25 (September 1980): 56-57, cited by Karl Hinterbichler in the *NITA* 8, no. 3 (April 1981): 32, discusses the evolution of jazz trombone styles and the principal influences on them.
Bio/ColoradoJazzParty/Fontana,C./Grey,A./Hampton,S./Havens,B./ Hinterbichler,K./Jazz-Blues/Watrous,B./Welk,L.

644. GIFFORD, Robert M., Jr. "A comprehensive performance project in trombone literature with an essay consisting of a survey of the use of the trombone in chamber music with mixed instrumentation composed since 1956." University of Iowa, DMA, 1978.

Gifford deals primarily with a body of chamber music with mixed instrumentation, composed from about 1956 through the mid-1970s and utilizing one trombone. See *Dissertation Abstracts* 39/09-A, p. 5198, AAD79-05662 and *RILM* 78/1639dd45. See also H.J. Arling, 395, Alan L. Arnold, 396, James W. Erdman, 431, Robert E. Gray, 648, Michael Struck-Schlön, 762, and James D. Willis, 780.
Arling,H./Arnold,A./ChamMus-Trb/Diss/Eastman/Erdman,J./Gray,R./ Hindemith,P./IowaU/Struck-Schlön,M./TrbMus-20thC/Willis,J.

645. ————. "The music and performance practices of the medieval wind band." *Journal of Band Research* 10, no. 2 (Spring 1974): 25-32.

Gifford discusses the possible early beginnings of the trombone in the wind bands. See Martha R. Nicholas, 717, Keith Polk, 725, and Edmund A. Bowles, 802.

Bowles,E./Instruments-14thC/Instruments-15thC/Instruments-16thC/Medieval/Nicholas,M./Polk,K./Waits

646. GLENDENING, Andrew R. "The use of the trombone in Schubert's mature symphonies and symphonic fragments, D.729, D.759, D.944, and D.936a." Indiana University, DM, 1992.

See *RILM*1992-03857-dd. See also Kelly C. McKay, 709, and William Taylor, 767.

Diss/IndianaU/McKay,K./Orchestra/Schubert,F./Taylor,W./TrbMus-19thC

647. GLOBOKAR, Vinko. "The creative interpreter." *JITA* 9 (1981): 24-26.

Globokar is an outstanding European trombonist/composer who has mastered practically all of the avant-garde techniques required to perform works in that genre. He talks about interpretation, concrete and electronic music, improvisation, and instruments. For more references on Globokar, see John J. Bingham, 601.

Avant-Garde/Bingham,J./Improvisation/Instruments-20thC/Solos/TrbMus-20thC

648. GRAY, Robert E. "The treatment of the trombone in contemporary chamber literature." University of Rochester [Eastman], PhD, 1957.

See *Dissertation Abstracts*, publication no. AAC0207430 [listed as not available]. See also his article in *Brass Quarterly* 1, no. 1 (September 1957): 10-19, which, in spite of its age, remains a landmark study on the use of the trombone in chamber music. See Robert M. Gifford, Jr., 644, for more references.

ChamMus-Trb/Diss/Eastman/Gifford,R./RochesterU/TrbMus-20thC

649. GREEN, Michael. "A comparison of the bass trombone and the tuba as the lower voice in the brass quintet." University of Iowa, DMA, 1988.

See *RILM*1988-08682-dd. See Marta Hofacre, 462, Robert Lindahl, 696, and Robert Posten, 726.
BassTrb/Bib/BrassQuintet/ChamMus-Trb/Diss/Hofacre,M./IowaU/ Lindahl,R./Posten,R./Tuba

650. GRUBB, Marion. "Trombone town [Bethlehem], Pennsylvania." *Etude* 60 (1942): 378+.

See Wesley Branstine, 606, for more references on Moravian trombone music. For further information about the Moravians in Bethlehem, see Barbara Mitchell, *Tomahawks and Trombones*, Minneapolis: Carolrhoda Books, 1982.
Bethlehem/Branstine,W./Mitchell,B./Moravian/Pennsylvania/ Sacred/TrbChoir

651. GUION, David M. "French military music and the rebirth of the trombone." *Journal of Band Research* 21, no. 2 (Spring 1986): 31-36.

Guion chronicles the modest and dreary beginnings for the trombone in the military bands of France after the Revolution. He then shows how their use in France influenced their increased importance in Europe and the United States, initially in bands and opera orchestras, and later in symphonic scoring. See also Tibor Kozma, 686.
Bands/France/Kozma,T./Military

652. ———. *The Trombone: Its History and Music, 1697-1811*. New York: Gordon and Breach, 1988.

Guion's doctoral dissertation (see *Dissertation Abstracts* 46 [December 1985]: 1435A), written at the University of Iowa and on which this book is based, is cited in *RILM*1985-05368-dd, which gives the title dates incorrectly as "1607-1811." His study is based on the premise that the trombone did not change greatly as an instrument during the time surveyed but was utilized in different ways as the world of European music changed.

Paul Hunt reviewed Guion's book in his ongoing column "Literature reviews," in the *JITA* 17, no. 4 (Fall 1989): 50. Other reviews may be found in the *Instrumentalist* 43 (May 1989): 76; *Journal of the American Musical Instrument Society* 16 (1990): 192-196; *HBSJ* 1 (1989): 115-116; and *Music and Letters* 71, no. 2 (1990): 248-250.

Baroque/ChamMus-Trb/Diss/Hunt,P./IowaU/Reviews/TrbMus-17thC/TrbMus-18thC/TrbMus-19thC

653. HALE, Ted. "The influence of jazz on Eric Ewazen's *Sonata for Trombone and Piano.*" *JITA* 25, no. 2 (Spring 1997): 32-34.
      Ewazen's sonata is available from Eric Ewazen Publishing, 127 W. 96th St., Suite 8A, New York NY 10025.
      Ewazen,E./Jazz-Blues/Solos/TrbMus-20thC

654. HALL, Harry H. "The Moravian trombone choir: A conspectus of its early history and the traditional death announcement." *Moravian Music Journal* 26, no. 1 (Spring 1981): 5-8.
      Cited by Karl Hinterbichler in his ongoing column, "Literature announcements," in the *NITA* 8, no. 4 (September 1981): 37, Hall's article relates accounts of such performances with a discussion of specific chorale tunes chosen for the occasion. See also Hall's article, "Early sounds of Moravian brass music in America: A cultural note from colonial Georgia," *Brass Quarterly* 7, no. 3 (Spring 1964): 115-123. For more references on Moravian trombone music see Wesley Branstine, 606. Branstine,W./Chorale/DeathAnnouncement/Hinterbichler,K./Moravian/Sacred/TrbChoir/TrbMus-17thC/TrbMus-18thC

655. HALSELL, George K. "North Italian sacred ensemble music of the first third of the seventeenth century calling for participation by one or more trombones: An annotated anthology with historical introduction and commentary." University of Texas at Austin, DMA, 1989.
      See *Dissertation Abstracts* 50/06A, publication no. AAC 8920717. Halsell has transcribed sacred vocal and instrumental music in score form. Works include small and large-form concerti ecclesiastici, music for the Office, Mass, and instrumental works with possible sacred functions. Composers include: Luigi Balbi, Guilio Belli, Giovanni Battista Chinelli, Giovanni Croce, Archangelo Crotti, Lodovico Grossi da Viadana, Ignazio Donati, Amante Franzoni, Amadio Freddi, Alessandro Grandi, Ercole Porta, and Agostino Soderini.
      See Klaus Winkler, 590. See also Carl G. Anthon, "Music and musicians in northern Italy during the sixteenth century," Harvard

University, MA, 1943. Excerpts from his thesis appeared in the *Journal of Renaissance and Baroque Music* 1 (1946-1947). Anthon,C.G./Balbi,L./Belli,G./Chinelli,G./Croce,G./Crotti,A./ DaViadana,L./Diss/Donati,I./Franzoni,A./Freddi,A./Grandi,A./ Italy/Porta,E./Sacred/Soderini,A./TexasU-Austin/TrbMus-17thC/ Vocal/Winkler,K.

656. HANLON, Kenneth M. "The eighteenth-century trombone: A study of its changing role as a solo and ensemble instrument." Peabody Institute of the Johns Hopkins University, DMA, 1989.
See *RILM*1989-08382-dd. Hanlon discusses not only the solo works for trombone written in the eighteenth century but the solo obbligato literature. Some of the virtuosos of that period, such as Thomas Gschlatt (also spelled Gschlacht and Gschladt) of Salzburg (see Richard Raum, 196) and the Christians of Vienna, are also discussed. See John Marcellus, 504, for more references on eighteenth-century trombone music and performance practices. Albrechtsberger,J./AltoTrb/ChamMus-Trb/Christian,C./ Christian,H./Christian,L.,Sr./Christian,L.,Jr./Christian,L.F./ Concertos/Diss/Gschlatt,T./Haydn,M./JohnsHopkinsU/ Marcellus,J./Mozart,L./Peabody/Salzburg/Solos/TrbMus-18thC/ Vienna/Wagenseil,G.

657. HARRIS, Noreen E. "'Concerto for Trombone' by Georg Christoph Wagenseil: An analysis and performance practice study." California State University, Long Beach, MM, 1990.
See above David Bruenger, 609. See also John Marcellus, 504, for more references on eighteenth-century trombone music and performance practices. Albrechtsberger,J./AltoTrb/Bruenger,D./CaliforniaStateU-LongBeach/ChamberMus-Trb/Concertos/Salzburg/Solos/Theses/ TrbMus-18thC/Vienna/Wagenseil,G.

658. HARTMAN, Mark S. "The use of the alto trombone in symphonic and operatic orchestral literature." Arizona State University, DMA, 1985.
See *Dissertation Abstracts* 46/05-A, p. 1122; MBB85-14324; AAD85-14324 [order numbers from various citations]. See

Kenneth M. Hanlon, 656, Terry Pierce, 722, and Jay Dee
Schaefer, 743. For more references, see John Marcellus, 504.
AltoTrb/ArizonaStateU/Diss/Hanlon,K./Marcellus,J./Opera/
Orchestra/Pierce,T./Schaefer,J.

659. HARTZELL, L.W. "Trombones in Ohio." *Moravian Music
     Foundation Bulletin* 28, no. 4 (1983): 72-74.
     Hartzell discusses the earliest Moravian settlements in the state
     of Ohio. The article is followed by Jeff Reynolds's "News on the
     trombone front," pp. 74-75, which deals with the availability of
     "Moravian-sized" trombones. For more references on Moravian
     trombone music, see Wesley Branstine, 606.
     Branstine,W./Moravian/Ohio/Reynolds,J./Sacred/TrbChoir

660. HECKMAN, D. "Jazz trombone: Five views." *Down Beat* 32
     (January 1965): 17-19.
     Jazz-Blues

661. HEIDSIEK, Dietrich. "Die Geschichte der Entwicklung des
     Musiklebens im Kreis Lübbecke [The history of the development
     of musical life in the region around Lübbecke]." University of
     Cologne, PhD, 1968.
     See *RILM*1969-01318-dd. In the second half of the nineteenth
     century, Lübbecke was the scene of the development of several
     church-oriented trombone choirs which contributed to both the
     religious and musical life of the city. Heidsiek's dissertation is in
     German.
     Diss/CologneU/Germany/Lübbecke/Sacred/TrbChoir

662. HENSCHEL [no first name given]. "Von Turm-Musik,
     Trompeten und Posaunen [Of tower-music, trumpets and
     trombones]." *Die Sendung* 7 (1930): 44.
     Henschel's article is cited by Mary Rasmussen on page 163 of
     her "Brass bibliography: 1926-1930," *Brass Quarterly* 2, no. 4
     (June 1959): 158-166. See D.G. Miller, 513, and Ludwig Plass,
     724. See also Helmut Schultz, "Deutsche Bläsermusik von
     Barock bis zur Klassik [German wind music from the Baroque to
     the Classical period]" *Das Erbe Deutscher Musik*, Erste Reihe, 14
     (Wolfenbüttel: Georg Kallmeyer, 1940), 32-38; Pattee Edward

Evenson, "A history of brass instruments, their usage, music, and performance practices during the Baroque era," University of Southern California, DMA, 1960, 408-415; and Robert Thomas, "The nature of the *Turmmusik* of Johann Pezel," Southern Illinois University, MM, 1959.
Baroque/ChamMus-Trb/Europe/Evenson,P./Medieval/Miller,D./ Plass,L./Rasmussen,M./Renaissance/Schultz,H./Stadtpfeifer/ Thomas,R./TowerMusic/Trumpet

663. HERBERT, Trevor. "The sackbut and pre-Reformation English church music." *HBSJ* 5 (1993): 146-158.

Herbert, who is staff tutor and senior lecturer at Open University in England, and performs on trombone with the Taverner Players, addresses the mystery of why no English music from the sixteenth century is directly linked to trombones, in spite of the fact that, as he says, "Throughout the sixteenth century trombonists occupied a regular and important place in English musical life." See also his dissertation, "The trombone in England before 1800," Open University, PhD, 1984. See also Herbert, 859, Peter Goodwin, 143, David Lasocki and Roger Prior, 167, Anthony Baines, 794, Philip Bate, 797, Heinrich Besseler, 798, K. Brehm, 803, Joseph Dey, 824, and Francis Galpin, 846.

See also Galpin, *Old English Instruments of Music*, 4th ed., revised with supplement by Thurston Dart, London: Methuen [1965]; Geoffrey [Jeffrey] Pulver, *A Biographical Dictionary of Old English Musicians*, New York: E.P. Dutton, 1923; and Donald H. Van Ess, "The stylistic evolution of the English brass ensemble," Boston University, PhD, 1963.
Baines,A./Bassano/Bate,P./Besseler,H./Brehm,K./Dart,T./Dey,J./ DrawnTrumpet/England/Galpin,F./Goodwin,P./Instruments-15thC/ Instruments-16thC/Lasocki,D./Medieval/OpenU/Prior,R./ Pulver,G.[J.]/Sackbut/Sacred/TavernerPlayers/TrbMus-16thC/ TubaDuctilis/VanEss,D.

664. HERMELINK, Siegfried. "Belege für die Aufführung von Werken Lassus im 18. Jahrhundert [Documentary evidence for the performance of works by Lassus during the eighteenth century]." *Die Musikforshcung* 27, no. 4 (1974): 455-456.

Surviving parts for some of Roland de Lassus's Masses in the Benedictine foundation of Lambach have both a texted set of voice parts and an untexted set (minus the soprano) for three trombones and continuo. Hermelink's article is in German.
Austria/Baroque/Lambach/Lassus,R./Sacred/Vocal

665. HERRICK, Dennis R. "An investigation of the frequency modulations and intensity modulations of the vibrato on selected brass instruments." University of North Texas, PhD, 1983.

Herrick utilized performance recordings of ten trumpet and ten trombone players performing a musical exercise written in three different registers. See *Dissertation Abstracts* 44/08A, p. 2400, publication no. AAC8327038. See Addison C. Himes, Jr. 672, Dick Nash, 715, Jay Friedman, 1094, James W. Schrodt, 1244, and Donald H. Wittekind, 1301.
Diss/Friedman,J./Himes,A./Nash,D./NorthTexasU/Pedagogy/ Schrodt,J./Trumpet/Vibrato/Wittekind,D.

666. HIGHFILL, Joseph R. "The history of the trombone from the Renaissance to the early romantic period." University of North Texas, MM, 1952.

One of the earliest graduate papers that outlined what was then known about the history of the trombone, Highfill's thesis is cited by Mary Rasmussen on p. 99 of her "Brass bibliography: 1951-1955," *Brass Quarterly* 1, no. 2 (December 1957): 93-109.
Instruments/NorthTexasU/Rasmussen,M./Theses/TrbMus-Gen

667. HILDEBRANDT, Jay. "The bass trombone in the twentieth-century orchestra: Its use in twenty-seven representative scores." Indiana University, PhD, 1976.

See *Dissertation Abstracts*, publication no. AAC0324354 [listed as not available], and *RILM*76/1543dd5. See also J.D. Shawger, 746, and Hope Stoddard, 761.
BassTrb/Diss/IndianaU/Orchestra/Shawger,J./Stoddard,H./ TrbMus-20thC

668. ———. "*Le Quatuor de Trombones de Paris.*" *NITA* 8, no. 2 (December 1980): 19-20.

Hildebrandt gives a brief sketch, including the training, rehearsal techniques, and performance styles of a quartet of French trombonists, Michael Becquet, Jacques Fourquet, Alain Manfrin, and Gilles Milliere, who were a sensation at the 1980 International Trombone Workshop. See Thomas G. Everett, 433, for more references on the trombone quartet.

Becquet,M./Everett,T./Fourquet,J./France/Manfrin,A./Milliere,G./Pedagogy/*QuatuorTrombones*/TrbQuartet

669. HILL, John. "Performance practices of the sixteenth, seventeenth, and eighteenth centuries: A few practical references for the trombonist." *JITA* 9 (1981): 20-23.

Hill includes a select discography and bibliography. He was a distinguished trombone professor for many years at the University of Iowa. For more references, see John Marcellus, 504, and Arnold Fromme, 640.

Baroque/Bib/Discog/Fromme,A./Marcellus,J./TrbMus-16thC/TrbMus-17thC/TrbMus-18thC

670. HILLS, Ernie M., III. "The use of trombone in the Florentine Intermedii, 1518-1589." University of Oklahoma, DMA, 1984.

See *Dissertation Abstracts* 45/08-A, p. 2296; MBB84-25538; AAD84-25538 [order numbers from various citations] and *RILM*83/1210dd24. Hills discusses *intermedii*, musical productions given at the opening or ending of the acts of a Baroque opera. Some were performed in the 1539 court of the Medici and contain the earliest known surviving music for which a composer specified the use of trombones.

Florence/Instruments-16thC/Intermedii/Italy/Medici/Renaissance

671. HILLSMAN, Walter. "Instrumental accompaniment of plain-chant in France from the late eighteenth century." *Galpin Society Journal* 33 (March 1980): 8-16.

Several types of wind instruments, including trombones, accompanied plain-chant in France during the eighteenth century, while the organ was used primarily for interludes between portions of the chant.

Baroque/France/Plain-Chant/Sacred/Vocal

672. HIMES, Addison C., Jr. "Artistic trombone performance practices: Vibrato." *JITA* 13, no. 4 (October 1985): 30-32.

    Data from this article were taken from the author's doctoral dissertation, "A comparison of the acoustical properties in solo and ensemble performance of the trombone (vibrato, intensity, spectral)," University of North Texas, DMA, 1985. See *Dissertation Abstracts* 45/12-A, p. 3572, AAD85-01499, June 1985. See also Dennis R. Herrick, 665, Dick Nash, 715, Jay Friedman, 1094, James W. Schrodt, 1244, and Donald H. Wittekind, 1301.
    Acoustics/Diss/Friedman,J./Herrick,D./Nash,D./NorthTexasU/ Pedagogy/Schrodt,J./Vibrato/Wittekind,D.

673. "Historique du trombone." *Musique et Radio* 48 (1958): 443.
    France/Instruments/Radio/Studio

674. HOFFMAN, Klaus. "Zwei Abhandlungen zur Weihnachshistorie von Heinrich Schütz. I: Die konzertierenden Instrumente im 4. Intermedium. II: Introduction und Beschluss—Zur Besetzung des Instrumentalchors [Two essays on the *Weinachshistorie* of Heinrich Schütz. I: The concertante instruments in the fourth intermezzo. II: Introduction and closing section—the instrumentation for the instrumental choir]." *Musik und Kirche* 40, no. 5 (September/October 1970): 325-330, and 41, no 1-1 (January/February 1971): 15-20.

    Hoffman's study may be of interest to students of Baroque trombone writing because evidence is shown that indicates the trombone parts in part 2 were added by an unidentified editor. The text is in German. See Werner Breig, 408, Frederick S. Miller, 712, and Richard R. Ross, 738.
    Baroque/Breig,W./ChamMus-Trb/Diss/Ross,R./Sacred/Schütz,H./ TrbMus-17thC/Vocal

675. HOUGH, Robert. "Hot lips [trombonist Alain Trudel]." *Saturday Night* 105 (November 1990): 81-84.

    See M. Ginsberg, 141, for more information on Alain Trudel.
    Bio/Ginsberg,M./Jazz-Blues/Trudel,A.

676. HÜBER, Heinrich. "Die Posaunenzüge im Wandel der Zeit [The trombone: Changing times, changing slide positions]." *BBIBC* 11 (1975): 83-94.

Hüber traces the variations in slide positions as found in treatises by Praetorius, Mersenne, and Speer compared to an obscure treatise written around 1600 by Aurelio Virgiliano. His article is in German, French, and English. For more references see Arnold Fromme, 640. See also Daniel Speer, *Grundrichtiger . . . unterricht*, Ulm, 1697.

Fromme,A./Mersenne,M./Pedagogy/Praetorius,M./Slide/Speer,D./ TrbMus-15thC/TrbMus-16thC/TrbMus-17thC/Virgiliano,A.

677. HÜBLER, Klaus-K. "Die polyphone Posaune: Ein Vorschlag zur Notation [The polyphonic trombone: A suggested notation system]." *BBIBC* 45 (1984): 31-33.

Hübler describes a system of notation, particularly useful for avant-garde music, which allows for the recording of various independent components of tone production. The article is in German, French, and English and is located in *RILM*83/ 5582ap55. See David Loucky, 497, Per Brevig, 607, and Milton Stevens, 759.

Avant-Garde/Brevig,P./Loucky,D./Notation/Reynolds,R./ Stevens,M./TrbMus-20thC

678. HUTSON, Danny J. "The trombone choir in colleges and universities in the United States: Its organization, current practice, and repertoire." University of Oklahoma, DMA, 1992.

See *Dissertation Abstracts* 9223068 and *RILM*1992-09529-dd. See also Carl M. Lobitz, 496, Paul Tanner, 766, and Irvin L. Wagner, 774.

Diss/Lobitz,C./OklahomaU/Tanner,P./TrbChoir/Wagner,I.

679. IOAKIMIDIS, D. "Trombonisti di ieri e di oggi [Trombonists yesterday and today]." *Musica Jazz* 20 (June 1964): 26-31, and 20 (July 1964): 29-33.

Ioakimidis's articles are in Italian.

Jazz-Blues

680.   KERSCHAGL [no first name given] and WEIDEMANN [no first name given]. "Das Posaunen-Problem (Eine Wagner-Reminiszenz) [The trombone problem (a Wagner reminiscence)]." *Neue Musikzeitung* (Stuttgart) 42 (191?): 11, 14.
       This article is cited on p. 169 of Mary Rasmussen's "Brass bibliography: 1911-1915," *Brass Quarterly* 3, no. 4 (Summer 1960): 166-170, as having been "extracted from the periodical bibliographies which appeared in *Zeitschrift für Musikwissenschaft* from 1918 through 1933." It is also cited in *BRASSBIB*. See also K. Weber, 233.
       Germany/Opera/Rasmussen,M./Stuttgart/Wagner,R./Weber,K./Weidemann

681.   KINGDON-WARD, Martha. "In defense of the trombone." *Monthly Musical Record* 80 (1950): 228-233.
       See also her article in *Symphony* 5 (July-August 1951): 14-15.
       Orchestra

682.   KLUCAR, Ludomir. "Trombon jako koncertantnnastroj v chramove sonate 17. stolet [The trombone as a concertante instrument in the seventeenth-century church sonata]." *Sbornk Janackovy akademie muzickychumen* 6 (1972): 43-51.
       Klucar's article is listed by David Stuart, 18. His article is in Czech, German, and Russian. See also A. Graydon McGrannahan III, 510, and Jeffrey P. Williams, 584.
       Baroque/Czechoslovakia/McGrannahan,A./Sacred/Stuart,D./TrbMus-16thC/TrbMus-17thC/Williams,J.

683.   KOMORZYNSKI, Egon. "Die Posaunen bei Mozart." *Wiener Figaro* 16 (1947): H. 7/8.
       Komorzynski's article is in German. See Stan Adams, 387, B. Gugler, 450, and Don L. Smithers, 757.
       Adams,S./Austria/Gugler,B./Mozart,W.A./Opera/Sacred/Smithers,D./TrbMus-18thC/Vienna

684.   KÖNIG, Wolfgang. *Vinko Globokar: Kompositon und Improvisation* [Vinko Globokar: Composition and improvisation]. Wiesbaden: Breitkopf & Härtel, 1977.

In German, located in *RILM*77/16930ac86, and based on his PhD dissertation for the University of Cologne, König's book includes a biographical sketch and a survey of Globokar's compositional tendencies. He also discusses the compositional styles of Jean-Pierre Drouet and Carlos Alsina. For further information on the music of Drouet, see Richard Griscom, "Instrumental solo and ensemble music for percussion by Jean-Pierre Drouet . . . ," *Notes* 40, no. 3 (March 1984): 642. See John J. Bingham, 601, for more references on Vinko Globokar and *Discours II*.

Alsina,C./Avant-Garde/Bingham,J./CologneU/Diss/Drouet,J./ Globokar,V./Griscom,R./Improvisation/Instruments-20thC/Solos/ TrbMus-20thC

685. KORNDER, Wolfgang. "Posaunenchöre als Identittsträger: Eine Studie zum Posaunenchorwesen im Nordtanganyika der 20er und 30er Jahre [Trombone choirs as a source of identification: A study on the activities of trombone ensembles in northern Tanganyika during the 1920s and 1930s]." In *Musikgeographie: Weltliche und geistliche Bläsermusik in ihren Beziehungen zueinander und zu ihrer Umwelt*, vol. 2, 233-252 (Bochum, Germany: Brockmeyer, 1991).
      See *RILM*1991-06161-as. Kornder's study, in German, discusses both trumpet and trombone choirs in what is now Tanzania. It includes observations on the relationship between secular and sacred wind music.
      Africa/Sacred/Tanganyika/Tanzania/TrbChoir/Trumpet

686. KOZMA, Tibor. "The trombone in *Aïda*." *Opera News* 16 (March 1952): 30-31.
      After a short history of the construction and general performance practices of the trombone, Kozma explains how the trombones in opera generally, and in *Aïda* specifically, display what he considers the three main facets of their "musical individuality." He lists the following: the sheer strength of their fortissimo, the way their admixture can bring weight and body to the orchestral color no matter how loudly or softly the section is playing, and the majestic solemnity their "sustained chords convey in piano or mezzoforte." See also Hans Kunitz, 690.

In an interesting sidelight, Josef Loschelder has written an article about the childhood of one of the giants of Italian opera, "L'infanzia di Gioacchino Rossini [The childhood of Gioacchino Rossini]," located in the *Bollettino del centro di studi rossiniani* 1 (1972): 45-63, and 2 (1972): 33-53 (*RILM75/1253ap27*). The articles describe Rossini's father, Giuseppe, as a town trombonist and theater musician. Gioacchino Rossini's operas have many significant and technically difficult parts for trombone, perhaps as a result of his early exposure to the instrument. *Aïda*/Italy/Kunitz,H./Loschelder,J./Opera/Rossini,Gio./Rossini,Giu./ TrbMus-19thC/Verdi,G.

687. KRAFT, James D. "The development of theater techniques for use in solo trombone performance." Catholic University of America, DMA, 1982.

Cited in *Dissertation Abstracts*, publication no. AAC0377053, Kraft's lecture-recital is listed as not available. See Howard Buss, 416, Stuart Dempster, 621, and Peter M. Vivona, 772. Avant-Garde/Buss,H./CatholicU/Diss/Solos/Theater/TrbMus-20thC/Vivona,P.

688. KRIEGER, Franz. "Society blues: Zur Geschichte und Analyse der ersten schwarzen Jazz-Schallplattenaufnahmen [Society blues: History and analysis of the first black jazz recordings]." *Jazzforschung/Jazz Research* 24 (1992): 99-172.

Krieger includes an analysis of a transcription of one of six numbers recorded by the Kid Ory ensemble on the album *Ory's Creole Trombone*. His article is in both German and English. Bib/Discog/Jazz-Blues/Ory,K.

689. KRÖGER, E. *Die Posaune im Jazz* [The trombone in jazz]." Vienna: Universal, 1972.

Kröger's study is listed by David Stuart, 18. See also Rudolf Josel, "Review of *Die Posaune im Jazz* [*The Trombone in Jazz*] by E. Kroger," *Reihe Jazz* 5, Vienna: Universal, 1972. Jazz-Blues/Josel,R./Reviews/Stuart,D.

690. KUNITZ, Hans. "Vier Posaunen in Opern Verdis und Puccinis [(the use of) four trombones in the operas of Verdi and Puccini]." *Musik und Geschichte* (1957): 29.

    Kunitz's article is in German. See Tibor Kozma, 686. See also Alfred Baresel, 796, for more references to the large instruments used as fourth trombones in many nineteenth-century opera orchestras. Baresel,A./BassTrb/Italy/Kozma,T./Opera/Puccini,G./TrbMus-19thC/Verdi,G.

691. LAJARTE, T.E.D.F.d. "Introduction du trombone dans l'orchestre de l'opéra [The introduction of the trombone in the opera orchestra]." In *Curiosités de l'opéra*. Paris: C. Lévy, 1883.

    This monograph is in French and is cited on p. 36 of Mary Rasmussen's "Brass bibliography: 1880-1889," *Brass Quarterly* 5, no. 1 (Fall 1961): 34-36. It is also cited in *BRASSBIB*. France/Opera/Rasmussen,M./TrbMus-19thC

692. LAPLACE, Michel. "Le trombone dans le jazz et la musique populaire [The trombone in jazz and popular music]." 3 parts. *BBIBC*, no. 50 (1985): 36-40; no. 51 (1985): 40-46; and no. 52 (1985): 20-28.

    As with almost all articles in *BBIBC*, this one is in English and German, in addition to French. The three parts deal with LaPlace's view of jazz history in both Europe and the United States and the trombonists who helped contribute to the art form. The articles are in roughly chronological order. Part 1 deals with the period before the dominance of Louis Armstrong, and ends with a discussion of the performance style of Tommy Dorsey. The period from Armstrong's emergence through some of the bebop performers is covered in part 2, "La periode classique Armstrongienne (1927-1945)." Part 3 discusses the period after 1945 and includes many of today's leading jazz trombonists. Armstrong,L./Discog/Dorsey,T./Jazz-Blues/PopularMusic

693. ———. "Ravel et le 'nouveau' trombone [Ravel and the 'new' trombone]." *BBIBC* 47 (1984): 34-38.

    Laplace's article is in French, German, and English. See above Jean Douay, 623. See George Broussard, 92, for further information on the trombone solo in *Boléro*.

Arnaud-Vauchant,L./*Boléro*/Broussard,G./France/Orchestra/
Ravel,M./TrbMus-20thC

694. LEAMAN, Jerome. "The trombone choir of the Moravian
church." *JITA* 5 (1977): 44-48+.
Leaman's study was published by the Moravian Foundation
while he was a graduate student at Columbia University. His
JITA article was reprinted from the *Moravian Music Foundation
Bulletin* 20, no. 1 (1975): 2-7. See above Wesley Branstine, 606,
for more references on Moravian trombone music.
Bib/Branstine,W./Moravian/Sacred/TrbChoir/TrbMus-18thC

695. LENTHE, Carl. "One hundred years of trombone history—from
Paul Weschke to Horst Raasch," *JITA* 25, no. 3 (Summer 1997):
38-47.
Lenthe's article first appeared in the *IPV Journal* 4 (1996) in
German and was translated into English by Lenthe. See also
Robert Reifsnyder, 540.
Germany/Raasch,H./Reifsnyder,R./Solos/Weschke,P.

696. LINDAHL, Robert G. "Brass quintet instrumentation: Tuba
versus bass trombone." Arizona State University, DMA, 1988.
See *Dissertation Abstracts* 50/01A, p. 18, publication no.
AAC8907717 and *RILM*1988-08689-dd.
Lindahl emphasizes the lower voices of the brass quintet in his
study of these six contemporary works: *Music for Brass Quintet*
by Gunther Schuller, *Quintet for Brass Instruments* by Alvin
Etler, *Laudes* by Jan Bach, *Triptych* by Charles Whittenberg,
Brass Quintet by Elliott Carter, and *Morning Music* by David
Sampson. Marta Hofacre, 462, discusses the works by Schuller,
Etler, and Jan Bach. See also Michael Green, 649, and Robert
Posten, 726.
ArizonaStateU/Bach,J./BassTrb/BrassQuintet/Carter,E./ChamMus-
Trb/Diss/Etler,A./Green,M./Hofacre,M./Posten,R./Sampson,D./
Schuller,G./TrbMus-20thC/Tuba/Whittenberg,C.

697. LINDSAY, Robert. "Professional music in the 1920s and the rise
of the singing trombone." New York University, unpublished
independent research, 1986.

See also an interview with Trummy Young by Lindsay, 327.
Jazz-Blues/NewYorkU/Research/TrbMus-20thC

698. LÜCK, Rudolf. "Von der Tuba mirum zur verfremdeten Posaune: Ein Werkstattgesprach mit Vinko Globokar [From the tuba mirum to an unusual trombone: Studio conversation with Vinko Globokar]." *Neue Zeitschrift für Musik* 131, no. 9 (September 1970): 439-44.

Lück's article is a prepublication excerpt in German from his book, *Werkstattgesprache mit Interpreten Neuer Musik* [Studio conversations with performers of new music], which is located in *RILM*71/1138ap29. See John J. Bingham, 601, for more references to Globokar.
Avant-Garde/Bingham,J./Globokar,V./Improvisation/Instruments-20thC/Solos/TrbMus-20thC

699. MADEROSIAN, Ardash. "Precarious assignment in Warsaw (trombonist coaches Polish brass section)." *Musical America* 111 (July 1991): 34-36.

At the time of this article Maderosian was principal trombone with the Chicago Lyric Opera and had taught at the Chicago Musical College of Roosevelt University for eighteen years. See Juliusz Pietrachowicz, 1206.
Orchestra/Pedagogy/Pietrachowicz,J./Poland/Warsaw

700. MAGLIOCCO, Hugo. "The Renaissance trombone." *Brass and Percussion* 1, no. 3 (1973): 6-7.

See Arnold Fromme, 640. For more references on the Renaissance see Francis W. Galpin, 846.
Galpin,F./Instruments-Renaissance/Sackbut/TrbMus-16thC/TrbMus-17thC

701. MAHRENHOLZ, C. "Über Posaunenmusik [On trombone music]." *Musik und Kirche* 1 (1929): 132-137, 163-173, 261-267.

Mahrenholz's article is in German and is cited by Mary Rasmussen on page 163 of her "Brass bibliography: 1926-1930," *Brass Quarterly* 2, no. 4 (June 1959): 158-166, as containing "a good general discussion of the subject at hand." It apparently deals primarily with the music of the *Posaunenchöre* (brass

ensembles used in German church services). It is also cited in
BRASSBIB. See also "Posaunenmusik," 535.
Germany/Posaunenchor/Posaunenmusik/Rasmussen,M./Sacred

702. MALTERER, Edward L. "The employment of ornamentation in
present day trombone performance of transcriptions of Baroque
literature." Ball State University, DA, 1979.
Using the Galliard sonatas for bassoon and cello, the Marcello
sonatas, and some sonatas by Vivaldi, Malterer deals with the
ornamentation practices of Italy and France in the eighteenth
century and how they may best be executed on the trombone
when performing transcriptions of music from this period. See
Dissertation Abstracts 41/07-A, AAD81-02474 and *RILM*80/
5570dd52.
BallStateU/Baroque/Diss/France/Galliard,J./Italy/Marcello,B./
Ornamentation/Pedagogy/Solos/Transcriptions/TrbMus-18thC/
Vivaldi,A.

703. "Marschmusik und Posaunenregister [March music and the
trombone register]. *Schweizerische Instrumentalmusik* (1937):
561-563.
This article is in German and is cited on p. 77 of Mary
Rasmussen's "Brass bibliography: 1936-1940," *Brass Quarterly*
2, no. 2 (December 1958): 63-77. It is also cited in *BRASSBIB*.
Bands/Rasmussen,M./Switzerland

704. MASSON, Gabriel. "Historique du trombone." *Musique et Radio*
52, no. 619 (November 1962): 41.
Masson was one of the most well-known trombone performers
and teachers in France around the middle of the twentieth
century. His article is in French. See Masson, 902, and his earlier
article, "Le trombone," *Musique et Radio* 46 (1956): 467+, 471,
where the text is in both English and French.
France/Instruments/Pedagogy

705. MATER, Friedrich. "Die Behandlung der Posaune im
Symphonie- und Opernorchester [The handling of the trombone
in symphonic and opera orchestras]." *Deutsche Militär-Musiker-
Zeitung* 63 (1941): 51.

Mater's article is in German and is cited on p. 236 of Mary Rasmussen's "Brass bibliography: 1941-45," *Brass Quarterly* 1, no. 4 (June 1958): 232-239. It is also cited in *BRASSBIB*. See "Die Posaune und einer ihrer Pioniere [The trombone and one of its pioneers]," 105.
Germany/Opera/Orchestra/Rasmussen,M.

706. MAURER, Joseph A. "The Moravian trombone choir." *Historical Review of Berks County* 20 (October-December 1954): 2-8.
For more references on Moravian trombone music see Wesley Branstine, 606.
Bib/Branstine,W./Moravian/Sacred/TrbChoir/TrbMus-18thC

707. MCCLELLAN, Lawrence, Jr. "Pro session: Curtis Fuller's solo on 'Blues after all'—a trombone transcription." *Down Beat* 56 (July 1989): 56.
At the time of this article, Lawrence McClellan, Jr., was chair of the Professional Education Division at the Berklee College of Music. In his succinct analysis of Fuller's solo, McClellan characterizes Fuller's style as a model of "down home" blues. The cut was taken from Jimmy Smith's *Houseparty* album.
Fuller,C./Jazz-Blues/Smith,J.

708. MCCREADY, Matthew. "Euphonium/trombone doubling among service band euphoniumists and orchestral trombonists in the United States." Indiana University, DM, 1989.
See *Dissertation Abstracts*, publication no. AAC0381041, currently listed as not available. See Edward R. Bahr, 793, Larry D. Campbell, 1032, and Lee A. Drummer, 1059.
Bahr,E./Bands/Campbell,L./Diss/Doubling/Drummer,L./ Euphonium/IndianaU/Military/Orchestra

709. MCKAY, Kelly Collier. "The trombone's evolutionary usage and its inclusion into the modern symphony orchestra from 1750 to 1850." Ball State University, MA, 1992.
See John Drew, 625, Andrew R. Glendening, 646, Kenneth M. Hanlon, 656, Terry Pierce, 722, Jay Dee Schaefer, 743, and William Taylor, 767.

Drew,J./Glendening,A./Hanlon,K./Instruments-18thC/Instruments-19thC/Orchestra/Pierce,T./Schaefer,J./Taylor,W./TrbMus-18thC/TrbMus-19thC

710. MCRAE, Richard. "Up from the tailgate: Comparing the jazz styles of Charlie Green, Jimmie Harrison, and Benny Morton." *JITA* 23, no. 2 (Spring 1995): 20-23.

McRae includes transcriptions of sample trombone solos from three jazz artists, all of whom were members of the Fletcher Henderson Orchestra: Charlie Green (1925), "Shanghai Shuffle"; Jimmie Harrison (1928), "Oh Baby"; and Benny Morton (1931), "Clarinet Marmalade." Unfortunately, the citation numbers for McRae's endnotes were not printed in the article. For more information on Benny Morton, see Les Tomkins, 357.

Green,C./Harrison,J./Henderson,F./Jazz-Blues/Morton,B./Swing/Tomkins,L.

711. MEINERZHAGEN, Fritz. "Das Posaunenregister im Orchester [The trombone register in the orchestra]." *Deutsche Militär-Musiker Zeitung* 27 (1905): 105-106, 120-121.

Meinerzhagen's article is in German and is cited in Mary Rasmussen's "Brass Bibliography: 1900-1905," *Brass Quarterly* 4, no. 3 (Spring 1961): 129-132. It is also cited in *BRASSBIB*.

Germany/Orchestra/Rasmussen,M.

712. MILLER, Frederick S. "A comprehensive performance project in trombone literature with an essay on the use of trombone in the music of Heinrich Schütz." University of Iowa, DMA, 1974.

See *Dissertation Abstracts* 35/07-A, p. 4595, AAD75-01287. See also Werner Breig, 408, Klaus Hoffman, 674, and Richard R. Ross, 738.

Baroque/Breig,W./ChamMus-Trb/Diss/Hoffman,K./IowaU/Ross,R./Sacred/Schütz,H./TrbMus-17thC/Vocal

713. MONTGOMERY, James. "The use of the trombone by G.F. Handel." *JITA* 13, no. 3 (July 1985): 32-34.

See W.F.H. Blandford, 603.

Baroque/Bib/Blandford,W./Choral/Handel,G.F./Oratorio/TrbMus-18thC

714. MYERS, Richmond E. "Two centuries of trombones." *Etude* 73 (April 1955): 12+.
    Myers discusses the Moravian tradition of trombone choirs at Bethlehem PA. For more references on Moravian trombone music, see above Wesley Branstine, 606.
    Bethlehem/Branstine,W./Moravian/OldMill/Sacred/TrbChoir/ TrbMus-19thC

715. NASH, Dick. "Self-expression in ballad playing." *JITA* 13, no. 4 (October 1985): 38-39.
    Nash, one of Henry Mancini's favorite studio lead trombonists, writes a perceptive history and analysis of the ballad style on the trombone, from the viewpoint of one of the most successful practitioners of the art. Nash has credited Murray McEachern as being indirectly responsible for the development of his ballad sound and style. See also Helen McNamara, 329, Dennis R. Herrick, 665, Addison C. Himes, Jr., 672, Jay Friedman, 1094, James W. Schrodt, 1244, and D.H. Wittekind, 1301.
    Ballad/Dorsey,T./Friedman,J./Green,U./Harris,B./Herrick,D./ Himes,A./Howard,J./Johnson,J.J./Legato/Loper,C./Lusher,D./ McEachern,M./McNamara,H./Noel,D./Pedagogy/Rosolino,F./ Schrodt,J./Ulyate,L./Vibrato/Watrous,B./Welsch,C./Wittekind,D.

716. NASH, Harold. "Trombones on trial." *Sounding Brass and the Conductor* 1 (April 1972): 21-22.
    See also Nash, 916. See also Simon Hogg, "Harold Nash: A half century with the trombone on the British scene, "*BBIBC* 98, no. 2 (1977): 70+.
    England/Hogg,S./TrbMus-Gen

717. NICHOLAS, Martha R. "Establishing and expanding an early music consort." *Instrumentalist* 32 (March 1978): 36-39.
    Nicholas discusses early consorts made up of cornettos and sackbuts. See Robert Gifford, 645, Keith Polk, 725, and Edmund A. Bowles, 802.
    Bowles,E./ChamMus-Trb/Cornetto/Gifford,R./Medieval/Polk,K./ Renaissance/Sackbut/TrbMus-15thC/TrbMus-16thC

718. NICHOLSON, Joseph M. "Performance considerations of early music
      for the trombone with other instruments." *JITA* 4 (1976): 20-21.
      See Martha Nicholas, 717, for other references to early
      consorts. See also Arnold Fromme, 640.
      Baroque/Fromme,A./Instruments-15thC/Instruments-16thC/
      Nicholas,M./TrbMus-15thC/TrbMus-16thC/TrbMus-17thC

719. "Notice sur l'introduction des cors, des clarinettes et des
      trombones dans les orchestres français, extraite des manuscrits
      autographes de Gossec [Instructions on the introduction of horns,
      clarinets, and trombones in the French orchestra, as taken from
      the autograph manuscripts of Gossec (François Joseph, 1734-
      1829)]." *Revue musicale* 5 (1829): 217-223.
      This article is in French and was listed by Mary Rasmussen on
      p. 195 of her "Brass bibliography: 1820-1829," *Brass Quarterly*
      7, no. 4 (Summer 1964): 194-197. Though no author is given, the
      article appeared in François Fétis's *Revue musicale*. It is also
      cited in *BRASSBIB*. See William A. Taylor, 767.
      See also Georges Curcel, *Études sur un orchestre au XVIIIe
      siècle: L'instrumentation chez les symphonistes de la Pouplinière:
      Oeuvres musicales de Gossec, Schenker, et Gaspard Procksch*
      [Studies on an eighteenth-century orchestra: Instrumentation
      among the symphonists of the Pouplinière: Musical works of
      Gossec, Schenker, and Gaspard Procksch], Paris: Fischbacher, 1913.
      Curcel,G./Fétis,F./France/Gossec,F.J./Orchestra/Rasmussen,M./
      Taylor,W./TrbMus-18thC/TrbMus-19thC

720. PARADIS-HAGAR, Jennifer. "Talkin' with the master plunger:
      The Art Baron interview." *New York Brass Conference for
      Scholarships* (1991): 50-56.
      Art Baron is one of the specialists in the use of the plunger for
      jazz trombone solos. He is well-known for his years with the
      Duke Ellington orchestra. An experimentalist, Baron and his
      colleagues used composer Harry Partch's musical instruments on
      one of their recent recordings of compositions by Charles
      Mingus, produced by Hal Willner. The sessions were taped by
      PBS for a documentary. Paradis-Hagar's article is actually an
      amalgamation of several interviews which began in 1990. See
      Bob Bernotas, 260, [Ben Ivey], 316, and Gerry Sloan, 751.

Baron,A./Bernotas,B./Bio/Ellington,D./Grey,A./Ivey,B./
Jackson,Q./Jazz-Blues/Mingus,C./Mutes/Partch,H./PBS/Plunger/
Sloan,G./Willner,H.

721. PEEBLES, Will. "Johann Anton Wenzel Stamitz: Father of the tacet trombone." *JITA* 18, no. 3 (Summer 1990): 44-45.

Peebles gives a somewhat tongue-in-cheek analysis of the predominantly silent trombone sections in eighteenth-century orchestras. Unfortunately two footnotes did not get printed (probably a subliminal allusion to the tacet trombones in the works of Stamitz). See also Kenneth Hanlon, 656, and William A. Taylor, 767.

Hanlon,K./Orchestra/Stamitz,J./Tacet/Taylor,W.

722. PIERCE, Terry. "The trombone in the eighteenth century." *JITA* 8 (1980): 6-10.

Pierce discusses the use of trombones in various settings, as well as construction and conceptual use of the instruments during the eighteenth century. See also his article, "Monteverdi's use of brass instruments," *JITA* 9 (1981): 4-8. See John Marcellus, 504, for more references on eighteenth-century trombone music and performance practices.

Bib/ChamMus-Trb/Christian,L./Gschlatt[Gschladt],T./
Instruments-18thC/Marcellus,J./Monteverdi,C./Opera/TrbMus-
18thC/Wagenseil,G.

723. PIEREN, J. "Die Kirchenposauner im alten Adelboden [Church trombones in old Adelboden]." *Musik und Gottesdienst* 49, no. 4 (1995): 190+.

Pieren's article is in German and may deal with the Posaunenchöre, brass or wind ensembles. In the annotation of Wilhelm Ehmann, 629, there is a discussion of a Posaunenchor.

Adelboden/Germany/Sacred

724. PLASS, Ludwig. "Was die Geschichte der Posaunen lehrt: Studie über die ehemalige und gegenwartige Turmmusik [What the history of the trombones [and trumpets?] show: Studies on early and present-day tower music]." *Allgemeine Musikalische Zeitung* (Berlin) 40 (1913): 445-447, 477-479.

Plass's article is in German. For further information on specific music see D.G. Miller, 513.
Germany/Instruments/Miller,D./Störl,J./TowerMusic

725. POLK, Keith. "Instrumental music in the urban centres of Renaissance Germany," *Early Music History* 7 (1987): 159-185. Polk has written several related articles including "Wind bands of medieval Flemish cities." *Brass and Woodwind Quarterly* 1, nos. 3-4 (Spring-Winter 1968): 93-113, and its continuation, "Municipal wind music in Flanders in the late middle ages," *Brass and Woodwind Quarterly* 2, nos. 1-2 (Spring-Summer 1969): 1-15. See Polk, 930-931, Robert Gifford, 645, Hugo Magliocco, 700, Martha R. Nicholas, 717, and Edmund Bowles, 802.
Bowles,E./Flanders/Gifford,R./Magliocco,H./Medieval/Nicholas,M./ Sackbut/SlideTrumpet/WindBands

726. POSTEN, Robert. "A view from below." *JITA* 5 (1977): 43-44. Posten discusses the perceived benefits of utilizing a bass trombone instead of a tuba in a brass quintet. He was a member of the Annapolis Brass Quintet at the time of the publication of the article. See also Michael Green, 649, and Robert G. Lindahl, 696.
AnnapolisBrassQuintet/BassTrb/Bib/BrassQuintet/ChamMus-Trb/ Green,M./Lindahl,R./TrbMus-20thC/Tuba

727. PRYOR, Stephen. "Bass trombone jazz styles." *Instrumentalist* 31, no. 11 (1977): 63-65. Pryor explores four different jazz styles—dixieland, swing, bop, and progressive jazz-rock—from the perspective of the bass trombonist.
BassTrb/Bebop/Dixieland/Jazz-Blues/Jazz-Rock/Swing

728. QUICK, Jeffrey. "Which pitch?" *JITA* 14, no. 1 (Winter 1986): 10-11. David Fetter, 132, includes comparison tables for slide positions from Carse, Bate, Hüber, Sachs, and Speer, and a table of several Baroque trombone parts. For more references see Arnold Fromme, 640.
Baroque/Bib/Fromme,A./Instruments-16thC/Instruments-17thC/ Instruments-18thC/Intonation/Pitch/Speer,D.

729. RAUM, Richard. "The eighteenth-century musician in a changing society." *BBIBC* 95 (1996): 42-59.

In a presentation given at the 1996 International Trombone Federation in Vienna, Raum deals with the Christian family, who supplied several trombonists for the Viennese court. See Raum, 196, 537, and 729-731. For more references on eighteenth-century trombone music and performance practices, see John Marcellus, 504.

Albrechtsberger,J./AltoTrb/ChamMus-Trb/Christian,C./ Christian,H./Christian,L.,Sr./Christian,L.,Jr./Christian,L.F./ Concertos/Gschlatt[Gschladt],T./Haydn,M./Mozart,L./Marcellus,J./ Salzburg/Solos/TrbMus-18thC/Vienna/Wagenseil,G.

730. ———. "The eighteenth-century trombone: Rumors of its death were premature." 2 parts. *BBIBC* 77 (1992): 87+, and 78 (1993): 93-97.

Raum's article is in English, French, and German. See Raum, 729, for more references.

TrbMus-18thC

731. ———. "From the diary of a court trombonist, 1727." *BBIBC* 82 (1993): 56-59.

Raum has written an excerpt from an imaginary diary by Viennese court trombonist Leopold Christian, Sr. See Raum, 729, for further references on performance practices during the eighteenth century.

Christian,L.,Sr./TrbMus-18thC/Vienna

732. REICHEL, William Cornelius. *Something about Trombones and the Old Mill at Bethlehem.* Ed. J.W. Jordan. Bethlehem PA: Moravian Publications Office, 1884.

Reichel's volume contains the memoirs of three members of the "Old Trombone Choir," J. Weiss, C.F. Beckel, and J.C. Till. See Wesley Branstine, 606, for more references on Moravian trombone music.

Bethlehem/Branstine,W./Moravian/OldMill/Sacred/TrbChoir/ TrbMus-19thC

733. REYNOLDS, Harold A. "Performance problems in the *Concerto for Trombone and Orchestra* by Carlos Chávez." University of Rochester, Eastman School of Music, DMA, 1989.

Reynolds has included suggested studies to prepare for performing the concerto, a selected list of published trombone concertos, reviews of performances of the Chávez Concerto, correspondence between Chávez and William Cramer, interviews with Per Brevig (who premiered the work), and a cassette recording of the author's performance with the Greensboro Symphony in 1981. See *Dissertation Abstracts* 8909271 and *RILM*1989-08880-dd.

Brevig,P./Chávez,C./Concertos/Cramer,W./Diss/Eastman/Greensboro/Pedagogy/TrbMus-20thC

734. REYNOLDS, Jeff. "The Moravian Trombone Choir." *NITA* 8, no. 1 (September 1980): 24-25.

Reynolds gives a history of the performance traditions and suggestions for instrumentation of a trombone choir in the Moravian church. A select, annotated bibliography of Moravian trombone choir music appears in the *Newsletter* 8, no. 2 (December 1980): 24-26. See Wesley Branstine, 606, for other references to Moravian trombone music. See also articles by Mathis Chazanov in the *Los Angeles Times*, December 24, 1987, section II, p. 3, col. 1, and John Henken, *Los Angeles Times*, April 3, 1985, section VI, p. 3, col. 1, about performances of a Moravian trombone choir in Downey CA.

Branstine,W./Chazanov,M./DowneyCA/Henken,J./Instruments-18thC/Instruments-19thC/*LosAngelesTimes*/Moravian/Sacred/TrbChoir/Vocal

735. ———. "The trombone in Moravian life." *Moravian Music Journal* 32, no. 1 (1987): 7-11.

See Wesley R. Branstine, 606, for more references to Moravian trombone music.

Bib/Branstine,W./Moravian/Trbchoir

736. REYNOLDS, Sam. "Synthesis." *JITA* 15, no. 3 (Summer 1987): 40-43.

In the author's words, "This is the first of a number of articles dealing with computers and electronic music in relation to trombone playing and teaching."
Avant-Garde/Computers/ElectronicMusic/Pedagogy/Synthesis

737. RICHARDSON, William W. "Lecture-Recital: New directions in trombone literature and the techniques needed for its performance." Catholic University, PhD, 1970.
See *Dissertation Abstracts*, publication no. AAC0265317 [listed as not available]. See David Loucky, 497, Per Brevig, 607, Klaus-K. Hübler, 677, and Milton Stevens, 759.
Avant-Garde/Brevig,P./CatholicU/Hübler,K./Lecture-Recital/Loucky,D./Pedagogy/Solos/Stevens,M./TrbMus-20thC

738. ROSS, Richard R. "The use of the trombone in the *Symphoniae Sacre I* of Heinrich Schütz." Catholic University, DMA, 1977.
See *Dissertation Abstracts*, publication no. AAC0323801 [listed as not available]. See Werner Breig, 408, Klaus Hoffman, 674, and Frederick S. Miller, 712.
Baroque/Breig,W./CatholicU/ChamMus-Trb/Diss/Hoffman,K./Miller,F./Sacred/Schütz,H./Vocal

739. RUH [no first name given]. "Über die Verwendung der Posaunen [About the use of the trombone]." *Evangelische Musikzeitung* 21 (191?): 3.
This article is in German and is listed by Mary Rasmussen on p. 170 of her "Brass bibliography: 1911-1915," *Brass Quarterly* 3, no. 4 (Summer 1960): 166-170, as having been "extracted from the periodical bibliographies which appeared in *Zeitschrift für Musikwissenschaft* from 1918 through 1933." It is also cited in *BRASSBIB*. It probably deals primarily with performance practices for the *Posaunenchöre* (brass ensembles used frequently in German church services). For a discussion of the Posaunenchor, see Wilhelm Ehmann, 629.
Posaunenchor/Rasmussen,M./Religious/Worship

740. SAGER, D. "Of ear, heart and arm: A tale of the slide trombone in early jazz." *The Second Line* 37 (Winter 1985): 36-43.
Jazz-Blues

741. SAMBALL, Michael Loran. "The influence of jazz on French solo trombone repertory." University of North Texas, DMA, 1987.
    See *Dissertation Abstracts* 48/03-A, p. 509, publication no. AAD87-13977. See Nathaniel O. Brickens, 409, and Harold McKinney, 511.
    Brickens,N./Diss/France/Jazz-Blues/McKinney,H./NorthTexasU/ Solos/TrbMus-20thC

742. SANGER, Robert. "The evolution and growth of the trombone and its influence on musical composition and performance." Northwestern University, MM, 1953.
    Sanger's thesis was cited by Mary Rasmussen on p. 99 of her "Brass bibliography: 1951-1955," *Brass Quarterly* 1, no. 2 (December 1957): 93-109.
    Instruments/NorthwesternU/Rasmussen,M./Theses/TrbMus-Gen

743. SCHAEFER, Jay Dee. "The use of the trombone in the eighteenth century." 3 parts. *Instrumentalist* 22 (April 1968): 51-53; (May 1968): 100-102; and (June 1968): 61-63.
    For more references on eighteenth-century trombone music and performance practices, see John Marcellus, 504.
    AltoTrb/Christian,L.,Sr./Gschlatt[Gschladt],T./TrbMus-18thC

744. SCHLEMM, Horst Dietrich, ed. *Posaunen in der Bibel und bei uns vor 1843* [Trombones (or large trumpets) in the Bible and among us before 1843]. Gütersloh, Germany: Gütersloher Verlagshaus Gerd Mohn, 1989.
    Part of a series called Beiträge zur Geschichte evangelischer Posaunenarbeit, edited by Eduard Lohse and others, its contents include articles on trombones and *Posaunenchöre*, brass groups which have been popular in German churches for hundreds of years (see Wilhelm Ehmann, 629). The use of trombones in worship by the Moravian people is also explored (see Wesley Branstine, 606). This collection of articles was cited in *LASOCKI*.
    Bible/Branstine,W./Ehmann,W./Germany/Lohse,E./Moravian/ Posaunenchor/Sacred/TrbChoir/TrbMus-18thC/TrbMus-19thC/ TrbMus-20thC

745. SCHROCK, Bradley Alan. *Physical and Technical Demands upon the Trombonist in Performance Caused by Changing between the Three Types of Trombones Commonly Used Today, the Bass Trombone, Tenor Trombone, and Alto Trombone.* N.p., 1981.
    Schrock's book is cited in the OCLC World Catalog online. No publisher is given, but the book is accompanied by a sound cassette or tape reel.
    AltoTrb/BassTrb/Doubling/Pedagogy

746. SHAWGER, J.D. "The uses of the trombone in the modern symphony orchestra." University of Washington, MM, 1958.
    See Carl J. Christensen, 418, John Drew, 625, Jay Hildebrandt, 667, and Hope Stoddard, 761.
    Christensen,C./Drew,J./Hildebrandt,J./Orchestra/Theses/WashingtonU

747. SHIFRIN, Ken. "Trombone myth busters, no. 1: Dvořák wrote for alto trombone." *JITA* 25, no. 2 (Spring 1997): 30-31.
    Shifrin discusses his belief that Dvořák's intention was that tenor and bass valve trombones perform the trombone parts in his orchestral works. The article also includes a discussion of the technical problems in Václav Smita's *Concertino in E-flat Major for Trombone and Orchestra*, which was required as a test piece in the recent Prague International Trombone Competition.
    Shifrin's "Trombone myth busters, no. 2: Rossini wrote the *William Tell Overture* for valve trombones—NOT!!!," *JITA* 25, no. 4 (Fall 1997): 44-47, takes issue with the thesis of Philip Bate and other scholars that Rossini originally intended the technically challenging sections of his famous overtures to be performed on valved instruments.
    AltoTrb/Bate,P./Czechoslovakia/Dvořák,A./Hejda,M./Instruments-19thC/PragueCompetition/Rossini,G./Smita,V./ValveTrb

748. SLOAN, Gerry. "Another look at Jiggs." *JITA* 11, no. 2 (April 1983): 38-39.
    Sloan reviews Jiggs Whigham's first jazz master class at the International Trombone Workshop. The article includes a transcription of a solo from his album, *Jiggs Whigham—Hope* called "Absolutely Knot." Also included is a brief discography of

Whigham's jazz performances (up to 1983). See Edward J.
Ulman, 362, and Joe Weisel, 374. See also Carl Lenthe and Jiggs
Whigham, "The differences are actually similarities," *JITA* 26,
no. 1 (Winter 1998): 50-54.
Bio/Discog/ITA/Jazz-Blues/Lenthe,C./Ulman,E./Weisel,J./
Whigham,J./Workshops

749. ———. "J.J. now and then." *JITA* 16, no. 4 (Fall 1988): 14-15.
Some of J.J. Johnson's classic jazz bebop stylings and those
performers who preceded him in the genre are discussed.
Included are transcriptions of solos from "Naked as a Jaybird,"
and "Little Benny." For more references on J.J. Johnson, see
Louis George Bourgois, 267.
Bourgois,G./Jazz-Blues/Johnson,J.J.

750. ———. "Something old, something new." *NITA* 4, no. 2
(February 1977): 12-13.
In what became an ongoing column in the *Newsletter*, Sloan
discusses transcriptions and analyses of recorded solos,
contrasting jazz styles from many famous jazz trombonists. His
first article includes Vic Dickenson (characterized by Benny
Morton as "the Will Rogers of the trombone) on "Jingle Bells,"
originally recorded in 1946 on Signature (1004) and reissued on
Flying Dutchman (later *re*-reissued on Bob Thiele BBM 1-0940,
Pre-Bop). Also included is a performance by Urbie Green on
"Slidework in A-flat," from *The Urbie Green Sextet*, Command
RS 857 SD. Sloan points out that those these two jazz greats
were very different in their styles, a comparison could "prove to
be enlightening as well as entertaining."
Later articles included 5, no. 1 (September 1977): 28-30,
featuring Benny Morton, "Out the Window," 1937, reissued on
The Best of Count Basie, Decca DXSB 7170, and Kai Winding,
"Danish Blue," 1976, from the album of the same name,
Glendale GLS 6003.
5, no. 2 (December 1977): 6-7, features Dicky (Dickie) Wells,
"Hollywood Hop," 1954 on the Tops label, and Jimmy Knepper,
"Kansas City Style," (see tribute by Whitney Balliet in *The New
Yorker* 67, no. 13 [May 1991]: 52).

Vol. 5, no. 3 (April 1978): 6-8, features Joe Yukl, "Sugar," (1944), Jump 7 (78 rpm), and Matthew Gee. [See the *Newsletter*, 7, no. 1 (December 1979): 2 for a short obituary of Matthew Gee (d. 1979)]. Also included is "Wow," Prestige P-24058. Vol. 6, no. 3, (April 1979): 24-26, features George Chisolm, "In a Mellotone," Rediffusion Stereo 1500001, and Torolf Mølaard, "Night in Tunisia," Artist LP 508. Vol. 7, no. 1 (December 1979): 3-6, features Jack Teagarden, "Pennies from Heaven," RCA Victor LPM 1443, and Carl Fontana, "Strike Up the Band," Bethlehem BCP-48. Balliet,W./Chisolm,G./Dickenson,V./Discog/Fontana,C./Gee,M./ Green,U./Jazz-Blues/Knepper,J./Mølaard,T./Morton,B./Teagarden,J./ Winding,K./Yukl,J.

751. ———. "The talking trombone in jazz." *JITA* 6 (1978): 12-15.

Sloan gives short sketches of outstanding jazz artists, including trombonists, who used verbal and plunger techniques and even more esoteric mutes in their jazz solos. See Bob Bernotas, 260, [Ben Ivey], 316, and Jennifer Paradis-Hagar, 720.

Sloan mentions the "infamous trombonist" who immortalized the *rink*, also called the *doink*, with the Spike Jones Band. Recently deceased West Coast trombonist and composer/arranger Tommy Pederson (see James Boltinghouse, 405) claimed credit for that achievement.

Archey,J./Baron,A./Bernotas,B./Bib/Boltinghouse,J./Burgess,B./ Dempster,S./Dickenson,V./Fulkerson,J./Glenn,T./Globokar,V./ Green,C./Green,J./Green,U./Grey,A./Irvis,C./Ivey,B./Jackson,P./ Jackson,Q./Jazz-Blues/Knepper,J./Lincoln,A./Lofton,T./ Mangelsdorff,A./Mutes/Nanton,T./Nelson,R./Ory,K./Paradis-Hagar,J./Pederson,T./Plunger/Robinson,J./Rodgers,I./Talking Trombone/Walker,J./Wells,D./White,H./Williams,S./Wood,B.

752. SLUCHIN, Benny. "Alto or tenor trombone: Open or closed case?" *HBSJ* 5 (1993): 309-317.

Sluchin debates the issue of whether to perform the first trombone part in the Cherubini *Requiem in D minor* on alto or tenor trombone. He gives a short account of his research but leaves the answer to the question up to the reader.

AltoTrb/Cherubini,L./Choral/TrbMus-18thC/TrbMus-19thC

753.   ———. "Eberlin and his contribution to the soloistic use of the
        trombone." *JITA* 13, no. 4 (October 1985): 36.
            Johann Ernst Eberlin (1702-1762) was a prolific composer
        apparently on friendly terms with Leopold Mozart, who admired
        him and compared his work to that of Scarlatti and Telemann.
        There is some evidence that the younger Mozart studied Eberlin's
        music (see Sluchin, 552). See Kenneth M. Hanlon, 656, Richard
        Raum, 196, 537, 729-731, and C. Robert Wigness, 583.
        AltoTrb/Eberlin,J./Hanlon,K./Raum,R./Salzburg/TrbMus-18thC/
        Wigness,R.

754.   ———. "Le trombone alto dans l'orchestre du Xxe siècle [The
        alto trombone in the twentieth-century orchestra]." *BBIBC* 75
        (1991): 52-57.
            Sluchin's article is in French, German, and English. See also
        Sluchin, 949, and Stephen Anderson, 788.
        AltoTrb/Anderson,S./Orchestra/TrbMus-20thC

755.   ———. "Playing and singing simultaneously on brass
        instruments." *BBIBC* 37 (1982): 20-28.
            See an earlier two-part article by Sluchin on this subject in
        BBIBC 35 (1981): 5-7+ and 36 (1981): 18-23. See also Joachim-
        Ernst Berendt, 600, Michelle Castellengo, 617, Stuart Dempster,
        621, Bruce Fowler, 639, Milton Stevens, 759-760, Paul Warnex,
        775, and R.W. Bowles, 1022. For more information on
        multiphonics in jazz, see George Broussard, 271.
        Avant-Garde/Berendt,J./Bowles,R./Broussard,G./Castellengo,M./
        Dempster,S./Everett,T./Fowler,B./Mangelsdorff,A./Multiphonics/
        Stevens,M./Warnex,P.

756.   SMITH, David B. *Trombone Technique in the Renaissance.* San
        Francisco: David B. Smith, 1989.
            See *Dissertation Abstracts* 42/11-A, AAD82-08865 and
        *RILM*82/1432dd45. Based on Smith's doctoral paper, "Trombone
        technique in the early seventeenth century," Stanford University,
        DMA, 1982, his book gives some guidelines for approaching the
        literature of the period discussed, including a discussion of the
        acoustical properties and weaknesses of the typical instrument of
        the time and suggestions for articulation and ornamentation.

Smith's latest address (1989) is 1720 19th Avenue, San Francisco CA 94122. For more references see Arnold Fromme, 640.
Baroque/Cesare,G./Diss/Instruments-17thC/Ornamentation/ Pedagogy/StanfordU/TrbMus-15thC/TrbMus-16thC/TrbMus-17thC

757. SMITHERS, Don L. "Mozart's orchestral brass." *Early Music* 20, no. 2 (May 1992): 254-265.
Smithers discusses five lip-blown instruments, including trombones, written for by Mozart. See correspondence from Peter Downey in *Early Music* 21, no. 1 (1993): 171-172. See Stan Adams, 387, B. Gugler, 450, Egon Komorzynski, 683, and William A. Taylor, 767. See also Eugen Brixel, "Mozart and Brass Musicians: W.A. Mozart in his personal relations with trumpet players, hornists, and trombonists," *BBIBC* 78 (1991): 18-24 (continued in volume 74 (1991): 44-47).
Adams,S./Brixel,E./Downey,P./Gugler,B./Komorzynski,E./ Mozart,W.A./Mutes/Orchestra/Taylor,W./TrbMus-18thC

758. SMITHWICK, Shelley. "The twentieth-century trombone quartet." [Cited in *ROBERTS* as graduate research for the MM at the University of Nevada-Reno].
For more references on the trombone quartet, see Thomas G. Everett, 433.
Bark,J./Everett,T./NevadaU-Reno/Rabe,F./Research/TrbMus-20thC/TrbQuartet

759. STEVENS, Milton L., Jr. "New techniques required to perform recent music for the trombone." Boston University School for the Arts, DMA, 1976.
Compositions considered avant-garde at the time of the dissertation and cited for Stevens's study are included under their individual titles in the index of this book, along with other entries where information on them may be found: *Consecuenza* (1966) by Carlos Alsina, *Changes* (1975) by Larry Austin, *Bolos* (1962) by Jan Bark and Folke Rabe, *Sequenza V* (1966) by Luciano Berio, *Solo for Sliding Trombone* by John Cage, *Music for Trombone and Piano* (1966) by Barney Childs, *Animus I* (1966) by Jacob Druckman, *Music for a Sliding Trombone* (1968) by Rob Du Bois, *Accord* (1966) and *Discours II* (1968) by Vinko

Globokar, *Three Sketches* (1967) by Andrew Imbrie, *Pour Quatre* (1968) by Wlodzimierz Kotonski, *Five Pieces for Trombone and Piano* (1967) by Ernst Krenek, *Cryptical Triptych* (1968) by Walter Ross, *Condensation* (1967) by Milan Stibilj, and *Eonta* (1963-64) by Iannis Xenakis.

Unpublished works (at the time of the completion of the study) include *Dialogues* (1979) by Dennis Good and *One Man* (1969-70) by Ben Johnston. No composition in the study utilizes more than six performers. See *Dissertation Abstracts* 36/09-A, p. 5632, AAD76-06651.

For references on multiphonics see Michelle Castellengo, 617. For more references on multiphonics in jazz, see George Broussard, 271. For references on theater techniques see Howard Buss, 416, Stanley R. Pethel, 532, Stuart Dempster, 621, James D. Kraft, 687, and Peter Vivona, 772.

Alsina,C./Austin,L./Avant-Garde/Bark,J./Berio,L./BostonU/ Broussard,G./Buss,H./Cage,J./Castellengo,M./ChamMus-Trb/ Dempster,S./Diss/Druckman,J./DuBois,R./ElectronicMusic/ Globokar,V./Good,D./Imbrie,A./Johnston,B./Kotonski,W./Kraft,J./ Krenek,E./Multiphonics/Pedagogy/Pethel,S./Rabe,F./Ross,W./ Solos/Stibilj,M./Tape/Theater/TrbMus-20thC/Vivona,P./Xenakis,I.

760.   ———. "Vocalization—an introduction to avant-garde trombone techniques." *Instrumentalist* 23 (February 1974): 44-46.

See Michelle Castellengo, 617, and George Broussard, 271, for more references on multiphonics.

Avant-Garde/Multiphonics/Pedagogy/TrbMus-20thC

761.   STODDARD, Hope. "The trombone in our orchestras." *New York Brass Conference for Scholarships Journal* (1978): 22-24.

Stoddard's article has been reprinted from the November 1949 issue of the *International Musician*. It contains photographs, biographical sketches, and performance styles of some of the most legendary North American orchestral trombone sections, including those in New York, Cleveland, St. Louis, Boston, and Chicago. See also Jay Hildebrandt, 667, and J.D. Shawger, 746.

BassTrb/Bio/Boston/Canada/Chicago/Cleveland/Hildebrandt,J./ NewYork/Orchestra/Shawger,J./StLouis

762. STRUCK-SCHLÖN, Michael. "Zwischen Möbelmusik und Zwölftonkonzert: Die Posaunen im Kammerensemble am Beginn der Neuen Musik (1913-1934) [Between wallpaper-music and twelve-tone music: The trombone in the chamber ensemble at the beginning of the new music (1913-1934)]." 2 parts. *BBIBC* 55 (1986): 6-14, and 56 (1986): 24-32.

   Struck-Schlön's article is in German, French, and English. Among the composers whose music is discussed are Satie, Milhaud, Stravinsky, Hindemith, Janáček, and Webern. See Robert M. Gifford, Jr., 644, Robert E. Gray, 648, and James D. Willis, 780.

   ChamMus-Trb/Gray,R./Hindemith,P./Janáček,L./Milhaud,D./ Satie,E./Stravinsky,I./TrbMus-20thC/Twelve-Tone/Webern,A./Willis,J.

763. STUART, David H. "A comprehensive performance project in trombone literature with an essay consisting of the use of the trombone in selected chamber compositions of Biagio Marini." University of Iowa, DMA, 1981.

   See also Stuart's article based on this dissertation, "The use of trombone in Biagio Marini's opus 1, *Affetti musicali*," *National Association of College Wind and Percussion Instructors Journal* 31, no. 1 (Fall 1982): 17-28. His dissertation is located in *RILM*81/6039dd52 and his article is located in *RILM*82/4586ap25. See also *Dissertation Abstracts* 42/05-A, p. 1847, AAD81-23382. Baroque/ChamMus-Trb/Diss/IowaU/Marini,B./TrbMus-17thC/ TrbMus-18thC

764. SUMERKIN, Viktor. *Trombon.* Moscow: Muzyka, 1975.

   In addition to brief descriptions of the history of the trombone in Europe, Sumerkin's monograph traces current tendencies in playing in the Soviet Union before its dissolution. The monograph, in Russian, is cited in David Stuart, 18. Pedagogy/PerfPrac/Russia/SovietUnion/Stuart,D./TrbMus-Gen

765. TANNER, James C. "Technical and musical uses of the trombone in selected original repertoire for the twentieth-century concert band." Columbia University Teachers College, EdD, 1983.

   Tanner includes a discussion of both the technical and musical uses of the trombone in the modern concert band. Topics

discussed include mutings and nontraditional playing requirements. A history of the trombone as used in the band is also included. See *Dissertation Abstracts* 44/05-A, p. 1239, AAD83-22247. See also Lucien Cailliet, 612.
Bands/Cailliet,L./ColumbiaU/Diss/Pedagogy/TrbMus-20thC

766. TANNER, Paul. "A versatile trombone ensemble." *Music Journal* 17 (April-May 1959): 36+.
    Tanner chronicles some of his experiences with his trombone choir at UCLA. See Carl M. Lobitz, 496, Danny J. Hutson, 678, and Irvin L. Wagner, 774.
    Hutson,D./Lobitz,C./TrbChoir/UCLA/Wagner,I.

767. TAYLOR, William A. "The orchestral treatment of the trombone in the eighteenth and nineteenth centuries." Eastman School of Music, MM, 1951.
    Taylor's thesis is cited by Mary Rasmussen on p. 99 of her "Brass bibliography: 1951-1955," *Brass Quarterly* 1, no. 2 (December 1957): 93-109. See William T. Collins, 421, Jonathan Holbrook, 464, Benny Sluchin and Raymond Lapie, 553, Hugh A. Callison, 613, John Drew, 625, Andrew R. Glendening, 646, Kenneth M. Hanlon, 656, Kelly C. McKay, 709, "Notice sur l'introduction . . . Gossec," 719, Will Peebles, 721, Terry Pierce, 722, Richard Raum, 729-731, and Jay Dee Schaefer, 743. See also Cecil B. Wilson, "Berlioz's use of brass instruments," Case Western Reserve University, PhD, 1971.
    Several entries in this book deal with the alto trombone, the favored solo and orchestral trombone in many areas of Europe during the eighteenth century. See C. Robert Wigness, 583, Stephen Anderson, 788, and Benny Sluchin, 949 for more references.
    Anderson,S./Berlioz,H./Callison,H./Collins,W./Drew,J./Eastman/ Gossec,F./Hanlon,K./Holbrook,J./Lapie,R./McKay,K./Orchestra/ Peebles,W./Pierce,T./Rasmussen,M./Raum,R./Saint-Saëns,C./ Schaefer,J./Sluchin,B./Stamitz,J./Theses/TrbMus-18thC/TrbMus-19thC/Wigness,R./Wilson,C.

768. TIMM, Willy. *Musik in Unna. Studien zu einer Kulturgeschichte der Stadt Unna* [Music in Unna. Studies relating to a cultural

history of the city of Unna]. *Beitrage zur westfalischen Musikgeschichte* 8. Hagen: Westfalisches Musikarchiv, 1971.

Located in *RILM*75/3384bm21, Timm's monograph is in German and discusses several types of town musicians and groups, including trombone choirs, since the thirteenth century.
Germany/Medieval/Posaunenchor/Stadtpfeifer/Unna/Westphalia

769. TUCKER, Wallace E. "The trombone quartet: Its appearance and development throughout history." 2 parts. *JITA* 7 (1979): 2-7, and 8 (1980): 2-5.

Tucker's article includes an appendix of original trombone quartet literature and a bibliography. For more references on the trombone quartet, see Thomas G. Everett, 433.
Bark,J./Bib/Everett,T./Marini,B./Pedagogy/*QuatuorTrombones*/Rabe,F./TrbQuartet

770. UNGER, Hermann. "Die Posaune: Ein Instrument des Überpersönlichen [The trombone: An instrument beyond personality (?)]." *Das neue Blasorchester* 10 (1951): 75.

Unger's article is cited by Mary Rasmussen on p. 99 of her "Brass bibliography: 1951-1955," *Brass Quarterly* 1, no. 2 (December 1957): 93-109.
Instruments/Rasmussen,M.

771. VANCE, John. "Posaune Wörterverzeichnis: A glossary of German terms and phrases found in the trombone parts of Mahler's symphonies." *JITA* 18, no. 2 (Spring 1990): 20-26.

Vance has compiled a helpful glossary which he has translated into idiomatic English. As an interesting aside, Eduard Reeser has written an article in *Nachrichten zur Mahler—Forschung* 20 (March 1993): 9-12, dealing with a previously unpublished sonnet dedicated to Mahler by the French trombonist Ferdinand du Pr. See also Wesley L. Hanson, "The treatment of brass instruments in the symphonies of Gustav Mahler," Eastman School of Music, DMA, 1977.
Hanson,W./Mahler,G./MusicalTerms/Orchestra/Poetry/Pr,F./Reeser,E.

772. VIVONA, Peter M. "Theater techniques in recent music for the trombone." *JITA* 10, no. 2 (1982): 20-25.

Part of a lecture-recital given in support of a DMA at the Eastman School of Music, Vivona's article includes a bibliography of theater techniques [see also p. 3 of the same issue of the *JITA* for a "Statement of correction" dealing with Vivona's article and an earlier one by Howard Buss, 416]. See James D. Kraft, 687, and Milton Stevens, 759, for more references on theater music.
Avant-Garde/Bib/Buss,H./Eastman/Heider,W./Kraft,J./Lecture-Recital/Moss,L./Pedagogy/Stevens,M./Theater/TrbMus-20thC

773. VOCE, Steve. "It don't mean a thing." *Jazz Journal* 28 (April 1975): 20-21.

Voce's ongoing column in this issue discusses the whereabouts of several prominent jazz trombonists of whom he had lost track, in addition to a discussion of some active groups who were led by or featured trombonists. Much of his information was courtesy of a letter from Tom Everett.
Everett,T./Jazz-Blues

774. WAGNER, Irvin L. "The organization and operation of the trombone choir." *JITA* 2 (1973-74): 63-67.

Wagner includes a short list of works performed by the University of Oklahoma Trombone Choir. See Carl M. Lobitz, 496, Danny J. Hutson, 678, and Paul Tanner, 766.
Bib/Hutson,D./Lobitz,C./OklahomaU/Tanner,P./TrbChoir

775. WARNEX, Paul D. "A comprehensive study of the technique of singing and playing simultaneously on the trombone." Central Missouri State University, MM, 1980.

See Michelle Castellengo, 617, for more references to multiphonics on trombone. See also George Broussard, 271, for references to multiphonics in a jazz idiom.
Avant-Garde/Broussard,G./Castellengo,M./CentralMissouriU/
Multiphonics/Pedagogy/Theses

776. WEINER, Howard. "The trombone: Changing times, changing slide positions." *BBIBC* 36 (1981): 52-63.

Weiner's article is in English, German and French.
Pedagogy/Slide

777. WESSELY, Othmar. "Obersterreichische Totenlieder aus dem Umkreis des Jungen Bruckner [Upper Austrian funerary music in the milieu of the young Bruckner]." In *Bruckner Symposium* (Linz: Anton Bruckner Institut, 1988): 73-83.
    See *RILM*1988-11766-as. Wessely includes Bruckner's two equales for trombone ensemble (WAB 114, 119). His article is in German. See Wessely, 581, and Andre Fiedler, 442, for a discussion of Beethoven's *Equale*.
    Austria/Beethoven,L./Bruckner,A./Equale/Sacred/TrbChoir/TrbMus-19thC

778. WESTRUP, J.A. "The misuse of the trombone." *Musical Times* 66 (1925): 524-525.
    TrbMus-Gen

779. WICK, Denis. "Personal viewpoint." *JITA* 2 (1973-74): 48-50.
    The former principal trombonist of the London Philharmonic gives his view of trombone performance opportunities in Britain in the early 1970s.
    Britain/Pedagogy

780. WILLIS, James D. "A study of Paul Hindemith's use of the trombone as seen in selected chamber compositions." University of Missouri-Kansas City, DMA, 1973.
    See *Dissertation Abstracts* 34/05-A, p. 2689, AAD-73-25951 and *RILM*74/1066dd45. See also Robert E. Gifford, 644, Robert E. Gray, 648, and Michael Struck-Schlön, 762.
    ChamMus-Trb/Diss/Gray,R./Hindemith,P./MissouriU-Kansas City/Struck-Schlön,M./TrbMus-20thC

781. WILSON, Phil. "Three great jazz trombone stylists." *Instrumentalist* 28, no. 7 (February 1974): 50-51.
    Wilson gives a stylistic analysis of Jack Teagarden, Vic Dickenson and Carl Fontana, all of whom have made major contributions "to the art and content of playing jazz trombone." See Rex Allen, 250, for references to Teagarden, Stanley Dance,

287, for references to Dickenson, and Jerry Atkins, 251, for references to Carl Fontana.
Allen,R./Atkins,J./Bio/Dance,S./Dickenson,V./Fontana,C./Jazz-Blues/Teagarden,J.

782. WINKLER, Klaus. "Die Posaune und ihr Repertoire: Wechselbeziehungen zwischen Musik und Umwelt vom 15. Jahrhundert bis zum 18. Jahrhundert [The trombone and its repertoire: Interconnections between music and milieu from the fifteenth century to the eighteenth century]." In *Musikgeographie: Weltliche und geistliche Bläsermusik in ihren Beziehungen zueinander und zu ihrer Umwelt.* Vol. 1 (Bochum: Brockmeyer, 1990): 17-55.
See *RILM*1991-08717-as. See Winkler's dissertation, 590.
ChamMus-Trb/Iconography/Instruments/TrbMus-16thC/TrbMus-17thC/TrbMus-18thC

783. YEAGER, William R. "A stylistic survey on the use of the trombone in jazz improvisation." University of North Texas, MM, 1976.
Yeager's thesis is cited in *KOHLENBERG II.* See also Bruce E. Melville, 512, Buddy Baker, 1007, Rob Boone, 1019, Samuel T. Daley, 1048, Henry Fillmore, 1081, Fortunato Sordillo, 1260, Les Tomkins [Kai Winding], 1278, and Edward Ulman, 1281.
Baker,B./Boone,R./Daley,S./Fillmore,H./Improvisation/Jazz-Blues/Melville,B./NorthTexasU/Rosolino,F./Sordillo,F./Theses/Tomkins,L./Ulman,E./Winding,K.

784. YEO, Douglas. "Me, myself, and I: Are orchestral brass players losing the concept of being team players?" *JITA* 25, no. 1 (Winter 1997): 21-23.
The bass trombonist of the Boston Symphony Orchestra questions the current trend toward larger instruments, larger mouthpieces, and larger egos among orchestral players.
Orchestra

785. ZWERIN, M. "Ca bouge dans la coulisse [There's movement (or stirring) in the slides]." *Jazz Magazine* 277 (July-August 1979): 46-47.
Zwerin's article is in French.
France/Jazz-Blues

6

INSTRUMENTS AND EQUIPMENT

786. AKSDAL, Bjorn. *Med piber og basuner, skalmeye og fiol* [With pipes and trombones, shawm and viol]. Trondheim: Tapir, University of Trondheim, 1982.

Aksdal's book is located in *RILM*82/3349 and is in Norwegian and English. Reviewer Jeremy Montagu in *Early Music* 11, no. 2 (April 1983): 241-243, has pointed out that its principal value is that it contains an appendix which is a summary checklist of important instruments in all Scandinavia plus a few other museums. See also reviews by Pandora Hopkins in the *Yearbook for Traditional Music* 15 (1983): 178-179; John G. Johnstone, *American Musical Instrumental Society Journal* 9 (1983): 124-125; and Anthony Baines, *Galpin Society Journal* 36 (March 1983): 135.
Baines,A./Hopkins,P./Johnstone,J./Montagu,J./Museums/Norway/
Reviews/Scandinavia

787. ALEXANDER, Ashley H. "A short history of the trombone with emphasis on construction innovations and performance modifications from 1945-70." University of North Texas, MM, 1971.

Alexander was a tragically short-lived jazz artist (1935-88), and ardent advocate of the Superbone, which he helped design. See his article, "The double trombone," *Instrumentalist* 35 (February 1981): 25-27. See also "Leblanc to offer . . . trombone," 886. For a list of obituaries see [Douglas Yeo], 382.
Instruments-20thC/Jazz-Blues/Leblanc/NorthTexasU/Obituaries/
Superbone/Theses/Valves/Yeo,D.

788. ANDERSON, Stephen C. "The alto trombone, then and now." *Instrumentalist* 40 (November 1985): 54+.

Anderson includes a list of music for alto trombone. See Mark Hartman, 658, Benny Sluchin, 755 and 949, Joel Elias, 831, Simon Karasick, 875, Christian Lindberg, 894, David Mathie, 904, William E. Runyan, 939, Ralph Sauer, 944, Max Thein and Heinrich Thein, 961, Donald Appert, 999, and Gloria J. Flor, 1086.
AltoTrb/Appert,D./Bib/Elias,J./Flor,G./Hartman,M./Karasick,S./ Lindberg,C./Mathie,D./PerfPrac/Runyan,W./Sauer,R./Sluchin,B./ Thein,H./Thein,M./TrbMus-18thC/TrbMus-20thC

789. ARFINENGO, Carlo. *La tromba e il trombone* [The trumpet and the trombone]. *Gli strumenti musicali. Storia della loro evoluzione tecnica en artista.* Ancona: Berben, 1973.
Arfinengo's monograph is in Italian and is cited in David Stuart, 18. See also *RILM*74/3728bm45.
Italy/Stuart,D./TrbMus-Gen

790. *Art du faiseur d'instruments de musique et lutherie* [The art of making musical instruments]. Geneva: Minkoff, 1984.
See *RILM*1989-07799-bf. This volume, in French, is a reprint of material published in 1785. It describes the manufacture of several instruments, including trombones. Most of the material appears to have been copied from Denis Diderot (see Diderot and d'Alembert, *Encyclopédie* [Paris, 1767/1776]).
D'Alembert/Diderot,D./Instruments-18thC

791. "B-flat trombone directory." *Sounding Brass and the Conductor* 4, no. 4 (1976): 124-125.
Directories/Instruments-20thC

792. BACKUS, J. "Input impedance curves for the brass instruments." *Journal of the Acoustical Society of America* 60, no. 2 (August 1976): 470-480.
Backus's experiments included muted and unmuted trumpets and trombones, and hand-stopped and unstopped horns. See Gloria Flor, 841, Ted Griffith, 851, David Langford, 885, and Benny Sluchin and Renè Caussè, 950.
Acoustics/Caussè,R./Flor,G./Griffith,T./Langford,D./Mutes/ Sluchin,B./Trumpet

793. BAHR, Edward R. "Idiomatic similarities and differences of the trombone and euphonium in history and performance." *JITA* 6 (1978): 31-36.
       See Matthew McCready, 708, Larry Campbell, 1032, and Lee A. Drummer, 1059.
       Bib/Campbell,L./Drummer,L./Euphonium/McCready,M./PerfPrac

794. BAINES, Anthony. "The fortunes of the trombone." *Symphony* 4 (March 1950): 7.
       Anthony Baines (1912-1997) was one of the leading authorities on the history and construction of instruments. His concise and well-written article contains a discussion of the etymology of the term *sackbut*. See his *Musical Instruments through the Ages* (Baltimore: Penguin Books, 1961), *European and American Musical Instruments*) New York: Viking Press, 1966), and his article, "Trombone," in *Grove's Dictionary of Music and Musicians*, 5th ed. (London: Macmillan, 1970), vol. 8, 552-559. See also Trevor Herbert, 663, Francis Galpin, 846, Geoffrey Pulver, 933, Alain Recordier, 935, and Kathleen Schlesinger, 945. For a tribute to Baines see Jeremy Montagu, "In memoriam: Anthony Baines (1912-1997)," *HBSJ* 9 (1997): 1-3.
       Galpin,F./Herbert,T./Orchestra/PerfPrac/Pulver,G.(J.)/ Recordier,A./Sackbut/Schlesinger,K./TrbMus-Gen

795. BARCLAY, Robert. "The Woodham-Rodenbostel slide trumpet and others, employing the 'clock-spring' mechanism," *Galpin Society Journal* 42 (August 1989): 112-120.
       Barclay discusses the slide trumpet which was designed and built by George (or George Henry) Rodenbostel and Richard Woodham in England in the last half of the eighteenth century. See also James Arthur Brownlow, Jr., 804, Günter Dullat, 828, Cynthia A. Hoover, 867, John Webb, 979, and Friedrich Anzenberger, 998. For further information see Adam Carse, *Musical Wind Instruments* (New York: Da Capo Press, 1965), Don L. Smithers, *The Music and History of the Baroque Trumpet Before 1721*, 2nd ed. (Carbondale IL: Southern Illinois University Press, 1988), and Edward Tarr, *The Trumpet*, trans. from the German by S.E. Plank and Edward Tarr, Portland OR: Amadeus Press, 1988 [originally published as *Die Trompete: Ihre*

Geschichte von der Antike bis zur Gegenwart (Bern: Hallwag, 1977]). See also Tarr's article on "Slide trumpet," *New Grove Dictionary of Musical Instruments*, vol. 3, (London: Macmillan, 1984), 404.
Anzenberger,F./Brownlow,A./Carse,A./ClockSpring/Dullat,G./ England/Hoover,C./Instruments-18thC/Plank,S./Rodenbostel,G./ SlideTrumpet/Smithers,D./Tarr,E./Webb,J./Woodham,R.

796. BARESEL, Alfred. "Die neue Kunitz'sche Bassposaune [The new Kunitz bass trombone]." *Instrumentbau-Zeitschrift* 20 (1965): 200-202.
      Cited and annotated in *JENKINS*, Baresel's study is concerned with the development of the "cimbasso." See Hans Kunitz, 690, Clifford Bevan, 799, Hans-Klaus Jungheinrich, 873, and Rudolf Lewy, 892. See also a discussion of Verdi's use of four trombones in *Instrumentenbau-Zeitschrift* 15 (1963): 497+, and vol. 17 (May 1964).
      BassTrb/Bevan,C./Cimbasso/Jungheinrich,H./Kunitz,H./ Lewy,R./Verdi,G.

797. BATE, Philip. *The trumpet and trombone: An outline of their history, development, and construction.* 2nd ed. London: Benn; New York: Norton, 1978.
      Located in *RILM*74/3729bf45, the first edition was published by Norton in 1966. Written by one of the most respected scholars in the world of brass instruments, Bate's book is especially strong in its discussion of the physical and acoustical properties of both trumpet and trombone. The book's appendix 2 deals with a fascinating experiment concerning the ongoing debate about the nature of J.S. Bach's *tromba-da-tirarsi*. See also Trevor Herbert, 663, and Curt Sachs, 941.
      Acoustics/Bach,J.S./Herbert,T./Instruments/Sachs,C./Sackbut/ TrombaDaTirarsi/Trumpet

798. BESSELER, Heinrich. "Die Entstehung der Posaune [The origins of the trombone]." *Acta Musicologica* 22 (1950): 8-35.
      One of the most thoroughly researched and concise articles written on the origins and development of medieval brass slide instruments, called by various names, which came to be known

as trombones, Besseler's article is published only in German. It is cited by Mary Rasmussen on p. 174 of her "Brass bibliography: 1946-1950," *Brass Quarterly* 1, no. 3 (March 1958): 168-181, as an article of the highest merit.
Instruments-Ancient/Instruments-14thC/Instruments-15thC/Instruments-16thC/Rasmussen,M./Trumpet

799. BEVAN, Clifford. "On the cimbasso trail." *Sounding Brass and the Conductor* 8, no. 2 (1979): 57-58.
Bevan's article is cited and annotated in *JENKINS*. See also his article in the *TUBA Journal* 23, no. 2 (Winter 1996): 50-53. See Alfred Baresel, 796, for more references on the cimbasso.
Baresel,A./BassTrb/Cimbasso

800. BIVRE, Guy de. "The improvisation moderator: An interview with Nicolas Collins." *Musicworks: The Journal of Sound Exploration* 49 (Winter 1991): 28-36.
Bivre discusses with Nicolas Collins his trombone propeller, which uses mechanical aspects of a trombone instead of the acoustical properties. It can be heard on Collins's recording, *One Hundred of the World's Most Beautiful Melodies* (Trace Elements TE 1018 C9, 1989).
Bib/Collins,N./TromPropeller

801. BLANCHARD, Henri. "M.C. Basler et M.A.-F.M. Leonard de la Tuilerie (Le Trombone et la resonnance du corps sonore [The trombone and the resonance of its body of sound])." *Revue et gazette musicale de Paris* 15 (1850): 355-356.
Mary Rasmussen cites Blanchard's article in her "Brass bibliography: 1850-1859," *Brass Quarterly* 6, no. 4 (Summer 1963): 187-189. She states that it is listed in Harold D. Rutan, "An annotated bibliography of written material pertinent to the performance of brass and percussion chamber music," University of Illinois, EdD, 1960. The article and Rutan's dissertation are also cited in *BRASSBIB*. See also Blanchard, 602.
Acoustics/Basler,M./France/Rasmussen,M./Rutan,H./ToneQuality/Tuilerie,L.

802. BOWLES, Edmund A. "Iconography as a tool for examining the
      loud consort in the fifteenth century." *Journal of the American
      Musical Instrument Society* 3 (1977): 100-121.
      Bowles includes a discussion on how the trombone was utilized
      in various types of consorts. See Robert Gifford, 645, Martha R.
      Nicholas, 717, and Keith Polk, 725.
      Gifford,R./Iconography/Instruments-15thC/Nicholas,M./Polk,K.

803. BREHM, K. "Die Zugposaune [The draw trombone (or
      trumpet)]." *Schweizerische Instrumentalmusik* 27 (1938): 7-8.
      An old name for a brass slide instrument (sometimes referred
      to in French as sacque-boute, or later in English as sackbut),
      Zugposaune translates as draw (or draught) trumpet (or
      trombone). "Draw or draught" roughly corresponds to the
      German word *zug*. *Posaune* can be a German term for a large
      trumpet, but the word has come to be identified with the slide
      trombone. For further discussion see Anthony Baines, 794, Philip
      Bate, 797, Heinrich Besseler, 798, and Francis W. Galpin, 846.
      Baines,A./Bate,P./Besseler,H./Galpin,F./Instruments-Renaissance/
      Sackbut/Switzerland/Zugposaune

804. BROWNLOW, James Arthur, Jr. *The Last Trumpet: A History of
      the English Slide Trumpet.* Stuyvesant NY: Pendragon Press, 1996.
      Brownlow has based his book on his doctoral paper from the
      University of Texas at Austin, 1994. See Robert Barclay, 795, for
      more references on the English slide trumpet.
      Barclay,R./Diss/England/Instruments-19thC/SlideTrumpet/
      TexasU-Austin

805. BUCHNER, Arno. "Musikinstrumente im Besitz schlesischer
      Kirchengemeinden [Musical instruments owned by Silesian
      parishes]. *Jahrbuch für schlesische Kirchenges* 56 (1977): 170-181.
      Buchner describes mid-eighteenth-century slide trombones
      which were commonplace in Silesian churches. His article is in
      German.
      Churches/Instruments-18thC/Silesia

806. BULEN, Jay C. "'Brightness' measures of trombone timbre
      (pitch, performance)." University of Washington, DMA, 1996.

See *Dissertation Abstracts* AAC 9609595, DAI-A 56/11, p. 4195, May 1996. See Karel Dekan, 822, James A. Franck, 844, R.L. Pratt and J.M. Bowsher, 932, William Thomas Walker, 977, and Klaus Wogram, 986.

Bowsher,J./Dekan,K./Diss/Franck,J./Pratt,R./Timbre/Walker,W./ WashingtonU/Wogram,K.

807. BUNIAK, Raymond. *A Twentieth-Century Treatise on the Trombone.* Bartlett IL: Raymond Buniak, 1986.

See *RILM*1989-08357-bm. Raymond Buniak's address, as of 1997, was 105 N. Western Ave., Barlett IL 60103.

Pedagogy/PerfPrac

808. [BUSER, Ernst-W.]. "An extraordinary document: The trombonist." *BBIBC* 11 (1975): 80-81.

The *BBIBC* has printed an illustration of the first known reproduction of a charcoal drawing (10" X 6") by Cornelius Saftleven of a trombonist, dated 1637. As of the date of the publication of this reproduction, the original was in the Kurt Meissner Gallery (private collection) in Zurich. The reproduction was courtesy of Ernst-W. Buser. See also Tom Naylor, 917.

Iconography/Instruments-17thC/Meissner,K./Naylor,T./Saftleven,C.

809. BÜTTNER, Manfred. "Die Trompete in Altertum und Mittelalter—Ursprung und Ausbreitung: Ein musikgeographisch-theologische Studie [The trumpet in the ancient world and the Middle Ages—origins and dissemination: A study in music geography and theology]." In *Musikgeographie: Weltliche und geistliche Bläsermusik in ihren Beziehungen zueinander und zu ihrer Umwelt*, vol. 2 (Bochum: Brockmeyer, 1991): 3-119.

See *RILM* 1991-08591-as. Büttner's study, in German, traces the development of the trumpet, starting about 6,000 years ago, and includes a discussion of the slide trumpet in the late Middle Ages and later the double-slide trombone.

AncientWorld/Europe/FarEast/Medieval/MiddleEast/Slide/ Theology/Trumpet

810. CAMPBELL, Larry. "A comprehensive sound and slide exhibit
      tracing the evolution of the trombone, euphonium, and tuba."
      Louisiana State University, independent research project, 1983.
      Cited in both *KOHLENBERG I* and *ROBERTS,* Campbell's
      project traces the development of present-day low brass
      instruments through the study of collections in museums in the
      United States and Europe.
      Collections/Euphonium/Instruments/LSU/Museums/Research/Tuba

811. ————. "An oral and pictorial survey of low brass instruments
      from the Renaissance to the present." Louisiana State University,
      independent research project, 1983.
      Campbell's study is cited in *KOHLENBERG I.*
      Iconography/Instruments/LowBrass/LSU/Renaissance/Research

812. CANEVA, Ernest O. "Trombone versus trombonium." *School
      Musician* 24 (May 1953): 8+.
      Caneva's article was written about the time of the release of J.J.
      Johnson and Kai Winding's LP (Columbia, CL892), *Jai[sic] and
      Kai Plus Six,* on which both Johnson and Winding performed at
      least one cut on tromboniums.
      Acoustics/Trombonium/Valves

813. CARTER, Stewart. "Contemporary sackbut makers: An update."
      HBSJ 1 (Summer 1989): 9-11, 13.
      Carter's article updates Henry Fischer's appendix 2 in his book,
      The Renaissance Sackbut and Its Use Today (New York:
      Metropolitan Museum of Art, 1984). See Fischer, 838.
      Fischer,H./Instruments-20thC/Reproductions/Sackbut

814. CASAMORATA, L.F. "Del trombone e dei suoi perfezionamenti
      e transformazioni in propositio della recente invenzione del
      bimbonifono [The trombone and its perfection and transformation
      in light of the recent invention of the bimboniphone]." *Atti dell'
      Accademia del R. Istituto musicale di Firenze* 13 (1875): 32-53.
      See also G. Bimboni, "La influenza della direzione dei
      padiglioni sulla espansione del suono nel trombone [The
      influence on the direction of the expanding sound of the

trombone]," *Atti dell'Accademia del R. Istituto musicale di Firenze* 18 (1880): 100-110.

Casamorata's article is cited on p. 115 of Mary Rasmussen's "Brass bibliography: 1870-79," *Brass Quarterly* 5, no. 3 (Spring 1962): 114-116, while Bimboni's article is cited on p. 35 of her "Brass bibliography: 1880-1889," *Brass Quarterly* 5, no. 1 (Fall 1961): 34-36.

Acoustics/Bimboni,G./Italy/Rasmussen,M.

815. CASE, George. "The contrabass trombone." *Musical News* 11, no. 299 (November 1896): 446.

See Gloria Flor, 842, Simon Karasick, 875, Arnold Myers, 914, Heinrich Thein, 960, and Bruce Tracy, 963.

ContrabassTrb/England/Flor,G./Karasick,S./Myers,A./Thein,H./ Tracy,B.

816. CECIL, Herbert M. "A treatise on the trombone." Eastman School of Music, MM, 1947.

Cecil's thesis is cited by Mary Rasmussen on p. 180 of her "Brass bibliography: 1946-1950," *Brass Quarterly* 1, no. 3 (March 1958): 168-181.

Eastman/Pedagogy/Rasmussen,M./Theses/TrbMus-Gen

817. ČIŽEK, Bohuslav. "Josef Kail (1795-1871), forgotten brass instrument innovator." 2 parts. *BBIBC* 73 (1991): 64-75, and 74 (1992): 24-29.

Čižek's biographical sketch mentions Czech brassmaker Kail's invention, which improved valve action and was used on valve trombones. Two examples are on instruments made by Vaclav Šámal. They are currently in the musical instrument collection of the Prague Conservatory, nos. 72 and 73.

Bio/Kail,J./Prague/Šámal,V./Valves

818. COFFEY, John. "The bass trombone." *Symphony* 2 (1949): 5.

Coffey's article is one of the earliest on the modern (post-nineteenth century) uses of the instrument. He was bass trombonist of the Boston Symphony and a distinguished teacher. His article is cited by Mary Rasmussen on p. 180 of her "Brass bibliography: 1946-1950," *Brass Quarterly* 1, no. 3 (March

1958): 168-181. Coffey (1907—1981) was given the ITA Award in 1977.
BassTrb/ITA/Pedagogy/PerfPrac/Rasmussen,M.

819. CREES, Eric. "Trombone evolution." *Sounding Brass and the Conductor* 4, no. 2 (1975): 83-84.
Crees's multipart article is continued in vol. 4, no 4 (1976): 106-108, vol. 5, no. 2 (1976): 45; vol. 5, no. 4 (1977): 116; and vol. 6, no. 2 (1977): 49-50. His articles trace the development of the trombone and its music from its earliest known appearance through the twentieth century. See also Joel Elias, 113.
Elias,J./Orchestra/PerfPrac/Research/TrbMus-Gen

820. CRIMMINS, Roy. "Holton TR-183 B-flat/F bass trombone." *Jazz Journal International* 38 (January 1985): 23.
Crimmins discusses a bass trombone for use in jazz ensembles that has a larger bore and bell than had been preferred by jazz bass trombonists in the past.
BassTrb/Holton/Jazz-Blues/Manufacturers

821. DAHLSTROM, Joseph F. "History and development of the trombone." *School Musician* 41 (March 1970): 64+.
Dahlstrom's article is third in a series of four articles on the origin of brass instruments used in American bands and symphony orchestras.
Pedagogy/PerfPrac

822. DEKAN, Karel. "Auswertung von musikalischen Dynamikbereichen bei verschiedenen Blachbles-Instrumentenspielern und die Klangfarbeanderungen bei Piano, Mezzo-forte und Forte [Evaluation of ranges of musical dynamics according to different wind instrument players and the timbral variations in piano, mezzoforte, and forte]." In *International Musicological Society: Report of the Eleventh Congress.* Copenhagen: International Musicological Society, 1972.
Located in *RILM*76/179, Dekan's study measures timbres of various homogeneous brasses in groups of three (including three trombones) during various volume levels in performance. The article is in German. See Anton Spelda, 67, Jay C. Bulen, 806.

James Franck, 844, R.L. Pratt and J.M. Bowsher, 932, William Thomas Walker, 977, and Klaus Wogram, 986.

See also a related article by Jurgen Meyer and Klaus Wogram, "Die Richtcharakteristiken von Trompete, Posaune und Tuba [The directional properties of sound in the trumpet, trombone, and tuba]," *Musikinstrument* 19, no. 2 (February 1970): 171-180, also in German, which discusses directionality of sound, seating arrangements, and reverberations.

Acoustics/Bowsher,J./Bulen,J./Dynamics/Franck,J./Meyer,J./ Pratt,R./SoundDirection/Spelda,A./Timbre/Walker,W./Wogram,K.

823. DENNIS, W. "The history of the trombone." *Metronome* 74 (March 1957): 34-35.

Dennis's article is cited by Mary Rasmussen on p. 14 of her "Brass bibliography: 1957," *Brass Quarterly* 2, no. 1 (September 1958): 12-19. An earlier unsigned article, probably not by Dennis, called "The story of the trombone" appeared in *Metronome* 40 (September 1924): 87+.

PerfPrac/Rasmussen,M./TrbMus-Gen

824. DEY, Joseph. "Tubas argenteas ductiles." *Die Musikforschung* 25, no. 3 (July/September 1972): 326-328.

Dey's study defines the biblical term *tuba ductilis* as a brass instrument made of silver or other embossed metal, not a slide trumpet or trombone. See Francis Galpin, 846.

Bible/Galpin,F./Sackbut/TubaDuctilis

825. DOWNEY, Peter. "The Renaissance slide trumpet." *Early Music* 12 (1984): 26-33.

For a response to this article, see Ross W. Duffin, 827.

See also Janet E. Griffith, 850, Janez Höfler, 865, Keith McGowan, 908, Herbert W. Myers, 915, Keith Polk, 931, Vivian Safowitz, 942, and Crispian Steele-Perkins, 952. For further information see Adam Carse, *Musical Wind Instruments* (New York: Da Capo Press, 1965); Don L. Smithers, *The Music and History of the Baroque Trumpet before 1721*, 2nd ed. (Carbondale IL: Southern Illinois University Press, 1988); and Edward Tarr, *The Trumpet*, translated from the German by S.E. Plank and Edward Tarr (Portland OR: Amadeus Press, 1988) [originally published as *Die Trompete: Ihre Geschichte von der Antike bis zur Gegenwart* Bern: Hallwag, 1977]. See also Tarr's article "Slide trumpet," *New Grove Dictionary of Musical Instruments*, (London: Macmillan, 1984), vol. 3, 404.

Carse,A./Duffin,R./Griffith,J./Höfler,J./Instruments-Renaissance/McGowan,K./Myers,H./Polk,K./Safowitz,V./SlideTrumpet/Smithers,D./Steele-Perkins,C./Tarr,E./TrompetteDesMenestrels

826. DUERKSEN, George L. "The history and acoustics of the trombone." University of Kansas, MM, 1956.

See also Duerksen, 626. For more references on acoustical topics relating to the trombone, see Karel Dekan, 822.

Acoustics/Dekan,K./KansasU/Theses

827. DUFFIN, Ross W. "The *trompette des menestrels* in the fifteenth-century *alta capella*." *Early Music* 17, no. 3 (August 1989): 397-402.

Duffin's article is a response to Peter Downey, 825 (where more references may be found). For another response see Edmund A. Bowles, "Blowing a trumpet," *Early Music* 18, no. 2 (May 1990): 350-351.

AltaCapella/Bowles,E./Downey,P./Instruments-Renaissance/SlideTrumpet/TrompetteDesMenestrels

828. DULLAT, Günter. *Fast vergessene Blasinstrumente aud zwei Jahrhunderten: vom Albisiphon zur Zugtrompete* [Almost forgotten wind instruments of the last 200 years: From the albisiphone to the slide trumpet]." Nauheim, Germany: Günter Dullat, 1992.

See Robert Barclay, 795, for more references on the slide trumpet.

Albisiphone/Barclay,R./Instruments-19thC/SlideTrumpet

829. DUTTENHOFER, Eva-Maria. *Gebruder Alexander: Zweihundert Jahre Musikinstrumentenbau in Mainz: Ein Beitrag zur Musikinstrumentenkunde* [Alexander Brothers: Two hundred years of music instrument manufacturing in Mainz: An essay on the science of making musical instruments]. Mainz: Schott, 1982.

Located in *RILM*83/3473bm45, Duttenhofer's study, in German, traces the history of the Alexander family from 1663. It deals specifically with the Baroque trombones made by the firm.
AlexanderBros/Baroque/Instruments-17thC/Instruments-18thC/ Instruments-19thC/Instruments-20thC/Manufacturers

830. EDWARDS, Robert. "A postal survey of trombone players in the London area." *JITA* 7 (1979): 15-19.

Edwards's purposes were to discover makes and models of trombones played by trombonists in the area of London and to discern attitudes about these instruments. His article was originally published as "The perception of trombones," *Journal of Sound and Vibration* 58, no. 3 (June 1978): 407-424.
Acoustics/England/London/Manufacturers

831. ELIAS, Joel. "Rediscovering the alto trombone." *Instrumentalist* 49 (October 1994): 50+.

See Stephen Anderson, 788, for more references on the alto trombone.
AltoTrb/Anderson,S.

832. ELIASON, Robert E. "The trombone in nineteenth-century America." *JITA* 10, no. 1 (January 1982): 6-10.

At the time of the writing of this article, Robert Eliason was the curator of the musical instrument collection at the Henry Ford Museum.
Collections/Instruments-19thC/Manufacturers/Museums

833. ELLIOTT, S.J., and J.M. BOWSHER. "Regeneration in brass wind instruments." *Journal of Sound and Vibration* 83, no. 2 (July 1982): 181-217.

The journal in which this article is found is published in the United Kingdom. Elliott and Bowsher are concerned with the production of musical notes by the interaction between the player's lips and the instrument. Both trombone and trumpet are used in the experiments. J.M. Bowsher has participated in several articles dealing with brass acoustics and materials; for more references see R.L. Pratt and Bowsher, 932, and P.S. Watkinson and Bowsher, 978. See also under Bowsher's name in the index.
Acoustics/Bowsher,J./Britain/Pratt,R.L./Trumpet/Watkinson,P.S.

834. EMSHEIMER, Ernst. "Zur Typologie derer schwedischen Holztrompeten [On the typology of Swedish wooden trumpets]." *Studia instrumentorum musicae popularis I.* Stockholm: Musikhistoriska museet, 1969.

Emsheimer's article, in German but located in a report from a Swedish symposium (see *RILM*71/154), deals with wooden trumpet-like instruments, some of which were similar to trombones, that were associated with village and farm life in Sweden. Sweden/WoodenTrumpets

835. ERVIN, Thomas R. "Trombone specifications." *JITA* 2 (1973-74): 13-16.

Ervin includes a comparison of various specifications, such as bore size, bell diameter, finish, and so forth, of several manufacturers of trombones. Instruments-20thC/Manufacturers

836. EVERETT, Thomas G. "Tunings for double-valve bass trombone." *Instrumentalist* 30, no. 10 (1976): 47-48, 50-52, 54.

Everett's article is one of the most thorough discussions of this controversial topic. See Gloria Flor, 843, Dwight D. Gatwood, 847, Alan Raph, 934, Bill Spilka, 951, Douglas Yeo, 988-990, Eliezar Aharoni, 994, Herbert Deutsch, 1053, Paul Faulise and Tony Studd, 1077, Alan Raph, 1213 and 1214, Robert D. Smith, 1256, M. Dee Stewart, 1264, and David Wilborn, 1295. Aharoni,E./BassTrb/Deutsch,H./Faulise,P./Flor,G./Gatwood,D./ Pedagogy/Raph,A./Slide/Smith,R./Spilka,B./Stewart,D./ Studd,T./Tuning/Valves/Wilborn,D./Yeo,D.

837. FARRAR, Lloyd P. [Reviews of various instrumental catalogs]. *Journal of the American Musical Instrument Society* 9 (1983): 112-117.

Farrar's series of reviews includes *Trompeten, Posaunen, Tuben.* Musikinstrumenten-Museum der Karl-Marx-Universität 3. See *RILM*80/2320 and Herbert Heyde, 861. Heyde,H./Reviews

838. FISCHER, Henry George. *The Renaissance Sackbut and its Use Today.* New York: Metropolitan Museum of Art, 1984.

Located in *RILM*83/5338bm45, Fischer's seventy-page booklet can be purchased from the Metropolitan Museum of Art Bookshop, Fifth Ave. at 82nd St., New York NY 10028. See also an article by Fischer, "Further comments on the Renaissance sackbut," in *Early Brass Journal* 2 (1985): 9-16.

See reviews by J. Michael Allsen in James Roberts's "Research," *JITA* 16, no. 4 (Fall 1988): 12-13, and John Webb in the *Galpin Society Journal* 39 (September 1986): 143-144. See Stewart Carter, 813, for an update of Fischer's appendix 2, "Contemporary makers of reproductions."

Allsen,M./Carter,S./Instruments-Renaissance/Reviews/Roberts,J./ Sackbut/Webb,J.

839. ———. "The tenor sackbut of Anton Schnitzer the Elder at Nice." *HBSJ* 1 (1989): 65-74.

Fischer makes a case that this instrument, dated 1581, is the oldest dated example of a sackbut. For information on another sackbut made by an Anton Schnitzer (possibly the son), see Raymond Parks, 925.

Collections/Instruments-17thC/Nice/Parks,R./Schnitzer,A.

840. FLANDRIN, G.P.A.L. "Le trombone." In *Encyclopédie de la musique et dictionnaire du Conservatoire*, part 2, vol 3 (1927). Paris: Delagrave, 1913-1931.

Flandrin's article is in French and is cited on p. 162 of Mary Rasmussen's "Brass bibliography: 1926-1930," *Brass Quarterly* 2, no. 4 (June 1959): 158-166. It is also cited in *BRASSBIB*.

France/Rasmussen,M./TrbMus-Gen

841. FLOR, Gloria J. "Brass workshop: The trombone mute [with history]." *School Musician* 51 (January 1980): 34-36.

See J. Backus, 792, Ted Griffith, 851, David Langford, 885, and Benny Sluchin and René Caussé, 950.

Acoustics/Backus,J./Caussé,R./Griffith,T./Langford,D./Mutes/ Sluchin,B./Trumpet

842. ———. "The contrabass trombone." *Woodwind World—Brass and Percussion* 23, no. 2 (1984): 10-12.

See George Case, 815, Herbert Heyde, 860, Simon Karasick, 875, Richard Lister, 895, Arnold Myers, 914, Heinrich Thein, 960, Bruce Tracy, 964, and Ben Van Dÿk, 975. The contrabass trombone web site URL is capella.dur.ac.uk/doug/contrabass_trombone.html.
Case,G./ContrabassTrb/Heyde,H./Karasick,S./Lister,R./Myers,A./Thein,H./Tracy,B./VanDÿk,B.

843.   ———. "In-line rotor: A new concept." *School Musician* 53, no. 3 (1981): 26-27.
Flor has devised a comparison chart of models with a slide chart for the various attachments. See her other article dealing with valves on bass trombone, "The bass trombone: Single rotor, double rotor, or in-line?" *Woodwind World—Brass and Percussion* 23, no. 2 (1984): 10-12. See also Thomas G. Everett, 836, Dwight D. Gatwood, 847, Alan Raph, 934, Bill Spilka, 951, Douglas Yeo, 988-990, Eliezar Aharoni, 994, Herbert Deutsch, 1053, Raph, 1213, Robert D. Smith, 1256, and M. Dee Stewart, 1264.
Aharoni,E./BassTrb/Deutsch,H./Everett,T./Faulise,P./Gatwood,D./In-line/Pedagogy/Raph,A./Slide/Smith,R./Spilka,B./Stewart,D./Studd,T./Tuning/Valves/Yeo,D.

844.   FRANCK, James A. "A comparative study of factors in trombone timbre." Ohio State University, MM, 1950.
See Jay C. Bulen, 806, Karel Dekan, 822, R.L. Pratt and J.M. Bowsher, 932, William E. Runyan, 939, William Thomas Walker, 976, and Klaus Wogram, 986.
Bowsher,J./Bulen,J./Dekan,K./OhioStateU/Pratt,R./Runyan,W./Theses/Timbre/Walker,W./Wogram,K.

845.   GAGNE, J. "Le sacqueboute." *Carnet Musical* 6 (December 1972): 19-20.
Gagne's article is in French.
Instruments-15thC/Instruments-16thC/Sackbut

846.   GALPIN, Francis William. "The sackbut: Its evolution and history," *Proceedings of the Royal Musical Association* 33 (1906-1907): 2-25.

In spite of its age, Galpin's study is still the most widely quoted and authoritative source on the origins of the trombone. It also deals with a misconception (fostered by such leading musicologists as Carl Engel and Edward Coussemaker) about the *sambuke* (a four-stringed harp-like instrument). The term *sambuke* is translated in the King James version of the Hebrew Bible (Daniel 3:5), and used in a poem from *Tales of a Wayside Inn* by Longfellow, as sackbut, or trombone.

Galpin also discusses another legend dealing with a supposed trombone discovered at Pompeii (or Herculaneum) and identified as a *tuba ductilis*, assumed by many to be a slide instrument. See Galpin's two-part article, "The sackbut," *Musical Times* 47, no. 766 (1906): 828-829; and 768 (1906): 110. See also Joseph Dey, 824, Kathleen Schlesinger, 945 (for another definitive study from the same time period as Galpin's article), and K. Weber, 981. Coussemaker,E./Dey,J./Engel,C./Instruments-Ancient/Instruments-15thC/Instruments-16thC/Sackbut/Sambuke/Schlesinger,K./TubaDuctilis/Weber,K.

847. GATWOOD, Dwight D. "Is 'dual in-line' really better?" *JITA* 12, no. 2 (April 1984): 24.

For a response see Douglas Yeo, 990 (see also Yeo, 988 and 989). See Thomas G. Everett, 836, and Gloria Flor, 843, for more references on in-line and other types of trigger attachments for trombone.
BassTrb/Everett,T./Flor,G./In-line/Pedagogy/Slide/Tuning/Valves/Yeo,D.

848. GOTTHOLD, J. "Reflexions sur le trombone basse [Reflections on the bass trombone]." *BBIBC* 39 (1982): 49-51.

Gotthold's article is in French, German, and English.
BassTrb/Pedagogy/PerfPrac

849. GREGORY, Robin. *The Trombone: The Instrument and Its Music*. New York: Praeger; London: Faber & Faber, 1973.

Gregory has put together a useful book, particularly for those people interested in the acoustical and scientific work that has been done in trombone construction and design before 1973.

Although the author was not a trombonist, he catalogs many thoughtful insights about the instrument.

The section on literature is not as complete or up to date as the section on the history, construction, and musical uses of the instrument. His book is located in *RILM*74/3744rb45.

For other comments on Gregory's opinions about trombone solo literature, see Joseph Nicholson, 525—527. See reviews by Joseph Wheeler in the *Galpin Society Journal* 27 (April 1974): 147-149, and by Dean Tudor in *American Reference Books Annual* 5 (1974): 402.

Acoustics/Nicholson,J./Reviews/TrbMus-Gen/Tudor,D./Wheeler,J.

850. GRIFFITH, Janet E. "The slide trumpet in the early Renaissance." University of Cincinnati, DMA, 1992.

See *Dissertation Abstracts* 9233224 and *RILM*1992-09511-dd.

Five pieces in Gustav Reese's *Music in the Renaissance* are examined as bases for tracing the development of the trumpet, particularly the slide trumpet. See Peter Downey, 825, for more references.

CincinnatiU/Diss/Downey,P./Instruments-Renaissance/Reese,G./ SlideTrumpet/TrbMus-15thC/TrbMus-16thC

851. GRIFFITH, Ted. "Confessions of a mutemaker." *NITA* 3, no. 2 (May 1976): 20,28.

At the time of the writing of this article, Griffith was the bass trombonist with the Montreal Symphony and trombone instructor at McGill University. See J. Backus, 792, Gloria J. Flor, 841, David Langford, 885, and Benny Sluchin and René Caussé, 950. Acoustics/Backus,J./Caussé,R./Flor,G./Langford,D./Mutes/ Sluchin,B./Trumpet

852. GUION, David. "The pitch of baroque trombones." *JITA* 8 (1980): 24-28

Guion discusses the controversy among orchestrators, scholars, and music historians about the key of the baroque trombone. He accedes to Speer's apparent contention that the tenor instrument was in A. See Keith McGowan, 908, Ephraim Segerman, 947, and Gerhard Stradner, 955. See Arnold Fromme, 640, for more references.

Baroque/Bib/Fromme,A./Instruments-17thC/Instruments-18thC/
McGowan,K./Pitch/Segerman,E./Stradner,G.

853. ———. "The seven positions: Joseph Frölich's new trombone method." *JITA* 14, no. 2 (Spring 1986): 50-53.

Guion discusses an article on the trombone taken from an early nineteenth-century work by Joseph Frölich, *Vollstandige theoretisch-pracktische Musikschule*, 4 vols. (Bonn: Simrock, 1811). Data from the article were taken from Guion, 452.
Frölich,J./Pedagogy/Pitch

854. GWYNN, Dominic. *Early Nineteenth-Century Trombones: Technical Notes, Drawings, and Photographs.* Welbeck, England: Martin Goetze and Dominic Gwynn, Organbuilders, 1993.
Iconography/Instruments-19thC/Manufacturers

855. HAGE, Kees van. "A day in Markneukirchen." 2 parts. *JITA* 19, no. 2 (Spring 1991): 20-26, and no. 3 (Summer 1991): 18-23.

Hage has written a fascinating and poignant account of a visit to a renowned city of musical instrument craftsmen, including trombone makers. The city is located in what used to be called East Germany. Hage is a free-lance trombonist, teacher, and writer who lives in Amsterdam. Arthur Moore provided the excellent translation of the article into English.
Instruments/Markneukirchen/Mönnich,K./Moore,A./Schmidt,W./
Voigt,H./Voigt,J.

856. HARLOW, Lewis. "We call them trombets." *Instrumentalist* 23 (August 1968): 73-76.

Harlow describes an E-flat alto trombone, designed with valves by Peter Edwards. Harlow used it in his instrumental groups to play second and third trumpet parts. See William T. Collins, 421. Benny Sluchin and Raymond Lapie, 553, deals with the valved alto trombone Berlioz favored for performing the first-trombone parts of some of his works.
AltoTrb/Berlioz,H./Collins,W./Edwards,P./Instruments-20thC/
Lapie,R./PerfPrac/Sluchin,B./Trombet/Valves

857. HAUPT, P. "Die Posaunen von Jerico [The large trumpets of Jericho]." *Wiener Zeitschrift für die Kunde des Morgenlandes* 23 (1909): 355.

The German word *Posaune* literally means "large trumpet." It is used in that context in German translations of both the Hebrew Bible and the New Testament. By the Middle Ages the word had become identified with the trombone in German-speaking countries. For more information on the *Posaunenchor* and the term *Posaune*, see Wilhelm Ehmann, 629. Haupt's article is cited by Mary Rasmussen on p. 94 of her "Brass bibliography: 1906-1910," *Brass Quarterly* 4, no. 2 (Winter 1960): 90-94.

Ehmann,W./HebrewBible/Instruments-Ancient/Jericho/Joshua/Kuhlo,J./Palestine/Posaune/Rasmussen,M./Trumpet

858. "Helikon-Posaune." *Zeitschrift für Instrumentenbau* 19 (1898/1899): 381.

The article is in German and is cited by Mary Rasmussen on p. 169 of her "Brass bibliography: 1890-1899," *Brass Quarterly* 4, no. 4 (Summer 1961): 168-172. A "Helicon-Bass" is in circular form and usually has its bell pointed skyward (they are known affectionately as "raincatchers"). Presumably the same shape and bell direction would be implied for a "helicon-trombone," or "helicon-trumpet." See Wilhelm Ehmann, 629, and P. Haupt, 857, for an explanation of the German term *Posaune*. See also Adam Carse, *Musical Wind Instruments* (New York: Da Capo, 1963), 304-306.

Carse,A./Germany/Helicon/Rasmussen,M.

859. HERBERT, Trevor. "The sackbut in England in the seventeenth and eighteenth centuries." *Early Music* 18, no. 4 (November 1990): 609-616.

Herbert discusses the contributions of James Talbot, professor of Hebrew at Cambridge during the seventeenth century, and chronicler of the performance practice of trombones in England during his day. See Herbert's dissertation, "The trombone in England before 1800," Open University, PhD, 1984. See also Herbert, 663, and Anthony Baines, "James Talbot's Ms.," *Galpin Society Journal* 1 (1948): 9.

Baines,A./Baroque/England/Handel,G.F./Sackbut/Talbot,J./
TrbMus-18thC

860. HEYDE, Herbert. "Brass instrument-making in Berlin from the
seventeenth to the twentieth century." *HBSJ* 3 (1991): 43-47.
   Translated by Steven Plank, Heyde's article mentions Hans
Schreiber, who apparently made a contrabass trombone in Berlin
in about 1615. See also Richard Lister, 895.
Berlin/Brass/ContrabassTrb/Germany/Instruments-17thC/
Instruments-18thC/Instruments-19thC/Instruments-20thC/
Lister,R./Plank,S./Schreiber,H.

861. ———. *Trompeten, Posaunen, Tuben: Katalog.* Musik-
instrumenten-Museum der Karl-Marx-Universität, no. 3. Leipzig:
VEB Deutscher Verlag für Musik, 1980.
   Located in *RILM*80/2320bm04 and cited in *BRASSBIB*. See
Lloyd Farrar, 837, for a citation of a review.
Collections/Farrar,L./KarlMarxUniversität/Museums/Trumpet/Tuba

862. HIMES, A.C., Jr. "A guide to trombone mouthpiece
comparisons." *JITA* 10, no. 2 (April 1982): 26-27.
   Himes includes most brands of mouthpieces distributed in the
United States. See [G.B. Lane], 1159. See also cceric@showme.
missouri.edu, for a mouthpiece specification chart by Eric
Nicklas, updated by Stanley Kling (kling@odpwcr.ucsd.edu).
Lane,G./Mouthpieces/Kling,S./Nicklas,E.

863. HINTERBICHLER, Karl, and Leigh GETTIER. "Heavy duty
case project." *NITA* 6, no. 4 (September 1979): 8.
   Hinterbichler and Gettier discuss a preliminary design for an
extremely protective trombone case. See Jerry Juhnke and G.B.
Lane, 872, and Rich Mays, 906. See also a report by Charles
Jones in the *NITA* 1, no. 2 (April 1974): 12-13.
Cases/Gettier,L./Jones,C./Juhnke,J./Lane,G./Mays,R.

864. "Historische Musikinstrumente [Historic music instruments]."
Musikhandel 17, no. 8 (1966): 386.
   The article is in German.
Collections/Europe/Instruments/Museums

865. HÖFLER, Janez. "Der 'Trompette de menestrels' und sein Instrument [The trompette de menestrels and his? instrument]." *Tidjschrift van der Vereniging voor Nederlandse Muziekgeschiedenis* 29, no. 2 (1979): 92-132.

Höfler discusses the trompette de guerre and the trompette des menestrels as documented in iconography during the early sixteenth century. The article is in German. See Peter Downey, 825, for more references.

Downey,P./Iconography/Instruments-16thC/TrompetteDeGuerre/
TrompetteDesMenestrels

866. HOGARTH, George. "Musical instruments: The trumpet, trombone, serpent and ophicleide." *Musical World* 4 (1837): 129-133.

George Hogarth (1783-1870) was an English lawyer, journalist, critic, composer, and general supporter of musical life in England during the nineteenth century. He achieved a modicum of fame by being the father-in-law of English novelist Charles Dickens. Hogarth's article is cited by Mary Rasmussen on p. 134 of her "Brass bibliography: 1830-1839," *Brass Quarterly* 7, no. 3 (Spring 1964): 133-136. See P.I. [only initials given], 923. For more information on Hogarth see John Warrack, "Hogarth, George," *New Grove Dictionary of Music and Musicians* (London: Macmillan, 1980), vol. 8, 638-639.

BassHorn/Iconography/Instruments-19thC/Ophicleide/P.,I./
Rasmussen,M./Serpent/Trumpet/Warrack,J.

867. HOOVER, Cynthia A. "The slide trumpet of the nineteenth century." *Brass Quarterly* 6, no. 4 (Summer 1963): 159-178 [with an illustrated supplement between pp. 190 and 191 of the issue].

Hoover discusses several English slide trumpets, including one at the Smithsonian, and artists who performed on the instrument in the latter half of the nineteenth century. Plates and illustrations are included in the supplement. See Robert Barclay, 795, for more references on the slide trumpet.

Barclay,R./England/Iconography/Instruments-19thC/Slide
Trumpet/Smithsonian

868. HUMFELD, Neill H. "How long is B-flat?" *JITA* 11, no. 2 (April 1983): 24-25.

Neill Humfeld, who was an outstanding trombone teacher, a former president of the International Trombone Association (1980-1982), and the 1984 recipient of the ITA Award, possessed an intelligence that was matched only by his fondness for whimsy. His article about a "herald trombone," which was designed by two of his instrument repairmen friends, Walter Pace and Larry Price, to graphically demonstrate the problems with breath control on the trombone, illustrates both facets of Humfeld's personality. See also "Humfeld's rare species," *Ovation* 4 (March 1984): 7.

Breathing/HeraldTrombone/Pace,W./Pedagogy/Price,L./Whimsy

869. JAHN, Fritz. "Posaunen-macher im 16. Jahrhundert, Beitr. zur Geschichte des Musikinstrumentenbaues [Trumpet and trombone-makers in the sixteenth century and a history of the development of musical instrument manufacturing]." Univerity of Leipzig, PhD, 1925.

Jahn's excellent work has been translated into English (in a rough form) from the German by Larry Weed and may be available from him (2221 Excalibur Dr., Orlando FL 32822). It deals primarily with the Nuremberg manufacturers, such as the families of Hans Neuschel and Albert Schnitzer. An article excerpted from this study is "Die Nürnberger Trompeten- und Posaunenmacher im 16. Jahrhundert," *Archiv für Musikwissenschaft* 7 (1925): 23-52. See Martin Kirnbauer, 878, George B. Lane, 884, Joseph M. Nicholson, 920-921, Ekkehart Nickel, 922, Gary M. Stewart, 953, and Willi Worthmüller, 987. See also Adam Carse, "The trumpet-makers of Nuremburg," *Monthly Musical Record* 67 (1937?): 203-204.

Baroque/Bauer,J./Carse,A./Diss/Germany/Instruments-15thC/ Instruments-16thC/Instruments-17thC/Kirnbauer,M./Lane,G./ LeipzigU/Neuschel,H./Nicholson,J./Nickel,E./Nuremberg/ Renaissance/Schnitzer,A./Stewart,G./Weed,L./Worthmüller,W.

870. JAMESON, R. Philip. "The Arthur Pryor trombone (1888-1988): A centennial tribute." *JITA* 16, no. 3 (Summer 1988): 30-31.

Jameson has provided pictures, with the assistance of Wayne Brill, of a gold-plated and engraved trombone made by C.G. Conn and presented to Pryor in the late 1880s. It is not known

when Pryor performed on this instrument. The trombone is now
housed at The National Music Camp at Interlochen. See Steve
Dillon, 107, for more references on Pryor.
Brill,W./Conn,C.G./Dillon,S./Instruments-19thC/Interlochen/
Pryor,A.

871. JAMESON, R. Philip, and A.C. HIMES. "An acoustical
      comparison among various trombone leadpipes." *JITA* 15, no. 1
      [mistakenly labeled as 14, no. 4] (Winter 1987): 50-52.
         See Tracy Miller, 912. For other references on trombone timbre
      see James A. Franck, 844.
      Acoustics/Franck,J./Himes,A.C./Leadpipes/Miller,T./Timbre

872. JUHNKE, Jerry, and G.B. LANE. "Airborne slushpumps." *JITA*
      1 (1972-1973): 28-29.
         Juhnke and Lane conducted one of the first surveys taken about
      the problem of the airline industry's handling of trombones as
      baggage. A report by Charles Jones on the results of the survey
      may be found in the *NITA* 1, no. 2 (April 1974): 12-13. See Karl
      Hinterbichler and Leigh Gettier, 863, and Rich Mays, 906.
      Airlines/Cases/Gettier,L./Hinterbichler,K./Jones,C./Lane,G./Mays,R.

873. JUNGHEINRICH, Hans-Klaus. "Der entfesselte Posaunenbass [The
      unbound bass trombone]." *Musik im Unterricht* 61 (1965): 122-123.
         Jungheinrich discusses Dr. Hans Kunitz's "cimbasso." The
      article is in German and is cited and annotated in *JENKINS*. See
      Alfred Baresel, 796, Clifford Bevan, 799, Rudolf Lewy, 892, and
      Bevan's "Any more for the cimbasso?" *TUBA Journal* 23, no. 2
      (Winter 1996): 50-53.
      Baresel,A./BassTrb/Bevan,C./Cimbasso/Kunitz,H./Lewy,R./
      Opera/Verdi,G.

874. KAPPEY, J.A. "Les trombones à pistones et les trombones à
      coulisses [Valve trombones and slide trombones]." *L'Echo
      musical* 20 (1890): 147-148, 160-161.
         Kappey's article is cited by Mary Rasmussen on p. 169 of her
      "Brass bibliography: 1890-1899," *Brass Quarterly* 4, no. 4
      (Summer 1961): 168-172, as having been reprinted from *The
      British Bandsman*. It is also cited in *BRASSBIB*. See also

Kappey's *Military Music: A History of Wind Instrument Bands* (London: Boosey, 1894), and his article, "Wind-Band," in *Grove's Dictionary of Music and Musicians*, 3rd ed. (New York: Macmillan, 1927-1928).
Britain/France/Rasmussen,M./Slide/Valves

875. KARASICK, Simon. "The alto and contrabass trombone." *Music Journal* 26 (January 1968): 30+.
For information on Simon Karasick see David Chamberlain, 98. See Stephen Anderson, 788, for more references on alto trombone and for more references on contrabass trombone, see Gloria Flor, 843. AltoTrb/Anderson,S./Chamberlain,D./ContrabassTrb/Flor,G.

876. KARSTÄDT, Georg. "Geschichte der Posaune [History of the trombone]." *MGG* 10 (1962): 1496-1506.
Karstädt's article is in German.
Acoustics/PerfPrac/TrbMus-Gen

877. "King creates the 'Flugabone.'" *Music Trades* 126 (June 1978): 70.
BRASSBIB cites a series of articles dealing with King instruments: "King Duo-Gravis bass trombone extends range to bottom of piano," *Music Trades* 118 (May 1970): 62; "King makes a special instrument for a very special person [handicapped person]," *School Musician* 45 (January 1974): 41; and "King makes a special instrument for a very special person [artificial arms]," *Music Trades* 122 (January 1974): 84. For further information about the last article cited, see Mark McDunn, 907. See also "New double-barrelled trombone," 919, and "Side-angle trombone," 948.
BassTrb/Duo-Gravis/Flugabone/Handicapped/Instruments-20thC/King/Manufacturers/McDunn,M./ShortArms

878. KIRNBAUER, Martin. "Die Nürnberger Trompeten- und Posaunenmacher vor 1500 im Spiegel Nürnberger Quellen [The Nuremberg trumpet and trombone makers before 1500 as reflected in Nuremberg sources]." In *Musik und Tanz zur Zeit Kaiser Maximilian I: Bericht der die am 21. und 22. Oktober 1989 in Innsbruck abgehaltene Fachtagung*, 131-142. Innsbruck: Helbing, 1992.

Kirnbauer's article is in German. See *RILM*1992-01269-bs. See above Fritz Jahn, 869, for more references on brass instrument manufacturing in Nuremberg.
Bauer,J./Instruments-15thC/Instruments-Renaissance/Jahn,F./ MaximilianI/Nuremberg

879. KITZEL, Larry. "The trombones of the Shrine to Music Museum." University of Oklahoma, DMA, 1985.
See *Dissertation Abstracts* 46/04-A, p. 832, AAD85-13847. The Shrine to Music Museum contains more than four thousand instruments, of which almost 250 are trombones, representing more than 150 European and American makers. Kitzel's study includes photographs and specific information on every trombone in the collection. See Randy B. Kohlenberg, 882. See also Gary Stewart, 953, where an account is given of the restoration of a 1608 trombone by Jacob Bauer of Nuremberg in the conservation laboratory of the Shrine to Music Museum (for more information on Bauer see Martin Kirnbauer, 878).
Bauer,J./Collections/Diss/Kirnbauer,M./Kohlenberg,R./Larson,A./ Museums/OklahomaU/ShrineToMusic/SouthDakota/Stewart,G.

880. KIZER, George A. "The bass trombone." *Instrumentalist* 10, no. 9 (1956): 25-27.
Kizer's article is cited in *JENKINS*.
BassTrb/Pedagogy/PerfPrac

881. KLEMENT, Miloslav. "Die historische Tenor-posaune in der heutingen Interpretationspraxis [The historical tenor trombone in present-day performance]." *Symposium zu Fragen des Musikinstrumentenbaus* (1983): 49-53.
Klement discusses a tenor trombone from the seventeenth century which was found in 1971 near Krivoklat Castle. It was later restored, with copies utilized by the chamber ensemble Symposium Musicum of Prague. His article is in German, and the symposium report is located in *RILM*84 681.
Instruments-17thC/Krivoklat/PerfPrac/Prague/SymposiumMusicum

882. KOHLENBERG, Randy B. "The Shrine to Music Museum." *JITA* 10, no. 2 (April 1982): 35-36.

See Larry Kitzel, 879. See also Gary Stewart, 953, where an account is given of the restoration of a 1608 trombone by Jacob Bauer of Nuremberg in the conservation laboratory of the Shrine to Music Museum is given.
Bauer,J./Collections/Kitzel,L./Larson,A./Museums/ShrineToMusic/ SouthDakota/Stewart,G.

883. KRAEMER, Ray L. "The slide French horn: Funnybone." *Experimental Musical Instruments* 3, no. 3 (October 1987): 10-11.
Experimental/Horn/Slide

884. LANE, George B. "The trombone: Its musical environment from the late Middle Ages through the late renaissance." University of Texas at Austin, DMA, 1976.
See *Dissertation Abstracts* 37/06-A, p. 3259, AAD76-26735. The book based on this study is no longer available. See Lane, "Instrument manufacturers and specifications," 2 parts, *JITA* 3 (1975): 13-14, and 4 (1976): 8-16. Both parts were excerpted from Lane's doctoral paper, which deals with the development of brass manufacturing, trombones in particular, and performance practices concerning trombones in Europe from the late Middle Ages through the eighteenth century.
It also contains a section dealing with instruments and performance practices in sixteenth- and seventeenth-century Mexico which features a transcription of a late seventeenth- or early eighteenth-century choral piece accompanied by two shawms and sackbut. The composer was Miguel Matheo de Dallo y Lanas, who was maestro di capella at the Puebla Cathedral from 1688 to 1705. A copy of the original manuscript was obtained from the Cathedral in Puebla, Mexico (see Robert M. Stevenson, *Renaissance and Baroque Musical Sources in the Americas* [Washington DC: General Secretariat, Organization of American States, 1970], 50).
Bib/Bio/DalloYLanas,M./Diss/Europe/Iconography/Instruments-15thC/Instruments-16thC/Instruments-17thC/Instruments-18thC/Medieval/Mexico/Nuremberg/PerfPrac/Puebla/Renaissance/ Stevenson,R./TexasU-Austin/TrbMus-15thC/TrbMus-16thC/ TrbMus-17thC

885. LANGFORD, David. "Selected trumpet and trombone mutes: An
      introduction." East Texas State University, MM, 1980.
      Langford's study is cited in *KOHLENBERG I.* See J. Backus,
      792, Gloria J. Flor, 841, Ted Griffith, 851, and Benny Sluchin
      and René Caussé, 950.
      Acoustics/Backus,J./Caussé,R./EastTexasStateU/Flor,G./
      Griffith,T./Mutes/Sluchin,B./Theses/Trumpet

886. "Leblanc to offer radical patented 'superbone' trombone." *Music
      Trades* 124 (May 1976): 64.
      See Ashley Alexander (who collaborated on the design of the
      "superbone"), 787. See also [Douglas Yeo], 382.
      Alexander,A./Leblanc/Manufacturers/Superbone/Yeo,D.

887. LEISENRING, John. "Who is your favorite trombone
      technician?" *JITA* 20, no. 2 (Spring 1991): 10-11.
      Leisenring has compiled an informal listing of trombone slide
      technicians, classified by geographic area, who are reputed to be
      good at their work. For an update, see the *JITA* 20, no. 3
      (Summer 1992): 10. See John Upchurch (my personal favorite
      slide technician—GBL), 973.
      SlideRepair/Upchurch,J.

888. LELOIR, Edmond. "Le trombone à six pistons indépendants [The
      trombone with six independent valves]." *BBIBC* 5/6 (1973): 97-105.
      Leloir's article, in French, German, and English, discusses
      Adolphe Sax's ingenuity in designing valved brass instruments,
      specifically the saxtrombone, which has six independent valves
      and was built in 1852.
      In the same issue of this journal is a short article by Albert
      Mertens, one of the most accomplished Belgian trombonists of
      the twentieth century, who tragically died at the age of thirty-
      three. In his "Le trombone en Belgique," he gives a capsule
      history of the rise and fall of the popularity of Sax's invention
      and his opinion of the reasons for the reacceptance of the slide
      trombone in Belgium around 1930.
      For more information on Adolphe Sax and his instruments see
      Malou Haines, *Adolphe Sax: Sa vie, son oeuvre et ses instruments
      de musique* [Adolphe Sax: His life, his work, and his musical

instruments] (Brussels: Editions de l'Université des Bruxelles, 1979), and Kenneth Deans, "A comprehensive performance project in saxophone literature with a essay consisting of translation source readings in the life of Adolphe Sax," University of Iowa, DMA, 1980. See also Adam Carse, *Musical Wind Instruments* (New York: Da Capo Press, 1965), 259-260.
Belgium/Brussels/Carse,A./Deans,K./Haines,M./Instruments-19thC/Mertens,A./Sax,A./Saxtrombone/Valves

889. LEVERMANN, A. "Aus dem 'Schneider'—Im Test: Die Posaune Schneider EL der Firma Amrein [The results of testing the 'Schneider': The Schneider trombone EL of the Amrein firm]." *Instrumentenbau-Zeitschrift* 49 (May-June 1996): 20-22.
Levermann's article is in German.
Amrein/Germany/Instruments-20thC/Manufacturers/SchneiderEL

890. LEVI, R. "Bass trombone." *Tatzlil* 15 (1975):136-141.
Levi's article is written in Hebrew and cited in *JENKINS* as being valuable as a reference to composers, though not necessarily revolutionary in its statements.
BassTrb/Israel

891. LEWIS, Maggie. "The sacbut, instrument of kings (once you get used to it)." *JITA* 10, no. 2 (April 1982): 12-13.
Lewis's article was reprinted from *The Christian Science Monitor*, 1981. She gives a brief history, including the musical philosophy and style, of The New York Cornet and Sacbut Ensemble from the viewpoint of its conductor and founder, alto sackbuteer and historic brass scholar, Ben Peck. Note the variant spelling of "sackbut." The word has gone through many permutations, including sagbut and sackbutt. See Francis Galpin, 846.
Galpin,F./NYCornetSacbutEnsemble/Peck,B./Sackbut

892. LEWY, Rudolf. "Cimbasso." *JITA* 6 (1978): 18.
Lewy discusses a contrabass trombone needed to correctly execute the lowest brass parts in Verdi's operas. *JENKINS* maintains that his article contains ideas which are "more a statement of beliefs than research." See Alfred Baresel, 796, Clifford Bevan, 799, and Hans-Klaus Jungheinrich, 873. See also

Bevan's "Any more for the cimbasso?" *TUBA Journal* 23, no. 2 (Winter 1996): 50-53), and a discussion in *Instrumentenbau-Zeitschrift* 15 (1963): 495+, and vol. 17 (May 1964). Baresel,A./Bevan,C./Cimbasso/ContrabassTrb/Jungheinrich,H./ Opera/Verdi,G.

893. ———. "Trombone basso." *JITA* 5 (1977): 10-22.
      Lewy's article is cited in *JENKINS* as being of value primarily because of the huge bibliography, citing 141 sources. It is based on Lewy's master's thesis from Tel Aviv, Israel, 1973. BassTrb/Bib/Israel/TelAvivU/Theses

894. LINDBERG, Christian. "Why a *B-flat* attachment on the alto trombone?" *JITA* 19, no. 3 (Summer 1991): 26.
      Trombone soloist Lindberg discusses the Conn 36H alto trombone and its B-flat attachment, which he helped design. He makes the case that the attachment is especially helpful in playing low Gs and in facilitating trills. See Stephen Anderson, 788, for more references on the alto trombone. Lindberg has also been involved in designing a new valve called the CL 2000 for the rotary valve systems on Conn trombones. AltoTrb/Anderson,S./CL2000/Conn,C.G./PerfPrac/Valves

895. LISTER, Richard. "The contrabass sackbut—a modern copy." *JITA* 9 (1981): 23.
      Lister discusses a copy made by Meinl and Lauber of a 1639 original contrabass sackbut by Johann Nikolaus Oller. The study was reprinted from *BBIBC* 31 (1980): 71+. See Gloria Flor, 842, and Herbert Heyde, 860. The contrabass trombone web site URL is capella.dur.ac.uk/doug/contrabass_trombone.html. ContrabassTrb/Flor,G./Heyde,H./Instruments-17thC/MeinlLauber/ Oller,J./Sackbut

896. LUMSDEN, Alan. "The sound of the trombone: A lecture on the history of the trombone." Edinburgh: Edinburgh University, Collection of Historic Musical Instruments, 1988.
      Lumsden is one of the leading performers of early trombone music in Britain. His monograph was reviewed by Trevor Herbert

in the *Galpin Society Journal* 42 (August 1989): 148-150. See *RILM*1988-07770-bm.
Britain/EdinburghU/Herbert,T./Reviews/Sackbut

897. MACCRACKEN, Thomas G. "Die Verwendung der Blechblasinstrumente bei J.S. Bach unter besonderer Berücksichtigung der Tromba da tirarsi [The use of brass wind instruments by J.S. Bach with special consideration for the tromba da tirarsi]," *Bach-Jahrbuch* 70 (1984): 59-89.

See a response by Don Smithers in the same periodical, 76 (1990): 59-89. MacCracken's response to Smithers is found in volume 73 (1992): 123-30. See Philip Bate, 797, and Curt Sachs, 941. See also Werner Menke's *History of the Trumpet of Bach and Handel*, translated by Gerald Abraham (Nashville: Brass Press, 1972) [reprint of the 1960 edition published by William Reeves, who also published the 1934 edition with German and English texts on facing pages], 84-87, and Fritz Piersig, *Die Einfürung des Hornes in die Kunstmusik und seine Verwendung bis zum Tode J.S. Bachs* [The introduction of horns in art music and their use up to the death of J.S. Bach] (Halle: Niemeyer, 1927).
Abraham,G./Bach,J.S./Bate,P./Menke,W./Piersig,F./Sachs,C./
Smithers,D./TrombaDaTirarsi

898. MAHILLON, Victor-Charles. "Le trombone." Brussels: 1906.

Mahillon's study, in French, is a monograph, very likely incorporating information from Mahillon's well-known *Les eléments d'acoustique musicale et instrumentale comprenant l'examen de la construction théorique de tous les instruments de musique en usage dans l'orchestration moderne* [Elements of musical and instrumental acoustics, including an examination of the theoretical construction of all musical instruments used in the modern orchestra]. 2nd and rev. ed. Brussels: Amis de la Musique, 1984 [originally published in 1874].
Acoustics/France/Instruments-19thC

899. ———. "Nouveau modèle de trombone ténor [New model of (a) tenor trombone]," *L'Echo musical* 4, no. 8 (August 1872).

V[ictor] C[harles] M[ahillon] is identified by Mary Rasmussen on p. 114 of her "Brass bibliography: 1870-1879," *Brass Quarterly* 5, no. 3 (Spring 1962): 114-116.
France/Instruments-19thC/Rasmussen,M.

900. MANZORA, Boris G. "Die Posaune mit Doppelaussenzug: Ein Museumstück mit Zukunft? [The double-slide trombone: museumpiece with a future?]." *BBIBC* 30 (1980): 33-42.
      Manzora discusses the potential technical advantages of the double-slide trombone, such as extending the number of positions, possibilities of glissandi, and legato articulations. The author is the trombone teacher at the L.V. Sobinov Conservatory located in Saratov in Russia. His article is in German, French, and English.
      A related story may be found in a 1996 article by Burlon Parsons in the *Houston Journal-Spectator*. A Wharton, Texas, resident, John Wanner, has designed what he calls a "quadro trombone slide," which takes the same amount of tubing ordinarily found in a regular trombone slide but doubles it over in a unique design so that the same amount of tubing fits in a horizontal plane. With his design, a player can execute the same scales utilizing exactly one-half the position differences of the regular slide. A similar instrument is now on the market.
      DoubleSlide/Parsons,B./QuadroTrb/Russia/Slide/Texas/Wanner,J.

901. MARTELL, Paul. "Zur Geschichte der Posaune [On the history of the trombone]." *Die Musik-Woche* 3, no. 4 (1935): 5-6.
      Martell's article is in German and is cited by Mary Rasmussen on p. 121 of her "Brass bibliography: 1931-1935," *Brass Quarterly* 2, no. 3 (March 1959): 117-125.
      PerfPrac/Rasmussen,M./TrbMus-Gen

902. MASSON, Gabriel. "Le trombone et ses différentes proportions [The trombone and its different proportions]." *Musique et Radio* 41 (1951): 147.
      See also Masson, 704. Earlier he wrote "Le trombone," *Musique et Radio* 46 (1956): 467+, 471, which is in both English and French. Masson was one of the most well-known trombone

performers and teachers in France around the middle of the twentieth century.
France/Instruments-20thC

903. MATHEZ, Jean-Pierre. "Branimir Slokar: Developpement d'un nouveau trombone [Branimir Slokar: Development of a new trombone]." *BBIBC* 91 (1995): 92-96.
   Mathez's interview is in French, German, and English. Slokar has worked with Klaus Wogram (see Wogram, 986) and Kühnl and Hoyer to develop two new models of trombones. One has a thinner bell and other features which differ. Slokar feels that one of the principal acoustical problems that afflicts most trombones is how the air column is affected by the curve in the tuning slide. He and his collaborators believe they have reduced that problem by utilizing an off-center bend in the tuning slide.
   Acoustics/Bells/Instruments-20thC/KühnlHoyer/Manufacturers/Slokar,B./Wogram,K.

904. MATHIE, David. "A survey of current alto trombone use in the United States." *JITA* 22, no. 4 (Fall 1994): 25.
   Mathie's survey is listed and summarized by George Broussard in his "ITW: Research presentations." It is based on Mathie's 1993 doctoral paper at the University of Georgia, "The alto trombone: Performance and pedagogy in the United States," AAC 9329811, DAI-A 54/06, p. 1994, December 1993. See Stephen Anderson, 788, for more references on alto trombone.
   AltoTrb/Anderson,S./Broussard,G./Diss/GeorgiaU/Instruments-20thC/ITA/ITW/Pedagogy/PerfPrac

905. MATZ, R. "Wilson-Posaunen mit neuen Rotax-Ventil [Wilson trombones with new Rotax-valves]." *Instrumentenbau-Zeitschrift* 48 (May 1994): 6-8.
   Manufacturers/Rotax/Valves/Wilson

906. MAYS, Rich. "The impossible dream." *NITA* 3, no. 2 (May 1976): 19-20.
   Mays's article contains a description of a special case designed by him for carrying his trombone on a plane in the passenger

area. See Karl Hinterbichler and Leigh Gettier, 863, and Jerry Juhnke and G.B. Lane, 872.
Airlines/Cases/Gettier,L./Hinterbichler,K./Juhnke,J./Lane,G.

907. MCDUNN, Mark R. "A slide trombone for short arms." *Music Journal* 24 (March 1966): 81+.

McDunn discusses his design of a tenor trombone with a G rotor, which allows young people with short arms to execute pitches ordinarily not playable except in the outer positions. See "King creates the 'Flugabone,'" 877, for more references.
G-rotor/Instruments-20thC/King/Pedagogy/ShortArms/Slide/Valves

908. MCGOWAN, Keith. "A chance encounter with a unicorn: A possible sighting of the Renaissance slide trumpet." *HBSJ* 8 (1996): 90-101.

McGowan deals with the theory that the typical Renaissance sackbut, which was collapsible and flat-stayed, could be and perhaps on occasion was converted to a single-slide trumpet. This instrument would sound at a pitch that would correspond to the tenor voice in an ensemble. See *HBSJ* 9 (1997): vi, for an errata to the endnotes on this article. See Peter Downey, 825, for more references to the slide trumpet. See also H.W. Schwartz, 946.
CollapsibleStays/Downey,P./Instruments-Renaissance/Sackbut/Schwartz,H.W./SlideTrumpet

909. ———. "The world of the early sackbut player: Flat or round?" *Early Music* 22, no. 2 (1994): 441-466.

McGowan's well-documented survey of research on the Renaissance trombone includes discussions of the instruments, problems in holding the sackbut, posture, and a section on the sackbut in A. See Francis W. Galpin, 846, David Guion, 852, and Ephraim Segerman, 947. For more references see Arnold Fromme, 640.
Baroque/Bib/Fromme,A./Galpin,F./Guion,D./Instruments-Renaissance/Instruments-17thC/Instruments-18thC/Pedagogy/PerfPrac/Pitch/Sackbut/Segerman,E.

910. MELKA, Alois. "Erfahrungen mit Posaunisten bei subjektiven Instrumententests [Findings concerning trombonists and subjective

evaluations of instruments]." In *Das Instrumentalspiel: Beiträge zur akustik der Musikinstrumente, Medizinische und Psychologische Aspekte des Musizierens*. Vienna: Doblinger, 1989.

Melka's study, in German, discusses the results of psychoacoustic investigations which determined whether or not professional trombonists are capable of making objective judgments regarding instruments. See *RILM*1989-11891-as. For another study which deals with psychological profiles of trombonists, see Albert Tucker, 73.
Psychoacoustics/Psychology/Tucker,A.

911. MEYER, Jürgen, and Klaus WOGRAM. "Die Richtcharakteristiken von Trompete, Posaune, und Tuba [The directional characteristics of trumpet, trombone, and tuba]." *Musikinstrument* 19, no. 2 (February 1970): 171-180.

Meyer and Wogram's article is in German. For more references on trombone timbre, see Jay C. Bulen, 806, and Karel Dekan, 822. For a related acoustical study see Anton Spelda, 67.
Bulen,J./Dekan,K./Masking/SoundDirection/Spelda,A./Timbre

912. MILLER, Tracy. "Trombone leadpipes." East Texas State University, MM, 1989.

See above R. Philip Jameson and A.C. Himes, 871. For other references on trombone timbre, see Jürgen Meyer and Klaus Wogram, 911, and James A. Franck, 844.
Acoustics/EastTexasStateU/Franck,J./Himes,A.C./Leadpipes/
Meyer,J./Theses/Timbre/Wogram,K.

913. MÜLLER, S. "Die Ventilposaune [The valve trombone]." *Evangelische Musik-Zeitung* 30 (1936): 33-34.

Müller's article is in German and is cited by Mary Rasmussen on p. 70 of her "Brass bibliography: 1936-1940," *Brass Quarterly* 2, no. 2 (December 1958): 63-77.
Germany/PerfPrac/Rasmussen,M./Valves

914. MYERS, Arnold. "A slide tuba?" *Galpin Society Journal* 42 (August 1989): 127.

The double-slide instrument Myers discusses was made by Besson in the 1860s. It is located in England at the Cliffe Castle

Museum, Keighly, West Yorkshire. See Myers, *Catalogue of the
Brass Musical Instruments at Cliffe Castle* (N.p.: 1988)
(Acquisition #8692). See George Case, 815, and Gloria Flor, 842,
for more references.
Besson/Case,G./CliffeCastle/ContrabassTrb/DoubleSlide/England/
Flor,G./Museums/Tuba

915. MYERS, Herbert W. "Slide trumpet madness: Fact or fiction?"
Early Music 17, no. 3 (August 1989): 383-89.
    For a response to this article see Edmund A. Bowles, "Blowing
a trumpet," *Early Music* 18, no. 2 (May 1990): 350-351. For
more references see Peter Downey, 825.
Bowles,E./Downey,P./Instruments-Renaissance/SlideTrumpet

916. NASH, Harold. "Instruments: A Bach with some bite." *Sounding
Brass and the Conductor* 1, no. 3 (1972): 96
    See also Nash, 716, and 1191, and Simon Hogg, 150.
Bach,V./Britain/Hogg,S./Manufacturers/Pedagogy

917. NAYLOR, Tom L. *The Trumpet and Trombone in Graphic Arts.*
Nashville TN: Brass Press, 1979.
    Naylor's well-documented and splendidly printed book contains
222 prints of various musical subjects dealing with trumpets and
trombones. It encompasses the period 1500 to 1800 C.E. and is
cited in *RILM*80/4272rb10. See reviews by Donald Scharfenberg
in the *NITA* 8, no. 1 (September 1980): 36, and Laurence Libin
in *Notes* 37, no. 1 (September 1980): 59-60.
GraphicArts/Iconography/Libin,L./Reviews/Scharfenberg,D./Trumpet

918. NETTO [no first name given]. "Von Hörnen, Posaunen, und
Trompeten aus alter and neuer Zeit [Of horns, trombones, and
trumpets from old and new time(s)]." *Deutsche Militär-Musiker
Zeitung* 28 (1906): 73-74.
    Netto's article is in German and is cited by Mary Rasmussen on
p. 91 of her "Brass Bibliography: 1906-1910," *Brass Quarterly*
4, no. 2 (Winter 1960): 90-94. The article is also cited in
BRASSBIB.
Bands/Military/PerfPrac/Rasmussen,M.

919. "New double-barrelled trombone eliminates long stretch." *Instrumentalist* 5 (May-June 1951): 26.

See also "A special trombone [adapted for player with artificial arms]," *Instrumentalist* 28 (February 1974): 86. See also "King creates the 'Flugabone,'" 877, Mark McDunn, 907, and "Side-angle trombone eliminates stretch," 947.

ArtificialArms/DoubleBarrelledTrb/Flugabone/King/McDunn,M./ShortArms/Slide

920. NICHOLSON, Joseph M. "The development and use of the Renaissance trombone." *Missouri Journal of Research in Music Education* 2 (Autumn 1967): 58-68.

For more references see Arnold Fromme, 640.

Baroque/Bib/Fromme,A./Instruments-14thC/Instruments-15thC/Instruments-Renaissance/Instruments-17thC/Instruments-18thC/Neuschel,J./Nuremberg/Pedagogy/PerfPrac/Pitch/Sackbut

921. ———. "The trombone: Its evolution and history." *Music Journal* 25 (October 1967): 70-73+.

See also Arnold Fromme, 640.

Fromme,A./PerfPrac/TrbMus-Gen

922. NICKEL, Ekkehart. *Der Holzblasinstrumentenbau in der Freien Reichsstadt Nürnberg* [The construction of (wood)wind instruments in the free imperial city of Nuremberg]. Giebing, Germany: Katzbichler, 1970.

Though primarily a study of woodwind manufacturing in Nuremberg, Nickel's book, which is in German, also includes some discussion of brass manufacturing, including trombones. It is located in *RILM*70/3958bm45. See Fritz Jahn, 869, Martin Kirnbauer, 878, George B. Lane, 884, Gary M. Stewart, 953, and Willi Worthmüller, 987. See also Adam Carse, "The trumpet-makers of Nuremberg," *Monthly Musical Record* 67 (1937?): 203-204.

Bauer,J./Brass/Carse,A./Germany/Jahn,F./Kirnbauer,M./Lane,G./Nicholson,J./Nuremberg/Stewart,G./Worthmüller,W.

923. P., I. [only initials given] "On the serpent, bass-horn and trombone." *Harmonicon* (1834): 234.

Mary Rasmussen cites this article on p. 134 of her "Brass bibliography: 1830-1839," *Brass Quarterly* 7, no. 3 (Spring 1964): 133-136. It is also cited in *BRASSBIB*. Rasmussen cites a similar article by George Hogarth (see 866).
BassHorn/Hogarth,G./Instruments-19thC/Ophicleide/PerfPrac/
Rasmussen,M./Serpent/Trumpet

924. PAQUETTE, Daniel. "La musique à Lyon au XVIe siècle [Music in Lyons in the sixteenth century]." *Revue Musicale de Suisse Romande* 35, no. 1 (March 1982): 2-9.
    Paquette's article is in French and mentions manufacturers of sackbuts in Lyons during the sixteenth century.
    France/Instruments-16thC/Lyons/Sackbut

925. PARKS, Raymond. *Technical Drawings from the Edinburgh University Collection of Historic Musical Instruments: Tenor Trombone (Anton Schnitzer, Nuremberg, 1594), Tenor Trombone (Joseph Huschauer, Vienna, 1794), Trumpet (Joseph Huschauer, Vienna 1974), Cornett (Anon., Seventeenth Century?)*. Edinburgh: Edinburgh University Collection of Historic Musical Instruments, 1993-1994.
    Parks's book is available from the publisher at Reid Concert Hall, Bristo Square, Edinburgh EH8 9AG, Scotland. Pictures from the collection may be available on the World Wide Web at http://www.music.ed.ac.uk/euchmi.index.html. See a review by Robert L. Barclay in the *HBSJ* 7 (1995): 203-205.
    Barclay,R./Collections/Cornett/EdinburghU/Huschauer,J./
    Instruments-17thC/Museums/Reviews/Schnitzer,A.

926. PAWLOWSKI, Józef. *Puzon od A do Z* [The trombone from A to Z]. Kraków: Wyd. Muz., 1978.
    Pawlowski discusses the origins (allegedly from the tenth century), performance practices, and music of the trombone. His book is in Polish. For references on the origins of the trombone see Galpin, 846.
    Bib/Galpin,F./Medieval/PerfPrac/TrbMus-Gen

927. PETNEKI, Aron. "Ikonographie der musikalischen Darstellungen des ungarischen Mittelalters [Music iconography of medieval Hungary]." *Studia Musicologica* 15 (1973): 175-185.

Petneki's study, in German, features a thematic catalogue of instruments, including trombones, depicted in the musical iconography of Hungary.

Hungary/Iconography/Medieval

928. PIERING, Robert. "Zur Richtigstellung über 'Robert Pierings Posaunen-Zug mit Führung' [Corrections (errata?)] for 'Robert Piering's trombone slide (slide trombone?) with guidance (instructions?)']." *Zeitschrift für Instrumentenbau* 19 (1898/1899): 282-283.

Piering's article is in German and is cited on p. 170 of Mary Rasmussen's "Brass bibliography: 1890-1899," *Brass Quarterly* 4, no. 4 (Summer 1961): 168-172.

Pedagogy/Rasmussen,M./Slide

929. PLENCKERS, Leo J. *Haags Gemeentemuseum: Catalogus van de muziekinstrumenten* [The Hague Gemeentemuseum: Catalogue of the musical instruments], Vol. 1, *Hoorn- en trompetachtige blaasinstrumenten* [Horn- and trumpet-like wind instruments]. Amsterdam: Frits Knuf, 1970.

Plenckers's catalog, written in Flemish, describes 136 instruments, including trombones.

Collections/HagueGemeentemuseum/Museums

930. POLK, Keith. "The trombone in archival documents, 1350-1500." *JITA* 15, no. 3 (Summer 1987): 24-31.

Polk's article contains an excellent overview and explanation of medieval records where terms which are presumed to be references to early trombones are found. The endnotes, though naturally not alphabetized, provide a listing of valuable resources for research in this period. See also Polk, 725, and 931.

Instruments-14thC/Instruments-15thC/Instruments-16thC/Medieval

931. ———. "The trombone, the slide trumpet, and the ensemble tradition of the early Renaissance." *Early Music* 17, no. 3 (August 1989): 389-397.

Polk discusses the wind bands, particularly the tradition of shawm and posaune ensembles, which were often regarded as status symbols of the nobility during the fourteenth and fifteenth centuries in Europe. For a response to this article, see Edmund A. Bowles, "Blowing a trumpet," *Early Music* 18, no. 2 (May 1990): 350-351. See also Polk, 725. For more references see Peter Downey, 825.
Bowles,E./Downey,P./Instruments-14thC/Instruments-15thC/
Instruments-Renaissance/PerfPrac/SlideTrumpet/WindBands

932. PRATT, R.L., and J.M. BOWSHER. "The objective assessment of trombone quality." *Journal of Sound and Vibration* 65, no. 4 (August 1979): 521-547.
The journal which published this article is edited in the United Kingdom. The same two authors also published "The subjective assessment of trombone quality," in vol. 57, no. 3 (April 1978): 425-35. For a related study, see Alois Melka, 910. See S.J. Elliott and Bowsher, 833, and P.S. Watkinson and Bowsher, 978. See also Jay C. Bulen, 806, Karel Dekan, 822, James A. Franck, 844, William Thomas Walker, 977, and Klaus Wogram, 986.
In *Acustica* 38 (1977): 236-46, Pratt and Bowsher, along with S.J. Elliott published "The measurement of the acoustic impedance of brass instruments," an article in English, German, and French which describes an apparatus which does not have the limitations of earlier methods of measuring input impedance of brass instruments [see *RILM*77/6067ap86]. In the journal *Nature* 271, no. 5641 (January 1978): 146-147, the two authors, along with R.A. Smith, published "Improving the timbre and responsiveness of a bass trombone."
Acoustics/BassTrb/Bowsher,J./Bulen,J./Dekan,K./Elliott,S./
Franck,J./Melka,A./Pratt,R./Smith,R./Timbre/Walker,W./
Watkinson,P./Wogram,K.

933. PULVER, Geoffrey. "The sackbut." *The Sackbut* 3, no. 8 (192?).
Pulver's article is cited on p. 70 of Mary Rasmussen's "Brass bibliography: 1921-1925," *Brass Quarterly* 3, no. 2 (Winter 1959): 67-72. See Arnold Fromme, 640, Francis W. Galpin, 846, Kathleen Schlesinger, 945, and K. Weber, 981. Pulver's name is cited in *BRASSBIB* as Geoffrey, but as the author of *A*

Biographical Dictionary of Old English Music and Musical Instruments (New York: E.P. Dutton, 1923), his first name is given as Jeffrey.

Fromme,A./Galpin,F./Instruments-15thC/Instruments-16thC/
Rasmussen,M./Sackbut/Schlesinger,K./Weber,K.

934. RAPH, Alan. "The 'now' trombone." *Instrumentalist* 25, no 3 (1970): 48.

Raph gives his reasons for preferring the D tuning of the double valve in first position, among other general thoughts about both tenor and bass trombone instruments and designs. See a reply from J. Back in the *Instrumentalist* 25 (December 1970): 8, in which Back takes the position that the instrument to which Raph refers is not a true bass trombone, but a large-bore tenor, since it is in B-flat. Back considers only instruments in F pitched a fourth below as bass trombones. See Thomas G. Everett, 836, Gloria Flor, 843, and Duane Gatwood, 847, for more references.
Back,J./BassTrb/Everett,T./Flor,G./Gatwood,D./In-line/Pedagogy/
Slide/Tuning/Valves

935. RECORDIER, Alain. "Sacquer, bouter [To sack, to butt]." *Marsyas: Revue de pedagogie musicale et chorographique* 14 (June 1990): 32-33.

Recordier's article is in French and the title alone is intriguing enough to incite translation to several other languages. See Anthony Baines, 794, which contains a discussion of the etymology of the term, *sackbut*. See also Francis Galpin, 846, Trevor Herbert, 859, Geoffrey Pulver, 933, and Kathleen Schlesinger, 945. For more references see Arnold Fromme, 640.
Baines,A./Etymology/France/Fromme,A./Galpin,F./Herbert,T./
Instruments-14thC/Instruments-Renaissance/Orchestra/PerfPrac/
Pulver,G./Sackbut/Schlesinger,K./TrbMus-Gen

936. RIDLEY, E.A.K. *Wind Instruments of European Art Music.* London: Inner London Education Authority, 1974.

Ridley has compiled a catalog of the Hornian Museum collection of wind instruments used in orchestras and military bands during the last three centuries. It includes the Adam Carse collection and representative trombones.

Carse,A./HornianMuseum/Instruments-18thC/Instruments-19thC/
Instruments-20thC/Museums

937. RODIN, Jared. "Bass trombone: Perspective." *School Musician*
      47 (May 1976): 20-21.
      Rodin addresses misconceptions about the bass trombone as an
      ensemble instrument, describes its various valve configurations,
      and laments its neglect as a legitimate instrument which could be
      taught in secondary school music programs.
      BassTrb/Pedagogy/Valves

938. ROSS, Denwood F. "Trombone geometry with emphasis on the
      bell." [cited in *ROBERTS* as undergraduate research for a BS in
      music and physics at Indiana University].
      Bells/Geometry/IndianaU/Physics/Research

939. RUNYAN, William E. "The alto trombone and contemporary
      concepts of trombone timbre." *BBIBC* 28 (1979): 43-50.
      Runyan discusses the revival of the alto trombone, the problems
      of its acceptance as a solo instrument, and the resistance to its
      rejoining the symphony orchestra. A few of the technical aspects
      of performing on the instrument are also examined. For more
      references on alto trombone, see Stephen Anderson, 788. For
      information on trombone timbre in general, see R.L. Pratt and
      J.M. Bowsher, 932.
      AltoTrb/Anderson,S./Bowsher,J./Orchestra/PerfPrac/Pratt,R./Timbre

940. RUSCH, Bob and H.J. RYAN. "Bob Enevoldsen." *Cadence* 17
      (April 1991): 5-16+.
      Bio/Enevoldsen,B./Jazz-Blues/PerfPrac/Valves

941. SACHS, Curt. "Bachs Tromba da tirarsi," *Bach-Jahrbuch* 5
      (1908): 141-143.
      Sachs discusses J.S. Bach's designation of "Tromba o corno da
      tirarsi," in the *Cantata No. 46* ("Schaüt doch und sehet"). He
      concludes that Bach meant the soprano trombone and that "corno
      da tirarsi" is another term for "tromba da tirarsi." See Philip
      Bate, 797, and Thomas G. MacCracken, 897, for more references.

Bach,J.S./Baroque/Bate,P./CornoDaTirarsi/MacCracken,T./
PerfPrac/TrombaDaTirarsi

942. SAFOWITZ, Vivian. "Trumpet music and trumpet style in the early Renaissance." University of Illinois, MM, 1965.

In spite of the title, which might lead one to think Safowitz's study had nothing to do with slide instruments, she discusses not only natural trumpets but also the brass slide instruments of the early Renaissance, including those that came to be known as trombones. There are copious musical examples, and the study is thoroughly documented. For more references see Peter Downey, 825.
AltoTrb/Bib/Downey,P./IllinoisU/Instruments-Renaissance/PerfPrac/
SlideTrumpet/Theses/Trumpet

943. SALMEN, Walter. "Musikanten auf Bilddarstellungen der Passion Christi [Musicians in pictorial representations of the Passion of Christ]. *Neue Zurcher Zeitung* 192, no. 471 (October 1971): 51.

Salmen's article, in German, shows musicians, including trombonists, in pictorial representations of the Passion dating from the fifteenth through the seventeenth centuries. They represent the musicians who were sometimes required to announce the execution of criminal sentences in Europe during the Middle Ages and later.
Germany/Iconography/Instruments-15thC/Instruments-16thC/
Instruments-17thC/PerfPrac

944. SAUER, Ralph. "The alto trombone in the symphony orchestra." *JITA* 12, no. 3 (July 1984): 41.

For more references see Stephen Anderson, 788.
AltoTrb/Anderson,S./Orchestra/PerfPrac

945. SCHLESINGER, Kathleen. "Sackbut." *Encyclopedia Britannica*, 11th ed. 23 (1911), 973-974.

For many years Schlesinger's was the definitive encyclopedia article on the trombone, and it is still one of the best researched and best written sources for information up to the turn of the twentieth century. Her article "Trombone" is located in vol. 27 of the same edition, pp. 302-304. Both articles are cited by Mary Rasmussen on p. 93 of her "Brass bibliography: 1906-1910,"

Brass Quarterly 4, no. 2 (Winter 1960): 90-94. See above for the other definitive article from the same time period, Francis W. Galpin, 846. For more references see Arnold Fromme, 640.

Fromme,A./Galpin,F./Instruments-Ancient/PerfPrac/ Rasmussen,M./Sackbut

946. SCHWARTZ, H.W. "Slip horn developed from trumpet tuning slide." *Metronome* 54 (March 1938): 17+.

See Keith McGowan, 908. For more references on slide trumpet see Peter Downey, 825.

Downey,P./McGowan,K./Slide/Trumpet

947. SEGERMAN, Ephraim. "The sizes and pitches of Praetorious's sackbuts." *FoMRHI Quarterly* 73 (October 1993): 50-51.

See David Guion, 852 and Keith McGowan, 909. For more references see Arnold Fromme, 640.

Baroque/Fromme,A./Guion,D./Instruments-16thC/Instruments-17thC/McGowan,K./Pitch/Praetorius,M./Renaissance

948. "Side-angle trombone eliminates 'stretch.'" *Instrumentalist* 5 (November-December 1950): 35.

This article gives a short description of an instrument designed and played by Davis Shuman, for many years the trombone teacher at the Juilliard School. The slide could be angled to the bell at forty degrees for young players with short arms, making it easier to reach the outer positions, or at twenty degrees, for older and more advanced players. The instruments were made by both the Reynolds Co. and the Buescher Co. For more references on designs which deal with trombonists who have problems reaching all the positions, see "King creates the 'Flugabone,'" 978, Mark McDunn, 907, and "New double-barrelled trombone," 919. See also "A special trombone [adapted for player with artificial arms]," *Instrumentalist* 28 (February 1974): 86.

AngledSlide/Buescher/Flugabone/King/Manufacturers/McDunn,M./ Reynolds/ShortArms/Shuman,D./Slide

949. SLUCHIN, Benny. "Le trombone alto [The alto trombone]." 2 parts. *BBIBC* 61 (1988): 70-71, and 62 (1988): 73+.

Sluchin's article is in French, German, and English. See a response by Howard Weiner in *BBIBC* 63 (1988): 77+. For more references on alto trombone, see Stephen Anderson, 788.
AltoTrb/Anderson,S./Weiner,H.

950. SLUCHIN, Benny, and René CAUSSÉ. "Sourdines des cuivres [Brass mutes]." *BBIBC* 57 (1987): 20-39.
Sluchin and Caussé include a discussion of trombone mutes. Their article is in French, English, and German. See J. Backus, 792, Gloria J. Flor, 841, Ted Griffith, 851, and David Langford, 885.
Acoustics/Backus,J./Caussé,R./Flor,G./Griffith,T./Langford,D./ Mutes/Trumpet

951. SPILKA, Bill. "Trombone conversion." *New York Brass Conference for Scholarships Journal* 4 (1976): 84-86.
Spilka describes tuning and technique for a bass trombone with F, E-flat, and G valves, in-line. For more references on multiple-valve designs, see Thomas G. Everett, 836.
BassTrb/Everett,T./In-line/Pedagogy/Slide/Tuning/Valves

952. STEELE-PERKINS, Crispian. "Practical observations on natural, slide, and flat trumpets." *Galpin Society Journal* 42 (August 1989): 122-27.
For more references, see above Peter Downey, 825. See also Frank Tomes, 963, and David Rycroft, "Flat trumpet facts and figures," *Galpin Society Journal* 42 (August 1989): 134-42.
Downey,P./FlatTrumpet/Instruments-Renaissance/Instruments-17thC/Instruments-18thC/NaturalTrumpet/Rycroft,D./ SlideTrumpet/Tomes,F.

953. STEWART, Gary M. "The restoration of a 1608 trombone by Jacob Bauer, Nuremberg." *Journal of the American Musical Instrument Society* 8 (1982): 79-92.
The instrument described by Stewart is from the Rosenbaum Collection in Scarsdale NY and is the only known surviving example of Bauer's (d. 1612) work. It was restored in the conservation laboratory of the Shrine to Music Museum, located in Vermillion, South Dakota. See Larry Kitzel, 879, and Randy Kohlenberg, 882. For more references, see Fritz Jahn, 869.

Baroque/Bauer,J./Carse,A./Instruments-17thC/Jahn,F./Kitzel,L./
Kohlenberg,R./Rosenbaum,R./ShrineToMusic/SouthDakota

954.   STIBLER, Robert. *"Cornett and Sackbut* [Review]." *International
       Trumpet Guild Newsletter* 6, no. 1 (1979): 15-16.
       Stibler reviews a periodical whose publication schedule is
       announced as irregular. It is edited by Paul Gretton and published
       its initial issue in February 1979 from Essen, Germany. The
       initial issue included an article by Philip Bate on draw-trumpet
       reconstructions (see 797). Stibler's article appeared in Kim
       Dunnick's ongoing column, "Book reviews."
       Baroque/Bate,P./Cornett/Dunnick,K./Gretton,P./Instruments-
       15thC/Instruments-16thC/Medieval/Reviews/Sackbut

955.   STRADNER, Gerhard. "The evolution of the pitch of cornetts
       and trombones at the time of Scheidt and Buxtehude." In *Dietrich
       Buxtehude and Samuel Scheidt: An Anniversary Tribute*
       (Saskatoon: University of Saskatchewan, 1988): 106-116.
       See *RILM*1992-09594-as. See Jeffrey Quick, 728, David Guion,
       852, and Ephraim Segerman, 947. For more references see
       Arnold Fromme, 640.
       Baroque/Buxtehude,D./Cornett/Fromme,A./Guion,D./Instruments-
       17thC/Instruments-18thC/Pitch/Quick,J/Scheidt,S./Segerman,E.

956.   STREETER, Thomas W. "The historical and musical aspects of
       the nineteenth-century bass trombone." 2 parts. *JITA* 4 (January
       1976): 33-36, and 5 (January 1977): 25-35.
       Streeter's article is cited in *JENKINS*. See also *Dissertation
       Abstracts*, publication no. AAC0237619 [listed as not available].
       Streeter served as the first treasurer (1972-1978) of the
       International Trombone Association. See Mary Rasmussen, 194,
       Werner Beyer, 403, Michael Lewis, 495, and Steve M.
       Wolfinbarger, 592.
       BassTrb/Beyer,W./Bib/CatholicU/Instruments-19thC/Lecture-
       Recital/Lewis,M./TrbMus-19thC/Wolfinbarger,S.

957.   ———. "Survey and annotated bibliography on the historical
       development of the trombone." *JITA* 7 (1979): 27-32.
       Bib/PerfPrac/TrbMus-Gen

958. TANNER, Paul, and Kenneth SAWHILL. "The differences between the tenor and bass trombones." *Instrumentalist* 23, no. 3 (1968): 50-53.

JENKINS cites Tanner and Sawhill's article as having been excerpted from a clinic. He further states that many aspects discussed in the clinic were omitted from the article.
BassTrb/Pedagogy/Sawhill,K.

959. THAYER, Orla Edward. "The axial flow valve update." *JITA* 10, no. 2 (April 1982): 34-35.

See also Thayer, "Thayer valve improves trombone sound," *Musik International—Instrumentenbau-Zeitschrift* 41 (June 1987): 439. For a further update on the Thayer valve see Ron Babcock, "The story of Ed Thayer and his axial-flow valve," *JITA* 26, no. 1 (Winter 1998): 38-42.
AxialFlow/Babcock,R./ThayerValve/Valves

960. THEIN, Heinrich. "Die Kontrabassposaune: Bild—Abriß unter besonderer Berücksichtigung der bautechnischen Aspekte (1973) [The contrabass trombone—pictures and sketches, taking particularly into account the principles of construction]." 2 parts. *BBIBC* 22 (1978): 53-60, and 23 (1978): 55-64.

Thein's article, in German, French, and English, deals with historical aspects in the first part, while the second part discusses modern construction aspects. Thein also includes a discussion of some of the music written for the instrument. Ben Van Dÿk, 975, also discusses the contrabass instrument as designed by the Thein brothers, Max and Heinrich. For more references on the contrabass trombone, see Gloria Flor, 842.
BassTrb/ContrabassTrb/Flor,G./Instruments-16thC/PerfPrac/
VanDÿk,B.

961. THEIN, Max, and Heinrich THEIN. "Neues über Alt-Posaune [News about the alto trombone]." *BBIBC* 45 (1984): 10-12.

The Thein brothers' article is in German, French, and English. See Stephen Anderson, 788, for more references on alto trombone.
AltoTrb/Anderson,S.

962.   "There's hope for trombonists with neck pain". *Weekly Telegraph*
       (New Zealand, N.d., n.p.).
       The article was submitted by Arthur Finch, a native of Great
       Britain living in New Zealand and appeared in Randy Campora's
       "General news," in the *JITA* 21, no. 3 (Summer 1993): 12. It
       recounts the experience of Ian Davies, formerly a trombonist with
       the English National Philharmonic Orchestra, who had to give up
       his position as a result of the neck pain he experienced during his
       performances with the symphony. Yamaha-Kemble, who were the
       makers of his trombone, devised a remote-control mechanism
       which proved successful in alleviating the pain. For a recent
       article dealing with repetitive strain injuries (RSIs), see Edward
       A. Wolff III, M.D., "Medical corner," *JITA* 26, no. 1 (Winter
       1998): 24-25.
       Campora,R./Davies,I./England/Finch,A./NewZealand/PainControl/
       RSI/Wolff,E./Yamaha-Kemble

963.   TOMES, Frank. "Flat trumpet experiments." *Galpin Society
       Journal* 43 (1990): 164-165.
       See above Crispian Steele-Perkins, 952.
       Baroque/FlatTrumpet/Steele-Perkins,C.

964.   TRACY, Bruce A. "The contrabass trombone: Its development and
       use." University of Illinois at Urbana-Champaign, DMA, 1990.
       See *Dissertation Abstracts* 9114442 and *RILM*1990-08021-dd.
       See George Case, 815, Gloria Flor, 842, Simon Karasick, 875,
       Arnold Myers, 914, Heinrich Thein, 960, Ben Van Dÿk, 975, and
       Herbert Deutsch, 1053. The contrabass trombone web site URL
       is capella.dur.ac.uk/doug/contrabass_trombone.html.
       Case,G./ContrabassTrb/Deutsch,H./Diss/Flor,G./IllinoisU-Urbana-
       Champaign/Karasick,S./Myers,A./Thein,H./VanDÿk,B.

965.   TRICHET, P. "De la saqueboute ou trompette harmonique (vers
       1640) [On the sackbut, or harmonic trumpet (about 1640)]."
       BBIBC 45 (1984): 10-12.
       Trichet's article is in French, German, and English. The term,
       "harmonic trumpet," is not widely used to describe any
       instruments of the seventeenth century. A reference to such an
       instrument was found in the index of Detlef Altenburg,

Untersuchungen zur Geschichte der Trompete im Zeitalter der Clarinblaskunst (1500-1800) [An examination of the history of the trumpet in the old times of the clarinplayers' art (from *clarino* or *clarion,* an S-shaped trumpet with a moveable sliding mouthpiece)], Regensburg: Gustav Bosse Verlag, 1973. However, a search of the page referenced (p. 27) did not reveal the word. A search of several other standard sources also failed to disclose the term being used to describe a trumpet or trombone of any sort, though the term *clarin* or *clarino* is used commonly. For more references on the slide trumpet, see Robert Barclay, 795, and Peter Downey, 825.
Altenburg,D./Barclay,J./Downey,P./HarmonicTrumpet/
Instruments-17thC/Sackbut

966. "The trombone." *American Musician* 29, no. 20 (1913): 10.
Cited by Mary Rasmussen on p. 169 of her "Brass bibliography: 1911-1915," *Brass Quarterly* 3, no. 4 (Summer 1960): 166-170.
PerfPrac/Rasmussen,M./TrbMus-Gen

967. "The trombone." *Metronome* 30, no. 6 (1914): 26; no. 11 (1914): 30-31.
Also cited by Mary Rasmussen in her "Brass bibliography: 1911-1915, *Brass Quarterly* 3, no. 4 (Summer 1960): 166-170.
PerfPrac/Rasmussen,M./TrbMus-Gen

968. "Trombone, Le." *Schweizerische Instrumentalmusik* 32 (1943): 363.
Cited by Mary Rasmussen on p. 236 of her "Brass bibliography: 1941-1945," *Brass Quarterly* 1, no. 4 (June 1958): 232-239.
PerfPrac/Rasmussen,M./TrbMus-Gen

969. "The trombone: A brief history." *Instrumentalist* 28 (February 1974): 41.
PerfPrac

970. ["Trombone videos"]. Elkhart IN: United Musical Instruments, USA, [1993].

Edward R. Bahr, in his column "Record reviews," in the *JITA* 21, no. 3 (Spring 1993): 38, lists three six-minute trombone video tapes pertaining to Benge, Conn, and King professional trombones. They are available from United Musical Instruments, USA, Inc., 1000 Industrial Parkway, Elkhart IN 46516.
Bahr,E./Benge/Conn,C.G./King/Manufacturers/UnitedMusical Instruments/Videos

971. TUERSOT, A. "Le trombone basse." *Musique and Radio* 51 (1961): 291+.
Tuersot's article is in both French and English. It is cited by Mary Rasmussen on p. 20 of her "Brass bibliography: 1961," *Brass Quarterly* 6, no. 1 (Fall 1962): 17-22, where she comments that the article is "uninformative."
BassTrb/France/Rasmussen,M.

972. TYACK, S.M. "Trigger happy." *Sounding Brass and the Conductor* 5, no. 2 (1976): 56-57+.
BassTrb/Valves

973. UPCHURCH, John. "Help . . . for sick slides and even good ones." *JITA* 21, no. 4 (Fall 1993): 48.
Upchurch's article contains helpful hints from one of the world's outstanding slide-repair people. See also his article, "So you'd like a faster slide?" *NITA* 4, no. 1 (September 1976): 8-9. See also John Leisenring, 887.
Leisenring,J./SlideRepair

974. VANCE, Stuart-Morgan. "Trombone slide position equivalence tables." *JITA* 6 (1978): 11-12.
Vance has compiled a set of tables "that show the amount of slide extension for the positions on trombones of different sizes, in terms of what that extension would be on a B-flat tenor trombone." See also Herbert Deutsch, 1053.
Deutsch,H./SlideEquivalenceTables

975. VAN DŸK, Ben. "New Thein bass trombone innovations." *BBIBC* 92, no. 4 (1995): 54-57.

Van Dÿk is currently bass trombonist with the Netherlands Radio Philharmonic Orchestra and a teacher at two conservatories in Holland. The Thein brothers' (Max and Heinrich) instrument is referred to by Van Dÿk as a contrabass trombone (see Heinrich Thein, 960, for further references on that instrument). It features a thinner bell, with a narrow rim (to minimize breaking up of the tone in loud dynamics), made of an alloy similar to the old Kruspe bells. The mouthpiece has a larger backbore and a more conical shape than the mouthpiece Van Dÿk had been using. See also Bruce Tracy, 963.
BassTrb/Bells/ContrabassTrb/Kruspe/Mouthpieces/Thein,H./ Thein,M./Tracy,B.

976. VENDRIES, Christophe. "Flûte transversière, cornemuse, trombone, et guimbarde dans la musique romaine impériale [Transverse flute, cornemuse [bagpipes], trombone and Jew's harp in the music of the Roman empire]," *Sources: Travaux Historiques* 2 (1985): 21-34.

Vendries's article is in French with a summary in English. See *RILM*1985-01135-ap. Though I have not seen the article, I believe the idea of a true trombone (as opposed to some brass instrument which merely had a sliding tube), even distantly related to the present-day instrument, in the musical panoply of the ancient Roman empire has little if any historical support.

One early account relates a tale of the Spartan bard Tyrtaeus, who supposedly got the idea of the slide in 685 B.C.E. (see Joseph Nicholson, 920, for more information).

Then there is the *tuba ductilis*, which, according to a legend, was discovered at Pompeii (or Herculaneum), was made of bronze, and had a mouthpiece of gold. For further information see Joseph Dey, 824, and Francis Galpin, 846. Galpin relates that several of these instruments were reported to have been found, and one specimen was reputed to have been presented to George III of England in 1738. However, though the relic was reported as late as 1856 to have been at Windsor Castle, there has been no record found of its cataloging and the instrument itself cannot be found in the royal collections. Galpin believed that this fabulous instrument was of the *buccina* class (large circular horns) and gives further reasons why other ancient writings which are

alleged to refer to slide-type brass instruments are either
mistranslations or have been corrupted by much later glosses.
Buccina/Dey,J./Galpin,F./Instruments-Ancient/Nicholson,J./
RomanEmpire/TubaDuctilis

977. WALKER, William Thomas. "The effects of an epoxy resin
surface coating on the characteristic sound of the trombone."
University of Northern Colorado, DA, 1988.
See *Dissertation Abstracts* 50/02A, p. 299, publication no.
AAC8909370, and *RILM*1989-12417-dd. See Jay C. Bulen, 806,
Karel Dekan, 822, James A. Franck, 844, and Klaus Wogram, 986.
Bulen,J./Dekan,K./Diss/EpoxyResin/Franck,J./Instruments-20thC/
NorthernColoradoU/SurfaceCoating/Timbre/Wogram,K.

978. WATKINSON, P.S., and J.M. BOWSHER. "Vibration
characteristics of brass instrument bells." *Journal of Sound and
Vibration* 85, no. 1 (November 1992): 1-17.
The journal from which this article is cited is edited in the
United Kingdom. Watkinson and Bowsher's study deals with
finite element techniques used to study the mode frequencies and
shapes of trombone bells. J.M. Bowsher has worked with several
people on various aspects of brass acoustics and materials. For
more references on trombone timbre, see S.J. Elliott and J.M.
Bowsher, 833, and R.L. Pratt and J.M. Bowsher, 932.
Acoustics/Bowsher,J./Elliott,S./Instruments-20thC/Pratt,R.L.

979. WEBB, John. "The English slide trumpet." *HBSJ* 5 (1993): 262-279.
See Robert Barclay, 795, Arthur Brownlow, 804, Cynthia A.
Hoover, 867, and Friedrich Anzenberger, 998.
Anzenberger,F./Barclay,R./Brownlow,A./England/Hoover,C./
SlideTrumpet

980. WEBER, K. "Die 'deutsche' Posaune [The 'German' trombone]."
Das Orchester 26 (July-August 1978): 566-570.
Weber's article is in German.
Germany

981. ———. "Die zweitältste Posaune (von 1557) [The second-oldest
trombone (from 1557)]." *Das Orchester* 35 (May 1987): 511-512.

Although I have not seen this article, which is in German, I feel certain that it deals with the Jorg Neuschel trombone, made in 1557 and discussed extensively in Canon Galpin's landmark study (see 846). Neuschel's instrument has long been considered to be the second-oldest extant trombone. The trombone that is allegedly the oldest was made by Erasmus Schnizter in 1551. Until recently, at least, it was located in the Germanic Museum of Nuremberg. See Henry George Fischer, 839, and Fritz Jahn, 869.
Fischer,H./Galpin,F./Instruments-16thC/Jahn,F./Neuschel,J./ Nuremberg/Schnitzer,E.

982. WEISSHAAR, Otto H. *Preventive Maintenance of Trombones.* Rockville Center NY: Belwin, 1966.

Weisshaar's monograph is taken from a larger volume, *Preventive Maintenance of Musical Instruments*, also published by Belwin. See also Les Benedict, 1015, Robert Giardinelli, 1101, and Frederick Snyder, 1258.
Benedict,L./Giardinelli,R./Maintenance/Repair/Snyder,F.

983. WENKE, Wolfgang. "Metallblasinstrumente im Bach-Haus Eisenach [Brass instruments in the Bach-Haus in Eisenach]." *Symposium zu Fragen des Musikinstrumentenbaus* (1983).

Wenke's article, in German, lists three trombones in the collection of the Bach-Haus, dating from the seventeenth to mid-eighteenth centuries. See also Miloslav Klement, 881.
Bach-Haus/Eisenach/Instruments-17thC/Instruments-18thC/ Klement,M./Museums

984. "The Wetherill trombone or slide flute." *Musical Standard* 31 (1928): 43-44, 59.

This article was cited by Mary Rasmussen on p. 162 of her "Brass bibliography: 1926-1930," *Brass Quarterly* (June 1959): 158-166, as having been obtained from a secondary reference. Though I have not seen the article, I believe the instrument named might be similar to one referred to by Hugh Davies in his article, "Swanee whistle," *New Grove Dictionary of Musical Instruments* (London: Macmillan, 1980) vol. 3, 480-481. The instrument is a flutelike cylinder with no finger holes. It is blown through a mouthpiece on its end with the pitch altered by an internal piston which is moved up and down. It was popular in light music of the 1920s, and several significant composers have written for its unique sound: Maurice Ravel in *L'enfant et les sortilèges*, Luciano Berio in his *Passaggio*, and Percy Grainger, who also constructed a "free music" machine which involved a slide flute. Davies found no connection with the famous "Swanee River."

Berio,L./Davies,H./FreeMusicMachine/Grainger,P./Rasmussen,M./Ravel,M./SlideFlute/SwaneeWhistle/Wetherill

985. WICK, Denis. "Performer's platform: The trombone." *Composer* (London) 50 (Winter 1976-1977): 36-39.

At the time of this article, Denis Wick was principal trombonist with the London Symphony and one of the most sought-after freelance performers and teachers in England.
England/PerfPrac

986. WOGRAM, Klaus. "Einfluss von Material und Oberflachen aus den Klang von Blechblasinstrumenten [The influence of material and surfaces on the sound of brass instruments]." *Instrumentenbau* 30, no. 5 (1976): 414-418.

Wogram's study involved the testing of eight trombones of identical bores and dimensions but made of different metals and with different surface coatings. Wogram has recently been working with trombonist Branimir Slokar in developing new trombone models. See Jay C. Bulen, 806, Karel Dekan, 822, James A. Franck, 844, Jean-Pierre Mathez, 903, R.L. Pratt and J.M. Bowsher, 932, and William Walker, 977.
Acoustics/Bowsher,J./Bulen,J./Dekan,K./Franck,J./Instruments-20thC/Mathez,J.P./Pratt,R./Slokar,B./SurfaceCoating/Walker,W.

987. WORTHMÜLLER, Willi. "Die Nürnberger Trompeten- und Posaunenmacher des 17. und 18. Jahrhunderts [The Nuremberg trumpet and trombone makers of the seventeenth and eighteenth centuries]." In *Mitteilungen des Vereins für Geschichte der Stadt Nürnberg* (Nuremberg), vol. 45 (1954): 208-325, and 46 (1955): 372-480.

These volumes are in German. See Fritz Jahn, 869, Martin Kirnbauer, 878, George B. Lane, 884, Joseph M. Nicholson, 920,

Ekkehart Nickel, 922, and Gary M. Stewart, 953. See also Adam Carse, "The trumpet-makers of Nuremburg," *Monthly Musical Record* 67 (1937?): 203-204.
Carse,A./Instruments-17thC/Instruments-18thC/Jahn,F./ Kirnbauer,M./Lane,G./Nicholson,J./Nickel,E./Nuremberg/ Stewart,G.

988. YEO, Douglas. "The bass trombone: Innovations on a misunderstood instrument." *Instrumentalist* 40 (November 1985): 22-26+.
BassTrb/Valves

989. ———. "Bass trombone equipment survey." *JITA* 11, no. 4 (October 1983): 22-23.
Yeo has compiled the results of a survey of the instruments favored by twenty-four bass trombonists in major U.S. symphony orchestras. See Thomas G. Everett, 836, and Gloria Flor, 843, for more references.
BassTrb/Everett,T./Flor,G./In-line/Orchestra/Pedagogy/Slide/ Tuning/Valves

990. ———. "In defense of the single valve bass trombone." *JITA* 12, no. 3 (July 1984): 20-22.
Yeo responds to an earlier article by Dwight Gatwood, 847 (see above for more references). His article also discusses the Thayer valve. There is a response by David J. Galloway at the end of Yeo's article. For an update on the Thayer valve, see Ron Babcock, "The story of Ed Thayer and his axial-flow valve," *JITA* 26, no. 1 (Winter 1988): 38-42. See Yeo, 988-989 for more references on multiple valves for bass trombones.
Babcock,R./BassTrb/Galloway,D./Gatwood,D./In-line/Thayer/Valves

991. ZOLA, Larry. "The trombone: The phenomenon of a musical sound." *JITA* 11, no. 2 (April 1983): 29-31.
Zola's article gives a succinct analysis of not only the makeup of a trombone sound and how it is produced but also how the ear responds to it.
Acoustics/Bib

992. "Zugposaune und Ventilposaune [Slide trombone and valve trombone]." *Schweizerische Instrumentalmusik* 32 (1943): 259.

This article is cited by Mary Rasmussen on p. 234 of her "Brass bibliography: 1941-1945," *Brass Quarterly* 1, no. 4 (June 1958): 232-239.

Rasmussen,M./Slide/Valves

7

PEDAGOGY

993. ACKERMAN, Bernard E. "Conversion method from B-flat tenor trombone to the trombone with an F attachment." State College of Washington, MM, 1957.

Ackerman's thesis is cited on p. 19 of Mary Rasmussen's "Brass bibliography: 1957," *Brass Bibliography* 2, no. 1 (September 1958): 12-19. See below Leon Brown, 1027, for more references.

Brown,L./"F"Attachment/Rasmussen,M./Theses/Valves/
WashingtonStateUniversity

994. AHARONI, Eliezar. "Locked triggers: A most helpful option for practicing and performing." *NITA* 5, no. 3 (April 1978): 33.

At the time of the writing of this article, Aharoni was bass trombonist with the Jerusalem Symphony Orchestra. He gives helpful suggestions about facilitating the rehearsal of extended passages which require the valves to be depressed, and ways to facilitate the manipulation of mutes during these same passages.

While agreeing to the worthiness of the idea, *JENKINS* believes that most of the time the locked triggers are not "worth the trouble in a practice session, unless one tires easily of holding the valves down." For more of Aharoni's concepts of the technique of working double triggers, see Aharoni, 996. For more references see Thomas G. Everett, 836, and Gloria Flor, 843.

BassTrb/Everett,T./Flor,G./Valves

995. ———. "New approach to teaching of the modern bass trombone." *JITA* 4 (1976): 29-33.

Aharoni's article contains excerpts from the first edition of his *New Method for the Modern Bass Trombone* (Jerusalem: Noga, 1975). See Aharoni, 996.
BassTrb

996.   ———. *New Method for the Modern Bass Trombone*, 4th ed. (Jerusalem: Noga, 1996).
See annotations to first edition (1975) in Thomas G. Everett, 432. Aharoni's book is intended for intermediate to advanced players and has a very helpful discussion on the uses of "double and independent rotary valve bass trombones." It is available in the United States from Lyceum, P.O. Box 747, Ithaca NY 14850, or in Europe from Schauer, 220 The Vale, London, NW11 8HZ. See also Everett, 836.
BassTrb/Everett,T./Valves

997.   ALESSI, Joseph. "Of slides, Sinatra, and trombone technique." *Instrumentalist* 47 (February 1993): 12-16.
Alessi, principal trombonist of the New York Philharmonic, outlines a practice routine which covers all aspects of technique and musicianship. His reference to Frank Sinatra is ascribed to a lecture by bass trombonist George Roberts in which Roberts credited Sinatra with outstanding phrasing and control of a musical line. Roberts, among many others, strongly suggests that students listen to recordings of Sinatra to learn techniques of musicianship.
Embouchure/Musicianship/PerfPrac/PracticeTechniques/ Roberts,G./Sinatra,F./Technique

998.   ANZENBERGER, Friedrich. "Method books for slide trumpet: An annotated bibliography." *HBSJ* 8 (1996): 102-114.
See also Anzenberger's "The earliest French tutor for slide trumpet," *HBSJ* 4 (1992): 106-111. See also Robert Barclay, 795, Arthur Brownlow, 804, Günter Dullat, 828, Cynthia A. Hoover, 867, and John Webb, 978.
Barclay,J./Bib/Brownlow,A./Dullat,G./Hoover,C./SlideTrumpet/ Webb,J.

999. APPERT, Donald. "The alto trombone: Its uses, problems, and solutions." *JITA* 8 (1980): 13-14.
For more references on alto trombone, see Stephen C. Anderson, 788.
AltoTrb/Anderson,S./Bib/PerfPrac/TrbMus-18thC/TrbMus-20thC

1000. ———. "Developing high register on the trombone." *JITA* 9 (March 1981): 9.
See Miff Mole, 1190, and Joseph Russell, 1236.
HighRegister/Mole,M./Russell,J.

1001. ———. "John Coffey's approach to teaching the trombone." *JITA* 14, no. 3 (Summer 1986): 46-47.
See Charles Colin, 102.
BassTrb/Bio/Coffey,J./Colin,C.

1002. ARMSTRONG, J., and J. COOMBES. "A two-star discussion of trombone troubles." *Melody Maker* 26 (June 1950): 8.
Armstrong and Coombes's article is cited by Mary Rasmussen on p. 179 of her "Brass bibliography: 1946-1950," *Brass Quarterly* 1, no. 3 (March 1958): 168-181.
Rasmussen,M./Technique

1003. ATWATER, D.F. "The development and trial of computer-based interactive videodisc courseware for teaching skills in the visual diagnosis of selected programs in trombone performance." University of Illinois at Urbana-Champaign, EdD, 1991.
Atwater's dissertation was reviewed by W.L. Berz in the *Council of Research in Music Education Bulletin* 120 (Spring 1994): 51-55.
Berz,W./Computers/Diss/IllinoisU-Urbana-Champaign/Interactive/PerfPrac/Reviews

1004. BACHELDER, Daniel F. "An investigation of trombone 'Tone Center.'" Brigham Young University, PhD, 1976.
See *Dissertation Abstracts* 37/08-A, p. 4681, AAD77-02174.
See also Charles Dalkert, 1050, and Joel Elias, 1061.
BrighamYoungU/Dalkert,C./Diss/Elias,J./ToneCenter

1005. BAER, Douglas. "Studio teaching: Improving pitch relationships between two trombones or euphoniums." *National Association of College Wind and Percussion Instructors Journal* 28 (Spring 1980): 44-46.

Baer shows a very simple way to teach students the concept of matching pitches through listening for the acoustic phenomenon of beats between two pitches (basically the same but not quite matched) played by similar instruments. See Thomas Beversdorf, 1016, for more references.

Beversdorf,T./Intonation/Overtones

1006. BAKER, Buddy. "Dealing with fear in performance." *NITA* 7, no. 2 (April 1980): 20-21.

Drawing upon his extensive experience as a performer and teacher, Baker outlines his ideas which he feels have worked for him and his students. He feels that too many articles which deal with this subject are not helpful because they are too technical, are too complicated, try to psychoanalyze, or all of the above. See John Swallow, 1269. See also Edward A. Wolff III, M.D., "Indereal and stage fright," *JITA* 24, no. 3 (Summer 1996): 20-21. Wolf edits an ongoing column in the *JITA* called "Medical corner."

Anxiety/Indereal/PerfPrac/Swallow,J./Wolff,E.

1007. ———. "Jazz improvisation: The beginning student and the inexperienced teacher." *JITA* 10, no. 1 (January 1982): 10-12.

See Bruce E. Melville, 512, William R. Yeager, 783, Rob Boone, 1019, Samuel T. Daley, 1048, Henry Fillmore, 1081, Fortunate Sordillo, 1260, Les Tomkins, 1278 [Kai Winding], and Edward J. Ulman, 1281.

Boone,R./Daley,S./Fillmore,H./Improvisation/Jazz-Blues/ Melville,B./Rosolino,F./Sordillo,F./Tomkins,L./Ulman,E./ Winding,K./Yeager,W.

1008. ———. "Performing with mutes on the trombone." *NITA* 7, no. 2 (April 1980): 23-24.

Baker recommends types of mutes for specific circumstances and gives advice on how to minimize the problems and noise that

mutes can cause. See Seymour Brandon, 1023, for more references.
Brandon,S./Mutes.

1009. ———. "Trombone demonstration." *JITA* 14, no. 1 (Winter 1986): 12-13.
Baker uses his ingenuity and love for children to create clever ways to interest fifth- and sixth-grade students in playing trombone. See another article by Ed Martin and Alice Campbell in *Director* [published by United Musical Instruments, USA] 3, no. 3-16 (1996): 3-5, which also deals with Baker's skills in working with children and showing them the wonders of the trombone world.
Beginners/Campbell,A./ElementarySchool/Martin,E./MusicEd

1010. ———. "Trombone talk." *National Association of Jazz Educators Educator Journal* 7, no. 2 (December/January 1974): 41.
Baker authored several other articles which appeared in various issues of this journal.
Jazz-Blues

1011. BANSCHBACH, Donald L. "Alternate slide positions." *Instrumentalist* 38 (February 1984): 55-56+.
See Antonio García, 642, for a discussion of alternate positions in a jazz context. See also Maurice Faulkner, 1078, Gloria Flor, 1085, Jeremy Kempton, 1144, Tom Malone, 1173, Marvin Rosenberg, 1232, James Smith, 1255, Albert Stoutamire, 1266, and John Swallow, 1269.
AlternatePositions/Faulkner,M./Flor,G./García,A./Kempton,J./ Malone,T./Rosenberg,M./Smith,J./Stoutamire,A./Swallow,J.

1012. ———. "Reducing pressure in the trombone embouchure." *Instrumentalist* 33 (October 1978): 54+.
See *Dissertation Abstracts* 48/06-A, p. 1410, AAD87-18613. Banschbach's study measures and discusses two types of mouthpiece forces which are observable during performance: direct force (where the mouthpiece pushes straight into the lips) and shear force (perpendicular to the direct force, induced if the player pulls the mouthpiece up or down).

See also A.C. Himes, Jr., 862, John Philip Froelich, 1096, James Fulkerson, 1098, [G.B. Lane], 1159, and Morris Sweatt and Gregg Magnuson, 1272. For a mouthpiece specification chart by Eric Nicklas, updated by Stanley Kling, contact them on the Internet at http://www.cceric/index.html, or by e-mail at cceric@showme.missouri.edu, and kling@odpwcr. ucsd.edu. Bib/Embouchure/Fulkerson,J./Himes,A./Kling,S./Lane,G./ Magnuson,G./MouthpiecePressure/Mouthpieces/Nicklas,E./Sweatt,M.

1013. BAUER, Paul D. "Bass trombone pedagogy as practiced by selected bass trombonists in major American symphony orchestras: Techniques and their origins." Northwestern University, DM, 1986.
See *Dissertation Abstracts* 47/07A, p. 2357, publication no. AAD86-24147. See also his article, "Focus on the excerpts," *JITA* 18, no. 1 (Winter 1990): 26-29, where chapter 2 of the dissertation is excerpted. Bauer's dissertation contains information gathered from interviews with five prominent American bass trombonists.
Five works were reviewed in the discussions: *Symphony No. 1* by Johannes Brahms, *Symphony in D minor* by César Franck, *Hary Janos Suite* by Zoltán Kodály, *Ein Heldenleben* by Richard Strauss, and "Ride of the Valkyries" from *Die Walküre* by Richard Wagner. The bass trombonists interviewed were Edwin Anderson, Cleveland Orchestra; Donald Harwood, New York Philharmonic; Edward Kleinhammer, Chicago Symphony; Jeffrey Reynolds, Los Angeles Philharmonic; and Charles Vernon, Philadelphia Orchestra.
See Thomas G. Everett, 301, 432, and 1071-1072, Donald Appert, 1001, Leon Brown, 1027, Robert G. Bruch, 1029, John Christie, 1035, John W. Coe, 1041, Reginald H. Fink, 1083, James Graham, 1105, James E. Hughes, 1123, Robert G. Hurst, 1129, Mike Kelly, 1142, Rich Mays, 1180, Allen Ostrander, 1196, Alan Raph, 1213, Traugott Rohner, 1229-1230, and David Wilborn, 1295. For an update on methods for bass trombone study see David William Brubeck, "An analysis of selected bass trombone methods," University of Miami, DMA, 1997.
Anderson,E./Appert,D./BassTrb/Brahms,J./Brown,L./Brubeck,D./ Bruch,R./Christie,J./Coe,J./Coffey,J./Diss/Everett,T./Fink,R./

Franck,C./Graham,J./Harwood,D./Hughes,J./Hurst,R./Kelly,M./
Kleinhammer,E./Kodály,Z./Mays,R./NorthwesternU/Orchestra/
Ostrander,A./Raph,A./Reynolds,J./Rohner,T./Strauss,R./
Vernon,C./Wagner,R./Wilborn,D.

1014. BAXTER, Leroy E. "The use of selected vocal materials from the classical and romantic periods as a method of teaching musical style characteristics to trombone students." Arizona State University, EdD, 1973.

Baxter's doctoral paper is located in *RILM*75/2490dd45. See also *Dissertation Abstracts* 34/12A, p. 7569, publication no. AAC7405456. See Glenn P. Smith, 555, Neill Humfeld, 1124, Randall T. Mitchell, 1189, and Benny Sluchin, 1253.

ArizonaStateU/Bordogni,M./Diss/Etudes/Mitchell,R./Musicianship/
PerfPrac/Rochut,J./Sluchin,B./Smith,G./Style/Transcriptions/
TrbMus-18thC/TrbMus-19thC/TrbMus-Gen/Vocal

1015. BENEDICT, Les. "How do you clean your 'bone'?" *Windplayer* 53 (1995): 41.

See Otto Weisshaar, 982, Robert Giardinelli, 1101, and Frederick Snyder, 1258.

Giardinelli,R./Maintenance/Snyder,F./Weisshaar,O.

1016. BEVERSDORF, Thomas. "Problems influencing trombone intonation." *Instrumentalist* 7 (October 1952): 24-25+.

Beversdorf, the 1979 recipient of the ITA Award, includes charts on overtones and their intonation tendencies on trombones. See *BRASSANTH* 109-110. See above Douglas Baer, 1005, Seymour Brandon, 1024, Charles Dalkert, 1051, David Fetter, 1079, A.C. Himes, 1117, Michael Keener, 1141, Gabriel Kosakoff, 1153, Brian Martz, 1174, Mark McDunn, 1182, Harry J. McTerry, 1184, and Albert Stoutamire, 1266.

Baer,D./Brandon,S./Dalkert,C./Fetter,D./Himes,A./Intonation/
Keener,M./Kosakoff,G./Martz,B./McDunn,M./McTerry,H./
Overtones/Stoutamire,A.

1017. BIDDLECOME, James. "Proper breathing and breath control." *JITA* 12, no. 3 (July 1984): 28-29.

At the time of the writing of this article, Biddlecome had bee n a regular member of the New York City Opera orchestra for eighteen years (not to be confused with Robert Biddlecombe, former bass trombonist with the American Symphony and the American Brass Quintet). See Roy Crimmins, 1045, Joel Elias, 1061, Lewis Van Haney, 1109, Kenneth H. Phillips and Karin H. Sehmann, 1205, and Herbert Schoales, 1241. See also Antonio J. García with José L. García Oller, M.D., "So why do I need my nose to breathe through my mouth?" *JITA* 22, no. 3 (Summer 1994): 32-34.
BreathControl/Crimmins,R./Elias,J./Haney,L.V./Phillips,K./ Schoales,H./Sehmann,K.

1018. BLAINE, Robert J., Jr. "Adaptation of the Suzuki-Kendall method to the teaching of a heterogeneous brass-wind instrumental class of trumpets and trombones." Catholic University, PhD, 1976.

   See *Dissertation Abstracts* 37/03A, p. 4010, publication no. AAC7619964 and *RILM*1978-05903-rd. Blaine's doctoral paper was reviewed by Charles A. Elliott in the *Council for Research in Music Education Bulletin* 56 (Fall 1978): 55-60.
CatholicU/Diss/Elliott,C./Kendall,J./Reviews/Suzuki,S./Trumpet

1019. BOONE, Rob. "Practicing jazz." *JITA* 23, no. 3 (Summer 1995): 20-21.

   Boone includes a list of jazz-related publications either written for trombone or available in bass clef. He also lists several helpful suggestions for setting up a jazz practice session, and includes an annotated page of jazz exercises. For more references see Buddy Baker, 1007.
Baker,B./Bib/Improvisation/Jazz-Blues

1020. BORDEN, Lawrence. "The doctrine of intent." *JITA* 25, no. 2 (Spring 1997): 24-28.

   Borden discusses his premise, "The goal of performance is for the audience to perceive the pure intent of the performer." Some of his basic ideas include, "It is the responsibility of performers to transmit the notated, implied or requested ideas of the composer to the best of their ability," and "The vast majority of

what performers wish to communicate is communicated via the sound itself."
PerfPrac/Philosophy

1021. ———. "Why trombones sound . . . late." *JITA* 22, no. 1 (Winter 1994): 18-21.
Borden presents a well-researched and documented study of the rubber-stamp lament from all conductors to trombonists (although he hastens to point out that the problem is not confined to trombonists). He gives several possible reasons for the phenomenon, with some practical suggestions for dealing with it in a constructive way. See John Seidel, 1246.
Articulation/Attacks/Musicianship/Precision/Seidel,J.

1022. BOWLES, R.W. "Multiphonics on low brass instruments." *Instrumentalist* 34 (October 1979): 52+.
See Michelle Castellengo, 617, and Stuart Dempster, 621, for more references. See also George Broussard, 271, for references to the use of multiphonics in a jazz context.
Avant-Garde/Broussard,G./Castellengo,M./Dempster,S./Multiphonics

1023. BRANDON, Seymour. "Muting the low brass." *Woodwind, Brass and Percussion* 20, no. 4 (1981): 4-5+.
See above Buddy Baker, 1008. See below Al Grey and M. Grey, 1107. In the index of this book under see entries under *Mutes* and *Plungers*.
Baker,B./Grey,A./Grey,M./Langford,D./Mutes/Paradis-Hagar,J./
PerfPrac

1024. ———. "Teaching trombone intonation." *Woodwind World-Brass and Percussion* 15, no. 4 (1976): 32+.
See Thomas Beversdorf, 1016, for more references.
Beversdorf,T./Intonation

1025. BRICK, John S. "An exploratory study of the effects of a self-instructional programme utilising the Pitch Master on pitch discrimination and pitch accuracy in performance of young trombonists." *Psychology of Music* 12, no. 2 (1984): 119-125.

Located in *RILM*83/7316ap82 Brick's article has been reprinted from the *Journal of the Society for Research in Psychology of Music and Music Education.* The conclusion of the article is that utilizing the Pitch Master did improve the level of pitch accuracy in student performances. See R. Philip Jameson, 1135, and Olin Parker, 1200.

Jameson,P./Parker,O./PitchDiscrimination/PitchMaster/Psychology

1026. BRIGHTWELL, James R. "The development of a standard for crediting the study of trombone at the college level." Ohio State University, MM, 1947.

Brightwell's thesis is cited by Mary Rasmussen on p. 179 of her "Brass bibliography: 1946-1950," *Brass Quarterly* 1, no. 3 (March 1958): 168-181. See Mark Hartman and Arved Larsen, 1112, William R. Haskett, 1114, and Robert Lee Kidd III, 1145.

Colleges-Universities/Hartman,M./Haskett,W./Kidd,R./Larsen,A./OhioStateU/Rasmussen,M./Theses

1027. BROWN, Leon. "Study literature for the F attachment and bass trombone." *Instrumentalist* 23, no. 11 (1969): 71-75.

Brown's study is cited by *JENKINS* as a useful and well-conceived article. See Bernard E. Ackerman, 993, Joel Elias, 1063, Thomas G. Everett, 1071, Reginald H. Fink, 1082, Gloria Flor, 1087, Jack Flouer, 1089, Neill Humfeld, 1126, and Alan Raph, 1214. For more information on bass trombone pedagogy see Paul Bauer, 1013. For references to using multiple valves or triggers, see Alan Raph, 1213, and David F. Wilborn, 1295.

Ackerman,B./Elias,J./Everett,T./"F"Attachment/Fink,R./Flor,G./Flouer,J./Raph,A./Valves/Wilborn,D.

1028. ——. "Trombone forum." *Southwestern Brass Journal* 1 (Spring 1957): 15-19.

BreathControl/Legato/Technique

1029. BRUCH, Robert G. "Fine tuning your bass trombonist." *Maryland Music Educator* (Spring 1977): 22-24.

Bruch's article is considered by *JENKINS* to be very basic. See Donald Appert, 1001, Paul Bauer, 1013, and Leon Brown, 1027.

For references to using multiple valves or triggers see Thomas G. Everett, 836, Alan Raph, 1213, and David Wilborn, 1295.
Appert,D./BassTrb/Bauer,P./Brown,L./Everett,T./Raph,A./ Wilborn,D.

1030. BUCHTEL, Forrest L. "Trombone problems in playing legato and slurring." *Educational Music Magazine* 19 (1939-1940): 43.
The subject of legato articulation on the trombone is one of the most frequently discussed and written about in the area of trombone pedagogy. The following list is representative: Richard Fote, 1091, James Graham, 1106, Mildred Kemp, 1143, Michael K. Mathews, 1177, David Mathie, 1178, June Phillips, 1204, James G. Poolos, 1207, Peter H. Riddle, 1224, Stewart L. Ross, 1234, William Shepherd, 1248, Robert D. Smith, 1257, and P. Young, 1305.
Articulation/Fote,R./Graham,J./Kemp,M./Legato/Mathews,M./ Mathie,D./Phillips,J./Poolos,J./Riddle,P./Ross,S./Shepherd,W./ Smith,R./Young,P.

1031. BUGLI, David. "Low brass master class at Peabody Conservatory." *JITA* 11, no. 2 (April 1983): 25-27.
The master class was led by the trombone section of the Baltimore Symphony Orchestra (David Fetter and James Olin, co-principals, Eric Carlson, second, and Douglas Yeo, bass) and David Bragunier, tubist with the National Symphony Orchestra. A list of audition material is included, classified according to tenor trombone, tenor tuba, bass trombone, and section audition passages. See also Eric Carlson, 1033.
Auditions/Bib/Bragunier,D./Carlson,E./Fetter,D./Olin,J./ Orchestra/Yeo,D.

1032. CAMPBELL, Larry D. "Why double on trombone and euphonium?" *TUBA Journal* 10, no. 4 (Spring 1983): 7-9.
See Matthew McCready, 708, Edward R. Bahr, 793, and Lee A. Drummer, 1059. See also Fortunato Sordillo, "Doubling on brass instruments," *Metronome* 42 (February 1926): 71-72, cited by Mary Rasmussen on p. 165 of her "Brass bibliography: 1926-1930," *Brass Quarterly* 2, no. 4 (June 1959): 158-166.

Bahr,E./Doubling/Drummer,L./Euphonium/McCready,M./
PerfPrac/Rasmussen,M./Sordillo,F.

1033. CARLSON, Eric. "Some thoughts on auditions." *JITA* 11, no. 4
(October 1983): 18-20.
At the time of the writing of this article, Eric Carlson was
second trombone with the Baltimore Symphony. See Charles
Hurt, 1130, Greg Lisemby, 1166, Milton Stevens, 1263, and
Douglas Yeo, 1302.
Auditions/Careers/Hurt,C./Lisemby,G./Orchestra/Stevens,M./Yeo,D.

1034. CATELINET, Barry. "Bass trombone: Byron McCulloh." *Accent*
4, no. 4 (1979): 8-11.
Catelinet interviews Pittsburgh Symphony bass trombonist
McCulloh in a master class format. See Bruce Tracy, 224. See
also a letter from Ralph Sauer, relating to McCulloh's comments
on the trend in bass trombone sounds, printed in "The eighth
position," *JITA* 15, no. 2 (Spring 1987). A short biographical
sketch of McCulloh appears in Ben Ivey's ongoing column,
"General news," in the *NITA* 7, no. 2 (April 1980): 4-5. It also
contains a brief bibliography of McCulloh's compositions up to
1980. See Byron McCulloh, 55.
BassTrb/Ivey,B./McCulloh,B./Orchestra/Pittsburgh/Sauer,R./Tracy,B.

1035. CHRISTIE, John M. "Teaching the bass trombone."
Instrumentalist 15, no. 7 (1961): 39-43.
Christie's article is one of the best early pedagogical studies on
bass trombone. He gives many valuable insights that are relevant
even for the present time. However, such problems as multiple
trigger techniques, which face today's performers more than those
of thirty years ago, are dealt with only briefly. The article is cited
and annotated in *JENKINS*. See also Christie's "Music for bass
trombone," on pp. 44-45 of the same issue. See Thomas G.
Everett, 836, and Paul Bauer, 1013, for more references.
BassTrb/Bauer,P./Everett,T.

1036. ČIMERA, Jaroslav. "Teaching the trombone." *Instrumentalist* 3
(September 1948): 11-14+

Čimera's approaches are ahead of his time, particularly in his suggestions for improving the upper register (they sound very much like Donald Reinhardt's "pivot system"). In the same issue of *Instrumentalist* on p. 34, see "Trombone materials." For a sketch of Čimera's life and teaching, see Keig E. Garvin and André M. Smith, 140, and [Traugott Rohner], 200.
Garvin,K./Reinhardt,D./Rohner,T./Smith,A.

1037. CLARK, Wayne R. "Teaching concepts and techniques utilized by three American trombone professors." University of Oklahoma, DMA, 1996.
The trombone teachers interviewed and discussed were Edwin D. "Buddy" Baker, University of Northern Colorado; Irvin Wagner, University of Oklahoma; and Vern Kagarice, University of North Texas.
Baker,B./Diss/Kagarice,V./NorthernColoradoU/NorthTexasU/ OklahomaU/Wagner,I.

1038. CLARKE, Ernest. "From a trombonist's viewpoint." *Tempo* 1 (February 1934): 21+.
Clarke's article is cited by Mary Rasmussen on p. 125 of her "Brass bibliography: 1931-1935," *Brass Quarterly* 2, no. 3 (March 1959): 117-125.
PerfPrac/Rasmussen,M.

1039. ———. "Hints for trombone players." *Metronome* 40 (March 1924): 66+.
Ernest Clarke was the trombonist brother of the famous cornet virtuoso Herbert Clarke and was considered a virtuoso in his own right. His article is cited by Mary Rasmussen on p. 72 of her "Brass bibliography: 1921-1925," *Brass Quarterly* 3, no. 2 (Winter 1959): 67-72. See also his *Clarke's Method for Trombone* (New York: Carl Fischer, 1913).
PerfPrac/Rasmussen,M./Technique

1040. ———. "Two perfect wind instruments—the voice and the trombone." *Jacobs' Band Monthly* 18 (December 1933): 5.

Clarke's article is cited by Mary Rasmussen on p. 125 of her "Brass bibliography: 1931-1935," *Brass Quarterly* 2, no. 3 (March 1959): 117-125. See also Michael Crist, 1046.
Crist,M./Rasmussen,M./Vocal

1041. COE, John W. "Developing bass trombonists in the public schools." *Selmer Bandwagon* 69 (1973): 24.
See Paul Bauer, 1013, for more references.
BassTrb/Bauer,P./PublicSchool/Selmer

1042. CRAMER, William F. "The fundamental and essential principles of trombone performance technique: Their teaching and application." *JITA* 13, no. 3 (July 1985): 12-15.
Reprinted from the *BBIBC* 49 (1985): 61-71, Cramer's article was originally a position paper for a three-hour seminar presented before the Second International Colloquium held in Paris, November 13-18, 1983.
France/PerfPrac/SecondInternationalColloquium

1043. ———. "Valsalva maneuver—why?" *BBIBC* 52 (1985): 36-38.
The "Valsalva maneuver," is defined in the tenth edition of *Webster's New Collegiate Dictionary* as "the process of making a forceful attempt at expiration while holding the nostrils closed and keeping the mouth shut for the purpose of testing the patency of the Eustachian tubes or of adjusting middle ear pressure." It was named after eighteenth-century Italian anatomist Antonio Maria Valsalva. For more references on breath control, see James Biddlecome, 1017.
Biddlecome,J./BreathControl/ValsalvaManeuver

1044. CRIDER, Joseph R., and F.H. NELSON. "The effectiveness of the buzz extension and resistance piece to tone, range, and intonation of beginning trombonists." *Dialogue in Instrumental Music Education* 14, no. 1 (1990): 35-47.
Crider and Nelson discuss a device known as the Buzz Extension and Resistance Piece (BERP), available from Musical Enterprises in California. See Tucker Jolly and Sherman Vanderark, 1136, Harold L. Leno, 1162, Ralph Sauer, 1239, and Peter M. Vivona, 1288.

BERP/Buzzing/Intonation/Jolly,T./Leno,H./Nelson,F./Range/
Sauer,R./ToneQuality/Vanderark,S./Vivona,P.

1045. CRIMMINS, Roy. "Strictly instrumental: Jazz is a warm
trombone." *Jazz Journal International* 37 (May 1984): 14-15.
Crimmins deals with breath control and technique in a jazz
context. See James Biddlecome, 1017.
Biddlecome,J./BreathControl/Jazz-Blues/Technique

1046. CRIST, Michael. "The expressive trombone: A singing
approach." *Dialogue in Instrumental Music Education* 16, no. 1
(1992): 1-11.
See Ernest Clarke, 1040.
Clarke,E./Legato/Musicianship

1047. CRUMP, Harold C. "Orchestral studies for trombone." University
of Michigan, MM, 1954.
See Glen C. Law, 1161.
Law,G./MichiganU/Orchestra/Theses

1048. DALEY, Samuel T. *Sure System of Improvising for Trombone*,
rev. ed. Akron OH: Samuel T. Daley, 1927.
I obtained a copy of this book, which was distributed by Alfred
Music Co. in New York, from my father-in-law, Robert
Grambling, who began studying trombone in the 1930s, played
with the Shreveport (Louisiana) Symphony for many years, and
was an active free-lance musician in the Shreveport area for over
forty years. It should be of special interest to anyone who is
interested in the history of jazz styles of the 1920s and 1930s.
The book has some fascinating terminology: For example, *weird
notes*—notes one half step above the principal notes of a chord;
the suggested practices are (1) don't use too many, and (2) they
should be accented. A thirty-bar example is given in which Daley
says nine hundred two-bar breaks of a C major chord are
possible. There are several pages of suggested ways to utilize
these "breaks."
Dirt choruses (sock choruses) are apparently choruses which
allow more *blue notes*, than *hot choruses*. Also a hot chorus us

es about one-half the original melody, while dirt choruses use very little of the original melodic line.

Improvisation is defined as "the ability to change the melody and not the harmony of one or more bars in a musical number." Other topics covered include keys, scales (including whole tone), chords (major, minor, diminished, augmented, seventh, and major ninths) and other melodic and rhythmic style features of the period. For more references see Buddy Baker, 1007.

Baker,B./DirtChorus/Grambling,R./HotChorus/Improvisation/ Jazz-Blues/WeirdNotes

1049. DALKERT, Charles. "Improved holding position—better sound." *Instrumentalist* 28 (February 1974): 48-49.

Dalkert explains how and why trombonists sometimes have problems with attacks and tone production, particularly in the outer positions. See Gene Stiman, 1265.

Articulation/HoldingPosition/Slide/Stiman,G./ToneQuality

1050. ———. "Some aids to tone production." *JITA* 8 (1980): 18.

See Daniel F. Bachelder, 1004, and Joel Elias, 1061. See also Gene Stiman, 1265.

Bachelder,D./Elias,J./Stiman,G./ToneQuality

1051. [———]. "Some thoughts on trombone tuning." *JITA* 6 (1978): 19.

See Thomas Beversdorf, 1016, for more references.

Beversdorf,T./Intonation/Overtones

1052. DESTANQUE, Guy. "Le pédaogie du trombone [Trombone pedagogy]." *Revue de musicothérapie* 8, no. 5 (1988): 64-71.

Destanque's article is in French. In 1979 Destanque was bass trombonist with the Orchestre de Paris. See Thomas G. Everett, 124.

BassTrb/Everett,T./France

1053. DEUTSCH, Herbert. "The trombone family." *Getzen Gazette* (December 1972).

Cited by Karl Hinterbichler in his ongoing column, "Literature announcements," in the *NITA* 6, no. 1 (September 1978): 22, Deutsch's article contains slide position charts for soprano (B-flat), alto (E-flat), tenor, tenor with "F" attachment, bass

trombone with double valve, bass trombone in F and G, and contrabass trombone (B-flat). See Stuart-Morgan Vance, 972. For more references, see Thomas G. Everett, 836.
AltoTrb/BassTrb/ContrabassTrb/Everett,T./Hinterbichler,K./ Slide/SopranoTrb/Valves/Vance,S.

1054. DE YOUNG, Derald Dwight. "A videofluorographic analysis of the pharyngeal opening during performance of selected exercises for trombone." University of Minnesota, PhD, 1975.
See *Dissertation Abstracts* 37/01-A, p. 22, AAD76-14881. See Kenton Ronald Frohrip, 1097. For further information on the use of videofluorography see A. Keith Amstutz, "A video-fluorographic study of the teeth aperture, instrument pivot and tongue arch and their influence on trumpet performance," University of Oklahoma, Doctor of Music Education, 1970. Articles based on Amstutz's study appear in the *Journal of the International Trumpet Guild* 2 (1977): 25-26, and the *Journal of Band Research* 11, no. 2 (1975): 28-39.
Amstutz,K./Diss/Frohrip,K./MinnesotaU/Videofluorography

1055. DICKINSON, Christian. "Effects of starting prospective elementary school trombone students on the euphonium/baritone." Indiana University (Pennsylvania), independent research, 1987.
Dickinson's study is cited in *KOHLENBERG I*. Though I am unaware of any written ideas by Thomas Beversdorf on this subject, on several occasions he expressed to me his belief that starting prospective trombone students on euphonium would be a positive strategy, particularly in developing tone quality and concepts on trombone.
Beversdorf,T./ElementarySchool/Euphonium/Indiana(Penn)U/Research

1056. DONNELL-KOTROZO, Carol. "Intersensory perception of music: Color me trombone." *Music Educators Journal* 65, no. 4 (December 1978): 32-37.
Donnell-Kotrozo's fascinating article addresses the concept of synesthesia (chromesthesia) among children and its relation to teaching and learning music. As early as February, 1921, a short article on what was then called *chromacousia* (hearing colors) appeared in *Etude*, vol. 39, no. 2. Donnell-Kotrozo cites

musicologist Albert Lavignac at the turn of the century as suggesting many instrument-color relationships. The trombone, for instance, was crimson with orange. One of the landmark studies on the phenomena of synesthesia and its related aspects is Lawrence E. Marks's *The Unity of the Senses* (New York: Academic Press, 1978).

Chromacousia/Chromesthesia/*Etude*/Lavignac,A./Marks,L./ Psychology/Synesthesia

1057. DOUAY, Jean. *L'A.B.C. du jeune tromboniste* [The ABCs of the young trombonist]. Paris: Billaudot, 1975.

Douay's volume is in French.

Beginners/France

1058. DRISCOLL, Anne. "The art of trombone playing: A conversation with Raymond Premru, and Ralph Sauer." *Instrumentalist* 40 (May 1986): 18-24.

Premru (d.1998) was for many years one of the top bass trombonists and a successful composer and arranger in London, England, before being appointed to the music faculty at Oberlin. Ralph Sauer is co-principal trombone with the Los Angeles Philharmonic.

Orchestra/PerfPrac/Premru,R./Sauer,R.

1059. DRUMMER, Lee A. "Euphonium performance opportunities [doubling]." *TUBA Journal* 17, no. 4 (Spring 1990): 8+.

See Matthew McCready, 708, Edward R. Bahr, 793, and Larry Campbell, 1032.

Bahr,E./Doubling/Euphonium/McCready,M./PerfPrac

1060. DUKER, Guy M. "A method for the trombone based upon the unit approach to the reading of rhythms, scales, and chords." University of Illinois, MM, 1942.

Duker's thesis is cited by Mary Rasmussen on p. 239 of her "Brass bibliography: 1941-1945," *Brass Quarterly* 1, no. 4 (June 1958): 232-239.

IllinoisU/Rasmussen,M./Theses/UnitApproach

1061. ELIAS, Joel. "Basics in breathing: An outline to a better sound."
BBIBC 32 (1980): 53.
See Daniel Bachelder, 1004, and James Biddlecome, 1017, for
more references.
Bachelder,D./Biddlecome,J./BreathControl/ToneQuality

1062. ———. "Developing the F-attachment range on tenor trombone."
*National Association of College Wind and Percussion Instructors
Journal* 41, no. 2 (1992-1993): 4-8.
See Leon Brown, 1027, for more references.
Brown,L./"F"Attachment/LowRegister/Valves

1063. ———. "The development of the alto and tenor clefs on the
trombone." *National Association of College Wind and Percussion
Instructors Journal* 42, no. 3 (1994): 16-17.
See John R. Melton, 1185.
Clefs/Melton,J.

1064. ———. "The middle school/high school trombone choir: A
conversation with Pat Crossen." *JITA* 19, no. 3 (Summer 1991): 28.
At the time of this interview, Pat Crossen was the band director
at St. Isidore's School in Danville CA. See Carl M. Lobitz, 496,
Danny J. Hutson, 678, Paul Tanner, 766, and Irvin L. Wagner, 774.
Crossen,P./Hutson,D./Lobitz,C./PublicSchool/Tanner,P./TrbChoir/
Wagner,I.

1065. ELIAS, Joel, and LaMar JONES. "The art of trombone section
playing." *Instrumentalist* 39 (February 1985): 36+.
See Robert K. Matchett, 1175, and Frederick Snyder, 1259.
Ensemble/Jones,L./Matchett,R./Musicianship/Precision/Snyder,F.

1066. ———. "Extending the trombonist's range." *Instrumentalist* 38
(September 1983): 90+.
Elias and Jones's article deals with balance and blend,
intonation, articulation, and precision within large ensembles.
Jones,L./Range

1067. ELLENRIEDER, M. *Unterricht für die Bass-, Tenor-, und Alt-
Posaune, nebst Übungen* [Practical lessons for the bass, tenor,

and alto trombone, together with exercises]. Regensburg: Reitmayr, [by 1832].

Ellenrieder's monograph is cited by Mary Rasmussen on p. 136 of her "Brass bibliography: 1830-1839, *Brass Quarterly* 7, no. 3 (Spring 1964): 133-136, as being listed in Kayser, *Vollständiges Bücher-Lexicon, 1750-1832.* It is also cited in *BRASSBIB.* Germany/Kayser/Methods/Rasmussen,M./TrbMus-19thC

1068. ERVIN, Thomas. "Precollegiate trombone workshops: A successful idea." *JITA* 13, no. 4 (October 1985): 40.

Ervin's article also appears in the *National Association of College Wind and Percussion Instructors Journal* 34, no. 1 (1985): 11. See also Benny Sluchin, 1254.
Pre-College/Sluchin,B./Workshops

1069. ———. "Some thoughts on differences between playing jazz and legit." No. 7 in the *Yamaha Wind Session Education Series.* Grand Rapids MI: Yamaha Corp. of America, 1990.

Ervin, one of the few outstanding trombonists who are almost equally successful as concert and jazz artists, has written a succinct and well-conceived pamphlet. It would be especially helpful to talented young trombonists who have not yet decided whether they wish to perform as a jazz or orchestral player or who are looking for exercises and suggestions which will assist them to prepare for both types of performances. See also Carl Lenthe and Jiggs Whigham, "The differences are actually similarities," *JITA* 26, no. 1 (Winter 1998): 50-54.
Jazz-Blues/Lenthe,C./PerfPrac/Whigham,J.

1070. ———. "Stuff to practice when you run out of stuff to practice." *NITA* 7, no. 1 (December 1979): 12.
PracticeMaterials

1071. EVERETT, Thomas G. "An annotated bibliography of methods and study for bass trombone with F attachment." *Brass World* 7, no. 1 (1972): 28-37.

Everett's bibliography is one of the articles which formed the basis for his *Annotated Guide to Bass Trombone Literature* (see

432). For more references, see Everett, 836, Paul Bauer, 1013, and Leon Brown, 1027.

BassTrb/Bauer,P./Brown,L./"F"Attachment/LowRegister/ Methods/PublicSchool/Valves

1072. ———. "Basic literature for bass trombone study." *Instrumentalist* 33, no. 5 (1978): 62-65.
See Everett, 1071, for references.
BassTrb/Bib

1073. ———. "A brief glimpse at the USSR." *BBIBC* 14 (1976): 16-18. Everett sketches activities in trombone classes at the Rimsky-Korsakov Conservatory located in what was then called Leningrad (now St. Petersburg), with Victor Venglovsky, professor of trombone at the conservatory and solo trombone with the Leningrad (St. Petersburg) Philharmonic Symphony Orchestra. See Heinz Fadle, 635, and Victor Venglovsky, 1287.
Fadle,H./Leningrad/Petrograd/SovietUnion/StPetersburg/Venglovsky,V.

1074. FADLE, Heinz. "A celebration of one hundred years of trombone in Hungary at the Franz Liszt Academy." *JITA* 26, no. 1 (Winter 1998): 34-36.
Professor Fadle relates an account of the historic movement of trombone teaching in Hungary as outlined by Franz Liszt Academy Professors Ferenc Steiner, Laszlo Ujfalussi, and Gustav Höna.
FranzLisztAcademy/Höna,G./Hungary/Steiner,F./Ujfalussi,L.

1075. ———. *Looking for the Natural Way: Thoughts on Trombone and Brass Playing.* Hannover, Germany: Edition Piccolo, 1997.
Heinz Fadle is professor of trombone in Detmold, Germany. His book is available in the United States from Kagarice Brass Editions, Box 5302, Denton TX 76203.
PerfPrac

1076. FALLENBERG, Jerry. "The sport of trombone playing?: Applying athletic peak performance techniques to your playing." *JITA* 25, no. 2 (Spring 1997): 21-22.

Fallenberg has coached basketball at the high school level and is a performing trombonist. He covers such topics as daily goal setting, mental rehearsal, and simulations, quoting such well-known sport psychologists as Terry Orlick, Barry Green, and Charles Garfield. See Stewart L. Ross, 1233, and John Swallow, 1271. See also David R. Kauss, *Peak Performance: Mental Game Plans for Maximizing Your Athletic Potential*, Englewood Cliffs NJ: Prentice-Hall, 1980, and Robert D. Weast, *Keys to Natural Performance for Brass Players* (New York: McGinnis & Marx, [1979]).
Athletics/Bib/Diss/Garfield,C./Green,B./Kauss,D./MentalPractice/ NorthwesternU/Orlick,T./PracticeTechniques/Ross,S./ Swallow,J./Weast,R.

1077. FAULISE, Paul and Tony STUDD. "Double rotor techniques." *Connchord* 14, no. 1 (1970): 3-5.
See Thomas G. Everett, 836, for more references.
BassTrb/DoubleRotor/Everett,T./Slide/Studd,T./Valves

1078. FAULKNER, Maurice. "Developing facility in the alternate positions." *Instrumentalist* 23 (November 1968): 61-62.
See above Donald L. Banschbach, 1011, for more references.
AlternatePositions/Banschbach,D./Technique

1079. FETTER, David. "The electronic tuner: A new practice tool for trombonists." *JITA* 15, no. 1 [mistakenly labeled as 14, no. 4] (Winter 1987): 49.
See also a letter from Fetter ("The eighth position," *JITA* 15, no. 2) explaining some points he felt were omitted from his article. See Thomas Beversdorf, 1016, for more references.
Beversdorf,T./ElectronicTuner/Intonation

1080. ———. "Slide exercises." *JITA* 12, no. 4 (October 1984): 36.
Fetter's article is included as part of Robert Reifsnyder's ongoing column, "Trombone pedagogy." See Donald Banschbach, 1011, Donald Hummel, 1127, Vern Kagarice, 1137, Guy Kinney, 1146, Ernest Lyon, 1170, Harold Nash, 1191, Robert Reifsnyder, 1218 and 1219, Milton Stevens, 1262, Robert W. Stroetz, 1268, and Jurij Usov, 1284 [Boris Grigoriev].

Banschbach,D./Grigoriev,B./Hummel,D./Kagarice,V./Kinney,G./
Lyon,E./Nash,H./Reifsnyder,R./Slide/Stevens,M./Stroetz,R./
Technique/Usov,J.

1081. FILLMORE, Henry. . . . *Jazz Trombonist for Slide Trombone,
Bass Clef . . . A Unique Treatise Showing How to Play Practical
Jazzes and How and Where to Insert Them in Plain Trombone
Parts.* Cincinnati: Fillmore House, 1919.
Cited in *BRASSBIB.* See Buddy Baker, 1007, for more
references.
Baker,B./Improvisation/Jazz-Blues

1082. FINK, Reginald H. "The 'F' attachment tenor trombone."
Instrumentalist 12, no. 7 (March 1958): 52-54.
See *BRASSANTH* 228-229. See also his update, "From tenor to
bass trombone." *Instrumentalist* 16, no. 5 (January 1962): 50-51,
cited and annotated in *JENKINS.* See Thomas G. Everett, 836,
Paul Bauer, 1013, and Leon Brown, 1027, for more references.
Fink was professor of trombone at Ohio University and editor of
Accura Music for many years. He passed away in 1996.
Bauer,P./Brown,L./Everett,T./"F"Attachment/LowRegister/
Methods/Valves

1083. ———. "The sound of a bass trombone." *Instrumentalist* 16, no.
10 (June 1962): 66-67.
Fink's article is cited and annotated in *JENKINS.* See also
BRASSANTH 315-316. See Paul Bauer, 1013, Leon Brown, 1027,
and Rich Mays, 1180, for more references.
BassTrb/Bauer,P./Brown,L./Everett,T./"F"Attachment/Mays,R./Valves

1084. ———. *The Trombonist's Handbook: A Complete Guide to
Playing and Teaching the Trombone.* Athens OH: Accura, 1977.
See reviews by Thomas G. Everett in the *NITA* 5, no. 1
(September 1977): 14-15, and by Donald A. Hummel in the
*National Association of College Wind and Percussion Instructors
Journal* 26, no. 1 (Fall 1977): 42. The book is located in
*RILM*77/5619rb45.
Bib/Discog/Everett,T./Hummel,D./Reviews

1085. FLOR, Gloria J. "Alternate positions on the trombone."
Woodwind World—Brass and Percussion 18, no. 3 (1979): 18-19.
See Donald L. Banschbach, 1011, for more references. For a
discussion on the use of alternate positions in a jazz context see
Antonio García, 642.
AlternatePositions/Banschbach,D./García,A.

1086. ———. "The alto trombone as a beginner's instrument."
Woodwind, Brass and Percussion 22, no. 5 (1983): 13.
See Donald Appert, 999, See Lee H. Kavanaugh, 1140, and
Traugott Rohner, 1231. For more references on alto trombone,
see Stephen C. Anderson, 788.
AltoTrb/Anderson,S./Appert,D./Beginners/Bib/Elias,J./
Kavanaugh,L./PerfPrac/Rohner,T./TrbMus-18thC/TrbMus-20thC

1087. ———. "The F attachment tenor trombone in the elementary
school music program, part I." 2 parts. *School Musician* 47, no.
3 (1975): 12, 14-15, and 47, no. 5 (1976): 16-18.
Part 2 of this valuable article contains a comparison chart of
instruments. See Leon Brown, 1027, and Jack Flouer, 1089.
Brown,L./ElementarySchool/"F"Attachment/Flouer,J./Low Register/
Methods/PublicSchool/Valves

1088. ———, ed. "Brass workshop: The pit orchestra trombonist." *The
School Musician* 50 (March 1979): 8+.
Flor discusses the equipment required for a pit orchestra
trombonist, especially mutes and special effects, and how to
determine which part may be called for when the trombonist is
expected to play parts originally written for other instruments.
Mutes/PerfPrac/Theater

1089. FLOUER, Jack. "Introducing the F attachment." *Instrumentalist*
35, no. 8 (1981): 56-58.
Flouer's article explores embouchure changes in the low
register and slide placement when using the attachment. His
article contains musical examples. See Gloria Flor, 1088, for
more references.
"F"Attachment/Flor,G./LowRegister/Valves

1090. FORTENBERRY, Robert E. "An evaluation of selected group
      methods for the trombone." Mississippi Southern College, MM, 1957.
      Fortenberry's thesis is cited by Mary Rasmussen on p. 19 of
      her "Brass bibliography: 1957," *Brass Quarterly* 2, no. 1
      (September 1958): 12-19.
      GroupMethods/Rasmussen,M./SouthernMississippiU/Theses

1091. FOTE, Richard. "Principles of trombone legato." *Instrumentalist*
      28 (February 1974): 47-48.
      Fote's article is one of the most logical and well-written on this
      subject. See Forrest L. Buchtel, 1030, for more references.
      Articulation/Buchtel,F./Legato

1092. FOWLER, Bruce. "Thoughts of a mother." *JITA* 4 (1976): 4-6.
      Fowler, one of the outstanding jazz stars in the 1970s and
      1980s, outlines his philosophy of "a creative approach to
      trombone playing," which covers what he calls the "controlled"
      period, "where the conscious mind is continuously aware of the
      basics," and the musically creative period, where "the music
      flows and the player tries to execute what he hears, not letting
      mistakes destroy the feeling and logic of what he is playing." He
      includes two etudes he composed which illustrate his points.
      Creativity/Technique

1093. FOWLER, William. "How to bone up on slip-horn changes."
      Down Beat 41, no. 20 (December 1974): 28.
      Fowler's article contains discussions on circular breathing,
      alternate positions, against-the-grain playing, and rhythmic
      manipulation, based on publications of David Baker, Tom
      Malone, and Bruce Fowler. *BRASSBIB* cites William Fowler as
      the author, while *Music Index* lists Bruce Fowler.
      AlternatePositions/Baker,D./BreathControl/CircularBreathing/
      Fowler,B./Jazz-Blues/Malone,T./Rhythm/Slide/Technique

1094. FRIEDMAN, Jay. "Random thoughts on the trombone." *JITA* 2
      (1973-1974): 3-11.
      The principal trombonist of the Chicago Symphony gives his
      ideas on breathing, vibrato, legato, sound, high register, tonguing,
      auditions, and public performance. For an insightful, clever, and

humorous updating of Friedman's ideas about trombone teaching and performance, see his "Thoughts to ponder," *JITA* 25, no. 1 (Winter 1997): 20-21, and no. 2 (Spring 1997): 16-18. Articulation/Auditions/BreathControl/HighRegister/Legato/ PerfPrac/ToneQuality/Vibrato

1095. ———. "Trombone: Beyond legato, vibrato, and slide technique." *Instrumentalist* 50 (August 1995): 148-150.
See Friedman, 1094.
PerfPrac

1096. FROELICH, John Philip. "Mouthpiece forces during trombone performance." University of Minnesota, PhD, 1987.
See *Dissertation Abstracts* 48/06-A, p. 1410, AAD87-18613. See also his article based on his dissertation in the *JITA* 18, no. 3 (Summer 1990): 16-23. His study is similar to that of Donald Banschbach, 1012 (for more references).
Banschbach,D./Bib/Diss/MinnesotaU/Mouthpieces/Mouthpiece Pressure/ShearForce

1097. FROHRIP, Kenton Ronald. "A videofluorographic analysis of certain physiological factors involved in performance of selected exercises for trombone." University of Minnesota, PhD, 1972.
See *Dissertation Abstracts* 33/10-A, p. 5763, AAD73-10555. See above Derald Dwight De Young, 1054.
DeYoung,D./Diss/MinnesotaU/Videofluorography

1098. FULKERSON, James. "Low register development for the trombone." *BBIBC* 13 (1976): 35-43.
Fulkerson discusses mouthpiece pressure versus shifting of the jaw to produce the low register. It contains musical exercises, and the article has been translated into French and German. See John Philip Froelich, 1096, and Daniel B. Tetzlaff, 1277.
Froelich,J./LowRegister/Tetzlaff,D.

1099. GALLOWAY, D. "A new L.R.S.M. trombone performers' diploma." *South African Music Teacher*, no. 107 (1985): 23.
A search through several sources, including library reference desks, led to a conclusion that the initials for this diploma stand

for Licentiate of the Royal School of Music or something similar. Galloway's article is cited in *BRASSBIB*.
L.R.S.M./SouthAfrica

1100. GEORGE, Stanley P. "An annotated bibliography of trombone methods and study materials." University of Northern Colorado, DA, 1982.
   Randy Kohlenberg [*KOHLENBERG I*] has cited an independent research project by Stanley George, "A teachers guide to trombone study books," Oral Roberts University, independent research, 1988, which is apparently a continuation of his doctoral project. See also *Dissertation Abstracts*, publication no. AAC0365345 [listed as not available].
   Diss/Etudes/NorthernColoradoU/OralRobertsU/Research

1101. GIARDINELLI, Robert. "Trombone care and maintenance." *Instrumentalist* 28 (February 1974): 51.
   See Otto H. Weisshaar, 982, Les Benedict, 1015, and Frederick Snyder, 1258.
   Benedict,L./Maintenance/Snyder,F./Weisshaar,O.

1102. GLASMIRE, David. "Trombone forum." *Southwestern Brass Journal* 1 (Fall 1957): 32-37.
   Technique

1103. GOROVOY, S.G. "Science and technology in trombone teaching." *BBIBC* 41 (1983): 37-38.
   Gorovoy's article is in French, German, and English.
   Science/Technology

1104. GOULD, James F. "The proposed use of string music as study etudes for the trombone; with selected transcribed examples." University of Southern California, MM, 1952.
   Gould's article is listed in Richard Roznoy, 16. It is also abstracted in the *Music Educators National Conference Journal*, 43 (September-October 1956): 60. See also Robert B. Conger, 422, Stanley P. George, 445, Chang-Yi Lai, 489, and Robin J. Zubeck, 594.

Bach,J.S./Conger,R./Etudes/George,S./Lai,C./Roznoy,R./
StringMusic/Transcriptions/Zubeck,R.

1105. GRAHAM, James. "Developing your bass trombonists."
Instrumentalist 21, no. 11 (1967): 49-52.
Graham's article is cited and annotated in *JENKINS* as a good
update for John M. Christie's article (see Christie, 1035). He
includes a list of tuba literature performable on bass trombone.
See Thomas G. Everett, 836, and Paul Bauer, 1013, for more
references.
BassTrb/Bauer,P./Everett,T./"F"Attachment/Solos/Tuba/Valves

1106. ———. "The legato style of the trombone." *Instrumentalist* 19
(May 1965): 79-80+.
See also *BRASSANTH* 390-394. There is probably as much or
more published material on this topic than on any other
pertaining to trombone pedagogy. See Forrest L. Buchtel, 1030,
for more references.
Articulation/Buchtel,F./Legato

1107. GREY, Al, and M. GREY. *Plunger Techniques: The Al Grey
Plunger Method for Trombone and Trumpet.* Introduction by I.
Gitler. New York: Second Floor Music, 1987.
The Greys' method is cited in *BRASSBIB*. See Bob Bernotas,
260, [Ben Ivey], 316, Jennifer Paradis-Hagar, 720, Gerry Sloan,
751, and Buddy Baker, 1008.
Baker,B./Baron,A./Bernotas,B./Gitler,I./Grey,M./Ivey,B./
Jackson,Q./Jazz-Blues/Mutes/Paradis-Hagar,J./Plunger/Sloan,G.

1108. HALL, Ben. *The Balanced Trombonist.* Gaithersburg MD:
Balanced Publications and Services, 1995.
Hall's monograph is advertised as a supplement to standard
method books, and claims endorsement by many outstanding jazz
and orchestral performers. The address of the publisher is 11122
Black Forest Way, Gaithersburg MD 20879.
PerfPrac/Technique

1109. HANEY, Lewis Van. "Some in's and out's of breathing." *JITA*
1 [1972-73]: 9-10.

Van Haney, long-time trombonist with the New York Philharmonic, and professor of trombone at Indiana University, was given the ITA Award in 1973. See James Biddlecome, 1017, for more references on breathing.
Biddlecome,J./BreathControl

1110. HARDIN, Anne F. "An instrument matching procedure as a factor in predicting success in beginning flute, trumpet, and trombone students." University of South Carolina, PhD, 1990.

Hardin's test groups involved ninety-three sixth-grade beginning band students enrolled in five demographically similar schools. Hardin was for many years editor of the *International Trumpet Guild Journal*.
Beginners/Diss/ElementarySchool/Flute/ITG/MusEd/PublicSchool/ SouthCarolinaU/Trumpet

1111. HARTMAN, Mark. ed. "Pedagogy: The young trombonist." *JITA* 16, no. 1 (Winter 1988): 18-19.

Mark Hartman took over as pedagogy editor for the *JITA* in 1988, and began a series of articles about how young, potential trombonists are being educated in private and public schools. A panel of eminent performers and teachers was engaged to provide input and answer pedagogical questions.

The initial column introduced the panel: Buddy Baker, William Harris, Jeannie Williams, and Gail E. Wilson. Part 1 appears in the *JITA* 16, no. 3 (Summer 1988): 14-16, and addresses the initial contact between the student and teacher. Part 2 appears in the *JITA* 17, no. 2 (Spring 1989): 10-15, and focuses on the structure of an applied lesson.
Baker,B./Harris,W./Williams,J./Wilson,G.

1112. HARTMAN, Mark, and Arved LARSEN. "Undergraduate trombone teaching survey." *JITA* 21, no. 1 (Winter 1993): 18-19.

Hartman and Larsen conclude that undergraduate trombone instruction, at least at the time of the questionnaire that was sent out, was in "relatively good health." See *Dissertation Abstracts* 40/04-A, p. 1740, AAD79-21237. See also James R. Brightwell, 1026, William R. Haskett, 1114, and Robert Lee Kidd, III, 1145.

Colleges-Universities/Haskett,W./Kidd,R./Larsen,A./
UndergraduateInstruction

1113. HASAN, Muhamed Ahmed Hasan. "K voprosu o razvitii
ispolnitel'skogo apparata trombonista [The development of the
trombonist's technique]." Moskovskaja konservatorija (Moscow
Conservatory), PhD, 1974.
See *RILM* 76/14978dd45. In addition to a discussion of basic
performance techniques and pedagogy, the author includes a set
of studies for the young student and six miniatures for trombone
and piano, based on the national music of Egypt.
Diss/Egypt/MoscowConservatory/SovietUnion/TrbMus-20thC

1114. HASKETT, William R. "Trombone performance at the collegiate
level: An assessment process evaluation." University of
Oklahoma, PhD, 1979.
See *Dissertation Abstracts* 40/04-A, p.1740, AAD79-21237. See
James R. Brightwell, 1026, Mark Hartman and Arved Larsen,
1112, and Robert Lee Kidd, III, 1145.
Assessment/Brightwell,J./Diss/Hartman,M./Kidd,R./Larsen,A./
OklahomaU

1115. HEATH, Fred. "Coping with problems in transferring to low
brass from trumpet." *TUBA Journal* 7, no. 2 (Fall 1979): 16-17.
Though Heath's article does not specifically deal with changing
to trombone from trumpet in the sense of the problems caused by
changing from a valved to a slide instrument, his discussions
about mouthpiece sizes, embouchure adjustments, breath control,
vibrato, and articulation on low brass instruments are germane to
the problems which would arise from shifting from a small-
mouthpiece brass instrument to a larger-mouthpiece instrument.
Articulation/BreathControl/Embouchure/Euphonium/LowBrass/
Trumpet/Vibrato

1116. HEY, Dean E., Jr. "Etudes for trombone using avant-garde
techniques." University of Miami, DMA, 1973.
See *Dissertation Abstracts* 34/08-A, p. 5229, AAD74-03489. See
Howard Buss, 416, Michelle Castellengo, 617, Stuart Dempster,

621, and Milton Stevens, 759, for more references on avant-garde techniques on trombone.
Avant-Garde/Buss,H./Castellengo,M./Dempster,S./Diss/Etudes/
MiamiU/Stevens,M./TrbMus-20thC

1117. HIMES, A.C. "Get into position for trombone intonation." *Instrumentalist* 36 (February 1982): 58+.
See Thomas Beversdorf, 1016, for more references.
Beversdorf,T./Intonation

1118. ———. "A trombone master class with Dean Werner." *JITA* 10, no. 4 (October 1982): 15-16.
In 1982 Werner was principal trombonist with the New Orleans Symphony and on the faculties of Loyola and the University of New Orleans. This master class was sponsored by the Bell System's "American Orchestras on Tour" program.
BellSystem/NewOrleans/Orchestra/Werner,D.

1119. ———. "A trombone master class with Keig E. Garvin." *JITA* 12, no. 1 (January 1984): 26-28.
Keig Garvin was solo trombonist with the U.S. Army Band for twenty-three years and later a clinician with C.G. Conn Corp. See Keig E. Garvin and André Smith, 140, and John Upchurch, 232.
Bands/Garvin,K./Military/Smith,A./Upchurch,J.

1120. HOFACRE, Marta Jean. "Getting into shape on trombone." *Instrumentalist* 40 (November 1985): 93-95.
Endurance

1121. HOLTON, Frank. "Pointers for those learning to play brass instruments." *JITA* 4 (1976): [inside back cover].
Holton's comments are reprinted from a 1914 issue of *Holton's Harmony Hints*. See Charles Stacy and Frank Holton, 1261.
Stacy,C.

1122. HOWEY, Henry E. "A comprehensive performance project in trombone literature with an essay consisting of a translation of Daniel Speer's 'Vierfaches Musikalishes Kleeblat' (Ulm, 1697)." University of Iowa, DMA, 1971.

Howey asserts that his dissertation is the first complete translation of Speer's 1697 musical treatise, which is frequently identified by William S. Newman and others as *A Musical Quatrefoil* [Howey explains that the information was organized into four sections or "cloverleafs"], to distinguish it from Speer's earlier treatise, published in 1687 and frequently called *A Fundamental Instruction.* Although *A Musical Quatrefoil* claims to be a complete method for composing for every string and wind instrument, it is of particular interest to trombonists because the third "cloverleaf" contains some of the earliest information about Baroque trombone performance practices and pedagogy. This information, along with other items in the treatise, was guarded jealously by the *Stadtpfeiffer* guild, to which Speer belonged. In order to publish his works, Speer apparently betrayed an oath of secrecy imposed on members in order to maintain the guild's monopoly.

Howey's study is located in *RILM*71/446dd25 and in *Dissertation Abstracts* 32/09A, p. 5267, publication no. AAC7208346. See also Howey's "The lives of *Hoftrompeter* and *Stadpfeiffer* as portrayed in three novels of Daniel Speer," *HBSJ* 3 (1991): 65-78.

See David Fetter, 132, David Guion, 452 and 852, Dale Voelker, 573, Arnold Fromme, 640, Heinrich Hüber, 676, and Jeffrey Quick, 728. For more information about the music of Daniel Speer, see Mitchell Neil Sirman, "The wind sonatas in Daniel Speer's *Musicalisch-Türckischer Eulen-Spiegel* of 1688," University of Wisconsin, PhD, 1972 [University Microfilms 72-29,512].

Baroque/ChamMus-Trb/Diss/Fetter,D./Fromme,A./Guion,D./ Hüber,H./IowaU/Newman,W./PerfPrac/Quick,J./Sirman,M./Speer,D./ TrbMus-17thC/Voelker,D.

1123. HUGHES, James E. "An annotated listing of studies for the bass trombone." *Instrumentalist* 36, no. 1 (1981): 54-57.

Hughes's listing is cited and annotated in *JENKINS.* See Paul Thomas G. Everett, 432, and 836, Paul Bauer, 1013, and Leon Brown, 1027, for more references.

BassTrb/Bauer,P./Brown,L./Everett,T./"F"Attachment/Solos/ Tuba/Valves

1124. HUMFELD, Neill. "Bordogni *Vocalise*: Exercise, etude or solo?" *JITA* 12, no. 1 (January 1984): 25-26.

Humfeld lists the number and keys of the Bordogni *Vocalises* in the Schirmer vocal editions (L.82 and L.432) and their corresponding numbers and keys in the Rochut trombone books, so that the accompaniments may be used if desired. See Glenn P. Smith, 555, Leroy E. Baxter, 1014, Randall T. Mitchell, 1189, and Benny Sluchin, 1253.
Baxter,L./Bordogni,M./Etudes/Mitchell,R./Rochut,J./Schirmer/ Sluchin,B./Smith,G./TrbMus-Gen/TrbMus-19thC/Vocalises

1125. ———. "The third T of trombone technique." *Instrumentalist* 28 (June 1974): 47-48.

Humfeld discusses the "three Ts" of technique as enunciated by Emory Remington—tonguing, tuning, and timing—with emphasis on the last T.
Remington,E./Slide/Timing

1126. ———. "What to do with the F attachment." *Connchord* 17, no. 2 (1973): 14.

Humfeld's article is similar to a pamphlet he authored in 1974, also published by Conn Corp. See Thomas G. Everett's book, annotated in 432, for a brief summary of both the pamphlet and article. For more references, see Leon Brown, 1027.
Brown,L./Conn,C.G./Everett,T./"F"Attachment/Valves

1127. HUMMEL, Donald A. "Continuity and fluctuation: Advanced concepts of slide technique." *National Association of College Wind and Percussion Instructors Journal* 25, no. 4 (1977): 41-47.

Hummel attempts to sort out and make coherent the "incredible maze of published articles, books, and methods of one sort or another which offer a variety of solutions to the brass player's problems," in this case dealing with trombone slide technique. Among other methods, he recommends the use of Robert Marsteller's *Advanced Slide Technique* (San Antonio TX: Southern Music Co., 1966), and Tom Malone, 1173. See also David Fetter, 1080, and Donald Banschbach, 1011, for more references.

AlternatePositions/Banschbach,D./Fetter,D./Malone,T./
Marsteller,R./Slide/Technique

1128. HUNSBERGER, Donald, comp. and ed. *The Remington Warm-up Studies for Trombone.* Athens OH: Accura Music, 1980.

These exercises include the text of interviews which Hunsberger conducted with Emory Remington before Remington's death in 1971.
Remington,E./Warmups

1129. HURST, Robert G. "An analysis of method books for the bass trombone." University of North Texas, MM, 1973.

Hurst's thesis is cited in *KOHLENBERG I.* See Paul Bauer, 1013, for more references.
BassTrb/Bauer,P./"F"Attachment/Methods/NorthTexasU/
Theses/Valves

1130. HURT, Charles. "New preliminary audition procedures for orchestras." *JITA* 12, no. 1 (January 1984): 19-23.

Hurt's article explains the tape-recorded preliminary audition system adopted by the St. Louis Symphony. Included are sample forms which the orchestra uses to reply to applicants. See Eric Carlson, 1033, Greg Lisemby, 1166, Milton Stevens, 1263, and Douglas Yeo, 1302.
Auditions/Careers/Carlson,E./Lisemby,G./Orchestra/Stevens,M./
StLouis/Yeo,D.

1131. "It's important to listen to what you're playing." *Melody Maker* 42 (November 1967): 15.

This article was cited in *BRASSBIB.*
Listening/Musicianship

1132. JACOBS, A. "Der Posaunist als Liederbläser [The trombonist as the player of a melodic wind instrument]." *Deutsche Militär-Musiker Zeitung* 62 (1940): 147.

Jacobs's article is cited by Mary Rasmussen on p. 77 of her "Brass bibliography: 1936-1940," *Brass Quarterly* 2, no. 2 (December 1958): 63-77.
Musicianship/Rasmussen,M.

1133. JAECKLE, Frank. "A method book for the alto trombone." [cited in *ROBERTS* as graduate research for the DMA at the University of Iowa with a projected completion date of 1982].
AltoTrb/IowaU/Research

1134. JAEGER, Jurgen. "Zu Grundfragen des Blechblaseransatzes am Beispiel der Posaune [Basic questions of embouchure in brass instruments, illustrated on the trombone]. *Beiträge zur Musikwissenschaft* 13, no. 1 (1971): 56-73.
Jaeger's article is in German and is cited in *RILM*71/4365ap45. In addition to a discussion of the aspects of embouchure, he includes acoustical factors and air pressure measurements taken during soft and loud playing. See also Earl L. Sherburne, 1249, and Peter M. Vivona, 1288.
AirPressure/Embouchure/Sherburne,E./ToneQuality/Vivona,P.

1135. JAMESON, R. Philip. "The effect of timbre conditions on the prompted and simultaneous pitch matching of three ability groups of trombone performers." Columbia University Teachers College, EdD, 1980.
See *Dissertation Abstracts* 41/01-A, p. 151, AAD80-15076, and *RILM*80/1710dd45. See John S. Brick, 1025, and Olin Parker, 1200.
Brick,J./ColumbiaU/Diss/Parker,O./PitchDiscrimination/Timbre

1136. JOLLY, Tucker, and Sherman VANDERARK. "Mouthpiece buzzing for low brass." *Instrumentalist* 38 (May 1984): 36.
See Joseph R. Crider and F.H. Nelson, 1044, Harold L. Leno, 1162, Ralph Sauer, 1239, and Peter M. Vivona, 1288.
BERP/Buzzing/Crider,J./Intonation/Leno,H./Mouthpieces/Nelson,F./Range/Sauer,R./ToneQuality/Vanderark,S./Vivona,P.

1137. KAGARICE, Vern. "Slide technique: Some basic concepts." *JITA* 12, no. 2 (April 1984): 23
Kagarice's article includes part of the discussion on the general subject of slide technique printed in the 1984 issues of the *JITA*. See David Fetter, 1080, for more references.
Fetter,D./Slide/Technique

1138. ———. "What instrument shall I play . . . or, I made my choice for all the wrong reasons." *JITA* 25, no. 2 (Spring 1997): 19-21. InstrumentChoice/ToneQuality

1139. KASTNER, J.-G. *Méthode élémentaire de trombone.* Paris: Troupenas, [ca. 1845].
Kastner's study is cited by Mary Rasmussen on p. 81 of her "Brass bibliography: 1840-1849," *Brass Quarterly* 7, no. 2 (Winter 1963): 78-81. It is also cited in *BRASSBIB.*
Beginners/France/Methods/Rasmussen,M./TrbMus-19thC

1140. KAVANAUGH, Lee H. "Babes in slideland." *JITA* 24, no. 4 (Fall 1996): 38-45.
Kavanaugh chronicles the teaching techniques of Astrid Nøkleby, a Norweigian trombonist and teacher. She has begun a controversial practice of teaching trombone to students as young as four years of age, using the alto trombone.
See Gloria J. Flor, 1086, and Traugott Rohner, 1231. See also in Randy Campora's "General news," *JITA* 22, no. 1 (Winter 1994): 10-11, the story of Ido Meshoulam, at that time aged three and a half years, who began seriously to work on a soprano trombone given to him by his father, Tel Aviv Big Band trombonist, Tovy Meshoulam. For more references on alto trombone see Stephen Anderson, 788, and Donald Appert, 999.
AltoTrb/Appert,D./Beginners/Campora,R./Flor,G./Israel/ Meshoulam,I./Meshoulam,T./Nøkleby,A./Norway/Pre-School/ Rohner,T./SopranoTrb

1141. KEENER, Michael. "Thoughts on intonation: Opening another 'can of worms.'" *JITA* 25, no. 3 (Summer 1997): 25-27.
See Thomas Beversdorf, 1016, for more references.
Beversdorf,T./Intonation

1142. KELLY, Mike. "Selecting and teaching the bass trombone player." *School Musician* 48, no. 9 (1977): 58.
Kelly's study is cited by *JENKINS* as a "good article written by a high school band director." See Paul Bauer, 1013, for more references.
BassTrb/"F"Attachment/PublicSchool/Valves

1143. KEMP, Mildred. "A review of legato as a means to an end."
JITA 3 (1975): 4-5.
Kemp discusses the always controversial topic of what role tonguing plays in trombone legato styles. There is probably as much or more published material on this topic on than any other pertaining to trombone pedagogy. See Forrest L. Buchtel, 1030, for more references.
Articulation/Buchtel,F./Legato

1144. KEMPTON, Jeremy. "Alternate positions on tenor trombone."
Instrumentalist 34 (February 1980): 51-52.
See Donald L. Banschbach, 1011, for more references.
AlternatePositions/Banschbach,D.

1145. KIDD, Robert Lee, III. "The construction and validation of a scale of trombone performance skills." University of Illinois, EdD, 1975.
See *Dissertation Abstracts* 36/09-A, p. 5905, AAD76/25147. Kidd's document was reviewed by Hal Abeles in the *Council for Research in Music Education Bulletin* 65 (Winter 1981). See above James R. Brightwell, 1026, Mark Hartman and Arved Larsen, 1112, and William R. Haskett, 1114.
Abeles,H./Assessment/Brightwell,J./Diss/Hartman,M./IllinoisU/
Larsen,A.

1146. KINNEY, Guy. "The wrist-arm leverage compromise."
Instrumentalist 36 (December 1981): 100-101.
For more references, see David Fetter, 1080.
Fetter,D./Slide/Technique

1147. KLEINHAMMER, Edward. *The Art of Trombone Playing.*
Evanston IL: Summy-Birchard, 1963.
Kleinhammer's book is considered by many trombonists and teachers as the magnum opus of trombone pedagogy. The techniques and ideas expounded by Kleinhammer, long-time bass trombonist with the Chicago Symphony, have become so popular and quoted so often that they have become a part of the general lore and legend of trombone teaching. Kleinhammer was given

the ITA Award in 1985. See Bruce Tracy, 228, and Douglas Yeo, 246. See Kleinhammer and Yeo's newest book, 1149.
PerfPrac/Technique/Tracy,B./Yeo,D.

1148. ———. "Thoughts to ponder." *JITA* 20, no. 4 (Fall 1992): 30-31.
The former bass trombonist with the Chicago Symphony gives some of his thoughts on breath control and an analysis of throat and tongue actions in trombone articulations.
Articulation/BreathControl/Throat

1149. KLINEHAMMER, Edward, and Douglas YEO. *Mastering the Trombone*. Hannover, Germany: Edition Piccolo, 1997.
The former bass trombonist of the Chicago Symphony, and the present bass trombonist of the Boston Symphony have combined to produce a contemporary text on trombone pedagogy. See Klinehammer, 1147.
PerfPrac/Technique/Yeo,D.

1150. KNAUB, Donald. *Trombone Teaching Techniques*. Rev. ed. Fairport NY: Rochester Music Publishers, 1977.
Knaub's essay at the beginning of the book would be especially helpful to teachers who are not performing trombonists. The book itself would be a good text for college music education classes dealing with teaching trombone. Knaub was for many years professor of trombone at Eastman, and is now on the music faculty at the University of Texas at Austin.
Colleges-Universities/Technique

1151. KNELLER, G.F. "The young trombonist." *Music Teacher and Piano Student* 41 (1962): 359+, 393+.
Kneller's article is cited by Mary Rasmussen on p. 49 of her "Brass bibliography: 1962," *Brass Quarterly* 7, no. 1 (Fall 1963): 45-49.
Beginners/Rasmussen,M.

1152. KNEPPER, Jimmy. "My approach to the trombone." *Crescendo International* 19, no. 9 (April 1981): 23-24.
See Whitney Balliet, 253, Gerry Sloan, 346, and Les Tomkins, 359.
Balliet,W./Jazz-Blues/PerfPrac/Sloan,G./Technique/Tomkins,L.

1153. KOSAKOFF, Gabriel. "Playing trombone in tune." *Instrumentalist* 14 (October 1959): 92-94. See *BRASSANTH* 249-250. See also Thomas Beversdorf, 1016, for more references.
Beversdorf,T./Intonation

1154. KRICKE, H. "Von Anfängerschulen bis zur Uraufführung: Das erstes Musikschulforum für Posaune fand in Dortmund statt [Concerning beginning students: The first music school forum for trombone held in Dortmund]." *Neue Musikzeitung* 44 (April-May 1995): 42.
Kricke's article is in German.
Beginners/Dortmund/Germany

1155. KUHLO, Johannes. *Posaunen-Fragen beantwortet* [Trombone questions answered]. Gütersloh, Germany: C. Bertelsmann, 1933.
See also Kuhlo's *Posaunen-Fragen, beantwortet* 3. Auflage Bethel (Bielefeld: Buchhalter de Anstalt Bethel, 1909). The earlier monograph is cited by Mary Rasmussen on p. 94 of her "Brass bibliography: 1906-1910," *Brass Quarterly* 4, no. 2 (Winter 1960): 90-94, and the later publication is listed in *BRASSBIB*. However, Rasmussen lists another publication by Kuhlo on p. 124 of her earlier bibliography, vol. 2, no. 3 (March 1959): 117-125, also dated 1933 and published by Bertelsmann, called *Das Wichtigste zur Schulung der Bläser* [The greatest importance of the training of wind(players)]. She does not list a 1933 version of *Posaunen-Fragen, beantwortet*. Both publications probably deal mainly with questions concerning Posaunenchöre, the brass choirs used in German churches, rather than just trombone pedagogy. See Wilhelm Ehmann, 629.
Ehmann,W./Germany/Posaunenchor/Rasmussen,M.

1156. LAFOSSE, André. *Traite de pedagogie du trombone a coulisse* [Pedagogical treatise on teaching slide trombone]. Paris: Alphonse LeDuc, 1955.
LaFosse's book is to be used in correlation with his method. Translations of the text are in German and English. See annotation in Roznoy, 16. LaFosse was for many years the

trombone instructor at the Paris Conservatory and the solo
trombonist with the Paris Opera.
France/Roznoy,R.

1157. LAGONDA, Rostislav. "A brief history of trombone teaching in
Belarus." *JITA* 21, no. 1 (Winter 1993): 20.
Lagonda's article was transcribed by Leonid Stukin and
prepared for publication by Hugo Magliocco. At the time of the
publication of the article, Lagonda was the professor of trombone
at the Belarus State Conservatory in Minsk.
Belarus/Magliocco,H./Minsk/Stukin,L.

1158. LAMMERS, Mark E. "An electromyographic examination of
selected muscles in the right arm during trombone performance."
University of Minnesota, PhD, 1983.
See *Dissertation Abstracts* 44/11-A, p. 3315, AAD84-04186
(May 1984). See also his article with Mike Kruger, "The right
arm of trombonists: A pedagogical reference," in the *JITA* 19, no.
3 (Summer 1991): 14-17. For more information on the uses of
electromyography in brass pedagogy research, contact Dr. Frank
Heuser, Department of Music, University of California at Los
Angeles, 405 Hilgard Avenue, Los Angeles CA 90024.
Diss/Electromyography/Heuser,F./Kruger,M./MinnesotaU/Slide

1159. [LANE, G.B.]. "Guidelines for selection of tenor trombone
mouthpieces." *National Association of College Wind and
Percussion Instructors Journal* 33, no. 3 (Spring 1975): 38-39.
Lane's article was published in A. Keith Amstutz's ongoing
column, "Brass forum," with Lane as guest editor (the article is
attributed to A. Keith Amstutz in both *Music Index* and
BRASSBIB). See A.C. Himes, Jr., 862, Donald L. Banschbach,
1012, John Philip Froelich, 1096, and Morris Sweatt and Greg
Magnuson, 1272. See also on the Internet http://www.missouri.
edu.cceric/index.html, e-mail cceric@showme.missouri.edu, for
a mouthpiece specification chart by Eric Nicklas, updated by
Stanley Kling (kling@odpwcr.ucsd.edu). See also Home Pages:
Trombone, 50.
Amstutz,K./Banschbach,D./Froelich,J./Himes,A./Internet/
Kling,S./Magnuson,G./Mouthpieces/Nicklas,E./Sweatt,M.

1160. LAUDENSLAGER, Samuel H. "Teaching the trombone." University of Michigan, MM, 1946.

Laudenslager's thesis is cited by Mary Rasmussen on p. 180 of her "Brass bibliography: 1946-1950," *Brass Quarterly* 1, no. 3 (March 1958): 168-181.

MichiganU/Rasmussen,M./Theses

1161. LAW, Glen C. "The development of trombone techniques through the study of orchestra excerpts." Columbia University, PhD, 1959.

See *Dissertation Abstracts*, publication no. AAC0209562 [listed as not available]. Law's thesis is also cited in *BRASSBIB*. See Harold C. Crump, 1047.

ColumbiaU/Crump,H./Diss/OrchExcerpts

1162. LENO, Harold Lloyd. "Lip vibration characteristics of selected trombone performers." University of Arizona, DMA, 1970.

Leno's work is the seminal landmark study utilizing sophisticated photographic techniques to view the actual workings of a trombone embouchure under performance conditions. Located in *RILM*70/2703dd86. See also *Dissertation Abstracts*, 31/09-A, p.4820, AAD71-06800.

Leno has also published articles based on the dissertation: "A study of lip vibrations with high-speed photography," *JITA* 15, no. 1 [mistakenly labeled as 14, no. 4] (Winter 1987): 46-48; and "Lip vibration characteristics of the trombone embouchure in performance," *Instrumentalist* 25 (April 1971): 56-62 (this article was later reprinted in the *BBIBC*. no. 7 (1974): 7-36, where it was also translated into French and German). See Joseph R. Crider and F.H. Nelson, 1044, and Tucker Jolly and Sherman Vanderark, 1136, Ralph Sauer, 1239, and Peter M. Vivona, 1288. ArizonaU/BERP/Buzzing/Crider,J./Diss/Embouchure/ Intonation/Jolly,T./LipVibration/Mouthpieces/Nelson,F./ Photography/Range/Sauer,R./ToneQuality/Vanderark,S./Vivona,P.

1163. LEWIS, Sam. "Tracking down the trombone." *Metronome* 48 (May 1932): 14+.

Lewis's article is cited by Mary Rasmussen on p. 125 of her "Brass bibliography: 1931-1935," *Brass Quarterly* 2, no. 3 (March 1959): 117-125.
PerfPrac/Rasmussen,M./Technique

1164. LINDAHL, Robert, and Andrew MILLAT. "To the mountain tops and back: The first annual Keystone Brass Institute." *JITA* 15, no. 1 [mistakenly labeled as 14, no 4] (Winter 1987): 26-28.
Lindahl and Millat outline the master classes taught by the trombonists of the Keystone Brass Institute: Joseph Alessi, Melvyn Jernigan, Ralph Sauer, and Gordon Sweeney.
Alessi,J./Jernigan,M./Keystone/Millat,A./Sauer,R./Sweeney,G.

1165. LINDELIEN, Doran Royce. "The design and use of video tape in teaching students the basic care and maintenance of the primary wind instruments." University of Oregon, DMA, 1979.
Lindelien's dissertation consists of nine color video tapes which deal with the care and maintenance of wind instruments, including the trombone. See also [Edward Bahr], 41.
Bahr,E./Diss/Maintenance/OregonU/VideoDesign

1166. LISEMBY, Greg. "Preparing for orchestral auditions." *JITA* 18, no. 3 (Summer 1990): 5.
Lisemby's article shows the likelihood of particular excerpts appearing on an audition for either principal or second trombone. See Eric Carlson, 1033, Charles Hurt, 1130, Milton Stevens, 1263, and Douglas Yeo, 1302.
Auditions/Careers/Carlson,E./Hurt,C./Orchestra/OrchExcerpts/
Stevens,M./Yeo,D.

1167. LUPICA, Benedict. *The Magnificent Bone.* New York: Vantage Press, 1974.
Leon Brown characterizes this treatise as "a clinical study of the muscular structure of the embouchure." See his review in the *NITA* 3, no. 1 (September 1975): 24.
Brown,L./Embouchure/Reviews

1168. LUSHER, Don. "My way." *Sounding Brass and the Conductor* 3, no. 4 (Winter 1974/75): 106-107.

Written by one England's top jazz and studio trombonists, Lusher's article features a list of six exercises that are of particular value for players who practice every day. PracticeTechniques/Warmups

1169. LUSHER, Don, and T. AITKEN. "Playing the trombone." *Brass International* 10, no. 3 (1982): 4-6.
Aitken,T./PerfPrac

1170. LYON, Ernest. "Improving slide technique." *Instrumentalist* 5 (January-February 1951): 18+.
See David Fetter, 1080, for more references.
Fetter,D./Slide/Technique

1171. ———. "Outline study of how to play the trombone." *School Musician* 21 (February 1950): 10-11.
Embouchure/PerfPrac/Technique

1172. ———. "Workshop notes on trombone." *JITA* 4 (1976): 16-20.
Embouchure/PerfPrac/Technique

1173. MALONE, Tom. *Alternate Position System for the Trombone.* New York: Synthesis Publications, 1974.
See Donald L. Banschbach, 1011, for more references.
AlternatePositions/Banschbach,D./Slide/Technique

1174. MARTZ, Brian. "Some reflections on intonation." *JITA* 13, no. 2 (April 1985): 39-40.
See Thomas Beversdorf, 1016, for more references.
Beversdorf,T./Intonation

1175. MATCHETT, Robert K. "Improving the trombone section." 2 parts. *Woodwind World—Brass and Percussion* 18, no. 1 (1979): 16-17+, and 18, no. 2 (1979): 34-35+.
See Joel Elias and LaMar Jones, 1065, and Frederick Snyder, 1259.
Elias,J./Ensemble/Jones,L./SectionPlaying/Snyder,F.

1176. ———. "Solving problems in the trombone section." *School Musician* 43 (January 1972): 28+.

See above Matchett, 1175, for references.
Ensemble/SectionPlaying

1177. MATHEWS, Michael K. "Teaching legato tonguing to the
trombone student." *Instrumentalist* 32 (May 1978): 69-70.
There is probably as much or more published material on this
topic than on any other pertaining to trombone pedagogy. See
Forrest L. Buchtel, 1030, for more references.
Articulation/Buchtel,F./Legato

1178. MATHIE, David. "Teaching legato to young trombonists."
Instrumentalist 40 (September 1985): 70+.
See Buchtel, 1030, for references.
Articulation/Buchtel,F./Legato

1179. MAXTED, George. *Talking about the Trombone.* London: John
Baker, 1970.
Maxted's short monograph deals with several aspects of
trombone history, pedagogy, and performance. It is located in
*RILM*70/2501bm45.
PerfPrac/TrbMus-Gen

1180. MAYS, Rich. "Bass trombone sound concept." *Instrumentalist*
35, no. 4 (1980): 54, 56-59.
Mays's article covers most of the important topics about bass
trombone pedagogy, including mouthpiece selection, breathing,
listening, equipment choices, design of instruments, and
performance practices. It is well-written and thought-provoking.
For more references, see Thomas G. Everett, 836, Paul Bauer,
1013, and Leon Brown, 1027.
BassTrb/Bauer,P./Brown,L./Everett,T./"F"Attachment/PerfPrac/
ToneQuality/Valves

1181. MCCHESNEY, Bob. "The doodle tongue technique." *JITA* 23,
no. 4 (Fall 1995): 40-41.
McChesney is a long-time practitioner of this technique of
articulation, which was used by only a few well-known jazz
artists in the past. It has become more and more popular in the
past few years. McChesney is the author of *Doodle Studies and*

Etudes, available from Chesapeake Music, 5300 Laurel Canyon Blvd., Suite 108A, North Hollywood CA 91607.
Articulation/DoodleTongue/Jazz-Blues

1182. MCDUNN, Mark. "51 + 2 = intonation." *Instrumentalist* 20 (January 1966): 7.
Provoked by a student's question, McDunn began a scientific study designed to pinpoint the positions of various notes on a trombone slide from the basic fundamentals up through sixteen overtones. See *BRASSANTH* 406-408. See Thomas Beversdorf, 1016, for more references. See also Albert Stoutamire, 1066, and Arthur L. Williams, 1296.
Beversdorf,T./Intonation/Slide/Williams,A.

1183. MCDUNN, Mark, and C.P. BARNES. *Trombone Artistry.* Kenosha WI: Leblanc, 1965.
Barnes,C./Musicianship/PerfPrac

1184. MCTERRY, Harry James. "Sliding into trombone intonation." *Music Journal* 26 (January 1968): 38+.
See Thomas Beversdorf, 1016, Seymour Brandon, 1024, Mark McDunn, 1182, Harry J. McTerry, 1184, A.A. Rockwell, 1228, and Albert Stoutamire, 1266.
Beversdorf,T./Brandon,S./Intonation/McDunn,M./Rockwell,A./ Slide/Stoutamire,A.

1185. MELTON, John R. "A comprehensive performance project in trombone literature with an annotated bibliography of clef studies for trombone and a guide to their selection." [Cited in *ROBERTS* as graduate research for the DMA at the University of Iowa].
See also Joel Elias, 1062.
Bib/Clefs/Elias,J.

1186. MEYER, Eileen. "Career counseling: Interviews with Arnold Jacobs and Frank Crisafulli." *JITA* 13, no. 4 (October 1985): 32-34.
See Paul Bauer, 86, Stewart Ross, 200, and Bob Rainer, 1212.
Bauer,P./Careers/Crisafulli,F./Jacobs,A./Orchestra/Rainer,B./Ross,S.

1187. MILAK, John J. "A comparison of two approaches of teaching brass instruments to elementary school children." Washington University [St. Louis MO], EdD, 1980.

Milak's study deals with two instructional methods—the Imposed Learning Method and the Subject Matter method, taught to a mixed group of fourth and fifth graders who played trumpets and trombones.

Beginners/Diss/ElementarySchool/ImposedLearning/MusEd/ SubjectMatter/WashingtonU

1188. MITCHELL, Arthur B. "The trombone: A short historical background with suggested methods and materials for its instruction in public schools." University of Wichita (Kansas), MM, 1954.

Mitchell's thesis is cited by Mary Rasmussen on p. 108 of her "Brass bibliography: 1951-1955," *Brass Quarterly* 1, no. 2 (December 1957): 93-109.

Instruments/PerfPrac/PublicSchool/Rasmussen,M./Theses/ TrbMus-Gen/WichitaU

1189. MITCHELL, Randall Thomas. "The use of selected *vocalises* of Marco Bordogni in the development of musicianship for the trombonist: A lecture-recital, together with three recitals of selected works by Eugène Bozza, Jacques Castrédè, Pierre Max Dubois, Christian Gouinguene, Axel Jørgensen, Richard Monaco, Lars-Erik Larsson, Erhard Ragwitz, and others." University of North Texas, DMA, 1989.

See *Dissertation Abstracts* 50/09A, p. 2700, publication no. AAC9005346. See Glenn P. Smith, 555, Leroy E. Baxter, 1014, Neill Humfeld, 1124, and Benny Sluchin, 1253.

Baxter,L./Bordogni,M./Diss/Humfeld,N./Lecture-Recital/ Musicianship/NorthTexasU/Rochut,J./Sluchin,B./Smith,G./ TrbMus-19C/Vocal/Vocalises

1190. MOLE, Miff. "Thoughts about trombone technique [practicing for range]." *JITA* 6 (1978): 15-16.

Mole (1898-1961), a well-known New York free-lance trombonist who performed for such diverse conductors as Paul Whiteman and Arturo Toscanini, wrote this article in 1940. The

original publication for the article is not given. See also Donald
Appert, 1000, and Joseph Russell, 1236.
Appert,D./Bio/HighRegister/Range/Russell,J.

1191. NASH, Harold. "The better half." *Sounding Brass and the
Conductor* 2, no. 2 (1973): 62-63.
Nash's article deals with "playing against the grain" and using
positions past fourth. It was also printed in *JITA* 2 (1973-1974):
73-74. See also David Fetter, 1080, for more references.
Fetter,D./Slide/Technique

1192. NEMETZ, A. *Neuste Posaunenschule* [Newest trombone
method]. Vienna: Diabelli, 1828.
Nemetz's book is in German and is cited in *BRASSBIB*. Mary
Rasmussen cites the book on p. 197 of her "Brass bibliography:
1820-1829," *Brass Quarterly* 7, no. 4 (Summer 1964): 194-197,
as being included in *The Orchestra from Beethoven to Berlioz,*
and *Musical Wind Instruments* by Adam Carse, and François
Fétis's *Biographe universelle.* Carse cites the book as describing
various brass instruments and their designs. According to Carse,
Nemetz names B-flat trombones as bass, tenor, or alto, "each
played with a different mouthpiece." Nemetz named the bass
trombone in F a *Quartposaune.*
Carse,A./Fétis,F./Germany/Instruments-19thC/Quartposaune/
Rasmussen,M./TrbMus-19thC

1193. NEPUS, Ira. "Lesson with Trummy Young." *New York Brass
Conference for Scholarships Journal* (1982): 36.
See Eddie Bert, 261, Mike A. Bloom, 263, Charles Colin, 280,
Gudrun Endress, 292, Thomas G. Everett, 302, and Robert
Lindsay, 327.
Bert,E./Bio/Bloom,M./Colin,C./Endress,G./Everett,T./Jazz-Blues/
Lindsay,R./Young,T.

1194. "New angle on the trombone." *Symphony* 4 (October 1950): 14.
This article is cited by Mary Rasmussen on p. 171 of her
"Brass bibliography: 1946-1950," *Brass Quarterly* 1, no. 3
(March 1958): 168-181.
Instruments-20thC/PerfPrac/Rasmussen,M.

1195. ORAM, P. "My way." *Sounding Brass and the Conductor* 9, no. 2 (1980): 23.
PerfPrac/Technique

1196. OSTRANDER, Allen. "From tenor to bass trombone." *Music Journal* 20, no. 2, (1962): 75.
See Paul Bauer, 1013, for more references on bass trombone pedagogy, and Leon Brown, 1027, for references to the "F" attachment. See Ostrander, 1197, for more references to him.
BassTrb/Bauer,P./Brown,L./"F"Attachment/ToneQuality/Valves

1197. ———. "Opinions." *JITA* 3 (1975): 4.
See a short article by Ryuichi Sagara, "Lessons with Allen Ostrander," which deals with Ostrander's teaching style, in the *New York Brass Conference for Scholarships Journal* (1982). See also Randy Kohlenberg and Robert Thomas, 164, Hal Reynolds, 197, Ronald G. Smith, 213, and Bruce Tracy, 223.
Kohlenberg,R./Reynolds,H./Sagara,R./Smith,R./Thomas,R./Tracy,B.

1198. ———. "Warming up." *Music Journal* 20, no. 4 (April 1962): 49.
See Ostrander, 1197.
Warmups

1199. OWEN, Herbert. "Trombone problems." *Instrumentalist* 4, no. 1 (September 1949): 16-17+.
A unique aspect of this article is the discussion about the use of extension handles on the slide for younger and smaller players. See Larry Wiehe, 242, for an account of his early experiences with the trombone, utilizing a special strap constructed by his father to extend his reach to the outer positions. See *BRASSANTH* 45-46. See also "King creates the Flugabone," 877.
Beginners/ShortArms/SlideExtension/Wiehe,L.

1200. PARKER, Olin. "Quantitative differences in frequency perceptions by violinists, pianists, and trombonists." *Bulletin of the Council for Research in Music Education* 76 (Fall 1983): 49-58.
Parker's study is cited in *KOHLENBERG II*. See also John S. Brick, 1025, and R. Philip Jameson, 1135.
Brick,J./GeorgiaU/Jameson,P./PitchPerception/Research

1201. PEER, Rex, and Roger BISSELL. "Advice to would-be professional trombonists (outline and transcript)." *NITA* 7, no. 1 (December 1979): 6-12.

The transcript is of Peer and Bissell's spoken presentation at the 1979 International Trombone Workshop. It elaborates on the outline.

Bissell,R./Careers

1202. PEIGHTEL, John W. "The development and comparison of two recorded programmed techniques in teaching the beginning trombone student." Pennsylvania State University, EdD, 1971. See *Dissertation Abstracts* 32/05-A, p. 2555, AAD71-28722.

Beginners/Diss/PennStateU/ProgramStudy

1203. PHILLIPS, Harvey. "Tips for trombonists from Bill Watrous." *Instrumentalist* 49 (September 1994): 18-22.

Phillips and Watrous, both outstanding performers (Phillips, of course, on tuba), have collaborated on one of the clearest and most articulate discussions on modern trombone performance, styling, and technique available. See Bill Watrous and Alan Raph, 1289. See also C. Colnot and B. Dobroski, 282.

Articulation/Ballad/Colnot,C./Dobroski,B./HighRegister/ Instruments-20thC/Jazz-Blues/Legato/Mouthpieces/Watrous,B.

1204. PHILLIPS, June. "The trombone slur." *Instrumentalist* 5 (May-June 1951): 20+.

See *BRASSANTH* 84-85. There is probably as much or more published material on this topic than on any other pertaining to trombone pedagogy. See Forrest L. Buchtel, 1030, for more references.

AlternatePositions/Articulation/Buchtel,F./Legato/Slur

1205. PHILLIPS, Kenneth H., and Karin H. SEHMANN. "A study of the effects of breath management instruction on the breathing mode, knowledge of breathing, and performance skills of college-level brass players." *Bulletin of the Council of Research in Music Education* 105 (Summer 1990): 58-71.

See James Biddlecome, 1017, for more references.

Biddlecome,J./BreathControl

1206. PIETRACHOWICZ, Juliusz. "Brass instrumentalists in Poland: Education and institution since 1945." *JITA* 5 (1977): 2-3.
See Ardash Maderosian, 699. See also Janusz Szewczuk, 222, and Pietrachowicz, 534.
Maderosian,A./MusEd/Orchestra/Poland/Szewczuk,J.

1207. POOLOS, James G. "Trombone articulation—legato style." *Instrumentalist* 27 (March 1973): 74-75.
There is probably as much or more published material on this topic than on any other pertaining to trombone pedagogy. See Forrest L. Buchtel, 1030, for more references.
Articulation/Buchtel,F./Legato

1208. POWELL, Richard E. "The tape recording: Gateway to the college studio teaching position." *JITA* 14, no. 3 (Summer 1986): 11.
Careers/Colleges-Universities/TapeRecording

1209. PULIS, Gordon. "On trombone technique." *Symphony* 2 (December 1948).
This or another article is also cited in *BRASSBIB* as having been published in *Symphony* 8 (June 1954): 13-14. The article cited from December 1948 has been reprinted in the 1978 *New York Brass Conference Journal*, p. 121. At the time of the writing of the article, Gordon Pulis was principal trombonist with the New York Philharmonic. See Randy Kohlenberg and Robert Thomas, 164, and Bill Spilka, 215. See also Harvey Phillips, "Musical stories," *Instrumentalist* 46 (January 1992): 4. An obituary of Pulis appeared in the *JITA* 11, no. 1 (January 1983): 7. He received the ITA Award in 1976.
ITA/Kohlenberg,R./NewYork/Obituaries/Orchestra/Phillips,H./Spilka,B./Thomas,R.

1210. PURCELL, Randy. "Playing trombone in the stage band." *Instrumentalist* 31 (June 1977): 60-63.
An earlier version of Purcell's excellent article was written for *Brass World* 8, no. 1 (1973): 30-32. Randy Purcell was the lead trombonist for the Navy Band Commodores.
Commodores/Jazz-Blues/StageBand

1211. RAINER, Bob. "Studying with Frank Crisafulli." *New York Brass Conference for Scholarships Journal* (1982): 42.

Rainer gives a student's view of the teaching style of Frank Crisafulli, who for many years was principal trombone, and later second trombone, with the Chicago Symphony. See Paul Bauer, 86, Stewart Ross, 200, and Eileen Meyer, 1186.

Bauer,P./Crisafulli,F./Jacobs,A./Meyer,E./Orchestra/Ross,S.

1212. RAMIN, Fritz. "Weg zu den Blechblasinstrumenten (Posaune) [The way of the brass instruments (trombone or trumpets?)]." In *Hohe Schule der Musik*, vol. 4, 156-178. Potsdam: N.p., 1936-1937.

Ramin's article is in German and is cited in *BRASSBIB*. It is also cited by Mary Rasmussen on p. 166 of her "Brass bibliography: 1926-1930 [with addenda, 1931-1955]," *Brass Quarterly* 2, no. 4 (June 1959): 158-166.

Germany/Rasmussen,M.

1213. RAPH, Alan. *The Double Valve Bass Trombone*. New York: Carl Fischer, 1969.

Raph's book is cited by Everett's *Annotated Guide to Bass Trombone Literature* as "probably the most complete and thorough exercise book on all aspects of bass trombone valve performance," at least at the time of its publication. A short article based on the book may be found in the *JITA* 2 (1974): 28-30. In addition, there are two pamphlets authored by Raph, and published by King Instrument Co., "Double valve bass trombone . . . and how to play it," and "Comprehensive guide to the possibilities of the 'F' attachment trombone," both based on Raph's method book. See Thomas G. Everett, 836, Gloria Flor, 843, Paul Bauer, 1013, and Leon Brown, 1027, for more references.

BassTrb/Bauer,P./Brown,L./DoubleRotor/Everett,T./Flor,G./ Slide/Valves

1214. ———. "Trombone—plus." *New York Brass Conference for Scholarships Journal* 4 (1976): 61.

Raph describes the uses of the "F" attachment, and how it expands the technical capabilities of the tenor and bass

trombones. See Thomas G. Everett, 836, Douglas Yeo, 990, and Leon Brown, 1027, for more references.
Brown,L./Conn,C.G./Everett,T./"F"Attachment/Valves/Yeo,D.

1215. RASMUSSEN, Mary. *A Teacher's Guide to the Literature of Brass Instruments.* 2nd ed. Durham NH: Appleyard Publications, 1968.

Rasmussen's systematic study of brass literature is one of the earliest and includes pedagogical materials, solos, and chamber music. Though the book is somewhat dated, the author's annotations and descriptions of the literature are still of value.
Bib/Brass/ChamMus-Trb/Etudes/Methods/Solos/TrbEnsemble/TrbMus-Gen

1216. RAYMOND, William F. *The Trombone and Its Player: A Theoretical and Practical Treatise on Both.* Cincinnati: Fillmore Music House, 1937.

Raymond was first trombonist of the U.S. Army Band. The pedagogy and style discussed date to the 1930s. Raymond's treatise is cited by Mary Rasmussen on p. 77 of her "Brass bibliography: 1936-1940," *Brass Quarterly* 2, no. 2 (December 1958): 63-77. See also an annotation in Roznoy, 16.
PerfPrac/Rasmussen,M./Roznoy,R./Technique

1217. REIFSNYDER, Robert. "Career patterns of professional trombonists." *JITA* 13, no. 1 (January 1985): 33-39.

Reifsnyder's article profiles the career patterns of a college teacher and an orchestral trombonist. It classifies teachers and schools according to influence and attendance and gives factors which rule aspects of each career choice. See also Douglas Yeo's "Another Point of View," in the *JITA* 14, no. 1 (Winter 1986): 26.
Auditions/Careers/Yeo,D.

1218. ———. "Differing slide movement in legato and staccato articulation." *JITA* 12, no. 1 (January 1984): 23-25.

Reifsnyder's article discusses the approach of several standard trombone pedagogy books and teachers to the problem of slide facility. See Reifsnyder, 1219, for a continuation of the discussion. See David Fetter, 1080, for more references on slide

technique. See also Robert Marsteller *Advanced Slide Technique*, San Antonio TX: Southern Music Co., 1966.
Fetter,D./Marsteller,R./Slide/Technique

1219. ———. "A discussion on slide technique." *JITA* 12, no. 3 (July 1984): 25-27.
This article appeared in Reifsnyder's ongoing column, "Trombone pedagogy." Allen Ostrander, Larry Wiehe, and Hal Janks are featured in this continuation of the article above. See David Fetter, 1080, for more references on slide technique.
Fetter,D./Janks,H./Ostrander,A./Slide/Technique/Wiehe,L.

1220. ———. "Trombone pedagogy." *JITA*.
Reifsnyder's column appeared in *JITA* 12, no. 3 (July 1984), continuing under Mark Hartman in vol. 16, no. 1 (Winter 1988).
Hartman,M.

1221. REYNOLDS, George E. "Thoughts for the young trombonist." *School Musician* 37 (October 1965): 42+.
Beginners/PerfPrac/Technique

1222. REYNOLDS, Sam. "Synthesis." *JITA* 15, no. 3 (Summer 1987): 40-43.
Reynolds's article is the first of a number intended to deal with computers and electronic music in relation to the trombone.
Computers/Synthesizers

1223. RICHARDSON, William. "Lecture-recital—new directions in trombone literature and the techniques needed for its performance." Catholic University of America, PhD, 1970.
See Richardson, 540, for citations of his continuing literature reviews in the *Instrumentalist*. See also Stuart Dempster, 621, and Milton Stevens, 759, for more references on new trombone performance techniques.
CatholicU/Dempster,S./Lecture-Recital/Stevens,M./TrbMus-Gen

1224. RIDDLE, Peter H. "Legato technique for the trombone." *School Musician* 43 (May 1972): 12+.

There is probably as much or more published material on this topic than on any other pertaining to trombone pedagogy. See Forrest L. Buchtel, 1030, for more references.
Articulation/Buchtel,F./Legato

1225. RISHAUG, Harry. "Trombonen." University of Trondheim, PhD, 1973.
Rishaug's dissertation is located in *RILM*75/2515dd45.
Acoustics/Diss/Norway/TrondheimU

1226. ROBERTSON, James D. "Low brass embouchure control." *Instrumentalist* 23 (December 1968): 65-67.
See John Swallow, 1270.
Embouchure/LowBrass/Swallow,J.

1227. ———. "The low brass instrumental techniques course: A method book for college level class instruction." University of Northern Colorado, DA, 1983.
Robertson includes works and discussions about both tenor and bass trombone.
Diss/LowBrass/NorthernColoradoU

1228. ROCKWELL, A.A. "Assuring accuracy in trombone positions." *Instrumentalist* 21 (October 1966): 30+.
For more references on alternate position pedagogy, see Donald Banschbach, 1011. For references on trombone intonation studies, see Thomas Beversdorf, 1016.
Banschbach,D./Beversdorf,T./Intonation/Slide/Technique

1229. ROHNER, Traugott. "The bass trombone for young beginners." *Instrumentalist* 6, no. 1 (1951): 46.
Although brief, Rohner's article gives a good idea of how the bass trombone was viewed in the 1950s. See Lucien Cailliet, 612. See also Paul Bauer, 1013, for more references.
BassTrb/Bauer,P./Beginners/Cailliet,L./"F"Attachment/Tone Quality/Valves

1230. ———. "Fingering the bass trombone and four-valve euphonium." *Instrumentalist* 8, no. 2 (1953): 30-31.

Annotated by *JENKINS*, who remarks that "fingerings" for the bass trombone with a single valve are a misnomer, since the valve is for the thumb. He then dismisses the term "valvings" as grammatically improper ["thumbings" would also be a misnomer, since that term means to soil or wear out, or to run over something, such as the pages of a book, with the thumb—GBL]. See *BRASSANTH* 142-143. For more references on bass trombone pedagogy, see Paul Bauer, 1013. For references on the "F" attachment, see Leon Brown, 1027.
BassTrb/Bauer,P./Brown,L./Euphonium/Valves

1231. ———. "Introducing the F alto trombone." *Instrumentalist* 4 (November 1949): 18-19.

Rohner discusses the value of using this instrument for students whose arms are too short to reach the outer positions on a regular tenor instrument. The instrument could also possibly bridge the tonal gap between trumpets and tenor trombones and could be used in performing extremely high register parts, particularly in jazz and dance orchestras. Performers such as Tom Ervin have experimented with the alto trombone in a jazz context. See Vern Kagarice's review of the 1982 International Trombone Workshop in the *JITA* 10, no. 3 (July 1982): 12, where he mentions Ervin's session, "Alto trombone as a jazz and serious instrument." See *BRASSANTH* 47-48. See also Gloria J. Flor, 1086, and Lee H. Kavanaugh, 1140. For more references on alto trombone, see Stephen Anderson, 788.
AltoTrb/Anderson,S./Ervin,T./Flor,G./HighRegister/Jazz-Blues/Kagarice,V./Kavanaugh,L.

1232. ROSENBERG, Marvin. "Alternate trombone positions: First year of study." *Instrumentalist* 26 (May 1972): 52-53.

See Donald L. Banschbach, 1011, for more references.
AlternatePositions/Banschbach,D.

1233. ROSS, Stewart L. "The effectiveness of mental practice in improving the performance of college trombonists." Northwestern University, DMA, 1985.

See *Dissertation Abstracts* 46/04A, p. 921; MBB85-11853. See Jerry Fallenberg, 1076. See also David R. Kauss, *Peak*

Performance: Mental Game Plans for Maximizing Your Athletic Potential, (Englewood Cliffs NJ: Prentice-Hall, 1980), and Robert D. Weast, *Keys to Natural Performance for Brass Players*, (New York: McGinnis & Marx, [1979]).
Bib/Diss/Fallenberg,J./Kauss,D./MentalPractice/NorthwesternU/Weast,R.

1234. ———. "Teaching trombone legato." *Instrumentalist* 30 (February 1976): 56-57.
There is probably as much or more published material on this topic than any other pertaining to trombone pedagogy. See Forrest L. Buchtel, 1030, for more references.
Articulation/Buchtel,F./Legato

1235. ROZNOY, Richard T. "Thoughts on contest performances: Music for trombone/euphonium." *Instrumentalist* 37 (February 1983): 73-77.
See also the continuation of this article, "Thoughts on contest performances: Tone and embouchure building for the trombone," *Instrumentalist* 37 (March 1983): 41-42+.
Competitions/Embouchure/Euphonium/ToneQuality/TrbMus-Gen

1236. RUSSELL, Joseph. "How I achieved a range of four and a half octaves on the trombone." *Etude* 48 (1930): 173+.
Russell had several other articles on trombone pedagogy published in *Etude:* "King trombone," vol. 52 (1934): 21+, "Putting heart into tone," vol. 50 (1932): 100+, and "Trombone secrets," vol. 54 (1936): 81+. All these articles are cited by Mary Rasmussen in the appropriately dated sections of her "Brass bibliography." For articles dated 1926-1930, see *Brass Quarterly* 2, no. 4 (June 1959); for 1931-1935, vol. 2, no. 3 (March 1959); and for 1936-1940, vol. 2, no. 2 (December 1958). See also Donald Appert, 1000, and Miff Mole, 1190.
Appert,D./Mole,M./Range/Rasmussen,M./ToneQuality

1237. ———. "Starting right on the trombone." *Metronome* 49 (February 1933): 13+.
Russell's article is cited by Mary Rasmussen on p. 125 of her "Brass bibliography: 1931-1935," *Brass Quarterly* 2, no. 3

(March 1959): 117-125. See 1236 for citations of other trombone articles by Russell published in *Etude*.
Beginners/Rasmussen,M.

1238. SANDIFER, Perry A. "A course of study for trombone at the college level." Texas Christian University, MM, 1952.
Sandifer's thesis is cited by Mary Rasmussen on p. 108 of her "Brass bibliography: 1951-1955," *Brass Quarterly* 1, no. 2 (December 1957): 93-109.
Rasmussen,M./TCU/Theses

1239. SAUER, Ralph. "Make your own practice pipe." *JITA* 16, no. 4 (Fall 1988): 37.
Sauer's device should not be confused with the B.E.R.P.
FART/PracticeMaterials

1240. ———. "Trombone basics." *JITA* 5 (1977): 3-5.
PerfPrac/Technique

1241. SCHOALES, Herbert. "Sniff breathing technique: Diaphragm impulse playing as applied to the low brasses." *Brass and Percussion* 2, no. 4 (1974): 20-21.
See James Biddlecome, 1017, for more references on breath control.
Biddlecome,J./BreathControl/DiaphragmImpulse

1242. SCHOOLEY, John. "A practice sheet for trombone students." *JITA* 10, no. 4 (October 1982): 13.
PracticeMaterials

1243. SCHREIBER, Earl A. "Quarter-tone scale, twenty-four note octave." *JITA* 9 (1981): 10.
Schreiber's study deals with problems in computing and finding quarter-tone intervals on the slide. See also his "An investigation into the application of the quarter-tone system to the trombone," independent research, Winona MN, 1989, cited in *KOHLENBERG II*. For more references on trombone intonation see Thomas Beversdorf, 1016.
Beversdorf,T./Intonation/QuarterTones/Research

1244. SCHRODT, James W. "Vibrato of the trombone soloist."
University of Illinois, MM, 1947.
      Schrodt's thesis is cited by Mary Rasmussen on p. 180 of her
"Brass bibliography: 1946-1950," *Brass Quarterly* 1, no. 3
(March 1958): 168-181. See Dennis R. Herrick, 665, Addison C.
Himes, Jr., 672, Dick Nash, 715, Jay Friedman, 1094, and Donald
H. Wittekind, 1301.
Friedman,J./Herrick,D./Himes,A./IllinoisU/Musicianship/Nash,D./
Rasmussen,M./Theses/Vibrato

1245. SEALE, Tommy Fred. "Advanced method for the slide
trombone." North Texas State College, MM, 1941.
      Seale's thesis is cited by Mary Rasmussen on p. 239 of her
"Brass bibliography: 1941-1945," *Brass Quarterly* 1, no. 4 (June
1958): 232-239.
NorthTexasU/Rasmussen,M./Theses

1246. SEIDEL, John. "The attack: Some fundamentals." *JITA* 12, no.
4 (October 1984): 36-38.
      Seidel's article is included in Robert Reifsnyder's ongoing
column, "Trombone pedagogy." See Lawrence Borden, 1021, Jay
Friedman, 1094, and Edward Kleinhammer, 1148.
Articulation/Attacks/Borden,L./Friedman,J./Kleinhammer,E./
Reifsnyder,R.

1247. SHAW, Gary. "Some observations on trombone playing in the
Soviet Union." *NITA* 3, no. 1 (September 1975): 11.
      Shaw has written a short but historically interesting account of
trombone performance and pedagogy under the old Soviet regime
during the Cold War. For more references see Heinz Fadle, 635,
Thomas G. Everett, 1073, and Victor Venglovsky, 1287.
Everett.T./Fadle,H./PerfPrac/SovietUnion/Venglovsky,V.

1248. SHEPHERD, William. "Beginning legato tonguing on trombone."
Woodwind World—Brass and Percussion 16, no. 6 (1977): 13.
      There is probably as much or more published material on this
topic than on any other pertaining to trombone pedagogy. See
Forrest L. Buchtel, 1030, for more references.
Articulation/Buchtel,F./Legato

1249. SHERBURNE, Earl L. "An analysis of the blowing pressure used for trombone tone and euphonium tone production." University of Minnesota, PhD, 1981.

See *Dissertation Abstracts* 42/10-A, p. 4197, AAD82-06423 and *RILM*81/3597dd45. See Jurgen Jaeger, 1134, and Peter M. Vivona, 1288.

AirSupport/Diss/Euphonium/Jaeger,J./MinnesotaU/Tone Production/Vivona,P.

1250. SHIFRIN, Ken. "Seeking employment in orchestras abroad." *NITA* 7, no. 2 (April 1980): 21-23.

Careers/International/Orchestra

1251. SHOEMAKER, John R. "The sackbut in the school." *Instrumentalist* 26 (September 1971): 40-42.

Instruments-Renaissance/PublicSchool/Sackbut

1252. SILBER, John J. "A critique of elementary trombone methods, and a suggested elementary trombone method." Eastman School of Music, MM, 1947.

Silber's thesis is cited by Mary Rasmussen on p. 180 of her "Brass bibliography: 1946-1950," *Brass Quarterly* 1, no. 3 (March 1958): 168-181.

Beginners/Eastman/Rasmussen,M./Theses

1253. SLUCHIN, Benny. "G[iulio] M[arco] Bordogni (1789-1856)." *JITA* 17, no. 2 (Spring 1989): 29-31.

Sluchin discusses the original *vocalises*, which, in their transcription for trombone by Johannés Rochut, have become a staple in trombone pedagogy. See Glenn P. Smith, 555, Neill Humfeld, 1124, and Randall Thomas Mitchell, 1189.

Bordogni,G./Humfeld,N./Legato/Mitchell,R./Rochut,J./Smith,G./ Vocalises

1254. ———. "Trombone workshops (their value and agendas)." *BBIBC* 52 (1985): 67-69.

Sluchin's article is in English, French, and German. See Thomas Ervin, 1068.

Ervin,T./Workshops

1255. SMITH, James. *Alternate Positions*. Fort Worth TX: Harris Music Publishers, 1971.
See Donald L. Banschbach, 1011, for more references.
AlternatePositions/Banschbach,D.

1256. SMITH, Robert D. "The double valve bass trombone." *National Association of College Wind and Percussion Instructors Journal* 23, no. 4 (1970): 10-12.
Cited by *JENKINS* as having great value in recognizing "the evolution of attitudes toward bass trombone performance." See Thomas G. Everett, 836, Gloria Flor, 843, Eliezar Aharoni, 994, Douglas Yeo, 988-990, Alan Raph, 1213, and David Wilborn, 1295.
Aharoni,E./BassTrb/DoubleRotor/Everett,T./Flor,G./Raph,A./ Slide/Valves/Wilborn,D./Yeo,D.

1257. ———. "Studies in legato." *Woodwind World—Brass and Percussion* 16, no. 3 (1977): 76+.
There is probably as much or more published material on this topic than on any other pertaining to trombone pedagogy. See Forrest L. Buchtel, 1030, for more references.
Articulation/Buchtel,F./Legato

1258. SNYDER, Frederick. "Cleaning and lubricating the trombone." *Brass and Percussion* 1, no. 5 (1973): 15+.
Synder includes advice on cleaning not only the slide section, but also the bell section. See Otto H. Weisshaar, 982, Les Benedict, 1015, and Robert Giardinelli, 1101.
Benedict,L./Giardinelli,R./Maintenance/Weisshaar,O.

1259. ———. "How to acquire a better trombone section." *Woodwind World—Brass and Percussion* 14, no. 2 (1975): 45+.
See Joel Elias and LaMar Jones, 1065, and Robert K. Matchett, 1175 and 1176.
Elias,J./Ensemble/Jones,L./Matchett,R./SectionPlaying

1260. SORDILLO, Fortunato. *Art of Jazzing for the Trombone; a Complete Treatise upon the Possibilities of the Slide*. Boston: G. Ditson, 1920.

See also Sordillo's articles in *Metronome* 41: "More possibilities on the trombone and other brass instruments," (January 1925); "Playing slurs on the slide trombone," (August 1925): 70-71; and "What the trombone player wants to know," (May 1925): 54-55. See Buddy Baker, 1007, for more references. Articulation/Baker,B./Improvisation/Jazz-Blues/PerfPrac/Slide

1261. STACY, Charles, and Frank HOLTON. "Some essentials of trombone playing." *JITA* 4 (1976): [inside back cover].

According to the *JITA* this is a reprint of material found in a 1914 issue of *Holton's Harmony Hints*. Mark Fasman in *BRASSBIB* dates it from 1906.

Fasman,M./Holton,F.

1262. STEVENS, Milton. "Neglected slide technique." *Instrumentalist* 48 (February 1994): 24-27+.

See David Fetter, 1080, for more references. See also Donald Hummel, 1127, Vern Kagarice, 1137, Guy Kinney, 1146, and Ernest Lyon, 1170.

Fetter,D./Hummel,D./Kagarice,V./Kinney,G./Lyon,E./Slide/Technique

1263. ———. "Winning an orchestral trombone audition." *JITA* 15, no. 1 [mistakenly labeled as 14, no. 4] (Winter 1987): 30-33.

At the time of the writing of the article Stevens had been principal trombonist of the National Symphony in Washington DC for almost ten years. See also Eric Carlson, 1033, Charles Hurt, 1130, Greg Lisemby, 1166, and Douglas Yeo, 1302. Auditions/Careers/Carlson,E./Hurt,C./Lisemby,G./Orchestra/ OrchExcerpts/Yeo,D.

1264. STEWART, M[erlin] Dee. "Material selected to assist a bass trombonist in developing playing facility utilizing the valve range." Northwestern University, MM, 1962.

See also Stewart's two-part article, "Material selected to assist a bass trombonist in developing playing facility utilizing the valve range," *JITA* 7 (1979): 11-12, and 8 (1980): 15-18. See Thomas G. Everett, 432 and 836, Gloria Flor, 843, and Leon Brown, 1027, for more references.

BassTrb/DoubleRotor/Everett,T./Flor,G./NorthwcsternU/Slide/
Theses/Valves

1265. STIMAN, Gene. "Problems in trombone tone production." *School
Musician* 41 (April 1970): 22+.
See also his other articles in the *School Musician:* "Slurs or
smears?" 39 (April 1968): 20+; and "Trombone left hand
technique," 38 (April 1967): 30+. See also Daniel F.
Bachelder, 1004, Charles Dalkert, 1049 and 1050, and Joel Elias, 1061.
Articulation/Bachelder,D./Dalkert,C./Elias,J./ToneProduction

1266. STOUTAMIRE, Albert. "Playing in first position."
Instrumentalist 20 (April 1966): 74+.
Stoutamire deals with how intonation needs to be adjusted by
the trombonist in first position as much as, or perhaps more than,
in any of the other positions. See *BRASSANTH* 410-412. See
another article by Stoutamire, "Altered positions on the
trombone," *Instrumentalist* 21 (March 1967): 76-77+. See Donald
L. Banschbach, 1011, for more references. See also Thomas
Beversdorf, 1016, for references on intonation.
AlternatePositions/Banschbach,D./Beversdorf,T./Intonation/Slide

1267. STROEHER, Michael. "A tonal approach to the trombone slide
positions." *JITA* 16, no. 1 (Winter 1988): 31-33.
Stroeher's article contains examples from several musical styles
and explores the various performance practices utilizing the slide
and the concept of alternate positions. See Donald Banschbach,
1011, and Albert Stoutamire, 1266, for more references.
AlternatePositions/Intonation/PerfPrac/Slide/Stoutamire,A.

1268. STROETZ, Robert W. "The slide technique." *Instrumentalist* 6
(October 1951): 35+.
See David Fetter, 1080, for more references.
Fetter,D./Slide/Technique

1269. SWALLOW, John. "Alternate trombone slide positions."
Instrumentalist 48 (June 1994): 32+.

See above Donald L. Banschbach, 1011, for more references on alternate positions. For more information on Swallow, see Thomas G. Everett, 119.
AlternatePositions/Banschbach,D./Everett,T./Slide

1270. ———. "Concepts of brass embouchure development." *Instrumentalist* 42 (August 1987): 12-15.
Swallow's article was later reprinted in *JITA* 17, no. 1 (Winter 1989): 18-20. See James D. Robertson, 1226.
Embouchure/Robertson,J.

1271. ———. "Stage fright, competitiveness, and dysfunction: Helping you to understand and overcome performance anxieties." *JITA* 26, no. 1 (Winter 1998): 26-33.
Swallow's article appears in an ongoing column in the *JITA* called "Thoughts to ponder." Among the sources he quotes is Walter Bonime, author of *Collaborative Psychoanalysis*, (Cranbury NJ: Associated University Press, Inc., 1989). See Buddy Baker, 1006. See also Edward A. Wolff III, M.D., "Indereal and stage fright," *JITA* 24, no. 3 (Summer 1996): 20-21. Wolf edits an ongoing column in the *JITA* called "Medical corner."
Anxiety/Baker,B./Competitiveness/Indereal/PerfPrac/StageFright/Wolff,E.

1272. SWEATT, Morris. and Gregg MAGNUSON. "Mouthpieces and wrists: Two tips for trombonists." *Instrumentalist* 28 (October 1973): 54-55.
See A.C. Himes, Jr., 826, John Philip Froelich, 1096, and [G.B. Lane], 1159. See also on the Internet http://www.missouri.edu. cceric/index.html, e-mail cceric@showme.missouri.edu, for a mouthpiece specification chart by Eric Nicklas, updated by Stanley Kling (kling@odpwcr.ucsd.edu).
Froelich,J./Himes,A./Internet/Kling,S./Lane,G./Magnuson,G./
Mouthpieces/Nicklas,E./Slide

1273. TANNER, Paul. "About trombone playing: A national consensus." *Instrumentalist* 24 (March 1970): 45-51.

Tanner's article is continued in vol. 24 (June 1970): 54-58, and
25 (September 1970): 75-78. Though written several years ago,
many of Tanner's observations are valid today.
NationalConsensus/PerfPrac

1274. ———. "Contemporary concepts of trombone playing."
Instrumentalist 20 (December 1965): 63-65.
Tanner discusses the changes and improvements in trombone
performance that were then, and are now, required to compete in
the professional world. He also includes helpful hints on
improving and expanding all areas of performance.
PerfPrac/Technique

1275. ———. *Practical Hints on Playing the Trombone*. Melville NY:
Belwin-Mills Publ. Corp., 1983.
Tanner's monograph was reviewed by Stan George in the *JITA*
11, no. 3 (July 1983): 57.
George,S./Reviews

1276. [TAYLOR, Stewart]. "Feedback: Slide movement." *JITA* 13, no.
1 (January 1985): 32.
Taylor responds to Vern Kagarice's article on "Slide technique"
in Reifsnyder's ongoing column, "Trombone pedagogy." There
is also a response by Reifsnyder in the same article. See David
Fetter, 1080, for other references on slide technique.
Kagarice,V./Reifsnyder,R./Slide

1277. TETZLAFF, Daniel B. "Trombone and trumpet low register."
International Musician 56 (August 1958): 28-29.
See the continuation of this article in the October 1958 issue,
pp. 26-27. See also James Fulkerson, 1098.
Fulkerson,J./LowRegister/Trumpet

1278. TOMKINS, Les. "The primary purpose of Kai Winding."
Crescendo International 19, no. 3 (October 1980): 12-13.
Kai Winding discusses his book, *The Kai Winding Method of
Improvisation*, breathing, versatility, his activities, and his work
with Chuck Mangione. The article is continued in *Crescendo
International* 19, no. 4 (November 1980): 23-24 under the title,

"Trombone topics discussed by Kai Winding." See Piet van Engelen, 293, Sue Mudge, 336, and Stan Wooley, 379.
Bio/Engelen,P./Jazz-Blues/Mudge,S./PerfPrac/Winding,K./Wooley,S.

1279. TRACY, Bruce. "A conversation with Charles Vernon." *JITA* 13, no. 1 (January 1985): 14-19.
Vernon discusses performance, training, background, his success on tenor and bass trombones, and his pedagogical ideas.
BassTrb/Bio/Doubling/Vernon,C.

1280. "Trombonist Roy Williams offers a few tips to beginners." *Jazz Journal International* 34 (March 1981): 21.
Roy Williams is an English traditional jazz trombonist. See Eddie Cook, 284.
Beginners/Cook,E./England/Jazz-Blues/Williams,R.

1281. ULMAN, Edward J. "A survey of modern jazz improvisation techniques as applied to the trombone." *JITA* 26, no. 1 (Winter 1998): 56-59.
Ulman surveys and analyzes several solos from notable jazz musicians, including Steve Turré, John Coltrane, Keith O'Quinn, and Conrad Herwig. See above Buddy Baker, 1007, for more references.
Baker,B./Coltrane,J./Herwig,C./Improvisation/Jazz-Blues/ O'Quinn,K./Turré,S.

1282. ULMER, J. Ross. "Philosophies of the warm-up as applied to the trombone." University of North Texas, MM, 1978.
Ulmer's thesis is cited in *KOHLENBERG II*. See Donald Hunsberger, 1128, and Allen Ostrander, 1198.
Hunsberger,D./NorthTexasU/Ostrander,A./Remington,E./Theses/ Warmups

1283. UPCHURCH, John D. "Communicating trombone skills." *JITA* 2 (1973-1974): 76-79.
Upchurch's article was reprinted from the *New York State School Music News*, 1973.
PerfPrac/Technique

1284. USOV, Jurij, ed. *The Methods of Instruction in Wind Instrument Playing, III.* Moscow: Muzyka, 1971.

Usov's book is in Russian and is found in *RILM*71/4369bc45. It contains an article by Boris Grigoriev, "Mastering positions and training the trombonist's right hand." See David Fetter, 1080, for more references.

Fetter,D./Grigoriev,B./Russia/Slide/SovietUnion/Technique

1285. ———, ed. *Metodika obucenija igre na dohuvyh instrumentah, IV* [Methodology of teaching the playing of wind instruments, IV]. Moscow: Muzyka, 1975.

Usov's book contains an article by A. Sedrakjan, "Modal sounds played on a trombone." The book is in Russian and is located in *RILM*76/3920bc45.

Modal/Russia/Sedrakjan,A./SovietUnion

1286. ———, ed. *Voprosy muzykal'noj pedagogiki. Sbornik statej, IV* [Problems in music pedagogy. A collection of articles, IV (wind instruments)]. Moscow: Muzyka, 1983.

Among the articles in this collection is "Osnovy racional'noj postanovki pri igre na trombone [Fundamentals of an effective position for playing the trombone]," by Victor Venglovsky (see 1287). The book is in Russian and is located in *RILM*83/1539bc45.

Posture/Russia/SovietUnion/Venglovsky,V.

1287. VENGLOVSKY, Victor. "Trombone school of the Petersburg-Petrograd-Leningrad Conservatory." *JITA* 12, no. 2 (April 1984): 26-28.

Venglovsky's article traces the legacy of the teachers and performers associated with the Petersburg-Petrograd-Leningrad Conservatory, "the oldest Russian performance school." He is the first trombonist of the First Orchestra of the St. Petersburg [Leningrad] Philharmonic and a professor at the Conservatory. See Heinz Fadle, 635, and Thomas G. Everett, 1073.

Bio/Everett,T./Fadle,H./Leningrad/Orchestra/Petrograd/Russia/SovietUnion/StPetersburg

1288. VIVONA, Peter M. "Mouth pressures in trombone players." *JITA* 15, no. 4 (Fall 1987): 28-31.

Vivona's article was the result of an experiment which served as a basis for a thesis at Ohio State University in 1965. The article was originally published by the New York Academy of Sciences in 1968. The stimulus for the study was provided by the research of Robert D. Weast. Vivona states that Weast in his book, *Brass Performance* (New York: McGinnis and Marx, 1965), claimed that various pitch levels on a brass instrument are the result of a relationship between membrane tension and air pressure in the mouth. See also Jurgen Jaeger, 1134, Harold L. Leno, 1162, and Earl L. Sherburne, 1249.
AirPressure/Jaeger,J./Leno,H./Sherburne,E./Weast,R.

1289. WATROUS, Bill and Alan RAPH. *Trombonisms*. New York: Carl Fischer, 1983.

Bill Watrous is one of the greatest living jazz trombonists, and Alan Raph is a long-time bass trombone virtuoso who has distinguished himself both in the symphonic and jazz worlds. Their book deals with several traditional trombone pedagogical topics, but also includes "da-dl-a-dl" tonguing, circular breathing, multiphonics, and other avant-garde and jazz techniques. A recording of the various techniques accompanies the book. See the index for other entries under Alan Raph and Bill Watrous.
Avant-Garde/CircularBreathing/Da-dl-a-dl/"F"Attachment/Jazz-Blues/Multiphonics/Raph,A.

1290. WEINER, Howard. *"André Braun's Gamme et méthode pour les trombonnes:* The earliest modern trombone method discovered." *HBSJ* 5 (1993): 288-308. For an update on the subject of trombone methods, see Benny Sluchin and Raymond Lapie, "Slide trombone teaching and method books in France (1794-1960)," *HBSJ* 9 (1997): 4-29. Sluchin and Lapie's article was translated into English by Anne Bonn, Peter Ecklund, and Jeffrey Snedeker.

See also Raymond Lapie, 166.
Bonn,A./Braun,A./Ecklund,P./France/Lapie,R./Sluchin,B./Snedeker,J./TrbMus-19thC

1291. WICK, Denis. "My way." *Sounding Brass and the Conductor* 5, no. 1 (1976): 8-9.
    Wick discusses his suggested practice routine.
    PracticeTechniques/Warmups

1292. ———. "Performer's platform: The trombone." *Composer* London 50 (Winter 1976-1977): 36-39.
    PerfPrac/Technique

1293. ———. "A practical aid to a beautiful sound." *JITA* 20, no. 2 (Spring 1992): 36.
    Wick gives his ideas on how to utilize a practice mute he designed to improve breath control through manipulation of the throat opening. By gaining an awareness of opening and closing the throat properly, one can learn to produce the best possible tone through all dynamic levels. See also Edward Kleinhammer, 1148.
    Kleinhammer,E./Mutes/Throat/ToneQuality

1294. ———. *Trombone Technique.* London: Oxford University Press, 1971.
    Located in *RILM*74/1065bm45, Wick's book is one of the most popular and useful treatises on trombone pedagogy ever written. The author was for many years the leading trombonist for many of the London-based orchestras and is the person for whom Gordon Jacob wrote his *Concerto for Trombone.* He is one of the most insightful musicians to ever play the instrument. A related volume has been published as *Die Posaune: Instrument und Spieltechnik* (Hannover, Germany: Edition Piccolo, 1997). Wick received the ITA Award in 1989.
    PerfPrac/Technique/TrbMus-Gen

1295. WILBORN, David F. "Introducing students to the bass trombone." *Instrumentalist* 52, no. 1 (August 1997): 54+.
    Wilborn's article is one of the best I have seen on this issue. It is concise and well-written and deals with such aspects as multiple triggers and tuning. He is currently on the music faculty of Eastern New Mexico University in Portales. See Thomas G. Everett, 836, Gloria Flor, 843, Paul Bauer, 1013, and Leon Brown, 1027, for more references.

1296. WILLIAMS, Arthur L. "Locating positions on slide trombones." *Music Journal* 27 (February 1969): 52+.
See Mark McDunn, 1182, James Smith, 1255, Albert Stoutamire, 1266, and John Swallow, 1269. For more references on trombone technique, see David Fetter, 1080.
Fetter,D./McDunn,M./Slide/Smith,J./Stoutamire,A./Swallow,J.

1297. WILLIAMS, Jeanne. "The trombonist as music educator." *JITA* 13, no. 2 (April 1985): 41-42.
MusEd

1298. WILLIAMS, M. "Thoughts on jazz trombone." *Down Beat* 29 (January 1962): 23-27.
See Tom Ervin, 1069. See also Carl Lenthe and Jiggs Whigham, "The differences are actually similarities," *JITA* 26, no. 1 (Winter 1998): 50-54.
Ervin,T./Jazz-Blues/Lenthe,C./Whigham,J.

1299. WINKEL, Hans. "Ventilposaunen in der Volksschule [Valve trombones in the public school]." *Junge Musik* (1957): 70-71.
Winkel's article is in German.
PublicSchool/ValveTrombone

1300. WITTEKIND, Donald H. "A guide to some aspects of trombone performance." *Woodwind, Brass and Percussion* 23, no. 6 (1984): 20-23.
Wittekind, who now resides in Woodside NY, is a former member of the National Symphony Orchestra and the Radio City Music Hall Orchestra. He also served on the faculty of New York University. See his book, *Patterns in Tonguing*, edited by Willard I. Musser (New York: Award Music Co., 1980).
Musser,W./PerfPrac

1301. ———. "On trombone vibrato." *Instrumentalist* 41 (March 1987): 46+.
See Dennis R. Herrick, 665, Addison C. Himes Jr., 672, Dick Nash, 715, Jay Friedman, 1044, James W. Schrodt, 1244, and Bill Watrous and Alan Raph, 1289.
Friedman,J./Herrick,D./Himes,A./Nash,D./PerfPrac/Raph,A./Schrodt,J./Vibrato/Watrous,B.

1302. YEO, Douglas. "So, you want to play in an orchestra?: A primer on audition readiness." *JITA* 15, no. 1 [mistakenly labeled as 14, no. 4] (Winter 1987): 38-45.

Yeo is bass trombonist of the Boston Symphony. He offers a different perspective from that of Milt Stevens, 1263.

See also Eric Carlson, 1033, Charles Hurt, 1130, and Greg Lisemby, 1166.

Auditions/Careers/Carlson,E./Hurt,C./Lisemby,G./Orchestra/OrchExcerpts/Stevens,M.

1303. ———. "What awaits you in a symphony orchestra?" *JITA* 17, no. 3 (Summer 1989): 32-33.

Yeo's article includes a chart of orchestra salaries, weeks in their seasons, vacation days, and annual budgets, reprinted with permission from the Symphony Department of the American Federation of Musicians.

AmericanFederationMusicians/Careers/Orchestra/Salaries

1304. YOUNG, Jerry A. "Duties of low brass instructors." *TUBA Journal* 9, no. 4 (Spring 1982): 13-16.

Colleges-Universities

1305. YOUNG, P. "Legato style and the student trombonist." *Woodwind World—Brass and Percussion* 16, no. 4 (1977): 26-27.

There is probably as much or more published material on this topic than on any other pertaining to trombone pedagogy. See Forrest L. Buchtel, 1030, for more references.

Articulation/Buchtel,F./Legato

APPENDIX I

SELECTED PERIODICAL LIST

Acta Mozartiana. Mitteilungen der Deutschen Mozart-Gesellschafte.V. Ulrich Konrad, ed. Karlstrasse 6/IV, 86150 Augsburg, Germany.

Acta Musicologica. Société Internationale de Musicologie. Rudolf Flotzinger, managing ed. Barenreiter, Neuweilerstrasse 15, CH-4015 Basel, Switzerland.

Adem: Driemaandelijks tijdschrift voor muziekcultuur. Paul Schollaert, ed. Het Madrigaal, Herestraat 53, 3000 Louvain, Belgium.

American Music. Josephine R.B. Wright, ed. University of Illinois Press, 1325 S. Oak St., Champaign IL 61820.

American Music Research Center Journal. Thomas L. Riis, ed. American Research Center, Campus Box 301, College of Music, University of Colorado, Boulder CO 80309-0301.

American Music Teacher. Francesca M. Blasing, ed. MTNA, The Carew Tower, 441 Vine St., Suite 505, Cincinnati OH 45202-2814.

American Organist, The. Official journal of the American Guild of Organists and the Royal Canadian College of Organists. Anthony Baglivi, ed. The American Guild of Organists, 475 Riverside Dr., Suite 1260, New York NY 10115.

American Record Guide. Donald R. Vroon, ed. Record Guide Productions, 4412 Braddock St., Cincinnati OH 45204.

American Suzuki Journal. Pamela Brasch, managing ed. SAA, P.O. Box 17310, Boulder CO 80308.

America's Shrine to Music Museum Newsletter. America's Shrine to Music Museum, 414 E. Clark, Vermillion SD 57069-2390.

Analisi: Rivista di Teoria e Pedagogia Musicale. Enrico Reggiani, ed. Società Italiana di Analisi Musicale, via Berchet 2, 20121 Milan, Italy.

Anuario Musical: Revista de Musicologia del Consejo Superior de Investigaciones Cientificas. Josep Marti y Perez, managing ed.

Servicio de Publicaciones del Consejo Superior de Inventigaciones Cientificas, Vitruvio, 8-28006 Madrid, Spain.

Archiv für Musikwissenschaft. Hans Heinrich Eggebrecht, et al., eds. Franz Steiner Verlag Wiesbaden, Sitz Stuttgart, Birkenwaldstrasse 44, D-70191 Stuttgart, Germany.

Arti Musices, Croatian Musicological Review. Stanislav Tuksar, editor-in-chief. Hrvatsko muzikolosko drustvo, Opaticka 18, HR-4100 Zagreb, Croatia.

Asian Music. Martin Hatch, ed. Society for Asian Music, Department of Asian Studies, 388 Rockefeller Hall, Cornell University, Ithaca NY 14853.

Audio: The Equipment Authority. Michael Riggs, editor-in-chief. Audio, P.O. Box 52548, Boulder CO 80321-2548.

Australian Journal of Music Education, The: The Official Journal of the Australian Society for Music Education. David Forrest, ed. Faculty of Education and Training, RMIT, P.O. Box 179, Coburg, Victoria 3058, Australia.

Bach: The Journal of the Riemenschneider Bach Institute, Baldwin-Wallace College. Elinore L. Barber, ed. Baldwin-Wallace College, 275 Eastland Rd., Berea OH 44017-2088.

Bach-Jahrbuch. Hans-Joachim Schulze and Christoph Wolff, eds. Evangelische Verlagsanstalt GmbH, 04007 Leipzig, Postfach 727, Germany.

Basler Jahrbuch für Historische Musikpraxis. Peter Reidmeister, ed. Schola Cantorus Basiliensis, Leonhardsstr. 6, CH-4051 Basel, Switzerland.

Batteries-Fanfares Magazine. Confédération Français des Batteries et Fanfares, B.P. 2, F-92420 Vaucresson, France.

Beethoven Journal, The. William Meredith, ed. The Ira F. Brilliant Center for Beethoven Studies, San Jose State University, One Washington Square, San Jose CA 95192-0171.

Beethoven-Jahrbuch. Martin Stähelin, ed. Verlag des Beethove-Hauses, Paul Zimnoch + Söhne GmbH, 5303 Impekoven, Bonn, Germany.

Billboard: The International Newsweekly of Music, Video, and Home Entertainment. Susan Nunziata, managing ed. BPI Communications, Inc., One Astor Plaza, 1515 Broadway, New York NY 10036.

Black Music Research Journal. Martha J. Reisser, managing ed. BMR Journal, Center for Black Music Research, Columbia College, 600 S. Michigan Ave., Chicago IL 60605.

Brahms-Studien. Martin Meyer, ed. Johannes Brahms Gesellschaft, Trostbrücke 4, 20457 Hamburg, Germany.

Brass Quarterly. Mary Rasmussen, ed. [Discontinued; back issues available from Appleyard Pub., Box 111, Durham NH 03824].

Brio: Journal of the United Kingdom Branch of the International Association of Music Libraries, Archives and Documentation Centres. Paul Andrews, ed. IAML(UK) Publications Office, Old Church Cottage, 29 Church Rd., Rufford, Ormskirk, Lancashire L40 1TA, England.

British Bandsman, The. Harold Charles House, managing ed. 64A London End, Beaconsfield, Buckinghamshire HP9 2JD, England.

British Journal of Music Education. Prof. John Paynter and Prof. Keith Swanwick, eds. Cambridge University Press, The Edinburgh Bldg., Shaftesbury Rd., Cambridge CB2 2RU, England.

Bulgarsko Muzikoznanie. Dimiter Christoff, editor-in-chief. Institute of Art Studies, Krakra St., No. 21, 1504 Sofia, Bulgaria.

Bulletin of Historical Research in Music Education, The. George N. Heller, ed. MEMT Division, 311 Bailey Hall, The University of Kansas, Lawrence KS 66045-2344.

Bulletin of the Council for Research in Music Education. Eunice Boardman and John Grashel, eds. School of Music, University of Illinois at Urbana-Champaign, 1114 W. Nevada St., Urbana IL 61801.

Cadence: The Review of Jazz and Blues: Creative Improvised Music. Bob Rusch, ed. Lisa Miller, Cadence Bldg., Redwood NY 13679-9612.

Canadian Musician. Shauna Kennedy, ed. Canadian Musician, Norris-Whitney Communications, Inc., 23 Hannover Dr., No. 7, St. Catharines, Ontario L2W 1A3, Canada.

Canadian University Music Review/Revue de musique des universités canadiennes. William R. Bowen and Marc-Andre Roberge, eds. Becker Associates, Box 507, Station Q, Toronto, Ontario M4T 2M5, Canada.

Chamber Music, A Publication of Chamber Music America. Gwendolyn Freed, ed. Chamber Music America, 305 Seventh Ave., New York NY 10001-6008.

Chigiana, rassegna annuale di studi musicologici. Guido Burchi, ed. Casa Editrice Leo S. Olschki, Casella posale 66, 50100 Florence, Italy.

Choral Journal. Barton L. Tyner, Jr., managing ed. American Choral Directors Association, P.O. Box 6310, Lawton OK 73506-0310.

Classic CD. Neil Evans, ed. Future Publishing Ltd., Cary Court, Somerton, Somerset TA11 6TB, England.

Classical Music Magazine. Derek Deroy, ed. Subscription Dept., Classical Music Magazine, Box 45045, 81 Lakeshore Rd. East, Mississauga, Ontario L5G 4S7, Canada.

Coda—Canada's Jazz Magazine: The Journal of Jazz and Improvised Music. William E. Smith, ed. Coda Publications, Box 1002, Station O, Toronto, Ontario M4A 2N4, Canada.

College Music Symposium. Herbert Lee Riggins, ed. The College Music Society, 202 W. Spruce St., Missoula MT 59802.

Computer Music Journal. Stephen Travis Pope, ed. Computer Music Journal, MIT Press Journals, 55 Hayward St., Cambridge MA 02142.

Computers in Music Research. John William Schaffer, editor-in-chief. Editors, c/o Computers in Music Research, School of Music, 455 N. Park St., University of Wisconsin, Madison WI 53706.

Concerto: Das Magazin für Alte Musik. Manfred Johann Böhlen and Johannes Jansen, eds. Concerto Verlag, Postfach 27 04 47, 50510 Cologne, Germany.

Consort, The: European Journal of Early Music. Jonathan Le Cocq, ed. The Dolmetsch Foundation, 'Jesses,' Grayswood Rd., Haslemere, Surrey GU27 2BS, England.

Contemporary Music Review. Nigel Osborne and Peter Nelson, eds. Harwood Academic Publishers, 820 Town Center, Langhorne PA 19047.

Crescendo and Jazz Music. Dennis H. Matthews, editorial director. 28 Lambs Conduit St., London WC1N 3LE, England.

Current Musicology. Emily Snyder Laugesen, editor-in-chief. Department of Music, Columbia University, 2960 Broadway, Box 1812, New York NY 10027.

Czech Music. Jindrich Bajgar, ed. Czech Music Information Centre, Besedni 3, 118 00 Prague 1, Czech Republic.

Dansk Årbog for Musikforskning. Dansk Selskab for Musikforskning, Åbenrå 30, postgiro 7 02 15 50, DK-1124 Copenhagen, Denmark.

Delius Society Journal, The. Stephen Lloyd, ed. Derek Cox, Treasurer, Mercers, 6 Mount Pleasant, Blockley, Gloscestershire, GL56 9BU, England.

Dialogue in Instrumental Music Education. Gerald B. Olson, ed. DIME, School of Music, Humanities Bldg., 455 N. Park St., University of Wisconsin, Madison WI 53706.

Diapason, The. Jerome Butera, ed. 380 E. Northwest Hwy., Des Plaines, IL 60016-2282.

Dissonanz/Dissonance. Christoph Keller, ed. Dissonanz/Dissonance, Möhrlistr. 68, 8006 Zurich, Switzerland.

Down Beat: Jazz, Blues and Beyond. John Ephland, managing ed. P.O. Box 906, Elmhurst IL 60126-0906.

Early Music. Tess Knighton, ed. Journals Subscriptions, Oxford University Press, Walton St., Oxford OX2 6DP, England.

Early Music America. Robin Perry Allen, ed. Early Music America, Inc., 11421½ Bellflower Rd., Cleveland OH 44106-3990.

Early Music History. Cambridge University Press, The Pitt Bldg., Trumpington St., Cambridge CB2 1RP, England.

Early Music News. Early Music Centre, Sutton House, 2-4 Homerton High St., Hackney, London E9 6JQ, England.

Early Music Today. Lucien Jenkins, ed. Early Music Today (Subs. Dept.), P.O. Box 47, Gravesend, Kent DA12 2AN, England.

Fanfare: The Magazine for Serious Record Collectors. Joel Flegler, ed. Fanfare, Inc., P.O. Box 720, Tenafly NJ 07670.

Fiati, I. v. Tullio Levi Civita, 29, I-00146 Rome, Italy.

Finnish Music Quarterly. Antero Karttunen, editor-in-chief. Pieni Roobertinkatu 16, FIN-00120 Helsinki, Finland.

FoMRHI Quarterly. FoMRHI [Fellowship of Makers and Restorers of Historic (Historical) Instruments], Jeremy Montagu, Hon. Sec., c/o Faculty of Music, St. Aldgate's, Oxford OX1 1DB, England.

Fontes Artis Musicae: Journal of the International Association of Music Libraries, Archives, and Documentation Centres. Susan T. Sommer, editor-in-chief. Allison Hall, Secretary General, Carleton University Library, 1125 Colonel By Dr., Ottawa K1S 5J7, Canada.

Galpin Society Journal, The. David Rycroft, ed. Alan Higgit, Membership Secretary, Ashdown Cottage, Chapel Lane, Forest Row, East Sussex RH18 5BS.

Gottesdienst und Kirchenmusik. Ruth Engelhardt, ed. Druckhaus Pegnitz GmbH, Postfach 1348, 91253 Pegnitz, Germany.

Gramophone. James Jolly, ed. Gramophone Publications, Ltd., 135 Greenford Rd., Sudbury Hill, Harrow, Middlesex HA1 3YD, England.

Horn Call: Journal of the International Horn Society. Johnny Pherigo, ed. Ellen Powley, Executive Secretary, 2220 N. 1400 E., Provo UT 84604.

IAJE: Jazz Research Papers. Larry Fisher, ed. IAJE Publications, P.O. Box 724, Manhattan KS 66502.

IAJRC Journal. Phil Oldham, ed. International Association of Jazz Record Collectors, Attn: Edward E. Nickel, P.O. Box 538, Wingate NC 28174.

IJAM: International Journal of Arts Medicine. Rosalie Rebollo Pratt, ed. IJAM/MMB Music, Inc., Contemporary Arts Building, 3526 Washington Ave., St. Louis MO 63103-1019.

Imago musicae. Duke University Press, P.O. Box 6697, College Station, Durham NC 27708.

Instrumentalist, The. Catherine Sell Lenzini, ed. The Instrumentalist Co., 200 Northfield Rd., Northfield IL 60093.

Instrumentenbau-Zeitschrift-musik international. Rainer Matz, ed. F. Schmitt, Kaiserstrasse 99-101, 53721 Siegburg, Germany.

International Journal of Music Education. Jack P.B. Dobbs and Anthony E. Kemp, eds. Elizabeth Smith, Administrator, ISME International Office, ICRME, University of Reading, Bulmershe Ct., Reading RG6 1HY, England.

International Musician. Jessica Roe, managing ed. American Federation of Musicians, 1501 Broadway, New York NY 10036.

International Review of the Aesthetics and Sociology of Music. Ivan Supicic, editor-in-chief. IRASM, Opaticka 18, HR-41000 Zagreb, Croatia.

Jazz Educators Journal, Official Magazine of the International Association of Jazz Educators. Antonio J. García, ed. IAJE, Box 724, Manhattan KS 66502.

Jazz Hot: La revue internationale du jazz. Yves Sportis, managing ed. Jazz Hot, BP 405, 75969 Paris Cedex 20, France.

Jazz Journal International. Eddie Cook, editor-in-chief. Jazz Journal Ltd., 1-5 Clerkenwell Rd., London EC1M 5PA, England.

Jazz Magazine. Philippe Carles, editor-in-chief. Jazz Magazine - Service Abonnements, 5 rue Maracci, 59884 Lille Cedex 9, France.

Jazz Podium. Gudrun Endress, ed. Jazz Podium Verlags GmbH, Vogelsangstr. 32, 70197 Stuttgart, Germany.

Jazzforschung/Jazz Research. Franz Kerschbaumer et al., eds. International Society for Jazz Research, Palais Meran, Leonhardstrasse 15, A-8010 Graz, Austria.

JazzTimes: America's Jazz Magazine. Mike Joyce, managing ed. JazzTimes, 8737 Colesville Rd., Fifth Floor, Silver Spring MD 20910-3921.

Journal of Band Research. Frances Conner, managing ed. Journal of Band Research, Troy State University Press, Troy AL 36082.

Journal of Musicological Research, The. Mary Hunter and James Parakilas, editors-in-chief. International Publishers Distributor, Postfach, 4004 Basel, Switzerland.

Journal of Musicology, The: A Quarterly Review of Music History, Criticism, Analysis, and Performance Practice. Marian C. Green, ed. The Journal of Musicology, University of California Press-Journals, 2120 Berkeley Way, Berkeley CA 94720.

Journal of New Music Research. Marc Leman and Paul Berg, eds. Swets & Zeitlinger, P.O. Box 825, 2160 SZ Lisse, The Netherlands.

Journal of Research in Music Education. Ella Wilcox, managing ed. Music Educators National Conference, 1806 Robert Fulton Dr., Reston VA 22091-4348.

Journal of the American Musical Instrument Society. Martha Novak Clinscale, ed. Dr. Albert R. Rice, AMIS Membership Registrar, 6114 Corbin Ave., Tarzana CA 91356-1011.

Journal of the American Musicological Society. Paula Higgins, editor-in-chief. 201 S. 34th St., Philadelphia PA 19104-6313.

Journal of the International Trumpet Guild. Anne F. Hardin, ed. International Trumpet Guild, Bryan Goff, School of Music, Florida State University, Tallahassee FL 32306-2098.

Journal of the Royal Musical Association. Andrew Wathey, ed. Journals Subscriptions Dept., Oxford Univerity Press, Walton St., Oxford OX2 6DP, England.

Key Notes: Musical Life in the Netherlands. Johan Kolsteeg, et al., eds. Donemus, Paulus Potterstraat 16, 1071 CZ Amsterdam, The Netherlands.

Kirchenmusikalisches Jahrbuch. Günther Massenkeil, ed. Luthe-Druck, Jakordenstrasse 23, 50668 Cologne, Germany.

Kirchenmusiker, Der: Zeitschrift des Verbandes evangelischer Kirchenmusikerinnen und Kirchenmusiker in Deutschland. Klaus-Jürgen Gundlach, ed. Verlag Merseburger Berlin GmbH, Motzstrasse 9, 34117 Kassel, Germany

Larigot: Bulletin de l'Association des Collectionneurs d'Instruments à Vent. 93, rue de la Chapelle, Apt. 166F, F-75018 Paris, France.

Living Blues: The Magazine of the African-American Blues Tradition. David Nelson, ed. Center for the Study of Southern Culture, University of Mississippi, University MS 38677-9836.

Medical Problems of Performing Artists. Alice G. Brandfonbrener, ed. Hanley & Belfus, Inc., 210 S. 13th St., Philadelphia PA 19107.

Mens en melodie. Wegener Tijl Tijdschriften Groep B.V., Jacques Valtmanstraat 29, 1065 EG Amsterdam, The Netherlands.

The Mississippi Rag: The Voice of Traditional Jazz and Ragtime. Leslie Johnson, ed. The Mississippi Rag, P.O. Box 19068, Minneapolis MN 55419.

Missouri Journal of Research in Music Education. John B. Hylton, ed. Martin Bergee, Associate Editor, Dept. of Music, 138 Fine Arts Bldg., University of Missouri-Columbia, Columbia, MO 65201.

Moravian Music Journal. Dr. Nola Reed Knouse, ed. Moravian Music Foundation, 20 Cascade Ave., Winston-Salem NC 27127.

Music and Letters. Nigel Fortune, et al.,, eds. Oxford University Press, Journals Subscriptions Dept., Walton St., Oxford OX2 6DP, England.

Music Educators Journal. Jeanne Spaeth, ed. Music Educators National Conference, 1806 Robert Fulton Dr., Reston, VA 20191-4348.

Music in New Zealand. William Dart, ed. 29 Prospect Terrace, Mount Eden, Auckland 3, New Zealand.

Music Perception. Jamshed J. Bharucha, ed. University of California Press, 2120 Berkeley Way, Berkeley, CA 94720.

Music Research Forum. Jennifer Lee Ladkani, managing ed. College-Conservatory of Music, University of Cincinnati, P.O. Box 21003, Cincinnati OH 45221-0003.

Music Review, The. A.F. Leighton Thomas, ed. Black Bear Press, Ltd., King's Hedges Rd., Cambridge CB4 2PQ, England.

Music Trades, The. Brian T. Majeski, ed. Music Trades Corp., P.O. Box 432, 80 West St., Englewood NJ 07631.

Musica. Clemens Kühn, managing ed. Bärenreiter-Verlag, Heinrich-Schütz-Allee 35, 34131 Kassel, Germany.

Musica Disciplina: A Yearbook of the History of Music. Frank A. D'Accone and Gilbert Reany, eds. American Institute of Musicology, Hänssler-Verlag, Bismarckstrasse 4, Postfach 1220, 73762 Neuhausen, Germany.

Musical Opinion. Denby Richards, eds. 2 Princes Rd., St. Leonards-on-Sea, East Sussex TN37 6EL, England.

Musical Quarterly. Leon Botstein, ed. Oxford University Press, Journals Fulfillment Dept., 2001 Evans Rd., Cary NC 27513.

Musical Times, The. Anthony Bye, ed. The Musical Times, 5 Riverside Estate, Berkhamsted, Herts HP4 1HL, England.

Musician. Robert L. Doerschuk, ed. Musician, Box 1923, Marion OH 43305.

Musicology Australia: Journal of the Musicological Society of Australia. Michael Noone, ed. The National Secretary, Musicological Society of Australia, GPO Box 2404, Canberra, A.C.T. 2601, Australia.

Musik: Tidningen för Klassiskt, Folkmusik och Jazz. Cecilia Aare, editor-in-chief. Box 1225, 111 82 Stockholm, Sweden.

Musik in der Schule: Zeitschrift für Theorie und Praxis des Musikunterrichts. Wolfgang Wunder, ed. Pädagogischer Zeitschriftenverlag GmbH & Co., Postfach 269, 10107 Berlin, Germany.

Musik und Bildung: Praxis Musikerziehung. Richard Jacoby, et al., eds. Schott Musik International, Carl-Zeiss-Strasse 1, 55129 Mainz, Germany.

Musik und Gottesdienst: Zeitschrift für evangelische Kirchenmusik. Andreas Mari and Hein-Roland Schneeberger, eds. Gotthelf Verlag, Badenerstrasse 69, 8026 Zurich, Switzerland.

Musik und Kirche. Klaus Röhring, ed. Bärenreiter-Verlag, Heinrich-Schütz-Allee 35, 34131 Kassel, Germany.

Musikern. Roland Almlen, ed. Svenska Musikerförbundet, Box 43 101 20 Stockholm, Sweden.

Musikforschung, Die. Bernd Sponheuer and Sabine Henze-Döhring, eds. Bärenreiter-Verlag, Henrich-Schütz-Allee 35, D-34131 Kassel-Wilhelmshöhe, Germany.

Musikhandel: Offizielles Fachblatt für den Handel mit Musikalien, Tonträgern, Musikinstrumenten und Zubehör. Hans-Hemming Wittgen, managing ed. Musik-Handel Verlagsgesellschaft mbH, Friedrich-Wilhelm Str. 31, 53113 Bonn, Germany.

Musikinstrument, Das. Verlag Erwin Bochinsky, Münchener Straße 45, D-60329 Frankfurt, Germany.

Musikpsychologie: Jahrbuch der Deutschen Gesellschaft für Musikpsychologie. Klaus-Ernst Behne, et al., eds. Florian Nötzel Verlag, Heinrichshofen Bücher, Postfach 580, D-26353 Wilhelmshaven, Germany.

Muziek & Wetenschap: Dutch Journal for Musicology. Henriette Straub, editor-in-chief, P.O. Box 11746, 1001 GS Amsterdam, The Netherlands.

Muzikoloski zbornik/Musicological Annual. Andrej Rijavec, ed. Oddelek za muzikologijo, Filozofska fakulteta, Askerceva 2, 61101 Ljubljana, Slovenia.

Muzsika. Maria Feuer, ed. HELIR, Lehel u. 10/a, 1900 Budapest XIII, Hungary.

Muzyka: Kwartalnik poswiecony historii i teorii muzyki. Katarzyna Morawska, editor-in-chief. Instytut Sztuki PAN, ul Dluga 26/28, 00-238 Warsaw, Poland.

Muzykal'naya Akademiya. Yu. S. Korev, ed. 103006, Sadovaya Triumfal'naya ul., Moscow, D. 14-12, Russia.

National Association of College Wind and Percussion Instructors Journal. Richard Weerts, ed. Executive Secretary-Treasurer, NACWPI, Division of Fine Arts, Truman State University, Kirksville MO 63501.

Nassarre: Revista aragonesa de musicología. Institución Fernando el Católico, Fundación Pública de la Diputación de Zaragoza, Palacio Provincial, Plaza de España, 2, E-50004 Zaragoza, Spain.

Neue Musikzeitung. Theo Geissler and Gerhard Rohde, eds. Verlag Neue Musikzeitung GmbH, Postfach 10 02 45, 93002 Regensburg 1, Germany.

Neue Zeitschrift für Musik. Rolf W. Stoll, ed. Schott Musik International, Vertriebsabsteilung, Carl-Zeiss-Strasse 1, D-55129 Mainz, Germany.

New Orleans Music. Mike Hazeldine, ed. 28 Stortford Hall Park, Bishop's Stortford, Herts CM23 5AL, England.

New Sound: International Magazine for Music. Mirjana Veselinovic-Hofman, editor-in-chief. Union of Yugoslav Composers' Organizations, Misarska 12-14, 11000 Belgrade, Yugoslavia.

New York Brass Conference for Scholarships Journal. Charles Colin, ed. 315 West 53rd St., New York NY 10019.

Nineteenth-Century Music. Christina Acosta, managing ed. Nineteenth-Century Music, University of California Press, 2120 Berkeley Way, Berkeley CA 94720.

Nordic Sounds. Anders Beyer, ed. Nordic Sounds, c/o Institute of Musicology, 2 Klerkegade, DK-1308 Copenhagen K, Denmark.

Norsk Musikerblad. Tore Nordvik, managing ed. Norsk Musikerblad, Youngsgate 11, 0181 Oslo, Norway.

Notes: Quarterly Journal of the Music Library Association. Daniel Zager, ed. Music Library Association, Inc., Business Office, P.O. Box 487, Canton MA 02021.

Nuova Rivista Musicale Italiana, trimestrale di cultura e informazione musicale. Giancarlo Rostirolla, ed. Nuova ERI — Edizioni RAI, Radiotelevisione Italiana, Via Arsenale, 41, 10121, Turin, Italy.

Nutida Musik. Arne Mellnaes, ed. Nutida Musik, Box 208, 135 27 Tyresoe, Sweden.

Orbis Musicae: Studies in the Arts. David Halperin, ed. Dept. of Musicology, Tel Aviv University, Ramat Aviv, Israel.

Österreichische Musikzeitschrift. Marion Diederichs-Lafite, ed. Hegelgasse 13/22, 1010 Vienna, Austria.

Orchester, Das: Zeitschrift für Orchesterkultur und Rundfunk-Chorwesen. Rolf Dünnwald, editor-in-chief. Schott Musik International, Postfach 3640, D-55026 Mainz, Germany.

Organ, The. Brian Hick, ed. Musical Opinion, 2 Princes Rd., St. Leonards-on-Sea, East Sussex TN37 6EL, England.

Organ Yearbook, The: A Journal for the Players and Historians of Keyboard Instruments. Peter Williams, ed. Laaber-Verlag, Regensburger Strasse 19, D-93164 Laaber, Germany.

Performance Practice Review. Roland Jackson, ed. 1422 Knoll Park Lane, Fallbrook CA 92028.

Performing Arts and Entertainment in Canada. Karen Bell, ed. Performing Arts and Entertainment Magazine, 104 Glenrose Ave., Toronto, Ontario M4T 1K8, Canada.

Perspectives of New Music. Jerome Kohl, managing ed. Perspectives of New Music, University of Washington, Music, Box 35340, Seattle WA 98195-3450.

Plainsong and Medieval Music. John Caldwell and Christopher Page, eds. Cambridge University Press, The Edinburgh Bldg., Shaftesbury Rd., Cambridge CB2 2RU, England.

Polish Music. Jan Grzybowski, ed. Authors' Agency, ul. Hpioteczna 2, 00-950 Warsaw, Poland.

Popular Music. Simon Frith, et al., eds. Cambridge University Press, The Edinburgh Bldg., Shaftesbury Rd., Cambridge CB2 2RU, England.

Psychology of Music. Jane W. Davidson, ed. Nicola Dibben, Membership Secretary, Department of Music, The University, Sheffield S10 2TN, England.

Psychomusicology: A Journal of Research in Music Cognition. Jack Taylor, ed. Center for Music Research, Florida State University, Tallahassee FL 32306-2098.

Quarterly Journal of Music Teaching and Learning, The. Diane Smice, managing ed. University of Northern Colorado, School of Music, 123 Frasier Hall, Greeley, CO 80639.

Recercare. Libreria Musicale Italiana Editrice, P.O. Box 198, I-55100 Lucca, Italy.

Revista Brasileira de Musica. Maria de Fatima Granja Tacuchian, ed. Universidade Federal do Rio de Janeiro, Escola de Musica, Rua do Passeio, 98-Lapa, 20021-290-Rio de Janeiro, Brazil.

Revista Musical Chilena. Miguel Aguilar Ahumada, et al., ed. Universidad de Chile, Facultad de Artes, Compania 1264, Casilla 2100, Santiago, Chile.

Revue Belge de Musicologie. Robert Wangermee and Henri Vanhulst, eds. Société Belge de Musicologie, Rue de la Rengence, 30, 1000 Brussels, Belgium.

Revue de Musicologie. Christian Myer, editor-in-chief. Société Francaise de Musicologie, 2, rue Louvois, F-75002 Paris, France.

Revue Musicale de Suisse Romande. Jacques-Michel Pittier, editor-in-chief. Evidence Communication, Airelle Buff, Ch. d'Entre-Bois 1, Case Postale 23, 1018 Lausanne, Switzerland.

RIdIM Newsletter. Research Center for Music Iconography of the City University of New York Graduate School, 33 W. 42nd St., New York NY 10036.

Rivista Italiana di Musicologia: Periodico della Società Italiana di Musicologia. Giorgio Adamo, et al., eds. Casa Editrice Leo S. Olschki, Viuzzo del Pozzetta (Viale Europa), 50126 Florence, Italy.

Sacred Music. Rev. Msgr. Richard J. Schuler, ed. Church Music Association of America, 548 Lafond Ave., St. Paul MN 55103.

Schütz-Jahrbuch. Werner Breig, ed. Bärenreiter-Verlag, Heinrich-Schütz-Allee 31-37, 34131 Kassel-Wilhelmshöhe, Germany.

Second Line, The. Donald M. Marquis, ed. New Orleans Jazz Club, Suite 265, 828 Royal St., New Orleans LA 70116.

Slovak Music. Olga Smetanova, ed. Music Information Centre of the Slovak Music Fund, Sturova 5, 811 02 Bratislava, Slovakia.

Sonneck Society Bulletin for American Music, The. George R. Keck, ed. Sonneck Society, P.O. Box 476, Canton MA 02021.

South African Journal of Musicology. Beverly Parker, ed. P.O. Box 29958, Sunnyside 0132, Pretoria, South Africa.

South African Music Teacher, The. Michael Whiteman, ed. The National Secretary, SASMT, P.O. Box 5318, Walmer 6065, South Africa.

Stereo Review. David Stein, managing ed. Stereo Review, P.O. Box 55627, Boulder CO 80322-5627.

Studi verdiani. c/o Broude Bros., Ltd., 141 White Oaks Rd., Williamstown MA 01267.

Studia Musicologica, Academiae Scientiarum Hungaricae. Zoltan Falvy, ed. Akademiai Kiado, P.O.Box 245, H-1519 Budapest, Hungary.

Studia Musicologica Norvegica. Finn Benestad, ed. Scandinavian University Press, Abonnementsseksjonen, Postboks 2959 Töyen, 0608 Oslo, Norway.

Studien zur Musikwissenschaft. Hans Schneider, D-82323 Tutzing, Germany.

Svensk tidkrift för musikforskning. Hans Berenskiöld and Ola Stockfelt, eds. Svenska samfundet för musikforskning, Statens musiksamlingar, Box 16326, 103 26 Stockholm, Sweden.

Symphony. Melinda Whiting, ed. American Symphony Orchestra League, Inc., 1156 15th St., N.W., Suite 800, Washington DC 20005-1704.

Tempo: A Quarterly Review of Modern Music. Calum MacDonald, ed. Boosey & Hawkes Music Publishers, Ltd., 295 Regent St., London W1R 8JH, England.

Tijdschrift voor oude muziek. Stichting Organisatie Oude Muziek Utrecht, Postbus 734, 3500 AS Utrecht, The Netherlands.

TUBA Journal for Euphonium and Tuba. John Taylor, ed. Steven Bryant, TUBA Treasurer, Dept. of Music, University of Texas at Austin, Austin TX 78712-1208.

Twentieth-Century Music. Twentieth-Century Music, P.O. Box 2842, San Anselmo CA 94960.

Variety. Elizabeth Guider, managing ed. Variety, P.O. Box 6400, Torrance CA 90504-0400.

Village Voice. Doug Simmons, managing ed. Village Voice, 36 Cooper Square, New York NY 10003.

Windplayer, for Woodwind and Brass Musicians. Daniel Miller, executive ed. Windplayer Publications, P.O. Box 2666, Malibu CA 90265.

Woodwind, Brass and Percussion. Evans Pub., 25 Court St., Deposit
    NY 13754.
*World of Music, The: Journal of the International Institute for
    Traditional Music (ITM).* Max Peter Baumann, ed. Florian Nötzel
    Edition, P.O. Box 580, D-26353 Wilhelmshaven, Germany.

APPENDIX II

This section lists short obituaries for trombonists who were primarily known as concert band and orchestral players, concert soloists, or teachers, or for other persons who were connected in some way with advancement of the trombone. Most are either not mentioned in connection with another article or have passed away recently.

OBITUARIES/GENERAL

Baines, Anthony (1912-1997). A distinguished historian and author of several books on the history of musical instruments, he was a frequent contributor on that subject to the most prestigious musical publications in the world including *The New Grove Dictionary of Music and Musicians*. See Jeremy Montagu, "In memoriam: Anthony Baines (1912-1997)," *HBSJ* 9 (1997): 1-3.

Clark, John (d.1984). Bass trombonist with the Metropolitan Opera Orchestra from 1958 until his retirement.

Fink, Reginald (d.1996) was a trombone professor at Ohio University and founder of Accura Music.

Giardinelli, Robert (d.1996) was the founder of the famous music store in New York which bore his name. Among his many contributions to the brass world was the concept of screw-rim mouthpieces. See Randy Campora's "General news," *JITA* 25, no. 4 (Fall 1997): 16.

Murray, Ian (d.1996?). Bass trombonist of the BBC Scottish Symphony Orchestra for twenty years and most recently bass trombonist of the Royal Seville Symphony. He died at age 35.

Nicar, Howard "Zeke" (d.1997). An honorary life member of the International Trombone Association who assisted Henry Romersa in organizing the early ITA Workshops. See Randy Campora's "General news," *JITA* 25, no. 2 (Spring 1997): 10.

Premru, Raymond (d.1998). Though born in the United States, Premru was one of the busiest orchestral bass trombonists and composer/arrangers in the London, England, area for many years. For the past few years he has served as professor of trombone at Oberlin College in Ohio.

Roderman, Teddy (1924-1980). Canadian trombonist, principal trombone with the CBC Symphony and a member of the Toronto Symphony. See the *NITA* 8, no. 3 (April 1981): 17.

Smith, Glenn P. (d.1997). Smith died on June 16, 1997, at the age of 85. He was professor of trombone at the University of Michigan from 1930-1980 and his writings are cited in this book. See Randy Campora's "General news," *JITA* 25, no. 4 (Fall 1997): 16.

Tchumakov, Pavel (d.1980?). Former trombone teacher at the Moscow Conservatory. See the *NITA* 8, no. 2 (September 1980): 7.

Varsalona, Bart (d.1985). New York bass trombonist who performed for many years with the Stan Kenton Orchestra and was later much in demand as a recording studio player. Among the albums on which he performed was the famous *Jay and Kai Plus Six* [see Bill Spilka, "The spit valve," *JITA* 13, no. 4 (October 1985): 37].

Yaxley, Donald C. (1921-1980). Former bass trombonist, professor of brass instruments, and acting dean of the School of Music at Stetson University. See the *NITA* 8, no. 2 (December 1980): 12.

Jazz, Popular, Studio

Brown, Marshall (1922-1984). See *Billboard* 96 (January 1984): 50; *Cadence* 10 (February 1984): 77; *Coda—Canada's Jazz Magazine* 194 (February 1984): 35; *International Musician* 82 (February 1984): 17; *Down Beat* 51 (March 1984): 12; and *Orkester Journalen: tidskrift for jazzmusik* 52 (May 1984): 34.

Brown, Vernon (1906-1979). See *NITA* 7, no. 1 (December 1979): 3.

Burgess, Bobby Dean (d.1997) played with most of the best-known jazz bands from 1950-1970, and is perhaps best remembered as lead trombonist with the legendary Stan Kenton bands of that period. See Chris Moncelli, "Remembering 'Butter'," *JITA* 25, no. 4 (Fall 1997): 48-54.

Byers, Billy (1927-1996). See the *JITA* 24, no. 4 (Fall 1996): 15-16. Byers was trombonist and arranger for some of the legendary big bands, including those of Count Basie, Buddy Rich, Quincy Jones, and Duke Ellington.

Carranza, Miguel (1955-1978). See the *NITA* 8, no. 1 (September 1980): 7.

Christie, Keith (1931-1980). British jazz trombonist who played with John Dankworth and Ted Heath. See the *NITA* 8, no. 3 (April 1981): 16-17.

Coker, Henry (1920-1979). See the *NITA* 7, no. 2 (April 1980): 3.

DiStacio, Gene (d.1996). See the *JITA* 24, no. 4 (Fall 1996): 19. DiStacio was a mainstay of the Boston jazz scene and also worked in a full-time orthodontic practice.

Fields, Ernie (d.1997) was the leader of the Territory Big Band, a regular at the Apollo Theater in Harlem during the 1930s and 1940s. See Randy Campora's "General news," *JITA* 25, no. 4 (Fall 1997): 16.

Hunt, Walter "Pee Wee" (1907-1979). See the *NITA* 7, no. 1 (December 1979): 3.

Jackson, Preston (1903-1984). New Orleans-style jazz trombonist who played with several famous bands, including Louis Armstrong's. See *Down Beat* 51 (March 1984): 12.

Jenkins, Les (d.1980). Former Los Angeles free-lance and commercial radio musician who played with Tommy Dorsey and Artie Shaw. See the *NITA* 8, no. 3 (April 1981): 16.

King, Leon B. (d.1996). See the *JITA* 24, no. 4 (Fall 1996): 19. King was a jazz trombonist, well-known in the St. Louis MO area.

Larsen, Kent (d.1979). Jazz and studio trombonist probably most well-known for his performances with the Stan Kenton Orchestra. See the *NITA* 8, no. 1 (September 1979): 7.

Pederson, Tommy (1920-1998). Pederson was a long-time performer, composer, and arranger in the studios of the West Coast. See Michael Millar, "In memoriam: Tommy Pederson (1920-1988)," *JITA* 26, no. 3 (Summer 1998): 22-23.

Raub, William (1904-1979). See *NITA* 7, no. 1 (December 1979): 3.

Roberts, John T. (1918-1984). See *Down Beat* 51 (December 1984): 14. A noted performer and educator, Roberts was a founder of the National Association of Jazz Educators and was also the principal trombonist of the Denver Symphony.

Shearer, Richard [Dick] (1940-1997). American trombonist who performed with the Stan Kenton Orchestra for thirteen years and later taught and performed in Michigan, California, and Oregon.

Stroup, Robert (1937-1996). See the *JITA* 24, no. 4 (Fall 1996): 16. Stroup was born in Michigan but moved to Edmonton, Canada, in 1975. He was a well-known free-lance performer and teacher who was renowned for his versatility in performing on trombone, vibes, piano, tenor sax, and flute.

APPENDIX III

ITA AWARD RECIPIENTS

The following received the International Trombone Association Award for outstanding contributions in the fields of trombone performance, teaching, research, or service.

1972 - Henry J. Romersa

1973 - Lewis Van Haney (1920-1992)

1974 - Edwin "Buddy" Baker

1975 - Robert King

1976 - Gordon Pulis (1912-1982)

1977 - John Coffey (1907-1981)

1978 - Stuart Dempster

1979 - S. Thomas Beversdorf (1924-1981)

1980 - Thomas G. Everett

1981 - Allen Ostrander (1909-1994)

1982 - George Roberts

1983 - Leon F. Brown

1984 - Neill Humfeld (1928-1991)

1985 - Urbie Green

1986 - Edward Kleinhammer

1987 - William Cramer (1919-1989)

1988 - J.J. Johnson

1989 - Denis Wick

1990 - Frank Crisafulli

1991 - Christian Lindberg

1992 - Juliusz Pietrachowicz

1993 - Larry Wiehe [posthumously] (1929-1992)

1994 - Robert Isele

1995 - Vern Kagarice

1996 - Carsten Svanberg

1997 - Irvin Wagner

1998 - Carl Fontana

APPENDIX IV

PRESIDENTS OF THE INTERNATIONAL TROMBONE ASSOCIATION

Thomas G. Everett (1972-1976)

Edwin "Buddy" Baker (1976-1978)

Thomas Ervin (1978-1980)

Neill Humfeld (1980-1982)

Irvin Wagner (1982-1984)

Robert Gray (1984-1986)

Steve Anderson (1986-1988)

John Marcellus (1988-1990)

Royce Lumpkin (1990-1992)

Hugo Magliocco (1992-1994)

Steve Wolfinbarger (1994-1996)

Heinz Fadle (1996-1998)

Paul Hunt (1998-2000)

INDEX

The index was compiled from the primary authors and the author/ subject/keyword (a/s/k) lines at the end of the each entry, with occasional references to related materials not annotated in the text. Titles of performance literature that are not mentioned in the annotations are indicated by asterisks (*). I particularly listed much of the significant (and perhaps not so significant) solo and chamber literature for trombone by referencing articles, dissertations, and other publications which supply annotations or comments. Most of these works are indexed by both title and composer, but some are listed only by title with the composer's name in brackets.

Materials cited and annotated under broad chapter headings are not indexed by the heading. For instance, *in the index* the entries listed under *Pedagogy* will be found in chapters other than the one titled "Pedagogy," since I have determined that pedagogy is an alternate emphasis for those particular entries. However, all entries are indexed by appropriate subcategories of the broad chapter headings, for instance, *Trombone Music-18th Century*, instead of simply *Music*.

Colleges and universities are identified by their current names, as closely as possible in the a/s/k line. I have chosen to leave the name of the institution at the time of the writing of the thesis or dissertation in the annotation. For instance, State College of Washington in the entry line will be identified as Washington State University in the a/s/k line and will be entered by that name in the index. Brass instrumental organizations and well-known academic and cultural institutions are cited mostly as acronyms or abbreviations. Further information on acronyms and abbreviations may be found in appendix 1, or in the preface under Standard Abbreviations.

Primary authors' names are indicated by all capitals. Numbers in italics immediately after their names indicate works they authored, or co-authored. Numbers after a semi-colon indicate either a reference to that person or a cross-reference to a related entry authored by the person. Authors' names whose works are mentioned but not annotated in separate entries are in small letters. Published materials referred to but not annotated in the text are also included after the author's name (except in the case of some individual musical or bibliographic material, as described in the first paragraph above). Examples of typical entries are given below:

DEMPSTER, Stuart [author's name], *621* [number of cited work by author]; 125,257,185,203 . . . [and so forth, indicate cross-references to works which are similar to the author's cited work, or in which the author is named].

*"Del fallo m'avvedo" from *La morte d'Abel* [Caldara], 616 [asterisk indicates a work by Caldara is discussed in 616, although not mentioned in the annotation].

Abeles, Hal, 1145 [small letters indicate that his work is not annotated as a separate entry but is mentioned in the annotation for 1145].

A

Aanraking [De Jong],
432,531
Abeles, Hal, 1145
Abraham, Gerald, 897
"Absolutely Knot," 748
Accord [Globokar], 601,759
ACKERMAN, Bernard E.,
993; 1027
Acoustics,67,617,672,792,
797,801,812,814,822,826,
830,833,841,849,851,871,
876,885,898,903,912,932,
950,978,986,991,1225
Acúfenos I [Lanza], 395
Adam, Eugene, 248
Adams, Joel, 307
ADAMS, Stanley R. [Stan]
80,385,386,387,388; 450,
683,757
Adelboden [Germany], 723

Adler, Samuel, 538
Adlgasser, Anton Catejan, 537
Advanced Slide Technique
[Marsteller], 93,116
AEBERSOLD, James D.
[Jamey], *249;* 307,324,333,
345,363,457,512
Affetti musicali [Marini], 763
Africa, 685
Agnus Dei from *Litanie*
[Eberlin?], 537
*"Ah se o da vivere" from
Gioas, Ré di Giuda
[Reutter], 616
AHARONI, Eliezer, *994,995,
996;* 124,129,619,836,843,
1256
Aïda [Verdi], 686,769
Air Pressure, 1134,1288
Air Support, 1249
Air Varie [Pryor], 538
Airlines, 872,906

AITKEN, T., *1169*
AKSDAL, Bjorn, *786*
Albert, Thomas, 531
Albisiphone, 828
Albrechtsberger, Johann
Georg, 504,537,538,583,
656,657,729
Alceste [Gluck], 625
ALESSI, Joseph, *997;* 229,
506,1164
ALEXANDER, Ashley H.,
787; 382,886
Alexander Brothers, 829
Alexei, Evtoushenko, 124
Allegro de Concert [Cools],
539,558
"Allemande," from *Suite no. 4*
for Unaccompanied
Violoncello [J.S.Bach], 551
ALLEN, Rex, *250;* 252,311,
348,781
ALLSEN, J. Michael, *389;*
395,467,838
Alma Redemptoris [Fux], 583
Alma Redemptoris [Reutter],
537
Alma Redemptoris Mater
[Harrison], 395
Alme ingrate [Joseph I], 395,
583,616
"Almo factori" from Motetto
de Tempore [Tůma], 595
Aloo, M., 247
Alpensinfonie, Ein
[R.Strauss], 769
ALSCHAUSKY, Josef
Serafin, *81;* 540,592
Alsina, Carlos Roqué, 515,
621,684,759

Alta Capella, 827
Altenburg, Detlef, 965
Alternate Positions,642,1011,
1078,1085,1091,1127,1144,
1173,1204,1232,1255,1266,
1267,1269
Alto Horn, 508
Alto Trombone, 196,391,392,
393,398,399,434,456,487,
504,508,533,537,553,554,
566,575,583,595,609,616,
656,657,658,722,729,743,
745,747,752,753,754,788,
831,856,875,894,904,939,
942,944,949,961,999,1053,
1086,1133,1140,1231
American Brass Quintet, 200,
205
American Federation of
Musicians [AFM], 1303
American Symphony-1938
[R.Harris], 587
American University, 445
Amrein, 889
Amstutz, A. Keith, 490,
1054,1159
"An den Wassern zu Babel
sassen wir und weineten
[Psalm 137]," 408
Analysis, 511
Ancient World, 809
. . . and then, toward the end
. . . [Erb], 621
Andante et Allegro [Barat],
479,538,539,558
"Andante" from *Divertimento*
in D Major [M.Haydn],
487,504,583
Anderson, Edwin, 88,225,1013

Anderson, Jeffrey, 239
Anderson, Leif, 128
Anderson, Miles, 115,129,
183,239
Anderson, Ray, 236,238,269,
325
ANDERSON, Stephen Charles,
*390,391,392,393,394,595,
788;*151,529,564,583,754,
767,831,875,894,904,939,
944,949,961,999,1086,1231
Andre, Wayne, 127
Andresen, Mogens, 124
Angled Slide, 231,948
*Animus I for Trombone and
Tape* [Druckman], 420,432,
531,538,551,579,621,759
Annapolis Brass Quintet,
726
Annie Laurie [Pryor], 478,
538
Anthon, Carl G., 590,655
Anthropology, 611
Antiphony IV (Poised)
[Gaburo], 395
Anxiety, 1006,1271
ANZENBERGER, Friedrich,
998; 795
APPERT,Donald,*999,1000,
1001;*102,788,1013,1029,
1086,1140,1190,1236
Arban, Joseph Jean Baptiste
Laurent, 1218
Archey, James [Jimmy], 751
[George] Arents Research
Library for Special
Collections, 392
Arentz, Ronald, 155
ARFINENGO, Carlo, *789*

Aria der Beate Virgine
[Joseph I], 538
Aria, Scherzo et Final, 558
Arizona, University of, 493,
565,1162
Arizona State University, 523,
658,696,1014
ARLING, Harry J., *395;* 396,
431,447,560,644
ARMSTRONG, J., *1002;* 692
Army Air Corps, 372
Army Blues, 587
Arnaud-Vauchant [Arnaud],
Leo, 92,115,129,623,693
ARNOLD, Alan L., *396;* 431,
447,644
Arnold, Denis, 401
Arnold, Malcom, 462
Arrieu, Claude, 558
Ars Antigua Trio, 434
Articulation,642,1021,1030,
1049,1091,1094,1106,1115,
1143,1148,1177,1178,1181,
1203,1204,1207,1224,1234,
1246,1248,1257,1260,1265,
1305
Artificial Arms, 919
ASHWORTH, Thomas, *38,
397;* 239
Assessment, 1114,1145
Athletics, 1076
ATKINS, Jerry, *251;* 273,
297,308,341,781
Atlanta [GA], 159
Attacks, 1021,1246
*Attendite, popule meus,
legem meam* [Schütz], 769
ATWATER, D.F., *1003*
Aubain, Jean, 558

Auditions, 75,1031,1033,1094,
1130,1166,1217,1263,1302
Auditui Meo [Tůma], 537
Aus den sieben Tagen
[Stockhausen], 614
Ausman, Sonny, 188,235,239
Austin, Larry, 621,759
Australia, 206
Australian Trombone
Association and
*AUSTRALIAN TROMBONE
EDUCATION MAGAZINE
[ATEM]*, 39
Austria, 219,344,456,510,583,
584,664,683,777
Autumn Music [Peruti], 395
Avant-Garde,25,165,182,183,
185,202,400,402,416,420,
430,437,441,444,446,460,
483,491,497,498,515,531,
570,601,607,614,617,621,
639,647,677,684,687,698,
736,737,755,759,760,772,
775,1022,1116,1289
Averte [Boog], 537
Axial-Flow, 959

B

BABCOCK, Ronald, *398;*
589,959,990
Bach, Jan, 462,696
Bach, Johann Sebastian, 422,
489,538,551,594,797,897,
941,1104
Bach, Vincent, 916
BACHELDER, Daniel Fred,
1004; 1050,1061,1109,
1205,1241,1265

Bachelet, Alfred, 539,558
Bach-Haus, 983
Bachmann, Friedrich, 629
Back, J., 934
BACKUS, J., *792;* 841,851,
885,950
BAER, Douglas, *40,1005;*
1016
BAHR, Edward R., *21,22,41,
399,793;*29,151,239,293,323,
708,970,1032,1059,1165
BAINES, Anthony, *794;* 583,
640,663,786,803,859,935
BAKER, David N., *596,597;*
264,301,342,343,488,1093
BAKER, Edwin [Buddy], *42,
82,83,400,1006,1007,1008,
1009,1010;*125,126,153,164,
175,176,227,235,239,515,
531,579,783,1019,1023,
1037,1048,1081,1107,1111,
1260,1271,1281
BAKER, Nicholson, 43
Balakirev, Mily Alexeivich,
625
Balbi, Luigi, 655
BALL, Donald, *84;* 164
Ball State University, 702
Ballad, 715,1203
*[The] Ballad of William
Sycamore* [D.Moore], 395
Ballade [Bozza], 409,413,476,
479,538,539,558; [Martin],
476,538,558; [Maxwell],395
Ballet, 108,247,627
BALLIET, Whitney, *252,253,
254;*250,287,311,319,346,
348,359,750,1152
Baltimore [MD], 177

Bands,71,145,163,187,207,
232,242,291,372,435,451,
485,530,546,612,620,651,
703,708,765,918,1119
Bänkelsängerlieder [Speer?], 132
BANSCHBACH, Donald L.,
1011,1012;642,1078,1080,
1085,1096,1127,1144,1159,
1173,1228,1232,1255,1266,
1269
Barat, Joseph Edouard, 96,
413,539,558
BARBOUR, William, 85
BARCLAY, Robert L., 795;
804,828,867,925,965,979,
998
Barenboim, Daniel, 568
BARESEL, Alfred, 796; 690,
799,873,892
Bargeron, David W., 301
Bark, Jan, 433,521,668,758,
759,769
BARNES, C.P., 1183
Barnes, Harrison, 322
Barnhill, Allen, 169
Baron, Arthur [Art], 720,
751,1107
Baroque,75,389,392,398,401,
408,422,445,467,475,502,
513,529,544,551,564,575,
583,584,589,603,638,652,
661,662,664,669,671,674,
682,702,712,713,718,728,
738,756,763,829,852,859,
869,909,920,941,947,953,
954,955,963,1122
Barron, Ed, 259
BARRON, Ronald, 598; 117,
129,248,424

BARTLETT, Clifford, 401;
590,640
Bartók, Bela, 619
Basie, William [Count], 255
Basler, M.C., 801
Bassano, 143,167,663
Bass Horn, 866,923
Bass Trombone, 7,37,50,76,
102,122,123,124,128,142,
147,181,194,197,200,205,
206,210,213,223,224,225,
226,227,244,245,246,268,
279,301,313,342,343,350,
358,399,413,419,432,436,
437,438,439,467,494,495,
509,510,517,520,548,563,
567,568,572,593,612,619,
649,667,690,696,726,727,
745,761,796,799,818,820,
836,843,847,848,873,877,
880,890,893,932,934,937,
951,956,958,960,969,971,
972,975,988,989,990,994,
995,996,1001,1013,1029,
1034,1035,1041,1052,1053,
1071,1072,1077,1083,1105,
1123,1129,1142,1180,1196,
1213,1229,1230,1256,1264,
1279,1295
*Bass Trombone, Bass
Clarinet, Harp* [Hibbard],
432
Bassett, Leslie, 156,236,469,
489,579
Batasev [Batashov], Viktor,
139,559
BATE, Philip, 797; 640,663,
747,803,897,919,941,954
Baudo, Serge, 538,558

Bauer, Jacob, 869,878,879, 882,922,953

BAUER,Paul,*86,255,256,1013;* 50,129,200,228,1029,1035, 1041,1071,1082,1105,1123, 1129,1180,1186,1196,1211, 1213,1229,1230,1295

BAXTER, Leroy E., *1014;* 1124,1189

Bay Bones, 56,407

Bayes, Jack Russell, 401,640

Bayreuth, 233

"Beautiful Friendship, A" 297

Bebop, 249,251,273,297,317, 341,370,642,727

Becquet, Michel [Michael], 209,237,424,668

Beethoven, Ludwig van, 442, 510,581,625,777

Beginners,1009,1057,1086, 1110,1139,1140,1151,1154, 1187,1199,1202,1221,1229, 1237,1252,1280

Behr, Carl, 248

Belarus, 1157

Belcke, Friedrich August, 145,148,194,403,426,495, 540,592

BELET, Brian, *402*

Belgium, 888

Bell, Rick, 129

Bell System, 1118

BELLAY, F., 599

Belli, Guilio, 655

Bellis, Richard, 435

Bells [brass instrument], 903, 938,975

Bemidji State University, 19

BENEDICT, Les, *1015;* 982, 1101,1258

Benge [instrument manufacturer], 970

Bennett, Richard Rodney, 462

BENSEL, James ten, *38*

BERENDT, Joachim-Ernst, *257,600;* 271,617,621,639, 755

Beres, Hagai, 619

Berghmans, José, 538,558

Berio, Luciano, 195,400,515, 531,538,579,621,759,984

Berklee School, 266

Berlin [Germany], 112,194, 426,860

Berlioz, Hector, 421,553, 767,856

BERNHARDT, Clyde, *258, 259*

BERNOTAS, Robert [Bob], *260;* 316,720,751,1107

Bernstein, Leonard, 413,531, 538,579

BERP, 1044,1136,1162

BERT, Edward [Eddie], *261;* 263,280,302,309,327,1193

Bertali [Bartali], Antonio, 475,538,583,616

Berz, W.L., 1003

Berzizia, Thomas de, 241

BESSELER, Heinrich, *798;* 663,803

Besson [instrument manufacturer], 914

Best of Count Basie, The, 750

*[Die] Beste Wahl die Christliche Seele [Eberlin], 537,753

Bethlehem [PA], 610,650,
  714,732
BEVAN, Clifford, *799;* 796,
  873,892
BEVERSDORF, S. Thomas,
  1016; 83,559,1005,1024,
  1051,1055,1079,1117,1141,
  1153,1174,1182,1184,1228,
  1243,1266
BEYER, Werner, *87,403;*
  194,495,540,577,592,956
Biber, Heinrich, 538
Bible, 744,824
Bibliographies,22,23,41,133,
  173,243,245,250,256,295,
  348,385,387,391,392,395,
  407,410,412,413,416,417,
  425,429,432,434,438,439,
  441,444,446,447,448,454,
  462,468,471,472,473,474,
  476,479,484,485,493,505,
  520,526,527,529,532,535,
  536,540,541,544,550,555,
  558,560,561,562,563,564,
  565,567,571,574,583,588,
  591,609,621,625,649,669,
  688,694,706,713,722,726,
  728,735,751,769,772,774,
  788,793,800,852,884,893,
  909,920,926,942,956,957,
  991,998,999,1012,1019,
  1031,1072,1076,1084,1086,
  1096,1185,1215,1233 [see
  also *1, General Reference/
  Bibliographies*]
Biddlecombe, Robert, 124,
  200,205
BIDDLECOME, James, *1017;*
  1043,1045,1061,1109,

  1205,1241
Big Apple, 353
Bigot, Eugène, 539,558
Bimboni, G., 814
BINGHAM, John J., *601;*
  498,579,614,647,684,698
*Biographie universelle des
  musiciens* [Fétis], 536,544
Biographies,2,8,10,23,24,41,
  66,70,76,245,246,306,407,
  417,435,454,457,489,493,
  512,514,516,540,549,569,
  583,592,594,618,629,643,
  675,720,748,761,781,817,
  884,940,1001,1190,1193,
  1278,1279,1287
  [see *2, Biographies/General,
  3, Biographies/Jazz,Popular,
  Studio,* and appendix 2,
  Obituaries]
*Biographisch-Biblio-
  graphisches Quellen-
  Lexikon* [Eitner], 536
Birmingham [England], 58
BISSELL, Roger, *1201*
Bitsch, Marcel, 558
BIVRE, Guy de, *800*
Björnson, Oddur, 191
Blacher, Boris, 538
*"Black and Tan Fantasy," 751
Black Music, 376,622
BLAINE, Robert J., *1018*
BLANCHARD, Henri, *602,
  801*
BLANDFORD, W.F.H., *603;*
  713
Blasel, Herionymus, 241
Blazhevich, Vladislav, 139,
  212,240,*413,*538

Bliege, Scott, 307
Blomquist, Bruce, 121
BLOOM, Michael A., *262,
263;* 261,327,1193
Blue Bells of Scotland [Pryor],
479,538,556
*[Der] blutschitzende Jesus
[Eberlin], 583,753
Bobcik, Brad, 121
Bobroff, David, 191
BOCK, E., *404*
BOGLE, Michael, *264;* 272,
369,380,604
Bohannon, Hoyt, 405
Bohanon, George, 329
Boléro [Ravel], 92,114,
623,693
BOLLINGER, Blair, *97;* 121,
229
Bologna [Italy], 75
Bolos [Bark and Rabe], 433,
481,521,621,759
Bolter, Norman, 117,248
BOLTINGHOUSE, James,
405; 751
*Bombardments No. 4
[Moran], 621
Bon, André, 531
Bondon, I., 558
Bonn, Anne, 1290
Bonneau, Paul, 558
Boog, Andreas, 583,616
Boog, Johann Nepomuk, 537
BOONE, Robert [Rob], *604,
1019;* 260,307,783,1007
Booth, William [Bill], 334
Bootz, William, 239
BORDEN, Lawrence, *1020,
1021;* 1246

Bordogni, Giulio Marco, 133,
555,1014,1124,1189,1253
Borodin, Alexander, 625
Bossa Nova, 604
Boston [MA], 79,117,244,247,
434,613,761
Boston University, 440,759
BOUCHARD, Fred, *265,266*
BOULTON, John, *605*
BOURGOIS, Louis George,
267; 24,274,299,300,303,
320,749
BOURNE, Michael, *268,269,
270;* 181,325
Boutry, Roger, 558
BOVERMANN, P., *406*
BOWELL, Jeffrey, *88;* 186,225
BOWLES, Edmund A., *802;*
645,717,725,827,915,931
BOWLES, Richard W., *1022;*
257,271,617,621,639,755
BOWSHER, J.M., *833,932,
978;* 806,822,844,939,986
Boyce, John, 463
Boyd, Frederick, 124
Boyd, Robert, 88
Bozza, Eugène, 409,413,462,
531,538,539,558
*B.P., A Melodrama [Moss],
772
Bradley, Jack, 287
Bradley, Will, 286
Bragunier, David, 1031
Brahms, Johannes, 625,1013
BRANDON, Seymour, *1023,
1024;* 1008,1016,1184
BRANSTINE, Wesley, *606;*
32,541,610,650,654,659,694,
706,714,732,734,735,744

BRANT, Henry, *407;* 56
Brass, 3,14,18,20,523,860,
922,1215
Brass Bands, 206
Brass Performance-19th
Century, 120
Brass Quarterly (later *Brass
and Woodwind Quarterly*)
[Rasmussen], 3,544
Brass Quintet, 200,205,449,
462,498,649,696,726
Brass Quintet [E.Carter], 696;
[Koetsier, op. 65], 462
Brass Trio, 477,478
Braun, André, 166,1290
Braun, Jean Christophe [Jean
Frédérick], 166
Braxton, Anthony, 328
Brazil, 367,507
Breath Control, 1017,1028,
1043,1045,1061,1093,
1094,1109,1115,1148,
1205,1241
Breathing, 868
BREHM, K., *803;* 663
BREIG, Werner, *408;* 415,
674,712,738
Bresgen, Cesar, 456
Breuninger, Tyrone, 229
BREVIG, Per, *607;* 151,211,
497,559,677,733,737
BRICK, John S., *1025;* 1135,
1200
BRICKENS, Nathaniel O.,
409; 511,741
BRIDGES, Glenn D., *89,90;*
10,120,125,135,145
"Brief Impression of
Brighton," 271

Brigham Young University,
1004
BRIGHT, Dudley, *91*
BRIGHTWELL, James R.,
1026; 1114,1145
Brill, Wayne, 870
Britain, 779,833,874,896,916
British Library, 514
British Trombone Society, 72
Brixel, Eugen, 757
BROUSSARD, George, *92,
271;* 28,115,196,257,296,349,
398,441,514,560,600,617,
621,623,639,693,755,759,
775,904,1022
BROWER, W.A., *272;* 264,
369,380
Brown, J.E., 531,538
Brown, James, 310
BROWN, Keith, *93;* 116,127,
151,473
Brown, Lawrence, 283,290,622
BROWN, Leon F.,*410,411,412,
1027,1028;*125,170,175,235,
237,443,471,479,526,527,
542,563,993,1013,1029,
1035,1041,1062,1071,1082,
1083,1087,1105,1123,1126,
1129,1142,1167,1180,1196,
1213,1214,1230,1295
Brown, Merrill, 413
Brown, Newell Kay, 489
Brown, Peter, 395,432,583
BROWN, R.S., *94;* 118,195
Brown, Steven R., 121
BROWNLOW, James Arthur,
804; 795,998
Brubeck, Christopher [Chris],
358

Brubeck, David William,
1013,1129
BRUCH, Robert G., *1029;*
1013
Bruckner, Anton, 442,466,
581,777
BRUENGER, David, *95,608,
609;* 487,504,554,657
Bruhns, August, 495
Brunis, George, 262,329
Bruns [Bruhns?], August, 403,
495,540
Brussels [Belgium], 888
BRUYNINCKX, Walter, *23*
BRYAN, Paul, *414*
*BTRB [Cope], 432,531
Buccina, 976
Bucher, Pia, 129
Buchman, Heather, 103,231,
236,238
BUCHNER, Arno, *805*
BUCHTEL, Forrest L., *1030;*
1091,1106,1143,1177,1178,
1204,1207,1224,1234,1248,
1257,1305
Buckholz, Chris, 290,493,567
Budin, Jeff, 121
Buescher [instrument
manufacturer], 947
Buffalo [NY], 104
BUGLI, David, *44,1031*
BULEN, Jay C., *806;* 822,
844,911,932,977,986
BUNIAK, Raymond, *807*
BUNTAIN, William E., *415*
*"Buon Gesú" from
Gerusalemme convertito
[Caldara], 616
Burgess, Bobby Dean, 256,751

Burkhart, Warren, 88,186
*Burlette [Brings], 395
BURNAP, Campbell, *273;* 251
BURNS, James [Jim], *274;*
24,267,370
BUSER, Ernst-W., *808*
BUSS, Howard J., *416;* 621,
687,759,772,1116
Büsser, Henri, 539,558
BÜTTNER, Manfred, *610,
611,809;* 32,606,629
Buxtehude, Dietrich, 955
Buzzing, 1044,1136,1162
Byrd, Robert, 121

C

Cadenzas, 118,195,511,556,
559,609
Cage, John, 298,531,579,621,
759
CAILLIET, Lucien, *612;* 765,
1229
Cairns, Walter, 90
Caldara, Antonio, 537,616
California State University-
Long Beach, 494,657
CALL, Glenn K., *96*
CALLISON, Hugh, *613;* 145,
767
*Camel Music [Buss], 772
Campbell, Alice, 1009
CAMPBELL, Larry, *810,811,
1032;* 151,708,793
CAMPORA, Randy, *275,276;*
50,121,142,172,290,334,
397,962,1140
Canada, 108,141,163,286,373,
499,761

CANEVA, Ernest O., *812*
Cantabile et Scherzando
[Büsser], 539,558
Cantilena Four [Gaburo],
395
Canto II [Adler], 432,479,
538
Canzon la Fineta à 2
[Riccio/G.Smith], 395
Canzon la Pichi à 2 [Riccio/
G.Smith], 395
Canzon la Venexiana
[Schiaffini], 528
*Canzona for Four
Trombones* [Marini], 769
Canzona IV [Frescobaldi],
479,538
Canzona la Sauoldi à 2
[Riccio/G.Smith], 395
Canzonas for Basso Solo
[Frescobaldi], 389,432,
467,538
Canzone [Bon], 531
Canzoni et Sonate
[G.Gabrieli], 640
CAPAB, 131
Cape Town [South Africa],
131
Cappa, Carlo Alberto, 145,243
Capriccio (solo):[Bonneau
and Boutry], 478,558
Capriccio (ens.): [Fitelberg],
395; [Janáček], 762
Capriccio da Camera [Krol],
538
Caramel mou [Milhaud], 762
Caravan, 239
CARDEW, Cornelius, *614;*
498,579,601

Careers,65,71,1033,1130,
1166,1186,1201,1208,1217,
1250,1263,1302,1303
CARLSON, Eric, *97,1033;*
177,229,1031,1130,1166,
1263,1302
"Caro trono ti abbandano"
from *Il zelo di Nathan*
[Porsile], 616
Carse, Adam, 795,825,852,
858,869,878,888,922,936,
953,987,1192
Carter, Elliott, 696
CARTER, J., *615*
CARTER, Stewart, *616,813;*
475,504,537,838
Carvalho, Urband, 530
CASAMORATA, L.F., *814*
Casati [Cassati?], [Pietro?], 537
CASE, George, *815;* 842,914,
960,964
Case Western Reserve
University, 421
Cases [instrument], 863,872,
906
CASTELLENGO, Michelle,
617; 621,639,755,775,759,
1022,1116
Castello, Dario, 394,395
Castérède, Jacques, 409,413,
538
CATALANO, Nicholas, *277;*
293,336,379
Catalogs, 545
CATELINET, Barry, *1034;*
55,224
Catholic University, 504,
547,687,737,738,956,
1018,1223

Catskills, 288
CAUSSÉ, René, *950;* 792,
    841,851,885
Cavatine, op. 144 [Saint-
    Saëns], 479,538,539,558
CBSO (City of Birmingham
    Symphony Orchestra), 58
CECIL, Herbert M., *816*
[La] cena del Signore [Fux],
    616
Centennial, 42
Central Missouri University,
    431,775
Cesare, Giovanni Martino,
    390,394,538,756
Cha Cha, 604
CHADBOURNE, Eugene,
    278; 285
Chamber Concerto No. 2
    [Townsend], 476
Chamber Music III: "Night
    Set," [Suderberg], 528
Chamber Music — Trombone,
    48,146,196,200,205,385,
    392,395,396,398,401,404,
    425,431,446,447,448,449,
    462,465,475,477,497,498,
    502,504,507,510,513,528,
    529,531,533,534,537,544,
    560,564,569,572,573,576,
    578,583,584,585,589,590,
    594,606,629,644,648,649,
    652,656,657,662,674,696,
    712,717,722,726,729,738,
    759,762,763,780,782,
    1122,1215
CHAMBERLAIN, David, *98;*
    875
CHAMBERS, Robert Lee, 417

Changes [Austin], 621,759
Chant et Danse [Bondon],
    558
CHASANOV, Elliott L., *99,*
    100; 127,129,207
Chase, Allen, 576
Chávez, Carlos, 528,733
Chaynes, J-M., 558
Chazanov, Mathis, 734
Cherubini, Luigi, 752
Chestnutt, Rod, 530
*"Chi ti conosco" from La
    deposizione della croce*
    [Fux], 616
Chicago [IL], 86,161,200,228,
    246,503,568,613,761
Chicago Loopers, 348
Childs, Barney, 538,579,621
Chinelli, Giovanni Battista,
    655
Chisolm, George, 750
"Chloe," 751
"Chop Suey," 264
Choral, 393,408,466,486,536,
    580,595,608,713,752
Chorale [religious or sacred
    music], 654
Chorale, Cadence, et Fugato
    [Dutilleux], 479,538,558
Choros No. 4 [Villa-Lobos],
    507
CHRISTENSEN,Carl J., *418;*
    746
Christian, Christian, 583,616,
    656,729
Christian, Hans Georg, 583,
    616,656,729
Christian, Leopold, Sr., 583,
    616,656,722,729,731,743

Christian, Leopold, Jr., 583, 616,656,729
Christian, Leopold Ferdinand, 583,616,656,729
Christianson, Michael, 307
CHRISTIE, John M., *419, 1035;* 432,436,439,1013
CHRISTMANN, Günther, *618;* 126
Christus-Petrus-Deborah u. Sarah [Eberlin], 537,753
Christus-Petrus-Joanes Phönissa [Eberlin], 537,753
Chromacousia, 1056
Chromesthesia, 1056
Churches, 805
Ciccarone, Rock, 121
Cimbasso, 796,799,873,892
ČIMERA, Jaroslav [Jerry], *1036;* 90,140,199,232,243
Cincinnati [OH], 147,613
Cincinnati, University of, 850
Cioffi, Felipe, 144,145
Circular Breathing, 639,1093, 1289
ČIŽEK, Bohuslav, *817*
"Clarinet Marmalade," 710
Clark, J. Bunker, 401
Clark, John, 124
CLARK, Wayne R., *1037*
CLARKE, Ernest, *1038,1039, 1040;* 90,243,1046
Clarke, Herbert, 135,207
Clefs, 1063,1185
Clergue, Jean, 539,558
Cleveland [OH], 88,186,225, 761
Cleveland, James [Jimmy], 127,329

Cliffe Castle Museum, 914
"Clock-Spring Mechanism," 795
CL 2000 valve, 894
Cobbett, W.W., 447
COE, John W., *420,1041;* 531,551,579,1013
COFFEY, John, *818;* 102, 124,235,248,1001,1013
COHEN, Albert, *101*
Cohen, Arthur, 530
Cohen, Gilbert, 164
Colegrove, John, 530
COLIN, Charles, *102,231, 279,280,281;* 261,313,327, 337,350,351,1001,1193
Collapsible Stays, 908
Collections, 392,810,832,839, 861,864,879,882,925,929
Colleges-Universities, 95,412, 413,1026,1112,1150,1208, 1304
Collins, Nicolas, 800
COLLINS, William T., *421;* 553,767,856
COLNOT, C., *282;* 1203
Cologne [Germany], and University of, 661,684
Colorado Jazz Party, 284,643
[La] colpa originale [I.Conti], 616
Coltrane, John, 1281
COLUMBE, Grahame, *283;* 254,287,290,318,319
Columbia University [NY], 627,765,1135,1161
Combinatoria II [Fulkerson], 395
Coming in Glory [Larosa], 395

Commedia IV [Bennett], 462

*Commedie, op. 42 [Campo], 395

Commodores [Navy Band], 1210

Competitions, 53,424,1235

Competitiveness, 1271

Composers Facsimile Edition-Basic Catalog: 1957, 536

Composers in America [Reis], 536

Computers, 312,402,736, 1003,1222

CONANT, Abbie, *103;* 172, 239

Concert Band, 217

*Concertino [Makris], 395; [Premru], 395,538

*Concertino Basso [Lieb], 432,479

Concertino d'hiver [Milhaud], 409,476,538

*Concertino for Large Trombone and Small Orchestra [McCulloh], 432

Concertino for Trombone and Orchestra, op.4 [David], 118,196,403,432,476,479, 495,538,551,577,592

*Concertino for Trombone and Strings, op. 45, no. 7 [Larsson], 476,478,538

*Concertino für Baßposaune [Kummer], 495; [Meyer], 432, 495; [C.G. Müller], 403,432,495

*Concertino in A-flat Major for Trombone [W.Rex], 403

Concertino in E-flat Major for Trombone and Orchestra [Smita], 747

*Concertino pour Trombone et Orchestre: [Berghmans and Spisak], 558

*Concerto [Spillman], 413, 432,478,538; [Van Dijk], 395; [Webern, op. 24], 762

Concerto for Alto Trombone (extracted from *Divertimento in D (1764)*] [M.Haydn], 487,503,538,566,583

Concerto for Alto Trombone and Orchestra [Bresgens], 456

Concerto for [Alto] Trombone and Orchestra [in E-flat Major] [Wagenseil],413,476, 504,538,554,583,609,656

Concerto for Alto Trombone and Strings [in B-flat Major] [Albrechtsberger], 476,503, 537,538,583,656

Concerto for Bass Trombone and Orchestra:*[George], 432,476,538;*[McCulloh], 432;[(Taafe)Zwilich],503,568

Concerto for Bass Tuba and Orchestra [Vaughan Williams], 413,479,538

*Concerto for Four Trombones [Dubois/Cohen], 530

Concerto for Horn [von Weber], 403,495

Concerto for Orchestra [Bartók], 619

Concerto for Tenor Trombone and Orchestra: [Alschausky], 476,592;*[Boutry],476,558;

[Chávez],528;*[Coker],432,
476;*[Gouinguene],478,538;
[Gräfe],476,478,592;
*[Gröndahl],476,478,538;
[Hovland],528;[Jacob],413,
476,478,538,569;[E.Reiche],
87,476;*[W.Ross],432,476;
[Rouse],506;[Serocki],423,476;
[Tomasi],409,423,476,538,558;
[G.Walker],530;*[A.Weber],
558;*[Wells],530;[(Taaffe)
Zwilich],503,530;*[Zwilich/
Chestnutt],530
*Concerto for Trombone and
Band* [Rimsky-Korsakov],
413,476,479,538,559
*Concerto für Trombone
[Posaune] oder Viola und
Orchester* [L. Mozart], 538
Concerto in f minor
[Handel], 413,538
Concerto in One Movement
[Lebedev], 413,479,538
*Concerto Lirico for Trombone
and Orchestra* [Bassett],
469
Concerto Militaire [David],
495
Concerto Palatino, 75
Concertos,138,194,196,231,
397,403,411,412,423,435,
456,469,476,480,485,487,
492,495,503,504,506,511,
528,530,533,538,540,554,
559,562,566,567,568,569,
583,609,613,656,657,722,
729,733
*Concerto no. 3 (Diran-The
Religious Singer)*

[Hovhaness], 476
Concert Sketch [Piece] No. 5
[Blazhevich], 413,479,538
Condensation [Stibilj], 395,
759
CONGER, Robert B., *422;*
594,1104
Conn, C.G., 870,894,970,
1126,1214
Conners, Charles [Chuck],
301
Consecuenza [Alsina], 515,
621,759
Contacts [Zbar], 531
Contemporary Techniques,
115,596
Contrabass Trombone, 815,
842,860,875,892,895,914,
960,964,975,1053
Conversation[s?] [Small],
353,432,538
COOK, Edward [Eddie], *284;*
1280
Cools, Eugène, 539,558
COOMBES, J., *1002*
COOPER, Isaiah, *104*
Cope, David, 531
Corelli, Arcangelo, 489
Cornell University, 502
Cornet [valves], 187
Cornett [pre-valves], 390,
513,925,954,955
Cornetto, 717
Corno da Tirarsi, 941
"Cosí a fiume" from Joaz
[Caldara], 616
*"Cosí fa splendor" from La
morte vinta sul Calvario*
[Ziani], 616

Couillaud, Henri, 553
Coulissiana [Dautremet], 558
Coussemaker, Edward, 846
Covington, Warren, 129
Cowell, Henry, 428
COX, Joseph L., 423
CRAMER, William, *424,*
  1042,1043; 125,127,153,
  174,178,723,733
Cravens, Terry, 128
*"[La] création du monde,"
  [Milhaud], 762
Creativity, 1092
*Credentials or think, think,
  lucky* [Haubenstock-
  Ramati], 395
CREES, Eric, *819;* 113
Creston, Paul, 116,530,538
CRIDER, Joseph R., *425,*
  1044; 1136,1162
CRIMMINS, Roy, *820,1045;*
  1017
Crisafulli, Frank, 86,154,200,
  228,1186,1211
CRIST, Michael, *1046;* 1040
Croce, Giovanni, 655
Crocé-Spinelli, B., 539,558
Crook, Hal, 265
CROOKS, Mack, *285;* 278
CROSBIE, Ian, 286
Crossen, Pat, 1064
Crotti, Archangelo, 655
CRUMP, Harold C., *1047;*
  1161
Cryder, Richard, 126
Cryptical Triptych [W.Ross],
  432,531,759
Crystal Records, 541,556,570
Cuatris [Balada], 395

Culpepper, Max C., 44
Cullum, Fred, 206
Cumbia, 604
Cunningbird, 253,346
Cuomo, James, 531
Cupid's Bow, 45
Curcel, Georges, 719
Czechoslovakia, 122,234,575,
  595,682,747
Czech Republic, 529,564

D

*"Da Christo ch'é pio" from
  Gesu Cristo negato da
  Pietro* [Fux], 616
Da Viadana, Lodovico Grossi,
  655
Da-dl-a-dl Tonguing, 1289
Dahl, Ingolf, 462
DAHLSTROM, Joseph F.,
  821
Dailey, John, 155
*"Dal limbo" from Cristo
  nell'orto* [Fux], 616
D'Alembert, 790
*"Dal tuo seglio luminoso"
  from Santa Elena al
  Calvario* [Caldara], 616
DALEY, Samuel T., *1048;*
  783,1007
DALKERT,Charles,*1049,1050,
  1051;*1004,1016,1061,1109,
  1205,1241,1265
Dallas [TX], 149
Dallo y Lanas, Miguel, 884
DANCE, Stanley, *287;* 254,
  318,319,781
Dangelmaier, Matthias, 121

Danish Blue, 750
Darmstadt [Germany], 460
Dart, Thurston, 663
Dautremet, Marcel, 558
Davenport, Roger, 80
David, Ferdinand, 118,195,
  403,495,538,551,577,592
Davidde Penitente, K.469
  [W.A. Mozart], 769
Davies, Hugh, 984
Davies, Ian, 962
DAVIS, Francis, *288;* 332,
  339,356
DAVIS, Micha, 619
Davison, John, 428,538
Deans, Kenneth, 888
Death Announcement
  [Moravian], 654
Dedrick, Art, 289
DEDRICK, Rusty, *289*
Defaÿ, Jean Michael, 409,
  530,558
Deffa, C., 361
*"Deh scogliere" from *Morte,
  e sepoltura di Cristo*
  [Caldara], 616
DEHN, *426*
DEISENROTH, F., *620*
DeJong, Conrad, 531
DEKAN, Karl, *822;* 806,826,
  844,911,932,977,986
*"Del fallo m'avvedo" from
  La morte d'Abel [Caldara],
  616
**D.E. Memorial* [Heider], 772
DEMPSTER,Stuart,*621;*126,
  151,185,202,237,257,271,
  298,400,617,639,751,755,
  759,1022,1116,1223

Denmark, 71,94,118,136,168,
  195,220,562
DENNIS, W., *823*
Dental, 5,45
Denver [Colorado], 155
DeSano, James, 88
Désenclos, Alfred, 558
De Souza, Raul, 367
Desportes, Yvonne, 528,539,
  558
DESTANQUE, Guy, *1052;*
  124
Detroit, 85
DEUTSCH, Herbert, *1053;*
  836,843,964,974
Deux Danses: [Defaÿ], 409,
  479,530,538;*[Defaÿ/
  Carvalho], 530
DEY, Joseph, *824;* 663,
  846,976
DE YOUNG, Derald Dwight,
  1054; 1097
*"Di al mio Ré" from *Il
  David pereseguitato*
  [F.Conti], 616
Dialogues [D.Good], 759
Diaphragm Impulse, 1241
Dibb, Jeremy, 514
Dickenson, Ray Clark, 383
Dickenson, Victor [Vic], 254,
  283,287,319,622,750,751,
  781
DICKINSON, Christian, *178,
  1055;* 174
Diderot, Denis, 790
Didjeridu, 621
Dieppo, Antoine, 145,553
DIETRICH, Kurt, *106,290,
  622;* 283

DILLON, Steve, *107;* 109,
135,171,243,556,870
DiLutis, John J., 121
D'Indy, Vincent, 625
*"Dio, qual sia la ria
sentenza" from *Naboth*
[Caldara], 616
*"Dio sol ne porge aita" from
Il Sacrificio d'Abramo
[Predieri], 616
Directories, 791
Dirt Chorus, 1048
Discographies,113,114,115,
118,128,135,142,146,171,
195,243,245,256,267,269,
271,278,281,293,297,298,
311,312,320,329,332,346,
348,362,373,381,391,479,
485,560,618,621,669,688,
692,748,750,1084
Discours [Globokar], 498,515,
532,579,601,759
.*Discourse [GUTs 2a]* I, 402
Dissertations,1,4,9,11,12,20,
21,135,213,267,290,392,395,
396,398,409,417,420,421,
425,428,440,452,458,467,
468,472,476,480,481,482,
491,492,493,498,502,506,
523,525,531,543,547,550,
551,564,565,567,582,583,
584,585,590,594,601,607,
609,627,638,640,644,646,
648,649,652,655,656,658,
661,665,667,672,674,678,
684,687,696,702,708,712,
733,738,741,756,759,763,
765,780,804,806,850,869,
879,884,904,964,977,1003,
1004,1013,1014,1018,1037,
1054,1076,1096,1097,1100,
1110,1113,1114,1116,1122,
1135,1145,1158,1161,1162,
1165,1187,1189,1202,1225,
1227,1233,1249
DiStasio, Eugene, 126
DITTMER, John, *109;* 107
Diversion [Peruti], 395
Diversions [Glass], 432
Divertimento: [Blacher], 538;
*[Layton], 395
Divertissement [Croley], 432
Dixieland, 262,314,727
DOBROSKI, B., *282;* 1203
Dodson, Glenn, 97,229
"Doink [rink]," 751
Doms, Johann, 112
Donati, Ignazio, 655
*Don Giovanni (Don Juan) [Il
Dissoluto punito]*, 387,450
DONNELL-KOTROZO,Carol,
1056
Doodle Tongue, 1181
Dorsey, James [Jimmy], 323,
587
Dorsey, Thomas [Tommy],
29,41,66,323,329,361,587,
692,715
Dortmund [Germany], 1154
DOUAY, Jean, *45,110,111,
427,623,1057;* 92,129,
154,184
Double-barrelled Trombone,
919
Double Rotor, 1077,1213,
1256,1264,1295
Double Slide [Doppel-
aussenzug], 900,914

Doubles sur un Choral
[Duclos], 539,558
Doubling, 708,745,1032,
1059,1279
*"Dov'é giá sviene" from *San
Pietro in Cesarea* [Caldara],
616
*"Dovunque il guardo" from
*La passione di Gesu Christo
Signor nostro* [Caldara],
616
Downey [CA], 734
DOWNEY, Peter, *624,825;*
757,827,850,865,908,915,
931,942,946,952,963,965
Draghi, Antonio, 616
Drake, Debra, 400
Drawn Trumpet, 663
Dreams, 275
Drei Equale [Beethoven],
769
Drei leichte Stücke
[Hindemith], 478,538
Dresden [Germany], 87
DREW, John Robert, *428,
625;*129,440,489,522,549,
709,746,767
DRISCOLL, Anne, 1058
Drouet, Jean-Pierre, 684
Druckman, Jacob, 420,531,
538,551,579,621,759
DRUMMER, Lee A., *1059;*
708,793,1032
Dry Ralph [Cuomo], 531
DSCH [Denisov], 395
Dualismos [Del Monaco],
395
Dubois, Pierre-Max, 530,538
Du Bois, Robert, 759

Dubois, Theodore, 539,558
Duclos, René, 539,558
DUDLEY, Paul, *291;* 372
DUERKSEN, George, *626,
826*
*Duet for Trombone and
Organ* [Holst], 463,514
Duett [Elgar], 395
DUFFIN, Ross W., *827;* 825
DUKER, Guy M., *1060*
DULLAT, Günter, *828;* 795,
998
Dunnick, Kim, 954
Duo-Gravis, 877
Durand, Pierre, 558
Dutilleux, Henri, 538
DUTTENHOFER, Eva-Maria,
829
Dvořák, Antonin, 747
Dynamics, 67,822

E

Eachus, Paul, 121
EASTER, Stanley, 627
Eastern Trombone Workshop
(ETW), 587
Eastman School of Music
[University of Rochester],
198,221,396,471,513,644,
648,733,767,772,816,1252
East Texas State University,
464,465,521,885,912
Eberlin, Johann Ernst, 196,
537,552,583,753
ECCOTT, D.J., *628*
Echanges [Globokar], 601
Ecklund, Peter, 1290
Eclipse Marching Band, 322

Edinburgh [Scotland],
    University of, 896,925
Educational Testing Service
    (ETS), 73
Edwards, Peter, 856
EDWARDS, Robert, *830*
Egypt, 74,1113
EHMANN, Wilhelm, *629,630,*
    631,632; 204,518,744,857,
    1155
EHRMANN, Alfred von, *633*
Einstein, Alfred, 545
Eisenach [Germany], 983
EISENBERG, Reinke, *112,429*
Eitner, Robert, 447,544
Electromyography, 1158
Electronic Music, 115,312,
    402,420,437,441,446,483,
    497,531,736,759
Electronic Tuner, 1079
Elegy for Mippy II
    [Bernstein], 413,479,531,
    538,579
Elementary School, 1009,
    1055,1087,1110,1187
ELIAS,Joel,*113,114,115,116,*
    831,1061,1062,1063,1064,
    *1065,1066;*92,93,109,183,
    788,819,904,944,949,961,
    993,1004,1017,1027,1050,
    1071,1081,1086,1087,1109,
    1126,1175,1185,1205,1214,
    1241,1259,1265
ELIASON, Robert, *832;* 145
ELLENRIEDER, M., *1067*
Ellington, Edward Kennedy
    [Duke], 290,622,720
Elliott, Charles A., 1018
Elliott, Douglas, 153

ELLIOTT, S.J., *833;* 932,978
Embouchure,45,897,997,1012,
    1115,1134,1162,1167,1171,
    1172,1226,1235,1270
EMI, 28
EMSHEIMER, Ernst, *834*
Encores for Stu [Wilding-
    White], 432 621
Encounters IV: Duel for
    Trombone and Percussion
    [W.Kraft], 395,570
Endgame [Peruti], 395
ENDRESS, Gudrun, *292;* 261,
    327,1193
Endurance, 1120
Enevoldsen, Robert [Bob], 940
[L']enfant et les sortilèges
    [Ravel], 984
Engel, Carl, 846
ENGELEN, Piet van, *293;*
    277,336,379,1278
England,58,69,72,113,114,
    150,165,167,284,357,417,
    463,520,605,614,663,716,
    795,804,815,830,859,867,
    914,962,979,985,1280   [*see*
    also Britain]
ENGLISH, Jon, *430*
English Language, 16
Ensemble, 37,1065,1175,
    1176,1259
Eonta [Xenakis], 759
Epigramme, op. 48 [Michael],
    528
Epoxy Resin, 977
Equale, 442,581,777
Equali for Three Tenor
    Trombones and Bass
    Trombone [Goosen], 769

Equipment, 40
Erb, Donald, 129,621
ERDMAN, James W. [Jim],
    431; 126,129,236,395,
    396,447,644
Erickson, Robert, 531,621
Ervin, Karen, 570
ERVIN, Thomas [Tom], *294,*
    835,1068,1069,1070; 127,
    151,190,239,375,570,1231,
    1254,1298
Erwin, Edward, 84,164
*Esorcismi No. 1 [Laneri],
    395
*Esque [Kellaway], 395
Etler, Alvin, 462,696
Eton, 69
Etude, 1056
*Etude de Concert [Büsser],
    539,558
Etudes, 133,411,412,1014,
    1100,1104,1116,1124,1215
Etymology, 794,935
EUBANKS, Robin, *634;* 236,
    312
Euphonium (Baritone horn),
    21,37,542,708,793,810,
    1032,1055,1059,1115,1230,
    1235,1249
Europe, 25,53,264,662,809,
    864,884
EVANS, David, *295*
Evensmo, Jan, 318
Evenson, Pattee Edward, 513,
    662
EVERETT, Thomas G. [Tom],
    1,2,24,25,117,118,119,120,
    121,122,123,124,125,126,
    127,128,129,296,297,298,
    299,300,301,302,327,432,
    433,434,435,436,437,438,
    836,1071,1072,1073; 94,151,
    152,162,195,234,251,257,
    261,267,271,307,308,327,
    419,439,468,478,481,521,
    524,550,560,579,593,600,
    617,618,621,635,639,668,
    755,758,769,773,843,847,
    934,951,989,993,994,996,
    1013,1027,1029,1035,1041,
    1052,1053,1063,1077,1082,
    1083,1084,1087,1105,1123,
    1126,1129,1142,1180,1193,
    1196,1213,1214,1229,1247,
    1256,1264,1269,1287,1295
*Evolution [Allison], 395,432
Ewald, Victor, 449
Ewazen, Eric, 653
ex tempore, 497
Experimental, 883
*Extase [Yoshioka], 538
*Ezechia [I.Conti], 616

F

"F" Attachment, 993,1027,
    1062,1071,1082,1083,1087,
    1089,1105,1123,1126,1129,
    1142,1180,1196,1214,1229,
    1289
*The Fabulous "Slide" Hampton
    Quartet,* 264
FADLE, Heinz, *130,635,*
    1074,1075; 237,1073,1247,
    1287
FALLENBERG, Jerry, *1076;*
    1233
FALLIS, Todd, *439;* 419,436

*False Relationships and the
Extended Ending* [Feldman],
395
Fanfare, Andante et Allegro
[Franck], 558
Fantaisie: [Desportes,
Stojowski], 539,558;
[Stojowski/Cohen], 530
Fantaisie Concertante
[Castérède], 413,432,479,538
Fantaisie Lyrique [Semler-
Collery], 558
Fantasie für Baßposaune
[Meyer], 495
*Fantasy for Trombone and
Orchestra* [Creston], 116,
476,538; *[Creston/ Cohen],
530
Far East, 809
FARNHAM, Dean A., *440;*
428,489
FARRAR, Lloyd P., *837;* 861
FART, 1239
FARWELL, Doug, *441*
Fasch, Johann Friedrich, 489
FASMAN, Mark J., *3;* 1261
FAULDS, John, *636*
FAULISE, Paul, *1077;* 301,
836,843
FAULKNER, Maurice, *1078;*
1011
FAUNTLEY, Basil J., *131*
[La] Favola d'Orfeo, 386
FEATHER, Leonard, *303,637;*
24,267,334
Fedchock, John, 237
Fedianin, Sergei, 121
Felten, Eric, 307
[La] Femme à Barbe

[Berghmans], 538
Féraud, M., 45
Ferdinand I, 241
Ferris, Glenn, 366
Fétis, François, 719,1192
FETTER,David,*132,133,1079,
1080;*177,452,573,640,1016,
1031,1122,1127,1137,1146,
1170,1191,1218,1219,1262,
1268,1284,1296
Fiction, 43,57
FIEDLER, Andre, *442;* 581
Fili mi, Absalon [Schütz],
538,769
Fillio, Lloyd, 128
FILLMORE, Henry, *1081;*
538,783,1007
Finch, Arthur, 962
FINK,Reginald H.,*1082,1083,
1084;*128,836,993,1013,
1027,1063,1071,1088,1126,
1180
Finland, 189
Finlayson, David, 99
Finton, Michael, 121
FISCHER, Henry George,
838,839; 813,981
Five Miniatures [McCauley],
395,432,476
Five Negro Spirituals
[Blacher], 395
*Five Pieces for Trombone and
Piano* [Krenek], 432,531,
538,621,759
Flanders, 725
FLANDRIN, G.P.A.L., *840*
Flat Trumpet, 952,963
FLOR,Gloria,*841,842,843,
1085,1086,1087,1088;*788,

792,815,836,847,851,875,
885,895,914,934,950,951,
960,964,989,993,994,1011,
1027,1053,1063,1071,1077,
1082,1089,1126,1140,1213,
1214,1231,1256,1264,1295
Florence [Italy], 670
FLOUER, Jack A., *638,1089;*
993,1027,1063,1071,1082,
1087,1126,1214
Flugabone, 877,919,948
Flute, 1110
FOCACCIA, Laura, *134*
Foley, David, 121
*Fond Memories of Frank
Rosolino*, 457
Fontana, Carl, 235,239,251,
273,297,308,341,643,750,
781
Fontana, Johann Fr., 583,616
Fontana, Silvano Angelo, 583,
616
FORBES, Vernon, *443;* 152,
410,471,479,539,558,563
Formata [Hellerman], 432
Forsang, Björn, 126
FORTENBERRY, Robert E.,
1090
FOTE, Richard, *1091;* 1030
Four Preludes (orig. piano)
[Shostakovich], 538
Four Songs [Kehrberg], 395
Fournier, Robert, 121
Fourquet, Jacques, 668
FOWLER, Bruce, *639,1092;*
128,365,617,621,755,1022,
1093
FOWLER, William, *1093*
Frackenpohl, Arthur, 538

France,46,92,96,101,110,111,
157,182,184,209,409,417,
451,493,539,558,567,582,
599,602,623,651,668,671,
673,691,693,702,704,719,
741,785,801,840,874,898,
899,902,924,935,971,1042,
1052,1057,1139,1156,1290
Franck, César, 1013
FRANCK, James A., *844;*
806,822,871,912,932,977,
986
Franck, Maurice, 558
FRANK, Robert, *304*
Franz Liszt Academy, 1074
Franzoni, Amante, 655
Freddi, Amadio, 655
"Free for All," 457
*Free Forms, Four Pieces for
Bass Trombone and Strings*
[Andrix], 395,432,476
Free Jazz, 288,339
Free Music Machine, 984
Frescobaldi, Girolamo, 389,
467,538
FRIEDMAN, Jay, *1094,1095;*
152,161,228,459,496,503,
665,672,715,1244,1246,1301
FRIZANE, Daniel E., *135;*
107,171
FROELICH, John Philip,
1096; 1012,1098,1159,1273
FROHRIP, Kenton Ronald,
1097; 1054
Frölich, Joseph, 452,853
. . . *From Behind the
Unreasoning Mask*
[Reynolds], 497,607,677
FROMME, Arnold, *640,641;*

132,401,590,669,676,700,
718,728,852,909,920,921,
933,935,945,947,955,1122
*"Fuggo d'una in altra selva"
from *Il David perseguitato*
[F.Conti], 616
FULKERSON, James, *444,
1098;* 751,1012,1277
Fuller, Curtis, 707
Funk, 310
Fux, Johann Joseph, 398,583,
589,616

G

Gabriel, Arnold, 175
Gabrieli, Giovanni, 401,
590,640
GADE, Per, *136,137,138;*
220
GAGNE, J., *845*
GAJDAMOVIC, Tat'jana,
139; 212,240
Galliard, Johann Ernst,
538,702
GALLOWAY, D., *1099;* 990
GALPIN, [Canon] Francis
William, *846;* 640,663,700,
794,803,824,891,909,926,
933,935,945,976,981
*Gamme et méthode pour les
trombonnes* [Braun], 166
GARCÍA, Antonio J., *642;*
1011,1078,1085,1144,
1173,1232,1255,1269
Garfield, Charles, 1076
GARVIN, Keig E., *140;* 129,
199,232,1036,1119
GATWOOD, Dwight D., *847;*

836,843,934,951,990
Gaubert, Philippe, 539,558
G-Bass Trombone, 206
Gee, Matthew, 750
Geminiani, Francesco, 638
General Speech [Erickson],
531,621,751
*Gentle Harm of the Bourg-
eoisie* [Rutherford], 165
Geography, 611
Geometry, 938
GEORGE, Stanley Paul, *445,
1100;* 594,1104,1275
George, Thom Ritter, 158,
538
Georgia, University of,
904,1200
Germany,60,81,87,105,130,
148,179,193,204,233,271,
296,349,362,374,417,453,
513,518,519,535,540,584,
592,600,618,620,629,630,
631,632,633,661,680,695,
701,705,711,723,724,744,
768,858,860,869,889,913,
922,943,809,980,1067,
1154,1155,1192,1212
GETTIER, Leigh, *863;*
872,906
Gewandhaus, 194,403,495,
540
GIARDINELLI, Robert,
1101; 982,1015,1258
Gibbs, Michael, 266
Gibson, David, 307
Gibson, William, 248,559
GIDDINS, Gary, *305,643;*
330,354,371,377,380,381
Giffels, A., 413

GIFFORD, Robert M., Jr.,
  644,645; 385,395,396,
  431,447,717,725,802
Gilbertson, James, 228
Gillen, Gerard, 624
Gillespie, John Birks [Dizzy],
  292
Gilmore, Patrick, 187
GINSBERG, M., *141;* 675
Girard, Yvelise, 111
Gitler, Ira, 281,337,351,1107
GLASMIRE, David, *1102*
GLENDENING, Andrew R.,
  646; 709
Glenn, Tyree, 751
Glinka, Michael Ivanovich,
  625
Glissandi, 619
Glissando [periodical], 46
GLOBOKAR,Vinko,*647;*128,
  236,400,498,515,532,579,
  601,614,621,684,698,751,
  759
"Glory of jazz . . . ," 306
Glover, Betty S., 124,147,
  237
GLOVER, Stephen L., *4;* 22
**go* [Kam], 395
Goatham, J., 336
Godlis, Abraham, 214
Goldkette, Jean, 338,360
Good, Dennis, 759
GOODWIN, Peter, *142,143;*
  167,226,663
GOROVOY, S.G., *1103*
Gossec, François Joseph,
  719,767
**Götterdammerung* [Wagner],
  769

GOTTHOLD, J., *848*
Gouinguene, Christian, 479,
  538
GOULD, James F., *1104;*
  422,594
Gräfe, Friedbald, 592
GRAHAM, James, *1105,
  1106;* 836,1013,1030,1305
Graham, Philip, 149
Grainger, Percy, 984
Grambling, Robert, 1048
[Grand] Concerto [Gräfe],
  476,478,592
Grandi, Alessandro, 655
Graphic Arts, 917
**Graphic I* [Goldstaub], 432
**Graphismes* [Bozza], 531
GRAY,Robert E.,*446,447,448,
  648;*127,230,237,395,396,
  431,560,644,762,780
Graz [Austria], 344
Green, Barry, 1076
Green, Bennett Lester
  [Bennie/Duke], 370
Green, Charles [Big Charlie],
  329,357,710,751
Green, Jake, 751
GREEN, Katherine, *47*
GREEN, Michael, *649;* 449,
  462,696,726
Green, Urban [Urbie], 41,
  129,281,294,329,337,351,
  715,750,751
Greenhoe, Gary, 106
GREENHOW, Ann, *449;* 462
Greensboro [NC], 733
GREGORY, Robin, *849*
Gregson, Edward, 462
GREINER, Anthony, *48*

Gretton, Paul, 954
GREY, Al, *1107;* 128,260,
643,720,751,1008,1023
GREY, M., *1107;* 1023
GRIFFITH, Janet E., *850;* 825
GRIFFITH, Ted, *851;*
124,154,792,841,885,950
Griggs, Alan, 131
Grigoriev, Boris, 139,1080,
1127,1137,1146,1170,1191,
1219,1262,1268,1284
Griscom, Richard, 684
GRISSOM, Eugene, *307;* 121,
249,512
GRISSOM, Nancy, *308,341;*
251
Grock, [Charles Adrien
Wettach], 400,531,621
Gröndahl, Launy, 138,538
G-Rotor, 907
Group Methods, 1090
*Grove's Dictionary of Music
and Musicians*, 536,640
"The Growl," 751
GRUBB, Marion, *650;* 32,
541,606
Grund-richtiger Unterricht . . .
[Speer], 132,676
GRUNO, Linda, *309,310*
Gschlatt [Gschladt], Thomas,
196,537,629,656,722,729,743
GUGLER, B., *450;* 387,683,
757
Guilford, Matthew, 121,239
Guilmant, Alexandre, 413,538,
539,558
GUION, David M., *144,145,
451,452,651,652,852,853;*
148,187,193,218,573,640,

909,947,955,1122
Gurin, Nathaniel, 85
GUTTRIDGE, Leonard, *311;*
250,252,348
GWYNN, Dominic, *854*

H

Haack, Don, 106
HAGE, Kees van, *855*
Hague Gemeentemuseum, 929
Haines, Malou, 888
HALE, Ted, *653*
HALL, Ben, *1108*
HALL, Harry H., *654;* 32,
541,606
Hall, Michael [Mike], 470
Hall, Ralph, 235
Hallberg, Gordon, 117,124,248
HALSELL, George K., *655;* 590
Halt, Fred, 104
Hamlet [A.Thomas], 553
Hammer, Matthias Joseph,
583,616
HAMMERBACHER, J., *453*
Hampe, Carl, 248
Hampton, Locksley
Wellington [Slide],
264,272,369,380,643
Hamrick, Robert, 100
Handbuch der Chormusik
[Valentin], 536
Handel, George Frederick,
413,538,603,713,859
Handicapped, 877
Handrow, Rolf, 236,495,540
HANEY, Lewis Van, *1109;*
82,125,126,129,154,164,176,
227,619,1017,1061,1205,1241

HANLON, Kenneth M., *656;*
196,251,464,486,504,537,
554,616,658,709,721,753,767
Hansbery, Richard, 159
Hansen, Anton, 136,137,220
HANSEN, J.E., *26;* 30
Hanson, Wesley Luther, 625,
771
Hansotte, Lucien, 248
Hansson, Anders, 128
HARDIN, Anne F., *1110*
HARLOW, Lewis, *856;* 421,
553
Harmonic Trumpet, 965
Harp, 404
Harper, Robert S., 124,210,
229
Harris, Craig, 332
HARRIS, Noreen, *657;* 504,
537,554
Harris, Roy, 29,323,587
HARRIS, S., *259*
Harris, William [Bill], 329,
715,1111
Harrison, James [Jimmy], 329,
357,710
Harry, Don, 104
HARTLEY, Walter S., *454;*
489,538
HARTMAN, Mark S., *658,*
1111,1112; 129,788,1026,
1114,1145,1220
Hartman, Scott, 237
HARTZELL, L.W., *659;* 32,
541,606
HARVEY, Martin, *455*
HARVISON, Emery, *146,147*
Harwood, Donald, 124,164,
1013

Hary Janos Suite [Kodály],
1013
HASAN, Muhamed Ahmed
Hasan, *1113*
HASKETT, William R., *1114;*
1026,1112
HAUPT, P., *857*
Havens, Robert [Bob], 643
Hawes, Randall, 236
Haydn, Johann Michael, 196,
487,504,538,566,583,609,
656,729
HEATH, Fred, *1115*
Heather, Cliff, 301
Hebrew Bible, 857
HECKMAN, D., *660*
Heider, Werner, 772
HEIDSIEK, Dietrich, *661*
Hejda, Miloslav, 122,234,747
[Ein] Heldenleben
[R.Strauss], 1013
Helicon, 858
HELLAND, David, *312;* 634
HELLER, Friedrich C., *456*
Helsinki, 189
Henderson, Fletcher, 710
Henken, John 734
Henry, Sunny, 322
HENSCHEL, *662*
HEPOLA, Ralph, *27*
Herald Trombone, 868
HERBERT, Trevor, *663,859;*
167,794,797,896,935
Herman, Edward, Jr., 164
HERMELINK, Siegried, *664*
HERRICK, Dennis R., *665;*
672,715,1244,1301
Herrington, Benjamin,
146,239

HERWIG, Conrad, *457;* 237,
249,307,1281
Heuser, Frank, 1158
HEY, Dean, *1116*
HEYDE, Herbert, *860,861;*
837,842,895
Hialmar [Loucheur], 558
[La] Hieronyma [Cesare],
538
Higginbotham, J.C., 329
High Register, 1000,1094,
1190,1203,1231
HIGHFILL, Joseph R., *666*
HILDEBRANDT, Donald Jay,
667,668; 126,433,746,758,
761,769
*Hi-Lites from the Carnivore
of Uranus for Trombone
and Tape* [London], 621
HILL, Elecia, *313;* 279,350
HILL, John, *669;* 235,616,
640,641,676
HILLMAN, Christopher, *314;*
321
HILLS, Ernie Marvin, III, *5,
670*
HILLSMAN, Walter, *671*
HIMES, Addison Choate, Jr.,
672,862,1117,1118,1119;
665,715,871,912,1012,1016,
1096,1159,1244,1272,1301
Hindemith, Paul, 395,396,428,
431,447,489,508,538,546,
644,762,780
Hines, Earl, 292
HINTERBICHLER, Karl G.,
149,458,459,460,461,863;
17,28,231,263,285,338,360,
372,410,479,496,643,654,

872,906,1053
[*L'*]*histoire du soldat*
[Stravinsky],465,585,625,
762
History, 68
*"Ho giá vinta" from La
morte vinta sul Calvario
[Ziani], 616
Hoena, Gustav, 128,151
HOFACRE, Marta, *462,1120;*
263,372,449,523,649,696
Hoffman, 537
HOFFMAN, Klaus, *674;* 408,
712,738
HÖFLER, Janez, *865;* 825
HOGARTH, George, *866;*
923
HOGG, Simon, *150,463;* 514,
716,916
HOLBROOK, Jonathan, *464;*
767
Holding Position, 1049
Holland, Bernard, 506
"Hollywood Hop," 750
HOLMAN, Peter, *401;* 590,
640
Holst, Adolph, 463
Holst, Gustav, 463,514
Holton [instrument
manufacturer], 820
HOLTON, Frank, *1121,1261;*
49,89,90,243
Holton's Harmony Hints, 49
Home Pages: Trombone, 50
Höna, Gustav, 128,151,1074
HOOPER, Jonathan, *465;* 585
HOOVER, Cynthia A., *867;*
795,998
Hopkins, Pandora, 786

Horgan, Maureen, 239
Horn [French Horn], 883
HORN, Erwin, *466*
Hornian Museum, 936
Horowitz, Marc David, 5
Hot Chorus, 1048
Houdy, Pierick, 558
HOUGH, Robert, *675;* 141
Houseparty [J.Smith], 707
Houston [TX], 76,169
Houston, University of, 512
Howard, Joseph [Joe], 276,
    715
HOWEY, Henry E., *1122;*
    132,452,573,640,948
HÜBER, Heinrich, *676;*
    132,640,1122
HÜBLER, Klaus-K., *6,677;*
    497,607,737
Hudson, Frank, 530
HÜGER, Florian H., *315*
HUGHES, James E., *1123;*
    1013
HUGHES, William M., *467;*389
Hugon, Georges, 558
HUMFELD,Neill,151,152,153,
    *154,868,1124,1125,1126;*125,
    129,133,162,555,993,1027,
    1063,1082,1088,1189,1214,
    1253
HUMMEL,Donald Austin,468,
    *1127;*434,478,524,1080,
    1084,1146,1170,1191,1262,
    1268,1284
Hummel, Sue, 298
Humor, 40,42,43,44,54,62,64,
    68,74
Hungary, 927,1074
HUNSBERGER, Donald,

1128; 198,1282
HUNT, Paul, *155,469,470;*
    29,223,432,493,501,532,
    567,652
Huntzinger, James Kenneth,
    Jr., 378
HURST, Robert G., *1129;*
    1013
HURT, Charles, *1130;* 1033,
    1166,1263,1302
Huschauer, Joseph, 925
Hutcheson, Jere, 531
HUTSON, Danny J., *678;*
    496,766,774,1064
HUXLEY, Aldous, *48*
HYLANDER, Martha A.,
    471; 410,443,478

I

Iceland, 191
Iconography, 640,782,802,
    808,810,854,865,866,867,
    884,917,927,943
Illinois,University of,Urbana-
    Champaign, 230,396,472,492,
    498,550,601,942,964,1003,
    1060,1145,1244
Image in the Snow
    [B.Weber], 395
Imbrie, Andrew, 621,759
Imposed Learning Method,
    1187
Impromptu: [Bigot], 539,558;
    [J.E.Brown], 432,478,531,
    538; [Clergue], 539,558
Improvisation, 283,512,618,
    647,684,698,783,1007,
    1019,1048,1081,1260,1281

Improvisations Sonoristiques
[Szalonek], 395
Impulsions [Chaynes], 558
"In a Mellotone," 750
In Memoriam Dylan Thomas
[Stravinsky], 769
Indereal, 1006,1271
Indiana, 343
Indiana University, 83,176,
227,395,420,476,506,638,
646,667,708,938
Indiana [PA] University,
1055
Indices, 8
In-line Valves, 843,847,934,
951,989,990
Innes, Frederick Neil, 90,145,
187,193,218,243
Innes and his Band: In
combination with scenes
from grand opera . . . , 193
Inno per il festo de s.
Theresia [Tůma], 595
Instrument Choice, 1138
Instruments,8,611,620,631,
632,666,673,704,714,724,
742,770,782,797,810,811,
855,864,1188
Instruments-Ancient, 798,846,
857,945,976
Instruments-14th Century,
645,798,920,930,931,935
Instruments-15th Century,
645,663,718,798,802,845,
846,869,878,884,920,930,
931,933,943,954
Instruments-16th Century,
645,663,670,718,728,798,
845,846,865,869,884,924,

930,933,943,947,954,960,981
Instruments-Renaissance,167,
700,803,825,827,838,850,
878,908,909,915,920,931,
935,942,952,1251
Instruments-17th Century,132,
167,728,756,808,829,839,
852,860,869,881,884,895,
909,920,925,943,947,952,
953,955,963,965,983,987
Instruments-18th Century,452,
709,722,728,734,790,795,
805,829,852,860,884,909,
920,936,952,955,983,987
Instruments-19th Century,194,
452,709,734,747,804,828,
829,832,854,860,866,867,
870,888,898,899,923,936,
956,1192
Instruments-20th Century, 89,
180,231,262,382,619,647,
684,698,787,791,813,829,
835,856,860,877,889,901,
902,903,904,907,936,977,
978,986,1194,1203
[see also *6, Instruments and*
Equipment]
Interactive, 1003
Interlochen [MI], 160,870
Intermedii, 670
International, 53,1250
International Computer
Association, 402
International Trombone
Association, *see* ITA
International Trumpet Guild,
see ITG
Internet, 50,1012,1096,
1159,1272

Interviews, 8
Intonation,728,1005,1016,
1024,1044,1051,1079,1117,
1136,1141,1153,1162,1174,
1182,1184,1228,1243,
1266,1267
Introduction et Allegro
[Hugon], 558
Invention [Helmschrott], 395
Inventum [Ammann], 395,492
*"Io ti do" from *Abele*
[Reutter], 616
IOAKIMIDIS, D., *679*
Iowa, University of, 447,452,
543,567,583,644,649,652,
712,763,1122,1133
Ireland, 624
Irvis, Charles [Charlie Plug],
751
ISAACSON, Charles F., *472;*
6,536,588
Isele, Robert, 90,99,207
Israel, 890,893,1140
ITA[International Trombone
Association],1,8,40,50,51,
52,69,77,82,83,91,94,102,
151,162,170,174,176,185,
190,197,215,222,226,230,
235,236,242,246,249,267,
279,294,307,329,337,350,
378,397,437,441,477,479,
501,504,514,534,592,604,
748,818,904,1209
ITA Scholarship, 121
Italy, 75,134,502,544,590,655,
670,686,690,702,789,814
ITG [International Trumpet
Guild], 4, 1110
"It's Only a Paper Moon," 260

ITW [International Trombone
Workshop], 209,441,904
IVEY, Stephen [Ben], *156,
157,158,316;* 55,96,224,
249,562,720,751,1034,1107

J

Jackson, Preston, 751
Jackson, Quentin [Butter],
316,720,751,1107
Jacob, Gordon, 413,538,569
JACOBS, A., *1132*
Jacobs, Arnold, 228,1186,1211
JAECKLE, Frank, *1133*
JAEGER, Jurgen, *1134;* 1249,
1288
JAHN, Fritz, *869;* 878,922,
953,981,987
JAMES, Betty A., *317,318*
JAMESON,R.Philip,*159,160,
473,870,871,1135;*107,484,
490,505,509,543,556,561,
574,1025,1200
Janáček, Leoš, 762
Janks, Hal, 127,1219
Japan, 25
Jazz-Blues,2,8,23,24,25,27,28,
29,31,33,34,35,41,66,70,141,
181,190,208,216,217,
235,405,409,457,488,511,
512,596,597,600,604,634,
637,639,642,643,653,660,
675,679,688,689,692,697,
707,710,720,727,740,741,
748,749,750,751,773,781,
783,785,787,820,940,1007,
1010,1019,1045,1048,1069,
1081,1093,1107,1152,1181,

1193,1203,1210,1231,1260,
1278,1280,1281,1289,1298
Jazz-Rock, 727
Jeffers, Jack, 301
Jeffs, Stan, 121
JENKINS, Grant B., *474*
JENKINS, Randal Mark
   [*JENKINS*], 7
JENNE, B., *341;* 251
JENSEN, Niels Martin, *475*
Jericho [Palestine], 857
Jernigan, Melvyn, 80,1164
JESKE, Lee, *319;* 254,283,
   287,332
[The] Jiggs Up, 362
Jiggs Whigham—Hope, 748
*"Jimmy's Blues," 751
"Jingle Bells," 750
JOHANSEN, David P., *161*
Johns Hopkins University,
   656
Johnson, Doug, 121
Johnson, J.J. [James Louis or
   Jay],24,153,260,267,274,
   299,300,303,320,329,715,749
Johnston, Ben, 621,759
Johnstone, John G., *786*
JOLLY, Tucker, *1136;* 1044,
   1162
Jones, Charles, 863,872
Jones, Keith David, 561
JONES, LaMar, *1065,1066;*
   1175,1259
Jones, Robert W., 428,538
Jones, Lindley Armstrong
   [Spike], *see* Spike Jones
Jorepi [W.Presser], 395
Jørgensen, Axel, 136,137,220
Jörgensen, Thorkild Graae, 138

Josel, Rudolf, 128,219,689
Joseph I [Emperor],538,583,
   616
Joshua, 857
JOYCE RECORDS, 29
JUHNKE, Jerry, *872;* 863,906
Juilliard, 192,211,231,607
JUNGHEINRICH, Hans-
   Klaus, *873;* 796,892
[The] Justice Variations
   [Zonn], 395

K

Kafalas, John, 118
KAGARICE,Vernon[Vern],51,
   162,163,476,477,478,479,
   *1137,1138;*52,77,108,128,
   129,152,237,247,410,434,
   443,468,485,524,1037,1080,
   1127,1146,1170,1191,1219,
   1231,1262,1268,1276,1284
Kahila, Kauko, 244,248
Kail, Josef, 817
KALBACHER, Gene, *320;*
   24,267
Kammerkonzert [Berg], 762
*"Kansas City Style," 750
Kansas, University of, 135,
   390,394,826
KAPLAN, Alan, *480;* 127,
   364,492
KAPPEY, J.A., *874*
KARASICK, Simon, *875;*
   98,788,815,842,960,964
Karl-Marx-Universität, 861
KARSTÄDT, Georg, *876*
KASTNER, J.-G., *1139*
Katarzynski, Raymond, 157

Kauss, David R., 1076,1233
KAVANAUGH, Lee H.,
   1140; 1086,1231
Kayser, 1067
*Kebyar [Aitken], 395
KEELING, Bruce N., *481;*
   433
Keen, Paul, 301
KEENER, Michael, *1141;*
   1016
KEHLE, Robert, *30;* 26
KEHRBERG, Robert, *9,482,*
   483,484; 473
KELLY, Michael [Mike],
   1142; 1013
KEMP, Mildred, *1143;* 1030
KEMPTON, Jeremy, *1144;*
   1011
Kendall, John, 1018
Kendor, 289,594
Kenfield, LeRoy, 248
Kenny, John, 238
Kenton, Egon, 401
Kenton, Stan, 256,363
Kentucky, University of, 428,
   531
"Keren" [Xenakis], 491
Kerner, L., 181,268
KERSCHAGL, *680;* 233
Ketting, Knud, 94,118,195
Kexel, Ted, 49
Keystone Brass Institute, 1164
KIDD, Robert Lee, III, *1145;*
   1026,1112,1114
KIDWELL, James K., *485;*
   443,476
Kimball, Richard [Dick], 106
King [instrument manufacturer],
   877,907,919,948,970

King, Thomas, 90
KINGDON-WARD, Martha, *681*
King's Musicians, 101
King's Musick, 143
KINNEY, Guy, *1146;* 1080,
   1127,1137,1170,1191,1219,
   1262,1268,1284
KIRNBAUER, Martin, *878;*
   869,879,922,987
KITZEL, Larry, *879;* 882,953
Kitzman, John, 149,236,238
KIZER, George A., *880*
Klaber, Thomas, 85
Klay, Eric, 239
Klee, J.H., 319
KLEINHAMMER, Edward,
   1147,1148,1149; 124,151,
   228,246,1013,1218,1246,1293
Kleinschuster, Eric, 344
KLEMENT, Miloslav, *881;*
   983
Kling, Stanley, 862,1012,
   1096,1159,1272
KLUCAR, Ludomir, *682;*
   510,575,584
KNAUB, Donald, *1150;* 126,
   548,593
KNELLER, G.F., *1151*
KNEPPER, James [Jimmy],
   1152; 126,253,346,359,750,
   751
Knight, Robert [Bobby], 301
Kodály, Zoltán, 1013
KOENIG, Karl, *321,322;* 314
Koetsier, Jan, 462
Kofsky, Allen, 88
KOHLENBERG, Randy B.
   [*KOHLENBERG*],*10,11,12,*
   164,486,487,882; 82,84,

120,176,197,213,215,223,
227,396,566,879,953,1197,
1209
Kölner Hochschule für Musik,
374
KOMORZYNSKI, Egon, *683;*
387,450,757
KÖNIG, Wolfgang, *684;*
498,579,601,614
Korall, Burt, 330
Kordus, Thomas, 307
KORNDER, Wolfgang, *685*
KOSAKOFF, Gabriel, *1153;*
1016
Kosinska, J., 94,118,195
Kotonski, Wlodzimierz, 759
KOZMA, Tibor, *686;* 651,690
*Krabogapa [Dobrowolski],
395
KRAEMER, Ray L., *883*
KRAFT, James D., *687;* 99,
416,621,772
Kraft, Robert, 99
Kraft, William, 570
Krenek, Ernst, 531,538,621,
759
KRICKE, H., *1154*
KRIEGER, Franz, *688;* 315
Krivoklat Castle, 881
KRÖGER, E., *689*
Krol, Bernhard, 538
Kromeriz Castle, 392,564
Krottendorfer [Krotendorfer,
Joseph?], 537
Kruger, Michael, 1158
Kruspe, 975
Kublock, Horst, 124
KUHLO, D. Johannes, *1155;*
204,629,857

Kuhlo, Eduard, 629
Kühnl and Hoyer, 903
Kummer, Friedrich August,
495
KUNITZ, Hans, *690;* 686,
796,873
KUZMICH, John, *488;* 597
Kyma System, 402

L

La Vere, 348
La Zorra, 354
Laber, Robert [Bob], 309
Laczko, Norbet, 121
LAFOSSE, André, *1156;* 110,
136,1218
LAGONDA, Rostislav, *1157*
LAI, Chang-Yi, *489;* 428,
440,516,549,594,1104
LAJARTE, T.E.D.F.d., *691*
LAKE, S., *165*
Lamar University-Beaumont,
489
Lambach, 664
Lambert, Robert, 161
LAMMERS, Mark E., *1158*
Lampinen, Olavi, 189
LANE, George Bertram [G.B.],
13,52,490,872,884,1159;
51,77,375,862,863,869,878,
906,922,987,1012,1096,1272
LANGFORD, David, *885;*
792,841,851,950,1008,1023
Langlitz, David, 192
*"Languire, morire" from
*Morte, e sepoltura di
Christo* [Caldara], 616
LaNormandin, Phil, 102

LAPIE, Raymond, *166,553;*
539,558,767,856,1290
LAPLACE, Michel, *692,693;*
623
"Larghetto à Trombone
Concerto" from *Sinfonia
No. 4* [M.Haydn], 487,566,
583,609
"Larghetto" from *Alma
Redemptoris Mater* [Ziani],
504,583
Largo and Allegro [G.West],
476
Largo et Toccata [Houdy],
558
LARSEN, Arved, *1112;* 1026,
1114,1145
Larson, André, 879,882
Larsson, Lars-Erik, 478,538
Laslo, Kalmar, 566
LASOCKI, David
[*LASOCKI*], *14,167;* 143,663
Lassus, Roland de, 664
Lassus Trombone [Fillmore],
538
Latin, 208,604
LAUDENSLAGER, Samuel
H., 1160
Laudes [Bach, Jan], 462,696
Lavignac, Albert, 1056
LAW, Glen C., *1161;* 1047
Lawrence, Mark, 152
Leadpipes, 871,912
LEAMAN, Jerome, *694;* 32,
541,606
Lebedev, A., 413,478,538
LEBENS, James C., *491*
Leblanc, 787,886
Leclerc, Michel, 462

Lecture-Recital, 398,422,423,
495,504,510,549,569,584,
606,737,772,956,1189,1223
Leduc, Alphonse, 96
LEE, Amy, *323;* 29,66,587
LEES, Gene, *324;* 249
Leftovers [Peruti], 395
Legal, 172
Legato,715,1028,1030,1046,
1091,1094,1106,1143,1177,
1178,1203,1204,1207,1224,
1234,1248,1253,1257,1305
Légende [Tournemire], 539,
558
Leipzig [(East) Germany],
194,403,540
Leipzig, University of, 869
LEISENRING, John Robert,
492,887; 480,973
Lejet, E., 558
LELOIR, Edmond, *888*
LEMKE, Jeffrey, *493;* 152,
539,558,567
Leningrad [Soviet Union] [St.
Petersburg, Russia], 1073,
1287
LENO, Harold Lloyd, *1162;*
151,1044,1136,1288
LENTHE, Carl, *53,695;* 540,
748,1069,1298
Lepetit, P., 539,558
LESTER, Raymond David,
494
Letsch, Frederick, 145,613
LEVENSON, Jeff, *325;* 269
LEVERMANN, A., *889*
LEVI, R., *890;* 327
Levilian, Guy, 317
Levin, Floyd, 327

Levy, Jules, 187
LEWIS, Alwyn, *326*
Lewis, George, 235,328
LEWIS, Laurie, *326*
LEWIS, Maggie, *891*
LEWIS, Michael, *495;* 194,
    403,540,592,956
LEWIS, Samuel [Sam], *1163*
LEWY, Rudolf, *892,893;*
    796,873
Libin, Laurence, 917
*[Il] libro con sette sigilli
    [Draghi], 616
Lieb, Richard [Dick], 301
Liechtenstein-C[K]astelkorn,
    Prince-Bishop Karl, 392,
    529,564
Lieb, Richard [Dick], 301
Lillebach, Hans Waldemar
    Durek, 248
Lillya, Clifford, 135
Lincoln, Abraham [Abe], 751
LIND, Michael, *168;* 220
LINDAHL, Robert, *696,1164;*
    449,462,649,726
LINDBERG, Christian, *894;*
    94,118,129,153,195,238,
    239,397,788
Lindberg, Roger, 128
LINDELIEN, Doran Royce,
    1165
LINDSAY, Robert, *327,697;*
    261,263,280,292,1193
*Line Studies [Gaburo], 395
*Lines from Shelly (and the
    "Requiem-Te Deum")
    [Gay], 395
Linz [Austria], 466
Lip Vibration, 1162

LISEMBY, Greg, *1166;*
    1033,1130,1263,1302
Listening, 1131
LISTER, Richard, *895;* 842,
    860
Liston, Melba, 239,355
Liszt, Franz, 625
"Little Benny," 749
LITWEILER, John B., *328;*
    165
LOBITZ, Carl M., *496;* 459,
    678,766,774,1064
Lofton, "Tricky," 751
Lohse, Eduard, 744
London [England], 91,113,
    142,226,830
London, Edwin, 621
"Long Ago and Far Away,"
    373
Loper, Charles [Charlie], 334,
    715
Lortie, Serge, 124
Los Angeles [CA], 93,188,
    276,313,335,352,405
Los Angeles Times, 734
Loschelder, Josef, 686
Loucheur, R., 539,558
LOUCKY, David, *497;* 153,
    607,677,737
Louisiana, 295,322
Louisiana State University
    (LSU), 213,810,811
Love, love, "Pepo Mtoto,"
    278
"Lover," 348
Low Brass, 811,1115,1226,
    1227
Low Register, 1062,1071,
    1082,1087,1089,1098,1277

L.R.S.M., 1099
Lübbecke, 661
Lube, Albert, 169
LUCAS, Donald [Don], *169*
LÜCK, Rudolf, *698;* 498,
    579,601
LUMPKIN, Royce, *170;* 175
LUMSDEN, Alan, *896*
Lunceford, James [Jimmy],
    292
LUND, Erik R., *498;* 515,
    532,579,601
LUPER, Loren, *171;* 107
LUPICA, Benedict, *1167*
LUSHER, Donald [Don],
    1168,1169; 127,336,357,715
LYON, Ernest, *1170,1171,*
    1172; 1080,1262
Lyons [France], 924

M

MACCRACKEN, Thomas G.,
    897; 941
MACHADO, Robert L., *31*
MacIntyre, Bruce, 537,616
MACKENZIE, Kirk, *499*
Maddox, Harry, 159
Maddy, Joseph, 160
MADEROSIAN, Ardash, *699;*
    1206
MAGLIOCCO, Hugo, *172,*
    500,501,700; 128,476,
    640,725,1157
Magnolia Plantation, 322
MAGNUSON, Gregg, *1272;*
    1012,1096,1159
MAHILLON, Victor-Charles,
    898,899

Mahler, Gustav, 538,625,771
MAHRENHOLZ, C., *701;* 535
Mahu, Stephan, 241
Main, Roy, 334
Maintenance, 982,1015,1101,
    1165,1258
Mainz [Germany], University
    of, 590
MALONE, Thomas [Tom],
    1173; 1011,1093,1127,1173
MALTERER, Edward L., *702*
Mambo, 604
Mandernach, Charles [Chuck],
    152
Manfrin, Alain, 668
Mangelsdorff, Albert, 28,153,
    235,257,271,296,329,349,
    600,617,621,639,751,755,
    1022
MANGSEN, Sandra J., *502;*
    544
MANSON, David, *173,503;*
    59,568
Mantia, Simone, 243,1218
Manufacturers, 820,829,830,
    832,835,854,877,886,889,
    903,905,916,948,970
Manuel universel de la
    littérature musicale,
    [Pazdirek], 536
MANZORA, Boris G., *900*
Marcello, Benedetto, 395,479,
    538,702
MARCELLUS, John, *54,154,*
    163,174,175,176,177,178,
    *329,504;*55,82,108,129,164,
    227,235,239,242,247,537,
    583,609,656,658,669,722,
    729

[La] Marche Héroïque
[Saint-Saëns], 553
Marconi, Guglielmo, 49
Marger, Jacques, 182
Margun, 548,593
Marine [Pichaureau], 395
Marini, Biagio, 763,769
Mariotti, Antonio, 145
Markneukirchen [Germany],
855
Marks, Lawrence E., 1056
MARKS, Steven, *330;* 305
Marsalis, Delfeayo, 304
MARSTELLER, Loren, *505,
509;* 152,435,473
Marsteller, Robert, 93,116,
1127,1218
MARTELL, Paul, *901*
Martin, Carroll, 90,243
Martin, Edward, 1009
Martin, Frank, 538,558
Martin, James, 307
MARTZ, Brian, *1174;* 1016,
1153
Maryland, University of,
College Park, 467,564
Masking, 67,911
Mason, Elliot, 307
MASSINON, Eileen, *506;*
121,249,307
Masso, George, 235
MASSON, Gabriel, *704,902*
MATCHETT, Robert K.,
1175,1176; 1065,1259
MATER, Friedrich, *705;* 105
MATHEWS, Michael K.,
1177; 432,1030
MATHEZ, Jean-Pierre, *179,
180,181,182,183,184,903;*

115,245,268,986
MATHIE, David, *160,507,
508,904,1178;* 788,1030
MATTA, Thomas, *509;* 473,
561,574
Matten, Chris, 129
Matteson, Richard [Rich], 642
Matthews, Michael K., 432
MATZ, R., *905*
MAURER, Joseph A., *706;*
32,541,606
Mäusebach, A., 248
Maximilian I, 878
MAXTED, George, *1179*
MAYS, Richard [Rich], *906,
1180;* 863,872,1013,1027,
1083
Mazellier, Jules, 539,558
M-BASE, 312
MCCARTY, Frank L., *185;*
202,621
McCarty, Patrick, 413,538
MCCHESNEY, Robert, *1181*
MCCLELLAN, Lawrence, Jr.,
707
McConnell, Robert [Rob], 373
MCCREADY, Matthew, *708;*
793,1032,1059
McCroskey, John, 169
MCCULLOH, Byron, *55;*
100,124,224,235,1034
McDougall, Ian, 153,154,239
MCDUNN,Mark,*907,1182,1183;*
877,919,948,1016,1066,
1153,1184,1266,1269,1296
McEachern, Murray, 331,715
MCENIRY, J.D., *26;* 30
MCGOWAN, Keith, *908,909;*
640,825,852,946,947

MCGRANNAHAN, A.
Graydon, III, *510;* 584,682
McHenry, Darren, 121
McKay, George F., 428,538
MCKAY, Kelly Collier, *709;*
646,767
McKee, Paul, 307
MCKINNEY, Harold, *186,*
511; 88,741
McLemore, Michael D., 121
MCNAMARA, Helen, *331;*
715
McQuary, Richard [Dick],
301
MCRAE, Richard, *710;* 357
MCTERRY, Harry James,
1184; 1016
Means, L., 278,285
Medical, 5,45
"Medical corner," 5
Medici, 670
Medieval, 101,582,624,645,
662,663,717,725,768,809,
884,926,927,930,954
Meinl and Lauber, 895
MEINZERHAGEN, Fritz, *711*
Meissner, Kurt, 808
MELKA, Alois, *910;*
73,932
Melodious Etudes for
Trombone [Bordogni/
Rochut], 133,555
MELTON, John R., *1185;*
1063
MELVILLE, Bruce E., *512;*
249,783,1007,1019,1048,
1081,1260,1281
Mendelssohn, Felix, 442
Menke, Werner, 897

Mental Practice, 1076,1233
Merengue, 604
Meridian Arts Ensemble, 146
MERLINO, Diane, *56;* 407
Mersenne, Marin, 640,676
Mertens, Albert, 888
Meshoulam, Ido, 1140
Meshoulam, Tovy, 1140
Messerer, Clemens, 583
Metcalf, Owen Wells, 119
Methods, 471,542,1067,1071,
1082,1087,1129,1139,1215
Metropolitan Opera, 192,211
Mexico, 418,884
Meyer, Carl Heinrich, 495
MEYER, Eileen, *1186;* 86,
200,1211
MEYER, Jürgen, *911;* 822,
912
MGG (Die Musik in
Geschichte und Gegenwart),
536,544,876
*"Mia compagna io la creda"
from *La colpa originale*
[F.Conti], 616
Miami, University of, 591,
1116
Michael, Frank, 528
Michigan, University of, 572,
578,1047,1160
Mickey Goes to School
[N.Lockwood], 395
Middle East, 809
Middleton, Arthur, 126
MILAK, John J., *1187*
Milhaud, Darius, 409,538,762
Military, 71,163,207,232,242,
291,372,451,620,651,708,
918,1119

MILKOWSKI, William, *332*
Millar, Michael, 276,405
MILLAT, Andrew, *1164*
MILLER, D[onald?] G., *513;*
    662,724
Miller, Donald, 104
MILLER, Frederick Staten,
    712; 408,738
Miller, Glenn, 41,291,372
MILLER, Tracy, *912;* 871
Milliere, Gilles, 668
Milwaukee [WI], 106
Mingus, Charles [Charlie],
    359,720
Minick, Larry, 235
Minneapolis-St. Paul [MN],
    317
Minnesota, 38
Minnesota, University of,
    1054,1097,1158,1249
Minsk [Belarus], 1157
Miraculous Mandarin
    [Bartók], 619
Miserere [Tůma], 537
Miss Trombone [Fillmore],
    538
Missa, Edmond J., 539,558
Mississippi, 295
Missouri, University of,
    Kansas City, 468,525,780
Mr. Nostalgia, 29,323,587
[Il] mistico Giobbe [Ziani],
    616
MITCHELL, Arthur B., *1188*
Mitchell, Barbara, 650
Mitchell, Grover, 255
MITCHELL, John C., *514;*
    463
MITCHELL, Randall Thomas,

1189; 133,555,1014,1124,
    1253
Mitchell, Thomas [Tom], 301
Mitsouka, I., 531
Moak, John, 307
Modal, 1285
Modogenesis [Delp and
    Weiss], 395
Moeller, Jan, 121
Mølaard, Torolf, 750
MOLE, Miff, *1190;* 1000,
    1236
Monaco, Richard, 428,489,
    538,549
Moncelli, Christopher, 256
Moncur, Grachan, III, 288,
    329,356
Mönnich, Karl, 855
Montagu, Jeremy, 786
Monte Carlo [Monaco], 45
Monteverdi, Claudio, 387,722
MONTGOMERY, James, *713;*
    603
Moore, Arthur, 855
Moran, Robert, 621
Moravian, 32,541,547,606,610,
    650,654,659,694,706,714,
    732,734,735,744
Morceau de Concours:
    [Bachelet, Missa], 539,558
Morceau Symphonique:
    [Gaubert], 478,539,558;
    [Guilmant], 413,479,538,
    539,558
Morgan, A., 319
MORGAN, Marty, *333;* 249
MORGAN, Robert P., *515;*
    614
Morgan, Sam, 321

Morning Music [Sampson], 696

Morrow, [Muni] Buddy [Moe Zudecoff], 361

[La] morte vinta sul Calvario [Ziani], 616

Morton, Benny, 329,357,710, 750

Moscow [Soviet Union/ Russia], 139

Moscow Conservatory, 1113

Moss, Lawrence, 772

Mouthpiece Pressure, 1012, 1096

Mouthpieces, 199,862,975, 1012,1096,1136,1159,1162, 1203,1272

Mouvement [Defaÿ], 558

Mouvements [Arrieu], 558

Moyer, William, 248

Mozart, Leopold, 196,504, 538,656,729

Mozart, Wolfgang Amadeus, 387,450,552,580,583,683,757

MPSsence, 28

MUDGE, Suzanne, *188,334, 335,336;* 107,171,277,293, 352,379,1278

Mueller, Robert, 90

Mulcahy, Michael, 151

MULLEN, Robert, *516,517;* 489

MÜLLER, Adolf, *518,519;* 204

Müller, C.G., 403,495

Müller, J.I., 538

Müller, Robert, 90,403,495, 540

MÜLLER, S., *913*

Multiphonics, 257,271,349, 600,617,621,639,755,759, 760,775,1022,1289

Munich [Germany], 172,424

Murphy, Turk, 33,383

Museums, 786,810,832,861, 864,879,882,914,925,929, 936,983

Music Education, 18,1009, 1110,1187,1206,1297

Music for a Sliding Trombone [R. Du Bois], 759

"Music for bass trombone," 520

Music for Brass Instruments [Dahl], 462

Music for Brass Quintet [Schuller], 462,696

Music for Trombone and Piano [Childs], 759

"Music for Wilderness Lake," [Shafer], 499

Musical Courier, 187

Musical Terms, 771

Musicalisch-Türckischer Eulen-Spiegel, 132

Musicianship, 997,1014,1021, 1046,1065,1131,1132,1183, 1189,1244

MUSIL, Frank J., *521;* 433, 668,758,769

Musique [Lejet], 558

MUSSELWHITE, Wayne, *522;* 625

Musser, Williard I., 1300

Mutes, 165,720,751,757,792, 841,851,885,950,1008,1023, 1088,1107,1293

"My Favorite Things," 597

"My Romance," 362

MYERS, Arnold, *914;*
  815,842,952,960,964
MYERS, Herbert W., *915;*
  825
Myers, Richard, 104
MYERS, Richmond E., *714;*
  32,541,606,610
Myers-Brigg Type Indicator
  (MBTI), 73
*Mysterious Horse before the
  Gate*, op. 205 [Hovhaness],
  395

N

Nabich, Moritz, 403,495,540
"Naked as a Jaybird," 749
Nanton, Joseph [Tricky Sam],
  290,316,751
NASH, Harold, *716,916,1191;*
  1080,1127,1137,1146,1170,
  1219,1268,1284
NASH, Richard [Dick], *715;*
  331,334,357,665,672,1244,
  1301
National Consensus, 1273
National Music Camp, 160
Natural Trumpet, 952
NAYLOR, Thomas, *917;* 808
NBC (National Broadcasting
  Co.), 223
Nebraska, University of,
  Lincoln, 443
NELSON, F.H., *1044;* 1136,
  1162
Nelson, Louis, 368,384
NELSON, Mark A., *523;* 462
Nelson, Richard, 751
NEMETZ, A., *1192*

Neoclassicism, 423
NEPUS, Ira, *1193;* 261,327
NETHERCUTT, Ronald, *524;*
  434,468,478
NETTO, *918*
Neudert, Jürgen, 307
Neumann, [Anton?], 537
Neumann, Hans, 869
Neuschel, Jorg, 836,920
Nevada, University of, Las
  Vegas, 378
Nevada, University of,Reno, 758
*New Grove Dictionary of
  Music and Musicians*, 640
New Orleans [LA], 262,314,
  315,321,368,1118
New York, 70,84,98,164,176,
  214,216,223,227,253,270,
  353,506,613,761,1209
New York Brass Conference,
  217,353
New York Brass Quintet, 119
New York City Opera, 123
New York Cornet and Sacbut
  Ensemble, 891
New York University, 480,
  640,697
New Zealand, 962
Newlin, Dika, 498,579,601
Newman, William S., 1122
Nice [France], 839
NICHOLAS, Martha R., *717;*
  640,645,718,725,802
NICHOLSON, Joseph M., *525,
  526,527,718,920,921;*410,
  443,471,479,640,849,869,
  878,922,976,987
NICKEL, Ekkehart, *922;*
  869,987

Nicklas, Erik, 50,862,1012, 1096,1159,1272
Nicolas, Rodolphe, 241
NIEMISTO, Paul, *189*
"Night in Tunisia," 750
Nightingale, Mark, 238
Nine Preludes for Flute and Trombone, op. 257A [Hewitt], 395
No Title [Sikorski], 395
Noel, Richard [Dick], 715
Nøkleby, Astrid, 1140
NOLAN, Herbert, *337;* 281, 351
"Non é giunta" from Il Sacrifizio d'Isacco [Ziani], 616
Norrell, Steve, 154
North America, 95
North Carolina, University of, Greensboro, 10,486,487,733
North Texas, University of, 170, 398,415,422,423,458,510,522, 549,569,584,606,609,665,666, 672,741,783,787,1037,1129, 1189,1245,1282
Northern Colorado, University of, 425,482,977,1037,1100, 1227
Northwestern University, 474, 742,1013,1076,1233,1264
Norvo, Red, 309
Norway, 211,786,1140,1225
Notation, 6,497,531,607,677
NOVA, Craig, *57*
Novel, 57
Nuremberg [Germany], 869, 878,884,920,922,981,987
Nux, Paul V. de la, 539,558

O

"O beata l'alme" from La cena del Signore [Fux], 616
"O! salutaris Hostia" from Motetto del santissimo [Tůma], 595
"O spirti di dite" from Le lacrime di San Pietro [Sances], 616
Obbligatos, 616
Obituaries, 83,92,102,120,123, 142,162,176,178,189,197, 198,215,231,249,256,259, 275,280,283,290,298,302, 316,319,327,336,340,345, 347,357,370,378,382,383, 384,405,457,512,787,1209
OBREGON, Richard, *190*
Offertorium [Adlgasser], 537
"Offesi, il veggo" from Elia [Reutter], 616
"Oh Baby," 710
Ohio, 659
Ohio State University, 267, 844,1026
Oklahoma, University of, 21, 392,417,481,485,678,774, 879,1037,1114
Old Mill, 714,732
Olin, James, 177,1031
Oliver, King, 258
Oliveros, Pauline, 621
Oller, Johann Nikolaus, 895
Olmütz, 196
[The] Olmütz Concerto for Alto Trombone and Orchestra [E.Raum], 195

O'LOUGHLIN, Niall, *528;*
601
Olson, Curtis, 129,238
"On Green Dolphin Street,"
634
*One Man for Trombonist and
Percussion* [B.Johnston],
621,759
Ontario [Canada], 499
Open University [England],
663
Opera, 108,123,233,247,387,
450,658,680,683,686,690,
691,705,722,873,892
Ophicleide, 866,923
Options I [Schwartz], 531
O'Quinn, Keith, 1281
*"Or conosco" from *Dio dul
Sinai* [F.Conti], 616
*"Or Iusinghiero" from *La
morte vinta sul Calvario*
[Ziani], 616
Oral History, 258
Oral Roberts University, 1100
ORAM, P., *1195*
Oratorio, 603,713
*Orbits—A Spatial Ritual for
Eighty Trombones*, 56,407
Orchestra,2,8,43,58,71,76,78,
79,80,84,85,86,87,88,91,92,
95,97,99,100,104,106,108,
112,113,114,115,116,117,
119,122,130,131,142,147,
149,150,155,157,159,161,
163,164,168,169,172,175,
176,177,184,186,188,191,
197,200,207,210,213,214,
215,217,219,220,222,223,
224,225,226,227,228,229,
230,231,233,234,244,245,
246,247,248,388,418,421,
464,490,506,522,553,568,
591,603,608,612,613,618,
619,622,623,625,627,646,
658,667,681,693,699,705,
708,709,711,719,721,746,
754,757,761,767,771,784,
794,819,935,939,944,989,
1013,1031,1033,1034,1047,
1058,1118,1130,1166,1186,
1206,1209,1211,1250,1263,
1268,1287,1302,1303
Orchestra Showcase: Iceland
Symphony Orchestra, 191
Orchestral Excerpts, 17,429,
473,484,505,509,543,561,
574,1161,1166,1263,1302
Ordman, Ava, 238
Oregon, University of, 1165
Organ, 6,463,472,514,588
Orlick, Terry, 1076
Ornamentation, 702,756
Orosz, Josef, 248
Ory, Edward [Kid], 315,329,
688,751
Ory's Creole Trombone, 688
Osmun Brass, 619
Österreichischer Rundfunk, 344
OSTRANDER, Allen, *1196,
1197,1198;*124,126,164,197,
213,223,1013,1027,1219,1282
Öttl, M., 537
OTTO, Craig, *529;* 392,564
"Out the Window," 750
Overtones, 1005,1016,1051
*Overture for Trombone and
Strings*, op. 76, no. 1
[Hovhaness], 476

OWEN, Herbert, *1199*

P

P., I., *866,923*
Pace, Walter, 868
Padua [Italy], 134
Pain Control, 962
Palestine, 857
Palmieri, Eddie, 275
PAQUETTE, Daniel, *924*
Par Monts et Par Vaux
  [LeClerc], 462
Parable for Brass Quintet
  [Persichetti], 462
Parable for Solo Trombone
  [Persichetti], 523
PARADIS-HAGAR, Jennifer,
  720; 316,751,1008,1023,
  1107
*Parcours [Durand], 558
Paris [France], 166
Paris Conservatory, 110,493,
  539,558
Parker, Derrick, 552,580
PARKER, Olin, *1200;* 1025,
  1135
PARKS, Raymond, *925;* 839
PARNELL, Michael, *530;* 59
Parsons, Anthony, 72
Parsons, Burlon, 900
Pärt, Arno, 195
Partch, Harry, 720
Pascal, Claude, 539,558
Passaggio [Berio], 984
*Pastorale Hèroïque [Pascal],
  539,558
Pauly, Reinhard, 566
PAWLOWSKI, Józef, 926

PBS (Public Broadcasting
  System), 720
Peabody Institute [of Johns
  Hopkins University], 132,
  656
Pearce, William [Bill], 126
Pearson, Norman, 239
Peck, Benjamin, 127,891
Pedagogy,2,8,54,64,81,83,91,
  102,105,109,110,112,119,
  132,133,135,150,162,166,
  168,170,171,174,178,185,
  189,190,192,197,199,200,
  203,210,213,219,221,223,
  224,225,226,230,271,280,
  282,301,342,377,386,388,
  391,412,419,443,471,479,
  482,488,490,493,539,542,
  551,555,556,563,567,586,
  594,596,597,598,604,607,
  621,637,639,640,642,665,
  668,672,676,699,702,704,
  715,733,736,737,745,756,
  759,760,764,765,769,772,
  775,776,779,807,816,818,
  821,836,843,847,848,853,
  868,880,897,904,907,909,
  916,920,928,934,937,951,
  958,989[see also *7, Pedagogy*]
Pederson, Tommy, 125,405,
  751
PEDICARIS, Steve, *58*
Peebles, Byron, 129,188
PEEBLES, Will, *721;* 729,767
PEER, Rex, *1201*
PEIGHTEL, John W., *1202*
*Penetrations VI [Lanza], 395
"Pennies from Heaven," 750
Pennsylvania, 650

Pennsylvania State University,
1202
Percussion, 385,431,570
Performance Practices,8,24,47,
61,65,75,78,81,92,105,107,
109,119,135,148,167,171,
179,182,183,194,196,208,
250,255,257,258,259,260,
264,267,271,282,283,285,
288,290,329,361,366,365,
370,377,392,393,394,398,
399,409,415,418,421,444,
449,458,462,480,482,483,
496,513,526,547,552,556,
582,583,584,594,764,788,
793,794,807,818,819,821,
823,848,856,876,880,881,
884,894,897,901,904,909,
913,918,920,921,923,926,
931,935,939,940,941,942,
943,944,945,957,960,966,
967,968,969,985,997,999,
1003,1006,1014,1020,1023,
1032,1038,1039,1042,1058,
1059,1069,1075,1086,1088,
1094,1095,1108,1122,1147,
1149,1152,1163,1169,1171,
1172,1179,1180,1183,1188,
1194,1195,1216,1221,1240,
1247,1260,1267,1271,1273,
1274,1278,1283,1292,1294,
1300,1301
[see also *5, Performance
Practices*]
Perger, Lothar Herbert, 566
Pergolesi, Giovanni Battista,
538
Periodical, 39,46,60,72
Periodicals, 13,18

Persichetti, Vincent, 462,
523,538
Persymfans, 212
PETHEL, Stanley, *531;* 420,
551,759
PETNEKI, Aron, *927*
Petite Suite [Baudo], 538,
539,558
Petrie, Phil W., 355
Petrograd [St. Petersburg],
1073,1287
Pezel, Johann, 513
Pfeiffer, G.-J., 539,558
Phelps, Roger P., 198,203,221
Philadelphia [PA], 97,161,
210,229,613
Philharmonia, 142
PHILLIPS, Harvey, *1203;*
215,282,1209,1289
PHILLIPS, Jeff, *532*
PHILLIPS, June, *1204;* 1030
PHILLIPS, Kenneth H., *1205;*
1017,1061,1109
Philosophy, 1020
Phoebus Variations, op. 87
[Büsser], 539,558
Photography, 1162
Physics, 938
Pickering, Roy, 121
Pièce Concertante:
[Rousseau], 478,538,539,
558; [Salzédo], 538,539,
558
Pièce de Concert [Lepetit],
558
*Piece for Bass Trombone
and Clarinet* [Trump], 432
*Piece for Clarinet and Bass
Trombone* [N.Owens], 432

Piece for Trombonist and Percussionist [Bachelder], 395,432

Piece for Violin, Cello, and Bass Trombone [Nisula], 432

Pièce in mi-flat mineur [mi bèmol]: [Barat], 478,539, 558; [Büsser, op. 55], 539, 558; [Ropartz], 538,539,558

[Le] Piège de la Méduse [Satie], 762

PIERCE, Terry, *533,722;* 464,658,709,729,743,767

PIEREN, J., *723*

PIERING, Robert, *928*

Piersig, Fritz, 898

[Una] pietá silenta [Anon.], 616

PIETRACHOWICZ, Juliusz, *534,1206*; 222,699

Pinard, Al, 90

Pioneers in Brass [Bridges], 90

Pitch, 728,852,853,909,920, 947,955

Pitch Discrimination, 1025, 1135

Pitch Master, 1025

Pitch Perception, 1200

Pittsburgh [PA], 100,224,1034

Plain-Chant, 671

Plain-Chant et Allegretto [Désenclos], 558

Plank, Steven E., 795,860,865

PLASS, Ludwig, *724;* 513, 662

PLENCKERS, Leo J., *929*

Plsek, Thomas [Tom], 153

Plunger, 260,316,720,751,1107

Poetry, 44,55,59,63,383,771

Poland, 222,423,534,618,699, 1206

Polic, Edward F., 291

Polichromia [Krauze], 395

POLK, Keith, *725,930,931;* 645,717,802,825

Poole, Donald, 102

POOLOS, James G., *1207;*1030

Popp, Harold, 530

Popular Music, 692

Porta, Ercole, 655

Posaune, 857

"[Die] Posaune und einer Ihrer Pioniere," 104

Posaunenchor, 204,518,519, 535,629,701,739,744,768, 1155

"Posaunenmusik," 535,701

POSTEN, Robert, *726;* 449, 462,649,696

Posture, 1286

Potpourri mit obligatur Baßposaune, [Meyer] 495

POTTER, Barrett, *338;* 360

Pour Quatre [Kotonski], 759

POWELL, Richard E., *1208*

Pr, Ferdinand du, 771

Practice Materials, 1070, 1239,1242

Practice Techniques, 997, 1076,1168,1291

Praeludium, Chorale, Variations, Fugue [J.I.Müller], 432,479

Praetorius, Michael, 640,676, 947

Prague [Czechoslovakia/Czech Republic], 817,881
Prague International Competition, 747
PRATT, R.L., *932;* 806,822, 833,844,932,939,978,986
Pre-Bop, 750
Precision, 1021,1065
Pre-College, 1068
Prelude and Allegro [Bozza], 413
Prelude, Chorale, Variations, and Fugue [J.Müller], 538
Prelude, Fugue, and Big Apple [W.Ross], 432,531, 538
Premru, Raymond, 124,142, 152,226,301,538,1058
Pre-School, 1140
Preservation Hall, 314,384
Presser, Theodore, 413
Pressler, Bernard, 125
Price, Harry, 338
Price, Larry, 868
Priester, Julian, 278,285
PRIMACK, Bret, *339;* 288, 356
PRINCE, Howard, *192*
PRIOR, Roger, *167;* 143,663
PRISMA, 239,530
Prix de Rome, 156
Proctor, Jerome, 90,243
Program Study, 1202
Prussing, Ron, 128
Pryor, Arthur, 90,107,109,135, 171,243,476,479,538,556,870
PRYOR, Stephen, *727*
Psychoacoustics, 910
Psychology, 73,910,1025,1056

Pteradactyls [Mitsuoka], 531
Public Broadcasting System (PBS), 720
Public School, 443,1041, 1064,1071,1087,1110,1142, 1188,1251,1299
Publishing, 114
Puccini, Giacomo, 690
Puebla [Mexico], 884
Pugh, James [Jim], 29,66,151, 154,323,587
PULIS, Gordon, *1209;* 126, 164,215
Pulitzer Prize, 156,506
PULVER, Geoffrey [Jeffrey], *933;* 663,794,935
PURCELL, Randy, *1210*

Q

Quadro Trombone, 900
"Qual del Libano" from *Le profezie evangeliche di Isaia* [Caldara], 616
"Quando amato non si pente" from *Il Ré del dolore* [Caldara], 616
"Quanto t'offesi" from *Bersabea, ovvero il pentimento di David* [Reutter], 616
Quarter Tones, 1243
Quartet [Diemente], 395
Quartposaune, 1192
Quatre [Grahn], 395
[Le] Quatuor de Trombones de Paris, 521,668,769
Queen Anna, 241

Queisser, Carl Traugott, 145,
148,194,403,495,540,592
*"Quell'amor" from *Santa
Ferma* [Caldara], 616
*"Quel sembiante" from *Il
mistico Giobbe* [Ziani], 616
QUICK, Jeffrey, *728;* 132,
640,955,1122
Quintet: [Arnold, op. 73],
462; [Blickhan], 395; [Gay],
395; [Goeb], 395; [Gregson],
462
Quintet for Brass Instruments
[Etler], 462,696
Quist, Emily, 298

R

Raasch, Horst, 540,695
Rabe, Folke, 521,621,758,
759,769
Rachmaninoff, Sergei, 538
RACKETT, A.H., *193;* 187
Radio, 599,673
Raga I [Cervetti], 395
Raichman, Jacob, 248
RAINER, Robert [Bob],
1211; 86,200,1186
RAMIN, Fritz, *1212*
Randall, Charles, 90
Random 7 [Brandon], 395
Range, 1044,1066,1136,
1162,1190,1236
Rank, William [Bill], 340
RAPH, Alan, *934,1213,1214,
1289;* 152,282,301,593,836,
843,993,1013,1027,1029,
1256,1301
RASMUSSEN,Mary,*194,447,*

*448,536,1215;*105,135,145,
148,204,230,243,403,426,
466,472,474,479,495,518,
536,540,560,590,592,599,
602,620,662,666,680,691,
701,703,705,711,719,739,
742,767,770,798,801,814,
816,818,823,840,857,858,
866,874,899,901,913,918,
923,928,933,945,956,966,
967,968,971,984,992,993,
1002,1026,1032,1038,1039,
1040,1060,1067,1090,1132,
1139,1151,1155,1160,1163,
1188,1192,1194,1212,1216,
1236,1237,1238,1244,1245,
1252
Raum, Elizabeth, 195
RAUM, J. Richard, *195,196,
537,729,730,731;* 94,504,
554,616,753,767
Rauscher, Daral, 149
Ravel, Maurice, 92,623,693,
984
RAYMOND, William F., *1216*
REAVER, Doc, *340*
Rebecca [P.Patterson], 395
RECORDIER, Alain, *935;*
794
Recording, 485
*Red Norvo and His Orchestra—
Live at the Blue Gardens*, 310
Reed, Richard [Dick], 155
Reese, Gustav, 850
Reeser, Eduard, 771
Rehak, Frank, 151,298,621
Rehak, Sandy, 298
Reiche, Eugen [*Concerto No.
2 in A Major*], 87,476

REICHEL, William Cornelius, *732;* 32,541,606

Reichenbach, William [Bill], 129,642

REIFSNYDER, Robert, *538, 539,540,1217,1218,1219, 1220;* 59,81,194,403,410, 443,475,479,493,495,558, 592,695,1080,1127,1137, 1146,1170,1191,1246, 1268,1276,1284

Reinhardt, Donald, 1036

Religious, 78,739

Remington, Emory, 154,198, 203,221,593,1125,1128,1282

Renaissance, 75,401,582,624, 662,670,717,811,869,884, 947

Renner, Richard, 27

Repair, 982

Repass, Morris, 334

Repetitive Strain Injuries (RSI), 962

Reproductions, 813

Requiem: [Berlioz], 625; [W.A.Mozart, K. 626], 552, 553; [Reutter], 583

Requiem in d minor [Cherubini], 752

Res/As/Ex/Ins-pirer [Globokar], 601

Research,1,4,9,11,12,15,16, 18,19,20,230,393,394,414, 441,443,464,486,487,560, 591,697,758,810,811,819, 938,1055,1100,1133,1200, 1243

Resnikoff, Robert, 164

Reutter, Georg, 537,583

Reviews (by entry number):
55 [*The Brass Larnyx*-McCulloh]
135 ["Arthur Pryor . . ."-Frizane]
167 [*The Bassanos . . .*-Lasocki and Prior]
290 [*Duke's 'Bones*-Dietrich]
294 [1974 ITA Workshop-Jazz]
318 [*The Night People: . . . Dicky Wells*-Wells and Dance, and . . . *The Trombone of Dicky Wells 1927-1942* . . . -Evensmo]
395 [*Trombone Chamber Music*-Arling]
429 [trombone literature]
432 [*Annotated Guide to Bass Trombone Literature*-Everett]
435 [*Concerto for Trombone and Band*-Bellis]
470 [Paul Hunt]
476 [*Annotated Guide to Trombone Solos with Band and Orchestra*-Kagarice]
479 [*Solos for the Student Trombonist*-Kagarice, et al.]
493 [*French Music for Low Brass Instruments*-Thompson/Lemke]
498 ["The 'Discours' of Vinko Globokar . . ."-Lund]

503 [*Concerto for Trombone and Orchestra-*(Taafe) Zwilich]

506 (Joseph Alessi performances of Rouse with NY Philharmonic)

515 [recording by Globokar]

528 [works by Chávez, Desporte, Hovland, Michael, Schiaffini, and Suderberg]

530 [*Concerto-*Walker]

567 [*French Music for Low Brass Instruments-*Thompson and Lemke]

576 [*Rondo for Eight Trombones-*Chase]

579 [*Suite for Unaccompanied Trombone-*Bassett and "New techniques required to perform recent music . . .,"-M.Stevens]

583 [*The Soloistic Use of the Trombone in Eighteenth-Century Vienna-*Wigness]

590 ["Selbständige Instrumentalwerk mit Posaune in Oberitalien von 1590 bis ca. 1650 . . ."-K.Winkler]

652 [*The Trombone . . .-*Guion]

689 [*Die Posaune im Jazz-*Kröger]

786 [*Med piber og basuner, skalmeye og fiol-*With

pipes and trombones, shawm and viol-B.Aksdal]

837 [*Trompeten, Posaunen . . .-*Heyde]

838 [*The Renaissance Trombone . . .-*Fischer]

849 [*The Trombone . . .-*Gregory]

896 ["The sound of the trombone . . ."-Lumsden]

917 [*The Trumpet and Trombone in Graphic Arts-*Naylor]

925 [*Technical Drawings from the Edinburgh University . . .-*Parks]

954 [*Cornett and Sackbut-*Gretton, ed.]

1003 ["The development and trial of computer-based interactive videodisc courseware . . ."-Atwater]

1018 ["Adaptation of the Suzuki-Kendall method . . ."-Blaine]

1084 [*The Trombonist's Handbook . . .-*Fink]

1167 [*The Magnificent Bone-*Lupica]

1275 [*Practical Hints on Playing the Trombone-*Tanner]

Rex, Franz [W?], 403,495,540

Reynolds [instrument manufacturer], 948

REYNOLDS, George E., *1221*

REYNOLDS, Harold [Hal],
197,733; 164,213,223,1197
REYNOLDS,Jeffrey,*541,734,
735;*32,124,188,235,238,239,
606,610,650,654,659,694,
706,732,1013
REYNOLDS, Mary E., *198;*
203,221
Reynolds, Roger, 497,607,677
REYNOLDS, Samuel [Sam],
736,1222
Reynolds, Verne, 462
Rhapsodie [Rueff], 558
Rhein, John von, 503
Rhythm, 1093
Ricercare [Bitsch], 558
Ricercare á 5 [Erickson],
432,621
RICHARDSON, William W.
[Bill], *542,737,1223;* 410,
443,479
Richmond, Lynne, 102
RIDDLE, Peter H., *1224;*
1030
"Ride of the Valkyries,"
1013
RIDLEY, E.A.K., *936*
RILEY, Dan, *59;* 173
Rimsky-Korsakov, Nicolai,
413,538,559,625
Rippert, H.J., 181,268,269
RISHAUG, Harry, *1225*
Ritual, 611
Roberts, George, 82,125,235,
279,301,313,350,593,997
ROBERTS, James Ernest
[*ROBERTS*], *15,543,544,
545;* 121,173,473,838
ROBERTSON, James D.,

1226,1227; 375,511,1270
Robinson, Jack, 121
Robinson, Janice, 126,751
Robinson, Nathan [Big Jim],
314,321
Robinson, William [Billy], 56,
407
Rochester, University of, *see*
Eastman School of Music,
471,513,648
Rochut, Johannes, 133,136,
248,555,1014,1124,1189,1253
Rock-Popular, 146
ROCKWELL, A.A., *1228;*
1184,1266
Rodenbostel, George
[Henry?], 795
Rodgers, Ike, 751
RODIN, Jared, *937*
Rodrigues, D.A., 283
Rogers, Barry, 275
Rogers, Douglas, 128
ROHNER, Traugott, *199,
1229,1230,1231;* 140,
1013,1027,1036,1086,1140
Roll [Rolle, Johann
Heinrich?], 537
Roman Empire, 976
Romance: [von Weber], 455;
*[von Weber/Hudson], 530
*Romance for Trombone and
Piano*, [Jørgensen], 137
Romersa, Henry [Hank], 125
Rondo for Eight Trombones
[Chase], 576
*Rondo for Trombone and
Strings* [W. Presser], 476
Roos, Ingemar, 127,238,239
Ropartz, J. Guy, 538

Robert Rosenbaum Collection,
  953
ROSENBERG, Marvin, *1232;*
  1011
Rosin, Armin, 128,179
Rosolino,Frank,31,50,249,
  307,324,329,333,345,363,
  457,512,642,715,783,1007,
  1019,1048,1081,1260,1281
ROSS, Denwood F., *938*
ROSS, Richard R., *738;* 408,
  674,712
ROSS, Stewart L., *200,*
  1233,1234; 86,1030,1076,
  1186,1211
Ross, Walter, 531,538,759
Rossini, Gioacchino, 686,747
Rossini, Giuseppe, 686
Rotax Valve, 905
Rouse, Christopher, 506
Rousseau, Samuel, 538,539,
  558
Roussel, Albert, 625
Roy, Klaus George, 428
ROZNOY, Richard T., *16,*
  546,1235; 127,474,525,594,
  1104,1156,1216
RUBINSTEIN, L., *201;* 205
Rudd, Roswell, 288,339,356
Rueff, Jeanine, 558
RUH, *739*
RUNYAN, William E., *939;*
  844,788
RUSCH, Robert [Bob], *341,*
  940; 251
RUSSELL, Joseph, *1236,*
  1237; 1000,1190
Russia, 139,212,240,417,
  635,764,900,1284,1285,

1286,1287
Rutan, Harold D., 801
Rutherford, Paul, 129,165
RYAN, H.J., *940*
Rycroft, David, 952
RYON, James P., *547*

S

*Sa Majestè le Trombone
  [Duclos], 558
SACHS, Curt, *941;* 797,898
Sackbut,75,101,143,663,700,
  717,725,794,797,803,813,
  824,838,845,846,859,891,
  895,896,908,909,920,924,
  933,935,945,954,963,965,
  1251
Sacrae Symphoniae (1597)
  [G.Gabrieli], 401
*Sacratissima from *Lytanie*
  [Eberlin], 537
Sacred,404,406,408,453,466,
  535,536,552,580,584,606,
  611,616,624,629,630,631,
  632,650,654,655,659,661,
  663,664,671,674,682,683,
  685,694,701,706,712,714,
  723,732,734,738,744,777
*[Il] Sacrifizio d'Isacco
  [Ziani], 616
SAFOWITZ, Vivian, *942;*
  825
Saftleven, Cornelius, 808
Sagara, Ryuichi, 1197
SAGER, D., *740*
Sagvik, S., 94,195
Saint Louis [MO], 80, 761,
  1130

Saint Mark's [Venice, Italy], 590
Saint Paul [MN], 397
Saint Petersburg [Russia], 635,1073,1287
Saint-Saëns, Camille, 538, 539,553,558,625,767
Sakakibara, Sakae, 124
Salaries, 1303
SALMEN, Walter, *943*
Salome [R.Strauss], 387
Salsa, 208,604
Salve from *Offertorium*, [Zechner], 536
Salve Regina: [Oettl], 537; [Reutter/Reitter?], 537
Salzburg [Austria], 196,456, 537,656,657,729,753
Salzédo, Carlos, 538,539,558
Šámal, Vaclav, 817
SAMBALL, Michael, *741;* 409,511
Sambuke, 846
Sampson, David, 696
SAMSON, Valerie, *202;* 185, 621
San Diego [CA], 103
San Francisco [CA], 56,383, 407
San Francisco Traditional Jazz Foundation, 33
Sanborn, Peter, 127
Sanders, Robert, 413
SANDIFER, Perry, *1238*
SANGER, Robert, *742*
Sares, 199
Satie, Eric, 762
Satterwhite, Dan, 121
Saturday Night Live, 270

SAUER,Ralph,*203,944,1239, 1240;*55,188,198,221,224, 235,239,788,1034,1044, 1058,1136,1162,1164
SAWHILL, Kenneth, *958*
Sax, Adolphe, 888
Saxhorn, 567
Saxony, 204
Saxtrombone, 888
Scandinavia, 786
Scerbinin, V.A., 139
SCHAEFER, Jay Dee, *743;* 464,504,658,709,729,767
Schafer, R. Murray, 499
Schallstück [Das], 60
Scharfenberg, Donald, 917
Scheidt, Samuel, 955
Schiaffini, Gian-Carlo, 528
Schirmer Music, 1124
SCHLEMM, Horst Dietrich, *744*
SCHLESINGER, Kathleen, *945;* 794,846,933,935
Schmidt, [Johann Christoph?], 537
Schmidt, M., 145,148,194
Schmidt, Werner Christoph, 855
SCHNABEL, Wolfgang, *204;* 629
SCHNECKLOCK, Timothy, *342;* 343
Schneider, Bernard, 80
Schneider EL, 889
Schnitzer, Anton, the Elder, 839,869,925
Schnitzer, Erasmus, 981
SCHOALES, Herbert, *1241;* 1017,1061,1109,1205
Schönberg, Arnold, 591

SCHOOLEY, John, *1242*
SCHREIBER, Earl, *61,62,
63,1243;* 55
Schreiber, Hans, 860
SCHROCK, Bradley Alan, *745*
SCHRODT, James W., *1244;*
665,672,715,1301
Schubert, Franz, 646
*[Die] Schuldigkeit des ersten
Gebots* [W.A. Mozart], 583
SCHULLER, Gunther, *343,
548;* 128,342,462,593,696
SCHULTE-HUERMANN,
Franz, *429*
Schultz, Helmut, 513,662
Schultz, Russ, 593
SCHULZ, Klaus, *344*
Schumacher, Stanley E., 550
Schütz, Henrich, 408,415,538,
674,712,738
*Schwann Long Playing
Record Catalogue,* 536
Schwartz, Elliot, 531
SCHWARTZ, H.W., *946;* 908
Science, 1103
Scott, Joseph, 131
SDTQ [Fulkerson], 432
*"Se dei pur senz'aita" from
La passione nell'orto*
[Ziani], 616
SEALE, Tommy Fred, *1245*
Section Playing, 1065,1175,
1176,1259
Second International
Colloquium, 1042
Sedrakjan, A., 1285
SEGERMAN, Ephraim, *947;*
640,852,909,955
SEHMANN, Karin H., *1205;*

1017,1061,1109,1241
SEIDEL, John A., *549,1246;*
1021
Seiter, Christopher, 307
Selfish Giant Suite [Knight],
395
Selmer [manufacturer], 1041,
1071
Semler-Collery, J., 558
SENFF, Thomas Earl, *550;*
375,438,579
Sequenza V [Berio], 400,479,
515,531,538,579,621,751,
759,772
Serenade No. 6 [Persichetti],
395,538
Serial, 516,517
Serocki, Kazimierz, 413,423,
538
Serpent, 866,923
"76 Trombones," [Willson/
Taylor], 530
"Shadow Waltz," 354
SHAKESPEARE, Margaret,
205; 200
"Shanghai Shuffle," 710
SHARPE, Margaret, *206*
SHAW, Gary, *551,1247;*
194,403,420,495,531,
540,579,592
SHAWGER, J.D., *746;* 418,
667,761,1096
Shear Force, 1096
SHEPHERD, William, *1248;*
1030
SHERBURNE, Earl L., *1249;*
1134,1288
Sheridan, Chris, 318
Sherman, Charles, 566

SHIFRIN, Ken, *207,747,1250;*
99,114
Shiner, Matty, 126,237
Shires, Steve, 619
SHOEMAKER, John R., *1251*
Short Arms, 877,907,919,
948,1199
Short Suite [Schwadron], 395
Shorter, Wayne, 634
Shostakovich, Dmitri, 538,591
Shrine to Music Museum,
879,882,953
Shroyer, Kenneth [Kenny],
301
SHUKMAN, Henry, *208;* 604
Shuman, Davis, 231,559,948
*"Si spezza il suolo," from *Il
libro con sette sigilli*
[Draghi], 616
Sigismundus [Eberlin], 537,
753
SILBER, John J., *1252*
Silesia, 805
Simons, Gardell, 90,243
Simpson, Carl, 530
Sinfonia [Pergolesi], 538
Sinfonia Sacra, op. 56, "Jesu
meine Freude," [Krol], 538
Sinatra, Frank, 997
Sirman, Mitchell Neil, 132,
452,573,1122
Six Bassoon Sonatas
[Galliard], 702
Six Sonatas (for violoncello
and continuo)[Geminiani], 638
*Six Studies in English
Folksong* [Vaughan
Williams], 538
Six Suites for Solo Violoncello

[J.S.Bach], 422,479,594
Six Violoncello Sonatas
[Marcello and Vivaldi], 702
Skrzynski, Joseph, 85
Slater, Muriel, 351
Slatkin, Leonard, 506
Slide,620,640,642,676,776,
809,836,843,847,874,883,
900,907,919,928,934,946,
948,951,989,992,1049,
1053,1077,1080,1093,1125,
1127,1137,1146,1158,1170,
1182,1184,1191,1213,1218,
1219,1228,1256,1260,1262,
1264,1266,1267,1268,1269,
1272,1276,1284,1296
Slide Extension, 1199
Slide Flute, 984
Slide Position Equivalence
Tables, 974
Slide Repair, 887,973
Slide Trumpet, 725,795,804,
825,827,828,850,867,908,
915,931,942,952,979,998
"Slidework in A-flat," 750
SLOAN,Gerald[Gerry],*34,345,
346,347,348,748,749,750,
751;*24,27,129,249,250,252,
253,267,311,316,359,720,
1107,1152
Slokar, Branimir, 126,180,
424,456,903,986
SLUCHIN,Benny,*209,552,553,
752,753,754,755,949,950,
1253,1254;*133,152,154,539,
555,558,580,617,621,639,
767,788,792,841,851,856,
885,1014,1022,1068,1124,
1189,1290

Slur, 1204

SMALL, Charles, *64,65;* 353,538

SMAR, Benedict J., Jr., *554;* 504

Smita, Václav, 747

SMITH, André, *210,211,212;* 139,140,199,229,232,240, 1036,1119

Smith, Clay, 90

SMITH, David B., *756;* 640

Smith, Gene, 152

SMITH, Glenn P., *555,556, 557,558,559;* 107,133,135, 152,237,410,443,493,539, 1014,1124,1189,1253

Smith, H. Dennis, 127,469, 640

SMITH, Henry Charles, *17;* 238

SMITH, James, *1255;* 1011, 1296

Smith, James [Jimmy], 707

Smith, Kilton Vinal, 248

Smith, Leonard, 135

Smith, Lindsey, 129

Smith, R.A., 932

SMITH, Robert D., *1256, 1257;* 836,843,1030,1197, 1218

SMITH, Ronald G., *213;* 164, 197,223

SMITH, William [Bill], *349;* 257,271,600,621

Smith College, 545

SMITHERS, Don L., *757;* 387,392,450,529,564,683, 795,825,897

Smithsonian Institution, 318,867

SMITHWICK, Shelley, *758;* 433

Snedeker, Jeffrey, 1290

SNYDER, Frederick ["Moe"], *66,1258,1259;* 29,192,323, 587,982,1015,1065,1101, 1175

*"Soapstick Blues," 751

Soderini, Agostino, 655

Solo [Stockhausen], 515

Solo de Concert (Concertpiece) [Dubois,T.], 539,558

Solo de Concert, No. 2 [Vidal], 476,539,558

Solo de Concours: [Crocé-Spinelli, Mazellier, de la Nux] 539,558

Solo de Trombone [Pfeiffer], 476,539,558

Solo for Sliding Trombone [Cage], 531,579,621,759

Solos,26,30,36,37,59,81,89, 94,115,118,144,148,158, 173,179,187,195,196,207, 231,242,243,386,389,396, 399,400,409,410,411,412, 413,417,420,422,423,425, 426,430,436,438,440,441, 443,445,458,467,469,471, 476,479,482,483,485,487, 489,491,493,498,500,504, 508,514,515,516,517,523, 526,527,528,531,533,538, 539,542,546,548,549,550, 551,556,558,562,563,567, 569,572,575,578,583,593, 594,598,601,606,607,621,

647,653,656,657,684,687,
695,698,702,722,729,737,
741,759,1105,1123,1215
Solti, Sir George, 503
*"Someone to Watch Over
Me," 715
Sonaré, 499
Sonata, 59,158,173,428,440,
489,508,516,538,546,548,593
*Sonata à 3: no. 1 in d minor
[Bertali],   395,538,583,616;
no. 2 in d minor, 395; no. 3
in a minor, 395
*Sonata à 3 [Biber], 395,538
*Sonata à 3 [Schmelzer], 395
*Sonata à Quattro [Fux], 583
*Sonata à 4 [Weckmann/
Lumsden], 395
*Sonata and Gigue [Speer/
G.Smith], 395
*Sonata Breve [Hartley], 432,
479,538
Sonata Concertante [Hartley],
479,489,538
*Sonata da Camera [Hartley],
395,432
*Sonata della la Vecchia
[Cazzati/D.Stuart], 395
Sonata for Alto Horn
[Hindemith], 508
Sonata for Bass Trombone
and Piano [Wilder], 432,
479,538,548,593
*Sonata for Bass Trombone
and Strings [P.McCarty],
395,413,432,476,538
*Sonata for Four Trombone
and Basso Continuo
[Speer], 769

Sonata for Trombone and
Basso Continuo [Anon./
Wagner,I.], 575
*Sonata for Trombone and
Percussion [Cahn], 395
Sonata for Trombone and
Piano:[Bassett],479,489,538;
[N.Brown],479,489;*[Childs],
432,479,538;*[Davison],413,
428,479,538;*[Giffels],413;
[Hindemith],413,428,479,489,
538;*[McKay],413,428,479,
538;*[Monaco],428,479,538;
[Roy],428;[H.Stevens],413,
428,538;[D.White],479,489,
516,538
*Sonata in a minor:
[Marcello], 395,413,479,
538; [Vivaldi], 538
*Sonata in d minor [Corelli],
395,479
*Sonata in E-flat [Sanders],
413,479
*Sonata in e minor [Tůma], 583
*Sonata in F major
[Marcello], 413,479
*Sonata in f minor
[Telemann], 413,479,538
Sonata No. 1:[J.S.Bach],
479,489; [Galliard], 413,479,
538; [Monaco], 428,489,549
*Sonata No. 5 [Galliard],
413,538
*Sonata No. 6 [Galliard], 413
Sonata No. 7 [Corelli], 489
Sonata No. 11 [J.F.Fasch], 489
Sonata (Vox Gabrieli):
[Šulek], 59,173,530,538;
*[Šulek/ Colegrove], 530

Sonatina: [Presser], 413,479;
[H.Stevens], 432,479,538;
[Watson], 428
*Sonatina for Trombone and
Orchestra* [Serocki], 413,
423,476,479,538
*Sonatina for Trombone and
Piano* [R.Jones], 413,428,
479,538
Sonatine: [Bozza], 462;
[Castérède], 409,413,479,538
Song and Dance [Lieb], 395
*Song for Trombone and
Percussion* [McKenzie], 395
Songs of a Wayfarer
[Mahler], 538
Soprano Trombone, 1053,1140
SORDILLO, Fortunato, *1260;*
783,1007,1032
Sorte, Bartolomeo, 134
[Un] souffle profound
[Desporte], 528
Soule, Matthew, 307
Sound Direction, 822,911
Sound Frames [Albert], 395,
531
[The] Sound of the Wasp
[P.Wilson], 531
Sousa, John Philip, 218
South Africa, 131,1099
South Carolina, University of,
1110
South Carolina Inter-State and
West Indian Exposition, 193
South Caroliniana Library, 193
South Dakota, 879,882,953
Southern, Eileen, 530
Southern Mississippi
University, 1090

"[La] sovrana eterna" from *Il
trionfo di Giuditta* [Posile],
616
Soviet Union [USSR], 764,
1073,1113,1247,1284,1285,
1286,1287
Spary, Claude, 90,243
Speer, Daniel, 132,452,573,
640,676,728,947,1122
SPELDA, Anton, *67;* 822,911
Spike Jones, 405,751
SPILKA,William [Bill],*35,68,
69,70,214,215,216,217,350,
351,352,353,951;*164,192,
279,281,313,316,334,337,
836,843,1209
Spillman, Robert, 413,538
Spisak, Michel, 539,558
STACY, Charles E., *1261;*
243,1121
Stadtpfeifer, 513,662,768
Stage Band, 1210
Stage Fright, 1271
Stamitz, Johann Anton
Wenzel, 721,767
Stanford University, 756
STANLEY, William, *560*
STEELE-PERKINS, Crispian,
952; 825,963
Steiman, Harold, 100
Steinbruckner, Andreas, 583,616
Steinbruckner, Ignaz, 583,616
Steiner, Ferenc, 1074
Steinmeyer, David, 153
Stevens, A., 319
Stevens, Halsey, 428,538,579
STEVENS,Milton,*561,759,
760,1262,1263;*99,153,235,
400,410,473,479,498,531,

579,601,617,621,639,677,
737,755,772,1022,1033,
1080,1116,1127,1130,1137,
1146,1166,1170,1191,1219,
1223,1268,1284,1302
Stevenson, Robert M., 884
STEWART, Gary M., *953;*
869,878,879,882,922,987
Stewart, George, 248
STEWART, [Merlin] Dee,
1264; 127,836,843
STEWART, Zan, *354;* 305
Stibilj, Milan, 759
STIBLER, Robert, *954*
STIMAN, Gene, *1265;* 1049,
1050
Stock, Jaxon, 294
Stockhausen, Karlheinz, 515,
614
Stockholm [Sweden], 195
STODDARD, Hope, *761;* 667
Stojowski, Sigismond, 530,
539,558
STOKES, W. Royal, *355*
Stone, Robert, 307
Stöneberg, Alfred, 473
Störl, Johann, 513,724
STOUTAMIRE, Albert, *1266;*
1011,1016,1184,1267,1296
STRADNER, Gerhard, *955;*852
Strassburg, Valentin von, 241
Strauss, Richard, 387,522,
625,1013
Stravinsky, Igor, 48,465,585,
591,625,762
STREETER, Thomas, *956,
957;* 127
STRICKLING, George F.,
218

"Strike Up the Band," 750
String Music, 1104
String Quartet, 560
STROEHER, Michael, *1267*
STROETZ, Robert W., *1268;*
479,1080
STRUCK-SCHLÖN, Michael,
762; 395,396,431,447,644,
780
STUART, David, *18,763;*
151,152,682,689,764,789
STUDD, Tony, *1077;* 836,843
Studio, 65,93,116,301,334,
335,337,352,364,405,599,673
Stukin, Leonid, 1157
Stuttgart [Germany], 680
Style, 1014
Subject Matter Method, 1187
Suderberg, Robert, 528
"Sugar," 750
Suite [Dubois], 538
Suite for Brass Quintet
[V.Reynolds], 462
Suite for Five Winds
[Hartley], 395
Suite for Four Trombones
[G.Jacob], 769
Suite for Unaccompanied
Trombone [Bassett], 478,
538,579
*Suite No. 2 for
Unaccompanied Violoncello*
[J.S.Bach], 538
Šulek, Stjepan, 59,173,530,
538
SUMERKIN, Viktor, *764*
Superbone, 382,787,886
SUPPAN, Wolfgang, *219*
Surface Coating, 977,986

Surgery, 45
Suzuki, Shinichi, 1018
SVANBERG, Carsten, *71,
220,562;* 127,153,154,168
SWALLOW, John, *1269,
1270,1271;* 119,128,1006,
1011,1076,1226,1296
Swanee Whistle, 984
SWANSON, Thomas L., *19*
Swanson, W.G., 31
SWEATT, Morris, *1272;*
1012,1159
Sweden, 118,195,375,834
Sweeney, Gordon, 1164
SWETT, James P., *36,563;*
410,443
SWIFT, Robert, *221;* 198,203
Swing, 286,370,376,710,727
*Swinging Music [Serocki], 395
Switzerland, 703,803
Sydney [Australia], 195
Symphoniae Sacre I [Schütz],
408,738
*Symphonie Funèbre et
Triomphale* [Berlioz], 553
*Symphonie Phantastique
[Berlioz], 625
**Symphony for Trombone and
Orchestra* [E.Bloch], 476
Symphony in d minor
[Franck], 1013
Symphony No. 1 [Brahms],
1013
*Symphony No. 3 [Saint-
Saëns], 553
Symphony No. 7, D.729
[Schubert], 646
Symphony No. 8 (Unfinished),
D.759 [Schubert], 646

Symphony No. 9 (The Great),
D.944 [Schubert], 646
Symposia, 3,38,402
Symposium Musicum, 881
Synanon, 298
*Syncretism [Lorentzen], 395
Synesthesia, 1056
Synthesis, 736,1222
Synthesizers, 1222
Syracuse, University of, 392
SZEWCZUK, Janusz, *222;*
534,1206

T

Taafe-Zwilich, Ellen, *see*
Zwilich
Tacet, 721
Tack, Ernest [Ernie], 301
Tafoya, John, 80
Tailgate, 262
Takemitsu, Toru, 397
Talbot, James, 859
"Talking trombone," 751
Tall, David, 239
"Tambourin" from *Concerto for
Trombone* [Tomasi], 409,511
Tanganyika, 685
TANNER, James C., *765;* 612
TANNER, Paul, *766,958,
1273,1274,1275;* 496,678,
774,1064
**"Tantum ergo" from
Pangelingua* [Tůma], 595
Tanzania, 685
Tape, 420,437,441,483,497,
531,759
Tape Recording, 1208
Tarr, Edward, 795,825

"Tautophonic" [Kehrberg], 483

Taverner Players, 663

Taylor, David, 153,181,245, 268,269

Taylor, Debra, 239

Taylor, Mark, 530

TAYLOR, Stewart, *1276*

TAYLOR, William A., *767;* 464,613,646,709,719,721, 757

Teagarden, Jack, 41,250,252, 311,329,348,750,781

Technique,641,997,1002,1028, 1038,1045,1078,1080,1092, 1093,1102,1108,1127,1137, 1146,1147,1149,1150,1152, 1163,1170,1171,1172,1173, 1191,1195,1216,1218,1219, 1221,1228,1240,1262,1268, 1274,1283,1284,1292,1294

Technology, 1103

*"Tecum principium" from *Dixit Dominus* [Tůma], 595

Teddy Trombone [Fillmore], 538

Tel Aviv, University of, 893

Telemann, Georg Philipp, 538

Television, 42,270

*"Tempo verrá" from *Il mistico Giobbe* [Ziani], 616

Ten Grand Hosery [Dempster], 621

TENNYSON, Robert S., *564;* 410,479

Tensta Emotions [Grahn], 395

TEPPERMAN, B., *356;* 288, 339

Tepser, Stephan [Stephen?], 583,616

TESCH, John A., *565*

[Il] testamento di nostro Signor Gesú Cristo sul Calvario [Fux], 616

Tetra Ergon [D.White], 432, 478,538

Tetrad [E.Walker], 395

TETZLAFF, Daniel B., *1277;* 1098

Texas, 900

Texas, University of, Austin, 409,421,585,594,655,804,884

Texas Christian University (TCU),1238

THAYER, Orla Edward (Thayer valve), *959;* 990

Theater, 202,416,531,621,687, 759,772,1088

Theater Piece for Trombone Player and Tape [Oliveros], 621

THEIN, Heinrich, *960,961;* 788,815,842,944,964,975

THEIN, Max, *961;* 788,975

Thelin, Eje, 294,375

Theology, 809

Theses,1,12,132,415,431,445, 449,465,471,474,489,494, 512,513,521,522,657,666, 742,746,767,775,783,787, 816,826,844,885,893,912, 942,993,1026,1047,1060, 1090,1129,1160,1188,1238, 1244,1245,1252,1264,1282

Things Are Getting Better All the Time, 260

Thomas, Ambroise, 553

Thomas, Dylan, 48
THOMAS, Robert, *164;* 82,
   84,176,197,213,215,223,
   227,513,662,1197,1209
THOMAS, T. Donley, *566;*
   487
Thomas, Wenzel, 583
THOMPSON, J. Mark, *567,*
   568; 493,503
Thorbergsson, Sigurdur, 191
Thoughts of Love [Love
   Thoughts] [Pryor], 479,
   538,556
Three Pieces [Cope], 432,
   479,531
Three Poems [J.Lewis], 395
Three Sketches [Imbrie], 621,
   759
Throat, 1148,1293
Tibi Redemptor, 537
Timbre, 806,822,844,871,911,
   912,932,939,977,1135
Times Five [E.Brown], 395
Timing, 1125
TIMM, Willy, *768*
Tinctoris, Johannes, 640
Tischer, [Johann Nikolaus?],
   537
Tizol, Juan, 41,290
Toccata Sonora [F.Stewart],
   395
Toledo [OH], 469
Tomasi, Henri, 409,511,538,
   539,558
TOMES, Frank, *963;* 952
TOMKINS, Les, *357,358,*
   359,1278; 253,277,334,336,
   346,379,710,783,1007,1152
Tommy Dorsey and His

Orchestra, 66
Tone Center, 1004
Tone Production, 1249,1265
Tone   Quality,801,1044,1049,
   1050,1061,1094,1134,1136,
   1138,1162,1180,1196,1229,
   1235,1236,1293
*"Too Little Time,"
   [Mancini], 715
Tournemire, C., 539,558
Tower Music [*Turmmusik*],
   513,662,724
TRACY,Bruce,*223,224,225,*
   226,227,228,229,230,964,
   1279; 55,82,88,97,164,176,
   197,210,213,246,815,842,
   960,975,1034,1147,1197
TRAILL, Sinclair, *360;*338,376
Traité d'Instrumentation et
   d'Orchestration [Berlioz],
   553
Trans-Atlantic, 49
Transcriptions, 422,445,459,
   489,496,508,546,594,638,
   702,1014,1104
Traulsen, Palmer, 168,220
TRICHET, P., *965*
Trimmer, Peter, 128
Trio 1967 [Alsina], 395
Trio No. 5 [R.Stewart], 395
Trio Sketches [McConnell],
   373
[Il] trionfo di Giuditta
   [Porsile], 616
Triptych [Whittenberg], 696
Trois Pieces [Bozza], 769
Tromba da tirarsi, 797, 897,
   941
Trombet, 421,553,856

Trombolympic Games, 42, 82

Trombone Choir, 32,405,407, 453,459,496,499,500,541, 606,610,636,650,654,659, 661,678,685,694,706,714, 732,734,735,744,766,774, 777,1064

Trombone Duet, 565

Trombone Ensemble, 557,576, 1215

*"Trombone Moanin' Blues," 751

Trombone Music-15th Century, 472,640,676,717,718,756, 850,884

Trombone Music-16th Century, 472,545,575,590,640,663, 669,676,682,700,717,718, 756,782,850,884

Trombone Music-17th Century, 132,387,389,391,392,408, 415,467,475,486,502,510, 529,545,547,564,573,575, 590,616,640,641,652,654, 655,669,674,676,682,700, 712,718,756,763,782,884, 1122

Trombone Music-18th Century, 32,166,196,387,390,391,392, 393,398,414,424,450,451, 452,486,487,504,533,537, 552,554,566,580,583,589, 590,595,606,609,616,652, 654,656,657,669,683,694, 702,706,709,713,719,722, 729,730,731,743,744,752, 753,757,763,767,782,788, 859,999,1014,1086

Trombone Music-19th Century, 32,144,148,187,193,194,204, 243,403,417,421,424,426, 442,448,452,455,458,463, 466,493,495,514,536,539, 540,551,553,555,558,559, 577,581,590,602,606,613, 629,646,652,686,690,691, 709,714,719,732,744,752, 767,777,956,1014,1067, 1086,1124,1139,1189,1192, 1290

Trombone Music-20th Century, 59,96,115,119,122,137,138, 156,158,173,182,183,185, 202,234,243,271,385,387, 391,395,396,397,399,400, 405,407,409,416,418,420, 423,424,425,428,430,431, 433,434,435,437,440,441, 444,446,447,448,454,456, 458,460,462,469,472,481, 482,483,491,492,493,494, 497,498,499,503,507,511, 515,516,517,521,523,528, 530,531,534,536,539,546, 549,551,558,562,570,571, 576,579,585,596,601,607, 614,621,629,644,647,648, 653,658,667,677,684,687, 693,696,697,698,726,733, 737,741,744,754,758,759, 760,762,765,772,780,788, 999,1113,1116

Trombone Music-General, 6,8, 21,22,26,30,37,47,61,79,112, 133,170,386,406,410,411, 412,419,427,429,432,439, 461,470,474,500,501,520,

525,535,542,586,605,615,
626,628,666,716,742,764,
778,789,794,816,819,823,
840,849,876,897,901,921,
926,935,957,966,967,968,
1014,1124,1179,1188,1215,
1223,1235,1294 [see also *4,
Music*]
*"Trombone Preaching
Blues," 751
Trombone propeller, 800
Trombone Quartet, 433,442,
481,521,530,581,636,668,
758,769
Trombone Quartet [W.Ross],
769
Trombone Quintet, 498,532
Trombone Trio, 434,468,477,
478,524
The Trombonist, 72
Trombonium, 812
Trombonology, 63
Trompetta, 582
Trompette de Guerre, 865
Trompette des Menestrels,
825,827,865
Trondheim [Norway],
University of, 1225
Trowbridge, Clinton W., 291
Trudel, Alain, 141,236,237,
239,675,950
Trumpet,448,630,662,665,
685,792,797,798,809,833,
841,851,857,861,866,885,
917,923,942,946,950,1018,
1110,1115,1277
Tuba [15th-16th centuries],
582
Tuba [19th-20th centuries],

240,567,627,633,649,696,
726,810,861,914,1105,1123
Tuba Ductilis [Ductiles],
663,824,846,976
TUCKER, Albert, *73;* 910
TUCKER, Wallace E., *569,
769;* 433
Tudor, Dean, 849
TUERSOT, A., *971*
Tuilerie, M.A.-F.M. Leonard
de la, 801
Tůma, Franz Ignaz, 393,537,
583,595
Tuning, 836,843,847,934,951,
989
Turetzky, Bertram, 621
Turk, Thomas [Tommy], 34,
347
Turner, Raymond, 85
Turré, Steve, 236,270,1281
Twelve-Tone, 516,517,762
Two Hymns, [Popp], 530
TYACK, S.M., *972*
TYCHINSKI, Bruce, *570*
Tyson, Edgar, 131

U

UBER, David, *571*
UCLA (University of
California at Los Angeles),
766
Ujfalussi, Laszlo, 1074
Ulbrich, Anton Michael, 583
Ulbrich, Ignaz, 583
Ulbrich, Johann K., 583
Ulbrich, Maximiliano, 537
ULMAN, Edward J., *362,
1281;* 374,748,783,1007

ULMER, J. Ross, *1282*
Ulyate, Lloyd, 128,335,715
Unaccompanied, 438,491,531,
  550,579
Undergraduate Instruction, 1112
UNDERWOOD, Lee, *363,
  364,365,366,367;* 249,480
*"[Der] Unflat Meiner Seele"
  from *Der verlorene Sohn*
  [Eberlin], 537,753
UNGER, Hermann, *770*
Unit approach, 1060
United Kingdom, *see* Britain;
  England
United Musical Instruments,
  USA, Inc., 970
United States (USA), 163
Universities, *see* Colleges-
  Universities
Unna [Germany], 768
**Untitled Piece No. IV*
  [Bruce], 395
**Up to a Point* [Pethel], 531
UPCHURCH, John D., *74,
  232,973,1283;* 126,140,
  887,1119
The Urbie Green Sextet, 750
USOV, Jurij, *1284,1285,1286;*
  1080,1127,1137,1146,1170,
  1191,1219,1268
USSR, *see* Soviet Union

V

VACHER, Peter, *368;* 384
Valsalva Maneuver, 1043
Valve Trombone, 373,620,
  747,1299
Valves,455,553,620,787,812,

817,836,843,847,856,874,
888,894,905,907,913,934,
937,940,951,959,972,988,
989,990,992,993,994,996,
1027,1053,1062,1071,1077,
1082,1083,1087,1089,1105,
1123,1126,1129,1142,1180,
1196,1213,1214,1229,1230,
1256,1264,1295
VANCE, John, *771*
VANCE,Stuart-Morgan, *974;*
  1053
VANDERARK, Sherman,
  1136; 1044,1162
VAN DOVER, David L., *572*
VAN DŸK, Ben, *975;* 237,
  842,960,964
Van Ess, Donald H., 663
Van Lier, Bart, 152
Van Lier, Eric, 152
Van Schaik, Harold, 121
**Variations* [Bigot], 558
**Variations on a March by
  Shostakovich* [Frackenpohl],
  538
**Variations on a Theme from
  Childhood* [Serebrier], 395
Vaughan Williams, Ralph,
  413,478,538
*"Vedi che il Redentor" from
  Il fonte della salute* [Fux], 616
Vejvanousky, Pavel Josef, 547
VENDRIES, Christophe, *976*
VENGLOVSKY, Victor,
  1287; 635,1073,1247,1286
Venice [Italy], 143,401
*"Venite, angioli" from Il testa-
  mento di nostro Signor Gesu
  Cristo al Calvario* [Fux], 616

Verdi, Giuseppe, 686,690,796,
873,892
VERGES, Robin, *369;* 264,
272,380
Vergnügliche Miniaturen
[Kubizek], 395
Vern, V., 94,195
Vernon, Charles, 124,128,229,
503,568,1013,1279
[Der] verurteilte Jesus
[Eberlin], 753
Veselack, John, 121
Vibrato, 665,672,715,1094,
1115,1244,1301
Vidal, Paul, 539,558
Video Design, 1165
Videofluorography, 1054,1097
Videos, 29,41,297,970
Vienna [Austria], 196,219,
241,537,583,616,656,657,
683,729,731
Village Gate, 70
Villa-Lobos, Heitor, 507
Vining, David, 239
Violoncello, 422
Virgiliano, Aurelio, 676
Virgo Music, 114
VITALI, Carlo, *75*
Vivaldi, Antonio, 538,702
VIVONA, Peter M., *772,
1288;* 239,416,621,687,759,
1044,1134,1136,1162,1249
Vocal,48,134,165,466,472,
486,536,555,580,582,583,
595,655,664,671,674,712,
734,738,1014,1040,1189
Vocalise [Rachmaninoff],
476,538
Vocalises, 1124,1189,1253

VOCE, Steve, *370,773;* 318
VOELKER, Dale, *573;* 132,
452,1122
VÖGEL, E.T., *371;* 305
Vogt, Nancy, 129
Voigt, Horst, 855
Voigt, Jürgen, 855
Vollrath, Carl, 127,399

W

WAGENKNECHT, Robert,
574; 473
Wagenseil, Georg Christoph,
413,504,533,538,554,583,
609,656,657,722,729
WAGNER, Irvin, *575,576,
774;* 126,410,479,496,678,
766,1037,1064
Wagner, Richard, 233,625,
680,1013
Waits, 645
Waldrop, Donald [Don], 301
Walker, George, 530
Walker, Jonas [Papa], 751
WALKER, Leo, *372;* 291
WALKER, William Thomas,
977; 806,822,844,932,986
[Die] Walküre [R.Wagner],
1013
WALTER, Cam, *373*
Wanner, John, 900
Ward, Charles [Chuck], 127
Warmups, 1128,1168,1198,
1282,1291
WARNEX, Paul, *775;* 617,
621,639,755,1022
Warrack, John, 866
Warsaw [Poland], 699

Warwick Music, 463,514
Washington [DC], 99
Washington State University
   [State College of
   Washington], 993
Washington, University of,
   491,746,806
Washington University [St.
   Louis MO], 1187
Wasson, John, 121
WATERS, David, *76;* 124,
   169
WATKINSON, P.S., *978;*
   833,932
Wather, Willi, 130
WATROUS, William [Bill],
   *1289;*27,125,128,152,154,
   239,282,294,305,330,336,
   354,371,377,381,642,643,
   715,1203,1301
Watson, Walter, 428
Weast, Robert D., 432,1076,
   1233,1288
WEBB, John, *979;* 795,838,
   998
Weber, Alain, 558
Weber, Carl Maria von, 403,
   455,495,530
WEBER, K., *233,980,981;*
   680,846,933
Webern, Anton, 762
Weckmann, Matthias, 415
WEED,Larry,*20,77,127,234,
   235,236,237,238,239,240,
   577,578;*51,122,125,127,128,
   139,194,212,403,495,540,
   551,592,869
WEEKS, Douglas, *579;* 400,
   438,498,531,550,551,601

WEIDEMANN, *680;* 233
Weinachshistorie [Schütz],
   674
Weiner, Andy, 354
WEINER, Howard, *776,1290;*
   166,552,580,949
WEINGARTNER, Felix, *580;*
   552
Weird Notes, 1048
WEISEL, Joseph [Joe], *374;*
   362,748
Weiss, Robert, 129
WEISSHAAR, Otto H., *982;*
   1015,1101,1258
Weldon, A.F., 90
Welk, Lawrence, 643
Wells, Donald, 159
Wells, Simon, 530
Wells, William [Dicky], 283,
   318,622,751
Welsch, Chauncey, 715
WENKE, Wolfgang, *983*
Werner, Dean, 1118
Werner Josten Library, 545
Weschke, Paul, 136,540,695
Wesley, Fred, 310
WESSELY, Othmar, *241,
   581,777;* 442
West, April, 383
Western Kentucky University,
   532
Western Michigan University,
   449
WESTIN, Lars, *375*
Westphalia (Germany), 768
WESTRUP, J.A., *778*
Wetherill, 984
*What Do You Know?
   [Grzesik], 432

Whatzit No. 6 [Wilding-White], 621
WHEAT, James R., *582*
Wheeler, Joseph, 849
Wheeler, Michael, 127
Whigham, Jiggs, 126,128,
151,237,239,362,374,748,
1069,1298
Whimsy, 62,868
Whiston, Harry, 376
White, Donald H., 489,516,
517,538
White, Harry, 624
White, Harry [Father], 751
Whitehead, Annie, 269
Whittaker, Leon [Peewee], 295
Whittenberg, Charles, 696
Wichita (Kansas), University
of, 1188
WICK, Denis, *779,985,1291,
1292,1293,1294;* 91,126,
153,154,1218
WIEHE, Larry, *242;* 90,125,
129,175,1199,1219
Wiest, Steve, 238
WIGNESS, Clyde Robert,
583; 127,196,475,486,
504,537,554,616,753,767
WILBORN, David F., *1295;*
836,843,1013,1027,1029,
1256
Wilcox, Spiegle, 338,360
Wilder, Alec, 538,548,593
Wilding-White, Raymond, 621
Wilhelm, Carl, 100
William Tell Overture
[Rossini], 747
WILLIAMS, Arthur L., *1296;*
1182

WILLIAMS, Jeanne, *1297;*
128,129,1111
WILLIAMS, Jeffrey Price,
584; 510,682
WILLIAMS, M., *1298*
WILLIAMS, Mark R., *585;*
465
Williams, Roy, 284,1280
WILLIAMS, Sandy, *376;* 751
Williard, Patricia, 327
WILLIS, James D., *780;* 395,
396,431,447,644,762
Willner, Hal, 720
Willson, Meredith, 530
Wilson [instrument
manufacturer], 905
Wilson, Art, 289
Wilson, Cecil, 421,767
Wilson, Gail E., 1111
WILSON, Phil, *781;* 82,125,
126,294,326,531,597
Wind Bands, 725,931
Wind Ensemble, 546
Winding,Kai,70,277,293,329,
336,379,750,783,1007,1019,
1048,1081,1260,1278,1281
WINKEL, Hans, *1299*
WINKING, Charles, *37,377,
586;* 305
WINKLER, Jonathan, *587;*
29,323
WINKLER, Klaus, *588,589,
590,782;* 398,401,472,544,
640,655
Wireless, 49
Wisconsin, University of,
Madison, 290,551,582
WISNER, Gary, *591*
Witser, Steve, 121,237

WITTEKIND, Donald H.,
  1300,1301; 665,672,715
Woelber, Henry, 135,243
WOGRAM, Klaus, *911,986;*
  806,822,844,903,912,932,977
Wogram, Nils, 307
Wolfer, J., 29
Wolff, Edward R., III, 5,962,
  1006,1271
WOLFINBARGER, Steve,
  243,378,592; 107,145,194,
  403,495,540,551,556,956
Women, 95,103,111,147,172
*Women Go to Heaven and
  Men Go to Hell* [R.Harris],
  395,432
Wonder Music IV
  [Hutcheson], 531
Wood, Mitchell [Booty], 751
Wooden Trumpets, 834
Woodham, Richard, 795
Woods, Phil, 265
Woodwinds, 396,431
WOOLEY, Stan, *379,380;*
  264,272,277,336,369,1278
*World Encyclopedia of
  Recorded Music* [Clough/
  Cuming], 536
World War II (WWII),
  291,372
World Wide Web, 50
Workshops,38,69,121,125,
  126,127,128,129,151,152,
  153,154,235.236,237,238,
  239,294,397,398,437,438,
  441,514,587,748,1068,1254
Worship, 518,519,739
WORTHMÜLLER, Willi,
  987; 869,878,922

"Wow," 750
Wozzeck [Berg], 769
Wright, Robert C., 123

X

Xenakis, Iannis,152,195,491,759

Y

Yamaha-Kemble, 962
YANOW, Scott, *381;* 305
Yaxley, Donald, 121,307
YEAGER, William R., *783;*
  512,1007,1019,1048,1081,
  1260,1281
YEO, Douglas, *78,79,244,245,
  246,247,248,382,383,384,
  593,619,784,988,989,990,
  1149,1302,1303;* 33,50,108,
  163,177,181,228,268,368,
  455,548,552,580,787,836,
  843,847,886,1031,1033,
  1126,1130,1147,1166,1214,
  1217,1256,1263
Yoder, Paul, 218
Yoshioka, E., 538
Young, H.T., 135
YOUNG, Jerry A., *1304*
YOUNG, P., *1305;* 1030
Young, P., 1030
Young, Trummy, 41,261,263,
  280,292,302,327,329,1193
Yukl, Joseph [Joe], 750

Z

ZADROZNY, Edward, *236*

Zahn, Johannes, 629
Zaliouk, Yuval, 469
Zbar, Michael, 531
Zechner, Johann Georg, 537
*Zeitschrift für
    Musikwissenschaft*, 680
Zentner, Si, 29
Ziani, Marc' Antonio, 504,
    583,616
Zimmerman, Leo, 243

Zinsmayr, Andreas, 537
ZOLA, Larry, *991*
ZUBECK, Robin J., *594;*
    1104
Zudecoff, Moe [Buddy
    Morrow], 361
Zugposaune, 803
ZWERIN, M., *785*
Zwilich, Ellen Taaffe,
    503,530,568

ABOUT THE AUTHOR

G.B. Lane has been a college teacher since 1965 and on the faculty of the School of Music at the University of South Carolina since 1972. During most of his academic career he functioned primarily as an applied trombone teacher but in 1991 began to emphasize teaching academic courses in music. He holds five academic degrees, including the Doctor of Musical Arts in trombone performance from the University of Texas at Austin and the Master of Library Science from Louisiana State University. He delivers papers on and has been published in the fields of brass pedagogy and history, historical brass instruments, and music education.